BASEBALL SKIPPERS AND THEIR CREWS

The History of Every Major League Manager and Coach, 1871–2007

BASEBALL SKIPPERS AND THEIR CREWS

The History of Every Major League Manager and Coach, 1871–2007

THOMAS W. BRUCATO

St. Johann Press
Haworth, NJ

ST. JOHANN PRESS

Published in the United States of America
by St. Johann Press
P.O. Box 241
Haworth, NJ 07641

Library of Congress Cataloging-in-Publication Data

Brucato, Thomas W.
    Baseball skippers and their crews : the history of every manager
and coach in the major leagues, 1871-2007 / Thomas W. Brucato.
        p. cm.
        ISBN 978-1-878282-50-7 (alk. paper)
        1. Baseball managers—United States—Biography. 2. Baseball
coaches—United States—Biography. 3. Baseball managers—United
States—Statistics. 4. Baseball coaches—United States—Statistics.
5. Baseball records—United States. I Title.

GV865.A1B76 2007
796.357092'2—dc22
[B]
                                                            2007060737

The paper used in this publication meets the minimum requirements of
the American National Standard for Informational Sciences—Permanence
of Paper for Printed Library Materials, ANSI/NISO Z39/48-1992

Cover design, printing and binding by G&H SOHO, Inc.; Hoboken, NJ
(www.ghsoho.com)

Manufactured in the United States of America

To Sue and Bud Westendorf —

It's always a good day for a ballgame

Contents

Introduction

The Managers

Baseball is the only sport in which the head of the team is referred to not as "coach" or even as "head coach," but as "manager." In baseball a coach teaches, drills, or assists; a manager makes decisions and implements those decisions. The job of major league baseball manager is one of the most coveted in the sports world, although some of those who have held the position have found themselves regretting ever having accepted it. A manager cannot win or lose a game by himself, and yet his actions can have a decided impact on the results. A manager is therefore under a great deal of pressure from his coaching staff, his players, the fans, and the press, and any losing manager can, if nothing else, expect to be consistently second-guessed and possibly roundly criticized for his actions or lack thereof.

Perhaps, then, it is no accident that managers are sometimes referred to as "skippers." Like the captain of a ship, the manager is responsible for making decisions that could ultimately lead to reaching or failing to reach a goal, and many eyes, including those of his crew, will be focused on him as he makes those decisions. He will cruise during times of calm, but must also weather the roughest seas. Like a captain, he will be on the bridge to experience moments of sun and glory. Like a captain, in the face of failure he may eventually have to go down with his ship.

As in any other aspect of life, some managers are better than others. Some are unfortunately saddled with poor teams and become scapegoats for failures over which they actually have little or no control. Others are blessed with superior squads and have to do very little to achieve victory. Still others are master strategists or are able to inspire their players to great heights, and only in so doing reach hard-fought and hard-won goals. This book does not provide an analysis or critique of managerial style, however. It simply presents a snapshot of each major league manager throughout history, providing a quick look at every man who has borne the moniker of "skipper" in major league baseball from 1871 to the beginning of the 2007 baseball season.

As the reader will see, the vast majority of these managers have been former players. Many, in fact, especially in baseball's early days, were both at the same time, functioning as player-managers. Some were former or future umpires, some were owners, and some were sportswriters. Some played minor league baseball but never reached the major leagues, and a very few had no professional playing experience at all. Their knowledge of the game varied widely, and their prowess at executing the dual functions of strategizing during games and managing the many and diverse personalities inhabiting a clubhouse differed as well. Some could handle the role and some could not. Some excelled at it, and others faded quickly into obscurity. At least one took his own life because of it.

Baseball is also the only major sport in which the head of the team is uniformed, like the players. A few throughout history have eschewed that tradition, however, most famous among them the incomparable Connie Mack, who managed in street clothes. Some were "interim" managers, usually coaches who briefly filled in when a manager was fired and his replacement had not yet arrived or been decided upon. Some managed thousands of games, others no more than one or two.

In 1961 and 1962 the Chicago Cubs conducted what is known as the "college of coaches" experiment. Rather than hiring a manager in the traditional sense, they appointed various coaches to take turns managing the team for limited periods of time. It is difficult to assess completely the results of the experiment, given that the team in that era performed just as poorly before the experiment as during it, although it did improve slightly when it was over. If nothing else, it is difficult to imagine that players and fans alike did not perceive some degree of a void in leadership.

Since 1871 there have been over 650 managers in major league baseball history. All of them are presented here in alphabetical order. Below each manager's name the reader will see the names of the teams he managed, together with the years and the leagues in which those teams played. Below that listing is the manager's all-time win-loss record for all teams combined. A capsule of the manager's life or career follows these headings.

In some cases a certain year may be listed more than once with the same team. Such a repetition indicates that a manager's tenure with a team during a specific season was interrupted (in most cases due to illness, suspension, or leave of absence), but that he later returned to the team the same year and continued as manager.

In looking back at the early years of baseball it is not always completely clear who served as the true manager of a team. Clubs frequently employed "team captains" who were also players, and the role of manager was more administrative in nature. Different sources credit different individuals with the records of those teams. This book relies on the eighth edition of *Total Baseball* (John Thorn et al., Sport Media Publishing, Inc., Toronto, Ontario, 2004) in such instances.

Leagues that are included here are those generally accepted by historians as being major leagues, with the addition of the original National Association. In total those leagues are the National Association (NA; 1871–75), National League (NL; 1876–present), American Association (AA; 1882–91), Union Association (UA; 1884), Players League (PL; 1890), American League (AL; 1901–present), and Federal League (FL; 1914–15).

This book uses the nine-point criteria established by Richard Topp and Robert Tiemann and spelled out in the eighth edition of *Total Baseball* (pages 2637–38) regarding how wins and losses are credited to managers. Records are complete through the 2006 season.

The Coaches

The onus on coaches, if not precisely the same, is similar to that placed on managers. Coaches comprise a skipper's crew, and like managers, they may bear a great deal of blame, whether justified or otherwise, if the ship is not sailing on smooth waters. At the same time they are perhaps the least appreciated of a team's uniformed personnel. With few exceptions they are rarely lauded for their accomplishments when a club is doing well. It is only in recent years, in fact, that teams have even begun compiling and publishing all-time rosters of their coaches.

Coaches' roles vary, and they have evolved greatly over time. There are even differing claims on exactly who was the first coach in the major leagues. The earliest one discovered and presented here is Arlie Latham, who served as a coach for the Cincinnati Reds in 1900 and then as a player-coach for the New York Giants in 1909. Several other clubs in the 1910s seem to have employed single coaches, and it makes sense to speculate that those coaches' duties involved assisting the manager with pregame and postgame practical chores. It is equally possible that they were brought on board to share their particular gifts and experience with the active players. In quite a number of cases, these men have even functioned as player-coaches, in some instances remaining active for entire seasons and in others being activated for limited numbers of games as circumstances required.

By the 1950s it was becoming rather standard practice for a team to employ four coaches: a hitting coach, a pitching coach, a first base coach, and a third base coach. Clubs later began to add bench coaches and bullpen coaches, and those six are the standard today, with Major League Baseball rules even stipulating that a maximum of six uniformed coaches may sit in a team's dugout during a game. Still, some clubs employ others whose primary functions are to assist during pregame warmups and off-day practices as well as to perform specific duties in the clubhouse. As a result there have been catching coaches, infield coaches, outfield coaches, baserunning coaches, administrative coaches, strength and conditioning coaches, mental skills coaches, and others.

Because of the diversity of roles and titles assigned to coaches, it was not always easy determining who should be included in this volume. As a general rule, this book attempts to include those who have borne titles containing the specific term "coach" and who have functioned as uniformed personnel. Therefore, as an example, an extra major league "catching instructor" would not be included, whereas an extra major league "catching coach" would be. An exception might be made where, for example, a team includes a "hitting instructor" among its six uniformed personnel who are qualified to sit in the dugout, but has no "hitting coach" on its staff. When in doubt, this book has preferred to err on the side of inclusion. In a few rare cases, a member of a coaching staff has borne the title "assistant manager" (such as Ray Knight with the 1995 Cincinnati Reds). These men are included as coaches.

There have been over 1300 coaches in major league baseball history; of those, more than 300 have also been managers. All of the coaches are presented in "The Coaches" section of this book in alphabetical order. Below each coach's name the reader will see the names of the teams he coached, together with the years and the leagues in which those teams played. Below that listing is a capsule of the coach's life or career. In the case of a coach who has also been a manager, the note *See Managers section* will appear.

The

Managers

Manny Acta
Washington Nationals (NL) 2007–
Record: 0–0
Played minor league baseball in the Houston Astros' system before becoming a minor league manager at the age of 25.

Acta attended Major League Baseball's scouting school and realized that he himself would not reach the major leagues as a player. He became a minor league coach and manager, and was named the Florida State League's Manager of the Year in 1999 when he guided the Kissimmee Astros to the championship.

Acta skippered the Licey Tigers of the Dominican Winter League from 2002–04, and his 2003 club won the Caribbean Series. He became the Mets' third base and infield coach following the 2004 season, and in 2006 he managed the Dominican Republic in the first World Baseball Classic. Following that season he was hired to replace Frank Robinson at the helm of the Nationals.

Bill Adair
Chicago White Sox (AL) 1970
Record: 4–6
Third base coach for the White Sox who filled in for 10 games in 1970 between the managerial reigns of Don Gutteridge and Chuck Tanner.

Adair never played in the major leagues, but in 1952 had served as player-manager for the Eau Claire Bears (a Milwaukee Braves' farm team) when Hank Aaron joined the club. He managed the Panama City Fliers to the Alabama-Florida League Championship in 1955, and later became a major league coach. He died in 2002.

Joe Adcock
Cleveland Indians (AL) 1967
Record: 75–87
Had a solid 17-year major league playing career with the Cincinnati Reds, Milwaukee Braves, Cleveland Indians, and Los Angeles/California Angels from 1950–66.

Adcock retired with a .277 lifetime batting average and 336 home runs. On July 31, 1954, he hit four home runs and a double in a game at Ebbets Field against the Brooklyn Dodgers.

He was considered a power hitter, often clubbing more than 20 home runs in a season and peaking with 38 in 1956. Later in his career he was usually platooned and was often injured, however.

After his retirement he was named manager of the Indians for the 1967 season, but was fired after his team finished in eighth place in the 10-team league.

Bob Addy
Philadelphia Phillies (NA) 1875; Cincinnati Red Stockings (NL) 1877
Record: 8–23
Player-manager for both the original Phillies and the Red Stockings of 1877.

Addy is credited with being the first player to use a slide to steal a base when he played for the Rockford Forest Citys in 1866. He managed the Phillies for only seven games in 1875, and was the second of three player-managers employed by the Red Stockings in 1877.

He was also an umpire in the National Association in 1875.

Bob Allen
Philadelphia Phillies (NL) 1890; Cincinnati Reds (NL) 1900
Record: 87–87
As player-manager was one of four men who led the Phillies in 1890, taking the reins for a mere 35 games, but continued to play shortstop for Philadelphia for five seasons.

Allen played briefly for the Boston Bostons in 1897, and managed an entire season for the Reds in 1900 while playing in five contests. His Cincinnati club finished seventh in the National League.

Felipe Alou
Montreal Expos (NL) 1992–2001; San Francisco Giants (NL) 2003–06
Record: 1033–1021
Had a 17-year playing career with 206 home runs with several teams.

Alou broke in in 1958 with the Giants and in 1966 with the Atlanta Braves he batted .327, hit 31 roundtrippers, and led the National League with 122 runs scored. He hit over .300 on three occasions.

Felipe's brothers, Matty and Jesus, were also major leaguers, and in 1963 all three played the outfield at the same time for the Giants. On September 10 the trio batted consecutively in the eighth inning against the New York Mets; unfortunately, none of them reached base. Felipe would later have the opportunity to manage his son, Moises.

After his retirement he became a coach and a minor league manager, and early in the 1992 season he was named the manager of the Expos, who had fired skipper Tom Runnells. In 1994 he won the Manager of the Year Award from both the Associated Press (AP) and the Baseball Writers Association of America (BBWAA) when his Expos had the best record in baseball during a strike-shortened season. The club was 74–40 when play halted. Unfortunately, there was no postseason, and no official divisional or league titles were awarded.

Following the 1998 campaign he nearly accepted an offer to manage the Los Angeles Dodgers, but at the last minute decided to remain in Montreal. The Expos eventually fired him early in the 2001 season.

In November of 2002 he took the helm of the Giants, where he remained until 2006.

Walter Alston
Brooklyn Dodgers (NL) 1954–57; Los Angeles Dodgers (NL) 1958–76
Record: 2040–1613

Had a major league playing career of one at-bat when, with the St. Louis Cardinals on September 27, 1936, he replaced the ejected Johnny Mize during a game and struck out.

Nicknamed "Smokey," Alston had a long and rather successful minor league career, some of it as a player-manager, before becoming a full-time manager. He was with the Portsmouth Cubs of the Piedmont League in 1940 and led the circuit in both home runs and runs batted in the following two seasons. He became player-manager with the Trenton Packers in the Brooklyn Dodgers' organization in mid-1944, and by 1949 was the skipper of the Montreal Royals, the top minor league club in the Brooklyn organization.

Branch Rickey named him the Dodgers' manager on November 24, 1953, and he would remain at that post for 23 seasons.

Alston won seven pennants and three World Championships during his managerial career, capturing the ultimate crown in 1955, 1963, and 1965. He was named the National League's Manager of the Year by the AP four times, and is among the 10 winningest managers in baseball history. He retired in 1976 with only four games left in the season, and was replaced by coach Tom Lasorda. The Dodgers retired his number 24 in 1977.

Alston was elected to the Hall of Fame in 1983, and he passed away a year later.

Joe Altobelli
San Francisco Giants (NL) 1977–79; Baltimore Orioles (AL) 1983–85; Chicago Cubs (NL) 1991
Record: 437–407

Played sparsely in three major league seasons before becoming a manager and coach.

Altobelli was named manager of the Giants in 1977, and a year later won the National League Manager of the Year Award from the AP when his club finished third. He was fired in 1979 after 140 games when his team was in third place, however.

He was hired to manage the Orioles in 1983 and promptly won the American League pennant and then defeated the Philadelphia Phillies in the World Series. He was fired during the 1985 campaign when the team slumped, and in 1991 he managed a single game for the Cubs on an interim basis—a game the team lost—between the tenures of Don Zimmer and Jim Essian.

Joey Amalfitano
Chicago Cubs (NL) 1979, 1980–81
Record: 66–116

Played 10 years as a utility infielder for several clubs before retiring from the playing field and becoming a coach.

Amalfitano was a Cubs' coach in 1979, and he managed the final seven games of the season as a temporary replacement for Herman Franks. In 1980, when manager Preston Gomez was fired, he was named manager. He held the reins through the 1981 season, but his team never finished higher than fifth and he was let go.

Sparky Anderson
Cincinnati Reds (NL) 1970–78; Detroit Tigers (AL) 1979–95
Record: 2194–1834

Light-hitting shortstop for the 1959 Philadelphia Phillies who gained prominence as one of the greatest managers in baseball history.

Sparky was only 36 years old when he became the manager of the Reds in 1970. His club immediately won the National League pennant, and would do so several more times during the decade as the Big Red Machine established itself under his reign as one of the most storied clubs in baseball lore. The Reds won five division titles under Anderson, resulting in four pennants and culminating in back-to-back World Championships in 1975 and 1976. Only once did they finish lower than second place.

Inexplicably fired following the 1978 campaign, Sparky was named to replace Les Moss at the helm of the Tigers early the following season. He would hold that job through 1995, and in 1984 he became the first manager to win the World Series in both the National and American Leagues when his Tigers went all the way.

Nicknamed "Captain Hook" because of his tendency to yank his starting pitchers early and go to his bullpen, Anderson routinely made good use of his entire pitching staff and pioneered many of the related managerial techniques commonly in use today.

Sparky was named NL Manager of the Year twice by the AP, and AL Manager of the Year twice by the BBWAA. His 2194 victories are among the top 10 in major league history. He was elected to the Hall of Fame in 2000, and the Reds retired his number 10 in 2005.

Cap Anson
Philadelphia Athletics (NA) 1875; Chicago White Stockings (NL) 1879, 1880–89; Chicago Colts (NL) 1890–97; New York Giants (NL) 1898
Record: 1296–947

One of the greatest players of the nineteenth century.

Anson began his career in 1871 with the Rockford Forest Citys, and in 27 major league seasons he failed to bat .300 on only three occasions, winning two batting titles and hitting .414 in 46 games in 1872. He had a .357 average in five years in the National Association, and a .329 lifetime average in 22 National League seasons. He was the first player to collect 3000 hits lifetime and amassed 3413 in his career.

Cap was player-manager for the Athletics for eight games in 1875, but would spend most of his later seasons as player-manager for the Chicago NL franchise, at first called the White Stockings and later the Colts. He managed most of 1879 before being sidelined in August due to a liver disorder. Silver Flint would take over for the rest of the season.

He managed the club through 1897, and he was regarded as such a father figure by the team that when he left, it renamed itself the Orphans.

Anson garnered five first-place finishes during his tenure. In an early version of the World Series against American Association clubs, his White Stockings tied the St. Louis Browns (today's Cardinals) in 1885, three games to three with one tie (the first game was called after eight innings because of darkness with the score knotted), and lost to those same Browns in 1886, four games to two.

Anson was one of the first managers to take his team to a warmer climate in the spring to practice for the approaching season, in a ritual that we refer to today as spring training. He died in 1922, and he was elected to the Hall of Fame in 1939.

Luke Appling
Kansas City Athletics (AL) 1967
Record: 10–30

Hall of Fame shortstop for the Chicago White Sox who finished off one dismal season as manager of the Athletics.

Appling had a 20-year career with the Sox, hitting over .300 sixteen times and winning two batting titles. He set major league records for games played and double plays turned by a shortstop, and American League records for putouts and assists by a shortstop.

Appling retired in 1950 and the White Sox eventually retired his number 4. He became a minor league manager and major league coach, and he won a pennant with the Memphis Chicks of the Southern Association in 1953 and another with the Indianapolis Indians of the American Association in 1962.

He became a coach with the Kansas City Athletics in 1964, and he replaced Alvin Dark as manager during the 1967 season. The club was in last place when he took over for the final 40 games, and they finished in the same spot.

Bill Armour
Cleveland Bronchos (AL) 1902; Cleveland Naps (AL) 1903–04; Detroit Tigers (AL) 1905–06
Record: 382–347

Minor league player who became a major league manager, and later a scout and executive.

In 1902 Armour managed the Cleveland Bronchos, who were renamed the Naps for player Nap Lajoie in 1903, and when Armour was fired following the 1904 season the club named Lajoie his successor. Bill was then hired by the Tigers, and was given credit for signing Ty Cobb.

He later returned to the minor leagues, where he became a part-owner of the Toledo Mud Hens, then a business manager for two other clubs. He died in 1922.

Ken Aspromonte
Cleveland Indians (AL) 1972–74
Record: 220–260

Journeyman infielder who played seven seasons with six teams before becoming manager of the Indians.

Aspromonte rarely stayed with one team for a full season, usually getting traded or sold somewhere during the course of a year. He won a batting title in the Pacific Coast League, but was never a strong hitter in the majors although he did play good defense.

As manager he never did better than a fourth-place finish, but his Indians' teams were never strong clubs.

Jimmy Austin
St. Louis Browns (AL) 1913, 1918, 1923
Record: 31–44

Eighteen-year major league veteran player who was a rather light hitter but an outstanding defensive third baseman.

Austin was a three-time interim player-manager during his long career with the Browns. In 1913 he managed a total of eight games between the reigns of George Stovall and Branch Rickey. He also filled in on Sundays for Rickey when the regular manager refused to go to the ballpark because of a promise he had made to his mother. In 1918 he took the helm for 16 more games between the tenures of Fielder Jones and Jimmy Burke. In 1923 he managed the last 51 games after Lee Fohl was let go, while playing but a single contest.

Del Baker

Detroit Tigers (AL) 1933, 1936, 1936, 1937, 1938–42; Boston Red Sox (AL) 1960

Record: 419–360

Light-hitting catcher who became a coach and later manager.

Baker had a long minor league playing career, although he spent only three active seasons in the major leagues. He was renowned for his ability to tip off batters to the types of pitches opposing hurlers were about to throw, having made quite a study of pitchers' habits and motions on the mound.

Baker was a coach for the Tigers from 1933–38. In 1933 he managed the final two games of the season when Bucky Harris was let go. He was interim manager on several occasions in 1936 and 1937, first when skipper Mickey Cochrane was suffering from a nervous breakdown and then when Cochrane was beaned and suffered a skull fracture. In August of 1938 he was named manager to replace Cochrane.

His club won the 1940 American League pennant, although they lost the World Series to the Cincinnati Reds. During the next two years the Tigers finished fourth and fifth, respectively, and Baker was fired.

Del was a coach for the Red Sox in 1960 when manager Billy Jurges left the team due to a reported illness. Baker took the reins for seven games, then the club fired Jurges and replaced him with Pinky Higgins.

Dusty Baker

San Francisco Giants (NL) 1993–2002; Chicago Cubs (NL) 2003–06

Record: 1162–1041

Played 19 years in the major leagues as an outfielder before his success as a manager.

After four short stints with the Atlanta Braves, Baker's first full season was 1972, and he promptly hit .321. While that average would not typify his career, he did win a Gold Glove, appear in two All-Star Games, and hit 242 home runs lifetime. In a game against the Cincinnati Reds in 1984, he stole second, third, and home, although he swiped only one additional base the entire year.

He managed the Giants from 1993 through 2002 and won two division titles. In 2000 his club captured the National League pennant, but lost a tough seven-game World Series to the Anaheim Angels. Baker was named NL Manager of the Year by the BBWAA on three occasions, but was let go following the 2002 season. He was immediately hired by the Cubs. In 2004 he was suspended for one game for arguing vehemently with an umpire about a call for batting out of order. He turned the reins over to

his pitching coach, Dick Pole, for that one contest. He was fired by the Cubs following the 2006 season.

George Bamberger

Milwaukee Brewers (AL) 1978–79, 1980, 1985–86; New York Mets (NL) 1982–83

Record: 458–478

Pitched 10 games in the 1950s before becoming a major league coach and manager.

Bamberger's greatest success as a pitching coach came with the Baltimore Orioles from 1968–77, when his hurlers won four Cy Young Awards. He became manager of the Brewers in 1978, but after two seasons he began to struggle with heart problems. In 1980 Buck Rodgers temporarily took the helm, and Bamberger returned for 92 games before Rodgers took over permanently. He managed the Mets in 1982, but was replaced by Frank Howard early in the 1983 season. He returned to the Brewers in 1985 and '86.

Bamberger died of cancer in 2004.

Dave Bancroft

Boston Braves (NL) 1924, 1924–27

Record: 228–336

Hall of Fame shortstop who was player-manager of the Braves for four seasons.

Bancroft played 16 years in the major leagues, beginning in 1915 with the Philadelphia Phillies. He was a switch-hitter and had garnered the nickname "Beauty" for himself in the minor leagues because of his tendency to yell that word whenever something went his team's way. As a manager he never accomplished more than a fifth-place finish, but he was elected to the Hall of Fame in 1971 because of his play.

He was known as a hard-nosed skipper, and his managerial style was not appreciated by many of his players. In 1927 during a game against the Pittsburgh Pirates, Bancroft got into an argument with Bucs' catcher Earl Smith, who had previously played under Dave in Boston. Smith punched Bancroft, and the Braves' manager had to be carried off the field.

Frank Bancroft

Worcester Ruby Legs (NL) 1880; Detroit Wolverines (NL) 1881–82; Cleveland Blues (NL) 1883; Providence Grays (NL) 1884–85; Philadelphia Athletics (AA) 1887; Indianapolis Hoosiers (NL) 1889; Cincinnati Reds (NL) 1902

Record: 375–333

Never played in the major leagues.

Bancroft managed seven different teams, all of them in the nineteenth century except for a 16-game stint he spent as interim manager of the Reds after Bid McPhee resigned. He finished higher than fourth place on only one occasion, when his 1884 Providence Grays dominated the National League and won the flag. In what may be termed the very first sanctioned World Series against the best of the American Association, the Grays then defeated the New York Metropolitans convincingly, three games to none.

Bancroft later became business manager for the Reds, a position he held for 30 years.

Sam Barkley
Kansas City Cowboys (AA) 1888
Record: 21–36

The second of three managers of Kansas City's American Association entry in 1888.

Barkley played six seasons, mostly in the AA and mostly at second base, and was player-manager for the partial season he managed. He was replaced as manager by Bill Watkins after steering the club for 57 games, but he continued to play for the Cowboys into the 1889 season.

Billy Barnie
Baltimore Orioles (AA) 1883–91; Washington Statesmen (NL) 1892; Louisville Colonels (NL) 1893–94; Brooklyn Bridegrooms (NL) 1897–98
Record: 632–810

Catcher who hit only .180 in 19 major league games, but managed for 14 years.

Barnie was technically a player-manager in 1883, but he saw action in only 17 games. During his tenure as manager he finished as high as third place only once, and had only two seasons above the .500 mark.

In 1900 he was the manager of the Hartford Indians of the minor Eastern League when, in the midst of the season, he died of asthmatic bronchitis.

Ed Barrow
Detroit Tigers (AL) 1903–04; Boston Red Sox (AL) 1918–20
Record: 310–320

Never played in the major leagues, but became most famous for his work as an executive.

Originally a newspaperman from Iowa, Ed Barrow entered the world of baseball through a concessions partnership. He later became a manager, general manager, and part-owner in the minor leagues, and was responsible for signing Honus Wagner.

A successful minor league skipper, Barrow was hired to manage the Tigers in 1903. A little more than halfway through the following season, he left the club because of a dispute with the general manager and was replaced by Bobby Lowe. He became the manager of the Red Sox in 1918 and responded by winning the American League pennant, then defeated the Chicago Cubs to win the World Championship.

Following the 1920 season Barrow became the general manager of the New York Yankees. It was there that he would garner his greatest fame, for he was responsible for building the great Yankee dynasty of that time period. His tenure as GM ran from 1921–45, and it included no fewer than 14 pennants and 10 World Championships.

Barrow was elected to the Hall of Fame in 1953, and he died in December of that same year.

Jack Barry
Boston Red Sox (AL) 1917
Record: 90–62

Player-manager for only one season who posted a .592 winning percentage.

Jack Barry had an 11-year major league career, spent mostly at shortstop and second base, and played on four pennant-winning teams with the Philadelphia Athletics, helping three of them to World Championships. He went to the Red Sox in 1915 while the A's were dismantling their club, and that team immediately won the World Series as well.

In 1917 he was named manager of the Sox when Bill Carrigan decided to retire. Boston went 90–62 under his control, but still finished in second place, nine games behind the Chicago White Sox.

His managerial reign ended when he spent all of 1918 in the military. When he returned the following season, Ed Barrow was at the helm and owner Harry Frazee was now dismantling his own club in order to fund his Broadway shows. In June Barry was traded back to the Athletics, but he decided to retire instead.

Joe Battin
Pittsburgh Alleghenys (AA) 1883, 1884; Pittsburgh Stogies (UA) 1884
Record: 9–23

Third baseman with a 10-year playing career who took the reins of two Pittsburgh clubs only briefly as a player-manager.

Battin was a light hitter who started out with the Cleveland Forest Citys in 1871. He got into only 480 games during his 10 seasons, and managed but 32 of them. He played for seven different clubs, and in 1884 was with the Chicago Browns of the Union Association when that team moved to Pittsburgh and became the Stogies. He filled in as manager there for six games, replacing Ed Hengle, who had guided them in Chicago, and won only one of them before being replaced by Joe Ellick.

Battin also umpired in the National Association in 1874, and in the National League in 1891.

Hank Bauer
Kansas City Athletics (AL) 1961–62; Baltimore Orioles (AL) 1964–68; Oakland Athletics (AL) 1969
Record: 594–544
Fourteen-year major league veteran who hit .277 lifetime with 164 home runs, spending 12 years with the New York Yankees.

Bauer was a solid player who possessed both power and speed, and he helped the Yankees to multiple World Championships during his time in New York. In December of 1959 he was sent to the Kansas City Athletics in a seven-player trade that also included Roger Maris, who would don Yankee pinstripes. In June of 1961, Athletics' owner Charlie Finley replaced Joe Gordon by making Bauer player-manager.

Bauer quit the playing field but continued as manager in 1962, although his club finished in a dismal ninth place. The following season he became a coach with the Orioles, and in 1964 he was named their manager and led them to the World Championship two years later. The AP named him American League Manager of the Year in both '64 and '66.

In July of 1968, the Orioles were in third place when Bauer was fired and replaced by Earl Weaver. He then returned to the A's, who were now in Oakland, and took the reins there, but he was fired in September and replaced by John McNamara with his team in second place.

Don Baylor
Colorado Rockies (NL) 1993–98; Chicago Cubs (NL) 2000–02
Record: 626–689
Solid major league player probably most renowned for setting records for most hit-by-pitches.

Don Baylor would often dig in and crowd the plate against opposing pitchers, and happily took his base on those frequent occasions when he could not get out of the way of a pitch. His 338 career home runs are a testament to his power, and in 1979 with the California Angels he led the American League with 120 runs scored and 139 runs batted in while slugging 36 roundtrippers en route to winning the Most Valuable Player Award.

He retired in 1988, and in 1993 was named the very first manager of the expansion Colorado Rockies. Incredibly, that club would post a winning record in only its third season, putting up a 77–67 mark in 1995 and winning a postseason berth as the National League wild card team. The BBWAA named him the league's Manager of the Year.

Unfortunately Baylor's relationship with Rockies' general manager Bob Gebhard had become rather strained, and at the end of the 1998 campaign he was let go. He later became a hitting coach with the Atlanta Braves, and in 2000 was hired to manage the Cubs. That club finished in sixth place his first year and in third the next, and they were foundering with a 34–49 record in 2002 when Baylor was fired and replaced by Bruce Kimm.

Buddy Bell
Detroit Tigers (AL) 1996–98; Colorado Rockies (NL) 2000–02; Kansas City Royals (AL) 2005–
Record: 450–631
Five-time All-Star third baseman and part of a three-generation major league baseball family.

Bell had a long playing career with the Cleveland Indians, Texas Rangers, Cincinnati Reds, and Houston Astros. His father Gus was an outfielder with the Reds, and his sons David and Mike also reached the majors, with Mike playing briefly for the Reds as well. Buddy was especially renowned for his glove work, winning six Gold Gloves at the hot corner while also amassing 2514 hits in his career.

As a manager he did not fare particularly well. He never had a winning season with the Tigers, and was fired toward the end of the 1998 season and replaced by Larry Parrish. With the Rockies his only winning year was 2000, when he was 82–80 and finished fourth, and after going 6–16 at the beginning of the 2002 campaign he was axed and replaced by Clint Hurdle.

In 2005 he was hired to manage the Royals when manager Tony Peña abruptly resigned.

John Benjamin
Elizabeth Resolutes (NA) 1873
Record: 2–21
Never played in the major leagues...and his team barely did so.

The Elizabeth Resolutes lasted only 23 games in the original National Association and won but 2 of those. Most clubs that year played a schedule of between 50 and 60 games. In the standings the Resolutes bested only the Baltimore Marylands, who lasted a mere six contests and lost them all, then Elizabeth disappeared from the scene.

Vern Benson
Atlanta Braves (NL) 1977
Record: 1–0
Spent many years in baseball in many facets of the game, most of them behind the scenes.

Benson was an instructor and coach with several major

league organizations. In 1977 he was the third base coach for the Braves under Dave Bristol when the club was suffering through a 16-game losing streak. Braves' owner Ted Turner gave Bristol a 10-day paid leave and decided to become the manager himself during that time.

After one game, however, which the Braves lost, National League president Chub Feeney created a rule stating that a team's manager may not have a financial stake in his club, and he relieved Turner of his field duties. An angry Turner lashed out at Feeney publicly, but he stepped down and named Benson manager for the next game. The Braves promptly snapped their losing streak by defeating the Pittsburgh Pirates, 6–1, and that would encompass Benson's entire managerial career.

Bristol was brought back the next day, and the Braves lost again.

Yogi Berra
New York Yankees (AL) 1964, 1984–85; New York Mets (NL) 1972–75
Record: 484–444
Famous as much for his "Yogi-isms" as for his Hall of Fame playing career.

Lawrence Peter Berra's nickname originated with a childhood friend who thought he resembled a Hindu yogi. Berra played both the outfield and catcher during an 18-year career with the Yankees and a subsequent four-game stint with the Mets. He retired with a .285 lifetime batting average and 358 home runs, and he played in 14 World Series and helped win 10 championships. He retired with World Series records for most games played with 75, most at-bats with 259, most hits with 71, and most doubles with 10. He was named American League Most Valuable Player three times during the 1950s, and he was an All-Star 18 times.

A player-coach for the Yankees in 1963, he became the team's manager the following season and guided them to the AL pennant by a single game over the Chicago White Sox. After a close, seven-game World Series loss to the St. Louis Cardinals, Yogi was fired.

He became a coach with the Mets, and in 1972 was made manager of that club. He guided them to a third-place finish his first year and to the National League pennant in 1973, but the Mets lost the World Series to the Oakland Athletics in seven games. The Mets fired him during the 1975 season, and in 1976 he returned to the Yankees as a coach.

He was again appointed Yankees' manager when owner George Steinbrenner fired Billy Martin following the 1983 campaign. The team finished third under Berra in 1984, and in 1985 they started 6–10 when Steinbrenner replaced him with Martin.

Yogi then coached the Houston Astros, and he retired in 1992. The Yankees retired number 8 for both Berra and Bill Dickey in 1972, the year Yogi was inducted into the Hall of Fame.

Terry Bevington
Chicago White Sox (AL) 1995–97
Record: 222–214
Third base coach with the White Sox who replaced the fired Gene Lamont in June of 1995.

Bevington never played in the major leagues, but during his three years as manager he garnered a third-place finish and two second-place showings.

His reign was almost immediately controversial when, on July 22, 1995, the White Sox got into a bench-clearing brawl with the Milwaukee Brewers and Bevington himself wound up in a fistfight with opposing manager Phil Garner.

Despite an American League Central Division second-place finish in 1997, with the team coming in six games behind the Cleveland Indians, the Chisox had only an 80–81 record. Bevington was replaced by Jerry Manuel the following season.

Hugo Bezdek
Pittsburgh Pirates (NL) 1917–19
Record: 166–187
Former Penn State football coach.

When the Pirates went 20–40 to start the 1917 season, manager Jimmy Callahan was fired and was replaced by Honus Wagner, who became player-manager. Hugo Bezdek, a Czechoslovakian, took charge of Pittsburgh's business affairs. Wagner resigned after posting a 1–4 record, however, deciding that management was not for him, and Bezdek was named his replacement.

After the Pirates finished in eighth place that season, Bezdek brought them in fourth the following two, his club finishing over .500 on both occasions. But he was replaced by George Gibson in 1920.

In 1937 the Cleveland Rams, who had played in the second American Football League the previous season, joined the National Football League and named Bezdek their head coach. The club failed to score more than 10 points in any game, however, and finished with a 1–10 record.

Bickerson
Washington Nationals (AA) 1884
Record: 0–1
First name unknown.

Bickerson remains one of the many mysteries of nineteenth century baseball. He took over for manager Holly

Hollingshead at the helm of the Washington Nationals of the American Association—the third of six teams to bear that name in major league history—for a single game, a game he lost. The Nationals finished in thirteenth and last place with a .190 winning percentage, 41 games behind the New York Metropolitans.

Joe Birmingham
Cleveland Molly McGuires (AL) 1912–14; Cleveland Indians (AL) 1915
Record: 170–191
Nine-year major league veteran for Cleveland who became a 28-year-old player-manager in 1912.

The Cleveland club, which was called the Molly McGuires in honor of the previous year's manager, Jim "Deacon" McGuire, was at first led by Harry Davis in 1912. The team was 54–71 when Davis was replaced by Birmingham, the club's center fielder who had a somewhat light bat but an excellent glove and a strong arm. The Molly McGuires went 21–7 the rest of the way to finish at 75–78.

The team finished a promising third in 1913, but dropped to eighth the following season. In 1915, the newly-renamed Indians were 12–16 and in sixth place when Birmingham was fired by owner Charles W. Somers and replaced by Lee Fohl.

Del Bissonette
Boston Braves (NL) 1945
Record: 25–34
Managed 60 games, one of which ended in a tie.

Bissonette played five years for the Brooklyn Dodgers at first base, hitting over .300 twice, and in 1928, his rookie season, he hit 25 home runs to set a new rookie record for the Bums.

Often injured, Del lasted only 604 major league games, mostly as a first baseman, and in 1945 he was a coach for the Braves when he was called upon to replace Bob Coleman for the final 60 games of the season as manager. He won only 25 of those games, and the Braves finished in sixth place.

Bud Black
San Diego Padres (NL) 2007–
Record: 0–0
Son of minor league hockey center Harry Black of the Los Angeles Monarchs.

A 17-game winner in 1984 with the Kansas City Royals, Black pitched for 15 seasons and won 121 major league games. He finished his career in 1995 with the Cleveland Indians before becoming a special assistant to the general manager with that club. In 1998 he was named

pitching coach of the Buffalo Bisons, the Indians' AAA affiliate, then returned to his previous post the next year.

In 2000 he was hired by the Angels as pitching coach, and in 2007 replaced Bruce Bochy as the manager of the Padres.

Lena Blackburne
Chicago White Sox (AL) 1928–29
Record: 99–133
Light-hitting major league shortstop with several teams.

Blackburne was a coach with the White Sox when he replaced Ray Schalk as manager in 1928 about halfway through the season. He finished sixth, then seventh the following year.

He later returned to coaching and became a scout, and is credited with the idea of rubbing mud on baseballs to remove the shiny, slick finish. He died in 1968 at the age of 81.

Ray Blades
St. Louis Cardinals (NL) 1939–40; Brooklyn Dodgers (NL) 1948
Record: 107–85
Solid-hitting, 10-year Cardinal outfielder who became a manager.

Hitting over .300 in 6 of his 10 years, Blades peaked with a .342 average in 1925. He finished at .301 lifetime, and was a player-coach from 1930–32. In 1939 he was named manager.

Ray managed the Redbirds to a second-place finish his first year at the helm, bringing them in 4½ games behind the Cincinnati Reds, but in 1940 they started out 14–24 when Blades was fired by owner Sam Breadon and replaced by Billy Southworth.

He later became a coach with the Brooklyn Dodgers, and in 1948 was named interim manager for one game—which he won—between the reigns of Leo Durocher and Burt Shotton. He eventually returned to the Cardinals as a coach, then coached the Chicago Cubs.

Walter Blair
Buffalo Blues (FL) 1915
Record: 1–1
Backup catcher for the New York Yankees who joined the Federal League in 1914 with the Buffalo Buffeds, later the Blues.

Blair hit only .217 lifetime in seven seasons. He was a catcher for the Blues in 1915 when he was named interim manager for two games between the tenures of Larry Schlafly and Harry Lord.

Ossie Bluege
Washington Nationals (AL) 1943–47
Record: 375–394
Infielder noted mainly for his defense, spending 18 years as a major league ballplayer.

Ossie Bluege (whose last name was pronounced "Bloogy," with a hard *g*) was a somewhat average hitter, batting .272 lifetime, but with his glove he led the American League in double plays three times and in assists on four occasions. His best season was 1928, when he batted .297 with 33 doubles, and in 1935 he was named to the All-Star team.

Bluege spent his entire career with Washington, and upon retiring from the playing field he became a coach with the club. He continued in that role through 1942, then was named manager. In five seasons Ossie managed two second-place finishes, then he became the club's farm director from 1948 through 1956. In 1957, when the Nationals returned to their old name of Senators, Bluege was named the team's comptroller, a position he would hold when the club moved to Minnesota and became the Twins in 1961 and on through the 1971 season.

Bruce Bochy
San Diego Padres (NL) 1995–2006; San Francisco Giants (NL) 2007–
Record: 951–975
First former San Diego player to become manager of the Padres.

A backup catcher during a nine-year playing career that included the Houston Astros and New York Mets in addition to the Padres, Bochy became a minor league manager after retiring from the playing field. He returned to San Diego as a coach in 1993, and after the club finished last the following season under manager Jim Riggleman, Bruce was named skipper in 1995.

In 1996 the Padres won 91 games under Bochy and Bruce became the first San Diego skipper to be named National League Manager of the Year by the BBWAA. Two years later the team went 98–64 and captured the NL pennant before being swept by the New York Yankees in the World Series. In both 2005 and 2006 they won the NL Western Division crown, but were swept by the St. Louis Cardinals in the Division Series on each occasion.

Bochy was still under contract with the Padres when the club gave permission for the Giants to interview him for the managerial vacancy in San Francisco caused by the firing of Felipe Alou. The Giants liked what they heard and hired him as their new skipper for 2007.

John Boles
Florida Marlins (NL) 1996, 1999–2001
Record: 205–241
Manager with the rare distinction of never having played professionally at any level.

John Boles managed in the minor leagues and worked in the front office of several teams before replacing Rene Lachemann in the midst of the 1996 season as manager of the Marlins. He responded with a 40–35 record, becoming the first Florida skipper to post a winning record. The following two seasons he returned to the front office while Jim Leyland took over (winning the World Series in 1997), but when Leyland left after the 1998 campaign Boles returned to the helm.

Unfortunately the Marlins were in the process of cutting their budget and dismantling their championship club, so Boles did not have much to work with. He was fired 48 games into the 2001 season and was replaced by Tony Perez.

Tommy Bond
Worcester Ruby Legs (NL) 1882
Record: 2–4
Outstanding nineteenth century pitcher and outfielder.

In 10 major league seasons Tommy Bond posted a record of 234–163 as a pitcher, and in 1877 and 1878 with the Boston Red Caps he led the National League with 40 victories each season. That 1877 campaign saw him win the league's first pitching Triple Crown, as he topped the circuit with 40 wins, a 2.11 earned run average, and 170 strikeouts, as well as with 6 shutouts.

In 1882 with the Worcester Ruby Legs he played only two games but managed six as a replacement for Freeman Brown before he himself was replaced by Jack Chapman. The Ruby Legs finished dead last that season, 37 games behind the Chicago White Stockings.

Bond would eventually become the last surviving participant of the NL's inaugural 1876 season.

Bob Boone
Kansas City Royals (AL) 1995–97; Cincinnati Reds (NL) 2001–03
Record: 371–444
With his father Ray and his sons Bret and Aaron, part of a three-generation major league baseball family.

A four-time All-Star catcher, Bob Boone put together a 19-year major league career with the Philadelphia Phillies, California Angels, and Kansas City Royals. He retired in 1990 as the all-time leader in games caught, a mark that was later eclipsed by Carlton Fisk although Boone still holds the National League record. He won seven Gold Gloves.

As a manager he never achieved a .500 record. With the Royals in 1996 he used 152 different lineups in 162 games. The following year, with the team 36–46, he was fired and replaced by Tony Muser. In 2001 he took the helm of the Reds, but suffered a similar fate two years later when his squad was meandering through a 46–58 record. He was fired in Cincinnati and replaced by Dave Miley.

In 2005 Boone became a special assistant to general manager Jim Bowden when the Montreal Expos relocated and became the Washington Nationals.

Steve Boros
Oakland Athletics (AL) 1983–84; San Diego Padres (NL) 1986
Record: 168–200
Minor league Most Valuable Player with a low-key managerial approach.

As a third baseman Boros managed only a .245 average in seven major league seasons, although he had started out well with the 1961 Detroit Tigers before a broken collarbone ended his season prematurely.

He managed the A's in 1983, but was fired in 1984 after starting out 20–24 and was replaced by Jackie Moore. With the Padres in 1986 he posted a 74–88 record and was promptly replaced by Larry Bowa.

On June 6, 1986, Boros was ejected from a game against the Atlanta Braves before the contest even started when he tried to give umpire Charlie Williams a videotape of a controversial play from the previous night's game.

Jim Bottomley
St. Louis Browns (AL) 1937
Record: 21–56
Hall of Fame first baseman with a 16-year major league playing career.

"Sunny Jim," as he was known, posted a .310 lifetime batting average. Most of his career was spent with the St. Louis Cardinals, although he spent several seasons with the Cincinnati Reds and two with the Browns. In 1925 he led the National League with 227 hits and 44 doubles, and the following season led with 40 doubles and 120 runs batted in. He garnered the 1928 NL Most Valuable Player Award when he batted .325 and topped the circuit with 31 home runs (tying him with Hack Wilson), 136 RBIs, and 20 triples.

He was playing and coaching for the Browns in 1937 when he was tapped to replace Rogers Hornsby as manager about halfway through the season. The club finished in last place, a whopping 56 games behind the New York Yankees.

Lou Boudreau
Cleveland Indians (AL) 1942–50; Boston Red Sox (AL)
1952–54; Kansas City Athletics (AL) 1955–57; Chicago Cubs (NL) 1960
Record: 1162–1224
Player-manager and eight-time All-Star.

Boudreau had played only two full seasons with the Indians when the club named him its player-manager. He was only 24 years old at the time, becoming the youngest person to manage an entire season in major league history.

Lou became known for his role in converting Bob Lemon from a third baseman and outfielder into a pitcher, and for creating a defensive shift against Boston's Ted Williams that would shortly be employed around the league.

He won the American League batting title in 1944 with a .327 mark, also leading the circuit for the second of three times with exactly 45 doubles. In 1948 he garnered the league's Most Valuable Player Award when he batted .355 with 34 doubles, a career-high 18 home runs, and 106 runs batted in. The Tribe finished in a tie with the Boston Red Sox in the standings, and in a one-game playoff Boudreau hit two home runs and two singles as the Indians topped the Bosox, 8–3. In the World Series Cleveland defeated the other Boston team of the time, the Braves, four games to two.

Boudreau signed with the Red Sox, solely as a player, following the 1950 season, but in 1952 he became Boston's player-manager, although he appeared in only four games.

He then quit the playing field but continued as manager through 1954. In 1955 he became the manager of the Kansas City Athletics, but his teams finished sixth and eighth his only two full seasons at the helm and were in eighth place in 1957 with a 36–67 record when Boudreau was replaced by Harry Craft. He was a broadcaster for Chicago in May of 1960 when the Cubs hired him to manage, and he guided that club to a seventh-place finish.

The Indians retired his number 5 in 1970, the same year he was inducted into the Hall of Fame.

Larry Bowa
San Diego Padres (NL) 1987–88; Philadelphia Phillies (NL) 2001–04
Record: 418–435
Excellent major league shortstop and five-time All-Star with a fiery temper.

After a 16-year playing career with the Philadelphia Phillies, Chicago Cubs, and New York Mets, Bowa became the manager of the Padres, but his aggressive personality and short temper did not endear him to his players. The club finished in last place in 1987, and was off to a 16–30 start the following year when he was fired and replaced by Jack McKeon.

In 2001 he took the reins of the Phillies and immediately led them to a second-place finish, a mere two games behind the Atlanta Braves. As a result the BBWAA named him the National League Manager of the Year. In succeeding seasons he never finished lower than third, but the Phillies fired him following the 2004 campaign and replaced him with Charlie Manuel.

Frank Bowerman
Boston Doves (NL) 1909
Record: 22–54

Fifteen-year catcher and first baseman with several major league teams.

Bowerman had a temper, as evidenced by the fact that he once got into an off-the-field fight with player-manager Fred Clarke of the Pittsburgh Pirates—an incident that earned him a $100 fine—and later punched a fan in Cincinnati who had been riding him during a game there.

Frank became player-manager of the Doves partway through the 1909 season, but managed only a .295 winning percentage.

Bill Boyd
Brooklyn Atlantics (NA) 1875
Record: 0–2

A .290 hitter during a four-year National Association career who became player-manager for only two games for a really bad team.

The Brooklyn Atlantics went 2–40 under previous manager Charlie Pabor in 1875, then 0–2 under Boyd to finish at 2–42. That computes to a winning percentage of .045, and the club ended up 51½ games behind the league champion Boston Red Stockings.

Ken Boyer
St. Louis Cardinals (NL) 1978–80
Record: 166–190

Along with Cloyd and Clete, one of three Boyer brothers to play in the major leagues.

Boyer was a good-hitting third baseman who won five Gold Gloves at the hot corner. A seven-time All-Star with the Cardinals, in 1964 he also won the National League Most Valuable Player Award when he batted .295 with 24 home runs, a league-leading 119 runs batted in, and 30 doubles. He was a major factor in the Redbirds' defeat of the New York Yankees in the World Series, smashing a grand slam in Game 4 in a 4–3 victory, and hitting another home run in the decisive seventh game. He also hit for the cycle in 1961 and did so again in '64.

He retired in 1969 and became a coach with St. Louis two years later. In early 1978 he was named the club's skipper, and he guided them to fifth- and third-place finishes his first two seasons but started off 18–33 in 1980 when he was let go.

Boyer died of lung cancer in 1982. In 1984 the Cardinals retired his number 14 on what would have been his fifty-third birthday.

Bill Bradley
Cleveland Naps (AL) 1905; Brooklyn Brookfeds (FL) 1914;
   Brooklyn Tip-Tops (FL) 1914
Record: 97–98

Outstanding third baseman with a 14-year major league career.

With the Cleveland Naps in 1905 (who were aptly named for player-manager Nap Lajoie), Bradley was called upon to take the reins as player-manager himself when Lajoie was spiked during a game and developed a nearly fatal case of blood poisoning. The Naps were 20–21 under Bradley, and Lajoie returned later in the season to a club that would finish just below .500.

Bradley jumped to the rival Federal League in 1914 as player-manager of the Brooklyn Brookfeds, who were renamed the Tip-Tops during the season for owner Robert B. Ward's Tip-Top bakeries. Bradley appeared in only seven games as a player, and the club finished 77–77. The following season he finished out his playing career with the Kansas City Packers of the FL.

Bobby Bragan
Pittsburgh Pirates (NL) 1956–57; Cleveland Indians (AL)
   1958; Milwaukee Braves (NL) 1963–65; Atlanta Braves
   (NL) 1966
Record: 443–478

Had a long major league career in many capacities.

Starting out in the 1940s as a shortstop and catcher, Bragan had a seven-year playing career in the majors before becoming a minor league manager. He would also serve as a scout, a major league coach, and the president of the minor Texas League. As a manager he was renowned for his altercations with umpires.

Hired to manage the Pirates in 1956, he was fired in August the following year after a dismal season and a half. He was then hired by Cleveland, but was fired midway through that season with a 31–36 record. Beginning in 1963 he managed three full seasons with the Milwaukee Braves, but although his club finished over .500 all three years, they could place no better than fifth. He was the team's first manager in Atlanta, but was fired partway through the 1966 season with a 52–59 record and was replaced by Billy Hitchcock.

In 2005 the Fort Worth Cats of the Central Baseball League signed Bragan to a one-game managerial contract, specifically so that he could break Connie Mack's record as the oldest manager in professional baseball history. At the age of 87 years, 9 months, and 16 days, he topped Mack's record by 7 days when he piloted the Cats on August 15. The game was suspended due to rain and continued the next day, and Bragan's record therefore now stands at 87 years, 9 months, and 17 days. Bobby did not get to manage the entire contest, however, because he was ejected from the game for arguing with the home plate umpire. He then proceeded into the stands and signed autographs for fans.

Bragan was assisted in the dugout by the Cats' regular manager, 80-year-old Wayne Terwilliger, who dropped a notch in the senior standings to become the third-oldest skipper in professional baseball history.

Bob Brenly
Arizona Diamondbacks (NL) 2001–04
Record: 303–262
Good defensive catcher with some power who played nine years for the San Francisco Giants and briefly for the Toronto Blue Jays.

Brenly's major league career began in 1981, and by 1984 he was the starting catcher for the Giants. He was named to the All-Star squad that year on the strength of a .291 season with 20 home runs and 80 runs batted in. For each of four consecutive seasons beginning that year, he banged at least 16 roundtrippers.

In a game in 1986 against the Atlanta Braves while he was filling in at third base, he committed four errors in one inning.

After retiring in 1989 Brenly became a coach with the Giants and later a broadcaster. In 2001 he became only the second manager of the Diamondbacks, replacing Buck Showalter, and he immediately took the team to the National League West title, ironically by two games over the Giants. They would eventually defeat the New York Yankees in a seven-game series to capture the World Championship.

They finished first again in 2002, but this time were swept by the St. Louis Cardinals in the Division Series. A third-place finish the following year was followed by a 29–50 start in 2004, at which point Brenly was fired and replaced by Al Pedrique.

Roger Bresnahan
St. Louis Cardinals (NL) 1909–12; Chicago Cubs (NL) 1915
Record: 328–432
Hall of Fame player who began his major league career in the late nineteenth century and eventually played every position.

Bresnahan began as a pitcher but later spent most of his time as a catcher. He had a lifetime .279 batting aver-

age with several teams, and is credited with pioneering much of the protective equipment now worn by backstops.

He was player-manager for both the Cardinals and the Cubs, but his teams generally did not do well. They came in over .500 only once, and never finished higher than fourth place. Bresnahan later coached for the New York Giants and the Detroit Tigers.

Dave Bristol
Cincinnati Reds (NL) 1966–69; Milwaukee Brewers (AL) 1970–72; Atlanta Braves (NL) 1976–77, 1977; San Francisco Giants (NL) 1979–80
Record: 657–764
Never played in the major leagues, and suffered through the burden of managing some rather dismal teams.

Bristol's best years were as the manager of the Reds, where he never failed to achieve a .500 winning percentage and finished in third place in 1969. He was replaced by Sparky Anderson following the season, however, and was then hired by the Seattle Pilots, who were moving to Milwaukee to become the Brewers. Two ninety-plus-loss seasons ensued, and the club was 10–20 in 1972 when Bristol was fired and replaced by Del Crandall.

He became the manager of the Braves in 1976, and the following year, after an 8–21 start, owner Ted Turner forced him to take a 10-day paid leave of absence and inserted himself as interim manager. When National League president Chub Feeney nixed Turner's plans after one game, creating a rule that prohibited managers from having a financial interest in their teams, Turner named coach Vern Benson manager for the next game and then brought Bristol back.

Things did not get much better for Dave, and he was fired in October and became a coach with the Giants. He would become skipper in San Francisco in 1979, replacing Joe Altobelli for the final 22 games of the season, and after a fifth-place finish in 1980 he was let go by the Giants.

Freeman Brown
Worcester Ruby Legs (NL) 1882
Record: 9–32
Had the misfortune of managing one of the most dismal teams in major league history.

Brown's Ruby Legs won only 9 of the first 41 games of the 1882 National League season. Brown was replaced by Tommy Bond for six games and then by Jack Chapman the rest of the way, but the club would win only nine more en route to an 18–66 overall record and a last-place finish.

Mordecai Brown
St. Louis Terriers (FL) 1914

Record: 50–63

Hall of Fame pitcher with a brief managerial stint.

Having lost part of his index finger and the use of his little finger to a farm machinery accident as a young man, Brown earned the nickname "Three Finger," but his disfigurement lent him the ability to throw a natural sinkerball. In a 14-year playing career he won 239 games, reaching 20 victories six consecutive times from 1906 through 1911. In 1909 he led the National League with 27 victories, after helping the Chicago Cubs to World Championships in 1907 and 1908.

In 1914 he managed 114 games for the Federal League's St. Louis Terriers while going 12–6 on the mound. His short managerial stint concluded, he went 17–8 pitching for the Chicago Whales in 1915, then returned to the Cubs for the last 12 games of his career the following season.

Tom Brown
Washington Statesmen (NL) 1897–98
Record: 64–72

Speedy outfielder who played 17 seasons for many teams.

Brown began his playing career in 1882 with the Baltimore Orioles of the American Association, and he hit .304 in 45 games. Always a threat to steal bases, he led the AA with 106 thefts in 1891 with the Boston Red Stockings (under slightly different rules, awarding a stolen base to a runner who advanced an extra base on a hit), and also topped that circuit with 189 hits, 177 runs scored, and 21 triples. Two years later he led the National League with 66 swipes while playing for the Louisville Colonels.

In 1897 and for a short time in '98 he was player-manager of the Washington Statesmen, but the club did not fare well. After a 12–26 start in 1898, Brown was replaced by Jack Doyle. He retired from the playing field with at least 657 stolen bases (they were not recorded during his first four seasons) and with 138 triples.

Earle Brucker, Sr.
Cincinnati Reds (NL) 1952
Record: 3–2

Former catcher who filled in as manager of the Reds for five games during the 1952 season.

Brucker had a sparse five-year playing career for the Philadelphia Athletics. He played 102 games in his rookie season of 1937, and the following year batted .374 in 53 games. In 1943 he retired with a .290 lifetime batting average in 241 contests.

He was a coach for the Reds in 1952 when he was called upon to manage the club on an interim basis when Luke Sewell was fired. He managed five games, and to his credit, the Reds won three of them. He then returned to coaching when Rogers Hornsby was hired as Sewell's replacement.

Al Buckenberger
Columbus Buckeyes (AA) 1889–90; Pittsburgh Pirates (NL) 1892, 1892–94; St. Louis Browns (NL) 1895; Boston Bostons (NL) 1902–04
Record: 488–539

Kind, gentlemanly manager who never played in the major leagues.

A minor league infielder who never made the cut at the game's top level, Buckenberger became a minor league manager in 1884 and would make his way to The Show in that manner. His first year at the helm of the National League's Columbus Buckeyes was rather unsuccessful, as the club finished sixth, and they were fifth the next year when he was let go. The Buckeyes would go on to finish second without him.

He had much more luck in Pittsburgh, failing to finish at .500 only once and managing a second-place showing in 1893. He was only 16–34 with the St. Louis Browns in 1895 when he was replaced by Chris Von der Ahe, and he would not manage in the majors again until the Boston Bostons made him their skipper in 1902. A third-place finish that first year would be his best in Beantown, and two subpar performances by the team after that would round out his managerial career.

Charlie Buffinton
Philadelphia Quakers (PL) 1890
Record: 61–54

Outstanding nineteenth century pitcher who posted 233 wins in his career.

One of the first pitchers permitted to use an overhand delivery, Buffinton threw an early version of what is today recognized as a curveball. He baffled hitters to the tune of a 2.96 lifetime earned run average and 1700 strikeouts in 11 seasons. He also played first base and the outfield for most of those years.

His best season was 1884 with the Boston Bostons, when he won 48 games (13 consecutively), pitched 587 innings, threw a no-hitter (despite losing the game), struck out 17 batters in one game, and pitched 16 innings in a 1–1 tie.

In 1890 Buffinton won a lawsuit against his previous team, the National League's Philadelphia Nationals, and was released from his contract. He then signed with the Philadelphia entry in the new rival Players League, the Quakers, and he became that team's player-manager after the first 16 games of the season as a replacement for Jim Fogarty. His club finished at 68–63, but the PL folded after that one season and Buffinton found himself blackballed by the NL because of his "traitorous" action. He caught on in the American Association the next year, and would eventually be accepted back into the NL although he would not manage again.

Jack Burdock
Boston Bostons (NL) 1883
Record: 30–24
Eighteen-year major league infielder nicknamed "Black Jack."

Burdock, as player-manager, was a temporary replacement for manager John Morrill for the Boston Bostons for the last 54 games of the 1883 season. In fourth place when Burdock took over, the club ended up winning the National League pennant by four games over the Chicago White Stockings.

Morrill returned the following season. Burdock continued to play second base for the Bostons, and in one game that year was knocked unconscious by Providence Grays' outfielder Paul Hines, who collided with Jack while trying to break up a double play. After 15 minutes Burdock came to, and he stayed in the game. Almost immediately, Hines took a big lead off second base and was picked off, with Burdock fittingly applying the tag.

Jimmy Burke
St. Louis Cardinals (NL) 1905; St. Louis Browns (AL) 1918–20
Record: 206–236
St. Louis native who played several years at third base for the Cardinals and managed two hometown teams.

A third baseman, Burke became player-manager for the Redbirds in 1905 after the team started 5–9 under Kid Nichols. His record was a mere 34–56 when he himself was then replaced by Stanley Robison.

He would not play again after that season, but he did become a minor league manager and a coach for the Detroit Tigers and was named skipper of the Browns in 1918, replacing Jimmy Austin partway through the season. He almost managed a .500 finish in 1920, missing by just one game, and then disappeared from the managerial scene and became a coach for the Boston Red Sox, the Chicago Cubs, and the New York Yankees.

Burke suffered a debilitating stroke in 1933, and he died an invalid in St. Louis in 1942.

George Burnham
Indianapolis Hoosiers (NL) 1887
Record: 6–22
The first of three men to manage Indianapolis in 1887.

The Hoosiers started out a dismal 6–22 under Burnham when George was replaced. The club did not fare well under its other two managers either, however, and finished in last place, 43 games off the pace.

Tom Burns
Pittsburgh Pirates (NL) 1892; Chicago Orphans (NL) 1898–99
Record: 187–170
Played 12 years for Chicago and one for Pittsburgh, mainly at third base.

Burns' last year as a player was 1892, when he was also called upon to fill in for Al Buckenberger as player-manager for 60 games. He later managed two seasons for the Chicago Orphans and finished over .500 both years, although the club ended up fourth in 1898 and a mere eighth (out of 12 teams) in 1899. He had replaced the extremely popular Cap Anson in Chicago; it was Anson's departure, in fact, that led to the team's name being changed from Colts to Orphans. Anson had been seen as a father figure by many of his players.

Bill Burwell
Pittsburgh Pirates (NL) 1947
Record: 1–0
Pitched 70 games in three seasons in the majors.

Burwell's only managerial experience came in the final game of the 1947 season, when he replaced player-manager Billy Herman. The Pirates won that game, although they finished in a tie for last place in the National League.

Donie Bush
Washington Nationals (AL) 1923; Pittsburgh Pirates (NL) 1927–29; Chicago White Sox (AL) 1930–31; Cincinnati Reds (NL) 1933
Record: 497–539
Longtime shortstop for the Detroit Tigers and Washington Nationals who would eventually serve as a player, minor league manager, major league manager, scout, and minor league owner.

Bush was an average to light hitter but a very speedy runner. He had 404 stolen bases in a 16-year career, and he set the then-rookie American League record in 1909 with 53. For the first 10 years of his career he stole fewer than 34 only twice, and only once in a full season. He led the league five times in bases on balls and once in runs scored.

As a manager he won the 1927 National League pennant with the Pirates, but his club was swept in the World Series by the New York Yankees. The Bucs were fourth the following year although they had a .559 winning percentage, and they were in second in August of 1929 when Bush resigned and was replaced by Jewel Ens.

He had two rather poor seasons with the White Sox the next two years, and after a pennant-winning season with the Minneapolis Millers of the minor American Association in 1932, Bush took over the Cincinnati Reds for one season. That club went 58–94, finishing in eighth and last place.

Bush continued managing in the minor leagues, and eventually became the owner of the Indianapolis Indians.

Ormond Butler
Pittsburgh Alleghenys (AA) 1883
Record: 17–36
Managed only 53 games.

The 1883 Pittsburgh Alleghenys of the American Association started out 12–20 under Al Pratt, who had guided them to a .500 finish in the league's inaugural season the year before. Pratt was replaced by Butler, who could manage only a 17–36 record before himself being replaced by Joe Battin for the final 13 games of the season. Pittsburgh finished in second-last place, 35 games off the lead.

Charlie Byrne
Brooklyn Atlantics (AA) 1885–87
Record: 174–172
Never played in the major leagues, but managed 2½ seasons in Brooklyn.

When the 1885 Atlantics started out 15–22 under Charlie Hackett, another Charlie, this one with the surname Byrne, a former journalist, took the reins. Byrne just happened to be the club president. The team was 38–37 under Byrne to finish out the year six games under .500. The following season they were a much stronger 76–61, but still ended up 16 games behind the American Association champion St. Louis Browns. After falling to 14 games under .500 and sixth place in 1887, Byrne replaced himself with Bill McGunnigle.

He worked on baseball's arbitration committee, handling disagreements between the AA and the National League, and was respected as a fine negotiator.

Nixey Callahan
Chicago White Stockings (AL) 1903; Chicago Uniques (AL) 1904; Chicago White Sox (AL) 1904, 1912–14; Pittsburgh Pirates (NL) 1916–17
Record: 394–458
Multitalented, versatile player who had little success as a manager.

Jim "Nixey" Callahan was a pitcher, infielder, and outfielder. He hit .273 lifetime as a position player and was always a threat on the bases, peaking in 1911 when he stole 45. In 1905, he swiped four in a single game.

As a pitcher he was a 20-game winner on two occasions and finished with a lifetime record of 99–73. At the plate he had three five-hit games in his career, all of them while he was pitching, becoming the only hurler to accomplish such a feat. In 1902 he also pitched a no-hitter.

In 1903 he became player-manager of the White Stockings, who would become the Uniques and then the White Sox the following year, and would return to manage them again in 1912. But with them and with the Pirates he would never garner better than a fourth-place finish. The Bucs were 20–40 out of the gate in 1917 when he was fired and replaced by Honus Wagner.

Bill Cammeyer
New York Mutuals (NL) 1876
Record: 21–35
Tanner who was the first to enclose a field specifically for baseball.

Cammeyer, who was the Mutuals' president from 1875–76, also managed the club for one season. The 21–35 record posted by the team (who had previously played in the National Association) represented nearly a full season in the National League's inaugural year of 1876. The club finished sixth of the eight teams in the circuit, 26 games behind the Chicago White Stockings. Bill decided not to take his team on its final road trip to finish out the season, and both he and the Mutuals were expelled from the league.

Count Campau
St. Louis Browns (AA) 1890
Record: 27–14
One of six managers for the Browns in 1890.

Charles "Count" Campau played three seasons in the major leagues (1888 with the National League's Detroit Wolverines, 1890 with the Browns, and 1894 for two games with the NL's Washington Statesmen).

As an outfielder in 1890 he led the American Association with 9 home runs (also clubbing 12 triples), and as player-manager for part of the season was 27–14.

Joe Cantillon
Washington Nationals (AL) 1907–09
Record: 158–297
Umpire who became the owner of the minor league Minneapolis Millers and then the manager of the Washington Nationals.

Cantillon's teams did not fare well, losing 102 games in 1907 and 110 in 1909. That '09 club, in fact, won only 42 games for a dismal winning percentage of .276. Managing only seventh- and eighth-place finishes, Cantillon was replaced by Jimmy McAleer in 1910.

Max Carey
Brooklyn Dodgers (NL) 1932–33
Record: 146–161
Hall of Fame center fielder for the Pittsburgh Pirates and Brooklyn Dodgers.

In a 20-year playing career, speedy Carey led the league in stolen bases 10 times, in triples twice, in walks twice, and in runs scored once. He amassed 738 steals lifetime, a National League record at the time, along with 2665 hits. In 1922 he stole 51 bases in 53 tries. Defensively he led the league in both putouts and total chances on nine occasions.

In 1932 he replaced the popular Wilbert Robinson as manager of the Dodgers. In two seasons his clubs finished third and sixth, and he was then replaced himself by Casey Stengel.

Carey later became a manager in the All-American Girls Professional Baseball League, taking the helm of the Milwaukee Chicks and the Fort Wayne Daisies and even becoming president of the league for a time. He then became a minor league manager and a scout and was inducted into the Hall of Fame in 1961.

Tom Carey
Baltimore Lord Baltimores (NA) 1873; New York Mutuals (NA) 1874
Record: 27–21
Nine-year major league infielder who played through all five seasons of the National Association's existence.

Thomas John Carey played for six different teams during those nine seasons, and was player-manager for two of them for two partial seasons. His 1873 Lord Baltimores finished in third place, and his 1874 Mutuals came in second. He was also one of the first players in the National League, taking the field in 1876 with the Hartford Dark Blues.

Bill Carrigan
Boston Red Sox (AL) 1913–16, 1927–29
Record: 489–500
Catcher who spent his entire playing career with the Red Sox.

In 1913, about halfway through the season, Carrigan was named player-manager to replace Jake Stahl with the team foundering in fifth place. They finished fourth, then came in second the following year. The next two seasons would mark the highlight of Carrigan's career, as he added a bright young hurler by the name of Babe Ruth to his pitching staff and led the Bosox to back-to-back World Championships. At that point he quit and went home to Maine to become a banker.

Bill returned to the fold in 1927, but this was not the same team. The Red Sox had finished last in 1926, and Carrigan was unable to help them, as they remained in the basement for the next three seasons as well. Carrigan then retired for good.

Bob Caruthers
St. Louis Browns (NL) 1892
Record: 16–32
Outstanding athlete as both a pitcher and an outfielder.

In a nine-year pitching career Caruthers posted 218 victories against 99 losses, leading the American Association with 40 wins in both 1885 and 1889. Five of his teams won pennants. He was also an excellent hitter, and after hurting his arm he turned to the outfield and continued to play. He finished his career with a .301 lifetime batting average and displayed speed on the bases as well, swiping 152 total.

He was player-manager for the Browns in 1892 (the last of five managers to take the helm that season), but the revolving door did not help and the team finished eleventh out of 12 clubs, 46 games behind the league leader.

Phil Cavarretta
Chicago Cubs (NL) 1951–53
Record: 169–213
Four-time All-Star first baseman who played 22 years, 20 of them with the Cubs.

A lifetime .293 hitter, Cavarretta tied Stan Musial for the National League lead in 1944 with 197 hits, then won the batting title and the Most Valuable Player Award the following season with a .355 batting average. In 1951 he became the Cubs' player-manager, replacing Frankie Frisch with the team 35–45 and in seventh place, although he was no longer a regular and used himself off the bench. In the second game of a doubleheader on July 29 against the Philadelphia Phillies, he inserted himself as a pinch-hitter with the bases loaded and promptly hit a grand slam home run as the Cubbies won by an 8–6 score. Still, the team finished eighth and last.

The Cubs improved to .500 the following season, but finished seventh in 1953. The following spring training saw Chicago post a 5–15 record, and Cavarretta told owner Phil Wrigley that he expected the team to finish in the second division of the NL. Wrigley fired Cavarretta for his negative outlook and replaced him with Stan Hack.

Cavarretta then caught on with the Chicago White Sox and played 77 games over the next two seasons to finish out his career. He later coached for the Detroit Tigers.

O. P. Caylor
Cincinnati Red Stockings (AA) 1885–86; New York Metropolitans (AA) 1887

Record: 163–182

Former lawyer, then sportswriter and editor of the *Cincinnati Enquirer*.

One of the founders of the American Association in 1882, Oliver Perry Caylor took the helm of the Cincinnati Red Stockings for two seasons, finishing second in 1885 but dropping to fifth the following year. In 1887 he became manager and part-owner of the New York Metropolitans, the last of three managers that season for a seventh-place club, but he was not allowed to attend the league meetings because of the fact that he was also a sportswriter.

He later wrote for the *New York Herald*, and he died of tuberculosis in 1897 at the age of 47.

Frank Chance
Chicago Cubs (NL) 1905–12; New York Yankees (AL) 1913–14; Boston Red Sox (AL) 1923
Record: 946–648

Of "Tinker to Evers to Chance" double play fame in the Franklin P. Adams poem "Baseball's Sad Lexicon" from 1910.

Frank Chance was a Hall of Fame first baseman with the Cubs for 15 seasons, finishing out his career in sparse appearances for 2 years with the Yankees. Player-manager for Chicago for 8 of those 15 years, he earned the nickname "The Peerless Leader" through his skillful handling of the club. As a player Chance batted .296 lifetime, hitting over .300 on four consecutive occasions. He led the National League twice in stolen bases and once in runs scored.

He became player-manager in August of 1905, when manager Frank Selee resigned, through a close vote among the other players. Chance had already been filling in for Selee on road trips, because the Chicago manager was suffering from tuberculosis.

Chance enjoyed great success at the helm in Chitown. His eight seasons resulted in three third-place finishes, two second-place finishes, and four pennants. The Cubs' 116 victories in 1906 were a major league record.

The Cubs lost the '06 World Series to the Chicago White Sox, but won championships the next two seasons. In the 1908 World Series, Chance himself led all hitters with a .421 batting average.

After another pennant in 1910, he suffered a blood clot in his brain in 1911, and that ended his playing career as a regular. He was fired as manager following the 1912 season, in spite of a third-place finish, and he was then hired to take over the Yankees.

His Yankee teams did not perform well, and he was forced to retire late in the 1914 season due to ill health. He later recovered and became a minor league manager

before leading the Red Sox to a last-place finish in 1923. He was hired to manage the White Sox for the 1924 season, but died in September of '23.

Ben Chapman
Philadelphia Blue Jays (NL) 1945; Philadelphia Phillies (NL) 1946–48
Record: 196–276

First batter for the American League in the very first All-Star Game, in 1933.

Chapman was initially an infielder who, because of his great speed, was converted to an outfielder. Playing for several teams in a 15-year career, he led the league in stolen bases four times, peaking with 61 in 1931 with the New York Yankees, in only his second season. In 1934 he topped the circuit with 13 triples, and he was a four-time All-Star who retired with a .302 lifetime batting average.

Unfortunately, he was also a racist, gaining notice on at least one occasion for yelling racial insults at a Jewish fan, and also being renowned for vehement protests of Jackie Robinson's presence in the major leagues.

As a manager he was rather unremarkable, taking over the Philadelphia Blue Jays (who later returned to their previous name of Phillies) as player-manager in 1945 for Fred Fitzsimmons, and never managing better than a fifth-place finish. He was let go during the 1948 season and replaced, eventually, by Eddie Sawyer.

Jack Chapman
Louisville Grays (NL) 1876–77; Milwaukee Grays (NL) 1878; Worcester Ruby Legs (NL) 1882; Detroit Wolverines (NL) 1883–84; Buffalo Bisons (NL) 1885; Louisville Colonels (AA) 1889–91, (NL) 1892
Record: 350–501

Light-hitting but slick-fielding outfielder for three seasons in the National Association and the National League.

Chapman's heyday actually occurred in the 1860s, before the advent of the first organized major league. Outstanding defensively, he garnered the nickname "Death to Flying Things" probably before anyone else did.

As a manager he had a mere .411 winning percentage, but his Louisville Colonels won the American Association pennant in 1890. In an early version of the World Series, the Colonels then faced off against the NL champions, the Brooklyn Bridegrooms, in a seven-game series. Each team won three contests and there was one tie, but a potentially tiebreaking eighth game was not scheduled because of cold weather.

Chapman would remain at the helm of the Colonels when the team joined the NL in 1892.

Hal Chase
New York Highlanders (AL) 1910–11
Record: 86–80
One of the most controversial figures in baseball history.

A very talented first baseman whose play was always nevertheless suspect, Chase somehow survived 15 years in the major leagues, batting .291 lifetime. In 1915 he led the Federal League with 17 home runs, and a year later won the National League batting title with a .339 average while leading the circuit with 184 hits.

One can only guess at what Chase's accomplishments might have been had he played honestly. Repeatedly accused of throwing games for cash and of betting on his own teams—usually to lose—"Prince Hal" drew the ire of many a manager and many a teammate. He somehow managed to beat most of the charges leveled against him, probably in part due to his charismatic personality, even though his play at times was blatantly subpar. He played for many teams during his career, and controversy followed him everywhere.

With the Highlanders (who would later become the Yankees) in 1910, Chase was accused by manager George Stallings of throwing games. In a twist of fate rather typical of Chase's story, Chase ended up replacing his skipper as player-manager for the final 11 games of the season, and he led his team to a second-place finish, rising a notch in the standings. A year later they played .500 ball under him and ended up sixth. Chase then resigned as manager, but stayed with the club as a player.

That was somewhat early in Hal's career—he would play until 1919—and he was eventually banned for life for throwing games and for attempting to bribe other players.

John Clapp
Middletown Mansfields (NA) 1872; Indianapolis Hoosiers (NL) 1878; Buffalo Bisons (NL) 1879; Cincinnati Reds (NL) 1880; Cleveland Blues (NL) 1881; New York Gothams (NL) 1883
Record: 174–237
Player-manager for a number of teams in the nineteenth century.

Mainly a catcher, Clapp began his major league career in 1872 as player-manager of the Mansfields, a horrid team that went 5–19. He bounced around between several clubs for the next six years before becoming player-manager of the Hoosiers in 1878.

His best year was 1879 when his Buffalo Bisons finished in third place in the National League, but other than that he never managed better than a fifth-place showing. The 1883 season would be his last as both a player and a manager.

Fred Clarke
Louisville Colonels (NL) 1897–99; Pittsburgh Pirates (NL) 1900–15
Record: 1602–1181
Hall of Fame outfielder and player-manager.

Fred Clarke debuted in 1894 with the Louisville Colonels and promptly rapped out five hits in his first game. In 1897, at the age of 24, he was named player-manager of the club by owner Barney Dreyfuss. He hit a career-high .390 that season, and would eventually retire after 21 seasons with a .312 lifetime average.

Dreyfuss owned both the Colonels and the Pittsburgh Pirates, and after the 1899 campaign his Pirates absorbed his Louisville club. Clarke was one of those transferred to Pennsylvania, and he retained his role as player-manager. Beginning in 1901 the Bucs then won three National League pennants in a row, including the 1903 flag when the first modern World Series was held. As a player Clarke batted .351 that season and ended the year in a three-way tie for the NL lead with 32 doubles. The Pirates lost the best-of-nine World Series to the American League's Boston Americans (also known as the Pilgrims, among other things), five games to three. Clarke batted .375 in the Series.

The Pirates won one more pennant under Clarke, in 1909. This time they bested the Detroit Tigers in what had become a best-of-seven World Series, four games to three. Clarke hit .571 in the seven games.

In 19 years as manager, Clarke won four pennants while also managing four second-place and three third-place finishes. His lifetime winning percentage as a skipper is an impressive .576.

He resigned in 1915, but he returned to Pittsburgh as a coach in 1925 and a vice president in 1926. After causing some consternation with some controversial front office moves, he went home to work on his ranch. In 1945 he was inducted into the Hall of Fame by a special veterans committee.

Jack Clements
Philadelphia Phillies (NL) 1890
Record: 13–6
One of four managers to skipper the Phillies in 1890.

A catcher for 17 seasons—most of them with Philadelphia—Clements was a lifetime .288 hitter who batted over .300 on seven occasions. His best season was 1895, when he hit .394 with 27 doubles and 13 home runs.

In 1890 the Phillies were managed by Harry Wright. When Wright developed eye problems in May of that year and temporarily lost his sight, the club was led for much of the season by Clements, Al Reach, and Bob Allen. Wright's eyesight was eventually restored and Harry was able to return to the team.

In spite of the turmoil, the Phillies finished in third place.

Jim Clinton
Brooklyn Eckfords (NA) 1872
Record: 0–11
Rather light-hitting outfielder who was player-manager for part of one season.

Clinton was totally winless as a manager, going 0–11 with the Brooklyn Eckfords before being replaced by Jimmy Wood. In truth it was not a good team, its final record being 3–26 for a .103 winning percentage. Clinton played for nine more seasons, totaling four in the National Association, two in the National League, and four in the American Association. His lifetime batting average was a mere .256, but he did hit .338 in 16 games in 1876, and .313 in 94 contests in 1883.

Ty Cobb
Detroit Tigers (AL) 1921–26
Record: 479–444
Nicknamed "The Georgia Peach," one of the greatest players of all time.

Ty Cobb was a Hall of Fame outfielder with a 24-year playing career that, when he retired, resulted in a great many new records. His .366 lifetime batting average remains the all-time record, and his 4189 career hits are second only to Pete Rose's 4256. (Recordkeeping errors over the years accounted for Cobb's having a .367 average and 4191 hits.)

Cobb won 12 American League batting titles, and failed to hit over .300 only in the 41 games of his first season, 1905, when he batted .240. He hit over .400 on three occasions, and won the Triple Crown in 1909 with a .377 average, 9 home runs, and 107 runs batted in. A speedy and aggressive baserunner, he also topped the circuit in stolen bases six times, finishing his career with 892 lifetime. At various times he also led the AL in many other offensive *and* defensive categories.

Cobb deliberately goaded opposing players and was fiercely competitive. He was not well-liked as a result, but popularity was not his concern. He always played hard and did whatever it took to win.

Named player-manager of the Tigers for the 1921 season, he would continue in that role through 1926. Only in that first season at the reins did he fail to produce a winning record at the helm; although he never won a pennant, his clubs regularly finished above .500 after that.

Cobb retired abruptly following the 1926 season amid allegations that he had helped fix a game in 1919 against the Cleveland Indians. He was cleared of the charges

when his accuser, Dutch Leonard, refused to testify, and he returned to play for Connie Mack with the Philadelphia Athletics for two more seasons. Mack had been one of Cobb's supporters and defenders, helping him get reinstated by Commissioner Kenesaw Mountain Landis.

Cobb retired for good in 1928 and was elected to the Hall of Fame in 1936.

Mickey Cochrane
Detroit Tigers (AL) 1934–36, 1936, 1936–37, 1937–38
Record: 348–250
Hall of Fame catcher and outstanding manager.

Mickey Cochrane was one of the greatest catchers of all time, hitting for a high average (.320 lifetime) while adding some power and even a little bit of speed on the bases.

A two-time All-Star, Cochrane failed to hit over .300 only four times in a 13-year career. One of those years was 1932, when he hit .293 with the Philadelphia Athletics with a career-high 23 home runs and 112 runs batted in.

He was named player-manager of the Tigers in 1934, and at the helm he would fail to produce a winning record only in his final season of 1938. In both 1934 and '35 his club won the American League pennant, and although they lost a seven-game World Series to the St. Louis Cardinals in 1934, they came back to win a six-game contest against the Chicago Cubs in their second go-round. In '34 Cochrane was also named the AL's Most Valuable Player for the second time. (The first was in 1928, when it was simply called the League Award.)

Unfortunately Cochrane was also rather high-strung. He suffered a nervous breakdown during the 1936 campaign, and twice had to turn the club over to coach Del Baker. In May of 1937 he was beaned by Bump Hadley of the New York Yankees and suffered a skull fracture, an injury that would end his playing career. Baker once again took over while Cochrane was convalescing, and in July Mickey would return as manager although he would no longer take the field.

In August of 1938, with the Tigers in fifth place, Cochrane was fired and replaced by Baker. He was elected to the Hall of Fame in 1947. In 1950 he would become a coach for and then general manager of the Athletics.

Andy Cohen
Philadelphia Phillies (NL) 1960
Record: 1–0
Interim manager for a single game.

Cohen played three rather unspectacular seasons for the New York Giants in the 1920s before becoming a minor league coach and manager. In 1960 he was a coach for the Phillies under manager Eddie Sawyer. On Opening Day of that season, the Phillies lost to the Cincinnati Reds, 9–4, and Sawyer abruptly quit the team. Cohen was named interim manager for the next game—a game he won—and Gene Mauch was then hired to take over.

Bob Coleman
Boston Braves (NL) 1943, 1944–45
Record: 128–165
Played 116 games over three seasons before becoming a longtime minor league manager.

Originally a catcher by trade, Coleman managed for many years in the Three-I League before becoming a coach with the Braves in 1943. When manager Casey Stengel was hit by a cab and injured his leg in April, Coleman took over for the first 46 games. The following year Stengel was fired, and Coleman became permanent manager. His clubs did not perform well, finishing in sixth place in 1944 and languishing in seventh in 1945 when Coleman was replaced by Del Bissonette.

Jerry Coleman
San Diego Padres (NL) 1980
Record: 73–89
Nine-year second baseman with the New York Yankees and later a broadcaster.

A World War II veteran, Coleman debuted in the major leagues in 1949 and became an American League All-Star in his second season when he hit .287 and displayed outstanding defensive prowess in the infield. He spent most of 1952 and 1953 back in the military during the Korean War, and after retiring from baseball in 1957 he became a broadcaster for the Yankees and later for the Padres. In 1980 he was hired to manage the Padres, but after a last-place finish he was fired as skipper and returned to the booth.

Eddie Collins
Chicago White Sox (AL) 1924, 1925–26
Record: 174–160
Hall of Fame second baseman in the early part of the twentieth century.

Eddie Collins was truly one of the greats not only of his era, but of all time. He played 25 seasons for the Philadelphia Athletics and Chicago White Sox and retired with a .333 lifetime batting average, 3315 hits, and 741 stolen bases. He led the American League four times in steals, three times in runs scored, and once in bases on balls. He hit over .300 in 20 of his 25 seasons. He never did win a batting title, however, because that crown was usually claimed by Ty Cobb.

In 1914 with the Athletics Collins won the AL's Chalmers Award, that era's version of the Most Valuable Player Award, when he hit .344 with 85 runs batted in and a league-high 122 runs scored.

Collins managed the White Sox on an interim basis for 27 games in 1924, and then became the club's regular manager (player-manager, actually) the next two seasons. Despite finishing over .500 both years, the team finished in fifth place, and he was released both as a player and a manager following the 1926 campaign.

Collins had played for the A's his first nine seasons before going to Chicago in 1915. When he was released by the White Sox he was invited back to Philadelphia by Connie Mack, and served the next four seasons as a part-time player and unofficial assistant manager.

He retired from the field after the 1930 season, coached for the A's for two years, and then became part-owner and general manager of the Boston Red Sox. He was elected to the Hall of Fame in 1939.

Jimmy Collins
Boston Americans (AL) 1901–06
Record: 455–376
A .294 lifetime hitter in 14 major league seasons, mainly at third base.

Collins began his career in 1895. He hit over .300 on five occasions, and in 1898 with the Boston Bostons he led the National League with 15 home runs.

In 1901 Collins was named player-manager of the Boston Americans in the brand new American League. In 1903 his club captured the pennant, easily outdistancing the Philadelphia Athletics, and then, in the first modern World Series, won the ultimate championship by defeating the NL's Pittsburgh Pirates in a best-of-nine series, five games to three.

The Americans repeated in 1904, edging out the New York Highlanders by a game and a half, but John McGraw of the New York Giants refused to allow his NL club to face Collins' team. What would have been the second modern World Series was therefore canceled.

Collins managed into the 1906 season but was suspended when he left the team without permission, ostensibly to take a vacation. He continued to play through 1908, however. He then became a minor league player and manager for the next three seasons before going home to Buffalo. He was elected to the Hall of Fame in 1945.

Shano Collins
Boston Red Sox (AL) 1931–32
Record: 73–134
Sixteen-year major league veteran at first base and in the outfield.

Breaking in with the Chicago White Sox as a first baseman, Collins was moved to the outfield when he proved to be a disappointment defensively. He quickly became an outstanding defensive fielder, and would play most of the rest of his career in the outfield. An average hitter, he was traded to the Red Sox in 1921 and would finish out his playing days by spending five seasons in Boston.

In 1931 he was hired to manage the club, but predictably did not fare well at the helm of a team that had finished in the American League basement the last six consecutive seasons. To his credit Collins helped break the streak by bringing them in sixth out of eight teams, but they were still 45 games behind the pennant-winning Philadelphia Athletics. Shano lasted only 55 games the following season, sporting a dismal 11–44 record, when he was replaced by Marty McManus. The Red Sox would go on to finish last again, losing 111 games total and coming in 64 games behind the New York Yankees.

Terry Collins
Houston Astros (NL) 1994–96; Anaheim Angels (AL) 1997–99
Record: 444–434
Fiery minor league shortstop-turned-manager who won several titles before taking the helm in the major leagues.

Debuting as a skipper in 1981, when he won an immediate California League championship at the head of the Class A Lodi Dodgers, Collins soon reached the AAA level and then became a coach with the Pittsburgh Pirates in 1992. In 1994 he was hired to manage the Astros, who hoped his aggressive demeanor would light a fire under their club.

The Astros finished only a half-game behind the Cincinnati Reds in the National League Central Division in the strike-shortened season of 1994, then came in second the next two seasons as well. The Astros fired Collins in October of 1996, and a month later the Angels hired him to lead in Anaheim.

Two more second-place finishes made it five in a row for Collins, but his players had begun expressing grave dissatisfaction with his fiery style. The 1999 campaign saw the Angels slide into the American League West basement, and despite support from the front office, Collins decided to resign in September.

Charlie Comiskey
St. Louis Browns (AA) 1883, 1884–89, 1891; Chicago Pirates (PL) 1890; Cincinnati Reds (NL) 1892–94
Record: 838–541
Renowned as a player and a manager, but mainly as an executive.

A 13-year major league playing career, which began in 1882, coincided with a 12-year managerial stint, which began a year later. Comiskey was a first baseman who was named player-manager of the American Association's St. Louis Browns, and a dozen seasons at the helm of several clubs would see him finish below .500 only once.

From 1885 through 1888 his Browns won four consecutive AA pennants and participated in an early version of the World Series against the champions of the rival National League. The 1885 affair was a best-of-seven series in which the Browns and the Chicago White Stockings each won three games and tied one. In 1886 they defeated the White Stockings, four games to two. A year later saw an odd best-of-15 series, with all 15 games to be played regardless of which team clinched first. The Browns lost to the Detroit Wolverines, 10 games to 5, then lost a similar 10-game series the following year to the New York Giants, 6 games to 4.

In 1890 Comiskey moved to the short-lived Players League as player-manager of the Chicago Pirates, but he returned to the Browns the following season. He would spend the next three years with the Cincinnati Reds before leaving both the playing field and the manager's position.

Ban Johnson purchased the minor Western League at the conclusion of the 1893 season, and the next year Comiskey purchased the Sioux City Cornhuskers of that circuit. He moved the team to St. Paul and renamed it the Saints, and in 1900 would transfer it to Chicago. The Western League was renamed the American League, and would declare itself a major league in 1901. Comiskey's team, originally called the Invaders (and very shortly thereafter the White Stockings), would eventually become the Chicago White Sox. Comiskey himself was one of the driving forces behind the league's reorganization, and today is seen as one of the founders of the AL.

It was eight members of Comiskey's White Sox who threw the 1919 World Series to the Cincinnati Reds, citing as their reason for doing so Comiskey's tightfistedness and refusal to pay them what they were worth. The Black Sox Scandal was a blot on what was an otherwise impressive career.

"The Old Roman" died in 1931, and was inducted into the Hall of Fame as an executive in 1939.

Roger Connor
St. Louis Browns (NL) 1896
Record: 8–37
Baseball's home run king prior to Babe Ruth.

With a playing career that lasted from 1880 to 1897, Roger Connor smacked 138 career homers in an era that was not renowned for the longball. Ironically, he led his league only one season in that category, in 1890 with the

New York Giants of the Players League when he hit 14. His season high was 17, a total he had reached three years earlier.

Connor was a .323 hitter lifetime, and also led the league once in doubles, twice in triples, once in runs batted in, once in hits, and once in walks. He won the batting title in 1885 with a .371 average while with the New York Giants of the National League. He amassed 2542 career hits. At 6-foot-3 and 220 pounds, Connor was large and strong for his time, and many of his home runs traveled impressive distances even by today's standards.

In 1896 he was playing for the St. Louis Browns when manager Harry Diddlebock was fired for drunkenness. Arlie Latham managed two games and owner Chris Von der Ahe managed three before Connor was named player-manager. After going 8–37, however, Connor surrendered the reins to Tommy Dowd and went back to playing full-time.

After his retirement in 1897 he became a minor league player, manager, and owner—all at the same time. He later worked as a school inspector. He passed away in 1931, and was inducted into the Hall of Fame in 1976.

Dusty Cooke
Philadelphia Phillies (NL) 1948
Record: 6–6
Played eight years for the New York Yankees, Boston Red Sox, and Cincinnati Reds, hitting .280 lifetime.

Cooke suffered some injuries early in his career and never lived up to his billing as a top prospect. He had some decent years in the majors as a part-time outfielder, and 10 years after his retirement he became a coach for the Phillies.

When manager Ben Chapman was fired in 1948 Cooke was named interim manager. He went 6–6 before Eddie Sawyer took the helm, and then went back to coaching through 1952.

Jack Coombs
Philadelphia Phillies (NL) 1919
Record: 18–44
Outstanding pitcher for 14 years who flirted only briefly with managing.

Nicknamed "Colby Jack," Coombs was a 20-game winner on three occasions. In 1910 with the Philadelphia Athletics he led the league in wins when he went 31–9, then won the victory title again the following year with a 28–12 record. He also topped the circuit in 1910 with 13 shutouts. In his rookie year of 1906, he had pitched all 24 innings of what was, up to that point, the longest game in American League history. Coombs and the A's won that game, defeating the Boston Americans, 4–1. He struck out

18 batters. His opponent, Joe Harris, also went the distance.

Coombs retired after the 1918 season and was hired to manage the Phillies. He resigned after going 18–44, however, with his club in last place. In 1920 he would pitch two games as a player-coach for the Detroit Tigers, totaling 5⅔ innings and posting a 3.18 earned run average.

Johnny Cooney
Boston Braves (NL) 1949
Record: 20–25
Both a pitcher and an outfielder.

Johnny Cooney pitched nine seasons, from 1921 through 1930, and posted a 34–44 record and a 3.72 earned run average. He occasionally played the outfield during this period, but arm problems caused him to give up pitching entirely and focus on being a position player. From 1931–34 he was in the minor leagues refining his hitting, and he returned to the majors in 1935 as an outfielder with the Brooklyn Dodgers. He lasted 20 major league seasons total, and had a respectable .286 batting average. Casey Stengel compared him to Joe DiMaggio as a fielder. From 1940–42 he served as a player-coach.

Cooney retired in 1944. In 1946 he became a coach with the Braves, and in August of 1949 he temporarily took over as manager when the club was experiencing turmoil in the clubhouse in the wake of its 1948 National League pennant. Manager Billy Southworth was pressured to take a leave of absence, and Cooney assumed control and managed them to a 20–25 record for the rest of the season. The Braves finished fourth, and the next season Southworth returned and Cooney went back to coaching.

Pat Corrales
Texas Rangers (AL) 1978–80; Philadelphia Phillies (NL) 1982–83; Cleveland Indians (AL) 1983–87
Record: 572–634
Backup catcher for several teams, spending a number of years behind Johnny Bench with the Cincinnati Reds.

A light hitter, Corrales lasted nine seasons in the major leagues before retiring in 1973. In 1976 he became a coach with the Rangers, and when manager Billy Hunter was fired prior to the final game of the 1978 season, Corrales was named his successor.

The Rangers won that game, and Corrales stayed at the helm for two more seasons. He was then hired to manage the Phillies, and after a second-place finish in 1982, he had the team in first place the following year when he was fired in July by general manager Paul Owens. In spite of its first-place standing, Owens claimed that the team was not living up to its potential under Pat, and he promptly named himself manager. The team did finish first.

Less than two weeks later the Indians fired their manager, Mike Ferraro, and hired Corrales to take over. Pat led the Tribe for several seasons but never managed better than a fifth-place finish. In 1987 he was let go at the All-Star break and was replaced by Doc Edwards, who had been the club's bullpen coach. He later coached the New York Yankees and the Atlanta Braves.

Red Corriden
Chicago White Sox (AL) 1950
Record: 52–72
Light-hitting shortstop and third baseman who played parts of five seasons in the major leagues.

Later a coach with many teams for many years, Corriden was hired to manage the White Sox in May of 1950 when the last-place club fired manager Jack Onslow. Corriden spent the rest of the season bringing them from eighth to sixth, and that was the end of his managerial career.

Chuck Cottier
Seattle Mariners (AL) 1984–86
Record: 98–119
Light-hitting second baseman who played nine seasons for four teams.

Eventually a coach with the Mariners, Cottier was called upon to replace Del Crandall in September of 1984. The team was in seventh place, and under Cottier they went 15–12 the rest of the way and climbed a notch to sixth.

Nineteen eighty-five would be Chuck's only full season at the helm, and the Mariners once again finished sixth as they won 74 games against 88 losses. The following season they were 9–19 to start the year and were once again foundering in sixth place in May when Cottier was fired and replaced by Dick Williams. The team would end up seventh.

Bobby Cox
Atlanta Braves (NL) 1978–81, 1990– ; Toronto Blue Jays (AL) 1982–85
Record: 2171–1686
Played two seasons for the New York Yankees before making his mark on the game as one of the winningest managers of all time.

After a playing career spent mainly in the minor leagues, Cox became a minor league manager in 1971. He would return to the majors as a Yankees' coach in 1977 before being handed the reins to the Atlanta Braves a year later.

His best finish during his first stint in Atlanta was fourth place, and he was fired at the conclusion of the

1981 campaign and was promptly hired to take over the Toronto Blue Jays. The Jays began a steady improvement under Cox, and in 1985 they won the American League Eastern Division title by two games over the Yankees. They lost the AL Championship Series to the Kansas City Royals, but Cox was named the league's Manager of the Year by the BBWAA.

Cox resigned after the season when he was offered the Braves' general manager post by owner Ted Turner. He remained in that position until June of 1990, when the Braves fired manager Russ Nixon and Cox returned to the dugout to take control himself.

Beginning in 1991 he would make first place an almost annual finish for his teams. They won the National League Eastern Division crown 14 times over the next 15 years, and captured NL pennants in 1991, 1992, 1995, 1996, and 1999. All those first-place finishes led to only one World Championship, however, in 1995.

In 1991 Cox was named the NL Manager of the Year by both the AP and the BBWAA, becoming the first ever to win the BBWAA award in both leagues. (In 2002 Tony LaRussa would become the second.) In 2004 he won career game number 2000 and was once again named Manager of the Year by the BBWAA. He won the award yet again in 2005.

Harry Craft
Kansas City Athletics (AL) 1957–59; Chicago Cubs (NL) 1961, 1961; Houston Colt .45s (NL) 1962–64
Record: 360–485
Outstanding defensive center fielder for the Cincinnati Reds' pennant-winning team of 1939 and World Championship team of 1940.

Craft played six seasons in the major leagues before eventually becoming the manager of the Kansas City Athletics in 1957 as a replacement for Lou Boudreau. He managed nothing better than three consecutive seventh-place finishes, however, and in 1961 was a member of the Chicago Cubs' "college of coaches" who took turns at the helm. In 16 games for Chicago Craft was 7–9.

He was then hired to manage the expansion Houston Colt .45s in 1962, but that team predictably floundered. In September of 1964, with the team mired in ninth place, Craft was fired and replaced by Lum Harris.

Roger Craig
San Diego Padres (NL) 1978–79; San Francisco Giants (NL) 1985–92
Record: 738–737
Major league pitcher for 12 seasons, and later a pitching coach, scout, and manager.

With several teams in his career Craig compiled a 74–

98 record and a 3.83 earned run average. He won at least 10 games on three occasions, and in 1959 with the Los Angeles Dodgers he was one of seven pitchers to lead the league with four shutouts.

Craig was a pitching coach for many years, and was especially renowned for his ability to teach the split-fingered fastball. He managed the Padres for two years, but had his greatest success at the helm of the Giants. In 1987 San Francisco won the National League Western Division title, and although they dropped the League Championship Series to the St. Louis Cardinals in seven games, Roger was named the NL Manager of the Year by the AP. In 1989 they captured the division flag again, and this time they defeated the Chicago Cubs in five games to take the pennant. They were then swept by the Oakland Athletics in what has been called the Bay Series, a World Series that was marred by a severe earthquake.

Del Crandall
Milwaukee Brewers (AL) 1972–75; Seattle Mariners (AL) 1983–84
Record: 364–469
Four-time Gold Glove winner and 12-time All-Star catcher.

An average hitter, Del Crandall was above the norm in his defensive ability. He played for 16 seasons, mainly with the Boston/Milwaukee Braves, and hit 179 home runs lifetime, three times topping 20 in a season.

As a manager he did not have much luck, never accomplishing more than a fifth-place finish. He piloted the Brewers for three complete seasons and one partial one, and the Mariners for two partial seasons, replacing Rene Lachemann in June of 1983 and being replaced by Chuck Cottier in September of 1984.

Sam Crane
Buffalo Bisons (NL) 1880; Cincinnati Outlaw Reds (UA) 1884
Record: 73–79
Not to be confused with a later Sam Crane, who played from 1914–22 and was convicted of murdering his girlfriend and her male companion.

This Sam Crane—Samuel Newhall Crane—played seven seasons as a second baseman, beginning in 1880 with the Buffalo Bisons, but, like his later namesake, was a very light hitter. He averaged only .204 over his career, collecting but 277 hits.

He could not do much to help the Bisons as player-manager, ending up in seventh place. He had a little better luck as player-manager of the Cincinnati Outlaw Reds of the Union Association in 1884, however. Replacing Dan O'Leary with the club in fifth place, he managed a 49–21

record and raised the team to third in the only season of the team's—and the league's—existence.

Gavvy Cravath
Philadelphia Phillies (NL) 1919–20
Record: 91–137
California slugger with a laid-back, easygoing manner.

An outfielder by trade, Cravath played 11 major league seasons in the early part of the twentieth century. With the Phillies for most of those years, he led the National League in home runs six times, peaking with 24 in 1915, during the deadball era. He also topped the circuit in runs batted in twice, in hits once, in runs scored once, and in walks once. In 1919 he hit .341 with a league-leading 12 roundtrippers, despite playing in only 83 games.

When manager Jack Coombs resigned in 1919 with his club in last place, Cravath was named player-manager. His easygoing demeanor failed to light a fire under the team, however, and the Phillies finished last in both 1919 and 1920.

Following his baseball career he became a justice of the peace in Laguna, California, but lost that job because of his laid-back style as well.

Bill Craver
Troy Haymakers (NA) 1871; Baltimore Lord Baltimores (NA) 1872; Philadelphia Pearls (NA) 1874; Philadelphia Centennials (NA) 1875
Record: 70–66
Infielder and catcher who played five seasons in the original National Association and then two years in the infant National League.

A Civil War veteran, Craver was player-manager of the Troy Haymakers during their amateur years. During an 1869 game against the undefeated Cincinnati Red Stockings, Craver got into a heated argument with the umpire over a foul tip call. With the game knotted, he pulled his team off the field and refused to go on, declaring the game a tie. The umpire awarded the contest to Cincinnati by forfeit, however. The Red Stockings claimed that Craver was trying to protect the bets of the gamblers who controlled the Haymakers, but that charge was never proven.

Player-manager for four of his five seasons in the NA—with four different teams—Craver led most of them fairly well, finishing at .500 twice and with a 27–13 record once. His only failure was the Philadelphia Centennials, with whom he was a mere 2–12. As a player he hit .311 during his years in the NA and led the league in triples in 1875 with 13.

When the NA gave way to the NL in 1876, Craver signed with the New York Mutuals. The following year he played for the Louisville Grays, and he ended up being one of four players banned from major league baseball for life because of a gambling and game-fixing scandal that surrounded that club. While not directly involved in the scandal, he refused to cooperate during a subsequent investigation and thus shared the fate of those who were found guilty.

Ironically, Craver became a police officer when his baseball career was over.

George Creamer
Pittsburgh Alleghenys (AA) 1884
Record: 0–8
The fourth of five managers to skipper the Alleghenys in 1884.

A second baseman who debuted in 1878, Creamer was a light hitter, averaging only .215 over a seven-year career. Six years later he was with the Alleghenys, who were struggling through a dismal season when he was named player-manager to replace Joe Battin. After losing eight games in a row, he was replaced by Horace Phillips, and he never did win a game as a manager.

Joe Cronin
Washington Nationals (AL) 1933–34; Boston Red Sox (AL) 1935–47
Record: 1236–1055
Hall of Famer who hit over .300 eleven times in a 20-year playing career and finished with a .301 lifetime average.

Named player-manager of the Nationals in 1933 by owner Clark Griffith at the age of 27, Cronin immediately took Washington to the World Series, guiding his team to 99 wins and a first-place finish, 7 games ahead of the New York Yankees. They lost a five-game Series to the New York Giants, but Cronin had turned some heads. He had also hit .309 for the season with 118 runs batted in, and led the American League with 45 doubles. He batted .318 in the World Series.

In 1934 Cronin married Griffith's niece, Mildred Robertson, but the Nationals fell to seventh place and Griffith traded Cronin to the Boston Red Sox.

Named player-manager in Boston as well, Joe managed four second-place finishes there in the next 11 years. On the field he continued to excel, hitting .307 in 1937 with 110 RBIs, .325 in 1938 as he led the league with 51 doubles, and .308 in 1939 with 107 RBIs.

In 1945 he broke his leg, and the injury ended his playing career, but he did continue to manage for two more seasons. In 1946 he led the Red Sox to the World Series, but they lost in seven games to the St. Louis Cardinals.

Following the 1947 season Cronin moved to Boston's front office, where he would remain through 1959. He then served two terms as AL president.

In 1956 Cronin was elected to the Hall of Fame. The Red Sox retired his number 4 in 1984. Three months later, Joe passed away.

Jack Crooks
St. Louis Browns (NL) 1892
Record: 27–33
Player-manager and the third of five managers for the Browns in 1892.

A somewhat light hitter, Crooks nevertheless had a good eye, leading the league in walks in 1892 with 136 and again the following year with 121. He had an eight-year playing career, and his short managerial stint with the Browns was unspectacular. That was not necessarily his fault, as the team finished in eleventh place out of 12 under its five managers, 46 games out of first.

Lave Cross
Cleveland Spiders (NL) 1899
Record: 8–30
Outstanding catcher-turned-infielder who played 21 seasons in the major leagues.

Cross hit .293 lifetime playing for a number of different teams, most of them in Philadelphia. He batted .317 in 54 games in his debut season of 1887 with the Louisville Colonels of the American Association. He hit over .300 on seven occasions, and at least .290 on eight others.

Amassing 2666 hits lifetime, Lave never led the league in a major offensive category, but in 1897 he set a record with 15 assists by a second baseman in a major league game. That game lasted 12 innings.

Named player-manager of the once-strong Cleveland Spiders in 1899, he managed the first 38 games of the season—of which the club won only 8—before being transferred to the St. Louis Perfectos by Frank Robison, who owned both teams. He hit .298 for the season, and was replaced on the Spiders by the unfortunate Joe Quinn. The Spiders won only 12 more games *the entire season*, losing 104 to become baseball's all-time worst team with a final record of 20–134, a whopping 84½ games out of first place.

Mike Cubbage
New York Mets (NL) 1991
Record: 3–4
Part-time third baseman with the Texas Rangers, Minnesota Twins, and New York Mets.

A coach with the Mets following his playing career, Cubbage was named interim manager for the final seven games of the 1991 season when Bud Harrelson was fired.

He won three and lost four, and that was enough to drop the Mets from third to fifth place.

Ed Curtis
Altoona Unions (UA) 1884
Record: 6–19
Managed a very short-lived franchise.

The Altoona Unions (also known as the Mountain Citys, the Pride, and the Ottowas) were one of the original teams in the National League's rival, the Union Association, in 1884. The club played only through the end of May, winning a mere 6 games out of 25, before folding due to poor attendance. That was the end of both the Unions and Ed Curtis' major league career.

Charlie Cushman
Milwaukee Brewers (AA) 1891
Record: 21–15
Never played in the major leagues and managed a grand total of 36 games.

Cushman was the skipper of the Milwaukee Brewers, the third of five big league teams to bear that name. This one originally played in the minor Western League in 1891 (not to be confused with the Western League formed in 1892 that eventually became the basis of the American League). Toward the end of the season the Cincinnati Porkers dropped out of the major American Association, and the Brewers were brought in to fill out their schedule. They actually did fairly well, going 21–15 with Cushman at the helm.

Ned Cuthbert
St. Louis Brown Stockings (AA) 1882
Record: 37–43
Early player who is credited with stealing the first base in baseball history.

With the amateur Philadelphia Keystones in 1863, Cuthbert is said to have reached first base and then, with the next batter at the plate, taken off for second before the ball had been hit. The other players at first laughed, supposing he had simply made a mistake, but Cuthbert informed the umpire that there was no rule against what he had just done. The umpire agreed, and over the protests of the opposing team, the stolen base stood.

Ned played professionally when the National Association was formed in 1871, manning the outfield for the Philadelphia Athletics. He eventually played 10 big league seasons, which were comprised of 5 in the NA, 2 in the National League, 2 in the American Association, and 1 in the Union Association. He hit .338 in 1872, and in 1873 he tied for the NA lead with 13 stolen bases, although he had swiped more than that on at least three other occa-

sions.

In 1882 he was player-manager of the AA's St. Louis Brown Stockings, and he had a rather dismal year all around as he hit a mere .223 and the club finished in fifth place. In 1887 he worked briefly as an umpire in the AA, then he opened some saloons in St. Louis.

Bill Dahlen
Brooklyn Superbas (NL) 1910; Brooklyn Trolley Dodgers (NL) 1911; Brooklyn Dodgers (NL) 1911–13
Record: 251–355
Managed one team with something of an identity crisis.

Bill Dahlen enjoyed a successful 21-year career as a major league player beginning in 1891 with the Chicago Colts. He eventually played for the Brooklyn Superbas, then the New York Giants and later the Boston Doves before returning to Brooklyn. He hit over .300 on three occasions and amassed 2460 hits in his career. In 1894 he put together a 42-game hitting streak, and in 1904 with the Giants he led the National League with 80 runs batted in.

Defense was his strong suit, and he set several NL fielding records at shortstop. In 1910 he returned to the Superbas primarily as their manager, although he did play in three games but did not collect a hit in two at-bats. In 1911 the team changed its name to Trolley Dodgers and later to Dodgers, and Dahlen played in a single game but struck out three times in three at-bats.

He continued to manage through 1913, but did not have much success, boasting only two sixth-place finishes and two seventh. He was then replaced by the legendary Wilbert Robinson.

Alvin Dark
San Francisco Giants (NL) 1961–64; Kansas City Athletics (AL) 1966–67; Cleveland Indians (AL) 1968–71; Oakland Athletics (AL) 1974–75; San Diego Padres (NL) 1977
Record: 994–954
Solid infielder with a good bat who played 14 seasons in the major leagues before becoming a skipper.

Dark debuted for the Boston Braves in 1946 in 13 games, but his first full season was 1948, when he batted .322 and won the National League Rookie of the Year Award. He would eventually bat .289 lifetime and become a three-time All-Star.

Upon his retirement he was hired to manage the San Francisco Giants, the team with whom he had become an All-Star while in New York. In 1962 they won the NL pennant under Alvin, although they would drop a seven-game World Series to the New York Yankees.

Dark was fired in 1964 following a fourth-place finish, and two years later became the manager of the Kansas

City Athletics under Charlie Finley. The A's were not exactly in their prime, finishing seventh in 1966 and languishing in tenth the following season when, in August, reports of unprofessional, rowdy behavior on a team flight caused Finley to fire Dark. In not atypical Finley fashion, a 24-hour period saw Dark fired, then rehired, then fired again. He was replaced by Luke Appling.

After managing the Indians, Alvin returned to the A's, who by now had relocated to Oakland. He had much more success this time around. Winning the American League Western Division title in 1974, the A's went on to capture the pennant in a three-games-to-one victory over the Baltimore Orioles, and then the World Championship in five games over the Los Angeles Dodgers. The following season they again won their division, but this time were swept by the Boston Red Sox in three games in the AL Championship Series. That performance was apparently not good enough for Finley, who fired Dark again.

Alvin would take over the Padres for John McNamara in May of 1977, but the club would manage only a fifth-place finish. In March of 1978, during spring training, Dark was fired and was replaced by pitching coach Roger Craig.

Jim Davenport
San Francisco Giants (NL) 1985
Record: 56–88
Thirteen-year major league veteran who played his entire career with the Giants.

An excellent defensive infielder and an adequate hitter, Davenport debuted in 1958 and enjoyed his best season in 1962, when he hit .297 with 14 home runs, won a Gold Glove for his work at third base, and was named to the National League All-Star team. After his playing career he became a longtime coach with the Giants, and in 1985 was named their manager. He did not last the season, however, being replaced by Roger Craig after going 56–88.

He also coached for the San Diego Padres, the Philadelphia Phillies, and the Cleveland Indians.

Mordecai Davidson
Louisville Colonels (AA) 1888, 1888
Record: 35–54
Miserly owner who never played in the major leagues.

After purchasing the lowly Louisville Colonels in 1888, Davidson made himself extremely unpopular with his players when he began to levy fines for losses and poor play.

The Colonels had been a decent team in 1887, but Davidson's overly frugal manner likely contributed to the 10–29 record with which they started the 1888 season.

Manager John Kelly offered to resign, and Davidson accepted and named himself manager. After only three games, however—only one of which he won—the Louisville owner named John Kerins skipper. Kerins lasted only seven games and went 3–4, at which point Davidson named himself manager for a second go-round. This time the club went 34–52, and they finished in seventh place out of eight teams, 44 games behind the league leader.

The following season Davidson left the field and oversaw a revolving door of managers. When he began to take fines out of his players' paychecks, most of the team threatened to strike, and only six players showed up for the next game. The holdouts returned to the field when American Association officials stepped in to mediate.

George Davis
New York Giants (NL) 1895, 1900–01
Record: 107–139
Hall of Fame third baseman and shortstop who played 20 years in the major leagues.

With a career spanning 1890–1909, George Davis batted .295 lifetime and amassed 2665 hits. He batted over .300 nine years in a row, from 1893–1901. In 1897 he led the National League with 136 runs batted in.

Most of his years were spent with the New York Giants, and for part of 1895 he was their player-manager. The team did not play particularly well, going 16–17 in 33 games, and Davis surrendered the reins to Jack Doyle with the club in eighth place. They would eventually finish a game over .500, but would end up in ninth place in a 12-team league.

Davis fared better as a player, batting .340 and knocking in 101 runs. Five years later, when Buck Ewing resigned as manager in the midst of the 1900 season, Davis would again take control, but would not do much better. Eighth- and seventh-place finishes were all he would have to show for two more years as manager.

In 1900 he and teammates Kid Gleason and Mike Grady helped rescue several people from a serious apartment fire while on their way to a game at the Polo Grounds. They then continued to the park and played the regularly-scheduled game.

Davis concluded his career with the Chicago White Sox, and in 1998 he was elected to the Hall of Fame by the Veterans Committee.

Harry Davis
Cleveland Molly McGuires (AL) 1912
Record: 54–71
Renowned for a solid 22-year major league career as well as for stealing first base.

Harry Davis played for many teams, but spent most of

his years with the Philadelphia Athletics. Playing from 1895 through 1917, he led his league four consecutive times in home runs (the totals during that era were 10, 8, 10, and 12), three times in doubles, once in triples, twice in runs batted in, and once in runs scored.

In a game against the Detroit Tigers in 1902, he was on first base while teammate Dave Fultz resided on third. Davis then attempted to steal second base, hoping to draw a throw so that Fultz could score. No throw resulted from his attempt, however, and he ended up on second base with Fultz still on third. On the next pitch, he ran back to first, and since there was no rule at the time prohibiting such an action, he was permitted to stay there. He then stole second again, and this time he drew a throw and Fultz scored from third.

Following the 1911 season Davis became player-manager of the Cleveland Molly McGuires, who had been so-named in honor of their previous manager, Jim McGuire. Harry inserted himself into only two games, and he attempted to enforce strict discipline among his players, but his efforts were not appreciated. The club was in sixth place when he decided to resign.

He returned to the A's as a player-coach, but appeared in only 19 games over the next five seasons. He also became a city councilman in Philadelphia while still with the club.

Spud Davis
Pittsburgh Pirates (NL) 1946
Record: 1–2
Catcher who hit .308 for his career and managed the Pirates for three games.

Virgil "Spud" Davis played 16 years in the major leagues for several teams, and he hit over .300 for 7 years in a row and 10 total. A player-coach with the Pirates from 1942–45, he turned strictly to coaching in 1946, then became interim manager for the final three games of that season as a replacement for Frankie Frisch. The Bucs won one of those three.

Davis later became a coach with the Chicago Cubs.

John Day
New York Giants (NL) 1899
Record: 29–35
Non-player who managed for only one partial season.

Massachusetts native John Day was a cigar manufacturer and part-owner of the Giants who ended up in dire financial straits. He sold off his shares and took a job as the team's manager in 1899. He led the club to a 29–35 record at the beginning of the season, a record that was good enough for only ninth place. His replacement, Fred

Hoey, could do no better, and the club ended up finishing tenth. Day later became an inspector of umpires.

Harry Deane
Fort Wayne Kekiongas (NA) 1871
Record: 2–3
Played two years in the National Association (1871 and 1874), but hit only .240.

Deane played only six games for Fort Wayne in 1871 and managed five, winning two of them. Having played since 1866 as an amateur club, the Kekiongas would last only 19 games in the professional NA before folding.

Bucky Dent
New York Yankees (AL) 1989–90
Record: 36–53
Three-time All-Star shortstop with a brief managerial tenure.

As a player Dent helped the Yankees to World Championships in 1977 and '78. In 1978, in fact, the team finished in a tie with the Boston Red Sox for the division title, and Bucky hit a home run in the one-game playoff that won it for the Yankees. In the World Series he batted .417 and was named the Series' Most Valuable Player.

Upon his retirement he became a manager in the Yanks' minor league system. He took over at the helm of the big club as a replacement for Dallas Green in 1989, but finished only fifth. The Yankees were in seventh place the following season when he himself was replaced by Stump Merrill. Dent then became a coach with several teams.

Bill Dickey
New York Yankees (AL) 1946
Record: 57–48
Louisiana native who spent his entire career with the New York Yankees as a catcher, player-manager, and coach.

In a 17-year playing career, Dickey hit over .300 eleven times and rarely struck out. He batted .313 lifetime, caught over 100 games for 13 consecutive seasons (setting an American League record), and in 1931 became the first catcher to go an entire season without allowing a single passed ball. He participated in eight World Series and helped to win seven championships.

He missed about half of 1943 and all of the next two seasons because he was serving in the Navy during World War II. He returned in 1946, and while he played only 54 games, he became the Yankees' player-manager 35 games into the season. He posted a 57–48 record at the helm, but was replaced by Johnny Neun for the final 14 games. The Yankees finished in third place.

Dickey returned as a Yankees' coach from 1949–57,

and was elected to the Hall of Fame in 1954. He scouted for the Yankees in 1959 and coached again in 1960.

In 1972 the Yankees retired uniform number 8 for both Dickey and Yogi Berra.

Harry Diddlebock
St. Louis Browns (NL) 1896
Record: 7–10
The first of five managers for the Browns in 1896.

Diddlebock was a sportswriter who started the managerial merry-go-round 17 games into the season. After going 7–10, he was fired because of intoxication and was replaced in succession by Arlie Latham, Chris Von der Ahe, Roger Connor, and finally Tom Dowd.

The Browns finished in eleventh place.

Larry Dierker
Houston Astros (NL) 1997–99, 1999–2001
Record: 435–348
Pitcher, broadcaster, and manager.

Dierker debuted in 1964 with Houston and would eventually win 139 games against 123 losses in a 14-year career. A two-time All-Star, he won 20 games in 1969 and pitched a no-hitter in 1976.

After pitching for the St. Louis Cardinals in 1977, Dierker retired and became a baseball broadcaster. In 1997, in spite of the fact that he had never managed professionally, the Astros hired him to be their skipper. His club immediately won the National League Central Division title, although they were swept in the Division Series by the Atlanta Braves.

In 1998 the Astros again captured the division crown, and Dierker won the NL Manager of the Year Award from the BBWAA. Houston lost the Division Series again, however, by a 3–1 margin to the San Diego Padres.

In 1999 Dierker suffered a grand mal seizure during a game and required brain surgery. He spent four weeks in recovery, during which Matt Galante took control of the team, but he eventually returned to the dugout and took the Astros to their third consecutive division title. Once again they lost the Division Series, however, falling to the Braves, three games to one.

The year 2000 marked the only season Dierker failed to finish first. The Astros lost 90 games and ended up fourth, 23 games behind the Cardinals. But they rebounded in 2001, winning the division crown for the fourth time in five years. They actually tied for first place in the standings with the Cardinals, and were awarded the division because of their winning season record against the Redbirds. St. Louis became the wild card team and went to the playoffs as well. In the Division Series, the Astros followed a now-predictable pattern and were swept by the Braves in three games.

Dierker was fired following the 2001 season with an all-time winning percentage of .553.

In 2002 the Astros retired his uniform number 49.

Larry Doby
Chicago White Sox (AL) 1978
Record: 37–50
First black player in the American League and a perennial All-Star.

Doby accomplished many firsts in his 13-year career. He was the first black player to lead his league in home runs, the first to hit a homer in the World Series, and the first to participate in winning a World Series.

Doby began his career with the Newark Eagles of the Negro National League, and contributed to that team's league championship in 1946. The following year he joined the Cleveland Indians, and the Tribe would go on to tie for the AL championship, win a one-game playoff against the Boston Red Sox to advance to the World Series, and then capture the ultimate championship by defeating the Boston Braves, four games to two.

In 1954 Doby led the league with 32 home runs and 126 runs batted in, and he finished second to Yogi Berra for the league's Most Valuable Player Award. The Indians once again won the pennant, but dropped the World Series to the New York Giants.

In all Larry led the AL twice in home runs, once in RBIs, and once in runs scored, and he was a seven-time All-Star. He finished his career with the Chicago White Sox, then played in Japan with the Chunichi Dragons.

He later became a coach with the Montreal Expos, the Indians, and the White Sox. In the midst of the 1978 season he was named the White Sox' manager as a replacement for Bob Lemon, but his record was a mere 37–50 and the club finished in fifth place.

In 1994 the Indians retired his uniform number 14. Doby was inducted into the Hall of Fame in 1998, and he passed away in 2003.

Bill Donovan
New York Yankees (AL) 1915–17; Philadelphia Phillies (NL) 1921
Record: 245–301
Pitcher nicknamed "Wild Bill" who won 186 major league games in an 18-year career.

Debuting in 1898, Donovan had the first of many outstanding seasons in 1901 with the Brooklyn Superbas. He went 25–15 that season and led the National League in wins and tied in games pitched and shutouts. He won 25 again in 1907, the only other season he surpassed the 20-victory mark, but he did win in double digits nine times.

In 1903 with the Detroit Tigers he tied for the American League lead with 34 complete games.

He was prone to wildness, serving up free passes at generous rates, but he retired with a 2.69 lifetime earned run average. He pitched sparsely toward the end of his career, totaling a mere 15 games in his last four seasons combined. He was primarily manager for the Yankees in 1915 and '16, and did not pitch at all in 1917 while leading the club to a sixth-place finish. He returned to the Tigers in 1918 as a player-coach and pitched two games.

Donovan became a minor league manager, and in 1921 was hired to manage the Phillies. He was replaced by Kaiser Wilhelm more than halfway through the season with the team in eighth place.

As manager of the Eastern League's New Haven Profs, he was killed in a train wreck in December of 1923 while on his way to baseball's winter meetings. He had traded positions on the train with George Weiss, the Profs' president, switching to a lower berth, and Weiss survived the crash with only minor injuries.

Patsy Donovan
Pittsburgh Pirates (NL) 1897, 1899; St. Louis Cardinals (NL) 1901–03; Washington Senators (AL) 1904; Brooklyn Superbas (NL) 1906–08; Boston Red Sox (AL) 1910–11
Record: 684–879
Lifetime .301 hitter and speedy baserunner.

An outfielder by trade, Patsy Donovan came to the United States from Ireland and began his major league career in 1890. In 17 years he would hit over .300 eleven times, peaking at .327 in 1903. Always a stolen base threat, he swiped at least 20 fourteen times, and stole 518 lifetime. He tied for the National League lead in 1900 with 45.

He was player-manager for a number of teams, and did not go strictly to the bench until 1908 with the Superbas and 1910–11 with the Red Sox. As a skipper he never managed better than a fourth-place finish. He then became a minor league manager and a scout.

Red Dooin
Philadelphia Phillies (NL) 1910–14
Record: 392–370
Fine defensive catcher and player-manager.

An average to light hitter, Dooin spent 15 years in the major leagues and was admired for his work behind the plate. He was reportedly the first catcher to wear shin guards, although his were made of papier-maché.

Dooin spent all but two years of his career with the Phillies, and for five years was also their manager. In 1913 he guided the club to a second-place finish as they went 88–63.

He suffered leg injuries in 1910 and 1911 that effectively ended his playing career as a regular, but he did continue as a backup catcher through 1916. He was also a good singer, and eventually performed in Philadelphia with Dumont's Minstrels, a group founded by tenor Frank Dumont in the late nineteenth century.

Mike Dorgan
Syracuse Stars (NL) 1879; Providence Grays (NL) 1880; Worcester Ruby Legs (NL) 1881
Record: 67–70
Player-manager of the amateur Syracuse Stars, who went 46–13 in 1876, before beginning his major league career in 1877.

Dorgan played 10 years, and was player-manager for parts of 3. He never did manage a full major league season, however.

In 1879 he managed the Stars for 43 games, and was in sixth place when he was replaced by Bill Holbert and later Jimmy Macullar. The team finished seventh. In 1880 he followed Mike McGeary and Monte Ward as manager of the Providence Grays. He managed 39 games. The club was in third place when he took over, and he brought them in second. In 1881 he managed the Worcester Ruby Legs for the first 51 games of the season before going to Detroit and being replaced by Harry Stovey. The team was in seventh when he left, and they finished eighth.

He played until 1890, when a knee injury ended his career. Dorgan was the first Syracuse native to play in the National League, and he was inducted into the Syracuse Hall of Fame in 1999.

Tommy Dowd
St. Louis Browns (NL) 1896–97
Record: 31–60
Ten-year major league outfielder and second baseman who was briefly a player-manager.

Dowd hit .271 lifetime, but had his finest season in 1895 when he batted .323 with 74 runs batted in and 32 stolen bases. That was the only season he hit higher than .284, although he swiped 368 bases in his career.

When manager Harry Diddlebock was dismissed for intoxication early in the 1896 season, Arlie Latham and owner Chris Von der Ahe each managed a few games on an interim basis before settling on Roger Connor to be player-manager. But Connor's record was a mere 8–37, and he was then replaced by Dowd. Tommy went 25–38, and then had the team at 6–22 the following season before himself being replaced by Hugh Nicol.

Jack Doyle
New York Giants (NL) 1895; Washington Statesmen (NL)

1898
Record: 40–40
Ireland native nicknamed "Dirty Jack."

A 17-year career for Doyle resulted in a .299 lifetime batting average. Jack played for many teams, but was rarely a regular. He hit over .300 for five seasons in a row and six total, and he topped the 100-RBI plateau twice.

He was player-manager on two occasions, both times being the second in a veritable revolving door of managers. In 1895 with the Giants he replaced George Davis with the team in eighth place, and after dropping with them to ninth was replaced by Harvey Watkins. Three years later with the Statesmen he took over for Tom Brown with the club in eleventh, but after going 8–9 and nevertheless raising them to tenth was replaced by Deacon McGuire, who was eventually replaced himself by Arthur Irwin.

Chuck Dressen

Cincinnati Reds (NL) 1934–37; Brooklyn Dodgers (NL) 1951–53; Washington Nationals (AL) 1955–56; Washington Senators (AL) 1957; Milwaukee Braves (NL) 1960–61; Detroit Tigers (AL) 1963–64, 1965–66
Record: 1008–973
Former major league quarterback for the Decatur Staleys and the Racine Legion before starting his baseball career as a third baseman in 1925.

Chuck Dressen played eight seasons, mostly as a reserve, and hit a respectable .272. He is most famous as a manager, however, having begun that phase of his career in 1934 with the Cincinnati Reds, with whom he had played seven of his eight seasons.

Dressen did not have great success at the helm of the Reds, but with the Brooklyn Dodgers in 1951 he finished second and then won back-to-back pennants the next two seasons. The Dodgers lost both World Series to the New York Yankees, but Dressen nevertheless felt confident in asking Brooklyn owner Walter O'Malley to go against his usual policy and grant him a multiyear contract. O'Malley promptly refused and replaced Dressen with Walter Alston.

Dressen later managed the Washington Nationals (who returned to their original name of Senators in 1957), the Braves, and the Tigers, but he never won another pennant. He did manage a second-place finish in 1960 with Milwaukee.

He served as a Dodgers' scout after being fired by the Braves following the 1961 season, but in 1963 was hired by Detroit in June to skipper the Tigers. In March of 1965 he suffered a mild heart attack, and coach Bob Swift took the reins for the start of the season. Dressen returned in May, but in May of 1966 he had a second heart attack and Swift had to take over once again. Chuck would not return to the dugout, and he died in Detroit on August 10.

Hugh Duffy

Milwaukee Brewers (AL) 1901; Philadelphia Phillies (NL) 1904–06; Chicago White Sox (AL) 1910–11; Boston Red Sox (AL) 1921–22
Record: 535–671
Hall of Fame outfielder who was outstanding both at the plate and in the field.

A true all-around player, Duffy began his career in 1888 with the Chicago White Stockings (now the Cubs), and would eventually post a .324 lifetime batting average in 17 seasons. He hit at least .300 eleven times, and in 1893 won the first of two batting titles. His second was the following year, when he hit an incredible .440 and also led the National League with 18 home runs, 51 doubles, and 237 hits. He later won the 1897 home run crown with 11 roundtrippers, after topping the circuit in runs batted in with 110 in 1891. He topped the 100 mark in that category eight times, and also stole 574 bases lifetime.

In 1890 he played for the Chicago Pirates of the short-lived Players League, and in its only year of existence led that loop in hits and runs scored.

As a manager he never finished better than fourth place, and topped the .500 mark on only two occasions. In 1901 with the Milwaukee Brewers (today's Baltimore Orioles), he slugged an umpire while arguing a foul ball call and was suspended indefinitely. He later worked as a scout for the Red Sox, having previously scouted for the Boston Braves.

Duffy was elected to the Hall of Fame by a special veterans committee in 1945.

Fred Dunlap

Cleveland Blues (NL) 1882; St. Louis Maroons (UA) 1884, (NL) 1885, 1885; Pittsburgh Alleghenys (NL) 1889
Record: 145–102
Excellent-fielding second baseman and outstanding hitter.

Dunlap debuted in 1880 with the Cleveland Blues and immediately led the National League with 27 doubles. He hit .325 the next season, and would eventually bat over .300 four times en route to a .296 lifetime average. He was named player-manager of the Blues partway through the 1882 season, but his most outstanding year by far was 1884. With the St. Louis Maroons of the Union Association in that league's only year of existence, he led the circuit with a .412 batting average, 13 home runs, 185 hits, and 160 runs scored. As manager he led his team to the one and only UA title as they went 94–19 (for an incredible .832 winning percentage), finishing 35½ games ahead of the second-place Milwaukee Cream Citys.

The Maroons were admitted into the NL upon the demise of the UA, and Dunlap remained at the helm as player-manager. Having defected from the NL the year before, he had to pay a $500 fine in order to be reinstated. The Maroons proved no match for the NL clubs, however, and finished eighth.

After a stint with the Detroit Wolverines, Dunlap ended up with the Pittsburgh Pirates in 1888. He became player-manager of that team partway through the 1889 season, replacing Horace Phillips, but after winning only 7 of 17 games he was in turn replaced by Ned Hanlon.

Leo Durocher
Brooklyn Dodgers (NL) 1939–46, 1948; New York Giants (NL) 1948–55; Chicago Cubs (NL) 1966–72; Houston Astros (NL) 1972–73
Record: 2008–1709
One of the winningest managers in major league baseball history.

As a shortstop for 17 years, Leo Durocher was a below-average hitter but a good fielder. He was a member of the St. Louis Cardinals' World Championship "Gashouse Gang" of 1934, and became a National League All-Star once with the Cards and twice with the Brooklyn Dodgers.

As a manager, he would eventually reach the Hall of Fame. He was the skipper of the Dodgers from 1939–46, functioning as player-manager for all but the final year of that tenure, and in 1941 took his club to the NL pennant. They lost the World Series to the New York Yankees, four games to one.

Prior to the 1947 season Durocher (who was not nicknamed "The Lip" for nothing) spoke out strongly against Dodgers' players who were beginning to foster negativity due to Jackie Robinson's imminent debut with the team. Robinson would soon break baseball's color line, becoming the first black player in the twentieth century, and Durocher said, "I don't care if the guy is yellow or black, or if he has stripes like a...zebra. I'm the manager of this team and I say he plays."

Durocher was friends with several actors, and he eventually married actress Laraine Day. Many of his friends were either gamblers or bookmakers, and many were said to have connections to the mob. In the spring of 1947 baseball Commissioner Albert "Happy" Chandler served Leo with a one-year suspension for, as he put it, "association with known gamblers." Clyde Sukeforth and Burt Shotton would take over the managerial reins until Durocher's return in 1948.

That return was short-lived, however. Experiencing friction with Dodgers' general manager Branch Rickey, Durocher was fired about halfway through the season, and he was immediately hired by the Dodgers' crosstown ri-

vals, the New York Giants. He took the Giants to the pennant in both 1951 and 1954, losing the World Series to the Yankees in '51 but sweeping the Cleveland Indians in '54.

He later managed the Cubs, beginning in 1966, and his best with Chicago was two second-place finishes. He was fired during the 1972 season and was immediately hired by the Houston Astros, and he finished second with them but would manage only one more year.

Durocher was named Manager of the Year by *The Sporting News* three times, and he was elected to the Hall of Fame in 1994.

Frank Dwyer
Detroit Tigers (AL) 1902
Record: 52–83
Pitched 12 years and won 177 games lifetime.

Dwyer was a 20-game winner twice—in 1892, when he went 22–18 with the St. Louis Browns and Cincinnati Reds; and in 1896, when he was 24–11 with the Reds. He won at least 16 during 9 of his 12 years.

After retiring as a player he spent only one season—a rather miserable one—as a major league manager, in 1902 with the Tigers. That club went 52–83 and finished in seventh place, 30½ games behind the Philadelphia Athletics.

He later scouted for the New York Giants and New York Yankees, and coached at Cornell University. In 1924 he was a pitching coach for the Giants, but only during spring training. He also served on the New York State Boxing Commission.

Eddie Dyer
St. Louis Cardinals (NL) 1946–50
Record: 446–325
Unspectacular pitcher, but had some fine years as a manager.

Dyer played from 1922–27 with the Cardinals, and upon his retirement he began managing in the minor leagues. Over the next 15 years he won nine minor league championships, and in 1942 was named Minor League Manager of the Year by *The Sporting News* while with the Columbus Red Birds of the American Association.

In 1946 he was hired to manage the Cardinals, and he guided the team to a tie in the standings with the Brooklyn Dodgers. St. Louis then won a best-of-three playoff, two games to none, to capture the National League pennant, and they went on to defeat the Boston Red Sox in a seven-game World Series.

After three consecutive second-place finishes, the Cardinals fell to fifth in 1950. Nevertheless Dyer was offered a one-year contract extension, but he declined and instead went into real estate and the oil business in Houston, Texas.

Jimmy Dykes

Chicago White Sox (AL) 1934–46; Philadelphia Athletics (AL) 1951–53; Baltimore Orioles (AL) 1954; Cincinnati Redlegs (NL) 1958; Detroit Tigers (AL) 1959–60; Cleveland Indians (AL) 1960–61
Record: 1406–1541

Extremely versatile infielder who played 22 seasons with the Philadelphia Athletics and Chicago White Sox.

Dykes reached the major leagues in 1918, and he would hit over .300 seven times and bat .280 lifetime. He was a two-time All-Star, and in 1924 was named the Athletics' Most Valuable Player when he hit .312. His award was a car.

Dykes was named player-manager of the White Sox in 1934, and in 1940 he would turn strictly to managing and would remain with Chicago into the 1946 season.

In 1949 he became a coach with the A's, and was named their manager two years later. He managed the Orioles during their first year in Baltimore, then became a coach with the Cincinnati Redlegs and took over for Birdie Tebbetts there on an interim basis toward the end of the 1958 season. In May of 1959 he became the manager of the Tigers, but in August of 1960 was actually traded to the Indians for their manager, Joe Gordon.

With his lively personality, Dykes kept his teams fired up but was often fined or suspended for arguing a little too vehemently with umpires. In 21 years of managing, he never finished better than third place.

Charlie Ebbets

Brooklyn Bridegrooms (NL) 1898
Record: 38–68

Longtime Brooklyn owner who tried his hand at managing for part of one season.

Charlie Ebbets was hired as a bookkeeper for the Brooklyn Atlantics, at that time a minor league team, in 1883. He began buying shares of the team, and by 1898 was its president. He named himself manager for the greater part of that season, but the team, now called the Bridegrooms, finished tenth and that was the end of that experiment.

Ebbets was renowned for his honesty and fairness. He proposed many innovations in the game, and is generally considered the inventor of the raincheck. He bought the Brooklyn franchise in 1905 when owner Ned Hanlon considered moving it to Baltimore.

Ebbets financed a new ballpark for his club in 1912, and that park would be named Ebbets Field in his honor. The team eventually became the Dodgers and later, as the Robins, won two pennants, in 1916 and 1920. Charlie died in 1925.

Doc Edwards

Cleveland Indians (AL) 1987–89
Record: 173–207

Former Navy medic and light-hitting but good defensive backstop with several teams.

Edwards played parts of five seasons in the major leagues before becoming a coach and a minor league manager. In 1981 his Rochester Red Wings of the International League played a 33-inning contest against the Pawtucket Red Sox. It was the longest game in professional baseball history and was won by the Red Sox, 3–2.

Edwards later became a bullpen coach with the Cleveland Indians, and in 1987 he was appointed manager when Pat Corrales was fired. In three years with Cleveland—only one of which saw him at the helm for a full season—sixth place was his best finish.

Kid Elberfeld

New York Highlanders (AL) 1908
Record: 27–71

Fiery, solid shortstop whose managerial tenure was not to his liking.

Nicknamed "The Tabasco Kid" because of his hard-nosed style of play and his hot temper, Elberfeld stood around five feet seven inches tall and weighed about 158 pounds. Nevertheless he could be a terror on the field, going head-to-head with many an opposing baserunner and, over the years, assaulting many umpires and receiving fines and suspensions as a result. Police had to remove him from a September 1906 game when he attacked arbiter Silk O'Loughlin.

In 1908, while he was with the New York Highlanders, manager Clark Griffith resigned, citing ownership's tightfistedness as his reason for doing so. The team was 24–32 at the time, and Elberfeld took over the reins. Kid's record ended up a mere 27–71, however, and the Highlanders, as of yet a long way from Yankee greatness, finished at 51–103, claiming last place as they ended up 39½ games behind the Detroit Tigers. Elberfeld went back to playing full-time the following year.

Upon his retirement he would become a minor league manager. In 1936, at the age of 61, he put himself in to pinch-hit for the Fulton Eagles of the Class D KITTY League and grounded out.

Lee Elia

Chicago Cubs (NL) 1982–83; Philadelphia Phillies (NL) 1987–88
Record: 238–300

Had minimal major league experience as a shortstop before his rather brief managerial tenure.

Elia played a total of 95 big league games in parts of two seasons with the Cubs and hit a mere .203. He later became a coach with the Phillies, then was hired to manage the Cubs. After a fifth-place finish in 1982, Chicago was once again in fifth the following season when, in August, Lee was fired and replaced by Charlie Fox.

He is probably most famous for a profanity-laced tirade he unleashed on reporters regarding Chicago fans on April 29, 1983. With a record of 5–14, the team had just lost a close game to the Los Angeles Dodgers because of a wild pitch thrown by Lee Smith in the ninth inning. Cubs' fans booed loudly, and a couple of them enticed some of the players to fight. When everything had settled and Elia got to his office and faced the media, he went off on Cubs' fans and accused them of being everything from fair-weathered to downright lazy…and not in terms nearly so kind. In three minutes, he used a certain FCC-banned word a total of 43 times.

After leaving Chicago he once again became a coach with the Phillies, and in June of 1987 took the place of John Felske with the team in fifth. They would finish fourth, and were in sixth place the next year when Elia was replaced by John Vukovich.

Joe Ellick
Pittsburgh Stogies (UA) 1884
Record: 6–6
Cincinnati native who played a total of 104 games in parts of four seasons in the nineteenth century at many positions.

Ellick took over for Joe Battin on the Union Association's Pittsburgh Stogies for the final 13 games of the 1884 season, accumulating six wins, six losses, and one tie. The club finished sixth, 42 games out of first place.

Bob Elliott
Kansas City Athletics (AL) 1960
Record: 58–96
Seven-time All-Star third baseman and outfielder.

Playing most of his career with the Pittsburgh Pirates and Boston Braves, Bob Elliott always hit for a decent average—topping .300 four times in 15 years—and also had good power, smashing at least 15 home runs five times and knocking in at least 100 runs six times. In 1948 he led the National League with 131 bases on balls while hitting .283 with 23 home runs and exactly 100 RBIs.

Elliott retired from the playing field in 1953, and later managed the A's for one season in Kansas City. He was let go after a last-place finish, although, in fairness to Elliott, the club had finished in the last two in the American

League for the previous four seasons and would do so again for the next two. He then became a coach with the expansion Los Angeles Angels.

Jewel Ens
Pittsburgh Pirates (NL) 1929–31
Record: 176–167
World War I veteran who played sparsely in the infield in four seasons with the Pirates before becoming a coach and manager.

Ens was coaching Pittsburgh in 1929 when, with the team in second place, manager Donie Bush resigned. Ens was named his replacement, and the Bucs would finish second.

Two consecutive fifth-place finishes spelled the end of Jewel's managerial career. He later coached the Detroit Tigers, the Cincinnati Reds, the Boston Braves, the Pirates again, and the Reds again.

Cal Ermer
Minnesota Twins (AL) 1967–68
Record: 145–129
Played a single game in the major leagues at second base with the Washington Senators.

Ermer went 0-for-3 in that game, and he eventually became a coach with his hometown Baltimore Orioles. In June of 1967 he was hired by the Twins to take over for manager Sam Mele. Minnesota was in sixth place at the time, and Ermer would eventually take them through a nearly heart-stopping pennant race. The Twins ended up in a tie for second place with the Detroit Tigers, one game behind the American League champion Boston Red Sox.

Ermer was fired after finishing seventh the following season. He would later go on to coach the Milwaukee Brewers and the Oakland Athletics.

Jim Essian
Chicago Cubs (NL) 1991
Record: 59–63
Major league catcher for 12 years and 5 teams.

A rather light hitter, Essian was usually a backup, and his busiest season was 1978 when he played 126 games for the Oakland Athletics.

In May of 1991 the Cubs hired him to replace Don Zimmer as their manager. They were fifth at the time and finished fourth, and Jim was fired in October.

Dude Esterbrook
Louisville Colonels (AA) 1889
Record: 2–8
Nineteenth century infielder who considered himself one of the game's best.

In reality Esterbrook was a decent player but not a superstar, averaging .263 lifetime. He played for a number of teams, and in 1889, still as an active player, he was the first of four men to manage the Louisville Colonels. After going 2–8 in the first 10 games, he was replaced by Chicken Wolf.

Esterbrook played into the 1891 season, then continued in the minors. His behavior became more and more erratic over the years, however, and he eventually began to brag about a flying machine he had supposedly invented and to claim that he could live to be 150 if he simply exercised and behaved like a little boy. He would attend league meetings and offer his services to various teams, but always at an exorbitant salary. He was not taken up on those offers.

In 1901 his brother was escorting him by train to a mental hospital in Middletown, New York. Esterbrook tried to escape through a lavatory window and fell from the train near Tuxedo. He died of his injuries later that night.

Johnny Evers
Chicago Cubs (NL) 1913, 1921; Chicago White Sox (AL) 1924, 1924
Record: 180–192
Of "Tinker to Evers to Chance" double play fame in the Franklin P. Adams poem "Baseball's Sad Lexicon" from 1910.

Evers (pronounced EE-vers) was the second baseman in that combination, and he played most of his 18-year career with the Cubs and the Boston Braves. He hit over .300 twice and stole at least 20 bases seven times, ending up with 324 total. In 1913 he was named the Cubs' player-manager, and the team finished third but Johnny was traded to the Braves before the start of the 1914 campaign.

That first year in Boston Evers hit .279 with 20 doubles and 81 runs scored, and he won the Chalmers Award, an early version of the Most Valuable Player Award. As a result he would drive away in a brand new car.

Johnny returned to manage again in 1921, but he was replaced in August with the team in sixth place. He became a coach with the White Sox and was named their skipper in 1924 when manager Frank Chance fell ill and eventually died. He was actually named interim manager, and he gave way to Ed Walsh and Eddie Collins after 21 games, but returned shortly thereafter and finished out the season. The team ended up last.

Evers later went on to coach the Braves, then ran a sporting goods store. He suffered a stroke in 1942, was elected to the Hall of Fame in 1946, and died in 1947.

Buck Ewing
New York Giants (PL) 1890; Cincinnati Reds (NL) 1895–99; New York Giants (NL) 1900
Record: 489–395
Hall of Fame catcher who played 18 seasons and hit .307 lifetime.

Beginning his career in 1880 with the Troy Trojans, Ewing hit over .300 eleven times, peaking at .365 in 1887. In 1883 he led the National League with 10 home runs, becoming the first player to reach double digits in that category. He topped the circuit with 20 triples the following season.

Buck played many positions during his career, including pitcher. It was as a backstop that he gained most of his notoriety, however, displaying outstanding defensive skills and a powerful throwing arm. He would routinely decoy opposing baserunners, deliberately allowing balls to get past him and then recovering them and throwing out the runners when they attempted to advance.

There have been two teams called the New York Giants in major league baseball history—one in the Players League and the other in the National League—and Ewing managed them both. In 1890 he was named player-manager of the PL's Giants, and he batted .338 while leading that team to a third-place finish. Those Giants were then absorbed by the other Giants, and Buck, having previously played for the NL Giants, returned to his former club. He did not manage again until 1895 with the Reds, and in five seasons he produced two third-place finishes. In 1900 he became the skipper of the NL Giants, but that club finished last and Ewing would not manage again.

Buck died in Cincinnati in 1906 of Bright's disease, and he was elected to the Hall of Fame in 1939. He is generally credited as having laid out the design of New York's Polo Grounds.

Jay Faatz
Buffalo Bisons (PL) 1890
Record: 9–24
Light-hitting first baseman who was briefly a player-manager of the Buffalo Bisons of the Players League.

After the first 19 games of the Bisons' season in the PL's only year of existence—and a 5–14 record—Faatz took over as player-manager for Jack Rowe. Faatz played 32 games and hit .189, and as a manager went 9–24 before surrendering the reins back to Rowe. The team finished eighth.

Bibb Falk
Cleveland Indians (AL) 1933
Record: 1–0

Excellent outfielder for the Chicago White Sox and Cleveland Indians for 12 seasons.

Falk hit over .300 eight times, and retired with a .314 lifetime average. He was a coach with the Indians in 1933 when he filled in for one game between the reigns of Roger Peckinpaugh and Walter Johnson, and he won that game. The following year he became a coach with the Boston Red Sox.

Jim Fanning
Montreal Expos (NL) 1981–82, 1984
Record: 116–103
Chicago native and member of the Canadian Baseball Hall of Fame.

A catcher who played only 64 games in the big leagues, Fanning spent many years in baseball in other capacities. Serving as a minor league manager, major league coach, scout, and assistant general manager after his playing career, he later worked as a scouting director for Major League Baseball and eventually became the first general manager of the Expos in 1968. He served as a vice president and scout with Montreal, and became the team's field manager during the 1981 season.

That season was split into two halves due to a players' strike. In the second half, Fanning's Expos won the National League Eastern Division title by a slim half-game over the St. Louis Cardinals. In a one-time divisional playoff series, they bested the Philadelphia Phillies, winners of the division's first half, three games to two, then lost the NL Championship Series to the Los Angeles Dodgers by an identical margin.

Fanning resigned after the 1982 season and went back to the front office. Late in 1984 he returned to the dugout to replace Bill Virdon, but that would be the end of his managerial career. He later joined a radio talk show on baseball in Montreal while residing in Dorchester, Ontario, and was inducted into the Canadian Baseball Hall of Fame in 2000.

Jack Farrell
Providence Grays (NL) 1881
Record: 24–27
Second baseman who played from 1879 through 1889 and was nicknamed "Moose."

Considered one of the best at his position in his day, Farrell had some power for the nineteenth century; his five home runs in 1881 were a National League record for a second baseman at that time.

That was the same year Farrell was named player-manager of the Grays, and he would play 84 games but would manage only 51 before turning over the reins to Tom York.

His hitting declined sharply during the second half of his career, although his fielding remained excellent. He eventually died in his native New Jersey in 1914.

Kerby Farrell
Cleveland Indians (AL) 1957
Record: 76–77
Played two rather mediocre seasons in the majors during World War II.

Farrell eventually became the manager of the Cleveland Indians, a team that, in 1956, had finished second in the American League under Al Lopez. Farrell's 1957 squad slipped to sixth, and that was the end of his big league managerial career.

Kerby later became a coach with the Chicago White Sox, and soon afterwards returned to the Indians in a similar role.

John Felske
Philadelphia Phillies (NL) 1985–87
Record: 190–194
Had several cups of coffee in the major leagues, but never caught on as a player.

Felske became a coach with the Toronto Blue Jays before going to work in the Phillies' organization. He was a coach under Paul Owens in 1984, and when Owens went to the front office he named Felske his successor.

The club finished fifth in 1985, but second the following year. They were struggling in 1987 at 29–32 when Felske was fired and replaced by his own third base coach, Lee Elia.

Bob Ferguson
New York Mutuals (NA) 1871; Brooklyn Atlantics (NA) 1872–74; Hartford Dark Blues (NA) 1875, (NL) 1876; Brooklyn Hartfords (NL) 1877; Chicago White Stockings (NL) 1878; Troy Trojans (NL) 1879–82; Philadelphia Nationals (NL) 1883; Pittsburgh Alleghenys (AA) 1884; New York Metropolitans (AA) 1886–87
Record: 417–516
Honest and well-respected infielder who was player-manager of every major league team for which he played.

Ferguson's play—and his notoriety—predated the original National Association. In 1870, when the Brooklyn Atlantics handed the Cincinnati Red Stockings their first defeat in two years, Ferguson was the one who knocked in the tying run and then scored the winning tally.

Beginning in 1872 and for several years after that while he played, Ferguson was also the president of the National Association. Generally considered to be baseball's first switch-hitter, he batted over .300 only once, but in 1880 he led the National League with 24 bases on balls.

While honest, Ferguson also had a short temper, and he was not beyond fighting with opposing players if he felt he had been physically slighted. As a manager he had one second-place finish with Hartford, but otherwise never climbed higher than third. He retired from playing in 1884 but continued managing. Throughout his playing and managing days, he also umpired many games.

Mike Ferraro
Cleveland Indians (AL) 1983; Kansas City Royals (AL) 1986
Record: 76–98
Played sparsely in the major leagues before becoming a coach with the New York Yankees.

Hired to manage the Indians in 1983, Ferraro was fired in July with the team in seventh place. He was a coach with the Royals when, in July of 1986, manager Dick Howser had to leave the club to receive treatment for a malignant brain tumor. Ferraro was named interim manager for the rest of the season, and the Royals finished third. Howser would not return.

Wallace Fessenden
Syracuse Stars (AA) 1890
Record: 4–7
Watertown, Massachusetts native who never played major league baseball.

Fessenden filled in for manager George Frazer for 11 games during the American Association's 1890 season with the Syracuse Stars. He won only four of them, and the club was in sixth place—where it would remain—when Frazer returned.

Freddie Fitzsimmons
Philadelphia Phillies (NL) 1943; Philadelphia Blue Jays (NL) 1944–45
Record: 105–181
Popular pitcher for the New York Giants and later the Brooklyn Dodgers.

Fitzsimmons debuted in 1925 and played 19 seasons in the big leagues. He became a 20-game winner for the only time in 1928 when he went 20–9 and fashioned a 3.68 earned run average. In 1935 he tied for the National League lead by tossing four shutouts. He won 217 games lifetime against 146 defeats, for a .598 winning percentage. In 1941 he even umpired a game.

Fitzsimmons became a coach with many teams, and was a player-coach with the Dodgers for several years. In mid-1943 he took over the manager's job for the Phillies, a team that would change its name to Blue Jays the next two seasons. Freddie's teams played miserably, and he was let go about halfway through the 1945 season and went back to coaching.

In 1943 and '44 he also served as general manager of Brooklyn's National Football League entry, called the Dodgers in '43 and the Tigers the following year.

Art Fletcher
Philadelphia Phillies (NL) 1923–26; New York Yankees (AL) 1929
Record: 237–383
Good-hitting, slick-fielding shortstop for the New York Giants and Philadelphia Phillies.

Fletcher played for 13 years before being named Phils' manager in 1923, the year following his retirement. Four uneventful years later he became a coach with the Yankees, a post he would hold until 1945.

Toward the end of the 1929 season, however, New York manager Miller Huggins fell ill, and Fletcher took over control of the team. Three days later, the regular skipper died of blood poisoning, and Fletcher would finish out the last 11 games of the season.

He then went back to coaching, and turned down several additional offers to manage again.

Silver Flint
Chicago White Stockings (NL) 1879
Record: 5–12
Catcher who filled in for manager Cap Anson at the end of the 1879 season.

Anson was in his first year as player-manager of the White Stockings when, in August, he was sidelined with a liver disorder. He left the team in order to recuperate, and Flint took over and finished out the season. In second place when Anson left, the club would finish fourth under Flint.

Anson would return the following season and go on to a long managerial career with Chicago. Flint continued to play and retired in 1889.

Jim Fogarty
Philadelphia Quakers (PL) 1890
Record: 7–9
Speedy outfielder with the Philadelphia Nationals before jumping to the Players League.

Fogarty played a total of seven major league seasons, six of them with the Nationals and all of them in Philadelphia. Stolen base records were not kept for the first two seasons he played, but from 1886 forward he never failed to steal at least 30. He swiped 102 in 1887, and two years later led the National League with 99. He totaled 325 in only five recorded seasons.

He also reached base a lot through walks, and led the league in that category in 1887 with 82, a season that also saw him hit .366.

Joining the Philadelphia Quakers of the short-lived Players League in 1890 as player-manager, he put together a record of only 7–9 before being replaced at the helm by Charlie Buffinton. He did continue to play, although that would be his final season. Hired to manage the Philadelphia Phillies in 1891, he came down with tuberculosis and died in May at the age of 27.

Horace Fogel
Indianapolis Hoosiers (NL) 1887; New York Giants (NL) 1902
Record: 38–72
Pennsylvania native who served as a sportswriter, manager, and owner in major league baseball.

The Indianapolis Hoosiers hired sportswriter Fogel to take over for manager Fred Thomas in 1887, but the venture was far from a success. Fogel was the Hoosiers' third and final manager of the season, and they were last when he took over and they finished last.

In 1902 he was hired to manage the Giants, but an 18–23 record led to his being fired in June and replaced by Heinie Smith, who would in turn be replaced by John McGraw.

In 1909 Fogel headed a group that purchased the Philadelphia Phillies. Since he was still a sportswriter, he was not allowed to attend the league meetings, however. Three years later he accused several teams of going easy against the Giants, and claimed National League umpires were favoring the Giants as well. His accusations were found to be without merit and led to his being banned from the league for life.

Lee Fohl
Cleveland Indians (AL) 1915–19; St. Louis Browns (AL) 1921–23; Boston Red Sox (AL) 1924–26
Record: 713–792
Catcher who played only five games in the major leagues.

A player-manager in the minors, Fohl was hired by the Indians to replace Joe Birmingham as manager during the 1915 season. The club did not fare well until 1917, when they finished third, then they climbed to second in 1918, missing the pennant by a mere 2½ games.

During a game in 1919, Babe Ruth hit a home run to defeat the Indians, and Fohl was criticized for not having walked the Bambino intentionally. He was fired the next day.

Two years later he was hired to manage the St. Louis Browns. He brought the team in third in 1921, and the following season the Browns finished second, only a single game behind the New York Yankees. The team was in third place in July of 1923, but Fohl was nevertheless fired and replaced by Jimmy Austin.

He was hired to manage the Red Sox the next year, but the team had lost most of its best players and over the following three seasons would finish seventh, last, and last. Lee resigned after the 1926 campaign.

Lew Fonseca
Chicago White Sox (AL) 1932–34
Record: 120–196
Outstanding hitter who played many positions.

In a 12-year playing career, Fonseca hit over .300 six times, peaking in 1929 with the Cleveland Indians when he won the American League batting crown with a .369 average. In May of 1931 the Tribe traded Lew to the White Sox, and Chicago made him its player-manager the following season.

Often injured, Fonseca played sparingly the next two years and turned strictly to managing in 1934. Having once appeared in the 1927 motion picture *Slide, Kelly, Slide*, he pioneered the use of film to analyze his players, but nevertheless a sixth-place finish was his best. He was fired in May of 1934 with the club 4–11, and he later became a motion picture specialist for both the American and National Leagues.

Dave Foutz
Brooklyn Bridegrooms (NL) 1893–96
Record: 264–257
Outstanding pitcher, first baseman, and outfielder.

As a player, Foutz helped win many championships in both the American Association and the National League. In 1885 with the AA's St. Louis Browns he won 33 games, then tied for the league lead with 41 the next season. But his best year was probably 1887, when he hit .390 while going 25–12 on the mound. His career record was 147–66, good for an astounding .690 winning percentage.

As a manager he did not have nearly that level of success, never achieving better than a fifth-place finish.

Charlie Fox
San Francisco Giants (NL) 1970–74; Montreal Expos (NL) 1976; Chicago Cubs (NL) 1983
Record: 377–371
Played only three major league games as a catcher before becoming a manager.

Fox began his managerial career in the minor leagues, then became a scout. He was a coach with the Giants for four years, and in May of 1970 was named to replace Clyde King as manager. The following season he took San Francisco to the National League Western Division title, finishing a single game up on the Los Angeles Dodgers. The Giants were defeated by the Pittsburgh Pirates in the

NL Championship Series, three games to one, but the AP named Charlie its NL Manager of the Year.

That would be Fox's only first-place finish. In 1976 he was working in the Expos' front office when Karl Kuehl was fired and he became interim manager for the rest of the season. The same situation occurred in 1983 with the Cubs, when he filled in for the fired Lee Elia.

Terry Francona
Philadelphia Phillies (NL) 1997–2000; Boston Red Sox (AL) 2004–
Record: 564–570

Played 10 major league seasons in the outfield and at first base.

Francona played more than 100 games in a season on only three occasions, and after retiring in 1990 he became a minor league manager. He had success at the helm, leading the Birmingham Barons to the Southern League title in 1993. He returned to the majors as a coach, and in 1997 was hired to manage the Phillies.

A last-place finish was followed by two third-place showings, then another cellar dwelling. Francona was fired in October of 2000, but he would become the Red Sox' manager four years later.

It was in Boston in 2004 that he would gain his greatest fame. After taking his team to the wild card and then winning the American League Division Series, he would lead the Sox to the AL pennant in a seven-game Championship Series against the New York Yankees. He would then break an 86-year-old curse—popularly known as the Curse of the Bambino, supposedly caused when the Red Sox sold Babe Ruth to the Yankees—by leading the Red Sox to their first World Championship since 1918, a four-game sweep over the St. Louis Cardinals.

In 2005 the Red Sox again won the AL wild card. They finished second in their division to the Yankees although they had an identical 95–67 record; the Yankees were awarded the division title because of their better record against Boston during the season. In the ALDS the Red Sox were swept by the Chicago White Sox, who would go on to win their first World Championship since 1917.

Herman Franks
San Francisco Giants (NL) 1965–68; Chicago Cubs (NL) 1977–79
Record: 605–521

Light-hitting catcher with several teams before becoming a scout and a minor league manager.

Hired to skipper the Giants after the 1964 campaign, Franks managed four consecutive second-place finishes before being let go in 1968. He then retired from baseball and went into business, but he was coaxed out of retirement in 1977 by his friend Bob Kennedy, the general manager of the Cubs.

Herman managed two full seasons in Chicago, but he resigned in September of 1979 with only a week to go in the season, and had some unkind words about a number of his players.

George Frazer
Syracuse Stars (AA) 1890, 1890
Record: 51–65

Managed all but 11 games in two stints with the Stars in 1890.

A Syracuse native, Frazer was actually the owner of the club and had the backing of a local streetcar line and a brewery. He served as both president and manager during the 1890 season in the American Association, but could accomplish no more than a sixth-place finish.

His team played only the one major league season, although they had existed as a minor league franchise since 1885. In 1891 they reverted to minor league status with the Eastern Association, and during the 1892 campaign moved to Utica before folding.

Joe Frazier
New York Mets (NL) 1976–77
Record: 101–106

Part-time outfielder with a brief managerial career.

Basically a reserve for four seasons in the '40s and '50s, Frazier was hired to manage the Mets in 1976 and finished a respectable third. But his club started out 15–30 the following season, and in May he was fired and replaced by Joe Torre.

Jim Fregosi
California Angels (AL) 1978–81; Chicago White Sox (AL) 1986–88; Philadelphia Phillies (NL) 1991–96; Toronto Blue Jays (AL) 1999–2000
Record: 1028–1094

San Francisco native who spent most of his career with the Angels before becoming their manager.

Fregosi was one of the few players who hit for the cycle twice; he accomplished the feat in both 1964 and 1968. A shortstop and later a first baseman, he won a Gold Glove and was a six-time All-Star.

He had debuted with the expansion Los Angeles Angels and went with them to Anaheim. After 11 years with the club, which had become the California Angels, he spent the latter part of his career with the New York Mets, Texas Rangers, and Pittsburgh Pirates.

Fregosi played 20 games with the Pirates in 1978 before being offered the manager's job with the Angels. He accepted and led the club to a second-place finish, then in 1979 took them to the top of the American League Western Division by three games over the Kansas City Royals. They lost the AL Championship Series to the Baltimore Orioles, three games to one.

That was his best season at the Angels' helm, and after a 22–25 start in 1981 he was replaced by Gene Mauch.

In 1986 he became the manager of the White Sox and could do no better than three consecutive fifth-place finishes. He became the Phillies' skipper in 1991, and two years later he guided that team to the National League Eastern Division Championship. They defeated the Atlanta Braves, four games to two, to win the NL flag, then lost the World Series to the Toronto Blue Jays. The AP named Fregosi its Manager of the Year, at a time when they chose only a single manager as the best of both leagues.

Fregosi stayed in Philadelphia through 1996, and in 1999 became the manager of the Blue Jays for two years. The Angels retired his uniform number 11 in 1998.

Jim Frey
Kansas City Royals (AL) 1980–81; Chicago Cubs (NL) 1984–86
Record: 323–287

Cleveland native who became a coach and then a manager before moving to the front office.

Hired to take the helm of the Kansas City Royals in 1980, Frey immediately led his team to the American League Western Division title by an impressive 14 games over the Oakland Athletics. They then swept the New York Yankees to capture the AL pennant before losing a six-game World Series to the Philadelphia Phillies. In 1981, a year that featured a split season because of a players' strike, the team finished fifth in the first half and then was in second place in the second half at 10–20 when Frey was fired and replaced by Dick Howser.

In 1984 he became the manager of the Cubs and once again took his team to the division title. They would lose a tough five-game National League Championship Series to the San Diego Padres, but Frey was named NL Manager of the Year by the BBWAA and overall Manager of the Year by the AP.

After a fourth-place finish the following year, the Cubs were in fifth in June of 1986 when Frey was fired. He then became a broadcaster before moving into the front office as director of baseball operations.

Frankie Frisch
St. Louis Cardinals (NL) 1933–38; Pittsburgh Pirates (NL) 1940–46; Chicago Cubs (NL) 1949–51
Record: 1138–1078

Lifetime .316 hitter and Hall of Fame second baseman.

Nicknamed "The Fordham Flash" because he excelled in several sports at Fordham University, Frankie Frisch was an exceptional athlete who never played in the minor leagues. Debuting with the New York Giants in 1919, he would hit over .300 thirteen times, would become a three-time All-Star, and would amass 2880 hits in his career. The speedy Frisch led the National League three times in stolen bases, as well as once in hits and once in runs scored. In 1931 with the Cardinals he won the first modern NL Most Valuable Player Award when he batted .311 with a league-leading 28 steals.

Named player-manager of the Redbirds in 1933, Frisch motivated his squad to play the same hard-nosed brand of ball that he himself practiced. In 1934 the Cardinals, nicknamed the "Gashouse Gang," finished two games up on the Giants to capture the NL pennant and then bested the Detroit Tigers in seven games to win the World Championship.

Frankie retired from playing in 1937, but he continued to manage the Cardinals for one more year and would later skipper the Pirates and the Cubs. A second-place finish with Pittsburgh in 1944 would be his best after leaving St. Louis.

Between managerial stints he briefly became a broadcaster, and later returned to the Giants as a coach. He was elected to the Hall of Fame in 1947.

Judge Fuchs
Boston Braves (NL) 1929
Record: 56–98

Owner who named himself manager for one season.

An attorney by trade, Judge Emil Fuchs was part of a group that included Christy Mathewson and purchased the Boston Braves in 1923. The club did not do well on the field, and in 1929 Fuchs, the team president, sought to cure its woes by naming himself manager. The tactic did not work, as the Braves finished last, and Fuchs removed himself from the dugout and hired Bill McKechnie.

During the Depression Fuchs began to have problems with his finances and received a loan from the National League. Desperate to raise flagging attendance, in 1935 he sought approval from the league to host dog races at the Braves' field, a request that was soundly denied. He then signed Babe Ruth to be a combination player, assistant manager, and vice president. The publicity stunt failed miserably, as Ruth was obviously past his prime and, despite a few impressive home runs, would retire before the end of the season. Fuchs himself resigned that year, and in 1938 he was forced to file for bankruptcy.

John Gaffney
Washington Statesmen (NL) 1886–87
Record: 61–101
Massachusetts native who injured his arm shortly before reaching the major leagues and never played at that level.

In 1884 Gaffney became a National League umpire, and he was so respected for his calls and his fairness that he earned the nicknames "Honest John" and "King of the Umpires."

So well-regarded was he that the Washington Statesmen offered him the managerial position with their club during the 1886 season. The club was not faring well, and although Gaffney took the job, he could not do much to improve its play either that year or the following season.

He returned to umpiring in 1888, although he switched from the NL to the American Association. The AA paid him a salary of $2500 plus expenses, making him the highest-paid arbiter in baseball. In 1890 he umpired in the Players League in that circuit's only season of existence, then returned to the NL.

This was an era that generally saw only one umpire per game, and both players and fans were notorious for taking out their frustrations on those umpires, no matter how well-respected. Gaffney began to drink excessively, and his alcohol abuse eventually led to his 1893 release by the NL.

He became an umpire in the minor Eastern League in 1894, but was released there because of his drinking. He was able to return to the EL for three years shortly thereafter, and in 1899 made a brief, two-year return to the NL.

He later became an umpire for college baseball, then worked as a night watchman. He died in New York in 1913, poverty-stricken, and Connie Mack would arrange an exhibition game between his Philadelphia Athletics and the Boston Red Sox to pay for a monument over Gaffney's grave.

Matt Galante
Houston Astros (NL) 1999
Record: 13–14
All-American at St. John's University who never played in the major leagues.

A strong defensive infielder when he played in college and the minor leagues, Galante worked his way up through the New York Mets' organization and eventually became a major league coach with the Astros. In 1999 he was with Houston when manager Larry Dierker suffered a grand mal seizure during a game. Dierker required brain surgery and spent four weeks in recovery, and during that time Galante filled in as interim manager. The team went 13–14 under Matt before Dierker returned.

Pud Galvin
Buffalo Bisons (NL) 1885
Record: 7–17
One of the greatest pitchers in baseball history.

Jim "Pud" Galvin received his nickname because he was said to turn batters into pudding. He played 15 major league seasons, his first full campaign being in 1879 with the Bisons when he went 37–27. He won 20 or more games 10 times, pitched two no-hitters, and was the first hurler to win 300 games in his career. He finished with 361 lifetime. He won 46 games in both the 1883 and 1884 seasons.

In 1885 he was named player-manager of the Bisons, but his record was a mere 7–17 before he turned the reins over to Jack Chapman. As a pitcher he went 13–19, and during the season he left Buffalo for the Pittsburgh Alleghenys of the American Association.

Galvin retired in 1892 and opened a saloon. He died of pneumonia on Thanksgiving Day of 1901, and he was inducted into the Hall of Fame by the Veterans Committee in 1964.

John Ganzel
Cincinnati Reds (NL) 1908; Brooklyn Tip-Tops (FL) 1915
Record: 90–99
One of five brothers to play major league baseball.

John played parts of seven seasons at first base and was an outstanding fielder. He was an inconsistent hitter, but in 1907 with the Reds he tied for the National League lead with 16 triples.

Ganzel played for several teams, but in 1904 he gained his release from the New York Highlanders and became a minor league player-owner. He returned to the majors in 1907 with the Reds, became their player-manager in 1908, and finished fifth. He returned to manage in the minor leagues, then resurfaced with the Federal League's Brooklyn Tip-Tops in 1915, replacing Lee Magee for the final 35 games of the season and finishing seventh.

Dave Garcia
California Angels (AL) 1977–78; Cleveland Indians (AL) 1979–82
Record: 307–311
Minor league infielder who never played a major league game.

Garcia became a coach with several major league teams when his playing days were over. It was in such a role that he found himself in July of 1977 when the Angels fired skipper Norm Sherry and named him manager. The team finished fifth, and they were third under Dave the following year when, in June, he was fired and replaced by Jim Fregosi.

He became a coach with the Indians the following year, and in July manager Jeff Torborg announced that he would be resigning at the end of the season. The Tribe waited only three weeks, however, before firing Torborg and replacing him with Garcia.

Dave remained with Cleveland through the 1982 season, but would not finish higher than fifth.

Ron Gardenhire
Minnesota Twins (AL) 2002–
Record: 455–354
Shortstop who played parts of five major league seasons, one of them as a starter for the New York Mets.

Gardenhire was a light hitter and never made his mark at the major league level. Playing mostly as a minor leaguer, he eventually spent time in the Twins' system, then became a Twins' coach before they named him their manager in 2002.

Ron promptly guided Minnesota to three consecutive American League Central Division titles, and a fourth in 2006. Only once in those four years did they get as far as the American League Championship Series, however, in 2002 when they lost the pennant to the Anaheim Angels.

Billy Gardner
Minnesota Twins (AL) 1981–85; Kansas City Royals (AL) 1987
Record: 330–417
Second baseman for 10 seasons with five major league teams.

Gardner did not hit for a high average, but he did tie for the American League lead with 36 doubles in 1957 while with the Baltimore Orioles. He became a coach for several years after retiring, and in May of 1981 was named manager of the Twins when skipper John Goryl was fired.

In 1984 he managed a second-place finish with a .500 winning percentage, but that was the only time he would reach that mark. He was fired in mid-1985.

In 1987 Gardner was supposed to hold a coaching position with the Royals, but manager Dick Howser, who had been attempting to come back from a brain tumor, gave up his bid during spring training and resigned in February. Gardner was named his successor, but with the team at 62–64 and in fourth place in August he was let go and replaced by John Wathan, who up to that time had been managing the AAA Omaha Royals.

Phil Garner
Milwaukee Brewers (AL) 1992–97, (NL) 1998–99; Detroit Tigers (AL) 2000–02; Houston Astros (NL) 2004–
Record: 927–981

Hard-nosed, three-time All-Star infielder with the Oakland Athletics and Pittsburgh Pirates.

Garner was an average hitter who nevertheless displayed a competitive fire that helped lead the 1979 Pirates to the World Championship. He was traded to the Astros in 1981 and spent several years in Houston before finishing out his career with the Los Angeles Dodgers and San Francisco Giants.

After coaching for the Astros, he was named manager of the Brewers in 1992 and led that club to a rare second-place finish. He was still at the helm when the team switched from the American League to the National League in 1998, and when he was fired in August of the following year he had become the winningest manager in Brewers' history.

He managed the Tigers for two full seasons, but was fired after losing the first six games of the 2002 campaign. He then returned to Houston to take the helm of the Astros in 2004. In 2005 his club won the NL wild card, then defeated the Atlanta Braves in the Division Series and the St. Louis Cardinals in the NL Championship Series to capture their first pennant ever. In the World Series, however, they were swept by the Chicago White Sox.

Cito Gaston
Toronto Blue Jays (AL) 1989–91, 1991–97
Record: 683–636
Outfielder who became one of the original San Diego Padres when he was selected in the expansion draft from the Atlanta Braves.

Gaston was an All-Star in 1970, only his second full season, when he hit .318 with 29 home runs and 93 runs batted in. Those were not to be typical numbers for him, however; he played eight more seasons but never matched any of those statistics.

He was the hitting coach for the Blue Jays when, in May of 1989, he was called upon to replace the fired Jimy Williams. He led the Jays to the American League Eastern Division crown by two games over the Baltimore Orioles, then lost the pennant to the Oakland Athletics.

In August of 1991 he was admitted to the hospital with a herniated disk, and coach Gene Tenace had to take over for the next 33 games. The Blue Jays were in first place when Gaston left, and happily, they were still in first when he returned. They went on to capture the division again, only to be bested by the Minnesota Twins in the AL Championship Series.

In 1992 the Jays again won their division, won the AL pennant by defeating the A's, and then took the World Championship in a six-game contest over the Braves. That title marked the first time a Canadian team had won the World Series and made Gaston the first African American manager ever to win the ultimate championship.

The following year the Blue Jays repeated, besting the Chicago White Sox for the AL flag and the Philadelphia Phillies for their second consecutive World Championship.

That was the last time the Jays would finish over .500 under Gaston. He was fired during the 1997 season, although in 1999 he would return to Toronto as a hitting coach. He was fired from that position in 2001.

In 2002 Cito was elected to the Canadian Baseball Hall of Fame.

Bob Geren
Oakland Athletics (AL) 2007–
Record: 0–0
Backup catcher for the New York Yankees and San Diego Padres.

A San Diego native, Geren went to work in the minor leagues after his playing days had ended. Starting as a roving catching instructor for the Boston Red Sox, he soon became a manager and eventually moved on to the Oakland system, where he won the California League Manager of the Year Award in 1999 when his Modesto A's made it to the semifinals. In 2003 he was promoted to Oakland as a coach, and following the 2006 season was named the club's manager.

Joe Gerhardt
Louisville Eclipse (AA) 1883; St. Louis Browns (AA) 1890
Record: 72–61
Rather light-hitting second baseman who played 15 seasons in the major leagues.

Gerhardt played for a number of different teams in three different leagues during his career. He was named player-manager of the Louisville Eclipse in 1883, and that team finished fifth in the American Association despite a respectable 52–45 record. In 1890 with the St. Louis Browns Gerhardt was again named player-manager, becoming the last of six skippers to manage the club that season. Despite the revolving door the Browns finished in third place with a decent 78–58 record.

Doc Gessler
Pittsburgh Pittsfeds (FL) 1914
Record: 3–8
Solid outfielder and first baseman at the beginning of the twentieth century.

In eight major league seasons Gessler topped the .300 mark only once, but he averaged .280 for his career. His managerial career was short-lived, as he skippered the Federal League's Pittsburgh Pittsfeds for only 11 games

and won but 3 of them before being replaced by Rebel Oakes.

John Gibbons
Toronto Blue Jays (AL) 2004–
Record: 187–187
Played only 18 major league games as a catcher before becoming a coach and eventual manager.

A Montana native, Gibbons was the Blue Jays' first base coach in 2004 when he was named to replace fired manager Carlos Tosca on an interim basis. After going 20–30 he was hired permanently and removed the "interim" label from his title for the 2005 season.

George Gibson
Pittsburgh Pirates (NL) 1920–22, 1932–34; Chicago Cubs (NL) 1925
Record: 413–344
Catcher for 11 seasons with the Pittsburgh Pirates and New York Giants.

Two years after his retirement, Gibson was hired to manage the Pirates, and the following season, 1921, he guided them to a second-place finish. The following year they were in fifth place after 65 games when he resigned.

In 1925 he was a coach for the Cubs, who had already replaced manager Bill Killefer with Rabbit Maranville during the season. Toward the end of the season Maranville, who was player-manager, was with the team on a train during a road trip when he splashed various passengers with the contents of a spittoon. Although Rabbit would play out the rest of the season with Chicago, he would not return after that as a player and was replaced as manager by Gibson for the final 26 games of the year.

In 1932 George came out of retirement to take the reins in Pittsburgh once again. He managed two consecutive second-place finishes, missing the National League pennant by four and five games, respectively, and was fourth in June of 1934 when he was fired and replaced by Pie Traynor.

Jim Gifford
Indianapolis Hoosiers (AA) 1884; New York Metropolitans (AA) 1885–86
Record: 74–136
Native of Warren, New York, who managed a couple of struggling teams.

Gifford was 25–60 with the Hoosiers in 1884 when he was replaced by Bill Watkins. The change would make no difference, as the club won only 4 games the rest of the season while losing 18, finishing 46 games out of first place.

The Metropolitans of 1885–86 were not much better,

and Gifford never accomplished more than a seventh-place finish.

Joe Girardi
Florida Marlins (NL) 2006
Record: 78–84
Catcher for 15 major league seasons.

Girardi started his career with the Chicago Cubs, but became an original member of the Colorado Rockies in 1993 when he was selected in the expansion draft. He later went to the New York Yankees and helped the club to three World Championships. In 1996 with New York he caught Dwight Gooden's no-hitter, and in 1999 caught David Cone's perfect game against the Montreal Expos.

Girardi returned to the Cubs in 2000 and was named a National League All-Star. He finished his career in 2003 with the St. Louis Cardinals, and he became a broadcaster the following season. In 2005 he returned to the Yankees as a coach, and was named Marlins' manager following that season when Jack McKeon retired. He was fired after one season, however, after not getting along with owner Jeffrey Loria and general manager Larry Beinfest. During a game in August, Loria began shouting at an umpire from the first row of seats and Girardi forcefully asked him to stop. That public confrontation nearly caused Loria to fire him, but the owner held off until after the season before dropping the axe. Girardi was fired despite the fact that he had two guaranteed years remaining on his contract. Shortly thereafter he was named the National League Manager of the Year by the BBWAA. His Marlins, loaded with rookies, finished at 78–84 after being expected to lose at least 100 games. Girardi thus became the first Manager of the Year with a losing record.

He then returned to broadcasting with the Yankees.

Jack Glasscock
Indianapolis Hoosiers (NL) 1889; St. Louis Browns (NL) 1892
Record: 35–35
Bare-handed, premier shortstop of the nineteenth century.

Glasscock played for 17 seasons, beginning in 1879 with the Cleveland Blues. He hit over .300 six times, amassing 2082 hits lifetime, and batted .294 for his career. In 1889 he became player-manager of the Hoosiers, replacing Frank Bancroft during the season, and he led the National League with 205 hits while batting .352 but finished in seventh place. With the New York Giants the following year he won the NL batting title with a .336 average and tied for the league lead with 172 hits.

He briefly managed the Browns in 1892, but turned control over to Cub Stricker after a 1–3 start.

Kid Gleason
Chicago White Sox (AL) 1919–23
Record: 392–364
Solid pitcher-turned-second-baseman with a 22-year major league career.

Gleason was an adequate hitter and a speedy baserunner, twice stealing more than 40 bases in a season and swiping 328 in his career. In 1900 he and teammates George Davis and Mike Grady helped rescue several people from a serious apartment fire while on their way to a game at the Polo Grounds. They then continued to the park and played the regularly-scheduled game.

He became a coach following his retirement in 1912, and was named manager of the White Sox for the 1919 season.

It was a powerful team he took over, and the club won the American League pennant by 3½ games over the Cleveland Indians. But many of his starting players then threw the World Series to the Cincinnati Reds in what has since been known as the Black Sox Scandal, due in large part to owner Charlie Comiskey's tightfistedness with some of his key players. Gleason reported to Comiskey that he was suspicious of some of his personnel. A 1920 investigation implicated eight of the White Sox, but evidence then mysteriously disappeared. Baseball Commissioner Kenesaw Mountain Landis nevertheless banned those eight for life, and what was probably the greatest scandal in baseball history came to an end.

Gleason felt betrayed by his players and never forgot what they had done. The team finished second in 1920 but was stripped of its best performers thereafter, and Gleason would not get better than a fifth-place finish out of the remnants after that.

Preston Gomez
San Diego Padres (NL) 1969–72; Houston Astros (NL) 1974–75; Chicago Cubs (NL) 1980
Record: 346–529
Played a mere eight games for the Washington Nationals in 1944.

A shortstop, Gomez went straight to the Nationals without ever playing in the minor leagues. After those eight games, however, he would spend the rest of his playing career at the bush league level.

He would return to the major leagues as a coach beginning in 1965. In 1969 he became the first skipper of the expansion Padres, and the team predictably finished last. They would fail to climb out of the cellar during Gomez's tenure, and 11 games into the 1972 season he was fired.

He fared little better with Houston, and no better with the Cubs. Twice—in 1970 with the Padres and in 1974 with the Astros—he put in pinch-hitters for pitchers who had no-hitters in progress. Fourth place would be the highlight of Preston's managerial career.

Fredi Gonzalez
Florida Marlins (NL) 2007–
Record: 0–0
Minor league catcher in the New York Yankees' system.

Gonzalez played six years before becoming a minor league manager late in the 1990 season with the Miami Miracle, an unaffiliated club. In 1992 he became the first minor league manager in the history of the Marlins when he took over the Erie Sailors. He managed for many years, and *Baseball America* named him the California League Manager of the Year in 1993 when his High Desert Mavericks won the championship, the Florida State League Manager of the Year in 1994 when his Brevard County Manatees finished 78–61, and the Eastern League Manager of the Year in 1997 when his Portland Sea Dogs finished in first place.

He was promoted to Marlins' coach from 1999–2001. He managed the Richmond Braves in 2002 before joining the Atlanta coaching staff, then returned to Florida as manager in 2007 to replace Joe Girardi.

Mike Gonzalez
St. Louis Cardinals (NL) 1938, 1940
Record: 9–13
Catcher who played 17 seasons with several teams before becoming a coach.

Gonzalez played three different times for the Cardinals, and ended his career with them in 1932. Two years later he became a Redbirds' coach, a position he would hold for 13 years.

Twice during those years he filled in as manager on an interim basis. In 1938 he replaced Frankie Frisch for the final 17 games of the season, and in 1940, when Ray Blades was fired, he took over for 6 games until Billy Southworth arrived as his permanent replacement.

Joe Gordon
Cleveland Indians (AL) 1958–60; Detroit Tigers (AL) 1960;
Kansas City Athletics (AL) 1961; Kansas City Royals
(AL) 1969
Record: 305–308
Played 11 years at second base and was an All-Star nine times.

Mainly a defensive whiz, Gordon also had power, cranking out at least 20 home runs seven times and ending his career with 253. In 1942 with the New York Yankees he was named the American League's Most Valuable Player when he hit .322 with 18 homers and 103 runs batted in.

Gordon retired in 1950 and became a minor league manager. In 1952, as player-manager of the Sacramento Solons of the Pacific Coast League, he used himself as a pinch-hitter in both games of a doubleheader and homered both times up. The first longball was a grand slam that accounted for all of his team's runs in a 4–1 victory.

He returned to the major leagues in 1956 as a coach with the Tigers, and became the manager of the Indians in 1958. The following year the club finished in second place. In 1960 he was traded to the Tigers for *their* manager, Jimmy Dykes. The Indians were fourth when he left and finished fourth; the Tigers were sixth when he took over and finished sixth.

He resigned at the end of the season because of interference from Bill DeWitt, the Tigers' president. He was hired to manage the A's in Kansas City, but was fired in June by owner Charlie Finley. Eight years later he would return to Kansas City to manage the Royals in their inaugural year, and resigned after the season.

George Gore
St. Louis Browns (NL) 1892
Record: 6–9
Outstanding hitter who played for 14 seasons and batted .306 lifetime.

Gore routinely scored over 100 runs per season, and he ended his career with 1327 in 1310 games. He is one of only three players to average more than a run scored per game in his career.

In 1880 he won the National League batting title with a .360 average, and would top the .300 mark nine times. In 1881 he stole seven bases in one game, setting a major league record. He led the league three times in bases on balls and twice in runs scored.

In 1892 he briefly became player-manager of the St. Louis Browns, becoming the fourth of five managers that year for the club. He went 6–9 and was then replaced by Bob Caruthers.

Johnny Goryl
Minnesota Twins (AL) 1980–81
Record: 34–38
Part-time infielder who spent many years in the Twins' organization.

Goryl's major league career consisted of six years, half spent with the Chicago Cubs and half with Minnesota. He would eventually become a minor league manager in the Twins' system, then a major league coach.

In August of 1980, Goryl took over when Gene Mauch resigned, and he brought the Twins from sixth all the way to a third-place finish. The following year, however, they were 11–25 when he was fired and replaced by Billy Gardner. The next year he became a coach with the Cleveland Indians.

Charlie Gould
New Haven Elm Citys (NA) 1875; Cincinnati Red Stockings (NL) 1876
Record: 11–77
Member of the original 1869 Cincinnati Red Stockings.

Gould was a Cincinnati native, and he began his playing career with the amateur Cincinnati Buckeyes in 1863. Charlie's father ran a business selling butter and eggs, and during the offseason Gould worked as a bookkeeper in that business. He played for the Buckeyes through 1867, then defected the following year to the Cincinnati Red Stockings, a rival team that had begun two years earlier as the Resolutes. In 1869 he was part of baseball's first professional team, a team that went undefeated in 57 games (68 if exhibition games are included).

In 1870 the Red Stockings were 68–6, and those few losses were enough to remove the magical aura from the team, for its owners decided they could no longer afford to field a club of professionals. Manager Harry Wright left for Boston, and Gould and several others went with him to play for the Red Stockings of the new, professional National Association.

Gould played two years there, and by 1875 was playing for the New Haven Elm Citys. As player-manager for part of the season he went 2–21 for a team that finished 7–40. In 1876 he returned to Cincinnati as player-manager of the restored Red Stockings in the brand new National League. Those Stockings were not nearly as glamorous as their forebears had been, however, and Gould's team was a dismal 9–56. Charlie no longer managed the following year but did continue to play, then he retired and eventually became a police officer in his hometown.

Hank Gowdy
Cincinnati Reds (NL) 1946
Record: 3–1
Solid-hitting catcher and first baseman who played his entire career with the New York Giants and Boston Braves.

Gowdy was the first major leaguer to enlist in the Army in World War I, and he missed the entire 1918 season. He returned the following year, and after retiring in 1925 he became a coach, although he served as player-coach for the Braves in 1929 and '30.

He was a coach for the Reds in 1946 when manager Bill McKechnie was fired with only four games remaining. Gowdy took over for those four contests, winning

three of them, then went to the Giants as a coach the next year.

Mase Graffen
St. Louis Brown Stockings (NL) 1876
Record: 39–17
Philadelphia native who never played in the major leagues.

Graffen managed the Brown Stockings during the National League's inaugural season of 1876. Despite a 39–17 record, he was succeeded by George McManus with only eight games to go. The Brown Stockings finished in second place, six games behind the champion Chicago White Stockings.

Alex Grammas
Pittsburgh Pirates (NL) 1969; Milwaukee Brewers (AL) 1976–77
Record: 137–191
Light-hitting but good-fielding shortstop for the St. Louis Cardinals, Cincinnati Reds, and Chicago Cubs.

After a 10-year career, spent mostly as a reserve, Grammas became a coach with the Pirates. When manager Larry Shepard was fired with only five games left in the 1969 season, Alex took over and won four of those games. The next year both he and Shepard joined the new coaching staff of Sparky Anderson in Cincinnati, at the beginning of what would become the Big Red Machine era.

Grammas was hired away from the Reds to manage the Brewers in 1976, but after two last-place finishes he returned to Cincinnati as a coach. He would later coach the Atlanta Braves, and then work again under Anderson with the Detroit Tigers.

Dallas Green
Philadelphia Phillies (NL) 1979–81; New York Yankees (AL) 1989; New York Mets (NL) 1993–96
Record: 454–478
Mediocre pitcher who later held a number of managerial and front office positions in major league baseball.

Green played for eight seasons before becoming the Phillies' manager in 1979. Only a year later he took the club to the National League pennant and then to its first World Championship in 65 years, defeating the Kansas City Royals four games to two.

In the strike-induced split season of 1981, the Phillies won the division title in the first half, but fell to the Montreal Expos in the divisional playoffs. Green resigned after the season when he was offered the general manager's position with the Chicago Cubs.

Dallas is credited with rebuilding a flagging Cubs' minor league system, and his work paid off when Chicago won the NL Eastern Division in 1984, although they fell short of the pennant.

Green resigned in 1987 because of differences with the Tribune Company, which owned the Cubs, and in 1989 was hired to manage the Yankees. His stay did not last long; in August, with the team in sixth place, he became one of owner George Steinbrenner's many managerial casualties. He later managed the Mets for several years before being replaced by Bobby Valentine in August of 1996.

Mike Griffin
Brooklyn Bridegrooms (NL) 1898
Record: 1–3
Outfielder with a .303 lifetime batting average.

As a rookie in 1887 Griffin stole 94 bases to set what was then a major league record for a rookie. He also batted .366, which was to be his highest average ever.

In 1889 he tied for the American Association lead with 152 runs scored, and two years later topped the National League with 36 doubles.

In 1898, his final year, he managed the Brooklyn Bridegrooms for four games when Billy Barnie was fired and before owner Charlie Ebbets took over as manager himself.

Sandy Griffin
Washington Statesmen (AA) 1891
Record: 2–4
Played parts of four season in the major leagues as an outfielder.

With the Washington Statesmen of the American Association in 1891, Griffin also managed the final six games of the season, becoming the last in a succession of managers that included Sam Trott, Pop Snyder, and Dan Shannon. The team finished last, 49 games off the pace.

Sandy later became a longtime player, manager, and owner of the Syracuse Stars of the minor New York State League. He managed that club from 1902–09, put together a 569–486 career record, and led them to the 1904 NYSL championship. He spent a total of 16 years with the organization.

In 2003 he became a member of the Syracuse Baseball Wall of Fame.

Clark Griffith
Chicago Invaders (AL) 1901; Chicago White Stockings (AL) 1901–02; New York Highlanders (AL) 1903–08; Cincinnati Reds (NL) 1909–11; Washington Nationals (AL) 1912–20
Record: 1491–1367
Pitcher-turned-manager-turned-owner.

An excellent hurler in the late nineteenth and early twentieth centuries, Griffith won 237 games in his career against 146 losses, good for a .619 winning percentage. He won at least 20 games seven times.

Nicknamed "The Old Fox," Griffith was a spitball pitcher at a time when using foreign substances on the ball was legal. He was a born leader, once convincing his fellow players to strike when he was with the Oakland Oaks of the Pacific Coast League and they were owed back pay, and finding them work as vaudeville performers. He led a major league strike in 1900, demanding an increase in players' base salary and insisting that owners pay for team uniforms. While this was going on, Griffith's friend Ban Johnson was on the verge of bringing his minor American League to major league status, making it a rival of the National League, and Clark set about convincing a large number of players to jump to the AL.

As a reward for his efforts he was named manager of the new league's Chicago Invaders (soon to be called the White Stockings) in 1901. He instantly led that team to the inaugural AL pennant, the only time in 20 years as a manager that he would finish in first place.

When Johnson moved the Baltimore Orioles to New York in 1903, he offered that managerial position to Griffith, who accepted. Griffith led the Highlanders until June of 1908, when he resigned because of his belief that the team's owners were not spending the money required to create a successful club.

He returned to the NL in 1909 at the helm of the Reds, but after three years Ban Johnson coaxed him back to his rival league with an offer to pilot the Washington Nationals. Griffith took him up on that offer, and in addition to becoming manager he purchased an interest in the team. He would eventually become the Nationals' principal owner, and would remain so until his death in 1955. The team, later called the Senators and then the Minnesota Twins, would remain in his family until his son and daughter sold it in 1984.

Burleigh Grimes
Brooklyn Dodgers (NL) 1937–38
Record: 131–171
Ill-humored pitcher who won 270 games in his career.

A spitballer who threw when it was legal to apply foreign substances to baseballs, Grimes debuted in 1916 and played for 19 years. He was a 20-game winner five times, and he tied for the National League lead in 1921 with 22 victories and again in 1928 with his career high of 25. He was also durable, leading twice in games pitched, three times in games started, and four times in complete games.

When the spitball was outlawed in 1920, Grimes was among a handful of pitchers who received an exemption from the new rule. When he retired in 1934, he was the last active legal spitballer in major league baseball.

Not usually affable on the baseball diamond, he managed the Brooklyn Dodgers for two unsuccessful seasons, bristling when owner Larry McPhail hired Babe Ruth as a coach and, more accurately, as a sideshow attraction. Grimes later became a longtime minor league manager, and coached the 1955 season with the Kansas City Athletics.

He was elected to the Hall of Fame by the Veterans Committee in 1964, and he died in 1985 at the age of 92.

Charlie Grimm
Chicago Cubs (NL) 1932–38, 1944–49, 1960; Boston Braves (NL) 1952; Milwaukee Braves (NL) 1953–56
Record: 1287–1067
Fun-loving, excellent-fielding first baseman who spent most of his career with the Pittsburgh Pirates and Chicago Cubs.

A solid, consistent hitter, Grimm batted over .300 in five of his full seasons and hit .290 for his career. In August of 1932 he was named player-manager of the Cubs when Rogers Hornsby was fired; in second place when he took over, the club went on to capture the National League pennant with a 15-game winning streak. They were then swept by the New York Yankees in the World Series.

The Cubbies won the pennant again in 1935, and this time they dropped the Series to the Detroit Tigers in six games. Grimm quit playing in 1936, but continued as manager until July of 1938, when he resigned because of a lack of control over his players. He moved to the broadcast booth while the Cubs won another pennant.

In that first go-round as skipper in Chicago, Grimm's teams never finished lower than third place. After calling games for a couple of years, Charlie returned to the dugout as a coach, then became a minor league manager.

In 1944 he once again took the Cubs' helm, and a year later won yet another NL pennant. This time his club dropped a tough seven-game Series, once again to the Tigers. The Cubs eventually began to flounder under Grimm, and he later returned to the minor leagues and then managed the Boston/Milwaukee Braves, where he would post two second-place finishes.

In 1960 he returned to the Cubs for a third round of managing, but after going 6–11 he went back to broadcasting, while Cubs' broadcaster Lou Boudreau took over as manager. The next two years Charlie was back in uniform as a Chicago coach. He then served in the front office, and died in 1983. His ashes were scattered over Wrigley Field.

Heinie Groh
Cincinnati Reds (NL) 1918
Record: 7–3
Solid hitter and infielder with the New York Giants, Cincinnati Reds, and Pittsburgh Pirates.

A .292 lifetime hitter, Groh led the National League twice in doubles, once in runs scored, once in hits, and once in bases on balls. He was with the Reds in 1918 when, with 10 games left in a season shortened by World War I, manager Christy Mathewson joined the Army. Groh was named his replacement as player-manager for the rest of the season.

He would play on the Reds' World Championship squad during the Black Sox Scandal of 1919, and would play on several others with the Giants and Pirates before retiring in 1927. He then became a minor league manager.

Ozzie Guillen
Chicago White Sox (AL) 2004–
Record: 272–214
Three-time All-Star shortstop with an excellent glove and a competent bat.

In 1985 Guillen won the American League's Rookie of the Year Award when he committed only 12 errors all season. He spent most of his career with the White Sox, winning All-Star accolades with them in 1988, 1990, and 1991. Fleet of foot early in his career, he stole at least 21 bases four of his first seven years before a knee injury suffered in an outfield collision effectively ended his running game.

Guillen retired after the 2000 season and coached the Montreal Expos and Florida Marlins before being named manager of the White Sox. In 2005 he led Chicago to the American League Central Division title, and his club then swept the defending World Champion Boston Red Sox in the Division Series and defeated the Los Angeles Angels of Anaheim for the AL pennant. In the World Series they swept the Houston Astros in four games to win the White Sox' first World Championship since 1917. The BBWAA named Guillen its AL Manager of the Year.

Don Gutteridge
Chicago White Sox (AL) 1969–70
Record: 109–172
Started his career as a third baseman with the St. Louis Cardinals, with whom he collected six hits in a doubleheader during his second day in the major leagues.

Gutteridge hit an inside-the-park home run and stole home twice that day, making it likely the most memorable of his life. Later playing for the St. Louis Browns, Boston Red Sox, and Pittsburgh Pirates, Don fashioned a respectable 12-year career before becoming a coach with the

White Sox.

He would manage two seasons, neither of them complete. When Al Lopez resigned in 1969 for health reasons, Gutteridge took over and led the team to a fifth-place finish. In sixth in September of 1970, he was fired and replaced by interim manager Bill Adair and eventually by Chuck Tanner.

Eddie Haas
Atlanta Braves (NL) 1985
Record: 50–71
Played a total of 55 games in the major leagues as an outfielder before eventually becoming a coach.

Haas spent two terms as a coach with Atlanta. The first was 1974–77, and the second lasted only a single season, 1984, before he was named manager to replace Joe Torre.

He didn't last a single season as skipper, however. The Braves were in fifth place in 1985 when Braves' owner Ted Turner fired Eddie and replaced him with Bobby Wine.

Stan Hack
Chicago Cubs (NL) 1954–56; St. Louis Cardinals (NL) 1958
Record: 199–272
Five-time All-Star third baseman with a .301 lifetime batting average.

Hack routinely scored over 100 runs in a season, and in a 16-year career—all of which was spent with the Cubs—he slugged at least 16 doubles 12 times. He led the National League twice in hits and twice in stolen bases, as well as five times in putouts, twice in assists, and twice in fielding average.

In three seasons as Cubs' manager he had little success, however, finishing seventh, sixth, and eighth. In 1957 he became a coach with the Cardinals, and was named their skipper for the last 10 games of the 1958 season when Fred Hutchinson was fired. He won only three of those, and he then became a manager in the minor leagues. He returned to the Cubs in 1965 as a coach.

Charlie Hackett
Cleveland Blues (NL) 1884; Brooklyn Atlantics (AA) 1885
Record: 50–99
Massachusetts native who never played in the major leagues and had a rather brief, unsuccessful managerial career.

Hackett piloted the Blues to a 35–77 record and a seventh-place finish in 1884. He was nevertheless hired to manage the Atlantics in 1885, a team that had finished ninth in the American Association the previous season.

After a 15–22 start, Hackett was fired by team President Charlie Byrne, who took over as skipper himself.

Bill Hallman
St. Louis Browns (NL) 1897
Record: 13–36
Infielder from Pittsburgh who played most of his career with Philadelphia.

Hallman actually played for two different Philadelphia franchises: the Nationals of the National League from 1888–89, and the Quakers of the Players League in 1890, who became the Athletics when they joined the American Association in 1891. In 1892 Bill returned to the NL franchise, which by then was called the Phillies.

During the 1897 season he joined the St. Louis Browns, a miserable team that won 29 games all season against 102 losses. He became player-manager, the third skipper for the club, and won only 13 of 50 games with one tie. That was the end of his piloting experience.

Four years later he returned to the Phillies, and would finish out his career with them in 1903. He was an actor and vaudeville performer in the offseasons.

Fred Haney
St. Louis Browns (AL) 1939–41; Pittsburgh Pirates (NL) 1953–55; Milwaukee Braves (NL) 1956–59
Record: 629–757
Played seven seasons in the majors as a third baseman, but only two full time.

Beginning his managerial career in the minor leagues, Haney was hired to manage the Browns in 1939, but he had some dismal years there with a dismal team. The club lost 111 games in 1939, and Haney would finish no better than sixth during those three seasons. He was fired with a 15–29 record in 1941.

Haney went back to managing in the minor leagues, then became a broadcaster for the Hollywood Stars of the Pacific Coast League. He was eventually named that team's manager and led them to two pennants, inspiring the Pittsburgh Pirates to hire him as their skipper. The Pirates were every bit as dismal as the Browns had been, but after leaving Pittsburgh Haney coached for the Milwaukee Braves and was soon named manager. He took them to a pennant in 1957 and then to a World Championship in seven games over the New York Yankees. Another pennant immediately followed, although this time the Yankees turned the tables in the Series, again in seven games.

Those results were apparently not good enough for some, because Haney was fired during the 1959 season with the club in second place. Soon afterwards he would become the first general manager of the expansion Los Angeles Angels.

Ned Hanlon

Pittsburgh Alleghenys (NL) 1889; Pittsburgh Burghers (PL) 1890; Pittsburgh Pirates (NL) 1891; Baltimore Orioles (NL) 1892–98; Brooklyn Superbas (NL) 1899–1905; Cincinnati Reds (NL) 1906–07
Record: 1313–1164

Outfielder and adequate hitter who gained great fame as a manager.

Hanlon's playing career lasted from 1880–92, and the last four years were spent as player-manager. He took over the Pittsburgh Alleghenys during the 1889 season, then helped form the rival Players League the next season and managed the Pittsburgh entry in that circuit, the Burghers. He returned to the National League in 1891 when the PL folded, and again managed his former team, which was now called the Pirates.

In 1892 he went to the Baltimore Orioles, and that would become one of the strongest teams in baseball history. After two rather miserable seasons, Hanlon guided them to three consecutive pennants, in part by using such tactics as the hit-and-run and having his groundskeeper keep the dirt around home plate hard so that his players could drive balls into the ground and run them out in a strategy that became known as the Baltimore chop.

The Orioles even participated in an early version of the World Series those three years, a contest known as the Temple Cup. In 1894 they were swept by the New York Giants in four games; in 1895 they lost to the Cleveland Spiders, four games to one; and in 1896 they swept the Spiders, four games to none.

In 1899 most of the Orioles were absorbed by the Brooklyn NL franchise, a process that would be completed by the end of that year. Hanlon went to Brooklyn as manager, and because there was a popular vaudeville act at the time called "Hanlon's Superbas," the team became known as the Brooklyn Superbas. In 1900 and 1901 Hanlon's club won consecutive NL pennants. In 1900 the NL was the only existing major league, but another early version of the World Series, the Chronicle-Telegraph Cup, pitted the league's first- and second-place finishers against each other. The Superbas participated and defeated the Pittsburgh Pirates, three games to one. There was no postseason in 1901.

Hanlon was fired in 1905 after finishing in last place, and he then managed the Reds for two years. He was elected to the Hall of Fame by the Veterans Committee in 1996.

Mel Harder

Cleveland Indians (AL) 1961, 1962
Record: 3–0

Nebraska native who spent 36 years with the Cleveland Indians as a player, coach, and manager.

For 20 of those years Harder was a pitcher, and his 223 victories made him one of the winningest in Indians' history.

He threw the first pitch at Cleveland's Municipal Stadium, and eventually became a four-time All-Star. After retiring he became the Indians' pitching coach, and he would spend 17 years in that role. On an interim basis he managed one game in 1961 and two in 1962, winning all three of them. After leaving the Tribe he would coach for several other teams. The Indians retired his number 18 in 1990.

Harder passed away in 2002.

Mike Hargrove

Cleveland Indians (AL) 1991–99; Baltimore Orioles (AL) 2000–03; Seattle Mariners (AL) 2005–
Record: 1143–1140

American League Rookie of the Year in 1974.

Hargrove hit .323 for the Texas Rangers that season, and that would be his career high although he would eventually top the .300 mark four more times. He hit .290 lifetime and was named to the 1975 All-Star team.

After retiring in 1985 he became a minor league manager in the Indians' system, and was named the big club's skipper in 1991. He and his team would hit their stride in 1995, beginning a run of five consecutive AL Central Division championships. They took the pennant twice—in 1995, when they dropped the World Series to the Atlanta Braves, and in 1997, when they lost to the Florida Marlins.

Despite his successes Hargrove was fired in 1999 following that fifth consecutive first-place finish, and he later managed the Orioles and the Mariners.

Toby Harrah

Texas Rangers (AL) 1992
Record: 32–44

Shortstop-turned-third-baseman and four-time All-Star.

In 17 years Harrah displayed some pop in his bat, hitting at least 20 home runs five times and peaking with 27 in 1977, the same year he led the American League with 109 bases on balls. He accomplished an odd feat that year, teaming with fellow Ranger Bump Wills in hitting back-to-back inside-the-park home runs. He also had good speed, stealing at least 15 bases in a season on nine occasions.

Harrah became a coach with the Rangers following his retirement, and in July of 1992 he managed the club for the second half of the year when Bobby Valentine was fired. The team finished fourth.

Bud Harrelson
New York Mets (NL) 1990–91
Record: 145–129
Good-fielding shortstop who played most of his career with the New York Mets.

Named to All-Star teams in 1970 and '71, Harrelson was a spark plug for the Mets, getting on base any way he could in spite of some low batting averages. He won a Gold Glove in 1971, and two years later helped the Mets to the National League Eastern Division crown. He is still well known for his fight with Pete Rose in the NL Championship Series, a battle that began when Rose slid hard into second base and that resulted in a bench-clearing brawl.

After retiring Harrelson became a coach with New York, and he was named skipper in May of 1990 when Davey Johnson was fired. After a second-place finish he returned to manage in 1991, but was fired late in September with the team in third place.

Bucky Harris
Washington Nationals (AL) 1924–28, 1935–42, 1950–54; Detroit Tigers (AL) 1929–33, 1955–56; Boston Red Sox (AL) 1934; Philadelphia Phillies (NL) 1943; New York Yankees (AL) 1947–48
Record: 2157–2218
Decent second baseman who played for 12 years and spent 29 seasons as a manager.

A .274 lifetime hitter, Harris received his first managerial job while still playing for the Nationals in 1924. Only 27 years of age, he received the nickname "The Boy Manager," but he showed great leadership ability by guiding his club to the American League pennant. And his team did not stop there, going on to capture the World Championship in seven games over the New York Giants. Harris himself hit .333 in that Series.

The Nationals were back the next year, finishing 8½ games ahead of the Philadelphia Athletics to take the AL flag, although they dropped a seven-game World Series to the Pittsburgh Pirates.

Bucky never again had that kind of success in Washington, although he would have three stints there as manager. He had two such tenures in Detroit with the Tigers, fifth place being his usual showing there.

But in 1947 he took the New York Yankees to the AL title, finishing 12 games up on the Tigers and then defeating the Brooklyn Dodgers in seven games for the World Championship. *The Sporting News* named him its Manager of the Year.

Harris had spent a season with the Red Sox and a partial season with the Phillies. After his second stint in Detroit he worked for the Red Sox as assistant general manager, then became a scout with the Chicago White Sox and the expansion Washington Senators.

Harris's 2157 victories place him in the top 10 all-time. He was inducted into the Hall of Fame by the Veterans Committee in 1975.

Lum Harris
Baltimore Orioles (AL) 1961; Houston Colt .45s (NL) 1964; Houston Astros (NL) 1965; Atlanta Braves (NL) 1968–72
Record: 466–488
Fair pitcher for some very bad teams in the 1940s.

Harris lost 21 games in 1943 with the Philadelphia Athletics, and he lasted only six major league seasons. But he spent many years as a coach, and had some success as a manager.

He took over the Orioles in September of 1961 when Paul Richards resigned, and he finished out the season with a 17–10 record and a third-place showing. Three years later he was a coach with the Colt .45s when Harry Craft was fired in September, and he went 5–8 for the final 13 games of the season—finishing ninth—and duplicated that finish the following year with the renamed Astros.

He took over the Braves in 1968, and in 1969 led that club to the very first National League Western Division title. In the first NL Championship Series, however, Atlanta was swept in three games by the New York Mets.

Harris could not duplicate that success afterwards, and was let go in August of 1972.

Jim Hart
Louisville Colonels (AA) 1885–86; Boston Bostons (NL) 1889
Record: 202–174
Hailed from Fairview, Pennsylvania, and never played a major league game.

Only 29 years old when he took control of the Colonels, Hart had two rather mediocre seasons before piloting the Bostons to a second-place finish in 1889. That team finished only a single game behind the pennant-winning New York Giants, who went on to defeat the Brooklyn Bridegrooms in an early version of the World Series.

John Hart
Cleveland Indians (AL) 1989
Record: 8–11
Tampa native who played minor league ball as a catcher and later became a major league executive.

After his playing career Hart coached high school baseball and then became a minor league manager in the Baltimore Orioles' system. With the Bluefield Orioles in 1982 he was named Appalachian League Manager of the Year. He eventually moved up to the Rochester Red

Wings, where he was named International League Manager of the Year in 1986.

He coached the major league Orioles in 1988, and was a scout with the Cleveland Indians in 1989 when he was named interim manager for the last 19 games of the season to replace Doc Edwards. He then became director of baseball operations, and eventually executive vice president and general manager. He was named Major League Executive of the Year by *The Sporting News* in both 1994 and 1995.

In November of 2001 he became the general manager of the Texas Rangers.

Gabby Hartnett
Chicago Cubs (NL) 1938–40
Record: 203–176
Six-time All-Star catcher and Hall of Famer.

A .297 lifetime hitter, Hartnett also slugged 236 career home runs and led the National League numerous times in various fielding categories. In 1935 he was named the NL's Most Valuable Player when he hit .344 with 13 home runs and 91 runs batted in while also leading all catchers in fielding average, assists, and double plays.

Halfway through the 1938 season, after serving as a player-coach, Gabby was named the Cubs' player-manager, replacing Charlie Grimm. He led the Cubs to the pennant in more ways than one. In a game late in September, the Cubs were playing the first-place Pittsburgh Pirates, a team they trailed in the standings by a mere half-game. The score was knotted at 5–5 as evening drew on, and in the bottom of the ninth inning darkness was setting in and the game was on the verge of being called. Hartnett then slugged a three-run homer to give the Cubs the win and put them in first place, and that blast has since been known as the "Homer in the Gloamin'." The Cubs clinched the pennant a few days later, although they would later be swept in the World Series by the New York Yankees.

Hartnett managed two more years but would not finish better than fourth. He closed out his career with the New York Giants in 1941, and was elected to the Hall of Fame in 1955. In 1965 he was a coach for the Kansas City Athletics.

Roy Hartsfield
Toronto Blue Jays (AL) 1977–79
Record: 166–318
Decent but oft-injured second baseman who spent three seasons with the Boston Braves.

Later a coach with the Los Angeles Dodgers and Atlanta Braves, Hartsfield became the very first manager of the Toronto Blue Jays at a time when it was generally understood that it would take an expansion team quite a few years to develop its talent. The Blue Jays exemplified that belief, finishing last all three years Hartsfield was at the helm. During those years they lost 107, 102, and 109 games, respectively.

Roy was fired following the 1979 campaign and replaced by Bobby Mattick.

Scott Hastings
Rockford Forest Citys (NA) 1871; Cleveland Forest Citys (NA) 1872
Record: 10–35
Civil War veteran who became a major league catcher.

Having served with the 145th Infantry Regiment in Illinois as a teenager in 1864, Scott Hastings became player-manager of the Rockford Forest Citys of the National Association in 1871, at the age of 23. He was a solid hitter, but Rockford went only 4–21 in what then qualified as a full season. Moving to the Cleveland Forest Citys in 1872 (a separate team despite the similar name), he went 6–14 for a squad that finished at 6–16, in seventh place out of 11 teams.

Hastings played for various teams until 1877 but no longer managed.

John Hatfield
New York Mutuals (NA) 1872–73
Record: 35–31
Played for the Cincinnati Red Stockings in 1868, the year before that club became baseball's first professional team.

Hatfield was with the New York Mutuals when the National Association was formed in 1871, and he was player-manager for parts of the 1872 and 1873 seasons. The team finished third and fifth, respectively, and Hatfield continued to play but not to manage. He concluded his career in 1876 in one game with the Mutuals in the brand new National League.

Grady Hatton
Houston Astros (NL) 1966–68
Record: 164–221
Infielder who played both second and third base.

Grady Hatton broke in with the Cincinnati Reds in 1946, and he was named to the National League All-Star team in 1952 despite hitting just .212. His playing career ended in 1960, and he became a coach with the Chicago Cubs and then a manager with the Oklahoma City 89ers of the Pacific Coast League, with whom he won two pennants. He was named Astros' manager in 1966, but finished eighth and ninth before being fired in June of 1968 with the team in tenth place. He returned to Houston as a coach from 1973–74.

Guy Hecker
Pittsburgh Innocents (NL) 1890
Record: 23–113
Outstanding pitcher, first baseman, and outfielder.

Hecker played eight of his nine major league seasons with the Louisville Eclipse/Louisville Colonels of the American Association. In 1883 he went 26–23 on the mound, then led the AA in victories the following year with a 52–20 record. The fact that the Eclipse won a grand total of 68 games that season means that Hecker accounted for 76 percent of the team's wins. He also led the league with 385 strikeouts and a 1.80 earned run average.

He won 30 games the next season, and in 1886 went 26–23 while winning the AA batting title with a .341 average. In a game against the Baltimore Orioles he went 6-for-7 with three inside-the-park home runs. Hecker remains the only pitcher ever to win a batting crown.

Securing 173 lifetime victories and a .290 career batting average, Hecker's only season outside Louisville was spent as player-manager of the Pittsburgh Innocents of the National League in his final year of 1890. He hit only .226 and won only 2 games on the mound, and the miserable Innocents lost 113 games en route to a last-place finish.

Don Heffner
Cincinnati Reds (NL) 1966
Record: 37–46
Light-hitting infielder, mainly for the New York Yankees and St. Louis Browns.

Heffner coached for several teams following his retirement, and was named manager of the Reds for the 1966 season. He did not last even a single year, however, posting a 37–46 record and foundering in eighth place when he was replaced in July by one of his coaches, Dave Bristol.

Louie Heilbroner
St. Louis Cardinals (NL) 1900
Record: 23–25
Business manager who briefly became a major league manager.

A native of Fort Wayne, Indiana, Heilbroner stood only four feet nine inches tall, and was the business manager of the Cardinals when manager Patsy Tebeau resigned in August of 1900. The Robison brothers, who owned the club, offered to make John McGraw player-manager, but McGraw turned them down. They then selected Heilbroner for the job, and Louie finished out the season nominally at the helm.

The fact was that many players would not take orders from Heilbroner, likely in part because of his size and in part because he never played a major league game.

McGraw made most of the decisions while playing third base, and the following year Patsy Donovan was hired to take over.

Tommy Helms
Cincinnati Reds (NL) 1988, 1989
Record: 28–36
Good-hitting, slick-fielding infielder and the National League's 1966 Rookie of the Year.

Helms won that award at third base, but the following season switched to second and became one of the best at that position. He was named to the NL All-Star team in both 1967 and 1968, and in 1972 was traded from the Reds to the Houston Astros in the deal that brought Joe Morgan, Cesar Geronimo, and others to the Reds and in essence completed the formation of the Big Red Machine.

Helms went into coaching when his playing career ended, and he served under Pete Rose with the Reds in the 1980s. He took over as interim manager twice: in 1988 when Rose was suspended for 30 days for shoving umpire Dave Pallone, and again in 1989 when Pete was suspended by Major League Baseball for gambling.

Solly Hemus
St. Louis Cardinals (NL) 1959–61
Record: 190–192
Solid infielder with the Cardinals and the Philadelphia Phillies.

A reliable hitter, Hemus was good at getting on base, in large part by getting hit by pitches, and in 1952 he tied with Stan Musial for the league lead with 105 runs scored. In 1959 he was named the Cards' player-manager, and he used himself sparingly while the team finished in seventh place. Hemus then retired from the playing field but remained at the helm, and after a third-place showing in 1960 the Cardinals were in sixth the next year when Solly was fired and replaced by Johnny Keane. He later coached for the New York Mets and the Cleveland Indians.

Bill Henderson
Baltimore Unions (UA) 1884
Record: 58–47
Managed the Unions in their only year of existence, in the Union Association's only year of existence.

Henderson skippered the Baltimore entry in the UA for the entire season, but in spite of an impressive .552 winning percentage the club finished in fourth place. They were still 32 games behind the pennant-winning St. Louis Maroons, who finished 94–19.

Jack Hendricks
St. Louis Cardinals (NL) 1918; Cincinnati Reds (NL) 1924–

29
Record: 520–528
Played briefly in the major leagues before becoming a minor league manager.

Beginning his managerial career in the bush leagues in 1906, Hendricks won consecutive Western League pennants with the Denver Grizzlies/Denver Bears from 1910–12. He was eventually hired to manage the Cardinals for two years, but resigned following the 1918 season and became the athletic director for the Knights of Columbus. He eventually returned to the major leagues as manager of the Reds when skipper Pat Moran died of Bright's disease during spring training of 1924.

Hendricks' Cincinnati club finished second in 1926, a mere two games behind the Cardinals, and that would be his best showing.

Ed Hengle
Chicago Browns (UA) 1884
Record: 34–39
Managed his hometown Chicago Browns during the Union Association's only year of existence.

The Browns spent most of the season in Chicago, but eventually, in sixth place, they moved to Pittsburgh and became the Pittsburgh Stogies. At that point Hengle turned the reins over to Joe Battin.

He umpired in the National League in 1887, and in the American Association in 1889. He died in 1927 in England.

Billy Herman
Pittsburgh Pirates (NL) 1947; Boston Red Sox (AL) 1964–66
Record: 189–274
Hall of Fame second baseman and 10-time All-Star.

Herman had a somewhat inauspicious start, having to be carried off the field in his second major league plate appearance when he fouled a ball off his own head. But it did not take him long to make his mark in a far more positive way. A .304 lifetime hitter, Billy topped the .300 mark eight times in his career. In 1935 with the Chicago Cubs he led the National League with 227 hits and 57 doubles, and in 1939 led with 18 triples. He routinely topped 20 doubles per season, and four times he scored over 100 runs. He frequently led the league in most fielding categories at second base.

As a manager he did not enjoy much success, however. Hired to skipper the Pirates in 1947, he led the team to eighth place in the standings and was fired prior to the final game of the season. The Pirates won that game and thus moved into a tie for seventh.

He took over the Red Sox with two games left in 1964, then managed one full season and was fired in September of 1966. He could do no better than eighth place in Boston.

For his play Herman was inducted into the Hall of Fame in 1975.

Buck Herzog
Cincinnati Reds (NL) 1914–16
Record: 165–226
Pugnacious infielder who spent three tours of duty with the New York Giants.

Herzog was frequently at odds with Giants' manager John McGraw, among others. He once failed to show up for a game while with Boston; he got into a fight with Ty Cobb when Cobb cut him with his spikes while sliding into second, prompting Herzog to meet Cobb at his hotel later that night; and he once refused to accompany the Giants on a road trip.

After his first two stays with the Giants he became player-manager of the Reds for 2½ seasons. The club did not perform well, and in July of 1916 he was traded back to the Giants. Christy Mathewson was a part of the deal for the Reds, and after Ivy Wingo filled in for two games, Mathewson would take over as the Reds' manager.

Whitey Herzog
Texas Rangers (AL) 1973; California Angels (AL) 1974; Kansas City Royals (AL) 1975–79; St. Louis Cardinals (NL) 1980, 1981–90
Record: 1281–1125
Part-time outfielder for eight major league seasons.

It was as a manager that Herzog truly made his mark. Nicknamed "The White Rat" because of the color of his hair, he was hired to manage the Rangers in 1973, but did not last the season. Replaced by Billy Martin in September, he became a coach with the Angels the following year. When manager Bobby Winkles was fired in June, Whitey took over on an interim basis for four games before Dick Williams was hired as Winkles' replacement.

With the Royals he won three consecutive American League Western Division titles, from 1976–78. His club lost the AL pennant to the New York Yankees all three years.

In June of 1980 he was named manager of the Cardinals, but in August was promoted to general manager. Red Schoendienst assumed his duties in the dugout, but in 1981 Herzog would serve as both manager and GM.

In 1982 he took the Cards to the National League Eastern Division title, then to the NL pennant with a three-game sweep of the Atlanta Braves and to the World Championship in a seven-game Series against the Milwaukee Brewers. In both 1981 and 1982, United Press International named him its Executive of the Year for his role as GM.

Another division title followed in 1985, as did the pennant when the Cardinals defeated the Los Angeles Dodgers. Despite a World Series loss to the Royals, Herzog was named Manager of the Year by the AP and NL Manager of the Year by the BBWAA.

In 1987 the Cardinals took yet another division championship, and then another NL pennant in a seven-game defeat of the San Francisco Giants. This time they would drop a seven-game World Series to the Minnesota Twins.

In July of 1990, with his team in sixth place, Herzog resigned because of the club's lackluster performance. His managerial credentials during his career totaled six division championships, three pennants, and one World Championship.

Walter Hewett
Washington Statesmen (NL) 1888
Record: 10–29
Washington native who took the reins of his hometown Statesmen in 1888.

Hewett did not even last a third of the season. In his mid-20s when he was named skipper, his club was in last place through the first 40 games when he was replaced by Ted Sullivan.

The Statesmen finished last anyway.

Nat Hicks
Philadelphia Pearls (NA) 1874; New York Mutuals (NA) 1875
Record: 59–67
Catcher who began his career with the amateur Brooklyn Eagles in 1866.

Hicks played several years for the Eagles, and became a professional in 1869 with the Washington Nationals. He eventually played four seasons in the National Association and parts of two in the National League.

He was player-manager of the Philadelphia Pearls for part of the 1874 season, and of the New York Mutuals for all of 1875. He retired in 1877, but was frequently seen as a spectator at major league games thereafter.

Pinky Higgins
Boston Red Sox (AL) 1955–59, 1960–62
Record: 560–556
Solid-hitting third baseman for the Philadelphia Athletics, Boston Red Sox, and Detroit Tigers.

A three-time All-Star, Michael Franklin "Pinky" Higgins hit .292 lifetime and topped the .300 mark four times. He hit at least 20 doubles 12 seasons in a row, and twice drove in 106 runs.

After retiring in 1946 Higgins became a minor league manager, and was hired to skipper the Red Sox in 1955. He boasted two third-place and two fourth-place finishes, and was fired in July of 1959 when his team was languishing in eighth.

His exile lasted less than a year, however, for when manager Billy Jurges was fired in June of 1960 Higgins was brought back to replace him. He then stayed through the 1962 season, and later became the team's vice president and general manager. Eventually he would scout for the Houston Astros.

Dick Higham
New York Mutuals (NA) 1874
Record: 29–11
Outstanding catcher and outfielder whose honesty was nevertheless always suspect.

Higham played for six different teams in eight years in the National Association and National League, and had three stints with the New York Mutuals. He was player-manager for part of the 1874 season when the Mutuals finished second and had a strong 29–11 record.

He frequently hit over .300, and in 1876 ended the season in a three-way tie for the NL lead with 21 doubles. In 1878 he led with 22 doubles and 60 runs scored, but in spite of those numbers there was much speculation that he was not always playing to the best of his ability and might be on the take with gamblers. Nothing was ever proven against him, however.

Higham had sometimes filled in as an umpire while playing in the NA, and when he retired from the playing field the NL hired him in that role. Rumors continued to mount that he was in league with some dishonest characters, and in 1882 William Thompson, Detroit's mayor and the president of the Detroit Wolverines, noticed that close calls made by Higham were frequently going against his team. He hired a private detective to investigate Higham, and the detective discovered a letter Higham had written to a known gambler laying out a system whereby the umpire would tell him when to bet and on whom.

Higham was confronted with the evidence and soon became the only umpire ever permanently banished from major league baseball because of dishonesty.

Vedie Himsl
Chicago Cubs (NL) 1961, 1961, 1961
Record: 10–21
Montana native who never played in the major leagues.

Himsl was a coach for the Cubs from 1960–64, and was a part of the team's "college of coaches" experiment that lasted from 1961–62, in which each of several coaches would take turns as manager. Himsl managed only in 1961, taking three turns as skipper and putting together an unimpressive 10–21 record. The records of the others were equally dismal, however.

Himsl later became the Cubs' director of scouting, and he died in 2004 at the age of 86.

Billy Hitchcock
Detroit Tigers (AL) 1960; Baltimore Orioles (AL) 1962–63; Atlanta Braves (NL) 1966–67
Record: 274–261
Light-hitting backup infielder with several teams for nine seasons.

Hitchcock debuted with the Detroit Tigers in 1942, but then lost three years to the Army in World War II. He earned the rank of major while serving in the military, while also being awarded a Bronze Star and three battle stars.

He returned to baseball in 1946 and played until 1953. Two years later he became a coach with the Tigers. In 1960, when the Tigers traded manager Jimmy Dykes to the Cleveland Indians for manager Joe Gordon, Hitchcock managed one game—and won it—while awaiting Gordon's arrival.

He later managed the Orioles for two seasons, where a fourth-place finish would be the best of his managerial career. He took over the Braves in August of 1966 when Bobby Bragan was fired, and was himself fired in September of 1967.

From 1971–80 he served as president of the minor Southern League.

Butch Hobson
Boston Red Sox (AL) 1992–94
Record: 207–232
Injury-prone third baseman with decent power who spent eight seasons in the major leagues.

Hobson was a regular for only three years—from 1977–79, all of which was spent with the Red Sox—and he peaked in '77 with 30 home runs and 112 runs batted in. Those were three pretty decent years (he hit 28 homers with 93 RBIs in 1979), but injuries and inadequate defensive play took their toll and he retired in 1982.

He managed the Red Sox for three years before being fired in 1994. He was managing the minor league Scranton/Wilkes-Barre Red Barons in 1996 when he was arrested because of cocaine possession.

Following his arrest and conviction Hobson became a motivational speaker on the dangers of drug use. He later managed the Class A Sarasota Red Sox, and then the independent Nashua Pride.

Gil Hodges
Washington Senators (AL) 1963–67; New York Mets (NL)
1968–71
Record: 660–753
Power-hitting first baseman who spent most of his career with the Brooklyn/Los Angeles Dodgers.

An eight-time All-Star, Hodges slugged over 20 home runs for 11 consecutive seasons, finishing with 370 lifetime, and garnered over 100 runs batted in seven straight times. He also won consecutive Gold Gloves in 1958 and 1959.

He finished his playing career in 1963 in 11 games with the Mets, who then traded him to the Senators. Washington was interested in him as a manager, and Gil would not return to the playing field.

After some lean years at the helm, Hodges was traded back to the Mets as a manager—in exchange for pitcher Bill Denehy and some cash—and his new club would finish ninth in 1968. The following year would make him nearly a legend, however.

The 1969 "Miracle Mets," as they became known, won the National League Eastern Division crown, climbing an incredible eight places in the standings from the year before. Hodges himself was dubbed the "Miracle Worker" as the team's skipper. In the NL Championship Series the Mets captured the pennant in a three-game sweep of the Atlanta Braves, and then won the World Championship in five games over the Baltimore Orioles. The AP named Gil its NL Manager of the Year.

That was his only shot at glory as a manager, but it was one that has endured. In 1972, during spring training, Hodges died of a heart attack following a golf game in West Palm Beach, Florida. The Mets retired his number 14 later that year.

Fred Hoey
New York Giants (NL) 1899
Record: 31–55
Managed his hometown New York Giants to a tenth-place finish in 1899.

Tenth place meant that two teams finished behind the Giants. Hoey had never played major league baseball, and the second half of the 1899 season marked his only stint as a manager when he replaced John Day at the New York helm.

Hoey died in Paris, France in 1933.

Glenn Hoffman
Los Angeles Dodgers (NL) 1998
Record: 47–41
Light-hitting shortstop with a good glove.

In nine years Hoffman spent only two seasons as a regular, and his .285 batting average in his rookie season of 1980 would be his career high. After retiring he became a minor league manager, and was hired to replace the deposed Bill Russell as manager of the Dodgers for the second half of the 1998 season.

A decent third-place finish would be his legacy. He remained with the Dodgers as a coach until 2005, however, and then became a coach for the San Diego Padres.

Bill Holbert
Syracuse Stars (NL) 1879
Record: 0–1
Catcher for 12 major league seasons with various teams.

Originally an umpire, Holbert batted only .211 lifetime, but he was one of the few members of the 1879 Syracuse Stars with previous major league experience. He was also interim manager for one game between the reigns of Mike Dorgan and Jimmy Macullar, a game the Stars lost. The team finished 30 games out of first place, and Holbert did not manage again.

Holly Hollingshead
Washington Nationals (NA) 1875; Washington Nationals (AA) 1884
Record: 16–66
Played only 58 major league games over three seasons, most of them as an outfielder.

John "Holly" Hollingshead was finished playing by the end of the 1875 season, a year he spent partially as player-manager of the miserable Washington Nationals of the National Association. His record was 4–16 with the club, and the team finished 5–23 overall.

In 1884 he managed another team by the same name, this one in the American Association. He did not fare much better this time around, going 12–50 for a team that ended up 12–51.

Tommy Holmes
Boston Braves (NL) 1951–52
Record: 61–69
Solid outfielder who batted .302 lifetime.

Spending 10 of his 11 seasons with the Boston Braves, Holmes enjoyed his best year in 1945, when he hit .352 while leading the National League with 28 home runs, 224 hits, and 47 doubles. He also drove in 117 runs and was an NL All-Star. He struck out only nine times all season, and from June 6 through July 8 he hit in 37 consecutive games, an NL record at the time.

That marked the second of five seasons in which he would hit over .300. In 1947 he led the league with 191 hits, and was an All-Star again in 1948.

Holmes became the Braves' player-manager in 1951, and finished fourth. In 1952 he turned strictly to managing, but was replaced by Charlie Grimm in May with the team in sixth place. He then signed on with the Brooklyn Dodgers as a reserve but did not perform well and retired.

Rogers Hornsby
St. Louis Cardinals (NL) 1925–26; New York Giants (NL) 1927; Boston Braves (NL) 1928; Chicago Cubs (NL) 1930–32; St. Louis Browns (AL) 1933–37, 1952; Cincinnati Reds (NL) 1952; Cincinnati Redlegs (NL) 1953
Record: 701–812
One of the greatest hitters of all time.

Nicknamed "The Rajah," Hornsby frequently led the National League in several hitting categories. He won seven batting titles, six of them consecutively, peaking with an incredible .424 average in 1924, an NL record. That was the second of three times he would top the .400 mark, and his lifetime average of .358 is also an NL record and is second in major league history only to Ty Cobb's .366.

In 1922 he won the Triple Crown, batting .401 with 42 home runs and 152 runs batted in while also leading the league with 250 hits, 46 doubles, and 141 runs scored. In 1925 he became the Cardinals' player-manager, and he is the only person in that position to win the Triple Crown. His .403 batting average, 39 homers, and 143 RBIs also earned him the NL's League Award, an early version of the Most Valuable Player Award.

He guided the Cardinals to his only pennant in 1926, finishing two games ahead of the Cincinnati Reds and then defeating the New York Yankees in seven games to capture the World Championship.

Hornsby owned stock in the Cardinals, but when he was traded to the Giants in 1927 he was forced to sell and made over $100,000. He filled in as player-manager for John McGraw for 33 games before moving on to Boston.

Hornsby had trouble with authority and also enjoyed betting on horse races. These two factors led to his frequently hopping from team to team in spite of his stellar play. With the Cubs in 1929 he won another League Award, hitting .380 with 39 homers and 149 RBIs. He became Chicago's player-manager the following year when Joe McCarthy resigned, but was fired in August of 1932. He returned to the Cardinals as a player, then became player-manager of the Browns. That St. Louis team fired him in 1937 for betting on the horses.

Hornsby later became a minor league manager, and he was inducted into the Hall of Fame in 1942. Ten years later he returned to manage the Browns, but was fired in June and then hired a month later by the Reds. Cincinnati, called the Redlegs in 1953, fired him in September of that year with eight games left in the season. He eventually coached for the Cubs and the New York Mets.

Hornsby died of heart problems in 1963.

Ralph Houk

New York Yankees (AL) 1961–63, 1966–73; Detroit Tigers (AL) 1974–78; Boston Red Sox (AL) 1981–84
Record: 1619–1531

Catcher who played only 91 major league games over eight seasons.

Houk is most famous for the 20 years he spent as a manager. After retiring as a player he became a minor league skipper and later a coach with the Yankees. In 1961 he followed Casey Stengel at the helm of the Bronx Bombers.

Houk won American League pennants his first three years, capturing World Championships the first two. In 1961 his Yanks bested the Cincinnati Reds in a five-game World Series, then took the San Francisco Giants in seven games the following year before being swept by the Los Angeles Dodgers in 1963.

Houk would never win another pennant, although in 20 years of managing he would never be fired. At the conclusion of the 1963 season he was promoted to Yankees' general manager, and in 1966 he fired manager Johnny Keane and reinstated himself as skipper. In 1973 he left to manage the Tigers, from whom he retired in 1978. Three years later he came out of retirement to lead the Red Sox, then retired for good in 1984.

The AP named him AL Manager of the Year in both 1963 and 1970.

Frank Howard

San Diego Padres (NL) 1981; New York Mets (NL) 1983
Record: 93–133

Power-hitting outfielder and first baseman.

Debuting in 1958, Howard played his first full season in 1960 with the Los Angeles Dodgers and won the National League Rookie of the Year Award when he batted .268 with 23 home runs and 77 runs batted in. He would split most of his career between the Dodgers and the Washington Senators, and he was named to four All-Star teams. He hit at least 15 home runs for 12 consecutive seasons, topping out at 48 in 1969. He led the American League with 44 in 1968, and 44 again in 1970 when he also led with 126 RBIs and 132 walks. He hit 382 career home runs.

Howard managed the Padres during the strike-shortened season of 1981, and his club finished last in both halves of the split-season format. He and his entire coaching staff were fired at the end of the year. He was a coach for the Mets in 1983 when George Bamberger resigned, and was named interim manager for the rest of the season. The Mets finished sixth, and he was fired again.

Art Howe

Houston Astros (NL) 1989–93; Oakland Athletics (AL) 1996–2002; New York Mets (NL) 2003–04
Record: 1129–1137

Solid infielder who played second, third, and even first.

Howe was dependable with both the glove and the bat, but in 11 years with the Pittsburgh Pirates, Houston Astros, and St. Louis Cardinals, had difficulty finding playing time at a single position.

He became a coach following his playing days and was hired to manage Houston in 1989. He finished third with them twice, then became a scout for the Los Angeles Dodgers and a coach with the Colorado Rockies. In 1996 he became the skipper of the A's, and he would eventually win two division titles with them, in 2000 and 2002.

In spite of his success the A's did not retain his services for 2003, and he went on to manage the Mets for two years.

As a coach Howe had spent the 1985–88 seasons with the Texas Rangers. Following the 2006 season he accepted a job as the Philadelphia Phillies' third base coach, but when his friend Ron Washington was hired to manage the Rangers he asked for and received permission to abandon Philadelphia and become the bench coach in Texas.

Dan Howley

St. Louis Browns (AL) 1927–29; Cincinnati Reds (NL) 1930–32
Record: 397–524

Catcher who played only 26 major league games and hit .125.

Howley had some success managing in the minor leagues, winning International League pennants with the Toronto Maple Leafs in both 1918 and 1926. At the major league level he managed the Browns for three years, finishing third in 1928, and the Reds for three, with whom he could accomplish no better than a seventh-place finish.

Dick Howser

New York Yankees (AL) 1978, 1980; Kansas City Royals (AL) 1981–86
Record: 507–425

Miami native who played eight seasons at shortstop and second base.

His rookie season of 1961 would be Howser's finest. He hit .280 with 108 runs scored, 37 stolen bases, and 171 hits, and was named to the American League All-Star team. He would never reach any of those highs again, but remained a spunky player with a good glove and a competent bat.

In 1978 he was a coach with the Yankees when manager Billy Martin was fired, and he filled in for one game—a game he lost—before Bob Lemon was named Martin's successor.

As the Yankees' full-time skipper in 1980 he guided the team to the American League Eastern Division title. But when the club was swept by the Royals in the AL Championship Series, he was fired by George Steinbrenner and replaced by Gene Michael.

In late 1981 he was hired to manage the Royals, and he took Kansas City to the AL Western Division title for the second half of the strike-shortened season. In the best-of-five divisional playoffs the Royals were swept by the Oakland Athletics.

After two consecutive second-place finishes, Howser led the Royals to two consecutive division titles. In 1984 they were swept in the best-of-five playoffs by the Detroit Tigers, but in '85 they took the flag in a best-of-seven set over the Toronto Blue Jays, four games to three, and then won by an identical margin over the St. Louis Cardinals to take the World Series.

Howser was diagnosed with a brain tumor in mid-1986, and he left the team to receive treatment and was replaced by Mike Ferraro for the remainder of the season. He tried to come back for spring training of 1987, but stepped down after only three days. He died on June 17 of that year. Sixteen days later, the Royals retired his number 10.

George Huff
Boston Red Sox (AL) 1907
Record: 2–6
The second of four managers to skipper the Red Sox in 1907.

A native of Champaign, Illinois, Huff never played major league baseball. He replaced Cy Young at the Boston helm after the first six games of the season, although Young continued to pitch for the club. Huff lasted only eight games himself, winning just two of them, before being replaced by Bob Unglaub.

Miller Huggins
St. Louis Cardinals (NL) 1913–17; New York Yankees (AL) 1918–29
Record: 1413–1134
Solid second baseman and Hall of Fame manager.

Standing only five feet six inches in height, Huggins' nickname was "The Mighty Mite." He had a 13-year playing career with the Cincinnati Reds and St. Louis Cardinals, and five of those in St. Louis were as player-manager. His highest batting average was .304 in 1912, and he led the National League four times in bases on balls.

With the Cardinals he had two third-place finishes as manager, but he truly made his mark with the Yankees. At the New York helm for 12 seasons, he won six American League pennants and three World Championships.

Huggins was sometimes frustrated with the antics of his biggest star, Babe Ruth, but he consistently asserted himself and did not hesitate to levy fines or suspensions on the Babe. He won his first flag with the Yanks in 1921 and promptly won two more, and after losing the first two World Series to the New York Giants his team bested that same club in 1923. In 1926 they embarked on a streak of three more pennants, and after losing to the Cardinals in seven games in '26 they would sweep the Pittsburgh Pirates the following year and the Cardinals the year after that to capture consecutive World Championships. Huggins' 1927 Yankees are often touted as one of the greatest teams of all time, boasting such names as Babe Ruth, Lou Gehrig, Earle Combs, Bob Meusel, Tony Lazzeri, Waite Hoyt, and Herb Pennock.

Huggins died of blood poisoning in September of 1929 as the result of a carbuncle. He was inducted into the Hall of Fame in 1964.

Billy Hunter
Texas Rangers (AL) 1977–78
Record: 146–108
Shortstop from Punxsutawney, Pennsylvania.

Excellent with the glove, Hunter was named to the American League All-Star team during his rookie year of 1953 while with the St. Louis Browns. He ended the season hitting only .219, however, and after six seasons that would end up being his lifetime average.

He eventually became a coach for the Baltimore Orioles, and was hired to manage the Rangers in June of 1977. Despite finishing second, and then having the team in second place in 1978, he was fired prior to the season's final game and replaced by Pat Corrales.

Clint Hurdle
Colorado Rockies (NL) 2002–
Record: 352–436
Number one draft pick of the Kansas City Royals.

An outfielder by trade, Hurdle won both the Rookie of the Year and Most Valuable Player Awards in the minor American Association in 1977. He did not have nearly that kind of success in the majors, however, and mainly served as a backup at several positions.

Clint became a coach when his playing career ended, and was hired to manage the Rockies in 2002.

Tim Hurst
St. Louis Browns (NL) 1898

Record: 39–111

Ill-tempered umpire for most of his baseball career.

Umpiring in the National League from 1891–97, Hurst was renowned for physically striking players and managers who dared to argue with him. In 1897 the NL fired him when a fan threw a beer stein at him and missed, and Hurst threw it right back and hit a different fan.

The Browns hired him to manage their club the following season, and his temper was just as bad. He had a miserable season in the win-loss department and, ironically, constantly rode umpires.

He was hired back as an umpire briefly in 1900, then switched to the American League from 1905–09. He attacked New York Highlanders' manager Clark Griffith following an argument in 1906, and in 1909 spat on Eddie Collins of the Philadelphia Athletics when Collins argued a call. Two weeks later Hurst was fired by the AL.

He became a boxing referee following his ouster from baseball, and died in 1915 at the age of 49.

Fred Hutchinson

Detroit Tigers (AL) 1952–54; St. Louis Cardinals (NL) 1956–58; Cincinnati Reds (NL) 1959–64, 1964
Record: 830–827

Solid major league pitcher who made his real mark as a manager.

A World War II Navy veteran, Hutchinson had a successful playing career with the Detroit Tigers. He won in double digits for six years in a row, and was named to the American League All-Star team in 1951.

In 1952 he was named Tigers' player-manager, replacing Red Rolfe. During the next three years he pitched less and less, and his best finish as a skipper was fifth place. He asked for a multiyear contract to continue as manager, but the Tigers refused and Fred departed.

In 1956 he was hired to manage the Cardinals, and the following season he led the Redbirds to a second-place finish. The Cardinals fired him in September of 1958, and halfway through the following season he was signed to manage the Reds.

In 1961 Hutchinson won his only pennant, guiding Cincinnati to the National League flag. Although the Reds lost the World Series to the New York Yankees, the AP named Hutchinson the NL's Manager of the Year.

Hutchinson was diagnosed with throat cancer in December of 1963, and he tried to keep his illness quiet. He continued to manage the Reds in 1964, but in July he was forced to step down to seek further treatment. He returned just over a week later, but stepped down again in mid-August. He resigned from the Reds in October and died in November.

In 1965 the Reds retired his uniform number 1.

Arthur Irwin

Washington Statesmen (NL) 1889; Boston Red Stockings (AA) 1891; Washington Statesmen (NL) 1892, 1898–99; Philadelphia Phillies (NL) 1894–95; New York Giants (NL) 1896
Record: 416–427

Toronto native who is reported to have invented the fielder's glove.

Irwin was a slick-fielding shortstop with a weak bat. In 1883 with the Providence Grays he broke two fingers on his left hand, so he bought a glove made of buckskin and modified it so that he could continue playing. The idea of such a glove caught on, and before long such mitts were the norm on the field.

Arthur managed a number of teams, including two separate squads called the Washington Statesmen. The second one, in fact, he managed twice. In 1891 his Boston Red Stockings won the final American Association pennant, and that was the only time he finished better than third place.

In 1921 Irwin committed suicide by jumping off the steamboat *Calvin Austin* somewhere on the route between Boston and New York. His body was never recovered. Following his death it soon became public that he had both a wife in Boston and a wife and family in New York.

In 1989 Arthur was inducted into the Canadian Baseball Hall of Fame.

Hughie Jennings

Detroit Tigers (AL) 1907–20; New York Giants (NL) 1924, 1925
Record: 1184–995

Hall of Fame shortstop and third baseman and lifetime .312 hitter.

With a playing career that began in 1891, Hughie Jennings never led his league in a single major offensive category in 17 seasons, but was a major part of the Baltimore Orioles' National League championship teams of the late 1890s. In 1896 he hit .401 and stole 70 bases, and three times he drove in over 100 runs.

Energetic and a strong leader, he suffered many an injury, not always on the baseball field. Those injuries included two skull fractures.

As a manager his best years were his first three, for he led the Tigers to American League pennants all three times. He never did capture a World Championship, dropping the first two World Series to the Chicago Cubs and the last to the Pittsburgh Pirates, but he would garner several second-place finishes over the ensuing years.

Following his tenure as Tigers' skipper Jennings became a coach with the New York Giants under John McGraw, and he filled in at the helm when McGraw was ill for 44 games in 1924 and for 32 more in 1925. In 1924 those Giants won the NL pennant.

Darrell Johnson
Boston Red Sox (AL) 1974–76; Seattle Mariners (AL) 1977– 80; Texas Rangers (AL) 1982
Record: 472–590
Backup catcher for several major league seasons.

After playing for seven different teams in six seasons, Johnson became a coach and then was hired to manage the Red Sox in 1974. The following season he guided his club to the American League pennant, although they dropped a brilliant seven-game World Series to the Cincinnati Reds. Johnson was named AL Manager of the Year by the AP.

During the 1976 season he was fired and replaced by Don Zimmer, and the following year he became the first skipper of the expansion Seattle Mariners. He lasted until August of 1980, then became a coach with the Rangers. With Texas in July of 1982 he was called upon to replace, ironically, former manager Don Zimmer for the rest of the season.

Davey Johnson
New York Mets (NL) 1984–90; Cincinnati Reds (NL) 1993– 95; Baltimore Orioles (AL) 1996–97; Los Angeles Dodgers (NL) 1999–2000
Record: 1148–888
Four-time All-Star second baseman and three-time Gold Glove winner.

Spending most of his playing career with the Baltimore Orioles and Atlanta Braves, Johnson frequently led the league in many fielding categories. An adequate hitter for average, he had an anomalous season in 1973 when he slugged 43 home runs with 99 runs batted in. His second-highest season home run total for his entire career was 18.

He played briefly in Japan before returning to the major leagues, and after retiring he became a minor league manager and won three consecutive pennants. He rose through the ranks to become the Mets' skipper in 1984, and two years later he took his club to the National League pennant and to a seven-game World Series victory over the Boston Red Sox.

The Mets won another division title in 1986, but this time they were bested in the NL Championship Series by the Dodgers. In May of 1990 Johnson was fired with his team struggling in fourth place.

He became the Reds' skipper in 1993, and the following season he had his club atop its division when the season ended abruptly due to a players' strike. The Reds repeated that performance in 1995, although, after defeating the Dodgers in the Division Series, they would drop the NLCS to the Atlanta Braves.

Johnson was let go by owner Marge Schott after that campaign, and he was immediately snatched up by the Orioles. In 1997 he took the O's to the American League Eastern Division crown, but in six games they lost the pennant to the Cleveland Indians. Nevertheless Davey was named AL Manager of the Year by the BBWAA.

Johnson resigned in November of that year, and in 1999 he was hired by the Dodgers and managed them for two seasons.

Roy Johnson
Chicago Cubs (NL) 1944
Record: 0–1
Solid outfielder for 10 major league seasons.

A .296 lifetime hitter, Johnson topped the .300 mark four times. In 1929 with the Detroit Tigers he tied for the American League lead with 45 doubles, and in 1931 he led with 19 triples.

A coach with the Cubs for many years following his playing career, Johnson managed a single game on an interim basis in 1944 when manager Jimmie Wilson resigned. The Cubs had won their first game that year and then lost nine straight, prompting Wilson's departure. After Johnson's one game, which resulted in a tenth consecutive loss, Charlie Grimm arrived to take over.

Tim Johnson
Toronto Blue Jays (AL) 1998
Record: 88–74
Light-hitting infielder with a decent glove for the Milwaukee Brewers and Toronto Blue Jays.

Johnson managed the Blue Jays for a single season, and it turned out to be a rough one. While posting a decent record, the Blue Jays suffered through a rather tumultuous clubhouse situation, with several players and coaches not getting along with Johnson and accusing the manager of favoritism. In particular Tim butted heads with Jays' pitching coach Mel Queen, for reasons that never came to light.

It was revealed during the season that Johnson had lied to his players about having served in Vietnam, and the Toronto skipper admitted to and later apologized for those actions. Negative sentiment grew during the offseason, and during spring training of 1999 Johnson was finally fired.

He became the manager of the Mexico City Red Devils of the Mexican League, where he won the league championship, and then served for a short time as a scout with the Brewers.

Walter Johnson
Washington Nationals (AL) 1929–32; Cleveland Indians

(AL) 1933–35
Record: 529–432
A true gentleman and one of the best pitchers of all time.

Nicknamed "The Big Train" because of his blazing fastball, Walter Johnson was discovered playing semipro ball in Idaho. He signed with Washington and debuted in 1907, but would not truly hit his stride until 1910. He won 25 games that year, and began a string of 10 consecutive 20-win seasons, peaking with an American League-leading 36 victories in 1913. That year, in fact, was the first of four straight seasons in which he would lead the league in wins. In all, his career consisted of 12 seasons of 20 or more wins (6 of which topped the AL), 2 seasons leading in games pitched, 4 in games started, 6 in complete games, 7 in shutouts, 5 in innings pitched, 12 in strikeouts, and 5 in earned run average. He fanned 3509 batters in his career, and his all-time victory total of 417 is second only to Cy Young's 511. He topped 30 wins twice and 300 strikeouts twice. His lifetime ERA was 2.17.

Upon his retirement Johnson became a minor league manager, then was hired to skipper the Nationals, with whom he had spent his entire 21-year playing career. A second-place finish in 1930 would be his best, and he was let go following the 1932 season. In June of 1933 he became the Indians' skipper, and he resigned in August of 1935. His winning percentage as a manager was a very respectable .550.

Walter was inducted into the Hall of Fame in 1936.

Fielder Jones
Chicago White Sox (AL) 1904–08; St. Louis Terriers (FL) 1914–15; St. Louis Browns (AL) 1916–18
Record: 683–582
Fifteen-year outfielder with a .285 lifetime batting average.

Fielder was Jones' real first name, and he lived up to it with an excellent glove. He also hit over .300 six times, and was named player-manager of the White Sox in 1904.

After third- and second-place finishes, Jones led the Sox to the American League pennant in 1906, and then to a four-games-to-two World Series victory over the crosstown Cubs. In 1908 the White Sox finished in third place, but ended up a mere game and a half behind the AL champion Detroit Tigers.

That was Fielder's last season in Chicago, and in mid-1914 he would take over the helm of the Federal League's St. Louis Terriers. That squad finished eighth and last, but the following season saw them miss the pennant by a single percentage point behind the Chicago Whales.

Jones then returned to the AL with the St. Louis Browns, and managed them for two full seasons and for 46 games into a third.

Eddie Joost
Philadelphia Athletics (AL) 1954
Record: 51–103
Shortstop who started out with a light bat and a shaky glove.

All areas of Joost's game improved with time, although he never did hit for a high average. His power numbers increased significantly halfway through his career, as did his eye at the plate. Never having hit more than 6 home runs during his first eight seasons, he suddenly belted 13 in 1947 and would reach double digits for six in a row, peaking with 23 in 1949. Never having walked more than 69 times for his first eight years, he would top the 100 mark for the next six straight. He was named an American League All-Star in 1949 and 1952.

Joost was named player-manager of the A's in 1954, but the club lost 103 games and he was replaced the following year.

Mike Jorgensen
St. Louis Cardinals (NL) 1995
Record: 42–54
First baseman with a 17-year major league career.

An inconsistent hitter, Jorgensen's best seasons were with the Montreal Expos, with whom he won a Gold Glove in 1973, hit .310 in 1974 (a truly anomalous average for him), and slugged 18 home runs (a career high) in 1975.

He played more than half his career as a backup, and upon retiring in 1985 he became a manager in the Cardinals' minor league system. In 1995, when skipper Joe Torre was fired, he took over on an interim basis for the rest of the season.

Bill Joyce
New York Giants (NL) 1896–98, 1898
Record: 179–122
Solid nineteenth century third baseman.

In eight major league seasons Joyce hit over .300 five times, four of them consecutively. In his debut season of 1890 with the Brooklyn Wonders he led the Players League with 123 bases on balls. In 1895 he tied for the National League lead with 96 walks, and in 1896 tied with 13 home runs. Twice before that he had slugged 17 round-trippers in a season. He was a lifetime .293 hitter.

As player-manager of the New York Giants his best finish would be third place. He was replaced by Cap Anson in 1898, although he continued to play for the Giants, and when Anson resigned 22 games later, Joyce was reinstated.

Billy Jurges
Boston Red Sox (AL) 1959–60
Record: 59–63
Three-time All-Star shortstop for the Chicago Cubs and New York Giants.

A moderate hitter, Jurges had a fine glove and an assertive personality on the field. In 1932, only his second year in the majors, he was shot twice in a hotel room by a former girlfriend, Violet Valli, who had apparently gone there with the intention of committing suicide. Jurges was shot while trying to wrest the gun away from her. He missed just over two weeks of action despite taking bullets to the hand and ribs.

He was hired to manage the Red Sox in July of 1959, and finished the season in fifth place. The next season he left the team in June because of a reported illness and was subsequently fired and replaced by Pinky Higgins, the same man he had replaced the previous season.

Eddie Kasko
Boston Red Sox (AL) 1970–73
Record: 345–295
Dependable infielder for 10 major league seasons.

Modest with a bat, Kasko was a solid fielder and was named a National League All-Star in 1961 while with the Cincinnati Reds. He retired in 1966, and in 1970 was hired to manage the Red Sox.

His teams finished third, third, and second, respectively, and despite being second in 1973 Eddie was fired with one game left in the season.

Johnny Keane
St. Louis Cardinals (NL) 1961–64; New York Yankees (AL) 1965–66
Record: 398–350
Managed his hometown St. Louis Cardinals.

After fifth- and sixth-place finishes his first two years at the helm, Keane led his club to second place in 1963 and earned the National League Manager of the Year Award from the AP. He went one better in 1964, winning the NL pennant and then taking the World Championship in seven games over the New York Yankees.

In spite of this success, Keane was upset that Cardinals' general manager Bing Devine, a friend of his, had been fired, and so he resigned his post. The Yankees, upset that they had lost the World Series to St. Louis, fired manager Yogi Berra and hired Keane in his place.

New York took a nosedive in the standings, however. After a sixth-place finish in 1965, they were 4–16 and in tenth place in 1966 when Yanks' general manager Ralph Houk fired Keane and replaced him with himself.

Joe Kelley
Cincinnati Reds (NL) 1902–05; Boston Doves (NL) 1908
Record: 338–321
Outstanding, speedy outfielder with a solid bat.

Kelley played for 17 seasons, beginning in 1891, and was one of the stars of the Baltimore Orioles' championship teams of that decade. He hit .317 lifetime and swiped 443 bases in his career, peaking with a National League-leading 87 in 1896. He stole in double digits 13 times (under somewhat different scoring rules), and hit over .300 eleven times.

As player-manager of the Reds and Doves his best finish would be third place, but as a player he was inducted into the Hall of Fame in 1971 by the Veterans Committee. He also worked as a minor league manager, scouted for the New York Yankees, and served on the Maryland State Racing Commission.

John Kelly
Louisville Colonels (AA) 1887–88
Record: 86–89
Unimpressive hitter who played four major league seasons for several clubs.

Nicknamed "Honest John," Kelly quit playing in 1884 and became an umpire. He worked in both the National League and the American Association, but in 1887 was hired to manage the Louisville Colonels. He lasted just over a season, then went back to umpiring. He eventually became a boxing referee, and then owned a gambling establishment.

Mike "King" Kelly
Boston Bostons (NL) 1887; Boston Red Stockings (PL) 1890; Cincinnati Porkers (AA) 1891
Record: 173–148
Hall of Famer who played every position in a 16-year major league career.

A native of Troy, New York, Kelly was a high-spirited, inspiring player. His aggressive baserunning and spectacular slides led to the coining of the now-famous phrase "Slide, Kelly, slide!" He played on many pennant-winners and hit .314 lifetime, in the process winning National League batting titles in 1884 and 1886 with averages of .354 and .388, respectively. He topped the .300 mark eight times, while also leading the league three times in doubles and three times in runs scored.

He was player-manager for the Bostons for most of the 1887 season, but was replaced with the club in fifth place. In 1890 his Boston Red Stockings won the one and only Players League pennant, finishing 6½ games ahead of the Brooklyn Wonders. With the demise of the PL Kelly went to the American Association and became player-manager of the Cincinnati Porkers, a team that, because of his leadership, was also called the Cincinnati Kellys. Nicknamed "Kelly's Killers," that squad would also be known by the moniker Cincinnati Killers, but they could do no better than seventh place.

Kelly played until 1893, then became a minor league player-manager for one season. He died of pneumonia in November of 1894, and he was inducted into the Hall of Fame in 1945.

Tom Kelly
Minnesota Twins (AL) 1986–2001
Record: 1140–1244
First baseman who played 49 games for the Twins and then managed the team for 15 years.

A Minnesota native, Kelly was a coach who was named interim manager when skipper Ray Miller was fired in September of 1986. In November he was named manager permanently, and he made his mark as a leader the very next season, guiding the Twins to the American League Western Division title. His team took the AL pennant over the Detroit Tigers, four games to one, then defeated the St. Louis Cardinals in an exciting seven-game World Series to capture the World Championship.

In 1991 the Twins repeated, taking their division, scoring a four-to-one AL Championship Series win over the Toronto Blue Jays, and capturing a crowning World Championship in seven games over the Atlanta Braves. Kelly was named the AL's Manager of the Year by the BBWAA.

Beginning in 1994 a series of player retirements and financial housecleaning moves would put Minnesota into a rebuilding mode, and Kelly played a large part in developing the new talent. He retired after a second-place finish in 2001, but his efforts were not in vain, for the Twins would go on to three consecutive division titles after that.

Bob Kennedy
Chicago Cubs (NL) 1963–65; Oakland Athletics (AL) 1968
Record: 264–278
Chicago native who played for his hometown White Sox and later managed the Cubs.

Kennedy actually played for several teams during a 16-year major league career, and he was a so-so hitter with a strong arm in the outfield. He was named the Cubs' manager in 1963, mercifully putting an end to the two-year "college of coaches" experiment. After some unspectacular years at the helm he became a coach with the Atlanta Braves, then managed the A's during their first season in Oakland and finished sixth, his best showing as a manager.

He later became the general manager of the Cubs and the Houston Astros.

Jim Kennedy
Brooklyn Gladiators (AA) 1890
Record: 26–73
New York native who managed his hometown Brooklyn Gladiators for a single season.

The Gladiators were short-lived, lasting only a single season and finishing in ninth place. That was the end of the team and of Kennedy's managerial career.

Kevin Kennedy
Texas Rangers (AL) 1993–94; Boston Red Sox (AL) 1995–96
Record: 309–273
Minor league catcher who managed the Rangers and Red Sox.

Kennedy's 1993 Rangers finished second, and in 1994 they were in first place in the American League Western Division, despite posting a mere 52–62 record, when the season was cut short by a players' strike. Kevin was fired, and he took the helm of the Red Sox in 1995.

Boston won its division under his leadership, but was eliminated in the AL Division Series. His club finished third in 1996 despite a decent 85–77 record, and Kennedy was let go.

He later became a sports show host for Fox on both television and radio.

John Kerins
Louisville Colonels (AA) 1888; St. Louis Browns (AA) 1890
Record: 12–12
Player-manager for only 24 games in the American Association.

After finishing in a six-way tie for the AA lead with 19 triples in 1887 with the Colonels, Kerins filled in for Mordecai Davidson as interim manager for seven games. In 1890 with the St. Louis Browns he was the second of six managers; that was his final year as both a player and a skipper, and the Browns somehow finished third despite the revolving door.

Kerins then became an umpire in the AA and later worked in a hotel.

Joe Kerrigan
Boston Red Sox (AL) 2001
Record: 17–26
Pitcher who played parts of four major league seasons.

Kerrigan became a pitching coach with the Montreal Expos and Boston Red Sox after his playing career, and he was serving in such a role in 2001 when Red Sox' manager Jimy Williams was fired. Joe was hired as his replacement for the rest of the season, and his club finished second. He was not rehired for 2002, however, and eventually went back to coaching with the Philadelphia Phillies.

Don Kessinger
Chicago White Sox (AL) 1979
Record: 46–60
Six-time All-Star shortstop who played most of a 16-year career in Chicago.

Twelve of those years were with the Cubs, where Kessinger was an outstanding fielder and adequate hitter. He led the National League multiple times in several fielding categories, including putouts, assists, double plays, and fielding percentage. After a year and a half with the St. Louis Cardinals, he finished his playing days with the White Sox.

His final year on the field was 1979, when he served as player-manager of the Pale Hose. He batted a mere .200, however, and as a manager won only 46 games while losing 60. He resigned in August and was replaced by Tony LaRussa.

Bill Killefer
Chicago Cubs (NL) 1921–25; St. Louis Browns (AL) 1930–33
Record: 524–622
Catcher for the St. Louis Browns, Philadelphia Phillies, and Chicago Cubs.

A .238 lifetime hitter, Killefer nevertheless batted .323 in 45 games for the 1921 Cubs, for whom he was named player-manager in August. He retired from the playing field after that season, but he continued to manage until 1925. He then became a coach with the St. Louis Cardinals and St. Louis Browns, and became the Browns' manager for several seasons. In his years as a skipper he never managed better than a fourth-place finish.

Killefer later returned to coaching with the Brooklyn Dodgers and the Philadelphia Phillies.

Bruce Kimm
Chicago Cubs (NL) 2002
Record: 28–46
Saw limited action as a catcher in four major league seasons.

Kimm became a minor league manager and a major league coach following his playing career, and he was named the Southern League Manager of the Year in 1995 with the AA Orlando Cubs. In 2001 he led the AAA Iowa Cubs to the Central Division championship of the Pacific Coast League.

In 2002 the Chicago Cubs fired manager Don Baylor and called Kimm up from Iowa to take over. He was installed as interim manager and was promised that he would be allowed at least to finish out the season. After a rather poor Cubs' showing, however, he was fired in September.

Clyde King
San Francisco Giants (NL) 1969–70; Atlanta Braves (NL) 1974–75; New York Yankees (AL) 1982
Record: 234–229
Relief pitcher for seven major league seasons.

Spending six of those years with the Brooklyn Dodgers, King rarely started. In 1951 he went 14–7 despite having only three starts, and he would post a 32–25 career record.

King both coached and managed following his retirement. He posted a second-place finish in his first year with the Giants, and that would be his best. He was dismissed in May of 1970 and later managed the Braves. In 1982 he was the third and final manager for the Yankees, but following the season he left the dugout and went to the front office.

Malachi Kittridge
Washington Senators (AL) 1904
Record: 1–16
Good-fielding backstop with a strong arm.

A lifetime .219 hitter, Kittridge would not have lasted the 16 seasons he spent in the major leagues without those defensive qualities. In 1894 he did hit .315, but that was in only 51 games, and his next-highest average was .252. Four times he failed to reach the .200 mark.

As a player-manager in 1904 he did not fare any better. His club went 1–16 out of the gate for a pitiful .059 winning percentage when Kittridge surrendered control to Patsy Donovan, although he would remain with the team as a player. The Senators would eventually lose 113 games and finish in last place.

After continuing to play in the minor leagues and coaching at Harvard, Kittridge became a traveling salesman.

Lou Klein
Chicago Cubs (NL) 1961, 1962, 1965
Record: 65–82
Infielder with a troubled playing career.

Debuting in 1943 with the St. Louis Cardinals, Klein hit a solid .287 and did not miss a single inning of play. He then lost time to military service in World War II, and when he returned in 1945 he was not the same hitter and lost his starting job. During the 1946 season he and a couple of other players left the Cardinals to play in Mexico, and as a result they were all banned for life by baseball Commissioner Happy Chandler.

Chandler later reduced those bans to five years each, but in 1949 he lifted them altogether. Klein returned to the Cardinals, and later played briefly for the Cleveland Indians and Philadelphia Athletics.

He was part of the Cubs' "college of coaches" experiment in 1961 and 1962, and was elevated to sole manager in 1965. He never did manage a full season.

Johnny Kling
Boston Braves (NL) 1912
Record: 52–101
Catcher and outstanding billiards player.

Kling began his career with the Chicago Orphans (later the Cubs) at the turn of the twentieth century. He was excellent defensively and possessed a strong and accurate throwing arm, making a habit of nailing potential basestealers. He led the National League several times in many defensive categories, and was a decent hitter as well.

Johnny left baseball following the 1908 season in order to become a professional billiards player. He won the 1908–09 pocket billiards world championship, then returned to baseball when he failed to retain that title the next year.

In 1912 he became the player-manager of the Boston Braves, but a 101-loss season would put an end to that aspect of his career. He finished playing in 1913 with the Cincinnati Reds.

Otto Knabe
Baltimore Terrapins (FL) 1914–15
Record: 131–177
Tough second baseman for 11 major league seasons.

Knabe played most of his career for the Philadelphia Phillies, but in 1914 jumped to the new rival Federal League as player-manager of the Baltimore Terrapins. Those seasons were mediocre for him at the plate, but as a manager he did finish in third place in 1914, a mere 4½ games off the pace.

He returned to the National League for one more season when the FL folded.

Lon Knight
Philadelphia Athletics (AA) 1883–84
Record: 127–78
Originally Alonzo P. Letti.

The son of Italian immigrants, Lon changed his surname to Knight when he entered college in an attempt to avoid the ethnic hostility that was sometimes visited upon Italian Catholics. He played baseball while in school and

developed as a decent pitcher. After graduating he became an apprentice to an accountant, but would soon become a professional baseball player.

Originally a pitcher and later an outfielder, Knight threw the first pitch in National League history on April 22, 1876, with the Philadelphia Athletics. He was a decent hurler but a weak hitter.

For a time he bounced around between the major and minor leagues, but in 1883 was named player-manager of another team that was also called the Philadelphia Athletics. This club won the American Association pennant, finishing a single game ahead of the St. Louis Browns. The following season they dropped to seventh, and Knight was through with managing.

He played for one more season, then became an umpire. He died in 1932 of gas poisoning when a line to his gas heater was severed.

Ray Knight
Cincinnati Reds (NL) 1996–97, 2003
Record: 125–137
Hard-nosed third baseman and first baseman for many teams.

Always a tough competitor, Ray Knight was a National League All-Star in 1980 at third base with the Reds, and at first base in 1982 with the Houston Astros. He hit over .300 twice in a 13-year career. In 1986 with the New York Mets he was named the Most Valuable Player of the World Series when his leadoff home run in the seventh inning of Game 7 touched off a three-run rally that would eventually win it for New York.

After his retirement Knight went into coaching, and in 1995 he was the Reds' assistant manager under Davey Johnson. He was being groomed for the manager's position, and was named skipper in 1996. A .500 record was followed by a 43–56 showing in 1997 when he was fired and replaced by Jack McKeon.

He later returned to the Reds as a coach under Bob Boone, and in 2003 when Boone was fired he managed one more game before Boone's replacement, Dave Miley, arrived.

Knight married professional golfer Nancy Lopez.

Bobby Knoop
California Angels (AL) 1994
Record: 1–1
Second baseman with a good glove and a not-so-good bat.

Knoop (whose last name is pronounced "kin-AHP") won three Gold Gloves for his defense, and was named an American League All-Star in 1966 when he belted an uncharacteristic 17 home runs and led the league with 11 triples. He retired in 1972 and became a minor league manager and an Angels' coach.

In 1994 when the Angels fired manager Buck Rodgers, Knoop took over as interim skipper for two games before the arrival of replacement Marcel Lachemann.

Jack Krol
St. Louis Cardinals (NL) 1978, 1980
Record: 1–2
Minor league manager and coach with the San Diego Padres and St. Louis Cardinals.

While with St. Louis Krol became interim manager twice—for two games in 1978 when Vern Rapp was fired, before the arrival of Ken Boyer, and for one game in 1980 when Boyer was fired, before the arrival of Whitey Herzog.

Krol died of oral cancer in 1994 due to dipping tobacco. The Padres later honored him by creating the Jack Krol Award, which recognizes the Player Development Man of the Year within their organization.

Karl Kuehl
Montreal Expos (NL) 1976
Record: 43–85
California native who never played in the major leagues.

Kuehl did not last a single season as a big league manager, losing almost twice as many games as he won with the Expos in 1976. About three-quarters of the way through the season he was replaced by Charlie Fox.

The following year Karl became a coach with the Minnesota Twins.

Harvey Kuenn
Milwaukee Brewers (AL) 1975, 1982–83
Record: 160–118
American League Rookie of the Year in 1953.

An outstanding shortstop and later outfielder, Kuenn won that award by hitting .308 and leading the AL with 209 hits while playing for the Detroit Tigers. He made the All-Star team and would eventually be named to eight such squads. He led the league four times in hits and three times in triples, and in 1959 won the batting title with a .353 average. He batted .303 lifetime.

From 1971–82 Kuenn served as a coach with the Brewers. He became interim manager for one game in 1975, when skipper Del Crandall was fired prior to the final contest of the season. In 1980 he suffered through several health problems, and ended up having part of his right leg amputated. He continued his duties with the Brewers, however, and in June of 1982, with the club in fifth place, he became manager on a permanent basis when Buck Rodgers was fired.

Under Harvey's leadership the Brewers climbed into first place and won the AL Eastern Division title by a single game over the Baltimore Orioles. In the AL Championship Series they defeated the Oakland Athletics, three games to two, before dropping a tough seven-game World Series to the San Diego Padres. The AP named Kuenn its AL Manager of the Year.

The Brewers finished fifth the following season despite an 87–75 record, and Kuenn was promptly fired.

Joe Kuhel
Washington Nationals (AL) 1948–49
Record: 106–201
Fine defensive first baseman with an inconsistent bat.

Signed as a prospect by Clark Griffith in 1930 for a then-considerable $65,000, Kuhel debuted with the Nationals that same year in 18 games. He eventually went from the Nationals to the Chicago White Sox, then back to the Nationals and back to the White Sox.

Always solid defensively, Kuhel had some good years at the plate. In 1933 he hit .322 with 11 home runs and 107 runs batted in. In 1936 he batted .321 while slugging 16 roundtrippers and knocking in 118. He hit .300 in 1939, and in 1940 slugged 27 homers.

Kuhel once had a run-in with Hank Greenberg of the Detroit Tigers, hurling anti-Semitic insults at the slugger that caused Greenberg to challenge him in the White Sox' clubhouse after the game. Kuhel declined the challenge, and the two coexisted peacefully on the field thereafter.

Joe retired in 1947 and became the Nationals' manager in 1948. His team was not a strong one, and finished seventh and eighth in the two seasons he was at the helm. He later managed the Kansas City Blues in the minor American Association.

Marcel Lachemann
California Angels (AL) 1994–96
Record: 160–170
Pitched 70 games over three major league seasons before becoming a coach and manager.

Lachemann started none of those games, pitching solely in relief with the Oakland Athletics. He had a fine year in 1970, appearing in 41 contests and going 3–3 with 3 saves and a 2.78 earned run average.

Most of his major league career after that was spent as a pitching coach. In 1993 he was named to that position with the Florida Marlins by their new manager, his brother Rene.

In 1994 Marcel left to take over as manager of the Angels when Buck Rodgers was fired. He managed all of 1995 and the Angels finished in second place, one game behind the Seattle Mariners. They were 52–59 the following season when Lachemann was replaced by John

McNamara. He then returned to coaching, and also spent time instructing minor leaguers.

Rene Lachemann

Seattle Mariners (AL) 1981–83; Milwaukee Brewers (AL) 1984; Florida Marlins (NL) 1993–96; Chicago Cubs (NL) 2002

Record: 428–560

Catcher for parts of three seasons with the Kansas City/Oakland Athletics.

Lachemann spent many years as a coach and manager following his playing career. Starting in the Athletics' minor league system, he also managed winter ball, and in 1978 led the Mayaguez Indians to the championship of the Caribbean Series, garnering Manager of the Year honors for himself in the process.

He became a major league manager in 1981 with the Mariners, and eventually spent a year with the Brewers before becoming the very first skipper of the Florida Marlins in 1993. He selected his brother Marcel to be his pitching coach.

Lachemann's best finish as a manager was third place. He was a coach with the Cubs in 2002 and was called upon to take over for a single game when Don Baylor was fired. The next day Baylor was replaced by Bruce Kimm.

Rene later returned to the A's as a coach.

Nap Lajoie

Cleveland Naps (AL) 1905, 1905–09

Record: 377–309

Hall of Fame second baseman for 21 seasons.

Napoleon Lajoie began his career in 1896 with the Philadelphia Phillies, and in 39 games he batted .326. From that point on he rarely hit below .300, falling under that mark only five times in his career.

Lajoie was an incredibly dominant player, winning three batting titles and leading his league in hits four times, in home runs once, in runs batted in three times, in doubles five times, and in runs scored once.

In 1901 he jumped from the Phillies to the Philadelphia Athletics of the new, rival American League. He immediately won the Triple Crown, hitting an incredible .426 with 14 home runs and 125 RBIs. In 1902 he was transferred to the Cleveland Bronchos because the Phillies had obtained an injunction preventing him from playing for any other team in Philadelphia. When he had another sensational year, the Bronchos renamed themselves the Naps in his honor, and two years later he became their player-manager.

Partway through the 1905 season Lajoie was spiked and suffered blood poisoning as a result. Bill Bradley took over for 41 games before Nap was able to return. In first place when Lajoie left, the Naps would finish fifth. A second-place showing in 1908 would be the skipper's best thereafter, but even after stepping down as manager in 1909 he continued to play. He returned to the A's in 1915, and ended his career the next year.

Lajoie's career batting average was .338, and he amassed 3242 hits lifetime. He was inducted into the Hall of Fame in 1937.

Fred Lake

Boston Red Sox (AL) 1908–09; Boston Doves (NL) 1910

Record: 163–180

Played several positions for 48 major league games during five scattered seasons.

Those five seasons were 1891, 1894, 1897, 1898, and 1910. Lake never played more than 19 major league contests in a year, and hit only .232 lifetime. His positions were first base, second base, shortstop, catcher, and outfielder.

As a manager he took the helm of the Red Sox in 1908 toward the end of the season as a replacement for Deacon McGuire. His club's third-place finish in 1909 would be his best. He moved to the National League's Doves in 1910, where he was technically player-manager because he appeared in three games.

Gene Lamont

Chicago White Sox (AL) 1992–95; Pittsburgh Pirates (NL) 1997–2000

Record: 553–562

Catcher who played 87 major league games over parts of five seasons.

Lamont homered in his first big league at-bat in 1970, but he would slug only three more roundtrippers at that level. After his retirement he became a manager in the Kansas City Royals' organization, and in both 1982 and 1983 his Jacksonville Suns finished in first place. In '82 he was named the Southern League Manager of the Year.

He became a coach with the Pirates in 1986, and was hired to manage the White Sox in 1992. The following year his club won the American League Western Division, and Lamont was named AL Manager of the Year by the BBWAA. The Sox were defeated in the AL Championship Series by the Toronto Blue Jays, four games to two, but they were first again in 1994 when the season was cut short due to a players' strike.

In 1995 he was fired partway through the season, and the following year returned to the Pirates as a coach. He became the Bucs' skipper in 1997, and a second-place finish that year would be his best in Pittsburgh.

Hal Lanier
Houston Astros (NL) 1986–88
Record: 254–232
Son of major leaguer Max Lanier.

An infielder with a good glove but a light bat, Lanier became a minor league player-coach after leaving the majors and then a minor league manager.

He was a coach with the St. Louis Cardinals from 1981–85, then took the managerial reins of the Astros for three seasons. His first year he guided Houston to the National League Western Division championship before they dropped the NL Championship Series to the New York Mets. For his efforts Lanier was named Manager of the Year by the AP and NL Manager of the Year by the BBWAA.

The Astros dropped to third the following season and then to fifth the next, and Hal was let go. In 1990 he became a coach with the Philadelphia Phillies.

Lanier became the manager of the independent Northern League's Winnipeg Goldeyes in 1996, and in a nine-year period he led his club to the postseason eight times and held the league's managerial record for best all-time winning percentage.

Henry Larkin
Cleveland Infants (PL) 1890
Record: 34–45
Outstanding outfielder and first baseman for 10 major league seasons.

A .310 lifetime hitter, Larkin topped the .300 mark six times, peaking at .371 in 1887. He led the American Association twice in doubles, with 37 in 1885 and 36 the following year.

In 1890 he started out as player-manager of the Players League's Cleveland Infants, but after a 34–45 record he turned the reins over to Patsy Tebeau. He remained with the club as a player, however, and hit .330.

When the PL folded he returned to the AA, where he played for three more seasons.

Tony LaRussa
Chicago White Sox (AL) 1979–86; Oakland Athletics (AL)
**   1986–95; St. Louis Cardinals (NL) 1996–**
Record: 2297–1986
One of the winningest managers in major league history.

An infielder who played only 132 games in six partial seasons, LaRussa turned to managing in the minor leagues and became a coach with the White Sox in 1978. A year later he replaced Don Kessinger at the helm despite being a mere 34 years of age. In 1983 he guided the team to the American League Western Division title before dropping a three-games-to-one playoff to the Baltimore Orioles.

LaRussa was named AL Manager of the Year by both the AP and the BBWAA.

With Chicago in fifth place just over a third of the way through the 1986 campaign, Tony was fired, but he was picked up shortly thereafter by the Oakland Athletics. The A's finished third that season and the next, then embarked on a string of three consecutive division titles. In 1988 they won the AL pennant but dropped the World Series to the Los Angeles Dodgers, in 1989 they won it all in a sweep over the San Francisco Giants, and in 1990 they took the pennant but were in turn swept by the Cincinnati Reds. In '88 the BBWAA once again named LaRussa its AL Manager of the Year.

The A's were back on top in 1992, and LaRussa was named Manager of the Year by the AP and AL Manager of the Year by the BBWAA. Oakland dropped the AL Championship Series to the Toronto Blue Jays, however.

LaRussa left Oakland for the Cardinals in 1996, and between that year and 2006 the Cards won seven division titles. Two pennants would result: the first in 2004, when St. Louis was swept by the Boston Red Sox in the World Series, and the second in 2006, when the Cardinals defeated the Detroit Tigers in five games to capture the World Championship. LaRussa thus became only the second manager in history (after Sparky Anderson) to win the ultimate title in both leagues.

The AP had named LaRussa Manager of the Year again in 1996, and the BBWAA had named him National League Manager of the Year in 2002. He thus became the first manager to win the BBWAA title four times (Bobby Cox was the second, accomplishing the feat in 2005), and only the second (Cox was the first) to win it in both leagues.

Tom Lasorda
Los Angeles Dodgers (NL) 1976–96
Record: 1599–1439
Successful minor league pitcher who lasted only 26 major league games.

After becoming a scout for the Dodgers in 1961, Lasorda turned to managing at the minor league level. Between 1965 and 1972 he won five pennants, and the following year became a Dodgers' coach under manager Walter Alston.

In 1976 Alston retired with four games left in the season, and Lasorda was named to take his place. He won two of those final four games, then won the National League pennant in both 1977 and 1978. He thus became the first NL manager to accomplish that feat in his first two seasons, but his club lost the World Series to the New York Yankees both years.

Lasorda took the Dodgers to the World Championship

in 1981. In a season that was split because of a players' strike, the team won its division in the first half and thus qualified for the postseason. They defeated the Houston Astros in a divisional playoff series, the Montreal Expos in the NL Championship Series, and finally the Yankees in the World Series.

First-place finishes would follow in 1983, 1985, 1988, and 1995, and in 1994 the Dodgers were in first place when the season abruptly ended due to another players' strike. The only World Championship that resulted was in 1988, when LA defeated a powerful Oakland Athletics team in five games.

The AP named Lasorda its NL Manager of the Year in 1977, 1981, and 1983, and its Manager of the Year in 1988 (choosing only one manager to represent both leagues). The BBWAA bestowed its similar title in 1983 and 1988.

Lasorda stopped managing during the 1996 season because of heart problems, and he went to work in the Dodgers' front office. In 1997 he was inducted into the Hall of Fame, and the Dodgers retired his uniform number 2.

In 2000 he returned to managing, this time in the Olympic arena as he guided the U.S. team to the gold medal in Sydney, Australia.

Arlie Latham
St. Louis Browns (NL) 1896
Record: 0–3
Good-humored, solid third baseman who managed very briefly.

Latham hit over .300 four times in his career, and he stole 742 bases. He led the American Association in that category in 1888 with 109, after leading in runs scored in 1886 with 152.

With the Browns in 1896, he played only eight games, and he was player-manager for three, losing all of them. Latham was the second of five managers to guide St. Louis that season, and the team finished in eleventh place. He is major league baseball's first known coach, having taken that role for one season with the Cincinnati Reds in 1900, and then in 1909 appeared in four games as a player-coach for the New York Giants.

Juice Latham
New Haven Elm Citys (NA) 1875; Philadelphia Athletics (AA) 1882
Record: 45–48
First professional player from Utica, New York.

George "Juice" Latham, who was given his nickname because of his lack of speed on the bases, began his professional career in 1869 with Ottawa at the age of 17. He reached the major league level in 1875 with the Boston Red Stockings of the National Association, and would become the player-manager of the New Haven Elm Citys of the same league that same year.

He frequently bounced between the major and minor leagues, and played for his hometown Utica Utes of the International Association in 1878. In 1882 he was back in the majors with the Athletics of the new American Association as player-manager, and his team finished in second place. He continued to play in the AA until 1884, and from 1886–87 returned home with the Utica Pent-ups of the New York State League. He later became a coach for another team by the same name.

Cookie Lavagetto
Washington Senators (AL) 1957–60; Minnesota Twins (AL) 1961, 1961
Record: 271–384
Four-time All-Star third baseman.

Always a solid player, Lavagetto is most famous for a single at-bat in the 1947 World Series, his final season as a player with the Brooklyn Dodgers. In Game 4, with his club being no-hit by the New York Yankees and down 1–0, Cookie came up as a pinch-hitter after Yankee pitcher Bill Bevens had walked two batters. Lavagetto promptly slammed a double off the right field wall, not only breaking up the no-hitter but winning the game for the Dodgers, 2–1.

After his retirement Lavagetto became a coach, and in 1957 he took the helm of the Washington Senators. A fifth-place finish would be his best, but he remained manager when the team moved to Minnesota in 1961 and became the Twins. In June, after a 19–30 start, Cookie was granted a week-long "vacation" by owner Clark Griffith, and coach Sam Mele took over the club. Lavagetto returned, went 4–6, and was fired by Griffith. Mele then assumed control for good.

Lavagetto later coached the New York Mets, and in 1963 he was involved in the only trade of coaches in major league history when he was swapped to the San Francisco Giants for Wes Westrum.

Bob Leadley
Detroit Wolverines (NL) 1888; Cleveland Spiders (NL) 1890–91
Record: 76–86
Brooklyn native who never managed a full season.

Never having played in the major leagues, Leadley managed a mere 166 games over three seasons. He replaced Bill Watkins during the 1888 season with the Wolverines and managed 40 games, replaced Gus Schmelz during the 1890 season with the Spiders and managed 58, and was replaced by Patsy Tebeau during the 1891 season with the Spiders after managing 68. His teams never finished better than fifth place.

Jim Lefebvre

Seattle Mariners (AL) 1989–91; Chicago Cubs (NL) 1992–93; Milwaukee Brewers (NL) 1999
Record: 417–442
Infielder for the Los Angeles Dodgers for eight seasons.

A switch-hitter, Lefebvre won the National League Rookie of the Year Award in 1965 when he hit .250 with 12 home runs and 69 runs batted in. He was named to the NL All-Star team the following season on the strength of a .274 average, 24 homers, and 74 RBIs, all career highs.

In the midst of his on-the-field accomplishments he was also making forays into television. Lefebvre appeared on the series *Batman* as one of the Riddler's henchmen, appeared with teammate Al Ferrara as a headhunter on an episode of *Gilligan's Island*, and later popped up on *M*A*S*H*, *Alice*, *St. Elsewhere*, and *Midnight Caller*.

He left the major leagues in 1972 to play in Japan, where he remained through 1976. He returned to the major leagues as a coach for several teams before becoming the manager of the Mariners in 1989. He spent three seasons there, during which he apparently had some conflicts with general manager Woody Woodward, then spent another two as manager of the Cubs. His best finish would be fourth place in Chicago. In 1999 he was a coach with the Brewers when he was called upon to replace the fired Phil Garner in August.

In 2003 Lefebvre returned to the Orient to become the manager of the Chinese national team.

Bob Lemon

Kansas City Royals (AL) 1970–72; Chicago White Sox (AL) 1977–78; New York Yankees (AL) 1978–79, 1981–82
Record: 430–403
Debuted with the Cleveland Indians as a third baseman in 1941.

After spending World War II in the Navy, Lemon returned to the major leagues in 1946 as a pitcher, although he also played occasional games in the outfield.

As a hurler he fashioned a Hall of Fame career, spending 13 seasons on the mound, all of them with the Tribe. He led the American League three times in victories, three times in starts, five times in complete games, once in shutouts, four times in innings pitched, and once in strikeouts. He was an AL All-Star seven years in a row, from 1948–54. He amassed 207 lifetime victories against 128 defeats for a .618 winning percentage.

After leaving the major leagues in 1958 Lemon pitched briefly in the Pacific Coast League, then became a scout and a coach. He returned to the Indians as a coach in 1960, and took a similar role with the Philadelphia Phillies in 1961. In 1966 he managed the Seattle Angels to the Pacific Coast League championship, and *The Sporting News* named him its Minor League Manager of the Year.

He was a coach with the Royals in 1970 when manager Charlie Metro was fired, and Lemon took the former skipper's place. He himself was dropped in 1972.

In 1976 he was a coach with the Yankees when he was inducted into the Hall of Fame. The following year he was hired to manage the White Sox, and when he was fired during the 1978 campaign he returned to manage the Yankees, who had fired Billy Martin. In third place when Lemon took over, the club finished in a tie for first with the Boston Red Sox, then won a one-game playoff to advance to the League Championship Series. There the Yankees defeated the Royals to take the AL pennant, then bested the Los Angeles Dodgers for the World Championship. Lemon was named the league's Manager of the Year by the AP.

As a Yankee manager Lemon had the typical tumultuous relationship with owner George Steinbrenner. During the 1979 season Bob was fired and replaced by the returning Billy Martin. During the 1981 campaign Lemon himself returned and replaced Gene Michael, and the Yankees won the AL pennant but lost the World Series to the Dodgers. In 1982, when the Yankees started 6–8, Lemon was fired and replaced by Michael.

In 1998 the Indians retired Bob's number 21. Lemon died in California two years later.

Jim Lemon

Washington Senators (AL) 1968
Record: 65–96
Outfielder with a strong arm and some decent power.

Jim Lemon debuted with the Cleveland Indians in 1950, but spent the next two years in the Korean War. He would not return to the major leagues until 1953, and would not become a regular until he went to the Washington Nationals (later the Senators) in 1956.

Lemon hit 27 home runs that year and finished the season in a four-way tie for the American League lead with 11 triples. In 1959 he slugged 33 roundtrippers while driving in 100 runs, and the following season became an All-Star in both games on the strength of 38 homers and another 100 RBIs.

After concluding his playing career in 1963, Lemon went into coaching. He became the manager of another Washington Senators team in 1968, finished last, and was fired. He then returned to coaching.

Bill Lennon
Fort Wayne Kekiongas (NA) 1871
Record: 5–9
Catcher for three seasons in the original National Association.

Lennon is credited with being the first catcher to throw out a baserunner trying to steal. That event occurred during the first game in major league baseball history, on May 4, 1871, in the seventh inning. The Kekiongas defeated the Cleveland Forest Citys in that game, 2–0.

As player-manager of the Kekiongas he went 5–9 for a team that would finish 7–12.

Jim Leyland
Pittsburgh Pirates (NL) 1986–96; Florida Marlins (NL) 1997–98; Colorado Rockies (NL) 1999; Detroit Tigers (AL) 2006–
Record: 1164–1198
Minor league catcher who became an excellent major league manager.

Leyland ended his playing career and became a minor league skipper at the age of 26, and in 11 years at the helm he won three Manager of the Year Awards. In 1982 he was tagged by Tony LaRussa to be a coach with the Chicago White Sox, a post he would hold for four seasons.

In 1986 he was hired to manage the Pirates, and he would do so for 11 seasons. His greatest success came from 1990–92, when his Bucs won three consecutive National League Eastern Division titles. Unfortunately, a pennant remained out of reach as the Pirates were eliminated in the playoffs all three times. In spite of that, the BBWAA named Leyland its NL Manager of the Year in both 1990 and 1992.

Leaving the Pirates voluntarily following the 1996 campaign, Jim signed on as skipper of the Marlins. His 1997 club finished second to the Atlanta Braves in the NL East but earned a wild card berth. They went on to defeat the San Francisco Giants in the NL Division Series, the Braves for the NL pennant, and the Cleveland Indians for the World Championship.

The Marlins began dismantling their club in 1998, and at the end of the season Leyland exercised an escape clause in his contract and bailed out. He took over the Rockies in 1999, then quit managing altogether in order to spend more time at home. He later became a scout for the St. Louis Cardinals, and in 2006 returned to the dugout to manage the Tigers. He took that club to its first winning record in 13 years and thence to the American League pennant, but the team then lost the World Series to La-Russa's St. Louis squad. Leyland was nevertheless named the AL Manager of the Year by the BBWAA, thus becom-

ing only the third manager (after Bobby Cox and La-Russa) to win the award in both leagues.

Nick Leyva
Philadelphia Phillies (NL) 1989–91
Record: 148–189
Californian who never played major league baseball.

An NAIA All-American out of the University of La Verne, Leyva played in the minor league system of the St. Louis Cardinals before becoming a minor league manager. He was the Texas League Manager of the Year in 1983 with the Arkansas Travelers, and became a coach for the Cardinals from 1984–88. He managed the Phillies for two full seasons and only 13 games of a third, then went back to coaching with the Toronto Blue Jays and once again managing in the minor leagues. In 2002 his Bristol White Sox won the Appalachian League championship.

Bob Lillis
Houston Astros (NL) 1982–85
Record: 276–261
Shortstop for 10 major league seasons.

Lillis debuted with the Los Angeles Dodgers in 1958, but after hitting .391 in 20 games that season he would never again bat over .268. His lifetime average, in fact, was a mere .236.

Drafted by the expansion Houston Colt .45s in 1962, he became the team's Most Valuable Player in their inaugural season. That team soon became the Astros, and after finishing his playing career with them, Lillis became a scout and instructor and later joined the major league coaching staff. He was named manager in August of 1982, and in the next three full seasons would never finish lower than third.

Fired in October of 1985, he then became a coach with the San Francisco Giants.

Johnny Lipon
Cleveland Indians (AL) 1971
Record: 18–41
Nine-year major league shortstop for several teams.

A .259 lifetime hitter, Lipon became a longtime minor league manager after retiring, and became a coach with the Indians in 1968. In July of 1971 the Indians fired manager Alvin Dark after going 42–61, and Lipon was tagged to take over for the rest of the season. He went 18–41 and was not brought back.

Grady Little
Boston Red Sox (AL) 2002–03; Los Angeles Dodgers (NL) 2006–
Record: 276–210

Longtime minor league manager who never played major league baseball.

Over 17 seasons, beginning in 1980, Little managed many competitive minor league teams. In 1981 his Hagerstown Suns won the Carolina League title and he himself was named the circuit's Manager of the Year. His 1985 Kinston Blue Jays made the playoffs in the same league, and Little was once again named Manager of the Year. His Pulaski Braves won the Appalachian League championship in 1986, and in 1989 his Durham Bulls made the playoffs with the best record in the Carolina League and Grady was yet again named Manager of the Year.

It did not stop there, as his 1992 Greenville Braves won their league championship, resulting in Little becoming the Southern League Manager of the Year, and his 1994 Richmond Braves did the same, winning him the title of International League Manager of the Year. The 1993 and 1995 Richmond clubs also made the playoffs.

Little took the helm of the Boston Red Sox in 2002, and the following season his team won the American League wild card berth. They bested the Oakland Athletics in the AL Division Series before losing the battle for the pennant to the New York Yankees. Little was fired following that 2003 season. In 2006 he became the skipper of the Los Angeles Dodgers. That club won the National League wild card, but was defeated in the Division Series by the New York Mets.

Hans Lobert
Philadelphia Phillies (NL) 1938, 1942
Record: 42–111
Speedy third baseman with a 14-year major league career.

Once considered the fastest man in the National League, Lobert stole 316 bases in his career, swiping at least 20 on eight occasions. A lifetime .274 hitter, he topped the .300 mark four times. A couple of knee injuries eventually took their toll on him, and he retired in 1917.

Hans became a minor league manager before joining the Phillies' coaching staff from 1934–41. When skipper Jimmie Wilson resigned with two games to go in the 1938 season, Lobert took over for those two contests, but lost both of them. In 1942 he was named full-time Phillies' manager, but 109 losses and a last-place finish ended his career in that arena.

Whitey Lockman
Chicago Cubs (NL) 1972–74
Record: 157–162
Outfielder and first baseman who homered in his very first major league at-bat.

Lockman topped the .300 mark only once, when he batted .301 in 1949, but he was always a decent hitter. In terms of power he peaked with 18 home runs in 1948 and reached double digits six times, but was generally not considered a longball threat. He was a National League All-Star in 1952 on the strength of a .290 average, 13 home runs, and 58 runs batted in.

Whitey coached several teams following his retirement, and was named Cubs' manager in 1972 when Leo Durocher resigned. His club finished second, and two years later he stepped down in July in order to become the organization's director of player development.

Tom Loftus
Milwaukee Cream Citys (UA) 1884; Cleveland Blues (AA) 1888; Cleveland Spiders (NL) 1889; Cincinnati Reds (NL) 1890–91; Chicago Orphans (NL) 1900–01; Washington Senators (AL) 1902–03
Record: 454–580
Had 33 major league at-bats before becoming a manager.

With a .182 average Loftus did not succeed as a big league player. As a manager he worked for nine seasons with several teams, including the Cleveland Blues of the American Association in 1888, who joined the National League and changed their name to the Cleveland Spiders with Loftus at the helm in 1889.

His Milwaukee Cream Citys finished second in the Union Association in 1884, and that would be his best showing. When he left the managerial arena he had the distinction of having managed in four different major leagues (the UA, the AA, the NL, and the AL). In 1903 he became the chairman of baseball's rules committee.

Ed Lopat
Kansas City Athletics (AL) 1963–64
Record: 90–124
Excellent left-handed pitcher for 12 major league seasons.

Lopat won 166 games in his career, most of them with the New York Yankees. He won in double digits 11 times, peaking with a 21–9 record in 1951, when he was named to the American League All-Star team. In 1953 he led the league with a 2.42 earned run average.

Lopat eventually became a coach following his playing career, and he was named manager of the Kansas City A's in 1963. He lasted only one full season, finishing eighth, and was in tenth place in June of 1964 when he was fired.

Davey Lopes
Milwaukee Brewers (NL) 2000–02
Record: 144–195
Speedy second baseman and outfielder with a proficiency for stealing bases.

Lopes swiped 557 bags in a 16-year playing career. Spending his best years with the Los Angeles Dodgers, he stole at least 20 for 11 years in a row and 13 total. He led the National League in 1975 with 77 and in 1976 with 63, and was named to the All-Star team every year from 1978–81. Not considered a power hitter, he nevertheless clubbed 28 home runs in 1979.

As a manager he guided the Brewers for two full seasons, finishing third and fourth, respectively, and when the club started out 3–12 in 2002 he was fired and replaced by Jerry Royster.

Al Lopez
Cleveland Indians (AL) 1951–56; Chicago White Sox (AL) 1957–65, 1968, 1968–69
Record: 1410–1004

Diminutive catcher who played 1950 games over 19 major league seasons.

An adequate hitter, Lopez was mainly valued for his work behind the plate. He was extremely durable and was strong defensively. He hit .309 in 1930 and .301 in 1933, the only two full seasons he topped the .300 mark, and was named to two National League All-Star squads.

Lopez became a minor league manager following his retirement, and soon afterwards was named skipper of the Indians. Six years at the helm produced one first-place and five second-place finishes. His 1954 Tribe won 111 games, an American League record at the time, before being swept in the World Series by the New York Giants.

Al resigned following the 1956 season and was immediately snatched up by the White Sox. His teams remained competitive, and in 1959 his club, nicknamed the "Go-Go Sox," took the pennant and then dropped the World Series to the Los Angeles Dodgers. The AP named Lopez its AL Manager of the Year. During that first tenure in Chicago, which encompassed nine seasons, he managed one first-place and six second-place finishes.

Lopez resigned following the 1965 campaign, but returned in July of 1968 to replace Eddie Stanky. Less than two weeks later he underwent an emergency appendectomy, and Les Moss filled in until he returned over a month later. In May of 1969 Lopez resigned for good due to health reasons. He was inducted into the Hall of Fame by the Veterans Committee in 1977.

Harry Lord
Buffalo Blues (FL) 1915
Record: 60–49

Rather inconsistent third baseman with several teams.

Lord did hit .315 in 1909 and .321 in 1911, but defensively he was almost a liability. His play was sometimes aggressive and sometimes lackluster, and after leaving the Chicago White Sox voluntarily in 1914 he joined the Buffalo Blues of the Federal League. About a quarter of the way through the season he was named player-manager, but his 60–49 record would not be enough to save a faltering club, and the Blues finished sixth.

Bobby Lowe
Detroit Tigers (AL) 1904
Record: 30–44

Solid player, mostly at second base, for 18 major league seasons.

Lowe hit over .300 three times and belted 17 home runs in 1894 with 115 runs batted in. He hit four of those home runs in a single game against the Cincinnati Reds. Three years later he hit only 5 roundtrippers but knocked in 106 runs.

With the Detroit Tigers in 1904, he was named player-manager during the season to replace Ed Barrow, but his club finished in seventh place. He would not manage again, but would play for three more years before retiring.

Frank Lucchesi
Philadelphia Phillies (NL) 1970–72; Texas Rangers (AL) 1975–77; Chicago Cubs (NL) 1987
Record: 316–399

Minor league outfielder who became a minor league manager at the age of 23.

Lucchesi reached the majors in 1970 as manager of the Phillies, then became a coach with the Rangers in 1974. The following year he was named Texas manager when Billy Martin was fired. In spring training of 1977 he was physically attacked by one of his own players, Lenny Randle, who was angry because Lucchesi had benched him. Lucchesi suffered several injuries, including a black eye and a fractured cheekbone, and Randle was suspended and was eventually arrested and charged with assault. Randle was found guilty and Lucchesi sued him, but the Rangers fired Frank in June.

Lucchesi would briefly manage the Cubs 10 years later, but in all his years of managing, a single third-place finish would be his best.

Harry Lumley
Brooklyn Superbas (NL) 1909
Record: 55–98

Played seven major league seasons, all with Brooklyn.

In his rookie year of 1904 Lumley led the National League with 9 home runs and 18 triples. Two years later he hit .324, a career high, and in 1909 he was named the Superbas' player-manager.

His team finished in sixth place, and Lumley played only eight games in 1910 and would not manage again.

Ted Lyons
Chicago White Sox (AL) 1946–48
Record: 185–245
Louisiana native who spent an entire 21-year playing career with the White Sox.

Lyons never pitched in the minor leagues, having been signed straight out of Baylor University where he had been studying law. He eventually won 260 games in his career, becoming a 20-game winner three times and leading the American League twice in victories, twice in complete games, once in shutouts, twice in innings pitched, and once in earned run average. In 1926 he pitched a no-hitter against the Boston Red Sox.

An arm injury in 1931 destroyed his fastball, but Ted developed a knuckleball and kept pitching successfully. In 1939 he was named to the AL All-Star squad, although he never again won more than 15 games in a season.

In 1942 Lyons joined the Marines, and he would not return to baseball until after World War II, when he pitched five games for the White Sox in 1946. Thirty games into the season he was named the team's manager. In three years he finished fifth, sixth, and eighth, then became a coach for the Detroit Tigers and the Brooklyn Dodgers.

In 1955 Lyons was inducted into the Hall of Fame. He died in Louisiana in 1986, and the following year the White Sox retired his number 16.

Ken Macha
Oakland Athletics (AL) 2003–06
Record: 368–280
Played sparingly for six major league seasons.

A power hitter in the minor leagues, Macha was used as a reserve in the majors until, in 1982, he departed for Japan. There he played for the Chunichi Dragons and once again displayed his home run form.

He played until 1985, and the following year became a coach with the Montreal Expos. He later coached the California Angels before becoming a minor league manager in the Boston Red Sox' system. His teams made the postseason his first three years at the helm, and in 1998 he was named International League Manager of the Year while with the Pawtucket Red Sox.

Macha then became a coach with the A's, and was named manager in 2003. He immediately led his club to the American League Western Division title, although they were eliminated in the first round of the playoffs by the Red Sox. He was technically fired in October of 2005, but was rehired a week later. In October of 2006 he was fired again, this time for good, despite the fact that the A's had made the playoffs.

Connie Mack
Pittsburgh Pirates (NL) 1894–96; Philadelphia Athletics (AL) 1901–37, 1938–39, 1940–50
Record: 3731–3948
Winningest manager in baseball history.

Also the losingest manager in baseball history, Connie Mack was a decent minor league catcher before reaching the major leagues in 1886 with the Washington Statesmen. He played 11 seasons and hit only .246, but was player-manager of the Pirates for three years.

Connie did not like the front office interference he had to endure in Pittsburgh, and in 1901 he took over the Philadelphia Athletics, where he would remain for the next 50 years. During that period he would win nine pennants and five World Championships. He disdained wearing a uniform while he managed, appearing in the dugout always in street clothes.

Becoming a member of baseball's rules committee as well as the Athletics' skipper in 1901, Mack took only a single year to capture his first pennant. There was no World Series in 1902, so his club reached its pinnacle. A 1905 pennant led to a Series loss to the New York Giants, but back-to-back pennants in 1910 and 1911 also led to back-to-back World Championships.

At that time Mack added his son Earle to the roster, and the younger Mack would play only five games but would primarily serve as assistant manager.

The A's repeated their back-to-back pennant performance in 1913 and 1914, but dropped the 1914 World Series. In need of cash and enduring several salary disputes with some of his players, Mack began dismantling his team. He thus, after managing some of the best teams in history, began to manage some of the worst.

He eventually rebuilt the club, and the A's took three consecutive AL pennants from 1929–31. Two World Championships also marked the 1929 and '30 seasons. In 1932 Connie started tearing it all down again, and he would never win another pennant.

In 1937, while he was still managing, Mack was inducted into the Hall of Fame. The following season the A's celebrated Connie Mack Day at Shibe Park as the club swept a doubleheader from the Chicago White Sox. Because of increasing illnesses, Connie's son Earle took over for him for several games in 1937 and 1939. In December of 1940, Connie purchased controlling interest in the A's.

In 1950 he finally stepped down as manager, but remained president of the club. Six years later he passed away at the age of 93.

Denny Mack
Louisville Eclipse (AA) 1882

Record: 42–38

Played in the original 1871 National Association.

Primarily a shortstop and first baseman, Mack also pitched a few games. In 1872 he led the NA with 23 bases on balls at the plate, and in 1882 became player-manager of the Louisville Eclipse of the American Association. He posted a decent third-place finish but hit only .182, and he would play just one more season.

In 1888, at the age of 37, he died from internal hemorrhaging and seizures after a fall at his home.

Earle Mack
Philadelphia Athletics (AL) 1937, 1939
Record: 45–77
Son of Connie Mack.

Earle played one game for the Athletics in 1910, two in 1911, and two more in 1914. Those five games, in which he totaled 16 at-bats, comprised his entire major league playing career. His primary role with the A's, however, was as assistant manager under his father beginning in 1924.

Due to illnesses suffered by Connie, Earle filled in as manager for 34 games in 1937 and for 91 in 1939. He was supposedly being groomed to replace Connie upon his father's eventual retirement, a retirement that did not come until 1950. At that time, however, Earle was instead assigned a scouting position, and Jimmy Dykes was named skipper.

Pete Mackanin
Pittsburgh Pirates (NL) 2005
Record: 12–14
Backup infielder who became a longtime minor league manager.

Mackanin managed in several big league organizations, and in 1995 won the International League championship with the Ottawa Lynx and was named Minor League Manager of the Year by *The Sporting News*. He amassed over 900 victories at the minor league level.

For a time he was a coach for the Montreal Expos, then managed in the Pirates' system before joining the Bucs as a coach. He was named Pirates' interim manager in September of 2005 when skipper Lloyd McClendon was fired.

Jimmy Macullar
Syracuse Stars (NL) 1879
Record: 5–21
Rather weak-hitting outfielder and shortstop for six major league seasons.

Macullar's highest average over those six years was .234; his lowest was .167. In 1879, his first season in the majors, he was named player-manager of the Syracuse Stars, becoming the third skipper of that team that year. He did no better than his predecessors, posting a mere 5–21 record for a team that would finish in seventh place.

Macullar did not manage again, but he played for five more seasons and then became an umpire in 1892.

Joe Maddon
California Angels (AL) 1996; Anaheim Angels (AL) 1999; Tampa Bay Devil Rays (AL) 2006–
Record: 88–125
Minor league catcher who became a major league coach and manager.

Maddon managed in the minors following his retirement as a player, winning the Manager of the Year Award in 1982 with the Northwest League champion Salem Angels. His experience as a major league skipper was first gained on an interim basis in two stints with the California/Anaheim Angels. His team finished fourth both years. Then, following the 2005 season, he was named manager of the Devil Rays to replace Lou Piniella.

Lee Magee
Brooklyn Tip-Tops (FL) 1915
Record: 53–64
Infielder and outfielder for nine seasons.

As a hitter Magee broke the .300 barrier only once, in 1915 when he was player-manager of the Federal League's Brooklyn Tip-Tops. He batted .323 that year, although he turned the managerial reins over to John Ganzel with 35 games left to go.

He did not manage again, and his playing career came to an end in 1919 when he admitted having bet against some of his own teams and having attempted to throw games.

Fergy Malone
Philadelphia Philadelphias (NA) 1873; Chicago White Stockings (NA) 1874; Philadelphia Keystones (UA) 1884
Record: 47–66
First left-handed catcher in major league history.

Born in Ireland, Ferguson Malone grew up playing cricket in Philadelphia. He turned to baseball in 1862 with the amateur Philadelphia Athletics, and was with that team when it turned professional as a member of the original National Association in 1871. He became one of the first catchers to wear a pair of gloves behind the plate, and continued playing through 1876. Along the way he was player-manager for parts of two seasons.

In 1884 he was hired to manage the Philadelphia Keystones of the Union Association, a team that finished 21–46. He then tried his hand at umpiring, but had a difficult time of it and was roundly criticized for his less-than-stellar efforts.

He left umpiring and managed for a time in the minor leagues, then became an inspector for the U.S. Treasury. He died in 1905 in Seattle.

Jack Manning
Cincinnati Red Stockings (NL) 1877
Record: 7–12
Decent outfielder and pitcher who played from 1873–86.

Spending those years with a variety of teams, Manning hit .346 in 1874 and .317 in 1877, the year he became player-manager of the Red Stockings. That Cincinnati club was not even a ghost of its former self, finishing last with a 15–42 record, and Manning was the last of three unsuccessful managers that season. He won only 7 of 20 games, tying one, and did not manage again. As a pitcher he had gone 18–5 in 1876, and he went 19–9 in three seasons overall.

Jimmy Manning
Washington Senators (AL) 1901
Record: 61–73
Outfielder with only a .218 lifetime average.

Manning played for five seasons, then worked for a time in the minor leagues before resurfacing as the manager of the Washington Senators in 1901. He lasted only one season, posting a 61–73 record and finishing in sixth place.

Charlie Manuel
Cleveland Indians (AL) 2000–02; Philadelphia Phillies (NL) 2005–
Record: 393–342
Minor league outfielder who played sparsely in the major leagues.

Spreading 242 appearances over six major league seasons, Manuel went on to his greatest success in Japan, where he won a Most Valuable Player Award and set a record for most home runs hit by an American. He returned to the United States as a scout, coach, and minor league manager, and was named Indians' skipper in 2000. After a second-place finish, he took the Tribe to the American League Central Division title in 2001, although the club was eliminated in the first round of the playoffs by the Seattle Mariners.

Manuel was fired with a 39–48 record in 2002, and three years later was hired to manage the Phillies.

Jerry Manuel
Chicago White Sox (AL) 1998–2003
Record: 500–471

Played only 96 major league games and never hit over .200.

Manuel went into coaching when his playing days were over, and he later became a minor league skipper. He was named Southern League Manager of the Year in 1990 when his Jacksonville Expos captured the league title. He worked for some time in the Montreal Expos' system, and his daughter even married Expos' outfielder Rondell White.

Manuel was a coach with the Florida Marlins during their 1997 World Championship season, but the next year he was hired away to manage the White Sox. After two consecutive second-place finishes, he led Chicago to the American League Central Division title in 2000. His club was swept by the Seattle Mariners in the AL Division Series, but Manuel was named AL Manager of the Year by the BBWAA and Manager of the Year by the AP.

After a third-place and two more second-place finishes, Manuel was fired.

Rabbit Maranville
Chicago Cubs (NL) 1925
Record: 23–30
Fun-loving, Hall of Fame shortstop for 23 major league seasons.

Walter Maranville was nicknamed "Rabbit" because of his speed and his agility in the field. An adequate hitter, he truly made his mark as one of the greatest fielders of all time, setting many records at shortstop and consistently leading the National League in many defensive categories.

Maranville debuted in 1912, and he lost most of the 1918 season due to service in the Navy. He did play 11 games for the Boston Braves when he was on leave in July, however, and batted .316 during that time.

Because of problems with alcoholism Maranville bounced around between many teams, but in 1925 he was named player-manager of the Cubs to replace Bill Killefer during a rather unsuccessful season. He lasted only 53 games in that position before being replaced himself.

In spring training of 1934 Rabbit broke his leg during a steal attempt, and he would never be the same player afterwards. He missed the entire season and attempted to come back in 1935 for 23 games, then he became a minor league player-manager.

He died in 1954, and was inducted into the Hall of Fame that same year.

Marty Marion
St. Louis Cardinals (NL) 1951; St. Louis Browns (AL) 1952–53; Chicago White Sox (AL) 1954–56
Record: 356–372
Eight-time All-Star shortstop.

Always outstanding defensively, Marion also led the National League with 38 doubles in 1942. As a member of the Cardinals he played on four pennant winners and three World Championship teams.

He played through 1950, and the Cards made him their manager the following season. Despite a third-place finish he was let go, and he became player-manager of the Browns during the following season after serving as player-coach. He was fired in 1953 after a last-place showing, then was hired by the White Sox. With Chicago he finished third for three straight seasons before resigning.

Jim Marshall
Chicago Cubs (NL) 1974–76; Oakland Athletics (AL) 1979
Record: 229–326
Backup first baseman for five seasons.

Playing for five teams during those five years, Marshall was but a .242 lifetime hitter. After finishing the 1962 season with the Pittsburgh Pirates, he played in Japan for three years with the Chunichi Dragons, where he averaged 24 home runs a season. He then became a minor league manager, and later a coach with the Cubs.

He was named Chicago's manager midway through the 1974 campaign when skipper Whitey Lockman stepped down to become the team's director of player development. In three years at the helm of the Cubs and one as manager of the A's, Marshall would never attain a .500 season.

Billy Martin
Minnesota Twins (AL) 1969; Detroit Tigers (AL) 1971–73; Texas Rangers (AL) 1973–75; New York Yankees (AL) 1975–78, 1979, 1983, 1985, 1988; Oakland Athletics (AL) 1980–82
Record: 1253–1013
Aggressive second baseman and fiery-tempered but highly successful manager.

In 1948 Martin played for the Oakland Oaks under Casey Stengel, and when Stengel went to the New York Yankees, he had the club acquire Martin. Billy debuted with New York in 1950, and in 1952 he made a World Series-saving, diving catch of a pop fly hit by Jackie Robinson of the Brooklyn Dodgers. The following season he was named Most Valuable Player of the Series, batting .500 with 12 hits and 2 home runs. His single in the bottom of the ninth inning of Game 6 drove in the winning run for the Yankees as they once again topped the Dodgers. In 1956 he became an American League All-Star.

Martin was traded after a nightclub scuffle for which he shouldered the blame. He bounced around between many teams until 1961, then he went to work in the Twins' organization and became a coach for them in 1965. In 1969 he was named manager, and his club took the AL Western Division crown but was swept in the playoffs by the Baltimore Orioles. Billy's temper caused him at one point to attack one of his own pitchers, Dave Boswell, and he had a penchant for ignoring the orders of owner Calvin Griffith. These factors combined to lead to his firing in spite of his on-field success.

In 1971 he became the skipper of the Tigers, and the following year he took that club to the AL Eastern Division title. They were defeated by the A's in the League Championship Series, however. Martin was fired in late 1973 and was immediately hired to finish out the season with the last-place Rangers.

In 1974 he brought the Rangers in second, improving their record from 57–105 to 84–76, and the AP named Martin the AL Manager of the Year. He was fired during the 1975 season, again because of problems with upper management, and he then began his tumultuous and rather infamous relationship with George Steinbrenner and the Yankees.

Martin led the Yanks to the AL Eastern Division Championship in 1976. They defeated the Kansas City Royals in five games to go to the World Series, and although they were swept by the Cincinnati Reds, the AP once again named Martin the AL's Manager of the Year. In 1977 the Yankees won their division again, and they once again defeated the Royals in a five-game playoff. This time, however, they defeated the Dodgers four games to two to win the World Championship. In 1978 Martin had public arguments with Reggie Jackson and Steinbrenner, and he was forced to resign midway through the season.

In July of 1979 Billy was hired back to replace Bob Lemon, then he was fired in October when he got into a fight with a marshmallow salesman. In 1980 he was hired to manage the Athletics, and he improved their record from 54–108 to 83–79 and was once again named the league's Manager of the Year by the AP. During the split season of 1981, his team won the first-half Western Division title by a game and a half over the Rangers, and finished only a game behind the Royals in the second half. They swept Kansas City in a three-game division playoff, but were in turn swept by the Yankees in three games for the pennant. For the fourth time, Martin was named the AP's AL Manager of the Year.

Martin was fired in 1982, and was hired back by Steinbrenner to manage the Yankees for a third time in 1983. He was then fired for the third time. Early in 1985 he was hired for a fourth time to replace Yogi Berra, then was fired for the fourth time. He was hired for a fifth time in 1988, and after getting into another nightclub fight, was fired for the fifth time in midseason. On Christmas Day of 1989, he was killed in an automobile accident.

The Yankees retired his uniform number 1 in 1986, between his fourth and fifth terms as manager.

Buck Martinez
Toronto Blue Jays (AL) 2001–02
Record: 100–115
Excellent defensive catcher.

Martinez's work behind the plate kept him in the major leagues for 17 seasons. As a batter he hit over. 253 on only one occasion, and fashioned a lifetime average of only .225. Defensively, however, he was considered invaluable.

After his playing career Martinez became a broadcaster, and was hired to manage the Blue Jays for the 2001 season. He lasted only a season and a half before being fired.

Marty Martinez
Seattle Mariners (AL) 1986
Record: 0–1
Infielder who eventually played almost every position on the diamond.

Orlando "Marty" Martinez played seven seasons as a utilityman, and after his retirement he eventually became a coach with the Mariners. He was in that role in 1986 when manager Chuck Cottier was fired, and Marty skippered a single game—a game he lost—before the arrival of Cottier's replacement, Dick Williams.

Charlie Mason
Philadelphia Athletics (AA) 1887
Record: 38–40
Played only 21 major league games as an outfielder, catcher, and pitcher.

Mason's main claim to fame was as a part-owner of the American Association's Philadelphia Athletics, a team that won the league pennant in 1883. One of the organizers of the AA, he acted as his own scout in order to build that championship team, and in 1887 named himself manager for part of the season.

Mason is said to have come up with the rule awarding first base to a batter hit by a pitch, and also for creating "Ladies' Day" at the ballpark. He died in 1936 at the age of 83.

Eddie Mathews
Atlanta Braves (NL) 1972–74
Record: 149–161
The only man to have played for the Braves in Boston, Milwaukee, and Atlanta.

An 11-time All-Star, Mathews finished his Hall of Fame career with 512 lifetime home runs. He led the National League twice in homers and four times in bases on balls. He hit over 20 home runs on 14 occasions and drove in more than 100 runs five times.

Mathews played for the Houston Astros and Detroit Tigers at the end of his career, but in 1971 he returned to the Braves as a coach. Partway through the 1972 season he replaced Lum Harris as manager. He finished fourth, then fifth in 1973, and the Braves were 50–49 in 1974 when Eddie was replaced by Clyde King.

The Braves retired his uniform number 41 in 1969. Mathews died in 2001 in California.

Christy Mathewson
Cincinnati Reds (NL) 1916–18
Record: 164–176
Hall of Fame pitcher with 373 lifetime victories.

One of the most dominating hurlers in major league history, Mathewson never won fewer than 22 games in a season between 1903 and 1914. He led the National League in victories four times, in shutouts four times, in games pitched once, in games started twice, in complete games twice, in innings pitched once, in strikeouts five times, and in earned run average five times. He won at least 30 games 4 times and at least 20 games 13 times. He also won the pitching Triple Crown twice—in 1905 when he went 31–8 with a 1.27 ERA and 206 strikeouts, and again in 1908 when he had a 37–11 record, a 1.43 ERA, and 259 whiffs.

Christy spent his entire career with the New York Giants, except for his final season of 1916 when he was traded to the Reds, who were primarily interested in him as a manager. He pitched a single game for Cincinnati—a game he won—then became a full-time manager. As a skipper he would be unremarkable, lasting only one full season and finishing fourth. Mathewson left the team in 1918 when he was commissioned as a captain in the Army. He was later accidentally gassed in a training exercise and contracted tuberculosis. In 1919 he returned to the Giants as a coach, where he would remain for three years, then he worked in the Boston Braves' organization. He died in 1925 at the age of 45.

Christy was one of the first five men inducted into the Hall of Fame in 1936.

Bobby Mattick
Toronto Blue Jays (AL) 1980–81
Record: 104–164
Played sparsely during five major league seasons as a shortstop.

Mattick was a regular once, in 1940 with the Chicago

Cubs, but he hit only .218. After his playing career he gained notoriety as an excellent scout, and he performed in that role for many years.

He managed only two seasons with the Blue Jays, and finished in seventh and last place both years.

Gene Mauch
Philadelphia Phillies (NL) 1960–68; Montreal Expos (NL) 1969–75; Minnesota Twins (AL) 1976–80; California Angels (AL) 1981–82, 1985–87
Record: 1902–2037
One of the losingest managers in major league history.

Mauch had an excuse, however; he managed for many years, totaling 3942 games, as well as having managed an expansion team (the Expos) at a time when free agency did not yet exist.

A light-hitting infielder for nine major league seasons, Mauch became a minor league manager at the age of 28 but then returned to playing. After retiring as a player he went back to managing, and landed his first big league job in 1960 with the Phillies.

In 26 years as a skipper Gene never won a pennant, although he did manage two division titles with the Angels. In both instances—the first in 1982, the second in 1986—his club was eliminated in the American League Championship Series.

In three of his non-championship seasons the AP named Mauch its National League Manager of the Year. Those years were 1962, when his Phillies improved from a 47–107 record to 81–80; 1964, when the same Phils nearly won the pennant, finishing only a game behind the St. Louis Cardinals in a second-place tie with the Cincinnati Reds; and 1973, when his Expos finished 79–83 in their fifth year of existence.

Gene died of cancer in 2005.

Lee Mazzilli
Baltimore Orioles (AL) 2004–05
Record: 129–140
All-around athlete who once won many speed-skating championships.

In baseball Mazzilli was an outfielder and first baseman who spent many years with the New York Mets. He was named a National League All-Star once, in 1979 when he hit .303 with 15 home runs and 79 runs batted in. His appearance in the Midsummer Classic was unforgettable, as he slugged a pinch-hit home run in the eighth inning to tie the game and then walked with the bases loaded in the ninth to win it.

As a manager Mazzilli posted a third-place finish in 2004, but he was fired with a 51–56 record in August of 2005 amidst rumors that he did not get along well with Orioles' owner Peter Angelos.

Jimmy McAleer
Cleveland Bluebirds (AL) 1901; St. Louis Browns (AL) 1902–09; Washington Nationals (AL) 1910–11
Record: 735–889
Outfielder during the latter part of the nineteenth century.

An adequate hitter, McAleer stole many bases, peaking with 51 in 1891. As a manager he used himself in seven games—three in 1901 with the Bluebirds, two in 1902 with the Browns, and two in 1907 with the Browns.

While he was at the helm his 1902 St. Louis club finished in second place, but he would never again manage better than a fourth-place showing.

In 1910 while with the Washington Nationals he reportedly convinced President William Howard Taft to become the first president to throw out a first pitch when Taft and his wife showed up unexpectedly on Opening Day.

McAleer later became president of the Boston Red Sox.

Dick McBride
Philadelphia Athletics (NA) 1871–75
Record: 161–85
Pitcher and manager from 1871–75.

The Athletics were a powerful team and became major league baseball's first champions in 1871 when they finished two games ahead of the Boston Red Stockings and Chicago White Stockings. Harry Wright's Boston club would begin to dominate the NA the following year, but McBride's A's put on a good show, failing to post a winning record only once.

As a pitcher Dick put up victory totals of 18, 30, 24, 33, and 44 during the NA's five-year run. In 1874 he led the league with a 1.64 earned run average.

In 1876 he joined Wright's Boston team, then called the Red Caps, but pitched only four games and lost them all.

George McBride
Washington Nationals (AL) 1921
Record: 80–73
Excellent defensive shortstop for 16 seasons.

A light hitter who nevertheless had a talent for coming through in the clutch, McBride built his career mainly with his glove, with which he led the American League in numerous defensive categories.

He played through 1920, mainly with the Washington Nationals, and was named the club's manager in 1921. One day during batting practice he was struck in the face by a batted ball, and afterwards suffered from vertigo and fainting spells. The stress caused by that event caused him to resign at the end of the season. McBride later became a coach with the Detroit Tigers.

Jack McCallister
Cleveland Indians (AL) 1927
Record: 66–87
Ohio native who never played a major league game.

McCallister became a coach with the Indians in 1920, and after seven seasons at that post he was named the team's manager. He lasted only a single season, however, finishing sixth, and later became a coach with the Boston Red Sox.

Joe McCarthy
Chicago Cubs (NL) 1926–30; New York Yankees (AL) 1931–46; Boston Red Sox (AL) 1948–50
Record: 2125–1333
One of only two managers to win seven World Championships.

The other was Casey Stengel, but McCarthy did it first. A minor league player who never reached the major leagues, Joe was the second batter to face Babe Ruth in the Bambino's first professional game, a game he pitched. McCarthy began playing in 1906 and managing in 1913, and he did reach the major league level in that role in 1926.

Joe won the 1929 pennant with the Cubs, the first of nine he would claim in a 24-year managerial career. Nevertheless fired in 1930, he became the first manager to win pennants in both the National and American Leagues when his Yankees took the AL flag in 1932. After ironically defeating the Cubs in the World Series, the Bronx Bombers would finish second three consecutive times before going on to win four straight World Championships between 1936 and 1939. They won again in 1941, and after being defeated by the St. Louis Cardinals in the 1942 Fall Classic, they came back to take the championship from those same Redbirds in 1943. That was McCarthy's ninth pennant and his seventh World Championship.

McCarthy was fired in 1946, but two years later he took over the Red Sox. After two second-place finishes, he was fourth in 1950 when he resigned. He remains the manager with the highest winning percentage in major league history at .614. In 1957 he was inducted into the Hall of Fame. He and Earl Weaver are the only two Hall of Fame managers who never played a major league game.

Tommy McCarthy
St. Louis Browns (AA) 1890, 1890

Record: 15–12
The only Hall of Famer to have played in the Union Association.

McCarthy was a speedy outfielder who had a very successful 13-year major league career, a career that began in 1884 with the Boston Unions of the UA. When that league collapsed he signed with the Boston Bostons of the National League, and he would eventually play for several teams in both the NL and the American Association. He hit over .300 four times, and was a .292 lifetime hitter. He stole 468 recorded bases in his career (records were not kept from 1884–85), peaking with 93 in 1888. In 1890 with the St. Louis Browns he led the AA with 83.

That 1890 season saw six Browns' managers, of which McCarthy, as a player-manager, was the first, for 5 games, and the fifth, for another 22. Despite the revolving door the team finished in third place. He later worked as a major league scout, a minor league manager, and a college coach.

McCarthy's main claim to fame was his innovative style of play, which included trapping balls in the outfield and making the hit-and-run an effective offensive weapon. He was inducted into the Hall of Fame in 1946.

Lloyd McClendon
Pittsburgh Pirates (NL) 2001–05
Record: 336–446
Reserve catcher, outfielder, and first baseman who played for the Cincinnati Reds and Chicago Cubs before finishing his career with the Pirates.

Those Pirates elevated McClendon to the level of big league coach in 1996, after he had worked for a year in their minor league system. Having decided toward the end of his playing career that his true calling was to manage, he got his wish in 2001 when he was named the Bucs' skipper. He was fired in September of 2005 with his team in last place. The following year he became a coach with the Detroit Tigers.

John McCloskey
Louisville Colonels (NL) 1895–96; St. Louis Cardinals (NL) 1906–08
Record: 190–417
Louisville native who founded five minor leagues, the first of which was the Texas League in 1888.

A semipro catcher, McCloskey never played in the major leagues. He did manage 30 different teams in 36 seasons.

At the major league level he skippered some miserable squads, never finishing better than seventh. He also spent some time as a minor league umpire, but he literally struck gold away from baseball. In 1906 a Colorado mine in which he had invested money paid off big with a major gold strike.

Jim McCormick

Cleveland Blues (NL) 1879–80, 1882
Record: 74–96
Native of Scotland and an outstanding pitcher.

McCormick's pitching career ran from 1878 to 1887, and the right-hander won 265 games lifetime. He led the National League with 45 wins in 1880 and with 36 in 1882, while also topping the circuit twice in games pitched, games started, innings pitched, and earned run average. He led three times in complete games, and was at least a 20-game winner eight times. In 1884 he won 19 games in the NL and *another* 21 in the Union Association.

McCormick spent two years as player-manager with the Blues, but decided to quit the helm in order to better focus on his pitching. He returned to the role of pilot for four games in 1882, but then switched permanently to playing.

Mel McGaha

Cleveland Indians (AL) 1962; Kansas City Athletics (AL) 1964–65
Record: 123–173
Never played major league baseball, but was a guard for the New York Knickerbockers of the Basketball Association of America (today's National Basketball Association) from 1948–49.

McGaha did play minor league baseball and eventually became a manager. As a minor league skipper he won pennants with three different clubs before becoming a coach with the Indians in 1961. He managed the Tribe to a sixth-place finish in 1962 and was fired, then became a coach with the Athletics. In mid-1964 he was named skipper of the A's, but that club finished tenth and started the next year 5–21 when McGaha was fired again. He went back to managing in the minors and eventually became a coach with the Houston Astros.

Mel passed away in 2002.

Mike McGeary

Philadelphia Phillies (NA) 1875; Providence Grays (NL) 1880; Cleveland Blues (NL) 1881
Record: 46–41
Catcher-turned-infielder who played for 11 seasons in the National Association and National League.

McGeary hit over .300 three times, and he led the NA with 20 stolen bases in 1871. While a backstop he also played some shortstop before eventually becoming primarily a second baseman, then a third baseman.

In 1880, while player-manager of the Providence Grays, he was given a 30-day "vacation" by team ownership when the club started out 8–7 and he himself was not playing well. He hit .136 before going to the Cleveland Blues and then becoming their player-manager the following season.

John McGraw

Baltimore Orioles (NL) 1899; Baltimore Orioles (AL) 1901–02; New York Giants (NL) 1902–24, 1924–25, 1925–32
Record: 2763–1948
Highly competitive infielder and fiery manager.

McGraw began his playing career with the Baltimore Orioles of the American Association in 1891, a club that joined the National League the following year when the AA collapsed. A lifetime .334 hitter, he peaked at .391 in 1899 as player-manager of the same team. During a 16-year playing career he hit over .300 nine consecutive times and led the league twice in runs scored and twice in bases on balls. He stole 436 bases lifetime.

Having won a couple of pennants as a player, McGraw eventually took 10 more as a manager. None of those came in Baltimore, however. When his Orioles were absorbed by the Brooklyn Superbas in 1900 McGraw was sold to the St. Louis Cardinals, then signed with a new Baltimore Orioles club in the new American League in 1901. He was player-manager there for two seasons but clashed with league president Ban Johnson, causing him to jump ship for the NL's New York Giants during the 1902 season.

All 10 of McGraw's pennants came with the Giants. The first was in 1904, and John refused to allow his club to face the AL champion Boston Americans in what would have been the second modern World Series. Both he and Giants' owner John T. Brush refused to acknowledge the AL as a major league, and both had ill feelings toward AL President Ban Johnson. They gave in a year later when McGraw's Giants repeated as NL champions and then bested the Philadelphia Athletics in five games.

From 1911–13 the Giants won three more league titles, but lost each World Series. In 1917 they finished 10 games ahead of the Philadelphia Phillies, but dropped the Series to the Chicago White Sox.

From 1921–24 they captured four straight NL flags, and this time McGraw's club won the first two World Series while losing the last two. Due to illnesses during the 1924 and 1925 seasons, Hughie Jennings took over for John for a number of games.

McGraw would not win another pennant, but he did continue to manage into 1932. Along the way he managed more future Hall of Fame players than anyone in baseball history. In 1933 he came out of retirement to manage the NL squad in the first All-Star Game.

McGraw died in 1934, and was inducted into the Hall of Fame posthumously in 1937. Among major league managers, only Connie Mack won more games than John McGraw.

Deacon McGuire

Washington Statesmen (NL) 1898; Boston Red Sox (AL) 1907–08; Cleveland Naps (AL) 1909–11
Record: 210–287
Played for an incredible 26 seasons.

The amazement caused by that number is lessened somewhat by the fact that McGuire played only 11 games in his last four seasons *combined*. Still, the fact that he was a catcher—and that he caught 1611 games—makes a true impression.

A solid hitter, McGuire played most of his career in the nineteenth century. As a manager he did not have much luck, never finishing better than fifth and never achieving a .500 record. His Cleveland club honored him the year after he left, however, renaming itself the Cleveland Molly McGuires in 1912.

Bill McGunnigle

Brooklyn Atlantics (AA) 1888; Brooklyn Bridegrooms (AA) 1889, (NL) 1890; Pittsburgh Pirates (NL) 1891; Louisville Colonels (NL) 1896
Record: 327–248
Firm but kind manager who played only 56 major league games.

An outfielder who also pitched, McGunnigle became a minor league manager and won a couple of pennants before being hired to skipper the Atlantics of the American Association in 1888. His club finished second, and upon changing their name to Bridegrooms they won the 1889 pennant. In 1890 they jumped to the National League and immediately won a pennant there as well.

They lost an early version of the World Series to the New York Giants in '89, and in a repeat appearance in '90 played to a three-games-to-three tie against the Louisville Colonels. That 1890 event also featured a tie game, and an eighth was not scheduled because of cold weather.

McGunnigle suffered a hip injury in 1897 when he was thrown out of a carriage, and it would plague him until he died in 1899.

Stuffy McInnis

Philadelphia Phillies (NL) 1927
Record: 51–103
Star first baseman who was part of the Philadelphia Athletics' "$100,000 infield."

Having debuted as a shortstop, John "Stuffy" McInnis excelled at his new position, leading the American League consistently in a variety of fielding categories. He was also an excellent hitter, batting over .300 twelve times and finishing his career with a .307 lifetime average.

As a manager he had no luck at all, taking the helm of the Phillies for a single, very disappointing season and producing but a .331 winning percentage. He quit after that and became a coach at Harvard University.

Bill McKechnie

Newark Peppers (FL) 1915; Pittsburgh Pirates (NL) 1922–26; St. Louis Cardinals (NL) 1928, 1929; Boston Braves (NL) 1930–35; Boston Bees (NL) 1936–37; Cincinnati Reds (NL) 1938–46
Record: 1896–1723
The only manager to win National League pennants with three different teams.

A so-so player for 11 seasons, McKechnie was an infielder who was most prized for his knowledge of the game. He had his first taste of managing in 1915 as player-manager of the Federal League's Newark Peppers, but he would not lead a club again until after his retirement as a player.

Tagged to manage the Pirates in 1922, his first pennant came in Pittsburgh in 1925. His Bucs finished 8½ games ahead of the New York Giants, then defeated the Washington Nationals in a seven-game World Series. He was fired the next year when the Pirates hired former manager Fred Clarke as a "management consultant" and clashes between Clarke and McKechnie resulted in the dugout.

Bill took over the Cardinals in 1928 and won the pennant, but after the Redbirds were swept by the New York Yankees in the World Series, McKechnie was demoted to the AAA Rochester Red Wings and replaced by former Rochester manager Billy Southworth. More than two-thirds of the way through the 1929 campaign, however, owner Sam Breadon realized he had erred, and he brought McKechnie back and sent Southworth back to Rochester.

McKechnie deserted St. Louis after the season to sign a long-term contract with the Boston Braves, who later became the Bees. His Boston clubs would never finish better than fourth, and in 1938 he signed to manage the Reds. He won his third pennant in 1939 with Cincinnati, but lost another Series to the Yankees. The Reds repeated in 1940, however, and this time bested the Detroit Tigers to take the World Championship.

Nicknamed "Deacon Bill" because he sang in his church choir and generally espoused clean living, McKechnie had a lifetime .524 winning percentage, and he was inducted into the Hall of Fame in 1962.

Jack McKeon

Kansas City Royals (AL) 1973–75; Oakland Athletics (AL) 1977, 1978; San Diego Padres (NL) 1988–90; Cincinnati Reds (NL) 1997–2000; Florida Marlins (NL) 2003–05
Record: 1011–940

Never played in the major leagues, but managed in the minors for 15 years.

McKeon reached the big league level as a skipper in 1973, and his Royals finished in second place. Oddly, in his career McKeon would never manage a first-place finish but would win a World Championship.

His Royals were once again second in 1975 when Jack was fired in July and replaced by Whitey Herzog. Two years later he took over the A's, but with the team in seventh place in June he was fired and replaced by Bobby Winkles. The following May Winkles abruptly quit with his team in first place and McKeon was brought back. Jack was fired again when the team sank to sixth place.

In 1980 he was hired to be the general manager of the Padres, and he would spend the next decade with the organization. He acquired the nickname "Trader Jack" because of his penchant for wheeling and dealing, at one point even trading his own son-in-law, Greg Booker, to the Minnesota Twins. McKeon became the club's vice president of baseball operations, and he also returned to the dugout in 1988, but quit that job in mid-1990. At the end of that season he lost his other position as well.

He would later manage the Reds, where his team very nearly won the 1999 National League wild card, losing a one-game playoff to the New York Mets. McKeon was nevertheless named Manager of the Year by the AP and NL Manager of the Year by the BBWAA.

In 2003 Jack's Florida Marlins finished in second place in the NL Eastern Division but won the wild card berth. They then proceeded to fight their way to the NL pennant and to the World Championship in a six-game series over the New York Yankees. The BBWAA once again named McKeon its NL Manager of the Year.

Alex McKinnon

St. Louis Maroons (NL) 1885
Record: 6–32

Hit .299 in four major league seasons.

A good-hitting first baseman, McKinnon briefly took over for teammate Fred Dunlap as player-manager of the Maroons during the 1885 season. After posting only a 6–32 record, however, he surrendered control back to Dunlap.

While playing for the Pittsburgh Alleghenys in July of 1887, McKinnon was forced to leave the team when he began to exhibit symptoms of typhoid fever. He died just

over two weeks later, exactly three weeks before his thirty-first birthday.

Denny McKnight

Pittsburgh Alleghenys (AA) 1884
Record: 4–8

One of the founders of the American Association.

McKnight, who never played major league baseball, was one of the men who called a meeting in Pittsburgh to plan the formation of a league that would rival the National League. In 1882 the AA was formed, and McKnight owned the Pittsburgh Alleghenys of that circuit. He was also named the league's first president, and it was he who reprimanded the Cincinnati Red Stockings for participating in the first, informal World Series, a contest that pitted the AA champion Red Stockings against the NL champion Chicago White Stockings. After each team won one game, the Series was called off because McKnight threatened the Cincinnati club with expulsion from the league.

In 1884 McKnight named himself manager of his Alleghenys, but after starting 4–8 he turned the reins over to Bob Ferguson and later to two other managers.

Dissatisfied with his handling of several issues, including his attempt to eject the New York Metropolitans from the league, the other owners replaced him as president with Wheeler Wyckoff in 1885.

George McManus

St. Louis Brown Stockings (NL) 1876–77
Record: 28–32

Irish-born manager who never played in the major leagues.

McManus took over the Brown Stockings during the National League's inaugural 1876 season. The club finished second, but dropped to fourth the following year. Late in the 1877 campaign, umpire Dan Devinney accused McManus of attempting to bribe him with $250 to allow St. Louis to win a game against the Louisville Grays. The Grays won the contest and McManus denied the charges, which were never proven.

Marty McManus

Boston Red Sox (AL) 1932–33
Record: 95–153

Played 15 major league seasons and hit .289.

A solid infielder, McManus hit over .300 four times (five if one includes the single game he played in 1920, when he went 1-for-3), peaking with a .333 average in 1924 with the St. Louis Browns. In 1925 he led the American League with 44 doubles, and in 1930 topped the circuit with 23 stolen bases while playing for the Detroit Tigers.

From 1932–33 he was player-manager of the Red Sox, but finished eighth and seventh, respectively. After retiring in 1934 he became a minor league manager.

Roy McMillan
Milwaukee Brewers (AL) 1972; New York Mets (NL) 1975
Record: 27–28
With Johnny Temple, part of a top double play duo with the Cincinnati Reds of the 1950s.

With McMillan at shortstop and Temple at second, the Reds had one of the best up-the-middle defenses in the game. Not a strong hitter, Roy won the first three Gold Gloves ever awarded at shortstop and was named to two All-Star teams.

After his playing career he became a coach with the Brewers, and in 1972 managed two games on an interim basis between the reigns of Dave Bristol and Del Crandall. He was a coach with the Mets three years later when Yogi Berra was fired, and McMillan was named interim skipper for the rest of the season.

John McNamara
Oakland Athletics (AL) 1969–70; San Diego Padres (NL) 1974–77; Cincinnati Reds (NL) 1979–82; California Angels (AL) 1983–84, 1996; Boston Red Sox (AL) 1985–88; Cleveland Indians (AL) 1990–91
Record: 1168–1247
Minor league catcher who spent many years as a major league coach and manager.

McNamara's first managerial job at the big league level came with the Athletics, a team he had joined as a coach in 1968. When Hank Bauer was fired the following season, McNamara was dubbed his successor, although he would last only the rest of that season and one more.

He would eventually manage six major league teams in his career, and in 19 seasons at the helm produced two first-place finishes. The first was in 1979 with the Reds, with whom he had replaced Sparky Anderson. That team won the National League Western Division crown, but was swept in the playoffs in three straight by the Pittsburgh Pirates. The other came in 1986 with the Red Sox, a club that went on to capture the American League pennant in a tough seven-game Championship Series over the Angels before losing an even tougher seven-game World Series to the New York Mets. The BBWAA named McNamara its AL Manager of the Year for that season.

Bid McPhee
Cincinnati Reds (NL) 1901–02
Record: 79–124
The last second baseman to play bare-handed.

McPhee spent his entire 18-year playing career with Cincinnati, while they were called the Red Stockings in the American Association and the Reds in the National League. He eschewed wearing a glove in spite of the fact that mitts were being used with regularity by 1886, but he continued to shine as the premier defensive second baseman of his day. He finally gave in and donned a glove in 1897, the third-last season of his career.

McPhee hit over .300 four times, and he led the AA with 8 home runs in 1886 and ended in a six-way tie for the league lead with 19 triples in 1887. He played until 1899, and in 1901 became the Reds' manager. He lasted only a season and a half, finishing eighth his first year and then languishing in seventh in 1902 when he decided to resign.

Bid was inducted into the Hall of Fame by the Veterans Committee in 2000.

Hal McRae
Kansas City Royals (AL) 1991–94; Tampa Bay Devil Rays (AL) 2001–02
Record: 399–473
Backup outfielder with the Cincinnati Reds who became a superb designated hitter with the Kansas City Royals.

The trade to Kansas City was the best thing that could have happened to McRae, for with the Royals he established himself as a dependable hitter and was eventually named to three All-Star teams. He hit over .300 seven times. In 1977 he led the American League with 54 doubles, and in 1982 he tied with 46 two-baggers and led with 133 runs batted in.

McRae became a Royals' coach following his playing career, and was eventually named the team's manager. Two third-place finishes would be his best showings. He later skippered the Devil Rays when their inaugural manager, Larry Rothschild, was fired.

Cal McVey
Baltimore Lord Baltimores (NA) 1873; Cincinnati Reds (NL) 1878, 1879
Record: 91–64
Member of baseball's first professional team, the 1869 Cincinnati Red Stockings.

Only 18 years of age when he joined Harry Wright in Cincinnati, McVey could play any position...and did so, although he was the regular right fielder on that squad. In 1871 he went with Wright to Boston when the National Association was formed, and he led that first major league with 66 hits in its inaugural season. He managed the Lord Baltimores for part of the 1873 campaign, but returned to Boston the following year and led the NA with 123 hits, 91 runs scored, and 71 runs batted in. In 1875 he led with 36 doubles and 87 RBIs. When the NA folded following that season, McVey was the all-time leader in RBIs with 276.

After that he played two seasons with the Chicago White Stockings when the National League was formed, then returned to Cincinnati and became player-manager of the Reds. His 1878 club finished second, then Deacon White took over for 1879. White returned control to McVey partway through the season with the club in fifth place, but the Reds would finish in that slot. McVey then went to California, where he ended his career in the minor Pacific Coast League.

Sam Mele
Minnesota Twins (AL) 1961, 1961–67
Record: 524–436
Outfielder who played for seven teams in eight years.

An average hitter, Mele tied for the American League lead with 36 doubles in 1951. He retired in 1956, and in 1959 became a coach with the Washington Senators, one of the teams for whom he had played (as the Nationals). In 1961 the team moved to Minnesota and became the Twins. In June, after a 19–30 start, manager Cookie Lavagetto was granted a one-week "vacation" by ownership, and Mele briefly took over and went 2–5. Lavagetto returned, went 4–6, then was fired and replaced by Mele permanently.

The following year Sam led the Twins to a second-place showing, and by 1965 had them atop the AL. They dropped a seven-game World Series to the Los Angeles Dodgers, but the AP named Mele its AL Manager of the Year.

After a second-place finish in 1966, the Twins were foundering in sixth in 1967 after the first 50 games of the season when Mele was fired.

Oscar Melillo
St. Louis Browns (AL) 1938
Record: 2–7
Second baseman for 12 major league seasons.

Spending most of those years with the Browns, Melillo fought a dangerous inflammation of the kidneys known as Bright's disease (today more commonly called nephritis) for much of his career. He was advised by a doctor to eat only spinach, and he did exactly that, earning himself the nickname "Spinach," although it is more than a little doubtful that the vegetable actually cured him.

His best year was 1931 when he hit .306. Although that was the only time he topped the .300 mark, he was generally dependable at the plate and even more reliable in the field.

He became a coach following his playing career, and was called upon to manage the Browns at the end of the 1938 season when Gabby Street was fired.

Bob Melvin
Seattle Mariners (AL) 2003–04; Arizona Diamondbacks (NL) 2005–
Record: 309–339
Catcher who played for seven teams in 10 years.

Excellent defensively with an arm aptly suited to nailing would-be basestealers, Melvin fashioned a career out of his work behind the plate, because he averaged only .233 lifetime in the batter's box.

He managed the Mariners for two seasons, fashioning one second-place finish. In 2005 he became the Diamondbacks' manager when their previous choice, Wally Backman, turned out to have a criminal record and was fired before ever managing a game.

Stump Merrill
New York Yankees (AL) 1990–91
Record: 120–155
Longtime minor league manager in the Yankees' system.

Beginning his managerial career in 1978 with the West Haven Yankees of the Eastern League, Carl "Stump" Merrill eventually won more than 1500 games at the professional level, including 120 in a season and a half with the major league club. Fired from that position in 1991, he continued to work as a skipper in the Yankee organization, having garnered eight first-place finishes at the minor league level.

Charlie Metro
Chicago Cubs (NL) 1962; Kansas City Royals (AL) 1970
Record: 62–102
Never managed a full season.

A backup outfielder for parts of three seasons, Metro also never hit over .210. He became a coach with the Cubs in 1962, and took over in June at the end of the "college of coaches" experiment. The Cubs finished ninth. Metro later coached the Chicago White Sox, then was hired to manage the Royals in 1970 but lasted only 52 games before being fired. He eventually coached the Oakland Athletics.

Billy Meyer
Pittsburgh Pirates (NL) 1948–52
Record: 317–452
Catcher who played 113 games in parts of three seasons.

Meyer became a very successful minor league manager after a long minor league playing career. He won pennants in four different leagues, and was named the

Manager of the Year in 1939 with the Kansas City Blues of the American Association.

In 1946 he was offered the managerial job with the New York Yankees, but he had suffered a heart attack a short time before that and did not believe he could handle the pressure. Two years later he became the skipper of the Pirates, a team that had finished in last place in 1947 with a 62–92 record. Meyer improved their record to 83–71 the following season and brought them in fourth, and *The Sporting News* duly named him its Manager of the Year.

That would be his best year at the Pittsburgh helm, for he would not again finish better than sixth. After stepping down as manager he continued to work in the organization, however, eventually becoming a scout and what ownership termed a managerial consultant.

The Pirates retired his uniform number 1 in 1954. Meyer died in 1957.

Gene Michael
New York Yankees (AL) 1981, 1982; Chicago Cubs (NL) 1986–87
Record: 206–200
Light-hitting shortstop who spent most of his career with the Yankees.

When his playing days were over Michael spent many years working in the Yankee organization. As a major league skipper in New York he was one of George Steinbrenner's many casualties...twice. After serving as general manager, he was appointed manager in 1981. In a season split by a players' strike, he led the Yanks to a first-place finish in the first half, but when the club sank to fifth in the second half he was fired and replaced by Bob Lemon. In April of 1982 Lemon was fired, and Michael was brought back to, in effect, replace his replacement. He was fired again in August after losing a doubleheader to the Chicago White Sox.

He returned as a Yankees' coach in 1984, then spent two partial seasons managing the Cubs.

Clyde Milan
Washington Nationals (AL) 1922
Record: 69–85
Speedy outfielder nicknamed "Deerfoot."

Clyde Milan played from 1907–22, and his entire career was spent with the Washington Nationals. Fleet of foot, he led the American League in stolen bases in 1912 with 88 and again in 1913 with 75. He swiped 495 in his career. A solid hitter as well, he topped the .300 mark four times, three of them consecutively.

In 1922 he was named player-manager of the Nats, but was criticized as being too laid back and finished in sixth place. He later returned to the Nationals as a coach, man-

aged in the minors for a while, and then became a Washington coach again. In spring training of 1953 he was hitting fungoes to the Nationals' fielders when he suffered a fatal heart attack.

Dave Miley
Cincinnati Reds (NL) 2003–05
Record: 125–164
Minor league catcher who later garnered over 1000 victories as a minor league manager.

Skilled at working with young players, Miley spent more than 17 seasons as an instructor, coach, and manager in the Reds' organization. He won several Manager of the Year Awards at the minor league level, and spent 1993 as a major league coach under Tony Perez. About two-thirds of the way through the 2003 season he was named Reds' skipper to replace Bob Boone. Saddled with a poor pitching staff, he never finished better than fourth and was fired in mid-2005.

George Miller
St. Louis Browns (NL) 1894
Record: 56–76
Mainly a catcher who played 13 major league seasons.

George Miller was a lifetime .272 hitter, but he topped the .300 mark twice. He especially shone in 1894 when, as player-manager of the Browns, he hit a career-high .339 with an equally exceptional 86 runs batted in. As a manager he did not fare nearly so well, however, finishing in ninth place with a .424 winning percentage.

Miller would not manage again, but he did play for two more seasons.

Joe Miller
Washington Nationals (NA) 1872
Record: 0–11
German-born second baseman who did not fare well in the major leagues.

Playing 29 games in parts of two seasons in the National Association, Miller batted a mere .139. As a manager he skippered 11 games and his team lost them all, and those 11 games constituted his club's entire 1872 season.

Miller did not manage again, but he did some umpiring in 1872 and 1873 and tried playing again in 1875.

Ray Miller
Minnesota Twins (AL) 1985–86; Baltimore Orioles (AL) 1998–99
Record: 266–297
Minor league pitcher who became an outstanding major league pitching coach.

Miller began coaching Orioles' pitchers in 1978, and his hurlers consistently performed well and usually posted victories in double digits. He was hired to manage the Twins during the 1985 season, but his club did not do well and he was fired during the 1986 campaign. He then coached the Pittsburgh Pirates for several years, and eventually returned to his old job with the Orioles.

Baltimore made him manager in 1998, but after two fourth-place finishes he was fired there as well. In 2005 he coached for the O's once again.

Buster Mills
Cincinnati Redlegs (NL) 1953
Record: 4–4
Speedy outfielder who played mostly as a reserve.

Mills became a coach with several teams following his retirement. He was in that role with the Redlegs in 1953 when manager Rogers Hornsby was fired with eight games remaining in the season. Buster took over for those last eight games and won half of them. He was not rehired the following year, and became a coach with the Boston Red Sox.

Everett Mills
Baltimore Lord Baltimores (NA) 1872
Record: 8–6
Hit .284 in six major league seasons, five of them in the National Association.

A first baseman, Mills was one of two player-managers for the Lord Baltimores in 1872, a club that finished second in the NA. The following year he led the league with nine triples. He was with the Hartford Dark Blues in 1875, the final year of the NA, and he remained with that team in 1876 when the club joined the new National League.

Fred Mitchell
Chicago Cubs (NL) 1917–20; Boston Braves (NL) 1921–23
Record: 494–543
Pitcher who became a catcher.

After posting a 31–50 lifetime record with a 4.10 earned run average as a hurler, Fred Mitchell disappeared from the major league scene and resurfaced five years later as a catcher. He hit only .230, and disappeared again until three years later, when he appeared in his final four games.

In 1917 he became the manager of the Cubs, and he led Chicago to the 1918 National League pennant. His team lost the World Series in six games to the Boston Red Sox, and he would not finish higher than third thereafter, either with the Cubs or with the Boston Braves. He was also the Cubs' president in 1919 while still managing.

John Mizerock
Kansas City Royals (AL) 2002
Record: 5–8
Backup catcher who became a longtime minor league manager.

Mizerock won three minor league Manager of the Year Awards, as well as capturing two league championships. He spent his entire minor league managerial career in the Kansas City system. In 2002 he was named bullpen coach with the Royals, and he became interim manager when Tony Muser was fired. He skippered 13 games and posted a 5–8 record before Muser's permanent replacement, Tony Peña, was hired.

Jackie Moore
Oakland Athletics (AL) 1984–86
Record: 163–190
Catcher and outfielder who played only 53 major league games.

Excellent defensively, Moore never caught on in the big leagues as a player, but spent 11 seasons in the minor leagues and then many years as a major league coach with several teams. He was manager of the A's for one complete season and two partial ones, but did not finish better than fourth place. He had much better success as a minor league skipper, where he earned many playoff berths, several division championships, and one league championship.

Terry Moore
Philadelphia Phillies (NL) 1954
Record: 35–42
Four-time All-Star outfielder.

Moore played his entire career with the St. Louis Cardinals, a team with whom he won two World Championships. He hit .304 in 1940, but lost the 1943–45 seasons to the military during World War II. He batted a solid .280 lifetime, and following his retirement in 1948 he became a coach with the Cardinals.

He coached through 1952, and midway through the 1954 season was hired to manage the Phillies on an interim basis to replace Steve O'Neill. He finished fourth, and in 1956 he returned to the Cardinals as a coach.

Pat Moran
Philadelphia Phillies (NL) 1915–18; Cincinnati Reds (NL) 1919–23
Record: 748–586
Light-hitting catcher who played from 1901–14.

Moran hit three triples in one game in 1905 with the Boston Bostons, but he truly made his mark as a manager. He was hired to manage the Phillies in 1915, and he immediately led them to the National League pennant. They lost the World Series to the Boston Red Sox, and would finish second the next two years.

In 1919 he became the Reds' skipper, and that team also captured the NL flag his first year and then went on to defeat the Chicago White Sox in a World Series forever marred by the Black Sox Scandal. Even though several of the Chicago players had conspired to throw the Series, Moran always contended that the Reds would have defeated the White Sox anyway.

After second-place finishes in 1922 and 1923, Moran died of Bright's disease during spring training of 1924.

Joe Morgan
Boston Red Sox (AL) 1988–91
Record: 301–262
Minor league outfielder who spent parts of four seasons in the majors.

Not to be confused with the Hall of Fame second baseman of the same name, this Joe Morgan hit only .193 but excelled as a minor and major league manager. A coach for the Red Sox in 1988, he was named to replace John McNamara on an interim basis and wound up leading Boston to the division title. They were swept by the Oakland Athletics in the American League Championship Series, but two years later were back on top. They were once again swept by the A's, and after a second-place finish in 1991 Morgan was fired. His lifetime winning percentage was .535.

George Moriarty
Detroit Tigers (AL) 1927–28
Record: 150–157
Spent 50 years in baseball.

As a player Moriarty was an adequate third baseman—good with a glove, fair with a bat, and very good at stealing bases. He routinely swiped over 20 a season. After retiring in 1916 he became an American League umpire. In 1927 he accepted an offer to manage the Tigers when Ty Cobb announced his retirement, but after two seasons and finishes of fourth and sixth place he resigned and returned to umpiring.

After a doubleheader in Cleveland in 1932 in which the Indians swept the Chicago White Sox, a number of Chicago players accused Moriarty of deliberately making poor calls against their club. The umpire challenged some of the players to a fight, and as a result ended up in the hospital.

He umpired through 1940 and then worked for the AL in public relations. He later became a scout for the Tigers.

John Morrill
Boston Red Caps (NL) 1882; Boston Bostons (NL) 1883, 1884–86, 1887–88; Washington Statesmen (NL) 1889
Record: 348–334
First baseman who spent many years as a player-manager.

After managing the Red Caps in 1882, Morrill stepped aside for Jack Burdock when the team was renamed the Bostons the following season, but he returned with the club in fourth place and guided them to the National League pennant. That would be his only one, but he did manage a second-place finish the following year. As a player he hit over .300 on three occasions.

He switched to the Washington Statesmen in 1889 but did not finish out the season. The next year he played two games for the Boston Red Stockings of the Players League and also scouted for them.

Charlie Morton
Toledo Blue Stockings (AA) 1884; Detroit Wolverines (NL) 1885; Toledo Maumees (AA) 1890; Toledo Black Pirates (AA) 1890
Record: 121–153
Light hitter who played parts of three major league seasons.

Morton was the manager of the Toledo Blue Stockings in 1884 when Moses "Fleetwood" Walker, an African American, played for the club. He witnessed racial epithets thrown Walker's way and himself received letters threatening Walker if Morton allowed him to play.

Morton did play Walker, but his team finished in eighth place. In two additional seasons with other clubs he would do no better than fourth.

Felix Moses
Richmond Virginians (AA) 1884
Record: 12–30
Skippered his hometown Richmond Virginians of the American Association in 1884.

Moses' club finished in tenth place and then left the AA for the minor Virginia League. That ended the major league career of the Virginians, and the major league managerial career of Moses.

Les Moss
Chicago White Sox (AL) 1968, 1968; Detroit Tigers (AL) 1979
Record: 39–50
Catcher for several teams over 13 seasons.

Seldom a regular, Moss became a coach, scout, and minor league manager after retiring as a player. He was a coach for the White Sox in 1968 when Eddie Stanky was fired, and he managed two games before Al Lopez took over. Less than two weeks later Lopez underwent an emergency appendectomy and Moss filled in for another 36 games before the regular manager's return.

He managed the Tigers for the first part of the 1979 season before being replaced by Sparky Anderson, and later coached the Chicago Cubs and the Houston Astros.

Tim Murnane
Boston Unions (UA) 1884
Record: 58–51
Originally an amateur player who became a professional and later a sportswriter.

Murnane began his career before professional baseball was a reality, and he played four years in the National Association. In 1875 he led the league with 30 stolen bases, then he played three years in the National League. In 1884 he managed the Boston Unions of the Union Association during their only year of existence; they finished fifth.

Murnane was one of the first players to employ the bunt, which he accomplished by using a flat-sided bat. Such a bat was legal at the time, and according to George Will in his book *Bunts*, the very term "bunt" may have come from Murnane's calling it "butting."

Murnane became an umpire after the UA folded, was later president of the New England League and the Eastern League, and also worked as a sportswriter and a scout. For a time he was the sports editor of the *Boston Globe*.

Billy Murray
Philadelphia Phillies (NL) 1907–09
Record: 240–214
Massachusetts native who never played in the major leagues.

Murray managed the Phillies for three full seasons in the early part of the twentieth century. His teams dropped steadily from third to fourth to fifth, and that was the end of his managerial career in spite of a decent .529 winning percentage.

Danny Murtaugh
Pittsburgh Pirates (NL) 1957–64, 1967, 1970–71, 1973–76
Record: 1115–950
Nine-year second baseman who became a very successful manager.

Murtaugh started his playing career in 1941 with the Philadelphia Phillies, with whom he led the National League in stolen bases with 18. He hit only .254 in his career but was a solid fielder, and he played until 1951, finishing his playing days with the Pirates, although he lost two seasons to World War II.

In 1952 he began managing in the Pirates' minor

league system, and in 1956 he rejoined the parent club as a coach. Late in 1957 he was named manager to replace Bobby Bragan.

In 1960 the Bucs won the NL pennant and then established themselves in an exciting seven-game World Series win over the powerful New York Yankees. The AP named Murtaugh its NL Manager of the Year. The team gradually faded in the following seasons, and Murtaugh stepped down in 1964 due to poor health.

He returned in 1967 to replace Harry Walker on an interim basis and finished out the season. In 1970 he came back for a third go-round, and his Pirates won the NL Eastern Division by five games over the Chicago Cubs. They dropped the League Championship Series to the Cincinnati Reds, but the AP named Danny its NL Manager of the Year for the second time.

In 1971 the Pirates finished first once again, and this time they defeated the San Francisco Giants in a four-game NLCS before overcoming the Baltimore Orioles for the World Championship.

Murtaugh retired once more, but he returned to replace Bill Virdon toward the end of the 1973 campaign. In 1974 the Pirates won their division again, although they dropped the NLCS to the Los Angeles Dodgers. They repeated as division champs the next year, but this time lost the pennant to the Reds. Danny's club finished second in 1976, and Murtaugh passed away in December of that year. His lifetime winning percentage was .540.

The Pirates retired his uniform number 40 in 1977.

Tony Muser
Kansas City Royals (AL) 1997–2002
Record: 317–431
Good defensive first baseman with several teams.

An adequate hitter, Muser became a coach following his playing career and was hired to manage the Royals in 1997. He never managed a winning record, however, and never finished better than third. He was fired 23 games into the 2002 season with his club 8–15.

Jim Mutrie
New York Metropolitans (AA) 1883–84; New York Giants (NL) 1885–91
Record: 658–419
Manager credited with naming the New York Giants.

Mutrie managed two New York teams, and the first, called the Metropolitans, won the 1884 American Association pennant. In an early version of the World Series, they then lost three straight games to the National League's Providence Grays.

In 1885 Mutrie took charge of the NL's New York team, and because some of the players were rather tall he called them his "giants" and the name stuck. That team won consecutive pennants in 1888 and 1889. In '88 they played a 10-game postseason against the AA champion St. Louis Browns and won, 6 games to 4. In '89 they played a best-of-11 series against the Brooklyn Bridegrooms and won that one as well, 6 games to 3.

George Myatt
Philadelphia Phillies (NL) 1968, 1969
Record: 20–35
Decent-hitting infielder nicknamed "Mercury" because of his speed.

Myatt hit .283 lifetime although he played only two seasons as a regular. When his playing career was over he served as a coach with many teams, and was in that role with the Phillies in 1968 when skipper Gene Mauch was fired. He managed one game before the arrival of Mauch's replacement, Bob Skinner.

Skinner resigned the following season citing a lack of support from the front office in enforcing player discipline, and Myatt was again named interim manager, this time for the final 54 games of the season.

Henry Myers
Baltimore Orioles (AA) 1882
Record: 19–54
Shortstop with a less-than-successful major league career.

Myers played one game for the Providence Grays in 1881, then became player-manager of the American Association's Baltimore Orioles the following season. He played 69 games, hitting .180, and even pitched six times, fashioning a 6.58 earned run average. As a manager he won only 19 of 73 games for a winning percentage of .260.

In 1884 he returned with the Wilmington Quicksteps of the Union Association, with whom he played six games and hit .125.

Jerry Narron
Texas Rangers (AL) 2001–02; Cincinnati Reds (NL) 2005–
Record: 260–290
Light-hitting catcher for the New York Yankees, Seattle Mariners, and California Angels.

Narron hit well in the minor leagues but never in the majors. His highest average was .247 in 1984. After his playing career he became a coach with the Rangers, and was promoted to manager when Johnny Oates resigned a month into the 2001 season.

Narron was fired after two consecutive fourth-place finishes. He was later hired to coach the Reds, and was promoted again when manager Dave Miley was fired in mid-2005.

Billy Nash
Philadelphia Phillies (NL) 1896
Record: 62–68
Solid third baseman for 15 major league seasons.

Nash's finest season came in 1887, when he batted .374 with the Boston Bostons. That was the only time he topped the .300 mark, but he was a consistent, reliable hitter who averaged .282 lifetime. In 1896 he was player-manager of the Phillies, who finished eighth.

Nash played until 1898, and in 1901 he became a National League umpire.

Johnny Neun
New York Yankees (AL) 1946; Cincinnati Reds (NL) 1947–48
Record: 125–143
Good-hitting, speedy backup first baseman.

While playing for the Detroit Tigers on May 31, 1927, Neun pulled off a rare, unassisted triple play against the Cleveland Indians. With two Cleveland runners on base, he caught a line drive for the first out, stepped on first base for the second, and then ran to second and stepped on that base for the third before the runner there could get back. It was only the seventh unassisted triple killing in major league history; oddly, the sixth had occurred the previous day.

Neun eventually became a minor league coach and manager in the Yankees' system, and as a coach with New York was called upon to take over the big league club for the final 14 games of the 1946 season when Bill Dickey resigned. He then managed the Reds for 1947 and most of 1948.

Jeff Newman
Oakland Athletics (AL) 1986
Record: 2–8
Catcher and first baseman who played mostly as a reserve.

Newman's best season by far was 1979, when he hit 22 home runs with 71 runs batted in for the A's and was named to the American League All-Star team. After his playing career he became an Oakland coach, and managed 10 games on an interim basis in 1986 when Jackie Moore was fired. He won only two of those games, and was soon replaced by Tony LaRussa.

Kid Nichols
St. Louis Cardinals (NL) 1904–05
Record: 80–88
Hall of Fame pitcher who won 361 games lifetime.

Nichols won 27 games in his rookie season of 1890, and for his first 10 years in a row he would never win fewer than 21. He was a 20-game winner 11 times and a

30-game winner on 7 occasions. He led the National League in victories each year from 1896–98 (tying with Frank Killen in 1896) and fashioned a 2.95 lifetime earned run average.

After winning 19 games in 1901 Nichols bought a part-interest in the Kansas City Cowboys of the minor Western League and became their player-manager. In 1904 he returned to the majors as player-manager of the Cardinals; he won 21 games as a hurler, but the team finished fifth. The following season he started out again as player-manager, but after going 1–5 on the mound and 5–9 as a skipper he was dealt to the Philadelphia Phillies. He played only one more season, then retired and became a professional bowler in Kansas City, where he won a Class A Championship.

Hugh Nicol
St. Louis Browns (NL) 1897
Record: 8–32
Quick outfielder who played 10 years in the National League and American Association.

Nicol stole 383 bases in the five years they were recorded during his career. In 1887 he led the AA with 138, although the rules were a bit different then concerning steals. (A runner going from first to third on a single, for example, was credited with a stolen base.)

In 1897 he was the second of four managers to take the helm of the St. Louis Browns, a hapless team that went 29–102. Nicol's record was 8–32 for a mere .200 winning percentage.

After working as a minor league owner and manager, he became the first athletic director at Purdue University and then scouted for the Cincinnati Reds.

Russ Nixon
Cincinnati Reds (NL) 1982–83; Atlanta Braves (NL) 1988–90
Record: 231–347
Decent catcher for a dozen seasons who later became a coach and manager.

Nixon hit over .300 only once, but he played only a couple of seasons as a true regular. After his playing career he became a coach with several teams, and with both the Reds and the Braves was elevated to the position of manager.

Russ did not have much success at the helm. His teams were always sixth when he took over and sixth when he left, and they always finished sixth.

Bill Norman
Detroit Tigers (AL) 1958–59
Record: 58–64
Played 37 major league games as a catcher before becoming a coach and manager.

Norman was named Tigers' skipper in June of 1958, replacing Jack Tighe. The team was in fifth place when he took over, and it finished fifth. The following year the club started out 2–15, and Bill was promptly fired and replaced by Jimmy Dykes.

Rebel Oakes
Pittsburgh Pittsfeds (FL) 1914; Pittsburgh Rebels (FL) 1914–15
Record: 147–145
Solid, dependable outfielder from 1909–15.

Oakes debuted with the Cincinnati Reds, and had his best season in 1914 as player-manager of the Pittsburgh Pittsfeds, with whom he hit .312. He took over as skipper for Doc Gessler 11 games into the season, and the Pittsfeds were soon renamed the Rebels in his honor. They finished seventh, but came in a more respectable third the following year.

Johnny Oates
Baltimore Orioles (AL) 1991–94; Texas Rangers (AL) 1995–2001
Record: 797–746
Catcher for several major league teams.

Mainly a backup as a player, Oates became a minor league skipper in the Orioles' system upon his retirement. In 1989 he was named an O's coach under Frank Robinson, and he was elevated to manager when Robinson was fired in May of 1991. The team gradually climbed from sixth to second, and was in that position when the 1994 season ended abruptly due to a players' strike. In spite of his three winning records over those three seasons, Oates was fired by owner Peter Angelos.

He was immediately snatched up by the Rangers, and in 1996 he led that squad to the American League Western Division title. The team was eliminated in the Division Series, but the BBWAA named Oates and New York Yankees' skipper Joe Torre its AL co-Managers of the Year. The Rangers then won back-to-back titles in 1998 and 1999, but both times were eliminated by the Yankees in the ALDS.

Oates resigned during the 2001 season. He passed away on Christmas Eve of 2004, and the Rangers retired his uniform number 26 the following year.

Jack O'Connor
St. Louis Browns (AL) 1910
Record: 47–107
Catcher who played 21 major league seasons.

O'Connor was technically player-manager of the Browns in 1910, because he appeared in one game. He is most famous, however, for his role in the 1910 American League batting race, in which Ty Cobb and Nap Lajoie were practically neck-and-neck during the final few days of the campaign. With a Chalmers automobile at stake, each man was determined to win.

Cobb was not well-liked, and the last day of the season saw Lajoie's Indians playing a doubleheader against O'Connor's Browns. O'Connor instructed his third baseman to play at the edge of the outfield grass, thus allowing Lajoie to reach safely on six bunts down the line and collect a total of eight hits on the day. An error in scoring gave the title to Cobb anyway by less than a percentage point, although later research has proven that Lajoie actually won. Chalmers awarded cars to both players.

O'Connor was soundly criticized for his actions, however, and in October he was fired and would not manage again in the major leagues. He did manage the St. Louis Terriers of the Federal League in 1913, however, a year before that circuit declared itself a major league. He later became a boxing promoter.

Hank O'Day
Cincinnati Reds (NL) 1912; Chicago Cubs (NL) 1914
Record: 153–154
Most famous as a longtime National League umpire.

O'Day pitched for several seasons but he was a 20-game loser three times. His best year was his last, when he played for the New York Giants of the Players League in 1890 and went 22–13.

He then went into umpiring, and would spend 35 years on the job. He was an arbiter at a time when umps could sometimes not leave the field without police protection, and endured abuse from players and fans alike. He was respected by the league, however, and was one of the umpires in the first modern World Series in 1903.

He left umpiring to manage the Reds in 1912 and again to skipper the Cubs in 1914. Both teams finished fourth, and O'Day returned to umpiring for good.

Bob O'Farrell
St. Louis Cardinals (NL) 1927; Cincinnati Reds (NL) 1934
Record: 122–121
Catcher for 21 major league seasons.

Always a decent hitter, O'Farrell topped the .300 mark several times but had his most memorable season in 1926 with the Cardinals, when he hit .293 with 68 runs batted in and caught 146 games, in the process helping to lead the Redbirds to the World Championship. For his efforts O'Farrell won the League Award for the National League, his era's version of the Most Valuable Player Award. The following year he was named player-manager, and he guided the team to a second-place finish, missing the pennant by a mere game and a half.

He returned strictly to playing in 1928, and in May was traded to the New York Giants. Six years later he became player-manager of the Reds, but after a 30–60 start he was relieved of his duties. He finished out his playing career back in St. Louis in 1935.

Dan O'Leary
Cincinnati Outlaw Reds (UA) 1884
Record: 20–15
Played 45 major league games over five seasons, 32 of them in 1884 with the Outlaw Reds.

A so-so outfielder, O'Leary was player-manager of Cincinnati during the only year of that team's existence. The club was strong and had an 18–9 record by May 30, but that was in spite of O'Leary's lack of leadership qualities. He did not enforce discipline, frequently took his players out drinking, and made a habit of betting on his own team.

An eight-game series against the league-leading St. Louis Maroons in June saw the Outlaw Reds go 2–6, and O'Leary was replaced by Sam Crane before things could deteriorate further. In fifth place when Crane took over, Cincinnati would finish third.

Steve O'Neill
Cleveland Indians (AL) 1935–37; Detroit Tigers (AL) 1943–48; Boston Red Sox (AL) 1950–51; Philadelphia Phillies (NL) 1952–54
Record: 1040–821
One of four brothers to play major league baseball.

The others were Jack, Jim, and Mike, but it was Steve who had the most success. In 17 years as a backstop he hit over .300 three times, batting .321, then .322, then .311 each season from 1920–22.

As a manager he won one pennant in 14 seasons, but amazingly he never had a finish below .500. His teams frequently ended up in the first division, and it was his 1945 Tigers who went all the way. That club won the American League pennant by a game and a half over the Washington Nationals, then went on to defeat the Chicago Cubs in a seven-game World Series.

Jack Onslow
Chicago White Sox (AL) 1949–50
Record: 71–113
Fiery manager credited, in part, with obtaining Nellie Fox for the White Sox.

Having caught a mere 45 major league games and hit .169, Onslow coached for many teams before being hired to manage the White Sox in 1949. He did not get along with General Manager Frank Lane, however, and the two were often heard arguing at post-game conferences. The Sox finished sixth in 1949, and they were off to an 8–22 start the following year when Onslow was fired.

Jim O'Rourke
Buffalo Bisons (NL) 1881–84; Washington Statesmen (NL) 1893
Record: 246–258
Collected the first hit in National League history.

Mainly an outfielder, O'Rourke played 4 years in the National Association and then 19 in the NL. Along the way he hit over .300 fifteen times, averaging .313 lifetime. In 1884 he hit .347 and tied for the league lead with 162 hits. In an era when home runs were far from the norm, he topped his circuit three times in that category (with single-digit totals). He also led once in triples, once in walks, and once in runs scored.

As a player-manager he posted several third-place finishes, but his 1893 Statesmen ended up twelfth. That was his final season as a player, although he played one game for the New York Giants in 1904 at the age of 54, a still-standing NL record. He was inducted into the Hall of Fame in 1945.

Dave Orr
New York Metropolitans (AA) 1887
Record: 3–5
Outstanding first baseman who never hit under .300 and averaged .346 for his career.

Orr's lowest average, in fact, was .305. He played eight major league seasons, most of them in New York, and peaked in 1887 at .406. He had already won the American Association batting title in 1884 with a .354 average, and he led the league twice in hits and triples and once in runs batted in.

He was the second of three managers for the 1887 Metropolitans, who eventually finished in seventh place. Those eight games were the only ones he would skipper. He continued playing until 1890, when, with the Brooklyn Wonders of the Players League, he suffered a stroke that ended his career.

Mel Ott
New York Giants (NL) 1942–48
Record: 464–530
Played his entire 22-year career with the New York Giants, 6 of them as player-manager.

Ott made his mark on the game in a big way, hitting .304 lifetime and frequently leading the National League in several offensive categories, especially home runs. He slugged 511 roundtrippers in his career and was named to 12 All-Star teams.

He was named the Giants' player-manager in 1942. In a typical year for him he led the league with 30 home runs and thus became the first player-manager ever to lead in that category. He also topped the NL with 118 runs scored and 109 walks. As a manager he was somewhat ill-tempered, often criticizing his own team in the press. In 1946 he became the first manager to be thrown out of both games of a doubleheader.

A third-place finish in his first year at the helm would be his best. In 1948 he retired from the playing field and turned strictly to managing, but he was replaced at mid-season by Leo Durocher with his club in fourth place.

The Giants retired his uniform number 4 in 1949, and he was inducted into the Hall of Fame two years later. He eventually became a minor league manager, and later a broadcaster for the Detroit Tigers.

Paul Owens
Philadelphia Phillies (NL) 1972, 1983–84
Record: 161–158
Minor league player who became a Phillies' executive.

Owens was the Phils' general manager in 1972 when he decided to take over in the dugout as well. The team finished sixth, and he went back to the front office, where he built a contending club over the next decade. In 1983 he managed again, dismissing skipper Pat Corrales in July with the team in first place, and he led the club to the National League Eastern Division title. The Phillies defeated the Los Angeles Dodgers to win the NL pennant before dropping the World Series to the Baltimore Orioles. Owens managed one more year before returning to the front office.

He had supposedly once completed a trade on a handshake at baseball's winter meetings with the Detroit Tigers, while he was drunk. The next day he said he did not remember anything about the deal, which had supposedly included Bob Boone and Bill Freehan, and it was off.

Owens spent 48 years in the Phillies' organization, and he died on the day after Christmas in 2003. He was nicknamed "The Pope" because he bore a physical resemblance to Pope Paul VI.

Danny Ozark
Philadelphia Phillies (NL) 1973–79; San Francisco Giants (NL) 1984
Record: 618–542
Minor league first baseman in the Los Angeles Dodgers' system who then became a minor league skipper.

Ozark rose through the ranks to become a Dodgers' coach in 1965, and would eventually manage the Phillies. The Phils improved each year under his guidance, until they won three consecutive division titles from 1976–78.

They were eliminated each year in the playoffs, losing to the Cincinnati Reds in 1976 and to the Dodgers in both '77 and '78. Danny was nevertheless named National League Manager of the Year by the AP in '76.

The Phillies were fifth in August of 1979 when Ozark was fired. He would later coach and then manage the Giants.

Charlie Pabor
Cleveland Forest Citys (NA) 1871; Brooklyn Atlantics (NA) 1875; New Haven Elm Citys (NA) 1875
Record: 13–64
Outfielder and one of the first left-handed pitchers in major league history.

A decent player, Pabor started out in amateur circles, but his professional career spanned all five years of the National Association's existence. As a manager he did not fare well. His 1871 Cleveland club went 10–19 under him, his 1875 Atlantics an embarrassing 2–40, and the Elm Citys 1–5 under his leadership the same season.

After retiring Pabor became a police officer in the city of New Haven.

Salty Parker
New York Mets (NL) 1967; Houston Astros (NL) 1972
Record: 5–7
Played only 11 major league games, and managed 12.

Parker was a minor league player who appeared briefly for the Detroit Tigers in 1936. He later became a longtime coach, serving with many teams, and was widely respected for his knowledge of the game.

He was an interim manager twice—in 1967 with the Mets, when he skippered the final 11 games of the season as a replacement for Wes Westrum; and in 1972 with the Astros, when he managed and won a single game between the reigns of Harry Walker and Leo Durocher.

Parker died in 1992.

Bill Parks
Washington Nationals (NA) 1875
Record: 1–7
Player-manager for one partial season in Washington.

Parks hit .179 in 29 games, and his winning percentage as a manager was an even worse .125. The other Nationals' manager that season, Holly Hollingshead, fared only slightly better, going 4–16 for a team that finished 40½ games out of first place.

Parks then played one game in the National League in 1876 for the Boston Red Caps and went 0-for-4.

Larry Parrish
Detroit Tigers (AL) 1998–99

Record: 82–104
Power hitter and strong defensive third baseman.

Eventually moved to the outfield and then to the role of designated hitter, Parrish spent most of his career with the Montreal Expos and Texas Rangers and was named an All-Star twice. He hit 256 career home runs in 15 seasons, and hit 70 more in 2 seasons in Japan.

After retiring he became a minor league manager in the Tigers' organization, and he eventually became a coach and was then named interim manager in 1998 when Buddy Bell was fired. He managed a full season the following year, but was fired when his team went 69–92.

He became a scout for a time, and then returned to managing in the minor leagues with the Toledo Mud Hens.

Dickey Pearce
New York Mutuals (NA) 1872; St. Louis Brown Stockings (NA) 1875
Record: 49–35
One of the earliest baseballers to play professionally.

Pearce debuted as early as 1856, when only select players were compensated for their talents. He played professionally for 22 seasons, 7 of them in the National Association and National League. He was one of the earliest bunters, and pioneered much defensive strategy at shortstop.

He was player-manager for two seasons in the NA, and after retiring as a player he became an umpire.

Roger Peckinpaugh
New York Yankees (AL) 1914; Cleveland Indians (AL) 1928–33, 1941
Record: 500–491
Solid shortstop for 17 major league seasons.

Peckinpaugh broke in with the Cleveland Naps (later the Indians) in 1910, but would spend most of his early career with the Yankees. In 1914, at only 23 years of age, he got his first taste of managing when skipper Frank Chance retired due to poor health and he was called upon to fill in as player-manager for the final 20 games of the season.

He would not manage again until his playing career was over, and that was a career that included the 1925 League Award for the American League (his era's version of the Most Valuable Player Award) when he hit .294 with 64 runs batted in for the Washington Nationals. He returned to Cleveland as skipper from 1928–33 and again in 1941, and his best finish was third place.

Al Pedrique
Arizona Diamondbacks (NL) 2004

Record: 22–61

Shortstop who played parts of three major league seasons before becoming a minor league manager.

Pedrique's minor league teams reached the postseason three times, and in 2000 his Michigan Battle Cats captured the Midwest League championship. He later became a coach with the Diamondbacks under Bob Brenly, and was named interim manager for the final three months of the season when Brenly was fired. His team finished fifth and he was not brought back.

Pedrique was one of the first Venezuelans to manage in the major leagues.

Tony Peña
Kansas City Royals (AL) 2002–05
Record: 198–285
Excellent catcher and five-time All-Star.

A reliable hitter, Peña was primarily noted for his defense and for his unique, one-legged crouch behind the plate. He won four Gold Gloves while displaying a strong arm and a prized ability to call games and handle pitchers.

He became the Royals' manager in May of 2002 when John Mizerock was fired. In June, when the Royals faced the Detroit Tigers in Kansas City, he and Luis Pujols became the first Dominican-born managers to face each other in major league history. The following year Peña was named the American League Manager of the Year by the BBWAA when he helped improve Kansas City's record from 62–100 to 83–79 and a third-place finish. The Royals suffered through 104 losses in 2004, and after an 8–25 start in 2005 Peña resigned, saying he simply could not take any more. He continued to work in the organization, however.

Tony Perez
Cincinnati Reds (NL) 1993; Florida Marlins (NL) 2001
Record: 74–84
Native of Cuba and a member of Cincinnati's Big Red Machine in the 1970s.

One of the best in history at driving in runs in the clutch, Perez was a third baseman and first baseman for the Reds and played on seven All-Star teams. He hit 379 home runs in his career, peaking with 40 in 1970. He was valued as much for his clubhouse leadership as for his bat.

He became a Reds' coach in 1987, and in 1993 he was named the club's skipper. He was fired by general manager Jim Bowden after only 44 games, however, posting a 20–24 record. He then went to work in the Florida Marlins' organization, briefly managed for them on an interim basis in 2001, and then returned to the front office.

Perez was inducted into the Hall of Fame in 2000, and the Reds retired his uniform number 24 that same year.

Cy Perkins
Detroit Tigers (AL) 1937
Record: 6–9
Catcher for many years, mainly with the Philadelphia Athletics.

Good with a glove but not as strong at the plate, Perkins was replaced when Mickey Cochrane came along. He coached for several teams following his playing career, and was in that role for the Tigers when he was called upon to manage on an interim basis. His tenure lasted 15 games, of which the Tigers won 6.

Sam Perlozzo
Baltimore Orioles (AL) 2005–
Record: 93–124
Minor leaguer who played 12 games in the major leagues at second base.

Perlozzo then played the 1980 season with the Yakult Swallows in Japan before retiring and becoming a minor league manager. He had considerable success, winning the 1983 Carolina League championship and Manager of the Year Award with the Lynchburg Mets, and the 1984 and 1985 Texas League championships with the Jackson Mets.

In 1987 he began his major league coaching career, and he was in his tenth year in Baltimore in that role when he was named manager in August of 2005 to replace Lee Mazzilli.

Johnny Pesky
Boston Red Sox (AL) 1963–64, 1980
Record: 147–179
All-Star infielder with a .307 lifetime batting average.

Excellent both in the field and at the plate, Pesky debuted with the Red Sox in 1942 and immediately led the American League with 205 hits. He lost the next three years to World War II, but returned to lead the league in both 1946 and 1947 with 208 and 207 hits, respectively. He hit over .300 during 6 of his 10 seasons.

After managing in the minor leagues Pesky became the Red Sox' skipper in 1963. After finishing seventh, his team was eighth in 1964 when he was fired with two games remaining in the season. He later coached the Pittsburgh Pirates, then became a broadcaster for several years. He returned to Boston as a coach in 1975, and filled in as interim manager for five games in 1980 when Don Zimmer was fired.

Fred Pfeffer
Louisville Colonels (NL) 1892
Record: 42–56
Second baseman who played for 16 seasons.

In 1884 Pfeffer hit 25 home runs, an astounding total for the time, with 101 runs batted in. What made the feat not so astounding was the fact that he played for the Chicago White Stockings at Lake Front Park, which had dimensions of 180 feet down the left field line and 196 down the right. In previous seasons, balls hit over those fences were counted as doubles, but an 1884 rule change caused them to be scored as home runs.

During the 1892 season, while continuing to play, he also replaced Jack Chapman as manager of the Louisville Colonels, but he returned strictly to playing the following year.

Lew Phelan
St. Louis Browns (NL) 1895
Record: 11–30
The last of four managers to guide the St. Louis Browns in 1895.

Phelan never played major league baseball, and there was not much he could do as a manager with the Browns of 1895. They did not perform well for any of their four skippers, and finished the season 39–92.

Bill Phillips
Indianapolis Federals (FL) 1914; Newark Peppers (FL) 1915
Record: 114–92
Pitcher who was once ejected for punching a batter who fouled off too many of his pitches.

Phillips played seven seasons and compiled a lifetime record of 70–76. His best season was 1899, when he went 17–9 for the Cincinnati Reds. He made his last appearance in 1903, and 11 years later he was hired to manage the Indianapolis Federals of the new Federal League. He led that club to the first FL championship, as they finished a game and a half ahead of the second-place Chicago Chifeds.

The following season the team moved to Newark and became the Peppers, and they were in sixth place at 26–27 when Phillips was replaced by one of his top players, Bill McKechnie. The team finished fifth under McKechnie, but even so they were only six games out of first place.

Horace Phillips
Troy Trojans (NL) 1879; Columbus Buckeyes (AA) 1883; Pittsburgh Alleghenys (AA) 1884–86, (NL) 1887–89
Record: 338–415
Ohio native who never played major league baseball.

Phillips managed several teams in the nineteenth century, although he never won a pennant. His best season was with the 1886 Pittsburgh Alleghenys, who finished second in the American Association. That club joined the National League the following season and finished sixth in

that circuit, however.

In late July of 1889 Phillips was suffering from exhaustion and was given a vacation from his managerial duties. He suffered a mental breakdown a week later, and was admitted to an asylum.

Lefty Phillips
California Angels (AL) 1969–71
Record: 222–225
Played only five games professionally, none of them in the major leagues.

Phillips suffered an arm injury shortly after beginning his career in 1939 with the Bisbee Bees of the Arizona-Texas League. He then went into scouting, and served with the St. Louis Browns, Cincinnati Reds, and Brooklyn Dodgers. He was credited with signing such notables as Don Drysdale and Ron Fairly, and in 1965 he became the Dodgers' pitching coach. The club had long since moved to his hometown of Los Angeles.

In late 1968 Phillips became the director of player personnel for the Angels, but in 1969 he was named to the coaching staff and then became manager in May to succeed Bill Rigney. Two third-place finishes were followed by a fourth-place showing in 1971, and Lefty was fired after that season.

Lip Pike
Troy Haymakers (NA) 1871; Hartford Dark Blues (NA) 1874; Cincinnati Red Stockings (NL) 1877
Record: 20–51
One of baseball's first professional players.

Pike was being paid under the table before professional baseball was legitimized. When it came to light that he was receiving $20 a week from the Philadelphia Athletics in 1866, in fact, the amateur National Association of Base Ball Players called a hearing to address the matter. No one showed up for the meeting, and Pike went about his business.

He managed the Troy Haymakers in the professional National Association's inaugural season of 1871, but the team went 13–15 although it finished only eight games out of first place. The teams that Pike managed generally did not perform well, but he himself was a truly legendary player. He routinely hit over .300, and four times in 10 years he led or tied for the lead in his respective league in home runs, although the totals were always in the single digits. When the NA folded following the 1875 season, he was the all-time home run king with 16.

A speedy runner, he frequently participated in foot races as publicity stunts (once racing a trotting horse), and thus earned himself some extra cash as well. At the end of his career he played in the minor leagues and even returned to amateur ball. He died of heart disease at the age of 48.

Lou Piniella

New York Yankees (AL) 1986–87, 1988; Cincinnati Reds (NL) 1990–92; Seattle Mariners (AL) 1993–2002; Tampa Bay Devil Rays (AL) 2003–05; Chicago Cubs (NL) 2007–
Record: 1519–1420
Solid outfielder nicknamed "Sweet Lou" for his sweet swing.

In 1969 with the Kansas City Royals Piniella was named the American League's Rookie of the Year when he hit .282 with 11 home runs and 68 runs batted in. In 1972 he was named to the AL All-Star team on the strength of a .312 average, 11 homers, 72 RBIs, and a league-leading 33 doubles. He was traded to the Yankees in 1974 and spent the rest of his career with them, a career that spanned 18 total seasons and saw him hit over .300 seven times.

After retiring he became a coach with the Yankees, and in 1986 he was appointed manager to replace Billy Martin, who had been fired for the fourth time. After the 1987 season he became the club's general manager and Martin was hired back, but when Billy was fired for the fifth time in June, Piniella replaced him again. Lou was fired in October after a fifth-place finish.

In 1990 he became the manager of the Reds, and that team became the first National League club to stay in first place from the first day of the season to the last. They went on to defeat the Pittsburgh Pirates for the NL pennant, then swept a heavily-favored Oakland Athletics squad to capture the World Championship.

In 1993 Piniella went to the Mariners, with whom he would eventually boast three first-place finishes. When they won the AL West in 1995, Piniella was named the league's Manager of the Year by both the AP and the BBWAA. They took another division title in 1997, and clinched a wild card berth in 2000. They won the division again in 2001, winning 116 games (an AL record, tying the major league mark set by the 1906 Chicago Cubs), and the BBWAA once again gave Piniella its managerial honor. While Seattle never won a pennant under his leadership, they did get as far as the AL Championship Series three times.

In 2003 Piniella left Seattle to become the manager of the Devil Rays so that he could be closer to his Tampa home. He was dissatisfied with the team's poor performance, however, and the Devil Rays bought out his contract after the 2005 season. Following the 2006 campaign he was hired to replace Dusty Baker at the helm of the Cubs.

Bill Plummer

Seattle Mariners (AL) 1992
Record: 64–98
Light-hitting catcher who batted over .200 only three times in a 10-year career.

Plummer spent most of his career with the Cincinnati Reds as a backup to Johnny Bench. After spending his last year with Seattle he became a Mariners' coach, and was named manager for the 1992 season. His club finished seventh and he would not manage again.

Eddie Popowski

Boston Red Sox (AL) 1969, 1973
Record: 6–4
Spent 65 years in the Boston Red Sox' organization.

Popowski never played in the major leagues, but served in many capacities in the Boston system. He was a minor league player and manager, a scout, a special instructor, and a major league coach and interim manager.

Nicknamed "Pop," Eddie's minor league clubs finished in first place 14 times and claimed four pennants. At the major league level, he was named interim skipper for the last nine games of the 1969 season when Dick Williams was fired, and for the last game of the 1973 campaign when Eddie Kasko was let go.

Popowski died in 2001.

Matt Porter

Kansas City Unions (UA) 1884
Record: 3–13
Had one very unsuccessful season in the major leagues.

In 1884 with the Kansas City Unions of the Union Association Porter hit .083 in three games as an outfielder. As a manager he went 3–13 for a winning percentage of .188.

In fairness, he was the second of three Unions' managers, and none of them produced respectable records. Harry Wheeler preceded Porter and went 0–4, and Ted Sullivan followed him and went 13–46. Kansas City finished a whopping 61 games out of first place.

Pat Powers

Rochester Hop-Bitters (AA) 1890; New York Giants (NL) 1892
Record: 134–143
Longtime minor league executive.

Having managed twice in the major leagues and never finished higher than fifth, Powers became president of the International League in 1893. In 1901 he was elected president of the National Association of Professional Baseball Leagues, an organization that still exists and that is today more commonly known as Minor League Baseball.

Al Pratt
Pittsburgh Alleghenys (AA) 1882–83
Record: 51–59
Native of Pittsburgh who pitched the first game in major league history.

Pratt's Cleveland Forest Citys lost to the Fort Wayne Kekiongas in that game, 2–0, a contest that launched the professional National Association in 1871. A Civil War veteran, he had previously pitched in amateur circles, and in 1871 led the NA with 34 strikeouts. He pitched only one more season, however, before returning to amateur ball.

He later became a bartender, and then helped bring the Pittsburgh Alleghenys into the new American Association. He managed the club for one season and part of another, then was named to the Board of Directors of the Union Association, a league that played only in 1884 before folding. He later became a major league umpire.

Jim Price
New York Gothams (NL) 1884
Record: 56–42
New York native who managed his hometown Gothams for most of the 1884 season.

Price set a record for a new manager by winning his first 12 games in a row, a mark that stood alone until Joe Morgan tied it with the 1988 Boston Red Sox. In fact, it stood as a North American sports record until it was broken by basketball's Lawrence Frank, whose New Jersey Nets of the National Basketball Association won his first 14 in a row in 2004.

Despite a .571 winning percentage, Price did not manage again.

Doc Prothro
Philadelphia Phillies (NL) 1939–41
Record: 138–320
Part-time infielder and dentist.

James Thompson Prothro's nickname was not bestowed lightly, as he really did practice dentistry in the offseason. As an infielder he played mainly backup for five seasons and hit .318. He managed the Phillies for three seasons, but the team was a perennial cellar-dweller and Prothro could do nothing to improve their situation.

Luis Pujols
Detroit Tigers (AL) 2002
Record: 55–100
Backup catcher with a weak bat.

Pujols spent most of his career with the Houston Astros, but never hit better than .239. He was a coach with the Tigers in 2002 when, after losing the first six games of the season, manager Phil Garner was fired. Pujols was named interim manager, then signed on as full-time skipper for the remainder of the season. In June, when the Tigers faced the Royals in Kansas City, he and Tony Peña became the first Dominican-born managers to face each other in major league history.

After posting a 55–100 record with Detroit, Pujols was fired.

Blondie Purcell
Philadelphia Nationals (NL) 1883
Record: 13–68
Pitcher and outfielder who played for many teams during a 12-year career.

Purcell went 15–43 as a hurler, and did not pitch at all the last three years of his career. As an outfielder he fared better, batting .274 lifetime and topping the .300 mark twice. He took over for Bob Ferguson as player-manager of the Nationals during the 1883 campaign, but the team finished 45 games out of first place.

Mel Queen
Toronto Blue Jays (AL) 1997
Record: 4–1
Outfielder-turned-pitcher.

As an outfielder Queen displayed a weak bat, so he turned to pitching and fashioned a 14–8 record with a 2.76 earned run average in 1967 with the Cincinnati Reds. He was inconsistent thereafter and bounced around between the majors and the minors, soon being relegated to the bullpen where he garnered nine saves for the California Angels in 1970.

He went into coaching when his playing career was over, and was with the Blue Jays in 1997 when manager Cito Gaston was fired with five games remaining in the season. Mel was named interim skipper and won four of the five.

Frank Quilici
Minnesota Twins (AL) 1972–75
Record: 280–287
Infielder who played for and then coached the Twins.

Quilici hit only .214 in five seasons, and he was later a coach under Bill Rigney, who was fired during the 1972 season. Frank was named the new manager, and he fashioned three consecutive third-place finishes. His managerial career ended with a fourth-place showing in 1975.

Joe Quinn
St. Louis Browns (NL) 1895; Cleveland Spiders (NL) 1899
Record: 23–132
First major leaguer born in Australia.

A mortician in the offseason, Quinn was an excellent second baseman who played for many teams during a 17-year career. He also had the misfortune of being player-manager for two of the worst teams in baseball history. His 1895 Browns were 39–92, but his 1899 Spiders were especially bad, having lost most of their talent to owner Frank Robison's other team, the St. Louis Perfectos, in a gradual absorption of the Cleveland club. Quinn was the second skipper for the team that season and went 12–104, for a winning percentage of .103. The team finished 20–134.

Doug Rader
Texas Rangers (AL) 1983–85; Chicago White Sox (AL) 1986; California Angels (AL) 1989–91
Record: 388–417
Third baseman with some power and an outstanding glove.

A five-time Gold Glove winner, Rader had a rather wild personality. He was fun-loving and unpredictable, and as a manager was somewhat intense. His first year with the Rangers saw him finish third, but his club would drop to seventh the next two seasons.

In 1986 he was a coach with the White Sox when he was called upon to manage two games between the reigns of Tony LaRussa and Jim Fregosi. In his first year with the Angels in 1989 he again finished third, but would not achieve that level again.

Willie Randolph
New York Mets (NL) 2005–
Record: 180–144
Played more games at second base than anyone in New York Yankees' history.

Randolph's career spanned 18 seasons, most of them with the Yankees. He was a six-time All-Star, enjoying his best season in 1987 when he hit .305. In 1980 he led the American League with 119 bases on balls.

He finished his career in 1992 with the Mets, and the following season he became the Yankees' assistant general manager. In 1994 he became a coach under Joe Torre, and spent the next 11 seasons in that role. In 2005 he returned to the Mets as manager. His 2006 squad made it to the National League Championship Series before being eliminated by the St. Louis Cardinals in seven games.

Vern Rapp
St. Louis Cardinals (NL) 1977–78; Cincinnati Reds (NL)
1984
Record: 140–160
Contentious manager who never played in the major leagues.

Despite being named Minor League Manager of the Year by *The Sporting News* in 1976 while at the helm of the Denver Bears, Rapp was reputed to have clashed with both his players and the front offices under which he managed. With his hometown Cardinals in 1977 he banned facial hair, creating some animosity among his players. Among them was pitcher Al Hrabosky, who was forced to shave his trademark Fu Manchu and was reported to have complained that he could not intimidate batters if he looked like a golf pro. In 1978 Rapp publicly called another of his players, Ted Simmons, a "loser," and he was fired the next day.

He coached the Montreal Expos from 1979–83, then was hired to manage the Reds. After going 51–70 he was replaced by a hometown hero who was also returning from the Expos: player-manager Pete Rose.

Al Reach
Philadelphia Phillies (NL) 1890
Record: 4–7
Founder of the AJ Reach Sporting Goods Company.

Born in London, England, Reach began to make himself known in baseball in Brooklyn as early as the 1850s. He was one of the first players to be paid, and eventually played for the Philadelphia Athletics for all five seasons of the National Association's existence.

One of the founders of the Philadelphia Phillies, he served as team president from 1883–1902, and in 1890 stepped in as one of three men to substitute for skipper Harry Wright when Wright temporarily lost his eyesight.

He founded his sporting goods company in the 1870s, and that venture made him a rich man. In 1883 he began to publish the annual *Reach's Official American Association Base Ball Guide*, which later became *Reach's Official Base Ball Guide*. He eventually became a part-owner of the Athletics, and he died in 1928 at the age of 87.

Phil Regan
Baltimore Orioles (AL) 1995
Record: 71–73
Excellent right-handed relief pitcher.

After garnering a career-high 15 wins with the Detroit Tigers in 1963, Regan began to struggle and was eventually moved to the bullpen. There he flourished, being named a National League All-Star in 1966 with the Los Angeles Dodgers and twice leading the NL in saves. Twice in 1968 he won both games of a doubleheader.

Regan became a coach following his retirement, and he managed the Orioles for one season and finished third.

Del Rice
California Angels (AL) 1972
Record: 75–80
Good defensive catcher who played for 17 seasons.

Rice was noted for his glove work and his handling of pitchers; with a bat he sometimes struggled to stay above .200 and averaged .237 for his career. In 1953 he was named a National League All-Star while playing for the St. Louis Cardinals despite a .236 season.

Following his playing career he coached for the Angels and then the Cleveland Indians. He later managed in the Angels' minor league system, and his 1971 Salt Lake City Angels won the Pacific Coast League pennant. Rice was rewarded with the managerial job of the major league club, but was fired when the team finished fifth.

Paul Richards
Chicago White Sox (AL) 1951–54, 1976; Baltimore Orioles (AL) 1955–61
Record: 923–901
Light-hitting backup catcher and later major league executive.

Richards played sparingly in the majors from 1932–35, then became a minor league manager. When World War II service claimed many star players from major league rosters, Richards caught on with the Detroit Tigers as a backstop and spent four more years at that level. He then went back to minor league managing.

In 1951 he was named skipper of the White Sox, but despite four straight winning seasons his club could not quite get over the top. He moved to the Orioles in 1955 as general manager *and* field manager. The seventh-place club gradually began to rise in the standings, and when it finished second in 1960 the AP named Richards its American League Manager of the Year.

Paul resigned in 1961 to become the general manager of the new Houston Colt .45s, then worked in the front office of the Atlanta Braves before returning to manage the White Sox for one more season in 1976.

Danny Richardson
Washington Statesmen (NL) 1892
Record: 12–31
Outfielder and infielder who even pitched several games.

In 1885 Richardson went 7–1 on the mound for the New York Giants while hitting .263. He pitched only six more games the rest of his career and played mainly at second base and shortstop. In 1887 he hit .331, the only time he topped the .300 plateau.

As player-manager he was the last of three skippers for the 1892 Washington Statesmen, who went 58–93 overall.

As a player Richardson soon began to experience problems with management that were likely alcohol related, at times disappearing from his team for days. He was finished after the 1894 season.

Branch Rickey
St. Louis Browns (AL) 1913–15; St. Louis Cardinals (NL) 1919–25
Record: 597–664
Most famous as a baseball innovator and pioneer.

Rickey had several cups of coffee as a major league player, mostly as a catcher. He totaled 120 games over four seasons, but was never able to catch on. He eventually became the manager of the Browns, then manager *and* president of the Cardinals. He managed a couple of third-place finishes, but his club's performances were usually mediocre.

As an executive he did work hard to assemble talent, however, and the Cardinals eventually became a force to be reckoned with. He pioneered the modern major league farm system as a way of developing talent, and pushed for such innovations as batting helmets, pitching machines, and batting cages.

From the Cardinals Rickey moved on to become an owner of the Brooklyn Dodgers, where the signing of Jackie Robinson broke baseball's color line and proved his most famous and enduring achievement. In 1950 he sold his interest in the club and went to work in the front office of the Pittsburgh Pirates.

Rickey died in late 1965, and he was inducted into the Hall of Fame as an executive in 1967.

Greg Riddoch
San Diego Padres (NL) 1990–92
Record: 200–194
Minor league player who retired to teach junior high school.

Riddoch eventually returned to the minor leagues as a manager, where he won two Northwest League championships with the Eugene Emeralds. He managed in the major leagues with the Padres from 1990–92, but 1991 was his only full season. He also suffered a concussion that year when he was accidentally struck by a batting helmet thrown in anger by Benito Santiago, who had just grounded out.

He later returned to managing in the minors and also coached for the Tampa Bay Devil Rays.

Jim Riggleman
San Diego Padres (NL) 1992–94; Chicago Cubs (NL) 1995–

99
Record: 486–598
New Jersey native who never played major league ball.

Riggleman was a coach with the St. Louis Cardinals before replacing Greg Riddoch as manager of the Padres at the end of the 1992 campaign. He lasted two full seasons, then managed the Cubs for five years. His 1998 Chicago squad finished in second place, but after dropping to sixth the following year Riggleman was fired.

Bill Rigney
New York Giants (NL) 1956–57; San Francisco Giants (NL) 1958–60, 1976; Los Angeles Angels (AL) 1961–64; California Angels (AL) 1965–69; Minnesota Twins (AL) 1970–72
Record: 1239–1321
Infielder and longtime manager.

Rigney played for eight seasons, only four of them as a regular. Not noted for his bat, he nevertheless clubbed a career-high 17 home runs in his sophomore season of 1947, and was named a National League All-Star in 1948 for the first of four times.

He spent his entire career with the Giants, and he eventually became their manager. He was at the helm when the team moved from New York to San Francisco, but he was fired in June of 1960 and was named manager of the expansion Los Angeles Angels the following season. That club had a first year typical of a new team, going 70–91 and finishing in eighth place in the 10-team league, then they rose to third place the next year with an 86–76 record. That performance earned Rigney the American League Manager of the Year Award from the AP. He would remain at the helm when the team relocated from Los Angeles to Anaheim, but was fired in 1969 while in sixth place.

The Twins hired him for 1970, and it was in Minnesota that year that Rigney won his only division title. His team was swept by the Baltimore Orioles in the AL Championship Series, however. He lasted with the Twins until mid-1972.

After coaching the San Diego Padres in 1975, Rigney returned to the Giants to manage for the 1976 season, and that would be his last.

Cal Ripken, Sr.
Baltimore Orioles (AL) 1985, 1987–88
Record: 68–101
Longtime Orioles' coach who never played major league baseball.

Ripken is probably most famous for his son Cal Junior, who broke Lou Gehrig's all-time record for consecutive games played. A coach with the O's from 1976–86,

Cal Senior got to work with his namesake and eventually manage both him and his other son, Billy Ripken, the Baltimore second baseman for several years. He managed one game in 1985 when Joe Altobelli was fired, before the arrival of Earl Weaver. He was then named full-time skipper in 1987, but the club finished in sixth place. After an 0–6 start in 1988, Ripken was fired, but he cannot be much faulted considering the fact that the team eventually set a record by going 0–21 before winning its first contest of the season.

Ripken returned as an Orioles' coach from 1989–92. He passed away in 1999.

Frank Robinson
Cleveland Indians (AL) 1975–77; San Francisco Giants (NL) 1981–84; Baltimore Orioles (AL) 1988–91; Montreal Expos (NL) 2002–04; Washington Nationals (NL) 2005–06
Record: 1065–1176
First black manager in major league baseball.

One of the greatest to play the game, Robinson won the National League Rookie of the Year Award in 1956 with the Cincinnati Redlegs at the age of 20. He went on to make his mark on the game in no small way, hammering 586 home runs lifetime, being named to 14 All-Star teams, and winning the Triple Crown in 1966 by hitting .316 with 49 home runs and 122 runs batted in with the Orioles. He hit over .300 nine times, won a Gold Glove in 1958, and was the only man to win the Most Valuable Player Award in both the National and American Leagues when he captured that crown with the Cincinnati Reds in 1961 and the Orioles in 1966. He hit over 20 home runs in a season 17 times, and he played for 21 years.

In 1975 Robinson was named player-manager of the Indians, and he would thus begin a second career of coaching and managing. He skippered the Indians, Giants, and Orioles, and was the manager of the Expos when they relocated from Montreal to Washington and became the Nationals.

In 1988, after taking over the Orioles for Cal Ripken, Sr., he suffered through 15 of the club's 21 season-opening losses, but in 1989 he led the squad to a second-place finish and won the AL Manager of the Year Award from the BBWAA and the Manager of the Year Award from the AP. Before going to Montreal he served for a time as Major League Baseball's vice president of on-field operations.

He was inducted into the Hall of Fame in 1982, and both the Orioles and Reds have retired his uniform number 20.

Wilbert Robinson
Baltimore Orioles (AL) 1902; Brooklyn Robins (NL) 1914–

31
Record: 1399–1398
Longtime, solid catcher and longtime Hall of Fame manager.

Nicknamed "Uncle Robbie" because of his likable personality, Wilbert Robinson played for 17 seasons. He hit over .300 five times and once set a record by collecting seven hits in a nine-inning game. He was player-manager of the Orioles in 1902, and that was his last season as a player.

He coached with the New York Giants under his friend John McGraw from 1911–13, then the two had a parting of ways that began when McGraw accused Robinson of missing a sign and therefore costing the Giants the 1912 World Championship. Robinson was hired to manage the Brooklyn Dodgers in 1914, and the team renamed itself the Robins in his honor.

In 18 seasons in Brooklyn he won two pennants. His 1916 club lost the World Series to the Boston Red Sox, and the 1920 squad lost to the Cleveland Indians. Robinson managed through 1931, then was let go. In 1933 he became a minor league skipper with the Atlanta Crackers, and he died the following year.

He was inducted into the Hall of Fame in 1945.

Stanley Robison
St. Louis Cardinals (NL) 1905
Record: 19–31
Most famous as a major league owner.

Stanley Robison and his brother Frank purchased the Cleveland Spiders of the National League in 1889, and that team became a powerhouse for a number of years. Prior to the 1899 season the pair also purchased the St. Louis Browns and changed their name to Perfectos. They then decimated the Cleveland squad by transferring the star players to St. Louis, believing they would get better attendance there. The Spiders suffered as a result and were eventually completely absorbed as the NL eliminated a number of clubs.

The Perfectos became the Cardinals in 1900, and Stanley assumed the reigns as manager for the final third of the 1905 season after two other managers led the team into sixth place. Robison could do no better, however, and the club finished there.

Frank Robison died in 1908, and Stanley passed away in 1911 and left the Cardinals to his niece.

Buck Rodgers
Milwaukee Brewers (AL) 1980, 1980–82; Montreal Expos (NL) 1985–91; California Angels (AL) 1991–92, 1992–94
Record: 784–773
Catcher who spent his entire career with the Los Angeles/California Angels.

Nicknamed "Buck" for the Buck Rogers comic strip and science fiction movie and serial character that first appeared in 1928, Robert Leroy Rodgers was a catcher who hit .232 lifetime. He retired in 1969 and soon became a coach and a minor league manager. He was a coach for the Brewers in 1980 when manager George Bamberger suffered a heart attack during spring training, and he took over as interim manager. Bamberger returned in June but then resigned in September, and Rodgers was named permanent skipper. In the split season of 1981 his Brewers won their division in the second half, but were eliminated in the divisional playoffs by the New York Yankees.

Buck later managed the Expos, then returned to the Angels in 1991. In May of 1992 the Angels' team bus crashed on the New Jersey Turnpike, and several members of the club, including Rodgers, were hospitalized. Buck suffered several broken bones, and John Wathan filled in as interim skipper while he recovered.

Rodgers was fired from the Angels in May of 1994.

Jim Rogers
Louisville Colonels (NL) 1897
Record: 17–24
Infielder who played only two major league seasons.

The second of those seasons was 1897, when Rogers was player-manager of the Louisville Colonels. He lasted only 44 games, scoring 17 wins, 24 losses, 2 ties, and 1 no-decision while batting .235, and he was replaced by Fred Clarke.

Cookie Rojas
California Angels (AL) 1988; Florida Marlins (NL) 1996
Record: 76–79
Five-time All-Star second baseman.

Always dependable, Rojas played 16 seasons and then served in many other capacities in major league and minor league baseball. In addition to working as a scout and special assistant to the general manager, Cookie was on several major league coaching staffs. During spring training of 1988 Angels' manager Gene Mauch took a leave of absence for health reasons, and Rojas filled in as skipper. Just over two weeks later Mauch announced his retirement, and Cookie became the permanent manager.

He did not last the season, however, being fired in September with the team in fourth place. He would go on to work in several other organizations, and was a coach with the Marlins in 1996 when Rene Lachemann was fired. Cookie managed one game and won it before new skipper John Boles arrived.

After working several more years as a coach, Rojas, who was born in Cuba, became a Spanish-language broadcaster for the Marlins.

Red Rolfe
Detroit Tigers (AL) 1949–52
Record: 278–256
All-Star third baseman for the New York Yankees.

Rolfe spent 10 years with the Yankees, although he played but a single game in his first season in New York. He was a consistent hitter, batting at least .300 on four occasions, and was equally competent defensively. Named to four All-Star teams, he tied for the American League lead with 15 triples in 1936 and had his best season in 1939, when he hit a career-high .329 with league-leading totals of 46 doubles, 213 hits, and 139 runs scored.

He managed the Tigers for four seasons after his playing career, and his best showing was second place in 1950.

Pete Rose
Cincinnati Reds (NL) 1984–88, 1988–89
Record: 412–373
Baseball's all-time hit leader.

Pete Rose played for 24 seasons, retiring with 4256 safeties. The only other player to top the 4000 mark was Ty Cobb, whose record Rose broke in 1985.

Pete was named to 17 All-Star teams, at five different positions—second base, right field, left field, third base, and first base. He was the National League's Rookie of the Year in 1963 when he hit .273 with 170 hits, but that was only a hint of things to come. In his career Rose hit over .300 fifteen times, retiring with a .303 lifetime average. He won three batting titles and collected over 200 hits in a season 10 times. He led the NL seven times in hits, five times in doubles, and four times in runs scored. In 1973 he was named the league's Most Valuable Player on the strength of a .338 batting average and 230 hits.

Rose played for the Reds for most of his career as a vital member of Cincinnati's Big Red Machine, helping the club to back-to-back World Championships in 1975 and 1976. But he departed for the Philadelphia Phillies as a free agent in 1979. He later played for the Montreal Expos, and returned to the Reds in 1984 in a deal for Tom Lawless, a deal that saw Rose become Cincinnati's player-manager.

The Reds finished second every year from 1985–88, and controversy soon began to cloud Pete's career. Having played his last game in 1986, Rose was suspended for a month in 1988 after getting into a shoving match with umpire Dave Pallone. Tommy Helms managed the club in his absence. In 1989 baseball Commissioner Bart Gia-

matti began an investigation into serious allegations that Rose had been betting on baseball. In August of that year Pete was banned from the game for life in a deal that saw Major League Baseball reporting no official findings. Once again Helms took over the Reds on an interim basis.

In 1990 Rose was convicted of income tax evasion and served a five-month prison sentence followed by 1000 hours of community service. In 2004 he finally admitted that he had indeed bet on baseball, but his lifetime ban has kept him out of the Hall of Fame.

Chief Roseman
St. Louis Browns (AA) 1890
Record: 7–8
Decent-hitting outfielder who played for seven years.

Roseman hit a career-high .339 in his final season of 1890, which saw him spend 15 games as player-manager of the Browns. He was one of six skippers that season, but despite the confusion the team finished in third place with a 78–58 record.

Larry Rothschild
Tampa Bay Devil Rays (AL) 1998–2001
Record: 205–294
First manager of the Tampa Bay Devil Rays.

A minor league pitcher, Rothschild got into seven major league games with the Detroit Tigers. He eventually became a successful pitching coach with several organizations, and was named skipper of the expansion Devil Rays in 1998. After three consecutive last-place finishes, the Rays were last again in early 2001 with a 4–10 record when Larry was fired and replaced by Hal McRae.

Dave Rowe
Kansas City Cowboys (NL) 1886; Kansas City Cowboys (AA) 1888
Record: 44–127
Once set a record by allowing 35 runs in a game.

Rowe was an outfielder who also pitched on four occasions in his career. In 1882 with the Cleveland Blues he hurled a complete nine-inning game, allowing 29 hits, walking 7, and allowing 35 runs (only 12 of which were earned).

A decent hitter until the end of his career, Rowe spent two seasons as player-manager of two rather bad and separate teams called the Kansas City Cowboys—one in the National League, and the other in the American Association, a club that was also known as the Blues. His winning percentage was a dismal .257.

Jack Rowe
Buffalo Bisons (PL) 1890, 1890

Record: 27–72

Catcher-turned-shortstop who hit .293 lifetime.

With the National League's Buffalo Bisons Rowe led the circuit with 11 triples in 1881 while batting .333. He topped the .300 mark five times in his career, and was considered one of the "Big Four" that also included Dan Brouthers, Hardy Richardson, and Deacon White. All four were acquired by the Detroit Wolverines from Buffalo for the 1886 season.

Rowe and White created some controversy when they bought the Buffalo Bisons of the minor International League in 1888. When the Wolverines sold the pair to the Pittsburgh Alleghenys, they refused to report to their new team. They held out for part of the 1889 season, but finally gave in because they learned of secret plans to create the Players League the following season. In 1890 they became part-owners of the new Buffalo Bisons of that league, and Rowe was the team's manager. That would be his final season, as his club finished last and the league collapsed.

Pants Rowland
Chicago White Sox (AL) 1915–18
Record: 339–247

Minor league catcher and executive.

Clarence Rowland received his nickname "Pants" when he was nine years old and ran the bases while wearing his father's overalls at games in Dubuque, Iowa, with the Ninth Street Blues. As an adult, after playing in the minor leagues, he became a scout and later a team owner. In 1915 he was named manager of the White Sox, and in the next three years he brought that club from third to second to first. In the 1917 World Series Chicago won it all in a six-game contest over the New York Giants.

Disagreements with owner Charlie Comiskey led to Rowland's being fired following the 1918 season—just in time for him to escape the Black Sox Scandal the next year. He became an American League umpire for five years, then returned to the minor leagues as an executive with the Los Angeles Angels. He eventually became president of the Pacific Coast League, and led an effort to bring that circuit to major league status, an attempt that won little support from the league's team owners.

Rowland died in Chicago in 1969. In 2005 he was inducted into the Pacific Coast League Hall of Fame.

Jerry Royster
Milwaukee Brewers (NL) 2002
Record: 53–94

Infielder who played 16 major league seasons.

Royster was an excellent hitter in the minor leagues but merely adequate in the majors. He was a regular for several seasons with the Atlanta Braves before being relegated mostly to utility duty.

He was named manager of the Brewers for most of the 2002 season when skipper Davey Lopes was fired in April. He himself was then fired at the conclusion of the season.

Dick Rudolph
Boston Braves (NL) 1924
Record: 11–27

Spitballer who went 121–109 lifetime.

Rudolph spent most of his career with the Boston Braves and fashioned a 2.66 earned run average. One of the few hurlers who was allowed to continue throwing the spitball after it was banned, he was a 20-game winner twice: in 1914, when he went 26–10 while helping the Braves to the World Championship, and in 1915, when he was 22–19 and led the National League with 43 starts.

He became a coach with the club from 1921–27, and even pitched a few games while in that role. In 1924 he filled in as manager for 38 games for regular skipper Dave Bancroft.

Muddy Ruel
St. Louis Browns (AL) 1947
Record: 59–95

Solid, dependable catcher for 19 seasons.

Nicknamed "Muddy" because of a mudball game he devised as a child, Herold Dominic Ruel was a .275 lifetime hitter who batted over .300 four times. He was notorious for hitting in the clutch and was consistently among the American League's top backstops defensively.

Possessing a law degree from Washington University, Ruel became a coach with the Chicago White Sox when his playing days were ended. He worked as an assistant to baseball Commissioner Happy Chandler and managed the Browns for one season, when his team finished in last place, 38 games behind the pennant-winning New York Yankees. He later coached for the Cleveland Indians and from 1954–56 he served as the general manager of the Detroit Tigers.

Tom Runnells
Montreal Expos (NL) 1991–92
Record: 68–81

Minor league infielder who appeared in 40 games at the major league level.

After spending 10 years in the minors as a player, Runnells became a minor league manager. In 1988 he was at the helm of the Chattanooga Lookouts when that team claimed the Southern League championship, and in 1989 he led the Indianapolis Indians to the American Association title. He then became a coach with the Expos, and was named manager in June of 1991 when Buck Rodgers was fired.

Runnells never managed a full season for the Expos. After finishing sixth in '91, his club was in fourth place in May of the following season when he himself was fired. He then became a minor league manager and roving instructor in the Detroit Tigers' organization before being hired to manage the Tulsa Drillers in the Colorado Rockies' system.

Pete Runnels
Boston Red Sox (AL) 1966
Record: 8–8
Consistent, versatile infielder who excelled at first base, second base, and shortstop.

Runnels played regularly at all three positions at various times during his career. A .291 lifetime hitter, he won the American League batting title in 1960 with a .320 average and again in 1962 with a .326 showing. He hit over .300 six times and was a five-time All-Star.

Runnels was a coach with the Red Sox from 1965–66, and was named interim manager for the final 16 games of the '66 season when Billy Herman was fired.

Bill Russell
Los Angeles Dodgers (NL) 1996–98
Record: 173–149
Originally a solid outfielder who became an excellent shortstop.

Appreciated for his outfield work, Russell was nevertheless converted to shortstop because the Dodgers needed a replacement for Maury Wills. Russell's first season at his new position was 1972, and he led the National League in errors at that spot, but he improved in 1973 and became an NL All-Star. He would be named to two more such squads during his 18-year career, all of which was spent with Los Angeles.

He became a Dodgers' coach under Tom Lasorda after his playing career, and in 1996 was named manager when Lasorda resigned in July after suffering a heart attack. The Dodgers finished second two consecutive years under Russell, but in 1998 new ownership was intolerant of the team's 36–38 start and fired both Russell and General Manager Fred Claire. Russell later coached for the Tampa Bay Devil Rays.

Connie Ryan
Atlanta Braves (NL) 1975; Texas Rangers (AL) 1977
Record: 11–22
Second baseman for 12 seasons with five different teams.

Ryan was an adequate hitter but not a great one. He batted a career-high .295 in 1944 with the Boston Braves and was named a National League All-Star. He was once ejected from a game in 1949 when it was raining and he came out to the on-deck circle wearing a raincoat.

Ryan became a coach following his playing career, and he was named interim manager twice: in 1975 with the Braves for the final 27 games of the season when Clyde King was fired, and in 1977 with the Rangers for 6 games when Eddie Stanky was let go.

Eddie Sawyer
Philadelphia Phillies (NL) 1948–52, 1958–60
Record: 390–423
Never had a chance to play in the major leagues after suffering an injury in the minors.

Sawyer did become a minor league manager, and replaced Ben Chapman at the helm of the Phillies in 1948. In 1951 his club captured the National League pennant, nearly blowing a seven-game lead when they lost 8 of their final 10 contests. They were swept by the New York Yankees in the World Series.

Sawyer was fired in mid-1952, but rehired six years later. The Phillies finished last both that year and the next, and when they lost the very first game of the 1960 season Eddie resigned. He said, "I'm 49 and I want to live to be 50."

Mike Scanlon
Washington Nationals (UA) 1884; Washington Statesmen (NL) 1886
Record: 60–132
Native of Ireland who never played major league baseball.

Scanlon managed one of the six teams to be called the Washington Nationals, this one in the Union Association, in 1884. That club finished seventh. Two years later he managed the Washington Statesmen of the National League, but they were 13–67 and in eighth place when he was replaced by John Gaffney.

Bob Schaefer
Kansas City Royals (AL) 1991, 2005
Record: 6–12
Minor league shortstop who worked in many capacities with several organizations.

Schaefer was a minor league manager for many years, and as such was named South Atlantic League Manager of the Year in both 1980 and 1981 with the Greensboro Hornets in the New York Yankees' system. In 1985 his Tidewater Tides won the International League championship in the New York Mets' organization.

Schaefer later worked in scouting and player development with several organizations before becoming a coach with the Royals. He managed one game in 1991 with Kansas City when John Wathan was fired, before the arrival of Hal McRae. He went back into scouting shortly thereafter, but returned as a Royals' coach in 2002. In 2005, when Tony Peña resigned, he managed another 17 games before Buddy Bell was hired as Peña's replacement.

Ray Schalk
Chicago White Sox (AL) 1927–28
Record: 102–125
Excellent defensive catcher.

Not a strong hitter, Schalk made his mark through his defense, with which he led the American League in many categories for many seasons, and with his handling of pitchers. He set a major league record by catching four no-hitters. Speedy for a catcher, he swiped bases in double digits 10 times, peaking with 30 in 1916, and he once hit for the cycle. He was one of the few White Sox' starters in the 1919 World Series who did *not* intentionally throw games.

He was named player-manager of the Sox in 1927, but resigned the following year. He later coached for the Chicago Cubs, and in 1955 he was elected to the Hall of Fame by the Veterans Committee.

Bob Scheffing
Chicago Cubs (NL) 1957–59; Detroit Tigers (AL) 1961–63
Record: 418–427
Catcher for the Chicago Cubs, Cincinnati Reds, and St. Louis Cardinals.

Generally an adequate hitter who displayed solid defense, Scheffing had his best season in 1948 when he hit .300 with 5 home runs and 45 runs batted in. He managed the Cubs from 1957–59 and resigned from that post. In 1961 he was hired to skipper the Tigers, who had finished in sixth place the preceding season with a 71–83 record. When they went 101–61 in 1961, finishing second to the New York Yankees (who won 109 games), Scheffing was named the American League Manager of the Year by the AP.

He never saw that kind of success again; the Tigers dropped to fourth in 1962, and were languishing in ninth in June of 1963 when Scheffing was fired. He later became the general manager of the New York Mets.

Larry Schlafly
Buffalo Buffeds (FL) 1914; Buffalo Blues (FL) 1915
Record: 93–99
Infielder who played sporadically over four seasons.

Schlafly played in the major leagues in 1902, 1906, 1907, and 1914. The Buffeds hired him as player-manager in 1914 despite the fact that he had not played in the majors for seven seasons, and he responded by hitting .260. The Buffeds finished fourth.

The team changed its name to Blues the following year, but they began to struggle early and Schlafly, who was no longer playing, was forced to resign as manager. In eighth when he left, the club would finish sixth.

Gus Schmelz
Columbus Buckeyes (AA) 1884; St. Louis Maroons (NL) 1886; Cincinnati Red Stockings (AA) 1887–89; Cleveland Spiders (NL) 1890; Columbus Buckeyes (AA) 1890, 1891; Washington Statesmen (NL) 1894–97
Record: 624–703
Columbus native who never played major league baseball.

A well-respected manager, Schmelz skippered many teams, including two in his hometown who were both called the Buckeyes. He treated his players well but fiercely opposed those who attempted to unify or form rival leagues.

He managed a couple of second-place finishes over the years, but never won a pennant.

Red Schoendienst
St. Louis Cardinals (NL) 1965–76, 1980, 1990
Record: 1041–955
Ten-time All-Star second baseman and longtime manager.

Schoendienst spent most of his career with the Cardinals. In his rookie season of 1945 he led the National League with 26 stolen bases, and as a fielder he would eventually lead the NL in fielding percentage seven times.

In 1950 he topped the circuit with 43 doubles, and in 1957, in playing time with the New York Giants and the Milwaukee Braves, he led the league with 200 hits. He hit .289 in his career, topping the .300 mark seven times. In 1959 he lost part of a lung due to tuberculosis, but he managed to come back and played four more years.

When his playing career was over Schoendienst returned to the Cardinals as a coach, and he was named skipper in 1965. The AP named him its NL Manager of the Year in both 1967 and 1968 when the Redbirds took the pennant both seasons. In 1967 his club defeated the Boston Red Sox in seven games to claim the World Championship, but in 1968 they lost to the Detroit Tigers despite some stellar pitching by Bob Gibson.

Red was fired in 1976 and became a coach with the Oakland Athletics. In 1979 he returned to the Cards as a coach, and in 1980, when skipper Whitey Herzog was promoted to the position of general manager, he took over as manager on an interim basis. In later years Herzog would serve as both manager and GM, and in 1990, when Whitey resigned, Schoendienst again filled in until he was replaced by Joe Torre. Red retired for good in 1995.

Schoendienst was inducted into the Hall of Fame in 1989. In 1996 the Cardinals retired his uniform number 2.

Joe Schultz
Seattle Pilots (AL) 1969; Detroit Tigers (AL) 1973
Record: 78–112

Only manager of the Seattle Pilots before they moved to Milwaukee.

A backup catcher for seven seasons, Schultz (actually Joe Schultz, Jr.) was the son of an infielder and outfielder who had an 11-year major league career. Joe Senior was the manager of the Houston Buffaloes of the Texas League with 13-year-old Joe Junior as a bat boy when, in a game against the Galveston Buccaneers, Senior put Junior in as a pinch-hitter. Junior promptly singled, then stole second and third and eventually scored.

Schultz, Jr. played in the major leagues from 1939–48, and he then became a minor league manager and a long-time major league coach. In 1969 he was named manager of the expansion Seattle Pilots and guided them to a predictable sixth-place finish. In 1973 he was a coach with the Tigers and took over when Billy Martin was fired, then went back to coaching the club the following year under Ralph Houk.

Mike Scioscia
Anaheim Angels (AL) 2000–04; Los Angeles Angels of Anaheim (AL) 2005–
Record: 609–525

Two-time All-Star catcher.

Merely adequate as a hitter, Scioscia could nevertheless deliver in the clutch and was especially noted for his ability to block the plate. He spent his entire 13-year playing career with the Los Angeles Dodgers.

He became the manager of the Angels in 2000. In 2002 his club earned a wild card berth to the postseason, and after capturing the American League pennant they went on to win the World Championship by defeating the San Francisco Giants in seven games. The BBWAA named Scioscia its AL Manager of the Year.

The Angels won their division in 2004 and again in 2005, but they were eliminated in the playoffs both years.

Frank Selee
Boston Bostons (NL) 1890–1901; Chicago Cubs (NL) 1902–05
Record: 1284–862

Hailed from Amherst, New York, and never played major league baseball.

Selee was nevertheless an extremely successful manager. He certainly did not overmanage, devising very little

in the way of strategy during the course of games and trusting his players to figure out plays for themselves. He had five first-place finishes, all of them with the Bostons. In three cases—1891, 1893, and 1898—standings determined the championships. In 1892, the season was split into halves, and the Bostons defeated the Cleveland Spiders in a postseason matchup of the winners of each half and defeated them, five games to none. One additional game resulted in a tie. In 1897 the championship was known as the Temple Cup and was determined by a best-of-seven series between the first- and second-place finishers, and the Bostons lost to the second-place Baltimore Orioles, four games to one.

Selee's clubs produced many second-place finishes as well, and the skipper's lifetime winning percentage was .598. His 1892 and 1898 clubs were the first ever to win 100 games in a season. In 1999 Frank was inducted into the Hall of Fame.

Luke Sewell
St. Louis Browns (AL) 1941–46; Cincinnati Reds (NL) 1949–52
Record: 606–644

All-Star catcher with a 20-year playing career.

Sewell began his major league career in 1921, but it was not until 1926 that he became a regular with the Cleveland Indians. His only All-Star season was 1937, when he hit .269 with the Chicago White Sox. On four occasions he led American League catchers in assists, and he caught three no-hitters.

As a manager he won his only pennant with the St. Louis Browns during the war year of 1944. The Browns lost the World Series in six games to the crosstown Cardinals, but *The Sporting News* named Sewell its Major League Manager of the Year.

He later coached and then managed the Reds.

Dan Shannon
Louisville Colonels (AA) 1889; Washington Statesmen (AA) 1891
Record: 25–80

Second baseman and shortstop who played parts of only three seasons with four teams.

A lowly .233 hitter, Shannon's managerial opportunities came with some rather bad teams. He was the third of four player-managers for the 1889 Colonels, who were eighth when Shannon took over, eighth when he surrendered the reins, and eighth when the season ended. He was also one of three player-managers and the third of four managers overall for the 1891 Statesmen, who were seventh when he took control, ninth when he was replaced, and ninth at the season's conclusion.

Bill Sharsig
Philadelphia Athletics (AA) 1886, 1888–90; Philadelphia Athletics (AA) 1891
Record: 238–216
Executive who helped organize the second Philadelphia Athletics.

There have been four teams by that name in major league history, and Sharsig managed two of them. The first he helped organize as a semipro team in 1880, and they joined the American Association in 1882. Dissatisfied with the team's performance over the years, Sharsig named himself skipper in 1886 as a replacement for Lew Simmons, and took over again from 1888–90. The club finished third twice before dropping to eighth place and then folding after the 1890 campaign.

In 1891 the rival Players League folded after its only season, and the AA took in the PL's Philadelphia entry. That club had been called the Quakers in 1890 but inherited the Athletics' name in the AA. Sharsig took over as manager but stepped aside in favor of George Wood with the club in seventh place.

In 1901 he became the business manager for the fourth Philadelphia Athletics, an entry in the brand new American League.

Bob Shawkey
New York Yankees (AL) 1930
Record: 86–68
Pitched the first game at Yankee Stadium.

Shawkey won that game 4–1 over the Boston Red Sox in April of 1923. He had made his debut in 1913 with the Philadelphia Athletics, and was sold to the Yankees during the 1915 season. During the course of his 15-year career he was a 20-game winner four times, peaking with a 24–14 record in 1916. In 1920 he led the American League with a 2.45 earned run average, and he won 195 games lifetime.

Shawkey retired in 1927 and became a coach with the Yankees two years later. In 1930 he was named manager, and that would be his only season at the helm despite a third-place finish. He later managed for many years in the minor leagues and eventually became a coach at Dartmouth College.

Tom Sheehan
San Francisco Giants (NL) 1960
Record: 46–50
Oldest rookie manager in major league history.

Sheehan pitched for several years between 1915 and 1926, fashioning a 17–39 record. He later coached the Cincinnati Reds and the Boston Braves, and in 1960 was named manager of the Giants to replace Bill Rigney. He set the record as major league baseball's oldest rookie manager at the age of 66 years, 2 months, and 18 days. In second when he took over, the Giants finished fifth, and Sheehan did not manage again.

Larry Shepard
Pittsburgh Pirates (NL) 1968–69
Record: 164–155
Ohio native who never played in the major leagues.

A right-handed pitcher, Shepard was a 20-game winner four times in the minors. As a minor league manager he won Western League pennants in both 1956 and 1957 at the helm of the Lincoln Chiefs in the Pirates' organization. He later became a coach with the Philadelphia Phillies, but in 1968 was named Pirates' manager. He guided the club to a fifth-place finish, and the Bucs were in third place the following season when Shepard was replaced by one of his coaches, Alex Grammas.

Both Shepard and Grammas would be named to Sparky Anderson's coaching staff the next year and would enjoy the Big Red Machine era of the 1970s. Shepard was the pitching coach for Cincinnati through 1978, and when Anderson was fired along with his entire coaching staff, Larry moved on to the San Francisco Giants.

Norm Sherry
California Angels (AL) 1976–77
Record: 76–71
Backup catcher for several seasons with the Los Angeles Dodgers.

Only a .215 lifetime hitter, Sherry had the privilege of catching his brother Larry, a Dodgers' pitcher in the early 1960s. Norm later became a coach with the Angels, and managed two incomplete seasons. He then went on to coach several other teams.

Sandy Koufax credited Sherry with helping him improve his control by reducing the power of his fastball.

Bill Shettsline
Philadelphia Phillies (NL) 1898–1902
Record: 367–303
Ticket seller who became a manager and an executive.

Bill Shettsline spent 44 years in baseball, beginning in 1884 when he sold tickets for the Philadelphia Keystones of the Union Association. He later joined the Phillies as an assistant secretary, and was tabbed to replace George Stallings as manager in 1898. He spent five pretty good years at the helm, with a second-place finish in 1901 being his best.

He later became the team's business manager, then club president, and then business manager again.

Burt Shotton
Philadelphia Phillies (NL) 1928–33; Cincinnati Reds (NL) 1934; Brooklyn Dodgers (NL) 1947, 1948–50
Record: 697–764
Outfielder for the St. Louis Browns, Washington Nationals, and St. Louis Cardinals.

Fleet of foot, Shotton played for 14 seasons and stole 293 bases in his career. He also had a good eye at the plate, leading the American League in walks in 1913 with 99 and again in 1916 with 110.

He became a coach and a minor league manager following his playing career, and was hired to manage the Phillies in 1928. In Philadelphia he could manage no better than a fourth-place finish, and he then became a coach with the Reds. When manager Bob O'Farrell was fired, Shotton managed and won one game before the arrival of O'Farrell's replacement, Chuck Dressen.

Shotton next became a scout with the Brooklyn Dodgers. Just before the 1947 season began, Dodgers' manager Leo Durocher was suspended for the season because of association with known gamblers. Owner Branch Rickey called Shotton and convinced him to lead the Dodgers for the year. Shotton refused to wear a uniform, however, manning his position in the dugout in street clothes. The Dodgers won the National League pennant, then lost a seven-game World Series to the New York Yankees.

Durocher returned the following year and Shotton moved to the front office, but when Leo was fired in July, Burt returned to the dugout, where he would stay until 1950. Brooklyn won the pennant again in 1949, and again dropped the Series to the Yankees.

After the 1950 season new Dodgers' ownership replaced Shotton with Chuck Dressen.

Buck Showalter
New York Yankees (AL) 1992–95; Arizona Diamondbacks (NL) 1998–2000; Texas Rangers (AL) 2003–06
Record: 882–833
Good minor league hitter who never made the major leagues.

After his playing career Showalter became a minor league coach at the Class A level, then he quickly became a manager and began to climb swiftly through the Yankees' system. By 1990 he was a coach with the big league club, and two years later he was named the team's skipper. In 1994 his club was in first place when a players' strike ended the season prematurely, and the BBWAA named Buck its American League Manager of the Year. The following year the Yankees earned a wild card berth but were eliminated in the Division Series by the Seattle Mariners.

Conflicts with owner George Steinbrenner predictably led to Showalter's departure like so many before him, and he was then signed to manage the expansion Arizona Diamondbacks two years before the team even took the field. In 1999, only their second year of play, the Diamondbacks won the National League Western Division crown, then were eliminated by the New York Mets in the Division Series.

Fired in 2000, Showalter was hired to manage the Rangers three years later. In 2004, when the Rangers improved from a 71–91 record to go 89–73, the BBWAA once again named Showalter its AL Manager of the Year. He was fired from Texas following the 2006 campaign.

Ken Silvestri
Atlanta Braves (NL) 1967
Record: 0–3
Catcher who played 102 games over eight seasons.

Just a .217 hitter in those games, Silvestri lost several years to World War II and became a coach with several different teams when his playing career was ended. He spent 10 years with the Braves, and his entire managerial career consisted of the final three games of the 1967 season, after Billy Hitchcock had been fired. The Braves lost all three, and Silvestri went back to coaching the next year.

Joe Simmons
Keokuk Westerns (NA) 1875; Wilmington Quicksteps (UA) 1884
Record: 3–28
Outfielder and first baseman who played 58 major league games, all of them in the National Association, over three seasons.

Simmons hit only .221 during that time, and only .170 in 1875 as the player-manager of the Keokuk Westerns. That club played only 13 games and went 1–12, finishing in last place.

By 1884 Simmons was no longer playing, but he did manage the Wilmington Quicksteps of the Union Association. That team played only 18 games and went 2–16, also finishing last.

Lew Simmons
Philadelphia Athletics (AA) 1886
Record: 41–55
Producer of and performer in minstrel shows.

Simmons never played major league baseball; he simply had an interest in the sport and owned the Philadelphia Athletics in 1882, a team he would manage for one partial season in 1886. With the team in sixth place he gave up that idea and then, after owning the A's again in 1887, dropped the baseball enterprise altogether, deciding that a baseball team could not be profitable.

Simmons possessed a great sense of humor and enjoyed drinking immensely. Ironically, he was struck and killed by a beer truck in 1911.

Dick Sisler
Cincinnati Reds (NL) 1964, 1964–65
Record: 121–94
Son of Hall of Fame first baseman George Sisler.

Dick was a first baseman and outfielder who debuted with the St. Louis Cardinals in 1946, and in 1950 became an All-Star with the Philadelphia Phillies when he hit .296. On the final day of the season in Brooklyn he hit a tenth-inning home run to capture the pennant for the Phillies.

Sisler played until 1953 and then went back to the minor leagues as a player and later manager. In 1961 he was named a Reds' coach under Fred Hutchinson. In 1964 Hutchinson revealed the fact that he was battling throat cancer, and when he was admitted to a hospital in July for further treatment Sisler took over the club. Hutchinson returned after six games, but left again in August and Dick took over for good. Hutchinson died shortly thereafter, and Sisler remained the Reds' manager through the 1965 season. In his two years at the helm his clubs finished second and fourth.

George Sisler
St. Louis Browns (AL) 1924–26
Record: 218–241
One of the greatest players of all time.

Much like Babe Ruth, George Sisler started out as a pitcher but was later moved to another position because his bat was simply too valuable and needed to be in the lineup every day. In his case his new position was first base, and he would play for 15 seasons and amass 2812 lifetime hits.

Spending most of those years with the Browns, Sisler hit over .400 twice and won the American League batting title both times. In 1920 he hit .407, and in 1922 batted .420 while also leading the league with 246 hits, 134 runs scored, 18 triples, and 51 stolen bases. During the season he had a 41-game hitting streak, and for his efforts he won the 1922 League Award, an early version of the Most Valuable Player Award.

George was a .340 lifetime batter. He hit over .300 thirteen times in 15 years, and also led the AL twice in hits, once in runs scored, twice in triples, and four times in stolen bases.

From 1924–26 he was player-manager of the Browns, a team that had a winning record only once in those years in spite of Sisler's bat. George was later sold to the Washington Nationals and finished his career with the Boston Braves, where he hit .309 as a player-coach in his final season of 1930. He then played in the minor leagues before going into the printing business in St. Louis and then opening his own sporting goods company.

In the 1940s Branch Rickey hired him as a scout and instructor, first in the Brooklyn Dodgers' system and then in the Pittsburgh Pirates' organization.

Frank Skaff
Detroit Tigers (AL) 1966
Record: 40–39
Played 38 major league games.

Six of those games were in 1935, when Skaff hit .545 with the Brooklyn Dodgers, and the other 32 were in 1943, when he batted .281 for the Philadelphia Athletics for a lifetime batting average of .320.

Skaff eventually became a coach with the Baltimore Orioles, then with the Tigers. In May of 1966 he was named Detroit's interim manager for the second half of the season when, in May, skipper Chuck Dressen suffered his second heart attack in two years, and two months later Dressen's replacement, Bob Swift, was hospitalized with cancer.

The Tigers finished third under Skaff, but he was never hired as manager permanently. He returned as a coach in 1971 and later became a scout for the team.

Bob Skinner
Philadelphia Phillies (NL) 1968–69; San Diego Padres (NL) 1977
Record: 93–123
Three-time All-Star outfielder.

Skinner was a .277 lifetime hitter with some power. In 1958 with the Pittsburgh Pirates he hit .321 with 13 home runs and 70 runs batted in, and in 1962 batted .302 with 20 homers and 75 knocked in.

After retiring Skinner became a minor league manager in the Phillies' system. In 1968 he was the skipper of the San Diego Padres of the Pacific Coast League, the Phils' top farm club, when he was called upon to replace the fired Gene Mauch in Philadelphia. He managed the rest of that season and much of 1969 before resigning in August due to what he cited as a lack of support from the front office in enforcing player discipline.

He then became a coach with the major league San Diego Padres and several other teams. He managed one game for the Padres in 1977 when John McNamara was fired, before the arrival of Alvin Dark.

Joel Skinner
Cleveland Indians (AL) 2002

Record: 35–40
Reserve catcher for nine seasons.

Good defensively, Skinner hit only .228 lifetime and spent only the 1986 season as something of a starter, when he garnered a career-high 315 at-bats. In 2002 he was a coach with the Indians when manager Charlie Manuel was fired, and Skinner took over for the rest of the season.

Jack Slattery
Boston Braves (NL) 1928
Record: 11–20
Coach with Boston College after a brief playing career.

Slattery was a first baseman and catcher who played only 103 major league games spread over four seasons. He hit only .212.

He coached the Braves for two seasons and was the baseball coach of Boston College when he was hired to manage in Boston, but his major league managerial career did not last long. In May, with his team in seventh place after winning only 11 of the first 31 games, Jack resigned and was replaced by Rogers Hornsby.

Bill Smith
Baltimore Marylands (NA) 1873
Record: 0–6
Outfielder, catcher, and second baseman for six major league games.

Smith was player-manager of the Baltimore Marylands, a National Association team that played only six games in its history and lost all of them. Smith himself went 4-for-23 for a lifetime batting average of .174. He also scored two runs and had one run batted in. He and the Marylands both disappeared from the scene after that.

Harry Smith
Boston Doves (NL) 1909
Record: 23–54
British-born, light-hitting catcher.

Smith played his entire career as a reserve and hit only .213. He kept both fans and teammates entertained with practical jokes, however, even victimizing umpires on several occasions.

In 1909 he was player-manager of the Doves, with whom he hit .168 as a player and registered only a .299 winning percentage before surrendering control to Frank Bowerman. He remained with the Doves as a player for one more season before becoming a minor league skipper.

Heinie Smith
New York Giants (NL) 1902
Record: 5–27
Good-fielding second baseman with a weak bat.

Smith was a minor leaguer who had four cups of coffee in the majors before becoming the Giants' regular second baseman in 1902. He was named player-manager when Horace Fogel went 18–23, but in six weeks with Smith at the helm the Giants won only 5 of their next 32 games and Heinie was replaced by John McGraw. He continued to play, but went back mainly to reserve status in 1903 with the Detroit Tigers. That was his last year in the major leagues.

Mayo Smith
Philadelphia Phillies (NL) 1955–58; Cincinnati Reds (NL) 1959; Detroit Tigers (AL) 1967–70
Record: 662–612
Outfielder who spent more than 20 years in the minor leagues and 73 games in the majors.

Smith's entire major league career consisted of the 1945 season, when he played those 73 games with the Philadelphia Athletics and hit .212. He became a minor league manager when his playing career was over, and in 1955 was named manager of the Phillies.

He spent three and a half years at the helm in Philadelphia, then went 35–45 with the Reds in 1959 before being fired and replaced by Fred Hutchinson. He became a scout with the New York Yankees before being hired to skipper the Tigers in 1967, where he finished second, then he guided his team to the American League pennant in 1968 and to a seven-game World Series victory over the St. Louis Cardinals. The AP named Smith its AL Manager of the Year.

The Tigers finished second the following year, then fourth in 1970. Smith was then fired and replaced by Billy Martin.

Jim Snyder
Seattle Mariners (AL) 1988
Record: 45–60
Second baseman who played 41 games in the major leagues and hit .140.

Snyder became a coach following his playing career, and was the first base coach with the Mariners in 1988 when manager Dick Williams was fired after starting the season 23–33. Snyder was named interim skipper for the rest of the year, and the club finished in seventh place.

He later worked in the minor league system of the Chicago White Sox.

Pop Snyder
Cincinnati Red Stockings (AA) 1882–83, 1884; Washington Statesmen (AA) 1891
Record: 163–122
Catcher for 18 major league seasons.

Possessing a strong arm but a weak bat, Charles "Pop" Snyder was appreciated for his work behind the plate but at the same time had more passed balls than any other catcher in the nineteenth century. He began his career in the National Association in 1873 and played for many teams during his 18 seasons. As player-manager of the Red Stockings in 1882 he guided his club to the very first American Association pennant, and Cincinnati then played two games of an unsanctioned World Series—the first one in history—against the National League champion Chicago White Stockings. Each team won one game, and when the AA threatened to oust Cincinnati from the league for playing the series, Snyder and his team gamely decided to play on, but the White Stockings withdrew in order to protect the other club.

Will White took over the Red Stockings in 1884, but two-thirds of the way through the season Snyder was once again given the helm. In 1885 he surrendered the managerial reins but continued to play for Cincinnati for two more years, then moved on and became an umpire in the Players League in 1890. In 1891 he was the second of four managers for the Washington Statesmen, then he began work as a National League and minor league umpire.

Allen Sothoron
St. Louis Browns (AL) 1933
Record: 2–6
Spitball pitcher who went 91–99 over 11 seasons.

Sothoron was a 20-game winner on one occasion—in 1919, when he went 20–12 for the Browns. When the spitball was outlawed after that season, he was one of several pitchers who were allowed to continue using it as long as they played.

He never won more than 13 games in a season again, but he ended the season in a six-way tie for the National League lead with four shutouts in 1924 while playing for the St. Louis Cardinals. He became a coach for the Cardinals after retiring, then a minor league manager and a coach for the Browns.

He managed the Browns for eight games on an interim basis during the 1933 season.

Billy Southworth
St. Louis Cardinals (NL) 1929, 1940–45; Boston Braves (NL) 1946–49, 1950–51
Record: 1044–704
Excellent outfielder and successful manager.

Southworth hit .297 in a 13-year major league career, topping the .300 mark six times. In 1919 with the Pittsburgh Pirates he tied for the league lead with 14 triples, and he stole more than 20 bases three years in a row.

Billy became a minor league manager following his re-

tirement, and in 1928 his Rochester Red Wings, a Cardinals' affiliate, won the International League pennant. The following season the Cardinals sent their manager, Bill McKechnie, to Rochester, and called on Southworth to take over in St. Louis. The major league team did not respond well to Billy's tactics, and in July the two managers were switched again. Southworth promptly won three more consecutive pennants in Rochester, but he and the Cardinals' front office did not get along and he left the organization to coach the New York Giants.

He was rehired to manage the Cards in 1940, and under his leadership St. Louis won consecutive National League pennants from 1942–44. In the World Series they defeated the New York Yankees in 1942, lost to the Yankees in 1943, and defeated the crosstown St. Louis Browns in 1944.

Southworth left in 1945 to become the manager of the Boston Braves. In 1948 he led them to the NL pennant, although they dropped the World Series to the Cleveland Indians. The following year the Braves suffered through some tumultuous clubhouse problems in the wake of their pennant, and in August Southworth was convinced to take a leave of absence. Coach Johnny Cooney managed the rest of the season, then Southworth returned until being fired in June of 1951.

Al Spalding
Chicago White Stockings (NL) 1876–77
Record: 78–47
Most famous for the A. G. Spalding and Brothers sporting goods company.

Spalding was originally an outstanding pitcher. He played amateur ball before the first professional league was formed, and he then continued with a seven-year major league career. He led the National Association in victories every year of its existence, from 1871–75, peaking with a 54–5 record in 1875. He led the Boston Red Stockings to the championship each of the last four years.

In 1876 he became player-manager of the Chicago White Stockings in the new National League, and he led the NL in victories as he went 47–12. He had pretty well worn out his arm by this time, so the next season he pitched only four games and played mostly at first base. As a pitcher he won 252 games in his career and lost only 65. As a hitter he batted over .300 five times. As a manager he led the White Stockings to the first NL pennant in 1876, although the club dropped to fifth the following year.

Spalding stepped down as manager in 1878 and played only one game, instead turning his energies to his sporting goods business. He eventually became the White Stockings' owner, and he served as president from 1882 until 1891. He was inducted into the Hall of Fame in 1939.

Tris Speaker
Cleveland Indians (AL) 1919–26
Record: 617–520
Hall of Fame outfielder who hit .345 lifetime.

Speaker played for 22 seasons, and in addition to leading the American League in many defensive categories year after year, he also led eight times in doubles, once in home runs, and twice in hits. He won the batting title in 1916 with a .386 average and holds the AL record with 792 lifetime doubles. He hit over .300 eighteen times and won the AL's Chalmers Award—an early version of the Most Valuable Player Award—in 1912 when he hit .383 with league-leading totals of 53 doubles and 10 roundtrippers (tying him with Frank "Home Run" Baker). He amassed 3514 hits lifetime.

Speaker began his career with the Boston Red Sox, but was traded to the Indians in 1916 when he objected to a salary cut. He was named player-manager of the Tribe in 1919, and the following year he led the team to the AL pennant and to a World Series victory over the Brooklyn Robins.

Amid rumors of a betting scandal involving Speaker and Ty Cobb, Tris was coerced to resign the helm by baseball Commissioner Kenesaw Mountain Landis. He was cleared early in 1927 and played two more seasons, although he would not manage again.

Speaker was inducted into the Hall of Fame in 1937.

Harry Spence
Indianapolis Hoosiers (NL) 1888
Record: 50–85
Virginia native who managed only one season.

Spence was at the helm of the Hoosiers for that entire season, a situation that was rather unusual for the team in that era. He went 50–85 and had one tie, and his club finished in seventh place. The following year he was replaced by Frank Bancroft.

Chick Stahl
Boston Americans (AL) 1906
Record: 14–26
Outstanding outfielder whose life ended tragically.

Stahl was a lifetime .305 hitter. In a 10-year career he hit over .300 on five occasions, and in 1904 he tied two other players for the American League lead with 19 triples while playing for Boston.

In 1906, when manager Jimmy Collins abruptly left the team to take an unauthorized vacation, Stahl was named player-manager. Collins had gone 35–79, and Stahl

went 14–26 as the Americans finished in last place.

Nevertheless Stahl was named manager for the 1907 season. In Indiana with the team during spring training, Stahl committed suicide by drinking carbolic acid. He had previously told Collins that he simply could not stand the pressure of managing, and he left a note saying that the team drove him to it.

Jake Stahl
Washington Nationals (AL) 1905–06; Boston Red Sox (AL) 1912–13
Record: 263–270
Catcher-turned-first-baseman.

Stahl played in the major leagues for nine years, four of them as a player-manager. He was a good fielder and in 1910 led the American League with 10 home runs.

As player-manager he led the 1912 Red Sox to the AL pennant, then to the World Championship in a four-games-to-three victory over the New York Giants. The following season the team was mired in fifth place and strife filled the clubhouse when, in July, Stahl resigned.

George Stallings
Philadelphia Phillies (NL) 1897–98; Detroit Tigers (AL) 1901; New York Highlanders (AL) 1909–10; Boston Braves (NL) 1913–20
Record: 879–898
Wealthy plantation owner who played seven major league games.

Mainly a catcher, Stallings spread those seven games out over a period spanning 1890 to 1898. He hit only .100 in 20 at-bats.

As a manager he was rather unspectacular except for one incredible season, when his 1914 Braves (often called the "Miracle Braves") went from last place in July to win the National League pennant and then capture an improbable World Championship by defeating the Philadelphia Athletics.

Stallings managed the Braves until 1920 but never enjoyed that level of success again. He later became owner and manager of the Rochester Tribe of the International League.

Eddie Stanky
St. Louis Cardinals (NL) 1952–55; Chicago White Sox (AL) 1966–68; Texas Rangers (AL) 1977
Record: 467–435
Second baseman and three-time All-Star.

Eddie Stanky was good at getting on base. He hit at least .300 twice and led the National League three times in bases on balls and once in runs scored. His 148 walks in 1945 set a since-broken NL record.

He finished his career as player-manager of the Cardinals, and shortly thereafter became a coach with the Cleveland Indians. He later managed the White Sox, then became a college coach.

Stanky returned to the major leagues in 1977 when the Rangers fired manager Frank Lucchesi. He managed one game (a victory), and then resigned because he decided he was homesick.

Joe Start
New York Mutuals (NA) 1873
Record: 18–7

First baseman who played many years as an amateur before professional baseball began.

Start helped the amateur Brooklyn Atlantics to several championships before the formation of the National Association in 1871, then played 16 seasons in the major leagues. He hit over .300 seven times, and in 1878 led the National League with 100 hits.

He was player-manager of the New York Mutuals for part of the 1873 season, a team that finished fifth. He played for them for two more years although he no longer managed. In 1874, when reserves were rare, he once missed a team train to Hartford, and the Mutuals had to face off against the Dark Blues with only eight players.

Start continued to play until 1886 and helped the Providence Grays to two championships along the way.

Casey Stengel
Brooklyn Dodgers (NL) 1934–36; Boston Bees (NL) 1938–40; Boston Braves (NL) 1941–42, 1943; New York Yankees (AL) 1949–60; New York Mets (NL) 1962–65
Record: 1905–1842

Nicknamed for his hometown of Kansas City, Missouri ("KC"), where he was born in 1890.

Stengel spent 54 years in professional baseball. Originally he was a decent outfielder, playing for 14 major league seasons and hitting .284 lifetime. Four times he topped the .300 mark.

It was as a manager that Casey really made his mark, however. He managed the Toledo Mud Hens of the American Association from 1926–31, then became a coach with the Brooklyn Dodgers. In 1934 he replaced Max Carey as Brooklyn skipper, and the rest is the stuff of legend.

Stengel achieved no better than a fifth-place finish in three years with Brooklyn, and in 1938 he took over the Boston Bees, who later returned to their previous name of Braves. The team was consistently bad, and in 1943 Casey missed the first 46 games when he was hit by a taxi and suffered a broken leg. Coach Bob Coleman assumed command on an interim basis.

Fired in January of 1944, Stengel returned to the minor leagues and led the Milwaukee Brewers to first place in the American Association. He later managed the Kansas City Blues, then the Oakland Oaks, who finished first in 1948.

Hired to manage the Yankees in 1949, Stengel proceeded to win five straight American League pennants. In the World Series his Yankees defeated the Dodgers in 1949, the Philadelphia Phillies in 1950, the New York Giants in 1951, and the Dodgers again in 1952 and 1953. Stengel's powerful New York club had taken five straight World Championships.

After finishing second in 1954 the Yankees won four more pennants in a row. In the World Series they lost to the Dodgers in 1955, defeated the Dodgers in 1956, fell to the Milwaukee Braves in 1957, and defeated those same Braves in 1958.

In 1960 the Yankees won the pennant again, but lost the World Series to the Pittsburgh Pirates. In 12 years Stengel had led his club to 10 pennants and 7 World Championships.

The Yankees fired Stengel because they claimed he was getting too old. Casey's remark was, "I'll never make the mistake of being seventy again."

The expansion New York Mets hired Stengel in 1962, and Casey would hold that job until he broke his hip and decided to retire in 1965. He was inducted into the Hall of Fame in 1966, and both the Mets and the Yankees retired his uniform number 37 in 1970.

George Stovall
Cleveland Naps (AL) 1911; St. Louis Browns (AL) 1912–13; Kansas City Packers (FL) 1914–15
Record: 313–376

Fiery first baseman who played for 12 seasons.

A .265 lifetime hitter, Stovall was player-manager of the Naps for most of 1911 and the Browns for two seasons after that. He then became the first big-name player to join the Federal League, and encouraged many others to follow him. For the two years the FL was on the scene, Stovall was player-manager of the Kansas City Packers.

In five years of managing, one third-place showing would be his best.

Harry Stovey
Worcester Ruby Legs (NL) 1881; Philadelphia Athletics (AA) 1885
Record: 63–75

Outstanding first baseman and outfielder for 14 seasons.

Strong and fleet of foot, Stovey consistently slugged home runs in double digits during an era when the longball was decidedly not the norm. He hit .295 lifetime and led his league five times in home runs, once in doubles, four times in triples, once in runs batted in, four times in runs scored, and twice in stolen bases. He hit over .300 five times.

As a player-manager he took over the Ruby Legs from Mike Dorgan during the 1881 season and finished eighth, then piloted the A's to a fourth-place finish in 1885.

Gabby Street
St. Louis Cardinals (NL) 1929, 1930–33; St. Louis Browns (AL) 1938
Record: 365–332
Walter Johnson's regular catcher.

In reality Street was a light hitter and spent only four years with the Washington Nationals, but while he was there he was Johnson's favorite. In 1908 he gained a good deal of notoriety by becoming the second person to catch a ball dropped from the Washington Monument. (The first was Pop Schriver, who did it in 1894.)

After his playing career Street served in World War I and eventually became a coach with the Cardinals. He managed one game in 1929 when skippers Billy Southworth and Bill McKechnie were switching places between St. Louis and Rochester. In 1930 he became the regular manager and proceeded to win two consecutive pennants. His Cardinals lost the 1930 World Series to the Philadelphia Athletics, but defeated those same A's in 1931.

Street was fired in 1933, and he left baseball until 1937, when he became a coach with the Browns and the team's manager the following year. He was let go with the team in seventh place, then he became a minor league manager and later a Cardinals' broadcaster.

Cub Stricker
St. Louis Browns (NL) 1892
Record: 6–17
The second of five managers for the St. Louis Browns in 1892.

Stricker was a second baseman whose career spanned 11 major league seasons. An average batsman, he played for several clubs, but his only opportunity as a skipper was as player-manager of the Browns. He had replaced Jack Glasscock, who lasted only four games, and he went 6–17, then departed for the Baltimore Orioles and was himself replaced by Jack Crooks.

George Strickland
Cleveland Indians (AL) 1964, 1966
Record: 48–63
Second baseman and shortstop for the Pittsburgh Pirates and Cleveland Indians.

After retiring in 1960 Strickland became a coach with the Minnesota Twins, then with the Indians. Just before the 1964 season began, manager Birdie Tebbetts suffered a heart attack, and Strickland took over until the regular skipper returned in July. Late in the 1966 season Tebbetts finally resigned for good, and Strickland finished out that season as well.

Moose Stubing
California Angels (AL) 1988
Record: 0–8
Had five major league at-bats and struck out four times.

Larry "Moose" Stubing was a power hitter in the minor leagues. He had turned down a football scholarship to Penn State in order to sign with the Pittsburgh Pirates' organization for a bonus of $400 and a monthly salary of $175. He was a well-respected slugger in the Texas League, and in 1964 with the El Paso Sun Kings hit .316 with 32 home runs and 120 runs batted in.

After playing for a season in Mexico Stubing retired and went into business, but in 1967 the Angels asked him to become player-manager of the Sun Kings. Stubing accepted, and he eventually won minor league championships in 1976 in the Midwest League, 1977 in the California League, 1978 in the Texas League, and 1984 in the Pacific Coast League.

He became a coach with the Angels in 1985, and in 1988 managed the last eight games of the season when Cookie Rojas was fired. Unfortunately, he lost them all and then went back to coaching.

Clyde Sukeforth
Brooklyn Dodgers (NL) 1947
Record: 2–0
Backup catcher for the Cincinnati Reds and Brooklyn Dodgers.

Sukeforth became a coach with the Dodgers following his retirement. Before the 1947 season began, Brooklyn manager Leo Durocher was suspended for the year for associating with known gamblers, and Clyde took over the club for two games before the arrival of replacement Burt Shotton. The Dodgers would go on to win the pennant.

Sukeforth later spent several years as a coach with the Pittsburgh Pirates.

Billy Sullivan
Chicago White Sox (AL) 1909
Record: 78–74
Catcher with excellent defensive and game-calling skills.

Sullivan excelled in every defensive aspect of the game, but at the plate hit only .213 in 16 seasons. He played most of his career with the White Sox, with whom he became player-manager in 1909 and finished fourth.

He did not manage again, but played until 1912 and then appeared in one game in 1914 and one in 1916, the last with the Detroit Tigers. In 1910 he caught a ball dropped from the Washington Monument, becoming the third person to perform that feat. (The first two were Pop Schriver in 1894 and Gabby Street in 1908.)

Haywood Sullivan
Kansas City Athletics (AL) 1965
Record: 54–82
Catcher who hit only .226 in seven seasons.

Sullivan played sparingly, performing as a regular only during the 1961 season with the A's. In 1965 he became the team's manager and the club finished last. He then resigned and eventually became the general manager of the Boston Red Sox.

In 1978 Sullivan was part of a group that purchased the Red Sox from Tom Yawkey, and he became the team's president.

Pat Sullivan
Columbus Buckeyes (AA) 1890
Record: 2–1
Managed the final three games of the 1890 season for the Columbus Buckeyes.

The Buckeyes had already been through two other managers that year—Al Buckenberger and Gus Schmelz. Under Sullivan the Buckeyes won two of the last three contests, but Schmelz returned as skipper the following season.

Ted Sullivan
St. Louis Browns (AA) 1883; St. Louis Maroons (UA) 1884; Kansas City Unions (UA) 1884; Washington Statesmen (NL) 1888
Record: 132–132
Excellent storyteller credited with coining the term "fan."

How and why Sullivan created the term is open to dispute. Ted himself told several versions of the story. In two of them the word was a shortened form of "fanatic," but in one it seems to have referred to certain people acting like "windbags" of a sort.

At any rate it is generally accepted that Sullivan invented the term in 1883, while he was managing the Browns. In 1884 he moved to the Union Association and had the Maroons in first place through 31 games, having won 28 of them, when he left for Kansas City and took charge of the Unions. In addition to managing he played three games for Kansas City and went 3-for-9 at the plate. He later managed the Washington Statesmen, but his main claim to fame was as a writer of books about baseball stories. His anecdotes were humorous, and only lightly based on true events.

Charlie Sweasy
St. Louis Red Stockings (NA) 1875
Record: 4–15
One of the original 1869 Cincinnati Red Stockings, baseball's first professional team.

Sweasy started out in amateur circles and in 1868 played for the Red Stockings' rivals, the Cincinnati Buckeyes. He was lured to the Stockings by manager Harry Wright, and played mostly at second base for that undefeated squad.

When Cincinnati decided to no longer field a professional team following the 1870 campaign, Sweasy joined the Washington Olympics of the new National Association. In 1873 he joined Wright on the Boston Red Stockings, but was released before the next season because of a disagreement with Wright. The disagreement fit Sweasy's character perfectly, because Charlie was known to be short-tempered and a heavy drinker.

Sweasy was player-manager for the St. Louis Red Stockings in 1875, a club that went 4–15 and finished 37 games behind Wright's Boston club of the same name. The following year he returned to Cincinnati and played for former 1869 teammate Charlie Gould. He retired after the 1878 season.

A hatmaker in the offseason, Sweasy became an oysterman following his playing days.

Bob Swift
Detroit Tigers (AL) 1965, 1966
Record: 56–43
Catcher for 14 seasons.

A light hitter, Swift was adroit at handling pitchers and made his career defensively. He was the catcher when the Chicago White Sox sent midget Eddie Gaedel to the plate as a pinch-hitter in 1951.

Following his retirement Swift became a coach with several teams. He was with the Tigers in 1965 when manager Chuck Dressen suffered a mild heart attack, and he took over as skipper for 42 games. In May of 1966 Dressen suffered another heart attack and Swift again took over, but Bob had cancer and after 57 games had to be hospitalized himself. Frank Skaff took over for him, and Swift died in October.

Chuck Tanner
Chicago White Sox (AL) 1970–75; Oakland Athletics (AL) 1976; Pittsburgh Pirates (NL) 1977–85; Atlanta Braves (NL) 1986–88
Record: 1352–1381

Outfielder who homered on the very first major league pitch thrown to him.

Only the third player to accomplish that feat as a pinch-hitter, Tanner played for eight years for various teams and hit .261 lifetime. He became a minor league manager following his retirement, and was hired to manage the White Sox in 1970. In 1972 his club finished second and the AP named him its American League Manager of the Year.

He managed the A's in 1976, then was traded to the Pittsburgh Pirates for catcher Manny Sanguillen and $100,000. With the Bucs he managed two consecutive second-place finishes before capturing the National League Eastern Division, sweeping the Cincinnati Reds in the playoffs, and defeating the Baltimore Orioles in the World Series.

That would be his only championship, although he remained at the Pittsburgh helm until 1985 and then managed the Braves for just over two years.

El Tappe
Chicago Cubs (NL) 1961, 1961, 1961–62
Record: 46–70
Part of the Cubs' "college of coaches" experiment in 1961 and 1962.

A catcher who hit only .207 lifetime, Elvin Tappe was a coach with Chicago from 1959–65, serving as player-coach in 1960 and 1962. In his stints as manager he finished out the 1961 season and started 1962 with a 4–16 record. The experiment would end later that year, and Tappe would not manage again although he did remain as a coach until 1965.

He then became a scout until 1975, and later worked as a broadcaster with his twin brother Melvin. The two also ran a sporting goods store.

George Taylor
Brooklyn Atlantics (AA) 1884
Record: 40–64
Editor of the *New York Herald* in 1883.

The Brooklyn Atlantics had been formed as a member of the Eastern Association in 1881, and played in the Inter-State League in 1883. Taylor had a hand in raising them to major league status, bringing them into the American Association in 1884, and he himself became the team's manager. After finishing in ninth place, he turned that job over to others.

Zack Taylor
St. Louis Browns (AL) 1946, 1948–51
Record: 235–410
Spent 50 years in baseball.

A catcher for 16 seasons, Taylor played for several teams before retiring and becoming a coach. He was with the Browns in 1946 when skipper Luke Sewell resigned, and he was named interim manager to finish out the season.

Zack became full-time manager in 1948, and was the instrument of several of owner Bill Veeck's rather imaginative promotions. He was the manager who inserted midget Eddie Gaedel into a game as a pinch-hitter in 1951. On another occasion Veeck allowed fans to vote on certain moves during a game, and it was Taylor's responsibility to carry out those decisions.

As a manager Taylor's teams never finished better than sixth place. Zack later became a major league scout.

Birdie Tebbetts
Cincinnati Redlegs (NL) 1954–58; Milwaukee Braves (NL) 1961–62; Cleveland Indians (AL) 1963, 1964–66
Record: 748–705
Four-time All-Star catcher.

Nicknamed "Birdie" because of his high-pitched voice, George Tebbetts played for 14 years with the Detroit Tigers, Boston Red Sox, and Cleveland Indians. Two years following his retirement he was hired to manage the Redlegs, and his best year as a skipper would come with that club in 1956, when Cincinnati finished in third place but was a mere two games behind the pennant-winning Brooklyn Dodgers.

Tebbetts resigned in August of 1958. He became an executive vice president with the Braves, and was named manager of that club in September of 1961. In 1963 he returned to the Indians as their skipper, but just before the next season began he suffered a heart attack and was out until July. Coach George Strickland filled in in his absence. Tebbetts returned and managed until August of 1966, when he resigned for good.

Patsy Tebeau
Cleveland Infants (PL) 1890; Cleveland Spiders (NL) 1891–98; St. Louis Perfectos (NL) 1899; St. Louis Cardinals (NL) 1900
Record: 726–583
Third baseman and first baseman who hit .280 lifetime.

Tebeau spent many of his 13 major league seasons as both a player and a manager. He hit over .300 three times, peaking at .329 in 1893.

As a skipper he made the postseason once, when his Cleveland Spiders finished first in the second half of the split 1892 season. His club faced off against the first-half champion Boston Bostons in a best-of-nine series, and were swept five games to none.

Tebeau remained at the Cleveland helm while the

Robison brothers, who owned both the Spiders and the St. Louis Perfectos, shifted most of the star players to St. Louis. Eventually the Cleveland club was completely absorbed and Patsy went as well, but in August of 1900 he resigned from the team, which had become known as the Cardinals.

In 1918 Tebeau committed suicide by shooting himself with a handgun in St. Louis.

Gene Tenace
Toronto Blue Jays (AL) 1991
Record: 19–14
Catcher and first baseman for 15 major league seasons.

Tenace did not hit for a high average, batting only .241 lifetime. He was good at getting on base, however, twice leading his league in walks and drawing over 100 in a season six times. He hit at least 15 home runs every year from 1973–80. He was named the Most Valuable Player of the 1972 World Series when he became the first player ever to homer in his first two Series at-bats and went on to club four roundtrippers in the Oakland Athletics' seven-game defeat of the Cincinnati Reds. In 1975 he was named an American League All-Star.

Tenace went into coaching after his playing career. He filled in as interim manager for the Blue Jays in 1991 when skipper Cito Gaston was hospitalized with a herniated disk. The Jays were in first place when Gaston left, and Tenace kept them there until Cito's return. Toronto would go on to win its division.

Fred Tenney
Boston Bostons (NL) 1905–06; Boston Doves (NL) 1907;
 Boston Rustlers (NL) 1911
Record: 202–402
First baseman who hit .294 lifetime.

Primarily a first baseman, Tenney played for 17 years and topped the .300 mark seven times. In 1908 he led the National League with 101 runs scored.

He played his first 14 years with Boston, then 2 with the New York Giants before returning to Beantown. He was player-manager from 1905–06, when the club was called the Bostons, and helped with the sale of the team to George and John Dovey, who renamed it the Doves and kept Tenney as manager. Fred was with the Giants in 1908 and 1909, but in 1911 returned to Boston, once again as player-manager. The team was now called the Rustlers, or the Heps, in honor of new owner William Hepburn Russell.

In his four years of managing Tenney finished seventh twice and eighth twice.

Bill Terry
New York Giants (NL) 1932–41
Record: 823–661
Outstanding player who spent his entire career with the New York Giants.

He debuted in 1923, and Terry was player-manager from 1932–36 before turning strictly to managing. A .341 lifetime hitter, he batted over .300 eleven times in 14 seasons, topping out in 1930 by winning the National League batting title with a .401 average. He also led the league with 254 hits, and the next year would top the circuit with 20 triples and tie Chuck Klein with 121 runs scored. He was named to three All-Star teams.

He became player-manager when skipper John McGraw stepped down in June of 1932 due to poor health. As manager Terry would lead the Giants to NL pennants in 1933, 1936, and 1937.

In the World Series Terry's Giants defeated the Washington Nationals in '33 but lost to the New York Yankees in '36 and '37. In 1942 Terry left the dugout to become the Giants' general manager.

He was inducted into the Hall of Fame in 1954, and the Giants retired his uniform number 3 (his player number, since he had actually switched to 30 when he turned solely to managing) in 1985.

Fred Thomas
Indianapolis Hoosiers (NL) 1887
Record: 11–18
Native of Indiana who never played major league baseball.

Thomas was the second of three managers to pilot the Hoosiers in 1887. None of them had much success. Thomas, for his part, went 11–18 for a team that posted a 37–89 record and finished last, 43 games out of first place.

A. M. Thompson
St. Paul Saints (UA) 1884
Record: 2–6
Played 11 games at the major league level.

Andrew Thompson was a catcher who had 41 major league at-bats with the Washington Nationals of the National Association in 1875 and hit .098. He then delved into minor league ball.

In 1884 Thompson was the manager of the St. Paul Apostles of the minor Northwestern League. That league was in its first season, but it collapsed in September with only four teams remaining. The Union Association, a major league, was rapidly losing franchises as well. When the UA's Pittsburgh Stogies folded, the Apostles were admitted to take their place and renamed the Saints. The club played nine games in the UA—winning two, losing six, and tying one—before the season ended and the entire league fell apart.

Jack Tighe
Detroit Tigers (AL) 1957–58
Record: 99–104
Spent 52 years in organized baseball.

A minor league catcher, Tighe became player-manager of the Michigan State League's Muskegon Reds in 1940. He eventually worked as a coach for the Tigers, and was named manager in 1957. His club finished fourth that season and was in fifth the next when Tighe was fired and replaced by Bill Norman.

He went back to work in the minor leagues, and in 1968 *The Sporting News* named him the Minor League Manager of the Year when his Toledo Mud Hens captured the International League championship.

He continued to work for the Tigers in various capacities until 1990.

Joe Tinker
Cincinnati Reds (NL) 1913; Chicago Chifeds (FL) 1914; Chicago Whales (FL) 1915; Chicago Cubs (NL) 1916
Record: 304–308
Of "Tinker to Evers to Chance" double play fame in the Franklin P. Adams poem "Baseball's Sad Lexicon" from 1910.

Tinker was the shortstop in that combination, and led the National League many times in many fielding categories. He and his teammates made an art of infield defense, and all three of them would eventually manage the Cubs. In 1905 he got into an argument with Johnny Evers over a taxi ride, and Evers did not speak to him again until 1938. In 1910 Joe became the first player to steal home twice in the same game.

Tinker was noted for salary disputes, and the Cubs traded him to Cincinnati following the 1912 season. He became player-manager of the Reds in 1913 and had his best season at the plate when he hit .317, the only time he would top the .300 mark. The Reds finished seventh and, tired of his salary complaints, sold him to the Brooklyn Dodgers. But Tinker jumped to the Federal League instead and became player-manager of the Chifeds, who finished second and then renamed themselves the Whales in 1915, when they won the FL pennant. He returned to the Cubs as player-manager for his final season of 1916.

Tinker later became president of the Columbus Senators of the minor American Association, and then owner of the Orlando Tigers of the Florida State League in 1921. He returned to the Cubs' organization as a scout.

Tinker was inducted into the Hall of Fame in 1946, and he died from complications related to diabetes on his sixty-eighth birthday, in 1948.

Jeff Torborg
Cleveland Indians (AL) 1977–79; Chicago White Sox (AL) 1989–91; New York Mets (NL) 1992–93; Montreal Expos (NL) 2001; Florida Marlins (NL) 2002–03
Record: 635–717
Catcher for 10 years who became a longtime coach and manager.

Torborg hit only .214 lifetime, and most of his major league career was spent as a backup. He nevertheless caught three no-hitters, one of them Sandy Koufax's perfect game in 1965.

Torborg replaced Frank Robinson as manager of the Indians in 1977. In July of 1979 he announced that he intended to resign at the end of the season, but the Tribe beat him to the punch and fired him before the end of the month. With the White Sox he managed two consecutive second-place finishes, and as a result of the first of those, in 1990, the AP named him Manager of the Year and the BBWAA named him American League Manager of the Year.

After managing the Mets and Expos, Torborg found himself at the helm of the Marlins. He was fired in 2003 after starting out 17–22, and Jack McKeon then took the club to the World Championship.

Joe Torre
New York Mets (NL) 1977–81; Atlanta Braves (NL) 1982–84; St. Louis Cardinals (NL) 1990–95; New York Yankees (AL) 1996–98, 1999–
Record: 1952–1687
Fast on his way to becoming one of the winningest managers of all time.

A consistent and versatile player, Torre excelled at several positions. He started his career as a catcher, where he won a Gold Glove in 1965, then gradually began to shift back and forth between first and third base. In 1971 he was named the National League's Most Valuable Player when he won the batting title with a .363 average and also led the league with 230 hits and 137 runs batted in while clubbing 24 home runs. A nine-time All-Star, he hit over .300 five times, slugged at least 20 homers six times, and topped the 100-RBI mark on five occasions.

Torre was named player-manager of the Mets in 1977, but stepped down as a player after only 18 games and turned strictly to managing. His first taste of success as a skipper did not come until 1982 with the Braves, when his club won the NL Western Division before being swept by the Cardinals in the playoffs.

It was with the Yankees that he would make his real mark, however. Named skipper by George Steinbrenner in 1996, Torre would finish in first place 10 times through the 2006 season, 9 of them consecutively. Those 10 first-place finishes netted 6 American League pennants and 4 World Championships.

In spring training of 1999 Torre learned that he had prostate cancer, and he turned the team over to coach Don Zimmer while he underwent treatment. He returned to the club in May and eventually guided the Yankees to the second of what would be three consecutive World Championships.

Torre was named NL Manager of the Year by the AP in 1982, when his Braves won the West. In 1996 he was named co-winner of the AL award by the BBWAA along with Johnny Oates when he guided the Yankees to the World Championship for the first time. In 1998 the BBWAA once again named him AL Manager of the Year and the AP named him Manager of the Year when he won his second Series with New York.

Carlos Tosca
Toronto Blue Jays (AL) 2002–04
Record: 191–191
Eighteen-year minor league manager.

Tosca won Gulf Coast League championships in both 1982 and 1985 with the Gulf Coast Yankees. Over the years his clubs made the playoffs seven times, and he won Manager of the Year Awards in 1985 with the Yankees and in 1996 with the Portland Sea Dogs.

Tosca was a coach with the Arizona Diamondbacks from 1998–2000, then managed the Richmond Braves before becoming a coach with the Blue Jays. He was named Toronto skipper in 2002. He finished third twice, and his club was 47–64 in 2004 when he was fired. He then returned to Arizona as a coach.

Dick Tracewski
Detroit Tigers (AL) 1979
Record: 2–0
Infielder who hit only .213.

Tracewski had a weak bat but an excellent glove, and it was his defense that kept him around for eight seasons with the Los Angeles Dodgers and the Detroit Tigers. After retiring he eventually returned to the Tigers as a longtime coach. In 1979 he was on the staff when Les Moss was fired, and he filled in for two games and won them both before the arrival of Moss's replacement, Sparky Anderson. He then continued to serve under Anderson.

Jim Tracy
Los Angeles Dodgers (NL) 2001–05; Pittsburgh Pirates (NL) 2006–
Record: 494–478
Outfielder who played only 87 major league games in two seasons.

Tracy spent many years in organized baseball, many of them as a minor league manager. In 1993 he was named Eastern League Manager of the Year by *The Sporting News* when he guided the Harrisburg Senators to the championship. He later coached for the Montreal Expos, and also served as a Dodgers' coach under Davey Johnson.

Tracy was named the Dodgers' skipper in 2001. In 2004 his club won the National League Western Division title, but was knocked out of contention in the first round of playoffs. He was fired following the 2005 season and was then hired to manage the Pirates.

Alan Trammell
Detroit Tigers (AL) 2003–05
Record: 186–300
Twenty-year major league shortstop.

Trammell spent all 20 years with the Tigers, and along with second baseman Lou Whitaker spent 19 of them forming the longest-lasting up-the-middle defensive combination in major league history. Trammell hit .285 lifetime while winning four Gold Gloves and being named to six All-Star teams. He hit at least .300 seven times.

In 2003 he became the Tigers' manager, but he had a disastrous season, winning only 43 games while losing 119. The Tigers maintained their faith in him, and the following year the team improved its record to 72–90. After going 71–91 in 2005, however, Trammell was fired and replaced by Jim Leyland.

Pie Traynor
Pittsburgh Pirates (NL) 1934–39
Record: 457–406
Hall of Fame third baseman who spent his entire 17-year playing career with the Pirates.

Harold Joseph Traynor likely received his nickname due to his fondness for pies when he was a child. As a major league baseball player he hit over .300 ten times, tied teammate Max Carey for the National League lead in 1923 with 19 triples, and was named to two All-Star teams. He batted .320 lifetime.

Named player-manager in 1934, he reduced his playing time and eventually turned solely to managing. His best finish would be in 1938, when the Bucs came in second. Following the 1939 season he became a scout in the Pittsburgh system, a position he held for many years.

Traynor was inducted into the Hall of Fame in 1948. He passed away in Pittsburgh in 1972, and the Pirates retired his number 20 later that year.

Tom Trebelhorn
Milwaukee Brewers (AL) 1986–91; Chicago Cubs (NL) 1994
Record: 471–461
Minor league catcher who became a coach and manager.

A schoolteacher in the offseason, Trebelhorn became the Brewers' skipper during the 1986 season when George Bamberger was fired. The following season his club won its first 13 games in a row, but shortly thereafter would go on a 12-game losing streak. His best finish would be third place, and he was fired following the 1991 campaign.

He then managed the Cubs during the strike-shortened season of 1994. He later coached for the Baltimore Orioles.

Sam Trott
Washington Statesmen (AA) 1891
Record: 4–7
Catcher who played from 1880–88 with several teams.

Trott was the first of four managers for the 1891 Washington Statesmen. He lasted only 12 games, one of which ended in a tie, and he was replaced with the team in sixth place. The club would eventually finish ninth and last.

Ted Turner
Atlanta Braves (NL) 1977
Record: 0–1
Controversial owner of the Atlanta Braves and a vast media empire.

Born in Cincinnati, Ted Turner took over his father's billboard business at the age of 24 when his father committed suicide, and from that he would build an impressive fortune. He eventually became owner of the Cable News Network (CNN), Turner Network Television (TNT), the Turner Broadcasting System (TBS), Metro-Goldwyn-Mayer (MGM), and many other properties, not to mention the Braves, the National Basketball Association's Atlanta Hawks, and the National Hockey League's Atlanta Thrashers. Once married to actress Jane Fonda, he has also had a penchant for making controversial and inflammatory statements, garnering for himself the nickname "The Mouth of the South."

He took a rather active role as owner of the Braves. In 1977, that activity reached a new height. When the club started the season 8–21 under manager Dave Bristol, Turner forced the skipper to take a 10-day paid leave of absence and inserted himself as interim manager. National League President Chub Feeney nixed Turner's plans after

one game, a game the Braves lost, creating a rule that prohibited managers from having a financial interest in their teams. Turner spoke out publicly against Feeney, but named coach Vern Benson manager for the next game and then brought Bristol back.

In 1996 Turner Broadcasting merged with Time Warner, and Ted became vice chairman and head of the cable networks division. In 2001 Time Warner merged with America Online (AOL), and two years later Turner resigned as vice chairman. The Braves renamed the former 1996 Olympic Stadium in his honor as Turner Field.

Bob Unglaub
Boston Red Sox (AL) 1907
Record: 9–20
The third of four managers for the 1907 Red Sox.

Unglaub hit only .258 in a six-year major league career, which was spent with three teams. A third baseman and later first baseman, he was hospitalized with blood poisoning during the 1904 season, and in 1905 recorded 31 putouts in a 20-inning game.

The 1907 Red Sox replaced skipper Cy Young with George Huff after only six games. Huff went 2–6 before being ousted for Unglaub, who took over as player-manager. Unglaub went only 9–20, however, and was replaced by Deacon McGuire.

Bobby Valentine
Texas Rangers (AL) 1985–92; New York Mets (NL) 1996–2002
Record: 1117–1072
Played many positions, in both the infield and the outfield, during a 10-year major league career.

A versatile player, Valentine spent his career with several teams and then went into coaching following his retirement. In 1985 he was hired to manage the Rangers, and a second-place showing in 1986 would be his best in Texas. In 1995 he went to Japan to manage the Pacific League's Chiba Lotte Marines, but was fired after a second-place finish because he did not get along with the club's general manager, Tatsuro Hirooka.

He returned to manage the Mets in 1996, and from 1998–2000 managed three second-place showings. He gained some notoriety in 1999 when he was ejected from a game and then returned to the dugout wearing a Groucho Marx disguise.

That 1999 club finished in a tie with the Cincinnati Reds for the wild card, and defeated Cincinnati in a one-game playoff to advance to the postseason. The Mets went on to defeat the Arizona Diamondbacks in the National League Division Series, but lost the pennant to the Atlanta Braves. The following year the Mets again won the wild card, and this time defeated the San Francisco Giants in the NLDS and the St. Louis Cardinals for the pennant. They then lost the World Series to the crosstown Yankees.

Following the 2002 season Valentine returned to Japan to take over the Marines once again. In 2005 he led them to the Pacific League championship.

George Van Haltren
Baltimore Orioles (NL) 1892
Record: 1–10
Started out as a pitcher but became an excellent outfielder.

Van Haltren went 40–31 on the mound lifetime, but in his rookie season of 1887 he once walked 16 batters in a game. Fleet of foot, he excelled in the outfield and at the plate, hitting over .300 twelve times in 17 seasons and batting .317 lifetime. In 1896 he tied for the National League lead with 21 triples, and in 1900 tied with 45 stolen bases. He swiped 583 bases lifetime.

In 1892 with the Orioles he started the season as player-manager, but after losing 10 of the first 11 games he was replaced by John Waltz. The team went on to finish in last place.

Gary Varsho
Philadelphia Phillies (NL) 2004
Record: 1–1
Outstanding pinch-hitter who played eight seasons.

Varsho debuted with the Chicago Cubs in July of 1988 and ended up leading the National League with a .393 pinch-hitting average. Although he hit only .244 lifetime with four different teams, he frequently led his club in pinch-hits.

In 1997 Varsho became a minor league manager, and in 2000 was named Eastern League Manager of the Year with the Reading Phillies. In 2001 he led Reading to a division championship and to an EL co-championship with the New Britain Rock Cats. (The championship series was scheduled to begin on September 11 but was canceled due to the terrorist attacks on the United States.) In both 2000 and 2001 *Baseball America* named Varsho the EL's Best Managing Prospect.

In 2002 Gary was promoted to Philadelphia as a coach. At the end of the 2004 season, when skipper Larry Bowa was fired with two games left to go, Varsho took over and went 1–1.

Mickey Vernon
Washington Senators (AL) 1961–63
Record: 135–227
Seven-time All-Star first baseman.

Mickey Vernon played in four different decades; his 20 major league seasons spanned 1939–1960, most of

which were spent with the Washington Nationals. He lost 1944 and '45 to World War II, but he returned in 1946 and won the American League batting title with a .353 average. He also led the league with 51 doubles and hit for the cycle in a game against the Chicago White Sox.

He won another batting crown in 1953 when he hit .337, and he led the league that season with 43 doubles and also the next with 33.

In 1961 Vernon was named manager of the expansion Washington Senators. The club predictably lost 100 and 101 games its first two seasons, respectively, and Mickey was fired during the 1963 campaign when the team started out 14–26. He also coached for several teams.

Bill Virdon
Pittsburgh Pirates (NL) 1972–73; New York Yankees (AL) 1974–75; Houston Astros (NL) 1975–82; Montreal Expos (NL) 1983–84
Record: 995–921
Solid, consistent outfielder for the St. Louis Cardinals and Pittsburgh Pirates.

Virdon debuted with St. Louis in 1955 and was named the National League Rookie of the Year on the strength of a .281 batting average, 17 home runs, and 68 runs batted in. He would never match those power numbers again, and he was hitting .211 in 1956 when the Cards traded him to the Pirates. He ended the season at .319, the only time he would top the .300 mark in a full season.

Virdon became a coach with the Pirates following his playing career, and he was named manager when Danny Murtaugh resigned due to health reasons. In 1972 he guided his club to the NL Eastern Division title, but they fell to the Cincinnati Reds in the NL Championship Series.

Bill was fired in September of 1973, and Murtaugh returned to take over. Virdon then managed the Yankees for a season and a half before being hired by the Astros. He led the 1980 Houston squad to a division title, but lost the NLCS to the Philadelphia Phillies. The AP named Virdon its NL Manager of the Year.

In the split season of 1981 Virdon's team finished first in the second half, then lost the divisional playoff to the Los Angeles Dodgers.

Virdon was fired in August of 1982, then briefly managed the Expos. He also coached in three more stints for the Pirates and in one for the Astros.

Ossie Vitt
Cleveland Indians (AL) 1938–40
Record: 262–198
Light-hitting outfielder-turned-infielder.

Once knocked unconscious when he was hit in the

head by a Walter Johnson fastball, Vitt lasted 10 major league seasons but never hit over .254. He averaged .238 lifetime.

He continued to play in the minors after his major league career, and eventually became a successful minor league skipper. In 1938 he was hired to manage the Indians. After leading the Tribe to third-place finishes the first two seasons, Vitt began to experience resistance from some of his players who disagreed with his tactics. The players went so far as to petition owner Alva Bradley for Vitt's dismissal, causing the public to jeer the players and cheer the manager. Bradley stuck with Vitt and the Indians finished the season in second place, a single game behind the Detroit Tigers. Nevertheless Bradley gave in and finally fired Ossie in November.

Chris Von der Ahe
St. Louis Browns (NL) 1895, 1896, 1897
Record: 3–14
German immigrant and entrepreneur.

Von der Ahe came to the United States as a teenager in 1867. He moved from New York to St. Louis shortly after his arrival and began to work in a grocery store. He eventually bought the store and opened a saloon in the back. When he noticed that many of his saloon patrons were on their way home from the ballpark, he bought the St. Louis American Association baseball franchise and eventually made a fortune.

His club was powerful as a member of the AA, but when the league folded he brought the team into the National League and it quickly began to falter. As a result he started to lose money. He moved the club to a larger ballpark, which he made part of an amusement park, but financial losses continued to plague him.

Von der Ahe went through a bevy of managers, and on three occasions he filled in himself—for 1 game in 1895, 2 in 1896, and 14 in 1897. He won only 3 of those 17 games at the helm.

He finally began to sell off most of his best players in an attempt to recoup some of his losses. He eventually lost the team, and was even kidnapped at one point because of his debts. He was divorced twice, and part of his ballpark burned down.

Von der Ahe lost his fortune and eventually ended up as a bartender. He died in 1913 of cirrhosis of the liver.

John Vukovich
Chicago Cubs (NL) 1986; Philadelphia Phillies (NL) 1988
Record: 6–5
Third baseman for 10 seasons who hit only .161.

Vukovich spent 7 of those 10 years with the Phillies. Mainly a utilityman, he never played more than 74 games

in a season and only twice reached the .200 mark in batting.

After retiring he became a coach with the Cubs, and he filled in as manager for one day when Jim Frey was fired. The Cubbies played a doubleheader that day and split it, then Gene Michael arrived to take over.

As a longtime coach with the Phillies he skippered the final nine games of the 1988 season when Lee Elia was fired and went 5–4. He then returned to coaching. In 2001 he had surgery to remove a brain tumor that had been discovered during spring training, but he died in 2007.

Heinie Wagner
Boston Red Sox (AL) 1930
Record: 52–102
Infielder who played 12 seasons, 11 of them with the Red Sox.

Not a particularly strong hitter, Wagner was a competent shortstop who could also play second and third base. At the conclusion of his playing career he had two stints as a coach with Boston, actually serving as a player-coach in 1916 and 1918. When manager Bill Carrigan resigned following the 1929 season after three consecutive last-place finishes, Wagner was named his replacement. But the team lost 102 games under Heinie in 1930 and finished last again, and he was let go.

Honus Wagner
Pittsburgh Pirates (NL) 1917
Record: 1–4
Hall of Fame shortstop who created a legendary career over 21 seasons.

One of the greatest players of all time, Wagner started his career with the Louisville Colonels but spent most of it with the Pittsburgh Pirates. He hit .328 lifetime and won eight batting titles, four of them consecutively. Nicknamed "The Flying Dutchman" because of his heritage and his speed, he led the National League five times in steals, as well as five times in runs batted in, seven times in doubles, three times in triples, twice in hits, and twice in runs scored.

On June 9, 1914, he became only the second player in history to reach 3000 hits (Cap Anson was the first) when he doubled off Erskine Mayer of the Philadelphia Phillies in the ninth inning of a game at the Baker Bowl. He would eventually retire with 3420 knocks.

Wagner's final year was 1917, and after the first 61 games of the season he was named player-manager to replace Nixey Callahan. He managed only five games, winning one and losing four, before determining that he did not like the job and stepping down. He was replaced by Hugo Bezdek. He soon left the Pirates and became a semipro player for the next seven years.

He returned to coach the Pirates from 1933–51, and in 1936 became one of the first five inductees in the Hall of Fame. The Pirates retired his uniform number 33 in 1956, a year after his death.

Harry Walker
St. Louis Cardinals (NL) 1955; Pittsburgh Pirates (NL) 1965–67; Houston Astros (NL) 1968–72
Record: 630–604
Excellent outfielder and two-time All-Star.

Walker played for 11 seasons, losing two years to World War II. He hit .296 lifetime, topping the .300 mark on six occasions. After spending his first five years with the Cardinals, he was traded in 1947 after only 10 games; he was batting .200. With the Phillies he went on to hit .371, winning the National League batting title with an overall average of .363, and led the circuit with 16 triples. It was the second time he was named to the All-Star team.

As a manager he posted a couple of third-place finishes, as well as a lifetime .511 winning percentage.

Bobby Wallace
St. Louis Browns (AL) 1911–12; Cincinnati Reds (NL) 1937
Record: 62–154
Spent 25 seasons as a major league player.

Wallace started his career as a pitcher, but then tried the outfield and third base before settling in at shortstop for many years. One of his best seasons was 1897, when he hit a career-high .335 for the Cleveland Spiders with 112 runs batted in. In 1899 he hit .295 with 108 RBIs for the St. Louis Perfectos, and in 1901 batted .324 for St. Louis, who had become the Cardinals. In 1902 he set a record with 17 chances at shortstop in a nine-inning game.

He was player-manager of the Browns in 1911 and part of 1912, but the team did poorly. He turned to umpiring in mid-1915, but late in the 1916 season he returned to the Browns. Wallace retired in 1918, then became a minor league manager.

He eventually became a coach and a longtime scout with the Reds. In 1937, when manager Chuck Dressen was fired, Wallace took over as skipper for the rest of the season, but posted a mere 5–20 record for a team that finished in last place. He refused to wear a uniform, managing in street clothes. After that season he returned to scouting.

Wallace was inducted into the Hall of Fame in 1953.

Ed Walsh
Chicago White Sox (AL) 1924
Record: 1–2
Coal miner who became a Hall of Fame pitcher.

Walsh played in the era of the spitball, and he mastered the pitch as few others did. At least a 24-game winner on four occasions, he peaked in 1908 with an American League-leading 40 victories, going 40–15 with a 1.42 earned run average. Spending all but one of his 14 seasons with the White Sox, Walsh also led the league twice in ERA, twice in strikeouts, five times in games pitched, three times in starts, twice in complete games, three times in shutouts, and four times in innings pitched. In 1905 he threw a five-inning no-hitter against the New York Highlanders, and in 1911 completed a nine-inning no-no against the Boston Red Sox. His lifetime ERA was 1.82.

Walsh went into coaching after his retirement, and also briefly tried umpiring. As a coach with the White Sox in 1924 he managed three games in a rather confusing morass of skippers. Frank Chance had been hired from Boston to manage the club, but died in September of the previous year. Johnny Evers stepped in on an interim basis and managed the first 21 games. Walsh then managed 3, and Eddie Collins piloted 27 before Evers took over again and finished out the season. Chicago ended up in last place.

Walsh was inducted into the Hall of Fame in 1946.

Mike Walsh
Louisville Eclipse (AA) 1884
Record: 68–40
Native of Ireland who never played major league baseball.

Walsh managed only one season, piloting a team that was named for a racehorse. The Eclipse had finished third and fifth the previous two seasons; despite another third-place finish in 1884, Walsh was replaced by Jim Hart in 1885 and the team was renamed the Colonels.

Bucky Walters
Cincinnati Reds (NL) 1948–49
Record: 81–123
Six-time All-Star pitcher.

Originally a third baseman, Walters started his conversion to pitcher in 1935, and by 1937 was a National League All-Star. Spending the greater part of his career with the Reds, Bucky led the league three times in victories, twice in earned run average, once in strikeouts, twice in starts, three times in complete games, and three times in innings pitched. In 1939 he won the pitching Triple Crown when he went 27–11 with a 2.29 ERA and tied Claude Passeau with 137 strikeouts. He was named the NL's Most Valuable Player, and he would help the Reds to the pennant and the following year to the World Championship.

Walters retired in 1948 and was named Reds' manager later that same year. The club finished seventh, and was seventh again with three games to go in the 1949 season when Bucky was fired and replaced by Luke Sewell. He then coached the Boston/Milwaukee Braves, also pitching one game for them in 1950, and later the New York Giants.

John Waltz
Baltimore Orioles (NL) 1892
Record: 2–6
Briefly managed a very bad team.

When the 1892 Orioles started out 1–10 under player-manager George Van Haltren, the O's consigned their skipper to the playing field exclusively and replaced him in the dugout with John Waltz. Waltz fared little better, going 2–6 before being replaced himself by Ned Hanlon.

The Orioles finished the season 46–101, in twelfth and last place.

Monte Ward
Providence Grays (NL) 1880; New York Gothams (NL) 1884; Brooklyn Wonders (PL) 1890; Brooklyn Bridegrooms (NL) 1891–92; New York Giants (NL) 1893–94
Record: 412–320
Pitcher, outfielder, shortstop, and second baseman.

John Montgomery Ward began his career in 1878 on the mound for the Providence Grays. He won 22 games his first season and led the National League with a 1.51 earned run average. The following year he topped the circuit with 47 victories and 239 strikeouts, and he won 39 games in 1880, his first year as player-manager. He also led the NL with eight shutouts and pitched a perfect game, only the second in major league history. In 1882 he pitched a complete-game 18-inning shutout, the longest by one pitcher in major league history.

As a hitter Ward batted .278 lifetime. He topped the league with 111 stolen bases in 1887 and with 88 in 1892, swiping 540 lifetime.

A natural leader, Ward fiercely opposed baseball's reserve clause, a rule that bound a player to one team for life. He formed the Players League in 1890 and was player-manager of the Brooklyn Wonders, but when that league collapsed after the season he returned to the NL. As a skipper he managed several second-place finishes but never won a pennant.

In 1911 he became a part-owner of the Boston Braves, and in 1914 he once again rebelled against the establishment when he became the business manager of the Federal League's Brooklyn Tip-Tops.

Ward was inducted into the Hall of Fame by the Veterans Committee in 1964.

Ron Washington
Texas Rangers (AL) 2007–
Record: 0–0
Major league shortstop for 10 seasons.

Washington played for five different clubs, mainly in a utility role, and hit .261 overall. He had played for nine minor league teams before sticking in the majors, one of them in Mexico. In 1988 with the Cleveland Indians he broke up a no-hitter that was being pitched by Odell Jones of the Milwaukee Brewers with one out in the ninth inning. Washington finished his professional career in the minors in 1990.

In 1991 he began coaching in the New York Mets' system, and spent a short time as a skipper before returning to a coaching role. In 1996 he became a longtime coach at the major league level for the Athletics, and in 2007 replaced Buck Showalter at the helm of the Rangers.

John Wathan
Kansas City Royals (AL) 1987–91; California Angels (AL) 1992
Record: 326–320
Catcher for the Royals for 10 years.

Playing mainly as a backup, Wathan also used his versatility to play some outfield and first base. He hit over .300 three times and, surprisingly for a catcher, had considerable speed. He swiped 36 bases in 1982 and another 28 the following year.

After retiring in 1985 Wathan briefly became a minor league manager, and was named Royals' skipper in August of 1987 when Billy Gardner was fired. He stayed until early 1991, then became a coach with the Angels. In May of 1992 he was named interim skipper in California when the team bus was involved in an accident, injuring several players and manager Buck Rodgers, who was hospitalized. Wathan managed 89 games before Rodgers returned.

Wathan later became a coach with the Boston Red Sox and a broadcaster before returning to the Royals to work in their minor league system.

Bill Watkins
Indianapolis Hoosiers (AA) 1884; Detroit Wolverines (NL) 1885–88; Kansas City Cowboys (AA) 1888–89; St. Louis Browns (NL) 1893; Pittsburgh Pirates (NL) 1898–99
Record: 452–444
Played only 34 major league games as a player-manager.

Those games came in 1884 with the Indianapolis Hoosiers, with whom Watkins hit .205 while playing second base, shortstop, and third base. He then turned strictly to managing with several teams.

In 1887 Watkins' Detroit Wolverines won the National League pennant, then engaged in a 15-game World Series against the American Association champion St. Louis Browns. All 15 games were to be played regardless of who clinched first, and the Wolverines took the Series, 10 games to 5.

Harvey Watkins
New York Giants (NL) 1895
Record: 18–17
Last of three managers for the 1895 Giants.

Watkins never played major league baseball. In 1895 the Giants started the season 16–17 under player-manager George Davis, who was replaced by player-manager Jack Doyle. Under Doyle they went 32–31, then Watkins came in and went 18–17. That all adds up to a not-so-bad 66–65 record, but that was good only for ninth place, and Watkins did not manage again.

Earl Weaver
Baltimore Orioles (AL) 1968–82, 1985–86
Record: 1480–1060
One of the only two managers in the Hall of Fame who never played a major league game.

Joe McCarthy is the other. A minor league infielder, Weaver became a minor league skipper following his playing days and in 1968 was named an Orioles' coach. He was elevated to manager about halfway through the season, and he would begin his Hall of Fame career by guiding his club to the American League pennant for the next three years in a row.

The Orioles lost the 1969 World Series to New York's "Miracle Mets," defeated the Cincinnati Reds in 1970, and fell to the Pittsburgh Pirates in 1971.

In 1973 the O's won their division again but lost the AL Championship Series. The AP named Earl its AL Manager of the Year for the first of three times. Another division title followed, with another ALCS loss.

Three straight second-place finishes would follow, but in the third of those years, 1977, the AP again selected Weaver as its AL Manager of the Year. The third nod would come two years later, when the club won 102 games, took the AL pennant, and then lost the World Series once again to the Pirates.

Notorious for his battles with umpires, Weaver was thrown out of an estimated 91 games and was suspended four times. He was once thrown out of both games of a doubleheader.

Earl retired in 1982, and the Orioles retired his uniform number 4 that year. He came back to Baltimore to manage again at the end of the 1985 season and for all of 1986, then he retired for good. He was inducted into the Hall of Fame in 1996.

Eric Wedge
Cleveland Indians (AL) 2003–
Record: 319–329
Played only 39 major league games.

Most of Wedge's appearances at the big league level were as a designated hitter. After retiring as a player he enjoyed a very successful minor league managerial career. In 1999 he was named Carolina League Manager of the Year when his Kinston Indians made the playoffs. Two years later he guided the Buffalo Bisons to a 91–51 record and was named International League Manager of the Year and *Baseball America* Triple A Manager of the Year. In 2002 he took the Bisons to the IL finals and was named Manager of the Year by *The Sporting News*.

In 2003 he was promoted to Cleveland to replace Joel Skinner.

Wes Westrum
New York Mets (NL) 1965–67; San Francisco Giants (NL) 1974–75
Record: 260–366
Catcher named to two All-Star teams despite hitting just .217 lifetime.

As a minor leaguer in 1949 Westrum set a record in the International League by hitting five grand slams. Amazingly, he accomplished that feat in just 51 games. As a major leaguer he rarely topped the .230 mark in batting average, although he slugged 23 home runs in 1950 and another 20 the following year. He was named an All-Star the next two seasons despite batting averages of .220 and .224 and home run totals of 14 and 12.

Westrum was hired as a Giants' coach in 1958, but in 1963 he was involved in the only trade of coaches in major league history when he was swapped to the Mets for Cookie Lavagetto. He took over the club when Casey Stengel broke his hip in 1965, and would later return to the Giants as a coach and then manager. A third-place finish in 1975 would be his best by far, and he resigned following that season.

Harry Wheeler
Kansas City Unions (UA) 1884
Record: 0–4
Played six seasons for nine different teams.

An outfielder who also pitched 14 games during his career, Wheeler hit a mere .228 while bouncing from team to team. His final season was 1884, when he played for four clubs. After starting out playing for the St. Louis Browns of the American Association that year, he jumped to the Union Association and was player-manager of the Kansas City entry for the first four games of their season. The club lost all four contests and he was replaced as skipper by Matt Porter, but he continued to play. After 14 games he went to the Chicago Browns, then to the Baltimore Unions to finish out the season.

Deacon White
Cleveland Forest Citys (NA) 1872; Cincinnati Reds (NL) 1879
Record: 9–11
First batter in major league history.

White also collected the first hit in major league history, because that first at-bat resulted in a double off pitcher Bobby Mathews of the Fort Wayne Kekiongas. The date was May 4, 1871, and in the National Association opener White's Cleveland Forest Citys would go on to lose to the Kekiongas, 2–0.

An actual deacon, James Laurie White served as player-manager of the Forest Citys for two games in 1872, and lost both. In 1873 he joined Harry Wright with the Boston Red Stockings and helped that club to three of its four consecutive championships.

White played many positions. Mainly a catcher for the first half of his career, he formed a battery with his brother Will with the Boston Red Caps and Cincinnati Reds. In 1879 he was named player-manager of the Reds, who had been managed by Cal McVey the previous season. After starting the season 9–9, however, White gave control back to McVey.

A .314 lifetime hitter, White played for several teams despite his strong, consistent performances. He won the NA batting title in 1875 with a .367 average, and the National League batting crown in 1877 when he hit .387. His career high was .390, which he reached in 1873. In addition he led his respective league once in triples, three times in runs batted in, and once in hits.

Spending the second half of his career as a third baseman, White deserted the NL to join the Buffalo Bisons of the Players League in 1890, his final season on the field.

Jo-Jo White
Cleveland Indians (AL) 1960
Record: 1–0
Speedy outfielder who spent most of his career as a backup.

Unable to crack the starting outfield of the Detroit Tigers, White began his major league career in 1932 and played for nine seasons. He hit .313 in 1934, the only time he would break the .300 mark, and also stole a career-high 28 bases.

After his retirement White eventually became a coach with the Indians. In 1960 when the Indians unexpectedly traded manager Joe Gordon to the Tigers for their skipper, Jimmy Dykes, White took the Tribe's reins for one game

until Dykes could arrive. The Indians won that game. White apparently rejoined Gordon in Detroit that season, because the Tigers do list him as a coach in 1960.

White went on to coach for a number of additional teams after that.

Warren White
Baltimore Lord Baltimores (NA) 1874
Record: 9–38
Civil War veteran who became an infielder.

Having served with the 14th Heavy Artillery Regiment New York from 1861–65, White turned to baseball after the war and was around for the founding of the National Association in 1871. He played one game that year for the Washington Olympics, and would eventually play six seasons for six different teams.

A third baseman by trade, White became player-manager of the Baltimore Lord Baltimores in 1874 but went only 9–38 for a team that finished in last place. The 1875 season was ostensibly his last, but nine years later he appeared in four games for the Washington Nationals of the Union Association.

Will White
Cincinnati Red Stockings (AA) 1884
Record: 44–27
First major leaguer to wear glasses regularly while playing.

A solid right-handed pitcher, White formed a battery with his brother Deacon with both the Boston Red Caps and the Cincinnati Reds. Will was at least a 30-game winner five times, on three of those occasions winning at least 40. In 1879 he won 43 while leading the National League with 76 games pitched, 75 starts, 75 complete games, and 680 innings pitched. His earned run average was a minuscule 1.99. In 1882 with the Red Stockings he led the American Association with 40 victories, 52 complete games, 8 shutouts, and 480 innings pitched. The following season he topped the circuit with 43 wins and a 2.09 ERA, and tied for the lead with 6 shutouts.

Named player-manager in 1884, White went 34–18 on the mound, but was replaced as skipper by Pop Snyder, the previous year's manager, partway through the season. The club finished fifth, and White played only two more partial seasons before retiring. He then went into business in Buffalo, New York.

Del Wilber
Texas Rangers (AL) 1973
Record: 1–0
Backup catcher for eight seasons.

Wilber went into coaching following his retirement

from the playing field and spent time with the Chicago White Sox and the 1970 Washington Senators. In 1973 he was a coach for the Rangers when skipper Whitey Herzog was fired, and he managed one victorious game before the arrival of Herzog's successor, Billy Martin.

Kaiser Wilhelm
Philadelphia Phillies (NL) 1921–22
Record: 83–137
Pitcher from Wooster, Ohio.

Irvin Key "Kaiser" Wilhelm pitched during nine seasons, but they were not all consecutive. He debuted in 1903 by appearing in nine games for the Pittsburgh Pirates, then played 1904–05 with the Boston Bostons, 1908–10 with the Brooklyn Superbas, 1914–15 with the Baltimore Terrapins of the Federal League, and 1921 with the Philadelphia Phillies.

When he appeared for the Phillies in 1921 as a player-coach it was only for four games, but he was 47 years old. As a manager from 1921–22 his team finished eighth and seventh, respectively.

Dick Williams
Boston Red Sox (AL) 1967–69; Oakland Athletics (AL) 1971–73; California Angels (AL) 1974–76; Montreal Expos (NL) 1977–81; San Diego Padres (NL) 1982–85; Seattle Mariners (AL) 1986–88
Record: 1571-1451
Fiery but successful manager with several teams.

Williams was a versatile outfielder who played for 13 seasons. He retired in 1964, and by 1967 found himself at the helm of the Red Sox. He would eventually have a 21-year managerial career with six different clubs, and of his five first-place finishes, four of them would come during his first six years as a skipper.

His Red Sox won the American League pennant in his first year as a pilot, although they dropped a tough seven-game World Series to the St. Louis Cardinals. The AP named Williams the AL Manager of the Year.

Williams often had problems getting along with both ownership and his players, and it was exactly that kind of situation that led to his firing during the 1969 season. He took over Charlie Finley's Athletics in 1971, and in three years at the helm he led his club to three division titles. That 1971 squad was swept by the Baltimore Orioles in the AL Championship Series, but the AP once again named Williams the league's Manager of the Year. In 1972 the A's took the Detroit Tigers for the pennant, then defeated the Cincinnati Reds in a close seven-game World Series. In 1973 they bested the Orioles for the pennant and the New York Mets for the World Championship. During that '73 Series, however, Finley made waves by

insisting Williams bench player Mike Andrews, who had made two errors in the twelfth inning of Game 2, and Andrews was instructed to claim an injury so that he could therefore be replaced on the roster. Williams refused and promised to resign following the World Series, and he lived up to that promise.

He later managed the Angels and Expos, and the AP named him the National League Manager of the Year in 1979 when his Montreal club finished second. In 1984 he took the Padres to their first World Series, but the team fell to Sparky Anderson's much stronger Detroit Tigers' squad.

Williams finished his managerial career with the Mariners, retiring about a third of the way through the 1988 season.

Jimmy Williams
St. Louis Browns (AA) 1884; Cleveland Blues (AA) 1887–88
Record: 110–169
Native of Columbus, Ohio, who never played major league baseball.

James Andrew Williams managed the St. Louis Browns in 1884, taking over for Charlie Comiskey, who had finished the previous season as skipper. Williams managed 85 games, then Comiskey took over again and would stay at the helm through 1889.

Jimmy later managed the Cleveland Blues, but he never had a team above fifth place.

Jimy Williams
Toronto Blue Jays (AL) 1986–89; Boston Red Sox (AL) 1997–2001; Houston Astros (NL) 2002–04
Record: 910–790
Played 14 major league games, mainly at shortstop.

Williams became a successful minor league manager following his playing career, winning the Pacific Coast League Manager of the Year Award in both 1976 and 1979 with the Salt Lake City Angels. In 1980 he became a coach with the Blue Jays, and would eventually be named their manager.

After a second-place finish in 1987 he began to experience some tumultuous relationships with some of his players, and he was fired in May of 1989 with the club in sixth place. Cito Gaston took over and led the club to the division title.

After coaching for a time with the Atlanta Braves, he took over the Boston Red Sox, and that team won the American League wild card every year from 1998–2000. In 1999 the BBWAA named Williams its AL Manager of the Year.

He was fired during the 2001 season due to a strained relationship with General Manager Dan Duquette, and he then managed the Astros for 2½ years.

Ted Williams
Washington Senators (AL) 1969–71; Texas Rangers (AL) 1972
Record: 273–364
One of the greatest hitters ever to play the game.

In a 19-year major league career, Williams *failed* to hit over .300 only once. He hit over .400 three times and won six batting titles, four home run crowns, and two Triple Crowns. Ted also led four times in runs batted in, twice in doubles, six times in runs scored, and eight times in bases on balls.

His first Triple Crown came in 1942, when he hit .356 with 36 homers and 137 RBIs. He then lost three seasons to World War II, serving as a Navy flight instructor from 1943–45. In 1946 he was named the American League's Most Valuable Player with a .342 average, 38 roundtrippers, and 123 RBIs. Oddly, none of those totals led the league.

In 1947 he won his other Triple Crown on the strength of a .343 average, 32 home runs, and 114 RBIs. Two years later he was again named MVP when he batted .343 with a league-leading 43 home runs and 159 RBIs, a total that tied him for the lead with Vern Stephens.

During his career Williams was named to 19 All-Star teams (appearing in both games in 1959 and 1960). He served as a fighter pilot in the Korean War and was shot down at one point and later contracted pneumonia. He returned to the baseball field in typical Williams fashion, but gradually began to suffer from injuries and retired in 1960. He hit a home run in his final at-bat.

The Red Sox retired his uniform number 9 that year, and in 1966 he was inducted into the Hall of Fame. He was hired to manage the Washington Senators in 1969, and although the team finished fourth, their record improved from 65–96 to a much more respectable 86–76, and the AP named Williams its AL Manager of the Year.

Ted stayed at the helm when the team moved from Washington to Arlington, Texas and became the Rangers. He retired after the 1971 season, and died in 2002.

Maury Wills
Seattle Mariners (AL) 1980–81
Record: 26–56
Speedy shortstop who spent most of his 14-year career with the Los Angeles Dodgers.

Wills had a shaky start in the major leagues, fielding terribly and hitting inconsistently, but he eventually won two Gold Gloves and hit over .300 twice. He led the Na-tional League six consecutive times in stolen bases and once in triples, and was named to seven All-Star teams.

Between 1960 and 1971 Wills never stole fewer than 15 bases in a season. Five times he swiped at least 50. In 1962 he set a since-broken record by stealing 104, and he batted .299, tied with three other players for the NL lead with 10 triples, and collected 208 hits en route to being named the league's Most Valuable Player.

Maury retired in 1972, and his managerial career consisted of two incomplete seasons with the Mariners. Taking over for Darrell Johnson in August of 1980, he had trouble controlling his players and finished seventh. In 1981 the club started out 6–18 and was again in seventh place when he was fired and replaced by Rene Lache-mann.

Jimmie Wilson
Philadelphia Phillies (NL) 1934–38; Chicago Cubs (NL) 1941–44
Record: 493–735
Eighteen-year major league catcher and two-time All-Star.

Wilson batted a solid .284 lifetime, several times hitting over .300, but his real strengths were his defense and his ability to handle pitchers. He was player-manager of the Phillies from 1934–38 but never finished higher than seventh. In 1939 he became a coach with the Cincinnati Reds, and he filled in as a catcher for a few games that season and also in 1940 when several Reds were injured and backstop Willard Hershberger committed suicide.

He became the Cubs' manager in 1941, but his best finish in Chicago would be fifth place. When his club started the 1944 season 1–9 he resigned and returned to the Reds as a coach until 1946.

Bobby Wine
Atlanta Braves (NL) 1985
Record: 16–25
Light-hitting shortstop who played 12 major league seasons.

Wine had a powerful throwing arm and was noted for his defense, as evidenced by his Gold Glove in 1963. He played his entire career with the Philadelphia Phillies and Montreal Expos, but never hit over .244 and batted .215 lifetime.

After retiring Wine became a Phillies' coach and later a scout for the Braves. He eventually joined the Atlanta coaching staff, and he took over as interim manager toward the end of the 1985 season when Eddie Haas was fired.

Ivy Wingo
Cincinnati Reds (NL) 1916

Record: 1–1

Catcher who set a National League record for most games caught.

His mark of 1231 has long since been surpassed, but Wingo was a durable backstop who played for 17 seasons. He hit .300 for the only time in 1914, but his .260 lifetime average was at least adequate.

In 1916 he managed the Reds for two games when skipper Buck Herzog was traded to the New York Giants. Christy Mathewson was part of that deal, and took over the Cincinnati club when he arrived.

Wingo retired in 1926, but returned as a Reds' coach from 1928–29, even filling in as a player for one game in '29 and garnering a single at-bat. He coached one more season for Cincinnati in 1936.

Bobby Winkles

California Angels (AL) 1973–74; Oakland Athletics (AL) 1977–78
Record: 170–213

Former coach at Arizona State University.

Winkles became a coach with the Angels in 1972, and the following season succeeded Del Rice as manager. He finished fourth. He was fired the following season with the team 30–44, then coached the Oakland Athletics and the San Francisco Giants.

In June of 1977 the A's fired manager Jack McKeon and appointed Winkles his successor. In May of the following year, however, with the club in first place, Winkles quit and was replaced by none other than McKeon.

He later coached the Chicago White Sox and the Montreal Expos.

Chicken Wolf

Louisville Colonels (AA) 1889
Record: 14–51

Lifetime .295 hitter.

Jimmy "Chicken" Wolf supposedly received his nickname from teammate Pete Browning. When the two were teenagers they both played for the Colonels, who at that time were a semipro team called the Louisville Eclipse. Before a particular game their manager instructed the team to eat lightly, but Wolf gorged on stewed chicken and then played poorly. Browning bestowed the name Chicken on him and it stuck.

An outfielder by trade, Wolf played 11 seasons, all but one of them with Louisville. He hit .300 in 1884 and .322 in 1887. In 1889 the Colonels started out under Dude Esterbrook and went 2–8. Esterbrook had begun levying fines against some of his players for not following his instructions, a tactic that owner Mordecai Davidson had tried unsuccessfully the previous season. Wolf openly opposed Esterbrook and even went to Davidson to complain. Ten games into the season Esterbrook was gone and Wolf himself was selected by his teammates to be player-manager.

Davidson himself soon began to impose fines once again, however, and Wolf resigned the managerial reins after going 14–51. Dan Shannon took over, then Jack Chapman, but the team finished last with a horrendous record of 27–111.

Wolf did continue to play, and in 1890 won the batting title with a .363 average while also leading the American Association with 197 hits. He played only three games in 1892, then played in the minor leagues through 1893.

The following year he became a firefighter in Louisville. Around the turn of the century he was involved in an accident while driving an engine to the scene of a fire and suffered head injuries that affected his sanity. In 1901 he was admitted to an asylum, and he died in 1903.

Harry Wolverton

New York Highlanders (AL) 1912
Record: 50–102

Third baseman who once hit three triples in a game.

Harry Wolverton batted .327 in 13 games in his debut season of 1898. With the Philadelphia Phillies he hit .309 in 1901, and .308 two years later. He was a .278 lifetime hitter.

Harry played through the 1905 season. In 1912 he was hired to manage the Highlanders, who did not fare well, but he also came out of retirement as a player, manning third base for several games and often employing himself as a pinch-hitter. In 50 at-bats he hit .300.

The Highlanders finished in last place, however, and Wolverton's managerial career was over.

George Wood

Philadelphia Athletics (AA) 1891
Record: 67–55

Boston native who played 13 major league seasons in the outfield.

A consistent performer, Wood debuted in 1880 with the Worcester Ruby Legs. In 1882 with the Detroit Wolverines he led the National League with seven home runs, and he batted over .300 three times.

In 1891 he took over the reins of the Philadelphia Athletics of the American Association as player-manager. This particular club was the third of four to bear the name, and had played the previous season in the Players League as the Philadelphia Quakers. Wood assumed control early in the season when skipper Bill Sharsig stepped aside, and he managed a fifth-place finish.

Wood played one more season but did not manage again.

Jimmy Wood
Chicago White Stockings (NA) 1871, 1874–75; Troy Haymakers (NA) 1872; Brooklyn Eckfords (NA) 1872; Philadelphia Philadelphias (NA) 1873
Record: 77–84
Second baseman who hit .333 in the National Association.

Wood played for the amateur Brooklyn Eckfords as early as 1860, and he was the player-manager of the original Chicago White Stockings (today's Cubs) in 1871. That club finished in a tie for second place, only two games behind the Philadelphia Athletics. When a fire destroyed the club's ballpark the team went on hiatus, and Wood moved on to Troy, back to Brooklyn, and to Philadelphia.

The White Stockings returned in 1874, and because of what had happened they were sometimes also known as the Chicago Remnants. Wood returned as manager but no longer played because of a leg injury (which led to eventual amputation of his limb). His club was not up to its previous near-championship form, finishing fifth and sixth, respectively.

Wood later opened a saloon.

Al Wright
Philadelphia Athletics (NL) 1876
Record: 14–45
Sportswriter who managed for one season.

Al Wright succeeded Henry Chadwick as a writer with the *New York Clipper*. He was a scorekeeper with the first Philadelphia Athletics of the National Association, and toured England with that team in 1874.

When the NA folded the A's joined the new National League, and Wright became the club's manager. After a 14–45 record and a seventh-place finish, however, he went back to sportswriting.

George Wright
Providence Grays (NL) 1879
Record: 59–25
Arguably the best player of his day.

The brother of Harry Wright, George was a star shortstop in amateur circles and was the first player Harry recruited for the 1869 Cincinnati Red Stockings. George was one of the anchors of that team, baseball's first professional club, which went undefeated in 68 games (57 of them official "league" matches).

When the National Association was formed in 1871 and Cincinnati decided to no longer field a professional team, George accompanied his brother to Boston, where the new Red Stockings proceeded to win four out of five

NA pennants. In 1874 George led the league with 15 triples, and he never hit below .329. When the NA folded Wright was the league's all-time leader in three-baggers with 41.

When the National League was formed George's performance began to drop dramatically. He was player-manager for the 1879 Providence Grays and led that team to the NL championship. There was no postseason. Despite his success that season he did not manage again.

Wright retired in 1882, but in 1884 helped form the Boston Unions, who played in the Union Association. He later left baseball altogether and opened a sporting goods company. He was later instrumental in promoting ice hockey and tennis in the United States.

Wright was inducted into the Hall of Fame in 1937.

Harry Wright
Boston Red Stockings (NA) 1871–75; Boston Red Caps (NL) 1876–81; Providence Grays (NL) 1882–83; Philadelphia Nationals (NL) 1884–89; Philadelphia Fillies (NL) 1890; Philadelphia Phillies (NL) 1890, 1890–93
Record: 1225–885
Baseball pioneer who helped form the 1869 Cincinnati Red Stockings.

Wright was born in England and came to the United States with his father, who was a cricket player and was hired by New York's St. George Cricket Club, named the Dragonslayers. By the age of 19 Harry himself was playing for the team, and he eventually made forays into baseball with the New York Knickerbockers.

Shortly after the Civil War Wright was hired by a group of Cincinnati businessmen who wanted to field a professional team. Harry was given the job of both recruiting and managing the club. Originally taking over the team in 1867, when it was a year-old amateur squad called the Resolutes, Harry recruited his brother George, a star shortstop, and set about creating a team that would soon become nationally known.

By 1869 the Red Stockings were entirely professional, and they toured the country and went undefeated in 68 games. (Fifty-seven of those contests were considered "official" by the loosely-constructed National Association of Base Ball Players, hence the disparity that sometimes appears in the reporting of the exact number.) The gentlemanly Wright not only pitched and managed but also spearheaded many innovations, including the style of uniform with bright red stockings that gave the team its name (and that were designed by George Ellard, a team official), defensive shifts, and pre-game fungoes. He even took his club to the West Coast to play a series of games against teams there.

In 1870 the Red Stockings lost their first game since

1868, having enjoyed a winning streak that lasted 130 contests, and they would eventually lose 5 more that year. At the conclusion of the season the team's owners decided they could no longer afford a professional squad, so Wright departed for Boston along with several of his players and formed the Boston Red Stockings of the new, professional National Association. The Philadelphia Athletics won the league's first championship, but Wright's Red Stockings won the rest, taking four consecutive pennants from 1872–75.

Harry played nearly every position on the diamond, but by 1875 he was nearly through playing and by 1877 was entirely finished. He continued to manage, however, and his Boston club, now called the Red Caps, won National League pennants in both 1877 and 1878.

Wright, who always kept detailed statistics, managed the Providence Grays for two years, then went to Philadelphia and took over a team that was called the Nationals, briefly the Fillies, and then the Phillies. In May of 1890 his club was in first place when his eyesight began to fail because of his constant poring over the team's numbers. Harry was forced to take a leave of absence and turned the reins over to Jack Clements, Al Reach, and Bob Allen. His eyesight eventually returned, but when he resumed his place at the helm the team had dropped to second and would end up in third.

Wright managed until 1893, and he died two years later. He was inducted into the Hall of Fame in 1953.

Rudy York
Boston Red Sox (AL) 1959
Record: 0–1
All-Star catcher who became an All-Star first baseman.

York was a power hitter who slugged 277 home runs in a 13-year career. Between 1937 and 1947 he never hit fewer than 17 in a season, although his career high of 35 came in his first full season of '37. In August of that year he set a record, since broken, by hitting 18 home runs in a single month. Named to seven All-Star teams, he played most of his career with the Detroit Tigers and in 1943 led the American League with 34 roundtrippers and 118 runs batted in. Six times he topped the 100-RBI mark, peaking with 134 in 1940, and three times he hit over .300.

York eventually became a coach with the Red Sox. In his first year in that role, 1959, he was named interim manager for one game when Pinky Higgins was fired, before the arrival of Billy Jurges. He then continued to coach until 1962.

Tom York
Providence Grays (NL) 1878, 1881
Record: 56–37

Outfielder who played in the original National Association.

York's career spanned 15 seasons, beginning in 1871 with the Troy Haymakers. A Brooklyn native, he played for seven different teams and was mostly a consistent performer. He hit over .300 four times, in addition to leading the National League with 10 triples in 1878 and with 37 bases on balls in 1883.

York spent that 1878 season as player-manager of the Grays, who finished in third place. George Wright took over the club in 1879, but Tom continued to play. After the club went through three managers in 1880 York took over again during the 1881 campaign, this time replacing Jack Farrell, and he helped the Grays rise from fourth to second place.

He did not manage again, but he played until 1885. He then went into independent baseball, and by the late 1880s was running a professional club in Albany.

Eddie Yost
Washington Senators (AL) 1963
Record: 0–1
Set records with 28 games leading off with home runs and with 2008 games played at third base.

Both of those records have since been surpassed, but Yost made his mark in solid, dependable fashion. In 18 seasons he hit only .254, but he nevertheless was patient at the plate, leading the American League six times in bases on balls and topping the 100-walk mark eight times.

In 1951 he tied with two other players for the league lead with 36 doubles, and in 1959 topped the circuit with 115 runs scored. He played until 1962, then became a coach for many years with many teams.

In 1963 he was a coach with the Senators when manager Mickey Vernon was fired. The Senators traded Jimmy Piersall to the New York Mets for Gil Hodges with the intention of making Hodges their manager, and Yost filled in as interim skipper for one game—a game the Senators lost—before Hodges' arrival.

Ned Yost
Milwaukee Brewers (NL) 2003–
Record: 291–356
Light-hitting backup catcher for six seasons.

Yost hit well in the Pacific Coast League but not in the majors, batting only .212 lifetime in limited action. When his playing days were over he became a minor league manager in the Atlanta Braves' system, then a major league coach for many years with Atlanta. In 2003 he was hired to manage the Brewers.

Yost once worked on the pit crew of NASCAR driver Dale Earnhardt before the racer's death. He donned uniform number 3 as a tribute to Earnhardt, whose car bore that same number.

Cy Young
Boston Red Sox (AL) 1907
Record: 3–3
Winningest pitcher in major league history.

Denton True Young won 511 games in his career, which spanned 22 seasons. He was nicknamed "Cy" by a catcher who helped him warm up during a minor league tryout and said that his pitches were as fast as a cyclone. Between 1891 and 1909 Young never won fewer than 13 games in a season, and he fell below 18 only once. He was a 20-game winner 15 times, and a 30-game winner on 5 of those occasions. Dominating the National League for the first half of his career and the American League for the second half, he led his respective circuit five times in victories, once in games pitched, once in starts, three times in complete games, seven times in shutouts, twice in innings pitched, twice in strikeouts, and twice in earned run average. In 1901 with the Boston Americans (later the Red Sox) he won the AL's pitching Triple Crown with a 33–10 record, 158 whiffs, and a 1.62 ERA. He threw three no-hitters in his career, one of them a perfect game in 1904 against the Philadelphia Athletics.

Young lost 316 games, also a record, but his lifetime winning percentage was .618. He was with the Red Sox when, just prior to the 1907 season, manager Chick Stahl committed suicide. Young was coerced into accepting the job as player-manager. He unhappily went 3–3 before being replaced by George Huff.

Young played until 1911. In 1913, when the Federal League was formed as a minor league, he managed the Cleveland Green Sox, but he would not stick around when the circuit declared itself a major league in 1914. He was inducted into the Hall of Fame in 1937, and in 1956 baseball honored him by naming an award after him. The Cy Young Award was originally given annually to the best pitcher in major league baseball, and is now awarded to the best pitcher from each league.

Nick Young
Washington Olympics (NA) 1871–72; Washington Nationals (NA) 1873
Record: 25–53
Executive who never played major league baseball.

Young helped organize the amateur Washington Olympics in 1867. He was also the one who suggested the meeting that led to the formation of the original National Association, and his Olympics became one of the entries in that first professional league. Young managed the club himself with modest results; the team went 15–15 the first season but only 2–7 in 1872 before folding during the season. In 1873 he took over the Washington Nationals of the same league but managed only an 8–31 record.

When the National League was formed in 1876 Young was elected secretary. He became league president in November of 1884, and would serve in that role until 1902.

Chief Zimmer
Philadelphia Phillies (NL) 1903
Record: 49–86
First catcher to consistently play directly behind the batter.

Most catchers of Zimmer's day backed up far behind the hitter when runners were on base. Zimmer stayed close on every play, and as a result led the league in many fielding categories many times. A lifetime .270 hitter, he hit over .300 four times in a 19-year career and peaked at .340 in 1895.

In 1900 he was elected president of the very first players' union, and he worked on discouraging National League players from jumping to the new, rival American League. His final season was 1903, when he was named player-manager of the Phillies. He batted only .220, and the team finished in seventh place.

In 1904 he served as an NL umpire, then spent three years as a minor league catcher, manager, owner, and umpire.

Don Zimmer
San Diego Padres (NL) 1972–73; Boston Red Sox (AL) 1976–80; Texas Rangers (AL) 1981–82; Chicago Cubs (NL) 1988–91; New York Yankees (AL) 1999
Record: 906–873
Cincinnati native who spent a long career in many capacities with many teams.

An infielder by trade, Zimmer played for 12 seasons and even filled in as a catcher at times, especially during his last season of 1965. He averaged only .235 over his career, but he hit a career-high 17 home runs in 1958 and was named a National League All-Star in 1961 (for both games that season) while playing for the Cubs.

Zimmer finished his playing career in Japan, then returned to the United States and became a minor league manager and a major league coach with many different clubs. He became a major league skipper for the first time in 1972 with the Padres. In 14 years as a manager, his only first-place finish came in 1989 with the Cubs, who then dropped the NL Championship Series to the San Francisco Giants, four games to one. The BBWAA named Zimmer its NL Manager of the Year, however.

After the 1991 season Zimmer turned strictly to coaching, and in 1996 became a longtime coach with the Yankees under Joe Torre. In March of 1999 Torre was diagnosed with prostate cancer, and when he went to seek treatment Zimmer filled in as skipper for the first 36 games of the season. He resumed his role as coach when Torre returned.

In 2004 he began work as a uniformed senior baseball advisor for the Tampa Bay Devil Rays.

The

Coaches

Tommie Aaron
Atlanta Braves (NL) 1979–84

Combined with his brother Hank to hit the most home runs among brother combinations in major league history.

Tommie played seven seasons with the Milwaukee/Atlanta Braves along with his brother, only one of them as a regular. He contributed 13 of the 768 roundtrippers smashed by the combo. After his playing career he coached for six seasons for the Braves.

Tommie both played for and managed the minor league Richmond Braves. He died of leukemia at the age of 45, and the Richmond club not only retired his number 23 but also named their Most Valuable Player Award the Tommie Aaron Award in his honor.

Spencer Abbott
Washington Nationals (AL) 1935

Chicago native and lifetime minor leaguer.

Displaying a rather contrary temperament, Abbott jumped from team to team and never did reach the major leagues. After playing he spent 34 years managing in the minor leagues, mostly in the system of the New York Giants. His longevity was a record at the time, and he piloted 24 different clubs and captured five pennants. He spent only a single season at the major league level as a Nationals' coach before returning to the minors as a skipper.

Oscar Acosta
Chicago Cubs (NL) 2000–01; Texas Rangers (AL) 2002

New Mexico native who managed successfully in the minor leagues.

Acosta's Lansing Lugnuts, a Chicago Cubs' affiliate, reached the playoffs in 1999, and their skipper became the big league club's pitching coach the following two seasons. After working in a similar capacity with the Rangers in 2002, he went to work in the New York Yankees' organization and managed the Gulf Coast Yankees to two consecutive championships.

In April of 2006 Acosta was killed in a car accident in the Dominican Republic near Santo Domingo, along with Yankees' field coordinator Humberto Trejo. He was 49 years of age.

Manny Acta
Montreal Expos (NL) 2002–04; New York Mets (NL) 2005–06
See Managers section.

Bill Adair
Milwaukee Braves (NL) 1962; Atlanta Braves (NL) 1967; Chicago White Sox (AL) 1970; Montreal Expos (NL) 1976
See Managers section.

Jerry Adair
Oakland Athletics (AL) 1972–74; California Angels (AL) 1975

Thirteen-year major league infielder.

Adair was only a .254 lifetime hitter, but he was gritty and played outstanding defense. In 1964 he set a second base record by committing only five errors, a mark later tied by Bobby Grich and Joe Morgan. He played through 1970, then played a season in Japan before returning to the United States as a coach for the A's and later the Angels.

Jimmy Adair
Chicago White Sox (AL) 1951–52; Baltimore Orioles (AL) 1957–61; Houston Colt .45s (NL) 1962–64; Houston Astros (NL) 1965

Shortstop who played only 18 games for the Chicago Cubs in 1931.

Nicknamed "Choppy," Adair hailed from Waxahachie, Texas. He batted .276 in his brief major league call-up, but eventually became a coach at that level with several clubs.

Rick Adair
Cleveland Indians (AL) 1992–93; Detroit Tigers (AL) 1996–99

Pitcher who never played in the major leagues.

Drafted by the Seattle Mariners out of Western Carolina University, Adair played for seven seasons in the minor leagues before becoming a pitching coach at that level in the Indians' system. He eventually became a roving pitching instructor for Cleveland, then a coach for the Tribe. After two seasons he went to work in the minor league system of the Tigers, and eventually reached the major league level as Detroit's pitching coach as well.

A big fan of former Atlanta Braves' pitching coach Leo Mazzone, Adair later worked in the Atlanta system and preached the "Mazzone way" before moving on to the Toronto Blue Jays' organization.

Bobby Adams
Chicago Cubs (NL) 1961–65, 1973

Solid infielder for 14 years, mostly as a backup.

Adams began his career in 1946 with the Cincinnati Reds. In 1958 with the Cubs he connected for six consecutive pinch-hits, and he would play only three games in 1959. He then coached the Cubs for several years.

Red Adams
Los Angeles Dodgers (NL) 1969–80
Pitched only 12 major league innings.

Spreading those innings out over eight games, Adams fashioned a miserable 8.25 earned run average and would not return to the major leagues as a player.

A California native, he did return to the top level as a coach, however, and spent 12 seasons with the Dodgers in that role.

Hank Aguirre
Chicago Cubs (NL) 1972–74
Pitched for 16 major league seasons before spending 3 as a Cubs' coach.

Aguirre spent most of his playing career with the Cleveland Indians and Detroit Tigers. In 1962 he went 16–8 and led the American League with a 2.21 earned run average. He won 14 games in both 1963 and 1965, and fashioned a 3.24 ERA lifetime. A horrendous batter, he managed a career average of only .085.

Jack Aker
Cleveland Indians (AL) 1986–87
Sidearmer who pitched for 11 seasons and posted a 3.28 lifetime earned run average.

Aker debuted with the Kansas City Athletics in 1964 and pitched for six teams in his career. He was solely a relief specialist and in 1966 led the American League with 32 saves. He went 8–4 that year with a 1.99 ERA en route to winning the AL Fireman of the Year Award. Always dependable, he underwent spinal surgery between the 1969 and 1970 seasons. He pitched with pain for the rest of his career but nevertheless he continued to be effective.

Of Native American ancestry, he ironically spent two seasons coaching the Cleveland Indians.

Darrel Akerfelds
San Diego Padres (NL) 2001–
Pitcher who spent five years in the major leagues.

Akerfelds appeared in 125 games in his major league career, which ended in 1991. In 1994 he pitched in Taiwan, and then returned to the United States and became a coach in the Padres' minor league system. He joined the big club in 2001 as bullpen coach.

Mike Aldrete
Seattle Mariners (AL) 2004; Arizona Diamondbacks (NL) 2005–06
Versatile outfielder who played 11 major league seasons.

Aldrete played for a number of teams between 1986 and 1996, and even pitched one scoreless inning for the New York Yankees in his final season. He then became a

minor league coach and later a minor league skipper before being hired to coach first base for the Mariners under Bob Melvin in 2004. The following season he joined the Diamondbacks as their hitting coach and remained in that position for two years.

Bob Alejo
Oakland Athletics (AL) 1996–97
Conditioning coach who worked in many arenas.

Having spent time in that role with UCLA, the Los Angeles Lakers, the U.S. national soccer and volleyball teams, and the U.S. Weightlifting Federation, Alejo worked for nine seasons with the A's but was listed as an official coach in only two of them. He later became the personal conditioning coach of the New York Yankees' Jason Giambi.

Carlos Alfonso
San Francisco Giants (NL) 1992, 1997–99
Minor league catcher and infielder who was converted to a pitcher but never reached the major leagues.

After his playing career Alfonso worked in the Houston Astros' bullpen (although the Astros do not officially list him as a coach), and then worked as a minor league manager and later pitching instructor. In 1981 his Daytona Beach Astros won the Florida State League Championship, and in 1983 he was named Manager of the Year in the Dominican League.

He eventually worked in a number of different major league organizations, winning co-Manager of the Year honors in 1985 with the second-place Columbus Clippers. In 1992 he joined the Giants as pitching coach, then returned to the minor leagues before rejoining San Francisco in 1997 as first base and administrative coach.

Alfonso also holds a black belt in Tae Kwon Do.

Luis Alicea
Boston Red Sox (AL) 2007–
Switch-hitting infielder from Puerto Rico.

In 13 seasons with five teams Alicea batted .260, spending time as both a starter and a backup. He had good range and decent speed, and in 2000 he hit .294 as the Texas Rangers' regular second baseman.

Alicea played the 1995 season with the Red Sox, and after his playing days he spent three years working as a minor league manager in the Boston organization. In 2007 he returned to the big league club as a coach.

Neil Allen
New York Yankees (AL) 2005
Troubled relief pitcher who played 11 major league seasons.

Allen debuted in 1979 with the New York Mets, and a few years later was struggling when he admitted to being an alcoholic. He lasted six more seasons but bounced around between several different teams, including the Yankees. He rejoined them for one season as a coach in 2005.

Gary Allenson
Boston Red Sox (AL) 1992–94; Milwaukee Brewers (NL) 2000–02
International League Most Valuable Player in 1978.

Allenson earned that honor with the Pawtucket Red Sox, but at the major league level he achieved only a .221 average in seven seasons, six of them with Boston. He later coached the Red Sox for three seasons and the Brewers for another three.

Sandy Alomar, Sr.
San Diego Padres (NL) 1986–90; Chicago Cubs (NL) 2000–02; Colorado Rockies (NL) 2003–04; New York Mets (NL) 2005–
Solid catcher who played 15 seasons at the major league level.

Alomar played for many teams, and in 1970 with the California Angels he was named to the American League All-Star team. After retiring in 1978 he coached the Puerto Rican national team for six years, then became a coach in the Padres' minor league system before joining the big club in that role. He also became involved with winter league programs in Puerto Rico and won two Manager of the Year Awards. From 1999–2000 he served as a general manager, then he joined the coaching staff of the Cubs before later moving on to the Rockies and the Mets.

Alomar's sons Robbie and Sandy, Jr. also excelled in the major leagues.

Felipe Alou
Montreal Expos (NL) 1979–80, 1984, 1992; Detroit Tigers (AL) 2002
See Managers section.

Jesus Alou
Houston Astros (NL) 1979
Fifteen-year major leaguer and brother of Felipe and Matty.

Jesus, like his brothers, was an outfielder. When he joined the San Francisco Giants late in the 1963 season, in fact, he and his siblings became the only all-brother outfield in major league history.

A solid .280 lifetime hitter, Alou served one season as a coach with the Astros, a team with whom he had had two stints as a player.

Joe Altobelli
New York Yankees (AL) 1981–82, 1986; Chicago Cubs (NL) 1988–91
See Managers section.

Nick Altrock
Washington Nationals (AL) 1912–53
Pitched for 16 years, many of which he spent as a player-coach.

Altrock started his career in 1898 with the Louisville Colonels. He won 19 games with the 1904 Chicago White Sox, then went 23–12 for them in 1905 and 20–13 in 1906. He hurt his arm shortly thereafter and was, for the most part, out of the game by 1909.

In 1912 he joined the Washington Nationals as a coach, a post he would hold for 42 years. Along the way he made many token appearances on the playing field, usually one per year. He created a clowning act in the coach's box and soon teamed up first with Germany Schaefer and later with Al Schact in inventing routines and entertaining players and fans alike.

In 1933, already a five-decade player, he made his last appearance as a player when he pinch-hit at the age of 57.

Joe Amalfitano
Chicago Cubs (NL) 1967–71, 1978–80; San Francisco Giants (NL) 1972–75; San Diego Padres (NL) 1976–77; Cincinnati Reds (NL) 1982; Los Angeles Dodgers (NL) 1983–98
See Managers section.

Ruben Amaro
Philadelphia Phillies (NL) 1980–81; Chicago Cubs (NL) 1983–86
Native of Mexico who played 11 seasons.

Never a strong hitter, Amaro got by on his versatility and excellent defense. Mainly a shortstop, he also played occasionally at all three bases and even appeared once in the outfield.

His last few years as a player were marred by injuries. His son, Ruben, Jr., also played major league baseball.

Rick Anderson
Minnesota Twins (AL) 2002–
Played only six games at the major league level.

Drafted by the New York Mets, Anderson pitched a no-hitter as a minor leaguer in 1979, but he would make only one appearance for the New York Yankees that year and five more for the Seattle Mariners in 1980. He spent the rest of his career in the minors, despite being named an International League All-Star in 1985.

In 1989 he became a coach in the Twins' organization, and eventually climbed through the ranks to become a pitching coach at the big league level.

Sparky Anderson
San Diego Padres (NL) 1969
See Managers section.

Brad Andress
Colorado Rockies (NL) 2000–
Holds a master's degree in exercise physiology.

Having worked for 4 years as strength/conditioning coach for the Athletic Department of the University of Michigan, Andress spent 10 years in a somewhat similar role for the Detroit Tigers. When the Rockies hired him they bestowed the titles Strength Coach and Quality Control Administrator upon him and entrusted him with several roles. He was put in charge of the strength and conditioning programs for the players, he assisted manager Clint Hurdle in the dugout during games, and he became involved in administrative areas such as scheduling and travel while also concentrating on players' attitudes and mental preparation for games.

Bob Apodaca
New York Mets (NL) 1996–99; Milwaukee Brewers (NL) 2000–01; Colorado Rockies (NL) 2003–
Solid relief pitcher who spent five seasons with the New York Mets.

Apodaca's entire professional career took place within the Mets' organization, and ended due to an elbow injury in 1981. He immediately went into coaching at the minor league level, and in 1986 was named Coach of the Year in the South Atlantic League when his Columbia Mets won the league championship.

In August of 1996 he was named pitching coach in New York, and he would hold that position through 1999 when he finally moved on to other organizations.

Rick Aponte
Washington Nationals (NL) 2007–
Minor league pitcher and longtime minor league instructor and scout.

After his playing days Aponte worked for a long time in the Houston Astros' organization. He spent 32 years in the Houston chain, 26 of them as a minor league instructor or a scout. It was in the Astro system that Aponte discovered Manny Acta, and Aponte took the youngster under his wing and served as a mentor to Acta.

Acta returned the favor in 2007 when, upon being named manager of the Nationals, he hired Aponte to be one of his major league coaches.

Luke Appling
Detroit Tigers (AL) 1960; Cleveland Indians (AL) 1961; Baltimore Orioles (AL) 1963; Kansas City Athletics (AL) 1964–67; Chicago White Sox (AL) 1970–71; Atlanta Braves (NL) 1981, 1984
See Managers section.

Brad Arnsberg
Montreal Expos (NL) 2000–01; Florida Marlins (NL) 2002–03; Toronto Blue Jays (AL) 2005–
Northern California Player of the Year with Merced Junior College in 1983.

Eventually pitching 77 major league games over four seasons, Arnsberg spent much of his career in the minor league system of the New York Yankees. He was named Yankees Minor League Pitcher of the Year and Eastern League Pitcher of the Year in 1985 when he won 14 games with the Albany-Colonie Yankees, and International League Pitcher of the Year in 1987 with the Columbus Clippers.

He began his coaching career in 1994 as a player-coach with the Wei-Chen Dragons in Taiwan. He then returned to the United States as a pitching coach in the Texas Rangers' organization before reaching the major league level with the Expos in 2000.

In 2003 he, along with manager Jeff Torborg, was fired by the Marlins. General Manager Larry Beinfest reported that Arnsberg became extremely angry when he was informed of the decision and that he became abusive, unprofessional, and "bordering on violent." Because of that Arnsberg was not even allowed back into the stadium to collect his belongings. Arnsberg accused someone on the Marlins' staff of being "vindictive," but would not go into detail.

He was hired by the Blue Jays' organization shortly thereafter, and returned to the major league level with Toronto in 2005.

Pierre Arsenault
Montreal Expos (NL) 1993–94, 1997–98, 2000–02; Florida Marlins (NL) 2003
Played only one professional season before going into coaching.

Arsenault actually studied sociology at Concordia University before returning to baseball, and in 1987 he became a part-time batting practice pitcher with the Expos. He then became the team's bullpen catcher and later bullpen coach, and over the years he would endure many title changes as other coaches and managers came and went.

Arsenault had good communication skills with pitchers, and the fact that he spoke French helped in Montreal as well. With personnel changes on the Expos' staff came changes for Arsenault; he went from bullpen coach to co-bullpen coach, back to sole bullpen coach, then went to the Florida Marlins when owner Jeffrey Loria sold his interest in the Expos and purchased the Florida franchise instead. In Florida he was named "bullpen coordinator," soon became bullpen coach again, and then, yet again, "bullpen coordinator." In truth his bullpen responsibilities did not change much, and as of 2006 he was still working in the bullpen while listed as a coordinator and not as an official coach.

Alan Ashby
Houston Astros (NL) 1997
Switch-hitting catcher who tied a major league record by catching three no-hitters.

Those gems were pitched by Ken Forsch in 1979, Nolan Ryan in 1981, and Mike Scott in 1986. In 1982 Ashby homered from both sides of the plate in the same game. A somewhat light hitter, he nevertheless played 17 seasons because of his defense and his ability to call games behind the plate. He spent most of those years with the Astros, and his playing career ended when he was traded to the Pittsburgh Pirates and refused to report.

He later returned to Houston for one season as a coach.

Tony Auferio
St. Louis Cardinals (NL) 1973
Never played in the major leagues.

A native of Orange, New Jersey, Auferio was a career minor league third baseman and a member of the 1971 division champion Three Rivers Eagles of the Eastern League. He coached only one season for the Cardinals, two years later.

Jimmy Austin
St. Louis Browns (AL) 1923–32; Chicago White Sox (AL) 1933–35, 1937, 1939–40
See Managers section.

Loren Babe
New York Yankees (AL) 1967; Chicago White Sox (AL) 1980, 1983
Third baseman who played 120 games at the major league level.

Those games were spread over two seasons—1952 and 1953—with the New York Yankees and Philadelphia Athletics. Babe hit only .223 and would not return to the major leagues except as a coach. He did work for the White Sox for many years as a scout, and in 1983, when he was dying of lung cancer, Charlie Lau surrendered his position as a Chicago coach to Babe so that Loren could qualify for his

10-year pension. Babe died in February of 1984, and Lau then died in March of colon cancer.

Lore Bader
Boston Braves (NL) 1926
Outstanding minor league pitcher.

Bader appeared in only 22 major league contests despite an impressive 2.51 earned run average. He hailed from Bader, Illinois, a town originally settled by his family. He spent some time in the Navy in the midst of his career, then became a coach, a scout, and a minor league manager. His nickname was "King."

Buddy Bailey
Boston Red Sox (AL) 2000
Minor league manager for the Red Sox for many years.

Bailey managed the Class A Lynchburg Red Sox as well as having two stints with the AAA Pawtucket Red Sox, with whom he became one of only four skippers in International League history to be named IL Manager of the Year twice. He accomplished the feat in 1996 and again in 2003, after having coached the major league Boston Red Sox for one season.

Mark Bailey
Houston Astros (NL) 2002–
Switch-hitting catcher who played for seven seasons.

Prone to striking out, Bailey nevertheless homered in three consecutive games during his rookie season of 1984 and later homered from both sides of the plate in a game the same year. He played many years with shoulder problems and retired in 1992.

After spending some time in private business, Bailey returned to baseball as a coach in the Astros' minor league system. In May of 2002 he was elevated to bullpen coach with the big league club as a replacement for Tony Peña, who had left the team to become the manager of the Kansas City Royals.

Bob Bailor
Toronto Blue Jays (AL) 1992–95
First pick of the Blue Jays in the 1976 expansion draft.

Bailor had played only 14 major league games previously with the Baltimore Orioles. A shortstop, he set a record by hitting .310 in 1977, the highest average ever for a player with an expansion team. His lifetime average was a more modest .264, but he was a versatile player who unfortunately suffered from many injuries.

In 1992 he returned to the Blue Jays as a coach for four seasons.

Harold Baines
Chicago White Sox (AL) 2003, 2004–
Six-time All-Star outfielder and designated hitter.

Baines played most of his 22-year career in three different stints for the White Sox. A .289 lifetime hitter, he hit over .300 eight times and in 1984 smacked a career-high 29 home runs while leading the American League with a .541 slugging average. He hit 384 homers lifetime and stroked 2866 hits. He also became the first player to register at least 1000 games as a DH and at least 1000 at another position. He set major league records for a DH with 1689 hits, 235 home runs, and 978 runs batted in. The White Sox retired his number 3 in 1989, while he was playing for the Texas Rangers and came to Chicago during a road trip. He thus became the only active player ever to receive such an honor.

After his playing career Baines served as an ambassador for the White Sox, making public appearances on the team's behalf. In 2002 he worked with the club's scouting and player development staffs, and in 2003 served as a special assignment instructor. He filled in for a short time as hitting coach when Greg Walker was recuperating from surgery to repair a broken arm. In 2004 he joined the coaching staff full-time.

Bill Baker
Chicago Cubs (NL) 1950
Part-time catcher for seven seasons.

A native of Paw Creek, North Carolina, Baker played for the Cincinnati Reds, Pittsburgh Pirates, and St. Louis Cardinals. He hit a mere .247, and the year following his retirement coached the Cubs for a single season.

Del Baker
Detroit Tigers (AL) 1933–38; Cleveland Indians (AL) 1943– 44; Boston Red Sox (AL) 1945–48, 1953–60
See Managers section.

Dusty Baker
San Francisco Giants (NL) 1988–92
See Managers section.

Floyd Baker
Minnesota Twins (AL) 1961–64
Third baseman for several major league teams.

Floyd Baker rejected a football scholarship so that he could play baseball. He lasted 13 seasons in the big leagues mainly because of his fielding prowess. He hit .317 in 83 games for the 1950 Chicago White Sox, but his lifetime average was a much humbler .251. He played a couple of seasons with the Washington Nationals, and returned to the franchise as a coach for several seasons in Minnesota.

Gene Baker
Pittsburgh Pirates (NL) 1963
Minor league shortstop who became a major league second baseman and third baseman.

Baker was a Pacific Coast League All-Star at shortstop, but he switched to second base in 1953 when he made his debut with the Chicago Cubs. In 1955 he became a National League All-Star at that position. He was eventually traded to the Pirates, with whom he switched to third base, and he ended his career with them after suffering a knee injury. He then became a coach and a scout with the Bucs.

Darren Balsley
San Diego Padres (NL) 2003–
Minor league pitcher in the organizations of the Oakland Athletics and Toronto Blue Jays.

After his playing career Balsley went into coaching and managing. He spent 10 years in the Blue Jays' system as a pitching instructor, coach, and advance scout before joining the Padres' organization. In May of 2003 he replaced Greg Booker as pitching coach in San Diego.

George Bamberger
Baltimore Orioles (AL) 1968–77
See Managers section.

Dave Bancroft
New York Giants (NL) 1930–32
See Managers section.

Chris Bando
Milwaukee Brewers (AL) 1996–97, (NL) 1998
Light-hitting backup catcher who spent most of his career with the Cleveland Indians.

Bando got by on his determination and his uncanny ability to catch the knuckleball. The Indians had two knuckleball pitchers—Tom Candiotti and Phil Niekro—and Bando proved adept at catching both of them. A switch-hitter, he averaged only .227 at the plate, and upon retiring coached for several seasons with the Brewers.

His brother, Sal Bando, had a long and somewhat storied major league career.

Sal Bando
Milwaukee Brewers (AL) 1980–81
Four-time All-Star third baseman.

Bando was a power hitter and the co-captain of the Oakland Athletics in the 1970s when that team captured five straight American League Western Division crowns and three consecutive World Championships. In 1973 he batted .287 and led the AL with 32 doubles, and he smashed more than 20 home runs six times, totaling 242 for his career.

He finished his playing days with the Brewers, spending the last two as a player-coach. On August 29, 1979, he was one of three position players to pitch for the Brewers in a game against the Kansas City Royals. The Brewers lost that game, 18–8, and Bando lasted three innings and surrendered two runs.

Jeff Banister
Pittsburgh Pirates (NL) 2000
Batted 1.000 in his major league career.

Banister went 1-for-1 with the Pirates in his single appearance as a pinch-hitter. He was called up from the minor leagues when catcher Don Slaught suffered an injury, but he did not appear in a game other than for that one at-bat.

He later coached the Pirates for one season and also served as a field coordinator.

Ernie Banks
Chicago Cubs (NL) 1967–73
Hall of Fame shortstop and first baseman.

Nicknamed "Mr. Cub," Banks was a 14-time All-Star and spent his entire 19-year playing career with the Cubs. His positive attitude was infectious, and he led the National League twice in home runs and twice in runs batted in. He was the NL's Most Valuable Player in both 1958 and 1959. He amassed 512 home runs lifetime, and between 1955 and 1960 clubbed more of them than anyone else in the major leagues. In 1960 he was awarded a Gold Glove at shortstop.

From 1967–71, at the end of his career, Banks served as a Cubs' player-coach. In 1972 and '73 he turned strictly to coaching, and in 1977 was inducted into the Hall of Fame. The Cubs retired his number 14 in 1982.

Banks had previously played for the Kansas City Monarchs of the Negro American League.

Jesse Barfield
Houston Astros (NL) 1995; Seattle Mariners (AL) 1998–99
Outstanding American League outfielder.

Barfield spent a 12-year career with the Toronto Blue Jays and New York Yankees. Offensively he topped the 20-home-run mark six times, peaking with a league-leading 40 in his All-Star season of 1986 when he also drove in 108 runs. Defensively he was equally adept, winning consecutive Gold Gloves in 1986 and 1987 and leading the AL in assists each season from 1985–87.

After retiring in 1992 he became a coach briefly with the Astros and the Mariners.

Mike Barnett
Toronto Blue Jays (AL) 2002–05; Kansas City Royals (AL) 2006–
Never played in the major leagues.

From 1982–87 Barnett worked for the New York Yankees with the title of Assistant Administrator of Baseball Operations and Video Director. He later became a coach in the minor league systems of the Chicago White Sox and Arizona Diamondbacks before being named the Blue Jays' hitting coach.

Following the 2005 season Barnett was hired by the Royals to serve as a roving hitting instructor. In early May of 2006 he became Kansas City's hitting coach when he switched roles with Andre David.

Dick Bartell
Detroit Tigers (AL) 1949–52; Cincinnati Redlegs (NL) 1954–55
Ill-tempered shortstop and two-time All-Star.

Bartell was an aggressive and skilled player who hit over .300 six times and averaged .284 for his career. In 1933 with the Philadelphia Phillies he tied a major league record by hitting four doubles in four at-bats in a game against the Boston Braves. Nevertheless his grating personality caused him to go from team to team during an 18-year career.

Nicknamed "Rowdy Richard," he retired in 1946 and later coached for Detroit and Cincinnati.

Tony Bartirome
Atlanta Braves (NL) 1986–88
Played one season at first base for the Pittsburgh Pirates.

That season was 1952, and Bartirome hit a mere .220. He served for a time in the military, but spent the rest of his time in the minor leagues until retiring in 1963. He then served as the Pirates' trainer for 19 seasons before accompanying manager Chuck Tanner to the Atlanta Braves and becoming one of his coaches for several years.

Monty Basgall
Los Angeles Dodgers (NL) 1973–86
Light-hitting second baseman with short stints in the majors.

Signing with the Brooklyn Dodgers as a 19-year-old in 1942, Basgall actually spent most of his playing career in the minor league system of the Pittsburgh Pirates. For three partial seasons he was with the big club but averaged only .215 for his career. He then became a longtime coach with the Dodgers, who by then were playing in Los Angeles.

Johnny Bassler
Cleveland Indians (AL) 1938–40; St. Louis Browns (AL) 1941

Solid, talented catcher who spent nine years in the major leagues.

Bassler hit over .300 four times, peaking at .346 in 1924 with the Detroit Tigers. His lifetime average was .304. After the 1927 season he decided that he loved California so much he preferred playing in the Pacific Coast League rather than the majors, and he therefore finished out his career on the West Coast.

He later became a PCL manager, but eventually spent a few years coaching the Indians and Browns.

Hank Bauer
Baltimore Orioles (AL) 1963
See Managers section.

Don Baylor
Milwaukee Brewers (AL) 1990–91; St. Louis Cardinals (NL) 1992; Atlanta Braves (NL) 1999; New York Mets (NL) 2003–04; Seattle Mariners (AL) 2005
See Managers section.

Larry Bearnarth
Montreal Expos (NL) 1976, 1985–91; Colorado Rockies (NL) 1993–95
Sinkerball pitcher with a degree in English literature.

Bearnarth spent five seasons playing at the major league level and many in the minors before becoming a pitching coach. After coaching the Expos he became the first pitching coach in Rockies' history in 1993. Following a three-year stint in Colorado he served as a scout for the Detroit Tigers for four seasons. On New Year's Eve of 1999 he died of a heart attack in Florida at the age of 58.

Tony Beasley
Washington Nationals (NL) 2006
Minor league infielder who became a successful minor league skipper.

A Carolina League All-Star in both 1990 and 1991 and a Southern League All-Star in 1996, Beasley took his first coaching job with the Gulf Coast Pirates in 1999. He eventually began to climb the ladder as a manager and won two Manager of the Year Awards at the Class A level and one at the AA level.

In December of 2005 he accepted a position with the New York Yankees as a minor league infield instructor, but he changed his mind when he was offered the third base coach position with the Washington Nationals. When manager Frank Robinson was fired following the 2006 season, he went to work in the Pittsburgh Pirates' minor league system.

Jim Beauchamp
Atlanta Braves (NL) 1991–98
Backup outfielder and first baseman in the major leagues.

An outstanding minor leaguer who displayed good defense, more-than-adequate speed, and power at the plate, Beauchamp spent most of his big league career coming off the bench. He hit only .231 with 14 home runs in 10 seasons at that level for several teams, and later became a coach with the Braves.

Walter "Boom Boom" Beck
Washington Senators (AL) 1957–59
Illinois native with a long professional career.

A right-handed pitcher, Walter Beck received his nickname in 1934 while pitching for the Brooklyn Dodgers. When manager Casey Stengel came to the mound to remove him from a game, Beck grew angry and hurled the ball into center field. The ball struck the tin-plated centerfield wall with a "boom," and Dodgers' center fielder Hack Wilson, who had started daydreaming when he saw Stengel emerge from the dugout, thought play had resumed. He fielded the ball off the wall and fired it back to the infield.

Beck spent 12 seasons in the major leagues, and pitched his last game while coaching in the minors for the Toledo Mud Hens at the age of 46. He later coached the Washington Senators.

Joe Becker
Los Angeles Dodgers (NL) 1958–64; St. Louis Cardinals (NL) 1965–66; Chicago Cubs (NL) 1967–70
Catcher who played 40 major league games.

Mainly a career minor leaguer, Becker spent parts of two seasons with the Cleveland Indians and hit .241. He served in the Navy during World War II, then became a minor league coach and later returned to the majors in that role with several teams.

Howie Bedell
Kansas City Royals (AL) 1984; Seattle Mariners (AL) 1988
Outfielder who never realized his potential in the major leagues.

Bedell had a long and successful minor league career, at one point tying a record by putting together a 43-game hitting streak while playing for the Louisville Colonels of the American Association. He played only 67 major league games, however, and batted a mere .193.

He coached one season for the Royals and one for the Mariners.

Buddy Bell
Cleveland Indians (AL) 1993–95, 2003–05
See Managers section.

Jay Bell
Arizona Diamondbacks (NL) 2005–06
Two-time All-Star infielder.

Bell played for several teams, but one of the highlights of his career came on the very first major league pitch he saw. Facing Bert Blyleven of the Minnesota Twins, he hit that pitch for a home run.

Having started out with the Cleveland Indians, Bell won a Gold Glove in 1993 with the Pittsburgh Pirates, and after making the All-Star team in both 1993 and 1999 he scored the Series-winning run in the 2001 World Series for the Diamondbacks.

He joined Arizona's minor league staff in 2004, and the following year became a coach for the big club.

Bell also has a pilot's license.

Rafael Belliard
Detroit Tigers (AL) 2006–
Seventeen-year major league veteran.

A light hitter (he averaged only .221 lifetime), Belliard got by on his solid defense at shortstop. He also played some second base, and he spent his entire career with the Pittsburgh Pirates and the Atlanta Braves. He suffered a broken left fibula several times early in his career.

Freddie Benavides
Cincinnati Reds (NL) 2003
Backup infielder with a good glove.

Benavides spent parts of four seasons in the major leagues, hitting .253, then he went to work as a manager in the Reds' minor league system. He made the playoffs in both 1999 with the Clinton LumberKings and 2000 with the Dayton Dragons. He later became a roving instructor, and in 2003 joined the major league club when Bob Boone was fired and replaced by Dave Miley. The following season he returned to the minor league side of the team's operations.

Chief Bender
Cincinnati Reds (NL) 1919; Chicago White Sox (AL) 1926; New York Giants (NL) 1931; Philadelphia Athletics (AL) 1951–53
Pitcher who won 212 major league games.

A 20-game winner twice, Charles "Chief" Bender was the first Native American inducted into the Hall of Fame. His father was German and his mother Chippewa, and he was raised on a reservation until his early teen years.

Debuting in 1903, Bender spent most of his career with the Athletics and was a 20-game winner twice. In 1910 he tossed a no-hitter against the Cleveland Naps, missing a perfect game because of a lone walk. In 1915 he jumped to the Federal League and posted a miserable 4–16 record

with the Baltimore Terrapins, then he pitched two seasons for the Philadelphia Phillies. He went on to coach for the Reds and to manage in the minor leagues. In 1925 he pitched a single game for the White Sox, then became a coach with them the following season. He eventually returned to the A's as a coach from 1951 until 1953, and he passed away in 1954.

Bruce Benedict
New York Mets (NL) 1997–99
Catcher and two-time All-Star.

A Birmingham native, Benedict spent his entire 12-year career with the Atlanta Braves. In 1981 he made the National League All-Star team, in 1982 he led the league's catchers in fielding average, and in 1983 he was named an All-Star again.

A rather light hitter, Bruce spent the next six years mainly as a reserve. In 1997 he became a coach with the Mets for three seasons.

Benny Bengough
Washington Nationals (AL) 1940–43; Boston Braves (NL) 1945; Philadelphia Phillies (NL) 1946–58
Talkative, likable catcher.

Bengough was a backup who played for 10 seasons, the first 8 with the New York Yankees and the last 2 with the St. Louis Browns. A .255 hitter, he played from 1923–32 and never swatted a big league home run. He eventually became a major league coach and spent many years in that role with the Phillies.

Vern Benson
St. Louis Cardinals (NL) 1961–64, 1970–75; Cincinnati Reds (NL) 1966–69; Atlanta Braves (NL) 1976–77; San Francisco Giants (NL) 1980
See Managers section.

Dick Berardino
Boston Red Sox (AL) 1989–91
Outfielder who never reached the major leagues as a player.

Berardino, a native of Cambridge, Massachusetts, spent several decades in the Red Sox' organization in a variety of roles, including major league coach and player development consultant.

Moe Berg
Boston Red Sox (AL) 1939–41
Most famous for his role as a pre-World War II spy.

A catcher and so-so hitter, Berg was recognized as being highly intelligent, having attended several universities and studied a variety of subjects. A lifetime .243 hitter, he was not the caliber player that would have been expected to accompany stars like Babe Ruth and Lou Gehrig on a tour of Japan in the 1930s, yet that was exactly what he did. It did not come to light until much later that he had done so as a spy for the United States government, having been entrusted with the task of taking strategic photographs and gathering critical pre-war information. His film of Tokyo was reportedly used by American bombers during the war.

On the baseball field Berg displayed a rapport with young pitchers and lasted 15 years at the major league level. He then coached the Red Sox for three seasons.

Carroll Beringer
Los Angeles Dodgers (NL) 1967–72; Philadelphia Phillies (NL) 1973–78
Minor league pitcher.

Beringer never reached the big time on the mound, but in 1959 was named Texas League Player of the Year. He later did reach the majors as a coach, spending 12 seasons with the Dodgers and Phillies.

Carlos Bernhardt
Baltimore Orioles (AL) 1998
Native of the Dominican Republic.

Bernhardt never played in the major leagues but spent a significant amount of time working in the Baltimore Orioles' organization. Rumor had it that he was brought to the major league level as a coach in 1998 in order to control the rather maverick ways of pitcher Armando Benitez, the reasoning being that they were both Dominican. Carlos was replaced in 1999, however, and became the Orioles' director of scouting in the Dominican Republic. He also ran the club's Dominican baseball school.

Yogi Berra
New York Yankees (AL) 1963, 1976–83; New York Mets (NL) 1965–71; Houston Astros (NL) 1986–89
See Managers section.

Ray Berres
Chicago White Sox (AL) 1949–66, 1969
Good defensive catcher who hit only .216.

Berres lasted 11 seasons because of his work behind the plate, spending those years with four different teams. He then became a longtime coach with the White Sox.

Charlie Berry
Philadelphia Athletics (AL) 1936–40
The second Charlie Berry to play major league baseball.

The first was his father, who played in the Union Association in 1884. This Charlie Berry lasted 11 seasons as a catcher, while also establishing himself with the Pottsville Maroons of the National Football League in 1925 and 1926. In '25, in fact, he led the NFL in scoring with 74 points.

Berry played for three teams in his big league baseball career, but he both started and finished with the Philadelphia Athletics. He became a coach for the A's in 1936 after playing 13 games for the club, and in 1938, still a coach, appeared in one game as a player and went 0-for-2.

In 1942 he became an American League umpire and would continue in that role for 21 years. At the same time he served as a head linesman in the NFL. In 1958 he accomplished the improbable task of umpiring the World Series and officiating the NFL championship game between the Baltimore Colts and the New York Giants.

Mark Berry
Cincinnati Reds (NL) 2003–
Minor league catcher for seven seasons.

Berry played in the Reds' organization and later went to work for the club in several capacities. He became a minor league coach and skipper and was named 1996 Southern League Manager of the Year with the Chattanooga Lookouts.

In 1999 he became the Reds' bullpen catcher, then was named to the coaching staff in 2003.

Sean Berry
Houston Astros (NL) 2006–
One of the original "Killer B's" with the Astros.

Together with Jeff Bagwell, Craig Biggio, and Lance Berkman, Berry helped Houston to division titles in 1997 and 1998. He actually played for five teams in an 11-year career, but those three years were among his best. After hitting .318 for the Montreal Expos in 1995, he batted .291 for the Astros in 1996 with career highs of 17 home runs and 95 runs batted in. He hit .314 in 1998, then moved to the Milwaukee Brewers.

Berry played until 2000 and later worked for the Astros as a minor league hitting coordinator. He was promoted to Houston as hitting coach in July of 2006 when Gary Gaetti was fired from that position.

Terry Bevington
Chicago White Sox (AL) 1989–95; Toronto Blue Jays (AL) 1999–2001
See Managers section.

Greg Biagini
Baltimore Orioles (AL) 1992–94
Chicago native who never played in the major leagues.

A first baseman and outfielder, Biagini became a minor

league coach and manager after playing for 10 seasons. As a skipper he guided the 1990 Rochester Red Wings to the International League championship and the 1996 Oklahoma City 89ers to the American Association title. Between those accomplishments he coached for three seasons with the Orioles.

Biagini later became a scout with the Boston Red Sox, and he died of kidney cancer in 2003 at the age of 51.

Dave Bialas

San Diego Padres (NL) 1993–94; Chicago Cubs (NL) 1995–99, 2002
Longtime minor league player and manager.

First managing in 1982, Bialas was player-manager of the Class A Springfield Cardinals the following season. He appeared in 33 games that year, most of them as a designated hitter. In both 1985 and 1987 he was named the Florida State League's Manager of the Year with the St. Petersburg Cardinals, and in 2000 became the Southern League Manager of the Year with the AA West Tenn Diamond Jaxx in the Chicago Cubs' system. Along the way he coached the Padres and the Cubs, and later served as a minor league field coordinator in the Chicago system.

Del Bissonette

Boston Braves (NL) 1945; Pittsburgh Pirates (NL) 1946
See Managers section.

Bud Black

Anaheim Angels (AL) 2000–04; Los Angeles Angels of Anaheim (AL) 2005–06
See Managers section.

Wayne Blackburn

Detroit Tigers (AL) 1963–64
Native of Mount Joy, Ohio.

A minor league outfielder, second baseman, and third baseman, Blackburn served as a scout for the Detroit Tigers before joining the major league club as a coach for two seasons.

Lena Blackburne

Chicago White Sox (AL) 1927–28; St. Louis Browns (AL) 1930; Philadelphia Athletics (AL) 1933–40, 1942–43
See Managers section.

Ray Blades

St. Louis Cardinals (NL) 1930–32, 1951; Cincinnati Reds (NL) 1942; Brooklyn Dodgers (NL) 1947–48; Chicago Cubs (NL) 1953–56
See Managers section.

Gary Blaylock

Kansas City Royals (AL) 1984–87
Right-handed pitcher from Clarkton, Missouri.

Blaylock reached the majors for only one season, 1959, when he pitched for the St. Louis Cardinals and later the New York Yankees. He later coached several seasons for the Royals.

Jack Bloomfield

San Diego Padres (NL) 1974; Chicago Cubs (NL) 1975–78
Texas native who played in Japan.

Bloomfield spent the 1960–64 seasons with the Kintetsu Buffaloes, and 1965–66 with the Nankai Hawks. He won two consecutive batting titles, peaking at .374 in 1962, and hit .315 for his career.

Following his playing career he later coached for the Padres and Cubs back in the United States.

Ossie Bluege

Washington Nationals (AL) 1940–42
See Managers section.

Bruce Bochy

San Diego Padres (NL) 1993–94
See Managers section.

Wade Boggs

Tampa Bay Devil Rays (AL) 2001
Hall of Fame third baseman.

A 12-time All-Star and 2-time Gold Glove winner, Wade Boggs won five batting titles and hit .328 lifetime. He also led the American League twice in doubles, once in hits, twice in runs scored, twice in bases on balls, and six times in on-base percentage. He accumulated 3010 hits in his career, and is the only player whose 3000th knock was a home run.

Boggs spent the vast majority of his career with the Boston Red Sox and New York Yankees, but finished it out in two seasons with the Devil Rays. His playing days ended in 1999, and Tampa Bay retired his uniform number 12 in 2000. He coached for the team the next year.

Ken Bolek

Cleveland Indians (AL) 1992–93
Longtime minor league manager.

Bolek made the playoffs four times—in 1986 with the Asheville Tourists of the South Atlantic League, in 1987 with the Osceola Astros of the Florida State League, and in 1990 and '91 with the Canton-Akron Indians of the Eastern League. He coached in Cleveland from 1992–93, then became the skipper of the Class A Daytona Cubs.

Marc Bombard
Cincinnati Reds (NL) 1996; Philadelphia Phillies (NL) 2005–06

Minor league pitcher for seven years in the Reds' system.

Bombard began his playing career in 1971, and three years later he was a player-coach with the Tampa Tarpons. After serving as a roving pitching instructor from 1977–81 he went on to a highly successful minor league managerial career. His 1983 Billings Mustangs won the Pioneer League championship, his 1988 Cedar Rapids Reds took the Midwest League title, and his 1994 Indianapolis Indians captured the American Association crown. He was named Manager of the Year by various agencies in 1994, 1995, and 2002.

He managed in the minor league organizations of the Reds, the Milwaukee Brewers, the Pittsburgh Pirates, and the Phillies. After coaching briefly for the Reds in 1996 he managed the AAA Scranton/Wilkes-Barre Red Barons, and was promoted to the major league Philadelphia coaching staff in 2005, where he stayed for two seasons.

Bobby Bonds
Cleveland Indians (AL) 1984–87; San Francisco Giants (NL) 1993–96

Three-time All-Star and three-time Gold Glove outfielder.

Bonds was the second player in history and the only player in the twentieth century to smack a grand slam as his first hit. He accomplished the feat on June 25, 1968, after it had first been done by William Duggleby of the Philadelphia Phillies in 1898.

Bonds cracked the 30 mark in both home runs and stolen bases five times, and he very nearly became a 40-40 player in 1973 when he finished with 39 homers and 43 steals. He also struck out consistently, however, leading the league several times, and consequently spent the latter part of his career jumping from team to team. He set a major league record with 35 leadoff home runs, a mark later broken by Rickey Henderson. He clouted 332 roundtrippers lifetime, and he and his son Barry are the majors' all-time leading father-son home run combination.

Bobby later coached the Indians and Giants, and he passed away in 2003.

Greg Booker
San Diego Padres (NL) 1997–2003

First baseman who was converted into a relief pitcher.

Booker had a tough time with the switch at first, in 1982 leading the California League in losses, walks, and wild pitches. He later became an effective major league reliever, however, and fashioned an eight-year career at the big league level.

Bob Boone
Cincinnati Reds (NL) 1994
See Managers section.

Steve Boros
Kansas City Royals (AL) 1975–79, 1993–94; Montreal Expos (NL) 1981–82; Baltimore Orioles (AL) 1995
See Managers section.

Chris Bosio
Tampa Bay Devil Rays (AL) 2003

Pitched for 11 major league seasons.

With a career that lasted from 1986–96, Bosio pitched for both the Milwaukee Brewers and the Seattle Mariners. With Milwaukee he won 15 games in 1989, 14 in 1991, and 16 more in 1992. In April of 1993, now with Seattle, he pitched a no-hitter against the Boston Red Sox.

Thad Bosley
Oakland Athletics (AL) 1999–2003

Speedy reserve outfielder who played for 14 years.

Bosley led the major leagues in pinch-hits in both 1985 and 1987, and in '85 clubbed six pinch-hit homers for the Chicago Cubs. He was also prone to injuries, however, and spent seven stints on the disabled list during his career. A .272 lifetime hitter, he retired in 1990 and later became a coach with the A's.

Dick Bosman
Chicago White Sox (AL) 1986–87; Baltimore Orioles (AL) 1992–94; Texas Rangers (AL) 1995–2000

Pitched from 1966–76.

In 1969 Bosman went 14–5 with the Washington Senators while leading the American League with a 2.19 earned run average. He won 16 games the following season before his numbers began to decline.

In 1974 with the Cleveland Indians he pitched a no-hitter against the Oakland Athletics. His own error was the only thing that prevented him from tossing a perfect game.

He later coached for the White Sox, Orioles, and Rangers.

Jim Bottomley
St. Louis Browns (AL) 1937
See Managers section.

Larry Bowa
Philadelphia Phillies (NL) 1988–96; Anaheim Angels (AL) 1997–99; Seattle Mariners (AL) 2000; New York Yankees (AL) 2006–
See Managers section.

Clete Boyer
Oakland Athletics (AL) 1980–85; New York Yankees (AL) 1988, 1992–94
Brother of Ken and Cloyd Boyer.

An outstanding defensive third baseman, Clete spent 16 years with the Kansas City Athletics, New York Yankees, and Atlanta Braves. He led the National League in fielding in both 1967 and 1969, and he clubbed 162 home runs in his career, peaking with 26 in 1967 with the Braves.

In 1964 with the Yankees he hit a homer in the seventh game of the World Series only two innings after his brother Ken had done the same for the St. Louis Cardinals. It was the only time that two brothers had homered in the same World Series game.

He was released by the Braves in 1971, then played in the Pacific Coast League before being traded to a Japanese team.

Cloyd Boyer
New York Yankees (AL) 1975, 1977; Atlanta Braves (NL) 1978–81; Kansas City Royals (AL) 1982–83
Brother of Ken and Clete Boyer.

Unlike his brothers, who were both third basemen, Cloyd was a pitcher. The eldest of the three, Cloyd threw for five seasons with the St. Louis Cardinals and Kansas City Athletics but never had a winning record. He only once had a *losing* record, however, going 0–0, 7–7, 2–5, 6–6, and 5–5.

Ken Boyer
St. Louis Cardinals (NL) 1971–72
See Managers section.

Bobby Bragan
Los Angeles Dodgers (NL) 1960; Houston Colt .45s (NL) 1962
See Managers section.

Jimmy Bragan
Cincinnati Reds (NL) 1967–69; Montreal Expos (NL) 1970–72; Milwaukee Brewers (AL) 1976–77
Brother of Bobby Bragan.

Jimmy never played major league baseball, but he did play in the minor league systems of the Brooklyn Dodgers and Cincinnati Reds. He later became a minor league coach, college coach at Mississippi State, and major league scout. From 1981–94 he served as president of the Southern League.

Bragan died of cancer in 2001.

Mickey Brantley
New York Mets (NL) 1999; Toronto Blue Jays (AL) 2006–
Played four seasons, mostly as a part-time outfielder.

Brantley hit .302 in 92 games for the 1987 Seattle Mariners. He clubbed 14 homers that season and 15 the next. He finished his playing career in 1993 with the Yomiuri Giants in Japan. In 1994 he became a minor league coach in the San Francisco Giants' organization, and later he briefly managed the Gulf Coast Mets. For many years he served as the Mets' minor league hitting coordinator, spending a year as a coach at the big league level and also briefly working as a minor league consultant before being named to the Blue Jays' staff in 2006.

Steve Braun
St. Louis Cardinals (NL) 1990
Third baseman and outfielder who developed into a pinch-hitting specialist.

Braun played for several teams during a 15-year career, hitting .271 overall, before retiring from the Cardinals in 1985 and becoming a coach in the club's minor league system. He spent 1990 as a coach at the big league level.

Harry Brecheen
Baltimore Orioles (AL) 1954–67
Two-time All-Star pitcher.

Brecheen spent 11 of his 12 seasons with the St. Louis Cardinals and the last with the St. Louis Browns. He won 133 games lifetime. Nicknamed "The Cat" because of his fielding prowess and cat-like reflexes, Harry had his best season in 1948 when he went 20–7 and led the National League with 149 strikeouts, a 2.24 earned run average, and 7 shutouts.

He retired in 1953 and became a longtime coach with the Orioles.

Joe Breeden
Florida Marlins (NL) 1995–96, 1999–2001; Toronto Blue Jays (AL) 2004
Minor leaguer in the Montreal Expos' system.

Breeden never reached the major leagues as a player, but worked as a coach in college baseball before managing in the Kansas City Royals' system and then spending time in the Marlins' organization as a roving catching instructor and major league coach. He later coached the Blue Jays and worked in the New York Yankees' system.

Scott Breeden
Cincinnati Reds (NL) 1986–89
Minor league and major league coach.

Breeden worked for many years in the Reds' minor league system before being promoted to the big club as pitching coach in the late 1980s under Pete Rose. He later held the same position in the minor league system of the

Toronto Blue Jays. Breeden died of a heart attack in February of 2006.

Bob Brenly
San Francisco Giants (NL) 1992–95
See Managers section.

Roger Bresnahan
New York Giants (NL) 1925–28; Detroit Tigers (AL) 1930–31
See Managers section.

Jim Brewer
Montreal Expos (NL) 1977–79
Reliever who pitched for 17 seasons.

Brewer debuted with the Chicago Cubs in 1960, and he racked up at least 14 saves every season from 1968–73 with the Los Angeles Dodgers. He totaled 132 in his career at a time when the role of closer was still a new concept. He was named a National League All-Star in 1973 and finished out his career with the California Angels in 1976. He then became a coach with the Expos.

Brewer was killed in a car accident in 1987, two days after his fiftieth birthday.

Rocky Bridges
Los Angeles Angels (AL) 1962–63; California Angels (AL) 1968–71; San Francisco Giants (NL) 1985
Utility infielder from Texas.

Bridges played for 11 seasons with various teams, hitting .247 but surviving well because of his versatility. In 1958 he was named an American League All-Star while playing for the Washington Senators. After finishing his playing career in 1961 with the Angels he became a coach for the club, then turned to managing in the minor leagues.

He became famous for his clever quotes and observations, and returned for a second stint as an Angels' coach in 1968. He later coached one season with the Giants.

Tommy Bridges
Detroit Tigers (AL) 1946; Cincinnati Reds (NL) 1951
Right-handed pitcher and six-time All-Star.

Bridges spent all of a 16-year career with the Tigers. He won 22 games in 1934, 21 in 1935, and 23 in 1936 to lead the American League. He also topped the circuit twice in strikeouts, twice in starts, and once in shutouts.

Having once struck out 20 batters in a minor league game, Bridges took no-hitters into the ninth inning several times at the major league level. In August of 1932 he was one out away from a perfect game against the Washington Nationals when pinch-hitter Dave Harris singled to spoil it.

Bridges lost some time to military service beginning in 1943, and when he returned the Tigers did not exactly welcome him with open arms. He pitched four games in 1945 and nine in 1946, when he was both a player and a coach. The following year, at the age of 40, he played in the Pacific Coast League for the Portland Beavers. He led the league with a 1.64 earned run average and finally achieved a no-hitter by blanking the San Francisco Seals.

He later spent one season coaching the Reds.

Ed Brinkman
Detroit Tigers (AL) 1979; San Diego Padres (NL) 1981; Chicago White Sox (AL) 1983–88
Outstanding shortstop who played for 15 seasons.

Brinkman was not especially strong with a bat, hitting only .224 lifetime, but he was steady and dependable with a glove. He won a Gold Glove in 1972 with the Tigers and the following season was named to the American League All-Star team while in the process of setting several fielding records for shortstops, including most consecutive errorless games.

Dave Bristol
Cincinnati Reds (NL) 1966, 1989, 1993; Montreal Expos (NL) 1973–75; San Francisco Giants (NL) 1978–79; Philadelphia Phillies (NL) 1982–85, 1988
See Managers section.

Gus Brittain
Cincinnati Reds (NL) 1937
Fiery-tempered catcher who played only three major league games.

Brittain was a lifetime minor leaguer who considered himself to be on good behavior if he limited himself to only three or four fistfights per year. He was suspended several times during a 17-year minor league career. His 1937 stint with the Reds lasted three games as a player and the rest as a coach.

He then became a minor league manager until 1949.

Gates Brown
Detroit Tigers (AL) 1978–84
Spent 13 years with the Tigers.

Brown debuted as a pinch-hitter in a 1963 game and promptly hit a home run. He eventually became something of a specialist in that role and led the American League in pinch-hits in both 1968 and 1974. He retired following the 1975 season and later returned to the Tigers as a coach, where he contributed to the team's wire-to-wire World Championship season in 1984.

Jackie Brown
Texas Rangers (AL) 1979–82; Chicago White Sox (AL) 1992–95; Tampa Bay Devil Rays (AL) 2002–05

Oklahoma native who debuted at the age of 27.

Brown pitched for seven seasons with various clubs, going 47–53 overall. He won 13 games in 1974 with the Rangers, but never again won more than 9. He and his brother Paul had starred in high school together, and Paul lasted for parts of four seasons with the Philadelphia Phillies but never won a game while posting eight losses.

Jimmy Brown
Boston Braves (NL) 1949–51
Switch-hitting infielder.

Jimmy Brown emerged from the minor league system of the St. Louis Cardinals to make his debut in 1937. He hit .276 that year and .301 the next. In 1941 he peaked with a .306 batting average and was named a National League All-Star the following season.

He lost most of 1943 and all of the next two seasons to the military, and when he returned in 1946 with the Pittsburgh Pirates he batted only .241 and was finished. He later became a coach with the Boston Braves.

Mace Brown
Boston Red Sox (AL) 1965
Iowa native and 10-year relief specialist.

Brown made his debut in 1935 for the Pittsburgh Pirates and appeared in 18 games. By 1938 he was a National League All-Star, and he established a lifetime earned run average of 3.46 while leading the league twice in games pitched. He lost the 1944 and 1945 seasons to military service and pitched just one season after that.

Mike Brown
Cleveland Indians (AL) 2002
Pitcher who struggled in six major league seasons.

Brown went only 12–20 during those years with the Boston Red Sox and Seattle Mariners and fashioned an unimpressive 5.75 earned run average. He later worked in the minor league system of the New York Yankees before becoming the Indians' pitching coach for one season.

Earle Brucker, Sr.
Philadelphia Athletics (AL) 1941–49; St. Louis Browns (AL) 1950; Cincinnati Reds (NL) 1952
See Managers section.

Clay Bryant
Los Angeles Dodgers (NL) 1961; Cleveland Indians (AL) 1967–74
Pitcher whose career ended due to arm problems.

Bryant pitched for only six seasons, all with the Chicago Cubs and the best of which was 1938. He went 19–11 that year with a 3.10 earned run average while leading the

National League with 135 strikeouts.

He would win only two more games against two losses the next two seasons, and then he was done.

Don Bryant
Boston Red Sox (AL) 1974–76; Seattle Mariners (AL) 1977–80
Backup catcher for three seasons.

Bryant played for the Chicago Cubs in 1966 and for the Houston Astros from 1969–70. He got only 59 major league games under his belt, but one of those came on May 1, 1969, when he was behind the plate for Don Wilson's second no-hitter.

Bill Buckner
Chicago White Sox (AL) 1996–97
Nineteen eighty National League batting champion.

A lifetime .289 hitter, Buckner captured the crown with the Chicago Cubs by hitting .324. It was one of seven times he hit over .300, and he also led the league in doubles twice.

In 1981 he was named an NL All-Star on the strength of a .311 average. He gutted out several injuries en route to a 22-year major league career with a number of teams. He retired in 1990 and later coached the White Sox for two years.

Don Buford
San Francisco Giants (NL) 1981–84; Baltimore Orioles (AL) 1988–94; Washington Nationals (NL) 2005
Infielder and outfielder from Linden, Texas.

Buford debuted in 1963 with the Chicago White Sox, and was eventually a member of the strong Orioles' teams of the late 1960s and early 1970s. In 1971 he was named an American League All-Star and hit .290 for the season while leading the league with 99 runs scored. He stole 200 bases in a 10-year career, but after a rough 1972 campaign he moved to Japan, where he played until 1976.

Al Bumbry
Boston Red Sox (AL) 1988–93; Baltimore Orioles (AL) 1995; Cleveland Indians (AL) 2002
Played 14 seasons, the first 13 of them with the Orioles.

An outfielder by trade, Al Bumbry debuted with the O's in nine games in 1972 and hit .364. The following year he batted .337 over a full season while tying Rod Carew for the American League lead with 11 triples en route to being named the AL Rookie of the Year. In a 1978 game he broke his leg while sliding into second base, but he recovered nicely. An All-Star in 1980, he stole 254 bases lifetime, twice topping the 40 mark.

Bumbry also won a Bronze Star as a platoon leader in the Vietnam War.

Lorenzo Bundy
Florida Marlins (NL) 1998; Colorado Rockies (NL) 1999; Arizona Diamondbacks (NL) 2004
Longtime minor league manager.

Bundy began his career as a skipper with the Gulf Coast Expos in 1990. His team had the best record in the league that season and made the playoffs. He continued to manage in the Expos' system and later that of the Marlins while also doing the same in the winter Mexican Pacific League. He joined the big league staff of the Marlins in 1998 before moving to the Rockies the following season. He then went to work in the Diamondbacks' system, where he was hitting coach for the Tucson Sidewinders before being promoted to bench coach at the big league level in July of 2004. He then returned to Tucson.

Lew Burdette
Atlanta Braves (NL) 1972–73
Two-time All-Star pitcher.

Burdette pitched for 18 seasons, and his finest years came with the Milwaukee Braves. He won at least 15 games on eight occasions, and was a 20-game winner twice. His 21 victories in 1959 put him in a three-way tie for the National League lead, and he also topped the circuit twice in shutouts, once in starts, once in complete games, once in innings pitched, and once in earned run average.

The Most Valuable Player of the 1957 World Series, when he hurled two shutouts, he opposed Harvey Haddix in 1959 when the Pirate threw 12 perfect innings of a nothing-nothing tie against Milwaukee. Haddix lost his gem in the thirteenth inning and soon lost the game as well; Burdette went the distance and got the win despite surrendering 12 hits. In 1960 he pitched a no-hitter of his own when he blanked the Philadelphia Phillies. He faced the minimum of 27 batters in that game, hitting a batter in the fifth inning to ruin his own perfect game although the batter was then retired on a double play.

Burdette returned to the Braves as a coach after they had moved to Atlanta.

Tom Burgess
New York Mets (NL) 1977; Atlanta Braves (NL) 1978
Outfielder and first baseman who spent most of his career in the minor leagues.

Burgess played 17 games for the St. Louis Cardinals in 1954, and 87 for the Los Angeles Angels eight years later. He batted only .177 in those stints. Beginning in 1968 he worked as a manager, coach, and instructor in the organizations of the Cardinals, Mets, Texas Rangers, Detroit Ti-

gers, and Kansas City Royals.

He then became an instructor with Baseball Canada and the Ontario Baseball Association. He was inducted into the Canadian Baseball Hall of Fame in 1992 and the London Sports Hall of Fame in 2003.

Tom Burgmeier
Kansas City Royals (AL) 1991, 1998–2000
Solid relief pitcher for 17 seasons.

Burgmeier started his career in 1968 with the California Angels, but was claimed by the Royals in the expansion draft afterwards. Eight times he posted earned run averages below 3.00, and he was named an American League All-Star in 1980 with the Boston Red Sox.

He pitched until 1984, when he retired due to tendonitis in his shoulder.

Jimmy Burke
Detroit Tigers (AL) 1914–17; Boston Red Sox (AL) 1921–23; Chicago Cubs (NL) 1926–30; New York Yankees (AL) 1931–32
See Managers section.

Jesse Burkett
New York Giants (NL) 1921
Hall of Fame outfielder.

Burkett began his professional career as a pitcher, once winning 30 games with Worcester of the Atlantic Association. As an outfielder he debuted in 1890 and played until 1905. He hit over .400 twice and won three batting titles, while also leading the National League three times in hits and twice in runs scored.

Nicknamed "The Crab" because of his sour demeanor and penchant for complaining, he followed his major league career by becoming the player-owner of the Worcester Busters of the New England League. He later became a minor league manager and college coach. He returned to the major leagues in 1921 as a coach with John McGraw's New York Giants. When the Giants won the World Series, the players refused to vote a share to the caustic Burkett, and McGraw gave him a bonus out of his own pocket.

Jesse was elected to the Hall of Fame by the Veterans Committee in 1946.

Rick Burleson
Oakland Athletics (AL) 1991; Boston Red Sox (AL) 1992–93; California Angels (AL) 1995–96
Four-time All-Star shortstop.

Solid both at the plate and in the field, Burleson hit .273 lifetime and won a Gold Glove in 1979. In 1980 he set a major league record for a shortstop by helping to turn

147 double plays. He was an American League All-Star from 1977–79 with the Red Sox and in 1981 with the Angels. A torn rotator cuff, which he injured twice, hampered his 1982–84 seasons and completely erased 1985, but he won the AL's Comeback Player of the Year Award in 1986 when he hit .284 in 93 games with the Angels.

He retired from the playing field a year later.

George Burns
New York Giants (NL) 1931
Early twentieth century outfielder.

George Joseph Burns began his career with the Giants and had his finest years with them. He hit over .300 three times and averaged .287 for his career. He led the National League twice in stolen bases, peaking with 62 in 1914 and swiping 383 lifetime. He also topped the NL five times in runs scored and five times in bases on balls.

He later played for the Cincinnati Reds and Philadelphia Phillies before returning to the Giants as a coach for one season.

Jack Burns
Boston Red Sox (AL) 1955–59
First baseman, mainly for the St. Louis Browns.

A consistent minor league hitter, Burns was no slouch at the major league level. He played eight games in 1930 and hit .300, and two years later posted a career-high .305 average. He lasted seven seasons and at his position he led the American League twice in assists and three times in double plays.

He finished his career with the Detroit Tigers and later became a coach and scout for the Red Sox.

Ray Burris
Milwaukee Brewers (AL) 1990–91; Texas Rangers (AL) 1992
Reliever who became a solid starter for the Chicago Cubs.

His third season in the major leagues saw Burris go 15–10 in 35 starts, and the next two years he won 15 and 14, respectively. Those years spanned 1975–77, but injuries would take their toll the next few seasons and Burris would not win in double digits again until 1984, when he garnered 13 victories with the Oakland Athletics. He won 108 games lifetime against 134 losses in 15 seasons.

Bill Burwell
Boston Red Sox (AL) 1944; Pittsburgh Pirates (NL) 1947–48, 1958–62
See Managers section.

Jim Busby
Baltimore Orioles (AL) 1961; Houston Colt .45s (NL) 1962–64; Houston Astros (NL) 1965–67; Atlanta Braves (NL) 1968–75; Chicago White Sox (AL) 1976; Seattle Mariners (AL) 1977–78
Speedy outfielder for 13 major league seasons.

A career .262 hitter, Busby batted a career-high .312 in 1953 with the Washington Nationals. In 1951 he was named an American League All-Star when he hit .283 and stole 26 bases for the Chicago White Sox.

A good fielder and the cousin of pitcher Steve Busby, Jim was a player *and* coach for the 1961 Orioles as well as for the 1962 expansion Colt .45s. He went on to coach a number of other teams.

Mike Butcher
Tampa Bay Devil Rays (AL) 2006; Los Angeles Angels of Anaheim (AL) 2007–
Veteran minor leaguer who pitched parts of four seasons in the majors.

Originally drafted by the Kansas City Royals, Butcher went 11–4 in those stints with the California Angels and played 14 professional seasons altogether. He later became a minor league coach and roving pitching instructor for the Angels as well as serving as pitching coach for the Arizona Fall League's Scottsdale Scorpions.

He was named pitching coach of the Devil Rays in November of 2005. One year later, he returned to the Angels as a pitching coach, this time at the big league level.

Sal Butera
Toronto Blue Jays (AL) 1998
Backup catcher for several clubs.

In addition to working behind the plate Butera threw batting practice, and that experience prompted his use as a pitcher on two occasions. In 1985 he pitched one scoreless inning for the Montreal Expos, and in 1986 threw another for the Cincinnati Reds while recording one walk and one strikeout. He retired with a 0.00 earned run average and a .227 batting average.

Brett Butler
Arizona Diamondbacks (NL) 2005
Quick outfielder and consistent hitter.

Butler spent a 17-year career with a variety of teams, but his dependability never wavered. He hit over .300 five times and retired with a .290 lifetime average. He stole over 20 bases 14 times and swiped 558 in his career. In 1985 he led all American League outfielders with a .998 fielding percentage, and in 1991 was named a National League All-Star while playing for the Los Angeles Dodgers. He led his respective league once in hits, four times in triples, twice in runs scored, and once in walks.

In the midst of the 1996 season he underwent two operations for throat cancer, but he was back in the Los Angeles outfield by the first week of September. Unfortunately, in his fifth game back he broke his hand when he was hit by a pitch in a game against the Cincinnati Reds. That ended his season, but he returned in 1997. That would be his final year despite a .283 average in 105 games.

Johnny Butler
Chicago White Sox (AL) 1932
Infielder nicknamed "Trolley Line."

That moniker was appropriate given the fact that Butler debuted with the Brooklyn Robins (later the Dodgers) in 1926. After two seasons he went to the Chicago Cubs, then to the St. Louis Cardinals. In those four seasons he batted .252, and he later coached one season for the White Sox.

Brian Butterfield
New York Yankees (AL) 1994; Arizona Diamondbacks (NL) 1998–2000; Toronto Blue Jays (AL) 2002–
Career minor leaguer.

Butterfield was the team Most Valuable Player of the Fort Lauderdale Yankees in 1981, but he never reached the major leagues. When his playing days ended he became a roving infield instructor in the Yankees' system, and later a coach and manager. He was named the Gulf Coast League's Manager of the Year in 1988, and worked as a manager, coach, and instructor in the following years before being named a coach at the major league level.

After one season in New York he was back working in the minors before being hired by the Diamondbacks and later the Blue Jays.

Chino Cadahia
Atlanta Braves (NL) 2007–
Minor league catcher-turned-manager.

Originally drafted by the Kansas City Royals in 1980, Cadahia never reached the major leagues as a player. He spent many years managing in the Texas Rangers' organization, and was named Gulf Coast League Manager of the Year in 1993. He is also credited with giving catcher Ivan Rodriguez his famous nickname, "Pudge."

In 1997 he became the Atlanta Braves' minor league field coordinator, a position he held until October of 2006 when he was named to the coaching staff of the big club.

Joe Camacho
Washington Senators (AL) 1969–71; Texas Rangers (AL) 1972
Minor leaguer who pitched a no-hitter in his final high school game.

Camacho played in the organizations of the St. Louis Browns, New York Giants, and Cleveland Indians, and also served two years in the Army. In 1952 he was named the Most Valuable Player of the G.I. World Series in Germany.

An ankle injury slowed his minor league career, and he eventually quit baseball and went into teaching. From 1963–68 he returned to baseball as the head of Ted Williams' baseball camp, and Williams himself, as skipper of the Senators (later the Rangers) offered Camacho a big league coaching position. Following the 1972 season Joe went back to education and became a principal until his retirement in 1986.

Doug Camilli
Washington Senators (AL) 1968–69; Boston Red Sox (AL) 1970–73
Son of Dolph Camilli.

Doug was a light-hitting backup catcher for the Los Angeles Dodgers and Washington Senators from 1960–67. His lifetime average was a mere .199, but he did catch Sandy Koufax's third no-hitter with Los Angeles in 1964. He then became a coach in Washington, and caught one more game for them in 1969, going 1-for-3. He later coached the Red Sox.

Bill Campbell
Milwaukee Brewers (NL) 1999
Relief pitcher for many teams.

In a 15-year career Campbell started only 9 of the 700 games he pitched, and all 9 of those came during his first three seasons. He garnered at least 19 saves on three occasions, leading the American League with 31 in 1977 with the Boston Red Sox. He was named an AL All-Star that year, after having posted a remarkable 17 wins the previous season, a league record for a reliever. He was the AL Fireman of the Year in both 1976 and '77. He twice led the league in games pitched.

Campbell played until 1987 and later coached one season with the Brewers.

Chris Cannizzaro
Atlanta Braves (NL) 1976–78
Catcher who played for two expansion teams.

Cannizzaro debuted in seven games for the St. Louis Cardinals in 1960, and the following season appeared in only six because of an appendectomy. Nevertheless he was drafted by the expansion New York Mets, for whom he served mainly as a backup until 1965. After a stint with the Pittsburgh Pirates he became the regular catcher for the expansion San Diego Padres in 1969 and was named a National League All-Star despite hitting only .220.

Jose Cardenal
Cincinnati Reds (NL) 1993, 2002–03; St. Louis Cardinals

(NL) 1994–95; **New York Yankees (AL) 1996–99; Tampa Bay Devil Rays (AL) 2000–01**
Native of Cuba and cousin of Bert Campaneris.

An outfielder who played for 18 seasons, Cardenal hit .275 lifetime and topped the .300 mark twice. He stole 329 bases, swiping more than 20 on nine occasions. In 1968 with the Cleveland Indians he became the fourth outfielder in history to execute two unassisted double plays in the same season.

He played for nine teams in his career and later coached four.

Rod Carew
California Angels (AL) 1992–96; Anaheim Angels (AL) 1997–99; Milwaukee Brewers (NL) 2000–01
Hall of Fame infielder from Panama.

Rod Carew played for 19 seasons and was an All-Star in 18 of them. Named the American League Rookie of the Year in 1967 on his way to a .292 average (one of only four times he hit under .300), he won seven batting titles and peaked with a .388 average in 1977 when he was named the AL's Most Valuable Player. He hit .328 lifetime while garnering 3053 hits, and he led the league three times in hits, twice in triples, once in runs scored, and four times in on-base percentage.

Both the Minnesota Twins and the California Angels retired his number 29, and he was elected to the Hall of Fame in 1991. The next year he began a coaching career with the Angels.

Max Carey
Pittsburgh Pirates (NL) 1930
See Managers section.

P. J. Carey
Colorado Rockies (NL) 1997
Played in the minor leagues for four years before becoming a coach and minor league manager.

A catcher by trade, Carey built a long career as a coach and skipper at the minor league level. He managed at least 13 minor league clubs and was twice named Manager of the Year of the rookie Arizona League while at the helm of the Arizona Rockies in Tucson. He spent one season at the major league level as a coach with Colorado before returning to the minors and eventually piloting the Casper Rockies.

Tom Carey
Boston Red Sox (AL) 1946–47
Infielder from Hoboken, New Jersey.

Thomas Francis Aloysius Carey (not to be confused with Thomas John Carey, the nineteenth century manager)

received a baptism by fire at second base with the St. Louis Browns in 1935. He had never played the position and had to learn it at the major league level, the result being that he led the American League in errors in 1936. He was used mainly in a utility role during his career and hit .275 lifetime in eight major league seasons.

After spending time in the military during World War II, Carey returned as a coach with the Red Sox from 1946–47, and appeared in three games for Boston in '46.

Fred Carisch
Detroit Tigers (AL) 1923–24
Catcher who played 226 games spanning eight seasons.

Carisch appeared in a handful of games for the Pittsburgh Pirates from 1903–06, then another handful for the Cleveland Indians from 1912–14. He later became a coach for the Tigers under Ty Cobb. In the first game of a doubleheader against the Cleveland Indians on July 4, 1923, the Tigers used all three of their catchers, the last of whom was ejected while arguing a call in the tenth inning. Cobb put Carisch in behind the plate. The Indians argued against the 41-year-old coach's insertion, since he was not on the Tigers' "eligible list" of players. Cleveland continued to play under protest, but won the game in the bottom of the inning.

Carisch appeared in one other game that season, but did not bat.

Dave Carlucci
Boston Red Sox (AL) 1996
Had a very brief career as a major league coach.

That career lasted only 25 games. When the Red Sox started out 6–19 in 1996, pitching coach Al Nipper took the heat and was demoted to coordinator of minor league pitching. He was replaced by Sammy Ellis. Carlucci, the bullpen coach, was also demoted, becoming the club's bullpen catcher and being replaced by Herm Starrette. The Sox ended up 85–77.

Dan Carnevale
Kansas City Royals (AL) 1970
Career minor leaguer who signed with the Buffalo Bisons in 1937.

With the Cornwall Bisons of the Canadian-American League the following season Carnevale gained attention by hitting .354 with 100 runs batted in. He played for 15 years with 14 different clubs in 9 leagues, reaching the .300 mark five times, hitting .284 lifetime, and leading his position in fielding average six straight times.

As a minor league skipper he was equally adept, winning five championships in six years. Those titles came with the 1948 Carbondale Pioneers, the 1949 Bradford

Blue Wings, the 1950 Terre Haute Phillies, the 1951 Wilmington Blue Rocks, and the 1953 Jamestown Falcons. He later became Buffalo's manager and general manager.

He scouted for the Oakland Athletics, Baltimore Orioles, and Cleveland Indians, and in 1970 coached the Royals at the big league level. In 1996 he was inducted into the Greater Buffalo Sports Hall of Fame.

Leonel Carrion
Montreal Expos (NL) 1988
Venezuelan who played for many years with the Zulia Eagles.

During the 1977–78 season Carrion became the only native Eagle to score at least 40 runs in a year when he crossed the plate 42 times. An outfielder, he later briefly became a coach with the Expos.

Dick Carter
Philadelphia Phillies (NL) 1959–60
Philadelphia native who coached his native Phillies for two seasons.

Carter had earlier managed in the club's minor league system, skippering the Schenectady Blue Jays from 1956–57 and the Williamsport Grays in 1958.

George Case
Washington Senators (AL) 1961–63; Minnesota Twins (AL) 1968
Speedy outfielder named for the first president of the United States.

George Washington Case was a native of Trenton, New Jersey. A four-time All-Star, he played from 1937–47 and led the American League six times in stolen bases, swiping 349 lifetime. He also hit over .300 three times and topped the circuit in 1943 with 102 runs scored. On July 4, 1940, he tied a major league record by collecting nine hits in a doubleheader.

He later coached for the Senators (the team that became the Texas Rangers) and the Twins.

Dave Cash
Philadelphia Phillies (NL) 1996; Baltimore Orioles (AL) 2005–06
Three-time All-Star second baseman.

Dave Cash played for 12 years and hit .283. With the Phillies he was named a National League All-Star from 1974–76, leading the NL with 213 hits in '75 and with 12 triples in '76. He set several fielding records.

After his playing career Cash became a minor league instructor in the Phillies' organization, then eventually moved up to minor league coach and finally to major league coach with Philadelphia. He then became a minor

league manager before moving to the Orioles' system and being named to their major league staff in August of 2005. In June of 2006 he was reassigned within the organization.

Bill Castro
Milwaukee Brewers (AL) 1992–97, (NL) 1998–
Relief pitcher from Santiago, Dominican Republic.

Castro pitched for 10 seasons and compiled a 31–26 record with a 3.33 earned run average. He pitched for the Brewers, the New York Yankees, and the Kansas City Royals from 1974–83, and attended spring training with the Detroit Tigers in 1984 when he was released. He then became a Brewers' scout for three years, the Brewers' minor league pitching coordinator for four years, and finally the Brewers' bullpen coach. He briefly served as the team's pitching coach from mid-August 2002 to the end of the season when Dave Stewart resigned.

Phil Cavaretta
Detroit Tigers (AL) 1961–63
See Managers section.

Orlando Cepeda
Chicago White Sox (AL) 1980
Ten-time National League All-Star.

Puerto Rican Orlando Cepeda played 17 seasons. He made his mark immediately, winning the NL Rookie of the Year Award in 1958 with the San Francisco Giants on the strength of a .312 batting average, a circuit-topping 38 doubles, and 15 stolen bases. In 1961 he batted .311 with NL-leading totals of 46 homers and 142 runs batted in, and in 1967 he was the league's Most Valuable Player when he hit .325 with 25 home runs, a league-leading 111 RBIs, and 37 doubles.

He coached for the White Sox in 1980. A .297 lifetime hitter, Cepeda was elected to the Hall of Fame in 1999, the same year the Giants retired his number 30.

Chris Chambliss
New York Yankees (AL) 1988, 1996–2000; St. Louis Cardinals (NL) 1993–95; New York Mets (NL) 2002; Cincinnati Reds (NL) 2004–06
Son of a U.S. Navy chaplain.

A solid-hitting first baseman, Chambliss spent 17 years as a major league player. After winning the American Association batting title in 1970 with a .342 average with the Wichita Aeros, he won the American League Rookie of the Year Award in 1971 with the Cleveland Indians by hitting .275 in 111 games. With the Yankees he was named an AL All-Star in 1976, and two years later he won a Gold Glove for his defense as he led the league's first basemen in fielding percentage. Toward the end of his career he was relegated to bench duty, but in 1986 he led the National League in pinch-hits with 20 for the Atlanta Braves. After retiring he became a coach with the Yankees, and he was activated for one game in 1988 but struck out in his only at-bat.

He then became a minor league skipper and was named 1990 Eastern League Manager of the Year with the London Tigers and 1991 Southern League Manager of the Year with the Greenville Braves. He later coached the Cardinals, the Yankees again, and the Mets.

Chambliss had been drafted twice by the Reds, in 1967 and 1969, but both times he decided to continue attending school and eventually signed with the Indians. He finally donned a Reds' uniform in 2004 when he became the club's hitting coach. He was fired following the 2006 season, however, when the team's offense began to sag.

Spud Chandler
Kansas City Athletics (AL) 1957–58
Four-time All-Star pitcher.

A right-hander, Chandler spent his entire 11-year career with the New York Yankees. His finest season by far was 1943, when he won the American League Most Valuable Player Award and led the circuit with a 1.64 earned run average while tying for the lead with 20 wins, 20 complete games, and 5 shutouts. He won 20 games again in 1946 and collected 109 victories lifetime.

He later became a coach for the A's in Kansas City.

Ben Chapman
Cincinnati Reds (NL) 1952
See Managers section.

Rafael Chaves
Seattle Mariners (AL) 2006–
Minor league pitcher from Puerto Rico.

Chaves pitched for 12 seasons in the organizations of the San Diego Padres, Baltimore Orioles, Florida Marlins, and Pittsburgh Pirates. He garnered 130 saves in 487 games lifetime. In 1998 he started coaching in the minors, and he rose through the ranks to become the Mariners' pitching coach in 2006.

Jack Chesbro
Washington Nationals (AL) 1924
Spitballer and Hall of Famer from the early twentieth century.

Chesbro actually began his career in the nineteenth century, debuting with the Pittsburgh Pirates in 1899. In 11 seasons he won 198 games, and from 1901–06 his victory totals were 21, a league-leading 28, 21, a league-leading 41, 19, and 23. He also topped the circuit twice in games

pitched, twice in starts, once in complete games, twice in shutouts, and once in innings pitched. His lifetime earned run average was 2.68.

Chesbro pitched the first game for the New York Highlanders (now the Yankees) after their relocation from Baltimore. He coached for the Nationals in 1924, and was elected to the Hall of Fame in 1946.

Dom Chiti
Cleveland Indians (AL) 1990–93; Texas Rangers (AL) 2006–
Son of major league catcher Harry Chiti.

Dom began a minor league pitching career in 1976 but retired in 1981 due to arm problems. He eventually became a roving pitching instructor and minor league coach for the Baltimore Orioles, then the bullpen coach and later a scout for the Indians.

He signed with the Rangers in 2002 and worked as a special assistant to the general manager and then as the director of player personnel before joining the dugout staff in 2006 as bullpen coach.

Galen Cisco
Kansas City Royals (AL) 1971–79; Montreal Expos (NL) 1980–84; San Diego Padres (NL) 1985–87; Toronto Blue Jays (AL) 1988, 1990–95; Philadelphia Phillies (NL) 1997–2000
Football champion with Ohio State University.

Cisco was co-captain and fullback on that 1957 team. As a baseball pitcher he had less success, lasting seven major league seasons, mostly as a reliever, and posting a 25–56 record with a 4.56 earned run average.

After his playing career he became a longtime and much-admired pitching coach.

Dave Clark
Pittsburgh Pirates (NL) 2001–02
Outfielder for many teams over 13 seasons.

One of those teams was the Pirates, and in a 1995 game Clark nearly ended his career in a frightening collision with teammate Jacob Brumfield. Clark blacked out just before his head struck the outfield wall, and he suffered a broken collarbone, a loose tooth, and various cuts.

He was able to come back, however, and played until 1998. After retiring from the Houston Astros he returned to the Pirates as a coach.

Jack Clark
Los Angeles Dodgers (NL) 2001–03
Injury-prone outfielder who nevertheless lasted 18 major league seasons.

Clark had power and was a feared clutch hitter. A four-time All-Star, he hit 340 home runs lifetime, reaching at least 20 eleven times. He led the league three times in bases on balls and hit over .300 twice.

Toward the end of his final season while with the Boston Red Sox, 1992, Clark filed for bankruptcy, citing debts of over $11 million and assets of over $4 million. He hit only .210 that season and would not play again, but he did coach the Dodgers from 2001–03.

Ron Clark
Chicago White Sox (AL) 1988–90; Seattle Mariners (AL) 1991; Cleveland Indians (AL) 1992–93
Backup infielder for seven seasons.

Clark got by mainly with his glove, because he hit only .189 in his career with several teams. A native of Fort Worth, Texas, he was also a rodeo rider and a Golden Gloves boxer.

His playing career ended in 1975, but he eventually returned to the major leagues as a coach.

Fred Clarke
Pittsburgh Pirates (NL) 1925
See Managers section.

Tommy Clarke
New York Giants (NL) 1932–35, 1938
Catcher in the early twentieth century.

A .265 lifetime hitter, Clarke played nine seasons for the Cincinnati Reds and only one game in a tenth season for the Chicago Cubs. He was excellent defensively and was no slouch at the plate.

A native New Yorker, he coached his hometown Giants for several years in the 1930s under John McGraw and Bill Terry.

Ellis Clary
Washington Nationals (AL) 1955–56; Washington Senators (AL) 1957–60; Toronto Blue Jays (AL) 1989–93
Infielder who played parts of four major league seasons.

Clary hit .263 in 223 games for the Washington Nationals and St. Louis Browns. A third baseman, he continued to play in the minor leagues when his major league career was over, then became a minor league coach and manager. From 1955–60 he coached the Washington Nationals, who changed their name to Senators in 1958. In 1961 he began to work as a scout for the team, which was now the Minnesota Twins, and later served in the same role for the Chicago White Sox.

He worked as an infielders' coach for the Blue Jays from 1989–93 and then retired. Clary died in 2000 at the age of 85.

Bob Clear
California Angels (AL) 1976–87
Minor league infielder-turned-pitcher who coached many years for the Angels.

Clear managed in the Pittsburgh Pirates' organization before joining the Angels' system in the same role in 1970. He was promoted to the big club as a coach in 1976 and spent 12 years in California, then he worked as a roving minor league instructor for the organization. He is credited with converting Troy Percival from a catcher into a pitcher after seeing Percival play in the minors. Unimpressed with the right-hander's hitting ability (or lack thereof) but very impressed with his knack for throwing out runners from behind the plate, Clear suggested Troy try pitching and, to the delight of the Angels, his advice was heeded.

Gene Clines
Chicago Cubs (NL) 1979–81, 2003–06; Houston Astros (NL) 1988; Seattle Mariners (AL) 1989–92; Milwaukee Brewers (AL) 1993–94; San Francisco Giants (NL) 1997–2002
Speedy outfielder for several teams.

After hitting .405 in 31 games for the Pittsburgh Pirates in 1970, Clines played nine more major league seasons. He batted .308 in 1971 and .334, his career high, the next year, while averaging .277 lifetime. He retired from the Cubs during the 1979 season but stayed on as the team's first base coach.

He later joined the Astros' system as a roving minor league hitting instructor before returning as a major league coach in Houston, Seattle, and Milwaukee. He then worked as a minor league hitting coordinator for the Giants before joining that big league club, and later returned to the Cubs.

Tony Cloninger
New York Yankees (AL) 1992–2001; Boston Red Sox (AL) 2003, 2004
North Carolina farmer.

Cloninger is perhaps most famous for the 1966 game in which he hit two grand slams, the only National Leaguer and the only pitcher to accomplish that feat. Those blasts and his nine runs batted in on the day paced the Atlanta Braves to a 17–3 victory over the San Francisco Giants.

Tony also held his own on the mound, however, winning 19 games in 1964 and 24 in 1965 en route to 113 lifetime victories. He retired in 1972 and later coached the Yankees and Red Sox. In 2003 with Boston he was replaced briefly in May by Glenn Gregson because Cloninger was recovering from bladder cancer and the Red Sox were preparing to travel to Toronto, which was experiencing an outbreak of severe acute respiratory syndrome (SARS). It was thought that Cloninger's immune system may not have been equipped to fight off SARS. In June he left the club for the rest of the season to seek further treatment. He was replaced in this instance by Dave Wallace, but he returned in 2004.

Bob Cluck
Houston Astros (NL) 1972–73, 1974, 1979, 1980, 1981, 1990–93; Oakland Athletics (AL) 1996–97; Detroit Tigers (AL) 2003–05
Minor league pitcher who eventually served in many roles.

Cluck played in the Astros' system and became a player-coach in 1972 and 1973. In 1974 he returned solely to playing, but was a full-time coach by the end of the year. He eventually worked for several organizations as a minor league field coordinator, instructor, manager, scout, coordinator, and director of minor league development. From 1979–81 he served several stints as the Astros' interim pitching coach. He then worked at the major league level in Houston again, in Oakland, and in Detroit.

Cluck has also written many books on baseball fundamentals.

Bill Clymer
Cincinnati Reds (NL) 1925
Philadelphia native who played only three games for the Athletics of the American Association in 1891.

A shortstop, Clymer went 0-for-11 in those three games. He later became a minor league manager and was nicknamed "Derby Day" because he used to clap his hands and try to encourage his players by exclaiming, "It's Derby Day today!" He eventually coached one season for the Reds.

Mickey Cochrane
Philadelphia Athletics (AL) 1950
See Managers section.

Alan Cockrell
Colorado Rockies (NL) 2002, 2007–
Played nine games for the Rockies and hit .625.

Cockrell spent five seasons with the Colorado Springs Sky Sox in the Rockies' system, and he retired as that team's all-time leader in games played, hits, doubles, runs batted in, and walks, as well as finishing second in home runs and runs scored. In 1990 he was named a Pacific Coast League All-Star, and the Sky Sox inducted him into their Hall of Fame and retired his number 31 in 1996.

Alan eventually returned to the major league club for two stints as a coach.

Andy Cohen
Philadelphia Phillies (NL) 1960
See Managers section.

Rocky Colavito
Cleveland Indians (AL) 1973, 1976–78; Kansas City Royals (AL) 1982–83
Power-hitting outfielder and nine-time All-Star.

Originally signed as a pitcher and outfielder, Colavito did eventually pitch two major league games in his career, but he also emerged as a prolific and highly valuable home run threat. He hit at least 21 home runs every year from 1956 through 1966, peaking with 45 in 1961 and clouting 374 lifetime. He tied for the American League lead with 42 in 1959, and in 1965 topped the AL with 108 runs batted in and 93 bases on balls. On June 10, 1959, he smashed four home runs in four consecutive at-bats. In 1965 he proved that his bat was not his only asset as he set a major league record by playing a full 162 games in the outfield and not committing a single error.

Colavito debuted with the Indians, and after being traded away he was eventually reacquired by them. He finished his career with the New York Yankees, but later returned to the Tribe as a coach and also coached the Royals.

Craig Colbert
San Diego Padres (NL) 2007–
Backup catcher and third baseman for the San Francisco Giants.

Colbert hit only .215 in limited playing time for the Giants during the 1992 and 1993 seasons, but spent 13 years as a professional player. He ended his playing career as a player-coach with the Las Vegas Stars in 1998, and he soon began to manage in the Padres' organization. His 2001 Lake Elsinore Storm won the co-championship of the California League when the final series was canceled due to the terrorist attacks on the United States.

One of Colbert's teammates on the Giants had been pitcher Bud Black, and when Black was named Padres' manager in 2007 he promoted Colbert to the big league club as a member of his coaching staff.

Jim Colborn
Los Angeles Dodgers (NL) 2001–05; Pittsburgh Pirates (NL) 2006–
California native who attended the University of Edinburgh on a Rotary Foundation Fellowship.

Colborn was All-Scotland in basketball at Edinburgh, but he became a major league baseball pitcher back in the United States. He threw for 10 seasons and achieved his greatest success in 1973 with the Milwaukee Brewers, when he went 20–12 and was named an American League All-Star. He won 18 games in 1977 with the Kansas City Royals.

After his playing career Colborn became a minor

league coach and manager, and he coached in Japan for four years with the Orix Blue Wave. He later scouted for the Seattle Mariners before being named a coach with the Dodgers and later with the Pirates.

Colborn also appeared in the Kevin Costner film *For Love of the Game.*

Dick Cole
Chicago Cubs (NL) 1961
Infielder who hit .249 lifetime.

Cole played second base, third base, and shortstop, mainly as a backup, for six major league seasons. His only year as a regular was 1954, when he appeared in 138 games for the Pittsburgh Pirates and hit a respectable .270. He later coached the Cubs for one season.

Bob Coleman
Boston Red Sox (AL) 1928; Detroit Tigers (AL) 1932; Boston Braves (NL) 1943
See Managers section.

Joe Coleman
California Angels (AL) 1987–90, 1996; St. Louis Cardinals (NL) 1991–94; Anaheim Angels (AL) 1997–99
Son of major league pitcher Joseph Patrick Coleman.

Joseph Howard Coleman combined with his father for 194 major league victories, third-highest among father-son combinations in history. The father lasted 10 seasons, the son 15. Joseph Howard posted 142 of those wins and garnered totals of 20, 19, and 23 from 1971–73. In 1972 he was named an American League All-Star while pitching for the Detroit Tigers.

He went on to coach for the Angels, the Cardinals, and the Angels again.

Dave Collins
St. Louis Cardinals (NL) 1991–92; Detroit Tigers (AL) 1996; Cincinnati Reds (NL) 1999–2000; Milwaukee Brewers (NL) 2002; Colorado Rockies (NL) 2003–06
Fast outfielder who stole 395 bases lifetime.

Collins made his debut with the California Angels in 1975, then was selected by the Seattle Mariners in the expansion draft for the 1977 campaign. After one season he was traded to the Reds, and later moved on to several other teams, including a second stint in Cincinnati.

He hit over .300 three times and batted .272 for his career. He swiped over 20 bases nine times, topping out with 79 in 1980. In 1984 he tied for the American League lead with 15 triples while playing for the Toronto Blue Jays.

After coaching for the Cardinals Collins scouted one season for the club. For the final two months of the 1996 season he was named bunting and baserunning coach of the

Tigers, then returned to the Reds as a minor league instructor and later major league coach. In 2001 he managed the Salem Avalanche to the Carolina League championship, and was then promoted to Brewers' coach before moving on to the Rockies. He resigned from Colorado following the 2006 season.

Eddie Collins
Philadelphia Athletics (AL) 1931–32
See Managers section.

Rip Collins
Chicago Cubs (NL) 1961–63
Pitched for 11 seasons and won 108 games.

Harry Warren "Rip" Collins was a four-sport star at Texas A & M, and most of his major league baseball career was spent in the 1920s. He was renowned for his lack of enthusiasm, his real passions being hunting, fishing, and partying.

He coached three years for the Cubs and eventually went into law enforcement in his home state of Texas.

Terry Collins
Pittsburgh Pirates (NL) 1992–93; Tampa Bay Devil Rays (AL) 2001
See Managers section.

Earle Combs
New York Yankees (AL) 1935–44; St. Louis Browns (AL) 1947; Boston Red Sox (AL) 1948–52; Philadelphia Phillies (NL) 1954
Speedy Hall of Fame outfielder.

"The Kentucky Colonel" played his entire career with the Yankees, spanning 1924–35. He hit .400 in 24 games his first year, and failed to hit .300 only twice—in 1926 when he batted .299, and in his final season of 1935, when he hit .282. He averaged .325 lifetime and led the American League three times in triples and once in hits.

Following his playing days he began a long career as a coach, starting with the Yankees. He was elected to the Hall of Fame in 1970.

Merl Combs
Texas Rangers (AL) 1974–75
All-Conference shortstop from the University of Southern California.

Mainly a career minor leaguer, Combs appeared in 140 major league games over five seasons. He hit only .202, and later coached the Rangers and spent many years as a scout.

Steve Comer
Cleveland Indians (AL) 1987
Seven-year major league pitcher.

Comer debuted with the Texas Rangers and won 11 and 17 games his first two seasons, respectively. A shoulder injury limited him to only 12 games and 2 victories the following season, and he never again won more than 8.

He finished his career with the Indians and then coached one season for them.

Mark Connor
New York Yankees (AL) 1984–85, 1986–87, 1990–93; Arizona Diamondbacks (NL) 1998–2000; Toronto Blue Jays (AL) 2001–02; Texas Rangers (AL) 2003–
Minor league pitcher whose career ended due to an arm injury.

At Columbia University Connor once struck out 20 batters in a game, and in the minor leagues he whiffed 108 in 109 career innings. He began his coaching career at the University of Tennessee from 1974–78, and he then became a scout with the Yankees and a minor league pitching coach. After serving two stints on New York's major league staff he became head coach at the University of Tennessee in Knoxville, then returned to the Yankees' system.

He worked as a coach in the Blue Jays' organization and as a scout and pitching coordinator for the Diamondbacks before returning to the major league level for Arizona. He was the Blue Jays' pitching coach from 2001 until June of 2002, when he resigned following the firing of manager Buck Martinez. He was hired by the Rangers in 2003.

Billy Connors
Kansas City Royals (AL) 1980–81; Chicago Cubs (NL) 1982–86, 1991–93; Seattle Mariners (AL) 1987–88; New York Yankees (AL) 1989–90, 1994–95, 2000
Pitched 26 major league games during three seasons.

Connors' 7.53 earned run average did not exactly distinguish him as a player, but he fashioned quite a career as a coach. He worked for a time in the New York Mets' organization as a pitching coach before reaching the major league level with the Royals, Cubs, Mariners, and Yankees.

He later served as the Yankees' vice president of player personnel.

Wid Conroy
Philadelphia Phillies (NL) 1922
Native of Camden, New Jersey.

Conroy was a shortstop who played briefly for the Paterson Giants of the Atlantic League before malaria nearly cut his career short. He recovered and ended up with the Milwaukee Brewers (today's Baltimore Orioles) in the brand new American League in 1901. He played for 11 seasons, having switched to third base early on with the New York Highlanders.

He retired in 1911 and later coached one season for the Phillies.

Billy Consolo
Detroit Tigers (AL) 1979–92
Light-hitting infielder who played for 10 major league seasons.

Consolo went from high school directly to the Boston Red Sox, where he played from 1953 until 1959. He finished his career in 1962 and hit only .221 lifetime, his season high being .270 in 1957 in 68 games.

He later became a longtime Tigers' coach.

Guy Conti
New York Mets (NL) 2005–
Minor league catcher-turned-pitcher.

Conti played from 1960–63, when his career was cut short by a shoulder injury. He eventually worked as a scout and coach in the Pittsburgh Pirates' organization, and as a coach and minor league pitching coordinator for the Los Angeles Dodgers. He then became a coach and minor league field coordinator in the Mets' system before being appointed bullpen coach for the big club.

Nardi Contreras
New York Yankees (AL) 1995; Seattle Mariners (AL) 1997–98; Chicago White Sox (AL) 1998–2002
Pitched eight games for the White Sox in 1980.

Those eight games constituted Contreras' entire major league career, and in $18^2/_3$ innings he fashioned a 5.93 earned run average. In 1989 he played in the Senior Professional Baseball Association with the St. Petersburg Pelicans.

After coaching the Yankees in 1995, Contreras went to the Mariners. He spent all of 1997 with the club and was fired only 11 games into the 1998 season. With the White Sox in 1992, he was "reassigned" in July and replaced by Don Cooper.

Dusty Cooke
Philadelphia Phillies (NL) 1948–52
See Managers section.

Jack Coombs
Detroit Tigers (AL) 1920
See Managers section.

Johnny Cooney
Boston Bees (NL) 1940; Boston Braves (NL) 1941–42, 1946–49, 1950–52; Milwaukee Braves (NL) 1953–55; Chicago White Sox (AL) 1957–64
See Managers section.

Cecil Cooper
Milwaukee Brewers (NL) 2002; Houston Astros (NL) 2005–
Five-time All-Star first baseman.

Good with both a bat and a glove, Cooper was a .298 lifetime hitter. He spent his entire 17-year career with the Boston Red Sox and Milwaukee Brewers, along the way hitting 241 lifetime home runs. He hit at least 20 five times, hit at least .300 nine times, and led the American League twice in doubles and twice in runs batted in. He also netted himself two Gold Gloves.

Cooper retired in 1987 and then worked for nine years as an agent. In 1997 he returned to the Brewers as their director of player development before becoming a special assistant to the general manager and roving minor league hitting instructor. Early in 2002 he became the team's bench coach, then managed the AAA Indianapolis Indians. In 2005 he was hired by the Astros as their bench coach.

Don Cooper
Chicago White Sox (AL) 1998, 2002–
Pitched 44 games in parts of four major league seasons.

Cooper was largely ineffective in his short big league stints, although at the minor league level he pitched a no-hitter in 1978 for the Fort Lauderdale Yankees against the Fort Myers Royals, and in 1983 was named an All-Star with the Syracuse Chiefs.

He worked in the White Sox' system for many years as a coach and pitching coordinator, spending most of 1998 as Chicago's pitching coach before being named to the position permanently in 2002.

Walker Cooper
St. Louis Cardinals (NL) 1957; Kansas City Athletics (AL) 1960
Upbeat, likable catcher.

An eight-time All-Star, Cooper played for 18 major league seasons and hit .285 lifetime. He hit over .300 nine times and was well respected for his work behind the plate. In 1947 with the New York Giants he hit 35 home runs with 122 runs batted in, and he slugged 20 roundtrippers in 1949.

Cooper's brother Mort was a pitcher with the Cardinals, and for a time the two were batterymates. Walker lost most of the 1945 season to the Navy, but the war was almost over and he was back in 1946.

Joey Cora
Chicago White Sox (AL) 2004–
Switch-hitting infielder for 11 seasons.

Cora played four of those years with the White Sox, but his best season came with the Seattle Mariners in 1997 when he batted .300 with 11 home runs and 54 runs batted in while being named an American League All-Star.

Joey concluded his playing career in 1998, and the following year he began working as a general manager in the Puerto Rican Winter League. He soon started coaching and managing in the minor leagues, and returned to the White Sox as a coach in 2004.

Pat Corrales
Texas Rangers (AL) 1976–78; New York Yankees (AL) 1989; Atlanta Braves (NL) 1990–2006; Washington Nationals (NL) 2007–
See Managers section.

Red Corriden
Chicago Cubs (NL) 1932–40; Brooklyn Dodgers (NL) 1941–46; New York Yankees (AL) 1947–48; Chicago White Sox (AL) 1950
See Managers section.

Chuck Cottier
New York Mets (NL) 1979–81; Seattle Mariners (AL) 1982–84; Chicago Cubs (NL) 1988–94; Baltimore Orioles (AL) 1995; Philadelphia Phillies (NL) 1997–2000
See Managers section.

Mike Couchee
California Angels (AL) 1996
Relief pitcher and native of San Jose, California.

Couchee was drafted three times. In 1976 he was picked by the San Francisco Giants and in 1978 by the Minnesota Twins, but both times he chose to attend college. In 1980 he finally signed with the San Diego Padres, and all of his big league games came with San Diego in 1983. He collected a hit in his first major league at-bat, but posted an 0–1 record and a 5.14 earned run average.

In 1986 he began coaching in the minor leagues in the Texas Rangers' organization, and later spent 15 years with the Angels, one of them as a big league coach at the end of the 1996 campaign. In 2003 he returned to the Padres as a minor league coach and pitching coordinator.

Clint Courtney
Houston Astros (NL) 1965
The first catcher to wear glasses.

Courtney was named American League Rookie of the Year by *The Sporting News* in 1952 when he hit .286 with

24 doubles and 50 runs batted in. He hit over .300 twice in an 11-year career and batted .268 lifetime.

Clint eventually coached the Astros for one year and also served as a minor league manager. He died in June of 1975 as the skipper of the Richmond Braves.

Bobby Cox
New York Yankees (AL) 1977
See Managers section.

Jeff Cox
Kansas City Royals (AL) 1995; Montreal Expos (NL) 2000–01; Florida Marlins (NL) 2002–05; Pittsburgh Pirates (NL) 2006–
Second baseman who played 61 major league games.

Mainly a career minor leaguer, Cox hit .311 in 1976 with the Modesto A's and .290 the following season with the Chattanooga Lookouts. In 1980 with the Ogden A's he hit .288 and was called up to the Oakland Athletics. He played 59 games but batted only .213, then got into only two the next season—with no at-bats—to end his major league experience as a player.

That experience continued as a coach, however, beginning in 1995 with the Royals.

Larry Cox
Chicago Cubs (NL) 1988–89
Light-hitting catcher who played for nine seasons.

Cox spent most of his career as a backup, beginning in 1973, and was one of the original Seattle Mariners in 1977. He spent a year with the Cubs but returned to Seattle the following season and became the regular backstop. In two seasons as a starter he hit only .215 and .202, respectively, and went back into a reserve role for two more seasons.

He then became a minor league manager in the Cubs' system and an eventual major league coach with Chicago. He died of a heart attack in February of 1990 while playing racquetball.

Estel Crabtree
Cincinnati Reds (NL) 1943–44
Outfielder with two distinct playing careers.

Crabtree made his major league debut in one game with the Reds in 1929, then he was a regular outfielder from 1931–32. Going to the St. Louis Cardinals in 1933, he lasted only 23 games before being relegated to the minor leagues for the next eight years.

He reappeared with the Cardinals in 1941, and played two more seasons for St. Louis and then two more for the Reds as a player-coach during the war years. He retired with a respectable .281 batting average.

Harry Craft
Kansas City Athletics (AL) 1955–57; Chicago Cubs (NL) 1960–61
See Managers section.

Roger Craig
San Diego Padres (NL) 1969–72, 1976–78; Houston Astros (NL) 1974–75; Detroit Tigers (AL) 1980–84
See Managers section.

Doc Cramer
Detroit Tigers (AL) 1948; Chicago White Sox (AL) 1951–53
Quick, excellent outfielder.

Cramer played for 20 major league seasons. Along the way he twice led the American League in putouts and in 1940 led with 200 hits. He was named to five All-Star teams and batted .296 lifetime, twice garnering six hits in a game and once hitting for the cycle. He hit over .300 eight times.

When his work as a regular was finished he continued as a pinch-hitter, and he topped the AL in that category in 1947. He was named a Tigers' coach in 1948 and also appeared in four games for them.

Del Crandall
California Angels (AL) 1977
See Managers section.

Doc Crandall
Pittsburgh Pirates (NL) 1931–34
Relief pitcher who won 102 games in 10 seasons.

Crandall led the National League in relief wins three years in a row. He garnered 17 victories overall in 1910, 15 in 1911, and 13 in 1912. In 1914 he jumped from the New York Giants to the St. Louis Terriers of the Federal League, and in 1915 went 21–15 while also leading the FL in relief wins with 6.

In 1918 with the Los Angeles Angels of the Pacific Coast League Crandall was one out away from a no-hitter against the Salt Lake City Bees when his brother Karl broke it up. Doc appeared in five games for the Boston Braves that year to finish out his major league career. He later coached several years for the Pirates.

Gavvy Cravath
Philadelphia Phillies (NL) 1923
See Managers section.

Mark Cresse
Los Angeles Dodgers (NL) 1974–98
Longtime Dodgers' coach.

After a long and productive coaching career in Los Angeles Cresse became most famous for the Mark Cresse School of Baseball. He helped found the training program, which teaches baseball fundamentals to children, in 1984, and after retiring from the Dodgers in 1998 began working full-time with the school. Beginning with one camp site and 140 ballplayers to help, the school soon expanded to six sites and over 2000 players.

Frank Crosetti
New York Yankees (AL) 1946–68; Seattle Pilots (AL) 1969; Minnesota Twins (AL) 1970–71
Longtime Yankees' infielder and coach.

A light hitter but outstanding fielder, Crosetti spent 37 consecutive seasons in a New York uniform. He played from 1932–48, spending the last three of those years as a player-coach, and then continued to coach until 1968. He hit only .245 lifetime but twice led American League shortstops in putouts and double plays. He was named an All-Star twice.

At the end of the 1942 season Crosetti shoved an umpire while arguing during a game, and as a result was suspended for the first 30 games of 1943. At the plate he led the league eight times in being hit by pitches.

When his Yankee career was finally concluded Crosetti coached a season for the expansion Pilots and then two years for the Twins.

Terry Crowley
Baltimore Orioles (AL) 1985–88, 1999– ; Minnesota Twins (AL) 1991–98
First designated hitter for the Orioles.

Crowley spent his entire career as a backup outfielder and DH. He became something of a pinch-hitting specialist, and toward the end of his career served almost exclusively as a DH with Baltimore. He played for several other teams between his two Baltimore stints and finished his career with the Montreal Expos.

Crowley then returned to the Orioles again, this time as a minor league batting instructor and very soon thereafter as major league hitting coach. He later became a minor league hitting instructor for the Boston Red Sox and a big league coach for the Twins before returning to the Orioles yet again in 1999.

Jose Cruz
Houston Astros (NL) 1997–
Brother of Hector and Tommy Cruz.

Jose spent the bulk of his career with the Astros, for whom he had great success. He hit over .300 seven times in 19 seasons and in 1983 tied for the National League lead with 183 hits. He stole more than 20 bases in a season eight times. He was a two-time All-Star, and when he retired he held many Houston offensive records. The club retired his number 25 in 1992.

Cruz briefly managed in the minor leagues after retiring and then returned to the Astros as a coach. During the 1999 season he missed 34 games because of an irregular heartbeat. In 2003 he was inducted into the Texas Baseball Hall of Fame.

He is also the father of major leaguer Jose Cruz, Jr.

Mike Cubbage
New York Mets (NL) 1990–96; Houston Astros (NL) 1997–2001; Boston Red Sox (AL) 2002–04
See Managers section.

Tony Cuccinello
Cincinnati Reds (NL) 1949–51; Cleveland Indians (AL) 1952–56; Chicago White Sox (AL) 1957–66, 1969; Detroit Tigers (AL) 1967–68
Excellent infielder and .280 lifetime hitter.

In 15 major league seasons Cuccinello led National League second basemen in assists three times and in double plays three times. At the plate he hit over .300 five times, including his final, All-Star season of 1945 when he batted .308. He had previously been named an All-Star in 1933 and 1938.

His brother Al played 54 major league games, and his nephew was Sam Mele.

Bobby Cuellar
Seattle Mariners (AL) 1995–96; Montreal Expos (NL) 1997–2000; Texas Rangers (AL) 2001; Pittsburgh Pirates (NL) 2006–
Minor leaguer who played four games at the major league level.

Cuellar was drafted by the Rangers in 1974, and he played 12 minor league seasons. In 1977 he pitched in relief four times for Texas and posted an excellent 1.35 earned run average, but he never made it back except as a coach. He became a minor league manager immediately following his retirement, and eventually coached several big league clubs in addition to the Rangers.

Benny Culp
Philadelphia Phillies (NL) 1946–47
Catcher who played 15 major league games over three seasons.

Those games spanned 1942–44 with the Phillies, and Culp then left for the military. When World War II was over he returned to Philadelphia, but this time as a coach. A Philadelphia native, he died in his hometown in October of 2000.

John Cumberland
Boston Red Sox (AL) 1995, 1999–2001; Kansas City Royals (AL) 2002–04
Reliever who became a starter with the San Francisco Giants.

Cumberland pitched for six seasons and posted a 3.82 earned run average. His career, which ended in 1974, was cut short due to an arm injury.

With the Red Sox in 2001 he was promoted from bullpen coach to pitching coach during the season, then was abruptly "reassigned" within the organization just minutes before a September game. An angry Cumberland lashed out at the Boston front office and refused to report. He was hired by the Royals the next season.

Bill Cunningham
Chicago White Sox (AL) 1932
Excellent defensive outfielder.

Cunningham manned center field for the New York Giants and Boston Braves from 1921–24. A part-timer his first three seasons, he hit .286 lifetime and later became a coach with the White Sox.

Joe Cunningham
St. Louis Cardinals (NL) 1982
First baseman and .291 lifetime hitter.

Cunningham debuted in 1954 with the Cardinals and promptly hit three home runs in his first two games. He batted .318 in 1957 and .312 the next year. In 1959 he became a National League All-Star when he batted .345 with a league-leading .456 on-base percentage. In 1962 with the Chicago White Sox he led all American League first basemen in fielding percentage. The following year he fractured his collarbone in a collision and never quite recovered from the injury. He lasted until 1966, but would never hit over .250 again.

He returned to the Cardinals as a coach for one season in 1982.

Kiki Cuyler
Chicago Cubs (NL) 1941–43; Boston Red Sox (AL) 1949
Speedy Hall of Fame outfielder.

Kiki (rhymes with "bye bye") got his nickname from the first syllable of his last name. While he was playing baseball in school, he would rush in for short pop flies and infielders would yell, "Cuy! Cuy!" intending for him to take the ball. The spelling became "Kiki."

Cuyler attended West Point during World War I, then worked for Buick and later for Chevrolet. He reached the major leagues with the Pittsburgh Pirates in 1921 and played 18 seasons. A .321 lifetime hitter, he led the National League once in doubles, once in triples, twice in runs

scored, and four times in stolen bases. He swiped 328 sacks in his career. In 1934 he was named an NL All-Star while playing for the Cubs. In a 1936 doubleheader he collected eight consecutive hits.

After his playing career he became a minor league skipper, then returned to the Cubs as a coach. He coached the Red Sox in 1949, and died suddenly in February of 1950, only 51 years of age.

Babe Dahlgren
Kansas City Athletics (AL) 1964
First baseman who replaced Lou Gehrig.

It was Dahlgren who manned first base the day Gehrig finally decided to sit down, ending his then-record streak of 2130 consecutive games played. Babe had actually debuted with the Boston Red Sox in 1935, had spent 1937 with the Newark Bears of the International League, and had gone to the New York Yankees in 1938 before that historic day the following year. Dahlgren hit a home run and a double in that contest.

He ended up playing for seven teams in a 12-year career, and was named a National League All-Star in 1943 with the Philadelphia Phillies. He was a .261 lifetime hitter.

Bruce Dal Canton
Chicago White Sox (AL) 1978; Atlanta Braves (NL) 1987–90
Semipro pitcher who reached the major leagues.

Signed by the Pittsburgh Pirates in 1967 after becoming a high school teacher, Dal Canton pitched for 11 seasons and posted a 3.67 earned run average. With the Kansas City Royals in 1972 he once retired 23 consecutive New York Yankees in a game. He was named the White Sox' pitching coach in June of 1978, and later became a roving minor league pitching instructor for the Braves. After serving four seasons as pitching coach in Atlanta, he returned to the Braves' minor league system in the same capacity at several levels for many years.

He also has a master's degree in biology.

Tom Daly
Boston Red Sox (AL) 1933–46
Backup catcher from Canada.

Daly played eight seasons but totaled only 244 major league games. A light hitter, he averaged just .239 lifetime, but did hit .311 in 44 games with the 1920 Chicago Cubs. He later became a coach with the Red Sox for many years.

Bill Dancy
Philadelphia Phillies (NL) 2005–06
Infielder who never played in the major leagues.

Dancy played for six years in the Phillies' minor league

system, his best season being 1977 when he hit .311 with the Oklahoma City 89ers. He had only one at-bat the following season before retiring and joining the AA Reading Phillies as a coach.

He served as a minor league coach, manager, or coordinator in the Phillies' system for all but two years between 1978 and 2004. Those years were 1996 and 1997, when he managed the Richmond Braves in the Atlanta organization. In 1983 he was named Eastern League Manager of the Year by *The Sporting News* when his Reading club posted a 96–44 record, best in the team's history. He won minor league championships in 1980, 1983, and 1995. In 2005 he was finally named a major league coach in Philadelphia, where he stayed for two seasons.

Alvin Dark
Chicago Cubs (NL) 1965, 1977
See Managers section.

Jeff Datz
Cleveland Indians (AL) 2002–
Catcher who played seven major league games.

Datz played in the minor league system of the Houston Astros from 1982–88, and in 1989 reached the Detroit Tigers and hit .200 in seven contests. He spent the next season with the Columbus Clippers before becoming a scout and later manager in the Indians' organization.

Jeff skippered the 1998 Buffalo Bisons to the International League championship, and following the 1999 season was named minor league field coordinator. During spring training of 2002 he replaced Grady Little as an Indians' coach when Little was hired to manage the Boston Red Sox.

Rich Dauer
Cleveland Indians (AL) 1990–91; Kansas City Royals (AL) 1997–2002; Milwaukee Brewers (NL) 2003–05
Infielder from San Bernardino, California.

Dauer spent 10 years in the major leagues, mainly as a second baseman and entirely with the Baltimore Orioles. He had once won the batting title in the minor International League with a .336 average, but in the majors he would hit .257.

Because of his successful career, the minor league San Bernardino Spirit in his hometown retired the number 25 he had worn with the Orioles. He later coached the Indians, Royals, and Brewers.

Darren Daulton
Tampa Bay Devil Rays (AL) 2001
Oft-injured catcher who played for 14 years.

Daulton injured his knees several times, and as a result was unable to crouch as low as most other backstops. A 1986 home plate collision did the most damage to his left knee. In 1991 he was in an auto accident while teammate Lenny Dykstra was driving him home from John Kruk's bachelor party. Dykstra had been driving under the influence and suffered some rather debilitating injuries, and Daulton got away with a broken left eye socket and a scratched cornea. In 1994 he injured his collarbone because of a foul tip, and in 1995 tore ligaments in his right knee.

Daulton persisted in spite of those injuries and was an All-Star on three occasions. One of those seasons was 1992, when he hit .270 with 27 home runs and a league-leading 109 runs batted in. He spent his entire career with the Philadelphia Phillies until the latter part of 1997, when he finished things out with the Florida Marlins. In 2001 he coached the Devil Rays.

Jim Davenport
San Francisco Giants (NL) 1970, 1976–82, 1996; San Diego Padres (NL) 1974–75; Philadelphia Phillies (NL) 1986–87; Cleveland Indians (AL) 1989
See Managers section.

Andre David
Kansas City Royals (AL) 2005–06
Played 38 games for the Minnesota Twins.

A native of Hollywood, California, David was a minor league outfielder who had cups of coffee in the majors in 1984 and 1986. He hit a home run in his first major league at-bat but never hit another. He retired in 1989 and became a minor league coach and manager in the organizations of the New York Mets and the Royals. Kansas City named him hitting coach in May of 2005, but reassigned him to the position of minor league roving hitting instructor in May of 2006.

Brandy Davis
Philadelphia Phillies (NL) 1972
Native of Newark, Delaware.

A minor league outfielder, Davis played 55 major league games in 1952 with the Pittsburgh Pirates and another 12 in 1953. He batted only .187. Following his playing career he became a scout and spent over 50 years in professional baseball altogether, one of them as a coach for the Phillies. He was inducted into the Delaware Sports Hall of Fame in 1989 and the Delaware Baseball Hall of Fame in 1999.

Davis died in 2005 in Newark.

Doug Davis
Florida Marlins (NL) 2003–04

Catcher who appeared in seven major league games.

Mainly a career minor leaguer in the California Angels' organization, Davis appeared in six games for California in 1988 and in one more for the Texas Rangers in 1992. He later became a minor league coach and then a skipper in the New York Mets' system. He won the South Atlantic League championship in 1998 with the Capital City Bombers, and *The Sporting News* named him its Minor League Manager of the Year. From May of 2003 through the 2004 season he was the Marlins' bench coach, and he spent 2005 as the club's minor league catching and baserunning coordinator. In 2006 he took the reins as manager of the New Hampshire Fisher Cats in the Toronto Blue Jays' organization.

Harry Davis
Philadelphia Athletics (AL) 1913–19
See Managers section.

Mark Davis
Arizona Diamondbacks (NL) 2003–04
Starting pitcher who became an outstanding reliever.

Davis won the 1980 Eastern League Most Valuable Player Award with the Reading Phillies when he went 19–6 with a 2.47 earned run average. He was soon called up to Philadelphia, and for his first few major league seasons he was a starter before being switched to the bullpen during the 1984 campaign with the San Francisco Giants. A curveballer who often struck out more than a batter an inning, he really hit his stride in 1988 with the San Diego Padres when he posted 28 saves and was named a National League All-Star.

In 1989 Davis won the NL Cy Young Award and again made the All-Star team on the strength of a league-leading 44 saves and 92 strikeouts in just over 92 innings.

His career inexplicably took a severe downturn thereafter, and he never again saved more than six games in a season. He continued to play until 1994, returned for 19 games with the Milwaukee Brewers in 1997, and eventually became a coach with the Diamondbacks.

Spud Davis
Pittsburgh Pirates (NL) 1942–46; Chicago Cubs (NL) 1950–53
See Managers section.

Tommy Davis
Seattle Mariners (AL) 1981
Native of Brooklyn, New York.

Davis signed with his hometown Dodgers in 1956, but would not reach the major leagues until the team had relocated to Los Angeles. He won two minor league batting titles and would eventually win two more with the Dodgers—in 1962, when he hit .346, and in 1963, when he batted .326. That 1962 season also saw him lead the National League with 230 hits and 153 runs batted in, and he clouted a career-high 27 home runs. Both that year and the next he was an NL All-Star, making both teams in '62.

Davis hit over .300 six times and batted .294 lifetime in 18 seasons. Toward the end of his career he became an extraordinary pinch-hitter.

He retired in 1976 and later coached the Mariners for one season.

Roly de Armas
Chicago White Sox (AL) 1995–96; Toronto Blue Jays (AL) 2000
New York native who spent many years in the Philadelphia Phillies' minor league system.

De Armas spent those years as a player, coach, and manager. His 1979 Helena Phillies had the best record in the Pioneer League. During the winters de Armas often worked at baseball academies in Venezuela and the Dominican Republic. He coached the White Sox and later the Blue Jays at the major league level before returning to the Philadelphia organization in 2001.

Cot Deal
Cincinnati Reds (NL) 1959–60; Houston Colt .45s (NL) 1962–64; New York Yankees (AL) 1965; Kansas City Athletics (AL) 1966–67; Detroit Tigers (AL) 1973–74; Houston Astros (NL) 1983–85; Cleveland Indians (AL) 1990–91
Pitcher for parts of four major league seasons.

Deal signed with the Pittsburgh Pirates while he was still in high school in 1940. He was originally an outfielder and third baseman in the minor leagues, but his professional career was interrupted by World War II, during which he served as a physical training instructor for the Air Corps. Upon his return he played for the Toronto Maple Leafs of the International League, and with them he was converted to a pitcher, a position at which he never felt truly comfortable. He actually preferred catching.

After reaching the Boston Red Sox in 1947, Deal hurt his arm during spring training the following year and would never completely recover. He pitched 45 major league games and posted a 6.55 earned run average. At the minor league level, however, he pitched an entire 20-inning game in 1949.

Once his playing career was over he spent many years with many organizations in many capacities, serving not only as a major league coach but also as a minor league coach and manager, a defensive coordinator, and an assistant farm director.

Dizzy Dean
Chicago Cubs (NL) 1941
Hall of Famer who pitched for 12 seasons.

A four-time All-Star, Dean led the National League twice in victories, twice in games pitched, once in starts, three times in complete games, twice in shutouts, three times in innings pitched, and four times in strikeouts. He won 150 games in his career against 83 losses and posted a 3.02 earned run average. In 1934 he was the NL's Most Valuable Player when he went 30–7 with a 2.66 ERA and a league-leading 195 strikeouts. He and his brother Paul (nicknamed "Daffy") pitched together for four seasons for the St. Louis Cardinals.

A toe injury changed Dizzy's delivery and eventually cut his career short. He pitched only one game for the Cubs in 1941 before becoming a coach, then he went into broadcasting with the St. Louis Browns. He pitched one game for them in 1947 when he became disgusted with the performance of the club's pitching staff.

Dean was elected to the Hall of Fame in 1953. The Cardinals retired his number 17 in 1974, shortly after he passed away.

Mark DeJohn
St. Louis Cardinals (NL) 1996–2001
Minor league infielder who played in 24 major league games.

The Connecticut native went only 4-for-21 in 1982 with the Detroit Tigers for a lowly .190 batting average. After his playing career he became a minor league manager, and coached the Cardinals for six seasons.

Billy DeMars
Philadelphia Phillies (NL) 1969–81; Montreal Expos (NL) 1982–84; Cincinnati Reds (NL) 1985–87
Shortstop who spent most of his career in the minor leagues.

DeMars appeared in 80 major league contests over three seasons with the Philadelphia Athletics and St. Louis Browns. Despite the fact that he hit just .237, he later became a well-respected and highly valued hitting coach at the big league level.

His playing career lasted from 1943–60, and he became a minor league skipper in the organization of the Browns, who transferred to Baltimore and became the Orioles. He then moved on to the Phillies as a major league coach and later to the Expos and Reds beginning in 1969.

Marty DeMerritt
San Francisco Giants (NL) 1989; Chicago Cubs (NL) 1999
Minor league pitcher for seven seasons.

DeMerritt grew up in San Francisco and, once his play-ing career ended, went to work for his uncle, who was a building contractor. Through coaching youth leagues he eventually met Jim Lefebvre, who was the Giants' field coordinator, and Lefebvre helped coax him into joining his hometown club as a scout. That was in 1982, and the following year he began to work as a coach in the Giants' minor league system. He reached the big league club at the end of the 1989 campaign, then he went to South Korea and coached the Samsung Lions. In 1991 he returned to the United States and coached in the minor league systems of the Giants, the Florida Marlins, and the Cubs.

He coached in Chicago in 1999 before becoming the Pittsburgh Pirates' minor league pitching coordinator and then a coach in the Tampa Bay Devil Rays' organization.

Steve Demeter
Pittsburgh Pirates (NL) 1985
Minor leaguer for many years.

Demeter led the Carolina League in doubles in 1954 with 48, and led the International League three times in the same category, from 1965–67. He never reached the major leagues as a player, but after managing in the Pirates' minor league system he coached the Bucs for one season and then returned to the minors as a skipper. His 1987 Salem Buccaneers won the Carolina League championship.

Rick Dempsey
Los Angeles Dodgers (NL) 1999–2000; Baltimore Orioles (AL) 2002–
One of only three catchers to play in four decades.

The other two were Tim McCarver and Carlton Fisk. Dempsey lasted 24 seasons, the majority of them with the Orioles. The son of a Vaudeville actor and a Broadway star, he became famous for entertaining players and fans during rain delays, including among his performances an imitation of an out-of-shape Babe Ruth.

In 1979 Dempsey led American League catchers in assists, and in both 1981 and 1983 he led in fielding percentage. In 1983 he was named the Most Valuable Player of the World Series when he batted .385 while knocking in the game-winning run in Game 2 and crushing a double and a home run in Game 5.

In 1992 he became a minor league manager, and his 1994 Albuquerque Dukes won the Pacific Coast League championship. He later became a scout for the Colorado Rockies, then a minor league skipper in the Dodgers' and New York Mets' organizations. He spent two years as a coach in Los Angeles, worked a year as a cable sports analyst, and then signed on as a coach back in Baltimore.

Gary Denbo
New York Yankees (AL) 2001

Career minor leaguer.

Renowned for his skills as a hitting instructor from a young age, Denbo's main strength was an ability to detect and correct flaws in a batter's swing quickly. He combined video with computer analysis of baseball swings to help hitters improve and battle out of slumps.

After playing for four years at the minor league level he became a coach in the Cincinnati Reds' organization, then a manager in the Yankees' system before coaching in New York. He later became a coach and then assistant manager of the Nippon Ham Fighters in Japan.

Bucky Dent
St. Louis Cardinals (NL) 1991–94; Texas Rangers (AL) 1995–2001; Cincinnati Reds (NL) 2006–
See Managers section.

Art Devlin
Boston Braves (NL) 1926, 1928
Speedy, brash third baseman in the early 1900s.

A native of Washington, D.C., Devlin debuted with the New York Giants in 1904 and played 10 seasons for them and the Braves. He hit a grand slam in his first major league at-bat, the first of only 10 home runs he would hit in his career. He stole at least 19 bases seven times, leading the National League with 59 in 1905.

Devlin frequently got into trouble for fighting, being suspended along with manager John McGraw for attacking an umpire in 1906, ending up in jail for attacking an abusive fan in 1910, and getting into a fight with Cincinnati Reds' third baseman Babe Pinelli while coaching for the Braves in 1926.

His big league playing career ended in 1913, but he continued for several years in the minors before returning to Boston as a coach.

Bobby Dews
Atlanta Braves (NL) 1979–81, 1985, 1997–2006
Longtime baseball man with the Braves.

A minor league outfielder from 1960–70, Dews became a player-manager in 1969 with the Lewis-Clark Broncs. In 1975 he joined the Atlanta organization as manager of the Greenwood Braves of the Western Carolinas League, and later worked as a minor league manager, director of player development (and assistant to same), roving minor league instructor, and minor league field coordinator, as well as serving three stints as a major league coach.

Dews reached the minor league playoffs three times as a skipper, and won the Southern League Manager of the Year award in 1978 when his Savannah Braves took the championship.

Dews has also published a couple of books, one of them a novel.

Bill Dickey
New York Yankees (AL) 1949–57, 1960
See Managers section.

Bob Didier
Oakland Athletics (AL) 1984–86; Seattle Mariners (AL) 1989–90
Switch-hitting catcher.

Didier's rookie season of 1969 was his only year as a regular, when he hit .256 with the Atlanta Braves and was named to the Topps All-Star Rookie Team. He lasted five more seasons as a backup but averaged only .229 lifetime. He later coached the A's and Mariners.

Joe DiMaggio
Oakland Athletics (AL) 1968–69
One of the greatest players of all time.

An outfielder by trade, DiMaggio was named an American League All-Star every year of his major league career, from 1936–51. He played his entire career with the New York Yankees, although he missed the 1943–45 seasons because of military service during World War II.

A .325 lifetime hitter, "Joltin' Joe" won two batting titles—hitting .381 in 1939 and .352 in 1940—and hit *below* .300 on only two occasions. He put together a major league record 56-game hitting streak in 1941, after setting a minor league record with a 61-game streak in 1933 with the San Francisco Seals of the Pacific Coast League. DiMaggio led the AL twice in home runs, twice in runs batted in, once in triples, and once in runs scored. He hit 361 career roundtrippers and was named the AL's Most Valuable Player in 1939, 1941, and 1947. He was also famous for his marriage to Hollywood actress Marilyn Monroe.

The Yankees retired Joe's number 5 in 1952, and three years later he was elected to the Hall of Fame. He had retired in 1951, and he returned to the majors as a coach with Oakland from 1968–69.

Walt Dixon
Chicago Cubs (NL) 1964–65
Sixteen-year minor leaguer.

Dixon lost three years to the military, but between 1940 and 1958 he led his league twice in home runs and once each in runs batted in and hits. He hit over 20 homers six times, and he drove in over 100 runs on five occasions. Originally a pitcher, he was converted to a position player in the late 1940s. In 1949 he became the player-manager of the Shelby Farmers of the Western Carolinas League, and he stopped playing in 1958 but continued managing. He coached for the Cubs for two years and managed in their farm system until 1986, when he retired.

Pat Dobson
Milwaukee Brewers (AL) 1982–84; San Diego Padres (NL) 1988–90; Kansas City Royals (AL) 1991; Baltimore Orioles (AL) 1996
One of four 20-game winners for the 1971 Orioles.

Dobson pitched for 11 seasons, only 2 of them for Baltimore. Those two were noteworthy, however, as he helped the club to a 1971 pennant and won 20 and 16 games, respectively. In 1972 he was named an American League All-Star.

Dobson won 19 games in 1974 with the New York Yankees, and 16 more in 1976 with the Cleveland Indians. His lifetime earned run average was 3.54.

Pat had once struck out 21 batters in a game in Puerto Rico, and in 1971 with the Orioles he pitched an exhibition no-hitter against the Yomiuri Giants in Japan.

Larry Doby
Montreal Expos (NL) 1971–73, 1976; Cleveland Indians (AL) 1974; Chicago White Sox (AL) 1977–78
See Managers section.

Bobby Doerr
Boston Red Sox (AL) 1967–69; Toronto Blue Jays (AL) 1977–81
Nine-time All-Star second baseman and Hall of Famer.

A native of Los Angeles, Doerr played his entire 14-year career with the Red Sox, losing the 1945 season to military service. An excellent fielder, he led the American League in putouts, assists, and double plays on many occasions. He hit .288 lifetime, topping the .300 mark three times, and in 1950 finished in a three-way tie for the league lead with 11 triples. He bashed 223 home runs in his career.

After his retirement Doerr eventually returned to Boston as a coach, and he later coached the Blue Jays. He was elected to the Hall of Fame in 1986, and in 1988 the Red Sox retired his number 1.

Cozy Dolan
New York Giants (NL) 1922–24
Seven-year outfielder and third baseman.

Debuting in 1909 with the Cincinnati Reds, Dolan played only two seasons as a regular. Those years were 1914, when he hit .240 in 126 games for the St. Louis Cardinals, and 1915, when he batted .280 for the Redbirds in 111 games. That was the end of his major league playing career, except for 1922, when he appeared in one game while coaching for the Giants.

Rich Donnelly
Texas Rangers (AL) 1980, 1983–85; Pittsburgh Pirates (NL) 1986–96; Florida Marlins (NL) 1997–98; Colorado Rockies (NL) 1999–2002; Milwaukee Brewers (NL) 2003–05; Los Angeles Dodgers (NL) 2006–
Catcher who played four minor league seasons.

Donnelly became a minor league manager following his playing career, and he was named the Western Carolinas League Manager of the Year for three consecutive seasons, from 1972–74. His 1974 Gastonia Rangers won the league championship. He managed in the Rangers' system until 1982, except for 1980 when he coached the big club, and rejoined the major league team from 1983–85. From 1986–99 he coached under Jim Leyland with three different clubs—the Pirates, Marlins, and Rockies—and remained in Colorado when Leyland left. He later moved on to the Brewers and then the Dodgers.

Donnelly is also an excellent racquetball player and trains in that arena with world-class athletes.

Bill Donovan
Detroit Tigers (AL) 1918
See Managers section.

Mickey Doolan
Chicago Cubs (NL) 1926–29; Cincinnati Reds (NL) 1930–32
Rather light hitter who played during the deadball era.

Doolan's career spanned 13 seasons, beginning in 1905 and ending in 1918. In 1917 he was player-manager of the Rochester Hustlers of the minor International League. A shortstop, Doolan never hit over .267 and averaged only .230 for his career, but it was his glove that kept him in the major leagues.

For a time he served as vice president of the Players' Fraternity, an early players' union, and from 1914–15 he played in the Federal League with the Baltimore Terrapins and Chicago Whales.

He was also a dentist.

Bill Doran
Cincinnati Reds (NL) 2001; Kansas City Royals (AL) 2005–
Solid second baseman who played 12 seasons.

A Cincinnati native, Doran led all National League second basemen in assists during his rookie season of 1983 while with the Houston Astros, and led his position in fielding percentage at .992 in 1987 and .987 in 1988. He hit .300 in 1990 while helping the Reds to the World Championship and averaged .266 for his career.

After finishing his playing days with the Milwaukee Brewers, Doran returned to the Reds as a minor league instructor and field coordinator. He replaced Buddy Bell as director of player development when Bell left to manage the Colorado Rockies, then became a special assistant to the general manager before joining the major league staff as a coach. He eventually became a minor league coach for the Tampa Yankees before being named to the Royals' staff by none other than Buddy Bell.

Luis Dorante
Florida Marlins (NL) 2005
Longtime minor league manager.

A minor league catcher in the Boston Red Sox' organization, Dorante debuted professionally in 1987, but in 1992 missed the entire season due to right knee surgery. In 1994 he was hired by the Montreal Expos to scout in Venezuela, and soon after became a minor league manager with the organization. He eventually joined the Marlins' system in a similar capacity, and spent the 2005 season as a major league coach. In 2006 he was named skipper of the AA Carolina Mudcats.

Harry Dorish
Boston Red Sox (AL) 1963; Atlanta Braves (NL) 1968–71
Consistent relief pitcher for several teams.

Dorish played from 1947–56 and posted a 45–43 record with a 3.83 earned run average. Four times he put up ERAs under 3.00, and he garnered 44 saves. He led the American League with 11 in 1952 with the Chicago White Sox, before the save became an official statistic. In a game in 1950 he stole home on the front end of a double steal, an extremely rare accomplishment for a pitcher.

Dorish eventually coached the Red Sox and the Braves, and for a time worked in the Cincinnati Reds' organization.

Otis Douglas
Cincinnati Reds (NL) 1961–62
Football player with the Philadelphia Eagles.

Also a college football coach at Akron and Arkansas, Douglas was hired by the Cincinnati Reds to be a sort of physical fitness coach. He was in charge of physical drills during spring training that seemingly had little to do with baseball, but apparently improved players' strength and coordination.

He was inducted into the Virginia Sports Hall of Fame in 1979.

Rick Down
California Angels (AL) 1987–88; New York Yankees (AL) 1993–95, 2002–03; Baltimore Orioles (AL) 1996–98; Los Angeles Dodgers (NL) 1999–2000; Boston Red Sox (AL) 2001; New York Mets (NL) 2005–
Minor league outfielder in the Montreal Expos' organization.

Down played for seven years and then coached in the

minors before leaving to coach baseball at the University of Nevada, Las Vegas from 1979–84. In 1985 he joined the Angels' organization as a roving hitting instructor and eventual big league coach. Shortly thereafter he became a minor league manager in the Yankees' system before being promoted to that staff in 1993. Under his leadership the AAA Columbus Clippers won three consecutive division titles and two straight Governor's Cup championships.

He moved around as a coach between several major league teams, even returning for a second stint with the Yankees after spending a year as their coordinator of instruction. In November of 2004 he was hired by the Mets.

Moe Drabowsky
Chicago White Sox (AL) 1986; Chicago Cubs (NL) 1994
Polish-born major league pitcher.

Drabowsky was born in 1935 and came to the United States with his parents in 1938. He once pitched a no-hitter in college, striking out 16 batters in the process, and soon signed on with the Cubs. He posted a 2.47 earned run average in his first season, and after 16 more he had managed a lifetime 3.71 ERA. He played with several teams, one of them the Kansas City Athletics, before being selected by the Kansas City Royals in the 1969 expansion draft, and he continued to pitch until 1972.

After coaching a season with the White Sox, one of the eight teams for whom he had played, he returned to Poland to help organize that country's first Olympic baseball team. He eventually returned to the United States and coached another season in Chicago, this time with the Cubs.

Chuck Dressen
Brooklyn Dodgers (NL) 1939–42, 1943–46; New York Yankees (AL) 1947–48; Los Angeles Dodgers (NL) 1958–59
See Managers section.

Rich Dubee
Florida Marlins (NL) 1998–2001; Philadelphia Phillies (NL) 2005–
Minor league pitcher in the Kansas City Royals' system.

Dubee pitched two no-hitters in high school, and he played for six years in the minor leagues and posted 26 complete games. He then became a pitching coach with several organizations, starting with that of the Royals, and spent a couple of years early as a roving pitching instructor. In 1998 he was promoted to the Marlins, and in 2002 joined the Phillies' system as a coach at the Class A level. In 2005 he was promoted to Philadelphia's major league staff.

Jean Dubuc
Detroit Tigers (AL) 1930–31

Controversial pitcher-turned-coach-turned-scout.

Dubuc pitched 34 games in 1908 and 1909 for the Cincinnati Reds, then went to the minors until 1912, when he resurfaced with the Tigers and promptly won 17 games. He won 73 games, in fact, between 1912 and 1916. He posted a lifetime 3.04 earned run average, and he was also a good hitter, being used frequently in a pinch-hitting role.

Jean finished his career in 1919 with the New York Giants, and the next year was implicated in the Chicago Black Sox Scandal that saw the White Sox throw the World Series to the Reds. While Dubuc was not involved in actually throwing the Series, he had what was termed "guilty knowledge" of the fix and did not report it. Apparently, Giants' teammate Hal Chase had approached Dubuc and Heinie Zimmerman and asked them to enlist other Giants in betting on the outcome of the crooked event. In 1922 Dubuc was supposedly banned for life, but he must have been reinstated because shortly thereafter he became a minor league manager, leading the Manchester Blue Sox to the 1926 New England League championship.

In 1930 Dubuc returned to the Tigers as a coach, where he remained for two seasons. He then became a scout with the organization and was responsible for signing such notables as Hank Greenberg and Birdie Tebbetts.

Hugh Duffy
Boston Red Sox (AL) 1931, 1939
See Managers section.

Oscar Dugey
Chicago Cubs (NL) 1921–24
Light-hitting infielder for the Boston Braves and Philadelphia Phillies.

Dugey played somewhat sparingly from 1913 to 1917, starting with the Braves, finishing with the Phillies, and resurfacing with Boston in 1920 for five games. He hit only .194 lifetime and never batted above .250. The year following the end of his playing career he became a coach with the Cubs.

Dave Duncan
Cleveland Indians (AL) 1978–81; Seattle Mariners (AL) 1982; Chicago White Sox (AL) 1983–86; Oakland Athletics (AL) 1986–95; St. Louis Cardinals (NL) 1996–
Catcher who became a pitching coach.

Duncan never hit over .259 in a season and averaged only .214 lifetime. He hit at least 10 home runs a year six times, however, and was named to the American League All-Star team in 1971 with the A's. He never matched the 46 home runs he hit in the California League in 1966, but he did hit the last roundtripper for the A's when they played in Kansas City and once hit four straight doubles in a game in 1975.

After 11 seasons Duncan retired due to knee injuries, and he then began a long career as a pitching coach.

Mariano Duncan
Los Angeles Dodgers (NL) 2006–
Versatile infielder who played mostly as a backup.

Originally a switch-hitter but later a righty, Duncan spent several years as a regular but was branded a utilityman and spent most of his career moving around the field with a number of teams. In 1990 he anchored second base for the Cincinnati Reds and helped them to the World Championship by hitting .306 with a league-leading 11 triples. In 1994 he was named a National League All-Star while playing for the Philadelphia Phillies, and two years later with the New York Yankees he hit a career-high .340.

He played through 1997 and then added one more season in Japan. Soon thereafter he became a minor league coach, and then ascended to the major league level with the Dodgers.

Harry Dunlop
Kansas City Royals (AL) 1969–75; Chicago Cubs (NL) 1976; Cincinnati Reds (NL) 1979–82, 1998; San Diego Padres (NL) 1983–87; Florida Marlins (NL) 2005
Career minor league catcher.

An excellent defensive backstop, Dunlop frequently led his league in various fielding categories. He also pitched 26 games. He played from 1952–68, except for the 1953–54 seasons, which he lost to military service during the Korean War, and the 1967 campaign, when he was a full-time skipper. In 1958 and from 1961–66 he was a player-manager, then turned to managing full-time in 1967. In 1968 he was a player-coach for the Seattle Angels of the Pacific Coast League, and the following year he became a major league coach.

Dunlop was named California League Manager of the Year in 1963, when his Stockton Ports won the title, and his San Jose Bees took the championship in '67.

After coaching the Reds for the second time in 1998, Dunlop stayed on as an instructor, then he retired. In 2005 he came out of retirement for one season with the Marlins.

Leo Durocher
Los Angeles Dodgers (NL) 1961–64
See Managers section.

Gene Dusan
New York Mets (NL) 1983
Nine-year minor leaguer.

Dusan played mainly in the organizations of the Oakland Athletics and Cleveland Indians before becoming a minor league manager. His 1977 Batavia Trojans posted the best record in the New York-Pennsylvania League. At the age of 33 he became the Mets' bullpen coach, then returned to managing in the minors.

Duffy Dyer
Chicago Cubs (NL) 1983; Milwaukee Brewers (AL) 1989–95; Oakland Athletics (AL) 1996–98
Light-hitting backup catcher.

Dyer never hit over .257 and averaged .221 lifetime. Before his professional career began he caught for Arizona State, who won the College World Series in both 1965 and 1966. As a major leaguer, he caught for the 1969 World Champion Mets. He retired in 1981 and later became a minor league manager and big league coach.

Jimmy Dykes
Philadelphia Athletics (AL) 1949–50; Cincinnati Redlegs (NL) 1955–58; Pittsburgh Pirates (NL) 1959; Milwaukee Braves (NL) 1962; Kansas City Athletics (AL) 1963–64
See Managers section.

George Earnshaw
Philadelphia Phillies (NL) 1949–50
Gentlemanly pitcher who played for nine seasons.

Earnshaw had a rather inconspicuous debut with the Philadelphia Athletics in 1928, but the following year he led the American League with 24 victories. The next season he topped the circuit with 39 starts and 3 shutouts. From 1929 through 1932 he posted records of 24–8, 22–13, 21–7, and 19–13. In 1933 he was fined by manager Connie Mack for being overweight and failing to get into proper condition.

After his retirement Earnshaw served as an officer in the Navy, where he won a Bronze Star during World War II. He then became a scout and a coach for the Phillies.

Mike Easler
Milwaukee Brewers (AL) 1992; Boston Red Sox (AL) 1993–94; St. Louis Cardinals (NL) 1999–2001
Good-hitting outfielder and designated hitter.

Easler spent a long time in the minor leagues before reaching the big time. Once in the majors, however, he made the most of his stay. His defense was a liability, but his bat was solid, and he was made a full-time DH in the American League.

Easler hit over .300 four times and batted .293 lifetime. In 1980 he hit for the cycle with the Pittsburgh Pirates, and in 1981 became a National League All-Star. He hit over 20 home runs twice.

Luke Easter
Cleveland Indians (AL) 1969
Negro Leaguer who reached the major leagues at the age of 34.

Easter's major league career spanned six seasons, all of them with the Indians. In 1953 he batted .303 in 68 games, then he continued his career for some time in the minors. In 1956 he became the first black player for the Buffalo Bisons since 1888, and after being released in 1959 despite impressive and league-leading power totals, he spent six years as a player-coach with the Rochester Red Wings. In 1969 he returned to Cleveland as a coach for one season.

Easter was murdered by thieves in 1979 in a bank parking lot while serving as chief union steward for the Aircraft Workers Alliance. His killers took the $40,000 in union funds he had on him at the time. The Bisons retired his number 25, and the Red Wings his number 36.

Dino Ebel
Los Angeles Angels of Anaheim (AL) 2006–
Minor league player, coach, and manager.

Ebel spent 17 years in the Los Angeles Dodgers' organization. The Gulf Coast League Player of the Year in 1988, he was a player-coach from 1991–95 before retiring from the playing field. After serving as a full-time minor league coach and manager, he worked with the Chinese National Team in 2000, Japan's Osaka Buffaloes in 2002, and Taiwan's Sinon Bulls the same year.

He joined the Angels' organization as a minor league manager in 2005 before being promoted to the major league staff as a coach.

Doc Edwards
Philadelphia Phillies (NL) 1970–72; Cleveland Indians (AL) 1985–87; New York Mets (NL) 1990–91
See Managers section.

Ben Egan
Washington Nationals (AL) 1924; Brooklyn Robins (NL) 1925; Chicago White Sox (AL) 1926
Catcher who played sparsely in the major leagues.

Egan spent two games in the majors in 1908, but would not surface again until 1912. In between he spent a great deal of time off and on with the minor league Baltimore Orioles, and *The Sporting News* once reported that he was the most popular player up to that time ever to have played in Baltimore. It even mentioned talk of a "Ben Egan Day" being planned by the city.

After playing 49 games in 1912 with the Philadelphia Athletics he played a few more in 1914 and 1915, then returned to the minors and ended up once again in Baltimore. He eventually became a minor league skipper and then a major league coach.

Dick Egan
Texas Rangers (AL) 1988–89
Pitched 74 major league games.

Egan appeared off and on in the majors with the Detroit Tigers, California Angels, and Los Angeles Dodgers between 1963 and 1967. He pitched only in relief, and posted a 1–2 record with a 5.15 earned run average. He struck out 68 batters in 101$\frac{1}{3}$ innings. He later became a coach with the Rangers for two years.

Lee Elia
Philadelphia Phillies (NL) 1980–81, 1985–87; New York Yankees (AL) 1989; Seattle Mariners (AL) 1993–97, 2001–02; Toronto Blue Jays (AL) 2000; Tampa Bay Devil Rays (AL) 2003–05; Baltimore Orioles (AL) 2006
See Managers section.

Bob Elliott
Los Angeles Angels (AL) 1961
See Managers section.

Sammy Ellis
New York Yankees (AL) 1982–84, 1986; Chicago White Sox (AL) 1989–91; Chicago Cubs (NL) 1992; Seattle Mariners (AL) 1993–94; Boston Red Sox (AL) 1996; Baltimore Orioles (AL) 2000
Pitcher from Youngstown, Ohio.

Sammy Ellis was a right-hander who had one really outstanding season, in 1965 when he went 22–10 for the Cincinnati Reds. He had won 10 games the previous season and he won 12 the next, but he never again posted double digits in the victory column.

Arm problems shortened his career, but he then began a successful career as a major league coach and a minor league pitching instructor.

Cal Emery
Chicago White Sox (AL) 1988
Most Valuable Player of the Three-I League in 1959.

Emery was an outfielder who played for the Des Moines Demons that season after having been voted the Most Outstanding Player of the College World Series in 1957. He played only 16 games at the major league level, in 1963 with the Philadelphia Phillies. He later coached a season with the White Sox.

Dave Engle
Houston Astros (NL) 1998; New York Mets (NL) 2001–02
Outfielder-turned-catcher who hit the first official home run in the Metrodome in Minneapolis.

Engle was never a good defensive backstop, but he hit .305 in 1983 and the following year was an American League All-Star. He was relegated to a reserve role thereafter and soon became an excellent pinch-hitter.

Jewel Ens
Pittsburgh Pirates (NL) 1926–29, 1935–39; Detroit Tigers (AL) 1932; Cincinnati Reds (NL) 1933, 1941; Boston Braves (NL) 1934
See Managers section.

Cal Ermer
Baltimore Orioles (AL) 1962; Milwaukee Brewers (AL) 1970–71; Oakland Athletics (AL) 1977
See Managers section.

Alvaro Espinoza
Pittsburgh Pirates (NL) 2004–05
Infielder and 12-year major league veteran.

A native of Venezuela, Espinoza played second base, shortstop, and third base, but averaged only .254 at the plate. After retiring in 1997 he became a minor league infield coordinator with the Montreal Expos, then worked as a minor league manager and roving infield coordinator in the Los Angeles Dodgers' system. He then became an infield instructor and later major league coach with the Pirates.

Duane Espy
San Diego Padres (NL) 2000–02; Colorado Rockies (NL) 2003–06
Most Valuable Player of the Midwest League in 1972.

Espy played one of his eight minor league seasons with the Danville Warriors that year and won the batting title with a .340 average, but he never reached the majors. After retiring he became a minor league coach and skipper, and in 1989 was named California League Manager of the Year when his San Jose Giants reached the playoffs for the second straight season. He later became the San Francisco Giants' coordinator of minor league hitting before reaching the major league staff of the Padres and later that of the Rockies.

The Rockies' official title for him was "hitting instructor" rather than "hitting coach," but they had no other hitting coach. Following the 2006 season he was reassigned within the Colorado organization.

Chuck Estrada
Texas Rangers (AL) 1973; San Diego Padres (NL) 1978–81; Cleveland Indians (AL) 1983
Pitcher who made a sensational start.

In his rookie season of 1960 Estrada led the American League with 18 victories with the Baltimore Orioles and was named to the All-Star team. He posted a 3.58 earned run average. The following year he notched 15 victories, but after winning 9 the next he would never again collect more than 3 in a season. Prone to wildness, he injured his elbow in 1963 and that was, more than anything, what started his downward spiral. By 1967 he was finished, but he later found new life as a major league coach.

Andy Etchebarren
California Angels (AL) 1977; Milwaukee Brewers (AL) 1985–91; Baltimore Orioles (AL) 1996–97
Two-time All-Star catcher.

Never a strong hitter, Etchebarren nevertheless did an adequate job behind the plate and became the Orioles' regular backstop in 1966 when catcher Dick Brown developed a brain tumor. In both 1966 and '67 he was named an American League All-Star, but he gradually began sharing time with Elrod Hendricks.

At a party in 1966, he and Charlie Lau saved teammate Frank Robinson from drowning when Robinson fell into a swimming pool.

In 1977 he was a player-coach for the Angels, and he retired from the Brewers in 1978 before eventually returning to them and later to the Orioles as a coach.

Darrell Evans
New York Yankees (AL) 1990
First player to hit 40 home runs in each league.

Evans was also the first 40-year-old to hit 40 homers, and became the oldest player to win a home run title. A two-time All-Star, he bashed 414 roundtrippers in his career. He hit at least 20 in a season 10 times and hit at least 40 twice. He led the National League in walks in both 1973 and 1974 and topped the American League in home runs in 1985 with 40. He was on first base when Hank Aaron hit his 715th home run to break Babe Ruth's all-time record.

He retired in 1989 and the next year became a coach for the Yankees.

Dwight Evans
Colorado Rockies (NL) 1994; Boston Red Sox (AL) 2002
Most Valuable Player of the International League in 1972.

Evans was with the Louisville Colonels when he won that title, but soon thereafter he began an outstanding major league career that lasted 20 years. Excelling at both offense and defense, he played all but his final year with the Red Sox, finishing off his career in 1991 with the Baltimore Orioles. In strike-shortened 1981 he finished in a four-way tie for the American League lead with 22 home runs, and he also led three times in walks and once in runs scored.

He was named to three All-Star teams and won eight Gold Gloves. In a game in 1984 he hit for the cycle, and on Opening Day of 1986 he became the first player ever to hit a home run on the very first pitch of a major league season. He hit at least 20 home runs 11 times, and crossed the 100-run-batted-in threshold 3 times.

Evans hit 385 lifetime home runs and batted .272, topping out with a .305 average in 1987. After retiring he spent one season as a coach with the Rockies and another as a coach with the Red Sox.

Bill Evers
Tampa Bay Devil Rays (AL) 2006–
Minor league catcher and first baseman.

Evers spent the 1976–79 seasons playing in the Chicago Cubs' organization before going to work in their minor league system for a year. He then moved on to the New York Yankees' system, the San Francisco Giants' organization, back to the Yankees', and then to the farm system of the Devil Rays. He spent many of those years as a manager, and his Durham Bulls won back-to-back Governor's Cup championships in 2002 and 2003.

In November of 2005 he was named bench coach for Tampa Bay.

Johnny Evers
New York Giants (NL) 1920; Chicago White Sox (AL) 1922, 1924; Boston Braves (NL) 1929–32
See Managers section.

Walter "Hoot" Evers
Cleveland Indians (AL) 1970
Two-time All-Star outfielder.

Evers played one game for the Detroit Tigers in 1941 before losing the next four years to World War II. When he returned in 1946 he broke his ankle and missed half the season. Finally becoming a regular in 1947, he batted .296 and then hit over .300 the next three seasons in a row. In 1950 he finished in a three-way tied for the American League lead with 11 triples, while also contributing 21 home runs and 103 runs batted in. He led AL outfielders in fielding percentage at .997, and on September 7 hit for the cycle.

Two years later he broke a finger and was not nearly the same hitter after that. He played until 1956, and resurfaced as a coach with the Indians in 1970.

Glenn Ezell
Texas Rangers (AL) 1983–85; Kansas City Royals (AL) 1989–94; Detroit Tigers (AL) 1996; Tampa Bay Devil Rays (AL) 2001–02
Longtime, well-respected minor league coordinator.

Ezell has worked for many years with several organizations, most notably that of the Tigers. After spending time at the major league level as a coach with the Rangers and Royals, he joined the Detroit system and was named a coach there in 1996. He then went back to work in their minor league organization before becoming a coach with the Devil Rays from 2001–02. In 2003 he returned to the Tigers as a minor league field coordinator.

Red Faber
Chicago White Sox (AL) 1947–48
Hall of Fame pitcher who played for 20 major league seasons.

Faber spent his entire career with the White Sox, and what is most striking is the fact that he established dominant statistics with a team that, for 16 of those years, finished in the bottom half of the standings. The year 1917 was one exception, when he won three games in the World Series to help Chicago to the World Championship.

Faber won more than 20 games four times, and he won at least 15 seven times. He posted 254 victories in his career and led the American League once in games pitched, twice in starts, twice in complete games, once in innings pitched, and twice in earned run average. His lifetime ERA was 3.15.

He left Chicago in 1933, but returned for two years in the 1940s as a coach. He was inducted into the Hall of Fame in 1964.

Bill Fahey
San Francisco Giants (NL) 1986–91
Reserve catcher for 11 seasons.

Fahey played from 1971–83 with various teams, but missed the 1978 season due to an injury. On only two occasions did he play more than 38 games in a season, and he batted .241 lifetime. He retired in 1983 and later coached the Giants for six seasons.

Bibb Falk
Cleveland Indians (AL) 1933; Boston Red Sox (AL) 1934
See Managers section.

Jim Fanning
Atlanta Braves (NL) 1967
See Managers section.

John Farrell
Boston Red Sox (AL) 2007–
Pitcher who went 36–46 over eight seasons.

Farrell pitched twice for the Cleveland Indians during his career, having his best season in his sophomore year of 1988 when he posted a 14–10 record in 31 games. He also spent two seasons with the California Angels and one with the Detroit Tigers, finishing with a 4.56 earned run average and 355 strikeouts in 698²/₃ innings.

After his playing career Farrell became an assistant baseball coach at Oklahoma State University, then the director of player development for the Indians before being hired as a pitching coach by the Red Sox.

Kerby Farrell
Chicago White Sox (AL) 1966–69; Cleveland Indians (AL) 1970–71
See Managers section.

John Felske
Toronto Blue Jays (AL) 1980–81; Philadelphia Phillies (NL) 1984
See Managers section.

Joe Ferguson
Texas Rangers (AL) 1986–87; Los Angeles Dodgers (NL) 1988–94
Catcher and San Francisco native.

Ferguson spent most of his 14-year career with the Dodgers, with whom he committed only three errors in 1973 while leading all National League backstops in fielding percentage and double plays. Often used in the outfield, he hit at least 20 home runs on two occasions and over 20 doubles on two others. He had two stints with the Dodgers and later returned to them again as a coach.

Mike Ferraro
New York Yankees (AL) 1979–82, 1987–91; Kansas City Royals (AL) 1984–86; Baltimore Orioles (AL) 1993
See Managers section.

Rick Ferrell
Washington Nationals (AL) 1946–49; Detroit Tigers (AL) 1950–53
Catcher in the first All-Star Game.

Ferrell played in eight Midsummer Classics in his career as a catcher, and retired as the then-all-time leader in the American League with 1806 games caught. For many years he and his brother Wes, a pitcher, were batterymates. Following the 1945 season he became a coach for the Nationals, then served as a player-coach the next year and batted .303 in 37 games before turning to full-time coaching for good.

He later coached the Tigers, and he was elected to the Hall of Fame in 1984.

Tom Ferrick
Cincinnati Redlegs (NL) 1954–58; Philadelphia Phillies (NL)

1959; Detroit Tigers (AL) 1960–63; Kansas City Athletics
(AL) 1964–65
Relief pitcher and New York native.

Ferrick went 40–40 in a nine-year major league career
spent with several teams. He pitched from 1941–52, losing
the 1943–45 seasons to military service. He started only 7
of 323 career games. In 1950 he led the American League
with nine relief wins. He later served as a pitching coach
with several clubs.

Dave Ferriss
Boston Red Sox (AL) 1955–59
Two-time All-Star pitcher.

Ferriss served in the military during World War II, but
was discharged because of asthma. He made his major
league debut in 1945 with the Red Sox and promptly went
21–10 and posted a 2.96 earned run average while being
named an American League All-Star. The following season
he was 25–6 and an All-Star again. He won 12 games the
next year and only 7 the next, and his final two seasons
encompassed only 5 games without a victory. He returned
to Boston as a coach in 1955.

Bruce Fields
Detroit Tigers (AL) 2003–05
Outfielder who played 58 major league games.

A Cleveland native, Fields hit .274 in three brief big
league seasons before becoming a successful minor league
manager. In 1997 he was named Manager of the Year of
the Midwest League when his West Michigan Whitecaps
finished with the best record in the league. The following
year his club captured the championship, and in 2000 they
once again posted the best record and Fields was once
again named Manager of the Year.

He managed the AAA Toledo Mud Hens in 2001 and
2002 before being named to the Tigers' major league staff.

Bill Fischer
**Cincinnati Reds (NL) 1979–83; Boston Red Sox (AL) 1985–
91; Tampa Bay Devil Rays (AL) 2000–01**
Former Marine drill instructor.

Fischer debuted in 1956 with the Chicago White Sox in
three games in relief, but started a third of his games the
next year. He had mixed results, but in 1962 he set a major
league record by going $84^1/_3$ straight innings without issu-
ing a walk. In 34 games and 16 starts, encompassing $127^2/_3$
innings, he served up only 8 bases on balls.

He later became a pitching coach with the Reds, Red
Sox, and Devil Rays.

Brad Fischer
Oakland Athletics (AL) 1996–
Longtime minor league manager and instructor.

A catcher by trade, Fischer played only the 1978 season
professionally before taking a year off and then returning
to the Oakland organization as a minor league skipper. His
1982 Madison Muskies won the Midwest League championship. In 1983 and '84 he appeared in several games as a
player, and in 1985 guided the Huntsville Stars to the
Southern League title. He later worked within the Oakland
system as an instructor and assistant director of player development before being named to the Athletics' staff in
1996.

Ed Fitz Gerald
**Cleveland Indians (AL) 1960; Kansas City Athletics (AL)
1961; Minnesota Twins (AL) 1962–64**
Catcher who played a dozen major league seasons.

Fitz Gerald played for the Pittsburgh Pirates from
1948–53, then moved to the Washington Nationals. In
1956 he batted a career-high .304 in 64 games, and in his
final season of 1959 he became the first player ever to hit
into a triple play on Opening Day. He finished that season
with the Indians, and became a coach the following year.

Joe Fitzgerald
Washington Nationals (AL) 1947–56
Native of Washington, D.C.

A catcher, Fitzgerald never reached the major leagues
as a player and therefore never got to play for his hometown club. He did reach The Show as a coach, however,
and spent 10 years in that role with the Nationals. He died
in Orlando, Florida, at the age of 70.

John Fitzpatrick
**Pittsburgh Pirates (NL) 1953–56; Milwaukee Braves (NL)
1958–59**
Catcher who never reached the major leagues.

A native of LaSalle, Illinois, Fitzpatrick did reach the
big time as a coach, spending four years with the Pirates
and two with the Braves. He died in 1990 at the age of 86.

Freddie Fitzsimmons
**Brooklyn Dodgers (NL) 1942; Boston Braves (NL) 1948; New
York Giants (NL) 1949–55; Chicago Cubs (NL) 1957–59,
1966; Kansas City Athletics (AL) 1960**
See Managers section.

Mike Flanagan
Baltimore Orioles (AL) 1995–98
Outstanding pitcher who played for 18 years.

Flanagan both started and finished his career with the
Orioles, spending several years with the Toronto Blue Jays
in between. He was called up in 1975 and by 1977 was a

force to be reckoned with. Over the next four seasons he won 15, 19, 23, and 16 games, respectively. In 1978 he tied for the American League lead with 40 starts and was named an AL All-Star, and the following season his 23 victories paced the circuit and he finished in a three-way tie with 5 shutouts en route to winning the league's Cy Young Award. He came within one out of a no-hitter in September when Gary Alexander of the Cleveland Indians hit a home run to break it up.

Knee and Achilles tendon injuries in 1983 and 1985 damaged his career as a starter, but he adjusted and began to work effectively in relief. In 1991 he teamed up with Bob Milacki, Mark Williamson, and Gregg Olson to pitch a four-man no-hitter against the Oakland A's, and later that year he was the last Oriole hurler to throw a pitch at Memorial Stadium before the club moved to Camden Yards.

He retired in 1992 but came back as a coach in '95.

Tim Flannery
San Diego Padres (NL) 1996–2002; San Francisco Giants (NL) 2007–
Infielder who spent 11 years with the Padres.

Flannery was mainly a utilityman who did spend several years as a starter at second base. A .255 lifetime hitter, he hit .281 and .280 two consecutive years when he was starting. He played until 1989, then went to work in television news. In 1992 he rejoined the Padres' organization as a minor league manager, and in 1994 he led the Rancho Cucamonga Quakes to the California League championship. Two years later he re-emerged in San Diego as a coach. When Padres' manager Bruce Bochy moved to the Giants as their manager in 2007, he hired Flannery as a member of his coaching staff.

Art Fletcher
New York Yankees (AL) 1927–45
See Managers section.

Jake Flowers
Pittsburgh Pirates (NL) 1940–45; Boston Braves (NL) 1946; Cleveland Indians (AL) 1951–52
Infielder for the St. Louis Cardinals, Brooklyn Dodgers, and Cincinnati Reds.

Flowers played for 10 years in the major leagues, and his career ended with the Reds when he was hit by a Daffy Dean pitch that broke his arm. He then became a minor league manager and major league coach for many years.

Jake's most auspicious season at the reins was that of his debut, in 1937 with the Salisbury Indians. After the team reeled off a 21–5 record and was firmly in first place by June, the league determined that the team's roster contained five players with previous professional experience;

league rules allowed four. One of the players had apparently signed a contract with the Harrisburg Senators but had been immediately suspended and never played. The league therefore declared all of Salisbury's 21 victories forfeit, and the team's record fell to 0–26. An angry Flowers, having lost multiple arguments with league officials, determined to climb back on top, and his club did just that, going 49–10 over its next 59 games and finishing first at 59–37. Without the forfeits the Indians would have been 80–16. They went on to capture the championship, and *The Sporting News* named Flowers its Minor League Manager of the Year.

Jake's team won another pennant in 1938. Soon he was coaching in the major leagues, and he eventually became the president and general manager of the minor league Milwaukee Brewers before turning to scouting for several teams.

Bobby Floyd
New York Mets (NL) 2001, 2004
Reserve infielder for the Baltimore Orioles and Kansas City Royals.

Floyd had a light bat, hitting only .219 lifetime, and he was used mainly to fill in around the infield. He played from 1968–74 and later coached two separate seasons with the Mets. He was valued for his skill in running baseball programs.

Marv Foley
Chicago Cubs (NL) 1994; Baltimore Orioles (AL) 1999
Highly successful minor league manager.

A backup major league catcher for five seasons, Foley became one of the best managers in AAA history. He won championships in three different leagues: the Pacific Coast League in 1989 with the Vancouver Canadians, the American Association in 1993 with the Iowa Cubs, and the International League (called the Governor's Cup) in 1997 with the Rochester Red Wings.

He later managed the Colorado Springs Sky Sox and then became a roving catching instructor in the Colorado Rockies' organization.

Tom Foley
Tampa Bay Devil Rays (AL) 2002–
Ambidextrous high school athlete.

Foley was a right-handed shortstop and a left-handed quarterback in school. In the major leagues he was capable of playing all four infield positions, and he even played one game in the outfield and one as a pitcher. In a game in 1986 he knocked himself unconscious while sliding into second base, and the next day broke his wrist when he was hit by a pitch.

After retiring he went to work for the Devil Rays as a field coordinator and then minor league manager. He was named Pioneer League Manager of the Year in 1996 with the Butte Copper Kings and continued as a field coordinator through 1999. He was then appointed director of minor league operations before being promoted to Tampa Bay's major league staff.

Tim Foli
Texas Rangers (AL) 1986–87; Milwaukee Brewers (AL) 1992–95; Kansas City Royals (AL) 1996; Cincinnati Reds (NL) 2001–03
Excellent defensive shortstop.

Foli played 16 years mainly because of his glove, because he hit .251 lifetime but led both leagues in several fielding categories on several occasions. He did hit for the cycle once in 1976, spreading the hits out over a two-day period in a game that was called on account of darkness and resumed the following day.

He retired in 1985 and the following year started a coaching career that began with the Rangers.

Barry Foote
Chicago White Sox (AL) 1990–91; New York Mets (NL) 1992–93
Light-hitting but strong-armed catcher.

Foote hit only .230 in his career, but was valued for his work behind the plate and once did hit 16 home runs in a season. In a 1980 game for the Chicago Cubs against the St. Louis Cardinals, he had eight runs batted in as he contributed four hits, two of which were home runs. One of those roundtrippers was a game-winning grand slam that came in the bottom of the ninth inning with two outs.

He finished his career with the New York Yankees in 1982 and then became a manager in their minor league system. He later coached the White Sox and Mets.

Whitey Ford
New York Yankees (AL) 1964, 1968, 1974–75
Winningest pitcher in Yankees' history.

Ford recorded 236 victories in his career. An eight-time All-Star, he led the American League three times in wins, twice in starts, once in complete games, twice in shutouts, twice in innings pitched, and twice in earned run average. In 1961 he won the AL Cy Young Award on the strength of a 25–4 record, 209 strikeouts, and a 3.21 ERA. He was also the Most Valuable Player of the World Series, going 2–0 against the Cincinnati Reds and allowing just 6 hits in 14 innings. He set many World Series records in his career, at one point pitching 33 straight scoreless innings.

A player-coach in 1964, he retired in 1967 and returned as a full-time coach the following season. He returned to coach again in 1974, and that same year he was inducted into the Hall of Fame and the Yanks retired his number 16.

Steve Foster
Florida Marlins (NL) 2007–
Dallas native who pitched 59 major league games.

Foster went 3–3 in those games for the Cincinnati Reds from 1991–93 with an excellent 2.41 earned run average. He once injured his shoulder throwing a ball at milk bottles on *The Tonight Show* and required surgery as a result. After his playing career he worked as the head baseball coach at the University of Wisconsin-Stevens Point, as the pitching coach at the University of Michigan, and as a scout for the Tampa Bay Devil Rays.

Foster spent the 2005 and 2006 seasons as the pitching coach for the Class A Greensboro Grasshoppers in the Marlins' system before being promoted to the big league staff for 2007.

Art Fowler
Minnesota Twins (AL) 1969; Detroit Tigers (AL) 1971–73; Texas Rangers (AL) 1974–75; New York Yankees (AL) 1977–79, 1983, 1988; Oakland Athletics (AL) 1980–82
Pitcher for the Cincinnati Redlegs and Los Angeles Dodgers.

Fowler was used somewhat equally as a starter and reliever during his first three major league seasons, and he won 34 games over that stretch. He was then used primarily out of the bullpen and won only 19 games the rest of his career, although he accumulated 32 saves.

At the age of 48 he was a player-coach for the Denver Bears of the American Association under Billy Martin, and he posted 9 victories, 15 saves, and a 1.59 earned run average. He had served as Martin's pitching coach with the Twins the previous season, and he then followed Billy to the Tigers, Rangers, Yankees, and A's in the same capacity.

Charlie Fox
San Francisco Giants (NL) 1965–68; New York Yankees (AL) 1989
See Managers section.

Nellie Fox
Houston Astros (NL) 1965–67; Washington Senators (AL) 1968–71; Texas Rangers (AL) 1972
Hall of Fame second baseman.

Fox played 19 seasons, most of them with the Chicago White Sox, and was a 15-time All-Star. He hit over .300 six times and led the American League four times in hits and once in triples. He won three Gold Gloves, and was named the AL's Most Valuable Player in 1959 when he hit

.306 and led the Sox to the World Series for the first time in 40 years.

Fox finished his career with the Astros as both a player and a coach in 1965. He later coached the Senators and accompanied them to Arlington, Texas, when they became the Rangers. He died in 1975, and the White Sox retired his number 2 the following year. The Veterans Committee inducted him into the Hall of Fame in 1997.

Jimmie Foxx
Chicago Cubs (NL) 1944
Three-time Most Valuable Player.

"Double-X" was one of the greatest players of all time. A nine-time All-Star, he was a .325 lifetime hitter and crushed 534 career home runs. He won the American League MVP Award in 1932, 1933, and 1938. He won two batting titles and led the AL four times in home runs, three times in runs batted in, three times in on-base percentage, five times in slugging percentage, once in runs scored, and twice in bases on balls. He was only the second batter in history (the first was Babe Ruth) to reach 500 career roundtrippers. He hit at least 30 home runs 12 consecutive times, peaking with 58 in 1932 and reaching the 50 mark twice. He reached the 100-RBI plateau 13 straight times. In 1933 he won the Triple Crown when he batted .356 with 48 home runs and 163 RBIs with the Philadelphia Athletics. He set a major league record in 1938 by walking six times in a game.

Foxx was a player-coach with the Cubs in 1944, appearing in only 15 games, and he ended his playing career the following year but did not coach again. He was inducted into the Hall of Fame in 1951.

Terry Francona
Detroit Tigers (AL) 1996; Texas Rangers (AL) 2002; Oakland Athletics (AL) 2003
See Managers section.

Herman Franks
New York Giants (NL) 1949–55; San Francisco Giants (NL) 1958, 1964; Chicago Cubs (NL) 1970
See Managers section.

Chick Fraser
Pittsburgh Pirates (NL) 1923
Major league pitcher from 1896–1909.

With the National League's Louisville Colonels Fraser once took a no-hitter into the ninth inning only to see it broken up. In 1903 with the Philadelphia Phillies he accomplished the feat, however, blanking the Chicago Cubs, 10–0.

Fraser was one of the early NL players who jumped to the new, upstart American League in 1901, signing with the Philadelphia Athletics and causing a court battle. In April of 1902 the Pennsylvania Supreme Court granted an injunction barring Fraser and several other players from performing for any other team in Pennsylvania than the Phillies. Chick returned to the Phils after having spent one season with the A's, and he remained with them until he was traded to the Boston Bostons in December of 1904.

After his playing career Fraser became a scout with the Pirates, being signed by his brother-in-law and former Louisville teammate Fred Clarke. He later coached the Pirates for one season, and also scouted for the Brooklyn Dodgers and New York Yankees.

George Freese
Chicago Cubs (NL) 1964–65
Brother of Gene Freese.

Unlike his sibling, who played a dozen major league seasons, George lasted only 61 games, spread over three years. His batting average was actually three points higher, however, at .257.

George worked for many years as a scout and minor league manager, and coached two seasons with the Cubs.

Jim Frey
Baltimore Orioles (AL) 1970–79; New York Mets (NL) 1982–83
See Managers section.

Owen Friend
Kansas City Royals (AL) 1969
Reserve infielder for parts of five seasons.

A light hitter, Friend averaged only .227 and spent only one year as a semi-regular, when he appeared in 119 games in 1950 for the St. Louis Browns. He played second base, third base, and shortstop, and played for five different teams.

His last major league season was 1956, and he resurfaced as a coach 13 years later with the Royals.

Frankie Frisch
New York Giants (NL) 1949
See Managers section.

Frank Fultz
Atlanta Braves (NL) 1992–
Strength and conditioning coach.

After earning a doctorate in health science from the University of Utah in 1976, Fultz became a pitching coach with Triton College and then with George Mason University. He spent seven years as head baseball coach at Texas Wesleyan University before becoming an assistant strength and conditioning coach with the Houston Astros in 1986, at the same time working as associate head baseball coach at the University of Houston.

From 1988–91 he worked as a strength and conditioning coach in the Pittsburgh Pirates' organization before joining the Braves' major league club in that capacity in '92. In 1998 he doubled as Atlanta's minor league fitness coordinator.

Frank Funk
San Francisco Giants (NL) 1976; Seattle Mariners (AL) 1980–81, 1983–84; Kansas City Royals (AL) 1988–90; Colorado Rockies (NL) 1996–98
Solid major league relief pitcher.

Funk played only four seasons and posted a 20–17 record with a 3.01 earned run average. He never started a single game. After his playing career he became a minor league manager and later re-emerged in the majors as a coach with several teams.

Gary Gaetti
Houston Astros (NL) 2004–06
Twenty-year major league veteran.

A two-time All-Star and four-time Gold Glove winner, Gaetti spent most of his career at third base, where he consistently led the American League in several fielding categories. He hit a home run in his first major league at-bat and clubbed 360 lifetime, cracking at least 20 eight times. In 1987 he was named the Most Valuable Player of the American League Championship Series when he hit .300 with two homers and five runs batted in as he helped the Minnesota Twins to the AL pennant and eventual World Championship.

In July of 1990 he started two triple plays in the same game at Fenway Park. In 1999 he even pitched in a game for the Cubs, who were being trounced by the Philadelphia Phillies, and he served up a home run on the mound.

Gaetti retired in 2000 and in 2002 became a minor league hitting coach. In July of 2004 he was promoted to the Astros in a coaching capacity, but was fired in July of 2006.

Augie Galan
Philadelphia Athletics (AL) 1954
First National League switch-hitter to homer from both sides of the plate in the same game.

Galan accomplished that feat in 1937, his fourth major league season. He had already led the league in runs scored and stolen bases in 1935, and led in steals again in '37 while being named an All-Star for the first of three times.

Somewhat prone to injuries, Galan was nevertheless a .287 lifetime hitter, batting over .300 seven times, and he topped the circuit twice in walks and once in on-base percentage. He also became the first regular to go an entire season without hitting into a double play. Toward the end of his career he gave up switch-hitting and became exclusively a left-handed batter.

Augie retired in 1949 and later coached one season with the A's.

Matt Galante
Houston Astros (NL) 1985–96, 1998–2001; New York Mets (NL) 2002–04
See Managers section.

Rich Gale
Boston Red Sox (AL) 1992–93
Starting pitcher from New Hampshire.

Gale was named Rookie Pitcher of the Year by *The Sporting News* in 1978 when he went 14–8 with a 3.09 earned run average for the Kansas City Royals. Unfortunately those would be his career highs. In 1980 he went 13–9, the only other time he would post a winning record, and his 3.92 ERA would be his second-best.

He pitched seven seasons and later spent two as a Red Sox' coach.

Mike Gallego
Colorado Rockies (NL) 2002, 2005–
Utility infielder who played 13 seasons.

Gallego spent five of those years as a regular, but he hit only .239 lifetime. He suffered through many injuries throughout his career, and after retiring from the playing field he joined the Boston Red Sox as a minor league infield instructor in 1999. He went to work for the Rockies the next year as a roving instructor and was promoted to the big league staff in May of 2002. He returned to his previous position from 2003–04, then was promoted to Colorado again.

Tom Gamboa
Chicago Cubs (NL) 1998–99; Kansas City Royals (AL) 2001–03
Center fielder in the Canadian Baseball League.

A two-time All-Star in Canada, Gamboa never reached the major leagues as a player. In 1973 he became a scout for the Baltimore Orioles, and later worked for the Major League Scouting Bureau. He soon served as an instructor, scout, and minor league manager in the Milwaukee Brewers' organization, then as a scout, minor league field coordinator, and minor league manager for the Detroit Tigers.

He eventually worked in the Cubs' system before being promoted to the major league staff, and in 2000 managed the Albuquerque Dukes, the Los Angeles Dodgers' AAA club. In 2001 he was named a coach with the Royals.

In the ninth inning of a game at Comiskey Park against the Chicago White Sox in 2002, Gamboa was standing in the first base coaching box when, for reasons unknown, he was suddenly tackled from behind by a 34-year-old man and his 15-year-old son. The two began pummeling Gamboa until Royals' players arrived to pull them off. The two claimed they had had a previous verbal confrontation with the coach, a charge Gamboa fervently denied. Tom seemed to escape with only minor cuts and bruises, but later claimed to have suffered hearing loss in one ear and frequent headaches because of the assault.

After leaving the Royals in 2003 he went back to managing in the minor leagues.

Jim Gantner
Milwaukee Brewers (AL) 1996–97
Dependable infielder who spent his entire career with the Brewers.

That career spanned 17 seasons, during which Gantner hit .274 while leading American League second basemen in total chances on three occasions. In a game in 1979 he even pitched an inning and did not give up a run.

He left the playing field in 1992, but returned to Milwaukee as a coach from 1996–97.

Carlos Garcia
Seattle Mariners (AL) 2005–
Venezuela native who played for several major league teams.

Seven of Garcia's 10 years were spent with the Pittsburgh Pirates, with whom he debuted in 1990. He hit his first home run in 1993, an inside-the-parker, and the following year was named a National League All-Star in the midst of a .277 season in which he played only 98 games. He finished his career in 1999 with the San Diego Padres.

In 2002 Garcia was a player-coach with the Buffalo Bisons, then he became a full-time hitting and infield coach with the club. In 2005 he was hired by the Mariners to coach third base at the big league level.

Dave Garcia
San Diego Padres (NL) 1970–73; Cleveland Indians (AL) 1975–76, 1979; California Angels (AL) 1977; Milwaukee Brewers (AL) 1983–84; Colorado Rockies (NL) 2000–02
See Managers section.

Ron Gardenhire
Minnesota Twins (AL) 1991–2001
See Managers section.

Billy Gardner
Boston Red Sox (AL) 1965–66; Montreal Expos (NL) 1977–78; Minnesota Twins (AL) 1981
See Managers section.

Mark Gardner
San Francisco Giants (NL) 2003–
Pitcher who won 99 major league games.

Mainly a starter, Gardner won in double digits five times in 13 seasons. He played for the Montreal Expos, Kansas City Royals, and Florida Marlins before finishing his career with the Giants. In 1991 with Montreal he pitched a nine-inning no-hitter against the Los Angeles Dodgers, but the game was scoreless and Gardner lost his bid in the tenth inning when he surrendered three safeties and dropped the game, 1–0.

He pitched his last in 2001, but in 2003 became a Giants' coach.

Phil Garner
Houston Astros (NL) 1989–91
See Managers section.

Adrian Garrett
Kansas City Royals (AL) 1988–92; Cincinnati Reds (NL) 2004
Florida native who hit only .185 in eight seasons.

Primarily an outfielder, Garrett could play many positions, including catcher. He was a power hitter in the minor leagues, winning two home run titles in the Texas League, one in the Pacific Coast League, and one in the American Association. He played only 163 major league games and slugged 11 roundtrippers, then became a minor league manager. He coached the Royals for five years, and was working in the Reds' minor league system in 2004 when he was called up to Cincinnati at the end of the season as one of several "extra" coaches.

Ford Garrison
Cincinnati Redlegs (NL) 1953
Outfielder and Navy veteran.

The 1944 season was Garrison's only one as a regular, when he played 13 games for the Boston Red Sox and 121 for the Philadelphia Athletics. He played a mere 51 games other than those and was a .262 hitter. He later coached one season with the Redlegs.

Cito Gaston
Toronto Blue Jays (AL) 1982–89, 2000–01
See Managers section.

Bob Gebhard
Montreal Expos (NL) 1982
Pitched 31 major league games over three seasons.

Gebhard posted an unimpressive 5.93 earned run average at the big league level, but eventually made his mark in other areas. He coached the Expos in 1982 and later worked in the minor league organizations of the Expos and the Minnesota Twins. He was the first general manager of the Colorado Rockies, serving from 1993–99. From 2000–04 he served as a vice president and special assistant to the general manager with the St. Louis Cardinals, and in 2005 was hired in a similar role with the Arizona Diamondbacks.

Charlie Gehringer
Detroit Tigers (AL) 1942
Hall of Fame second baseman and six-time All-Star.

Gehringer was potent both at the plate and at the keystone sack. He was a .320 lifetime hitter and he frequently led American League second basemen in several fielding categories. He played 19 seasons, the best of which was 1937 when he won the batting title with a .371 average and was named the AL's Most Valuable Player. He also led the league twice in hits, twice in doubles, once in triples, twice in runs scored, and once in stolen bases.

He ended his career in 1942 as both a player and a coach with the Tigers. He was inducted into the Hall of Fame in 1949, and from 1951–53 he served as Detroit's general manager. He soon became a club vice president, a position he held until 1959, and he then served on the Hall of Fame Veterans Committee. The Tigers retired his number 2 in 1983.

Bob Geren
Oakland Athletics (AL) 2003–06
See Managers section.

Dick Gernert
Texas Rangers (AL) 1976
Primarily a power-hitting first baseman.

Gernert spent 11 years in the major leagues, and four times hit more than 15 home runs in a season. He peaked with 21 in 1953 with the Boston Red Sox after having clubbed 19 the previous season. He was a schoolteacher in the offseason, and in 1976 coached the Rangers for one year.

Patsy Gharrity
Washington Nationals (AL) 1929–32; Cleveland Indians (AL) 1933–35
Catcher who could also play first base and the outfield.

Gharrity spent an entire 10-year career with the Washington Nationals. His finest season was 1921, when he hit .310 with 7 home runs and 55 runs batted in. He was a player-coach in 1929 and 1930, appearing in only five games as a player, then turned full-time to coaching for Washington and for the Indians.

John Gibbons
Toronto Blue Jays (AL) 2002–04
See Managers section.

Bob Gibson
New York Mets (NL) 1981; Atlanta Braves (NL) 1982–84; St. Louis Cardinals (NL) 1995
Hall of Fame pitcher with 251 victories.

A basketball player with the Harlem Globetrotters from 1957–58, Gibson debuted with the Cardinals in 1959 and spent an entire 17-year major league career in St. Louis. He was a 20-game winner on five occasions, and posted at least 15 victories 10 times. He struck out more than 200 batters in a season nine times, leading the National League with 268 in 1968 and registering 3117 lifetime. His 23 victories tied him with Gaylord Perry for the league lead in 1970, and he also led once in complete games and four times in shutouts. In 1968 he was named both the NL's Most Valuable Player and Cy Young Award winner when he went 22–9 with a league-best 1.12 earned run average and 13 shutouts. He was the World Series MVP in both 1964 and 1967, and he won nine Gold Gloves. In 1970 he won his second Cy Young Award on the strength of a 23–7 record, a 3.12 ERA, and 274 strikeouts. In 1971 he pitched a no-hitter against the Pittsburgh Pirates. The Cardinals retired his number 45 in 1975.

Gibson was hired by Joe Torre to coach the Mets in 1981, the same year he was inducted into the Hall of Fame. He then followed Torre to Atlanta for three years before going into broadcasting. He returned to the Cardinals as a coach for one season, in 1995, and shortly thereafter became a special instructor for the club.

George Gibson
Washington Nationals (AL) 1923; Chicago Cubs (NL) 1925–26
See Managers section.

Kirk Gibson
Detroit Tigers (AL) 2003–05; Arizona Diamondbacks (NL) 2007–
Baseball and football star from Michigan State University.

Gibson surprised many by choosing baseball over football, but it was baseball's good fortune that he did so. He created some of the most dramatic moments in baseball lore, helping to lead the Tigers to a 1984 World Championship by hitting two home runs in Game 5, and blasting an even more dramatic homer in Game 1 of the 1988 Series in the bottom of the ninth inning with two outs. His 1984 shot followed his being named the Most Valuable Player of the American League Championship Series. His 1988 blast came off relief ace Dennis Eckersley, when Gibson hobbled to the plate with his Los Angeles Dodgers down one run to the Oakland Athletics with a runner on first. Unable to play regularly in the Series because of knee problems, he winced as he fouled off four pitches and then connected to drive one into the right-field seats and limped around the bases an unlikely hero.

He was named the 1988 AL Most Valuable Player, having hit .290 during the season with 25 roundtrippers and 76 runs batted in.

He retired in 1995 after his second stint with the Tigers, but he would spend a third tour of duty in Detroit as a coach before moving on to the Diamondbacks.

Andy Gilbert
San Francisco Giants (NL) 1972–75
Outfielder who played eight major league games.

Six of those came before World War II, in 1942, and the other two after, in 1946. All were with the Red Sox, and Gilbert went 1-for-12 plus a walk.

He began to work in the New York Giants' organization in 1950, and stayed with the club through its move to San Francisco. He coached at the big league level for four years, then returned to the minors until 1980. He then moved on to the Atlanta Braves' system.

Jim Gilliam
Los Angeles Dodgers (NL) 1965–78
Negro League and National League All-Star.

Gilliam earned that honor three times in the Negro Leagues and twice in the NL. In 1953 he made his debut with the Brooklyn Dodgers and was named the league's Rookie of the Year when he hit .278 and led the NL with 17 triples. A switch-hitter, he also moved around the field because of his versatility and excellent defense, playing different infield and outfield positions at various times. He hit .300 in 1956, and in 1959 led the NL with 96 bases on balls.

Gilliam retired following the 1964 season and became a coach with the Dodgers, but his retirement from the playing field did not last long. He came out of retirement and played 111 games, batting .280 to help Los Angeles to the World Championship. He retired again and went back to coaching full-time in 1966, and once again came out of retirement to help the Dodgers repeat as World Champs. He then turned back to coaching full-time.

In 1978 the Dodgers won the NL pennant, and just before the World Series started Gilliam died of a brain hemorrhage. The Dodgers retired his number 19 shortly thereafter.

Fred Gladding
Detroit Tigers (AL) 1976–78
Relief pitcher who started only one game.

Gladding relieved another 449 times in his major league career with the Tigers and the Houston Astros. He garnered 109 saves and led the National League in 1969 with 29. He posted a 3.13 lifetime earned run average. He retired in 1973 and returned to Detroit for three years as a coach.

Kid Gleason
Chicago White Sox (AL) 1912–17; Philadelphia Athletics (AL) 1926–31
See Managers section.

Jim Gleeson
Kansas City Athletics (AL) 1957; New York Yankees (AL) 1964
Switch-hitting outfielder from Kansas City.

Gleeson lasted only five seasons despite hitting .313 in 1940. He went into the Navy during World War II, where he met Yogi Berra, and he would not return to play major league baseball after the war. He did later coach the A's in his hometown, however, and also coached under Berra for the Yankees in 1964. He also spent time as a minor league manager in the Yankees' organization and as a scout for the Milwaukee Brewers.

Gene Glynn
Colorado Rockies (NL) 1994, 1995–98; Montreal Expos (NL) 1999; Chicago Cubs (NL) 2000–02; San Francisco Giants (NL) 2003–06
Career minor leaguer and longtime coach.

Glynn played seven years in the minors, beginning in 1979 and ending in 1985 as a player-coach for the Indianapolis Indians. He then served as a minor league manager and coach in the Expos' system before joining the San Diego Padres' organization and winning the 1990 Northwest League Manager of the Year Award when he guided the Spokane Indians to the championship. He joined the Rockies' system in 1992 and was named to the big league staff two years later. In 1995 he began the season as Colorado's minor league coordinator, but when Don Zimmer resigned from the big club he was named the Rockies' first base coach. He later moved to the Expos, the Cubs, and the Giants.

Mike Goff
Seattle Mariners (AL) 2005–

Minor league player whose career ended because of a back injury.

Goff played in the Boston Red Sox' organization from 1984–87, and in 1988 he suffered the injury that caused him to miss the entire season and retire from the playing field. In 1989 he became an assistant coach at the University of South Alabama, then he signed on as a coach with the Jacksonville Suns. He later became a minor league skipper and then served many years as a minor league coordinator before being named a Mariners' coach at the end of the 2005 season.

Orlando Gomez
Texas Rangers (AL) 1991–92; Tampa Bay Devil Rays (AL) 1998–2000; Seattle Mariners (AL) 2003–04
Played 13 years in the minors as Juan Gomez.

A catcher who originally signed with the New York Yankees, Gomez never reached the major leagues as a player. He began managing in the minor leagues in 1977, and in 1989 was named South Atlantic League Manager of the Year when his Gastonia Rangers posted the league's best record. He soon coached two years in Texas before returning to the minors as a skipper and later coaching the Devil Rays and Mariners.

Preston Gomez
Los Angeles Dodgers (NL) 1965–67, 1977–79; Houston Astros (NL) 1973; St. Louis Cardinals (NL) 1976; California Angels (AL) 1981–84
See Managers section.

Fredi Gonzalez
Florida Marlins (NL) 1999–2001; Atlanta Braves (NL) 2003–06
See Managers section.

Mike Gonzalez
St. Louis Cardinals (NL) 1934–46
See Managers section.

Johnny Gooch
Pittsburgh Pirates (NL) 1937–39
Switch-hitting catcher who batted .280 in an 11-year career.

Gooch was competent with a bat and very dependable behind the plate. He hit .329 with the 1922 Pirates in his first full season, and in an 18-inning July game against the New York Giants collected six hits.

After his playing career he became a minor league manager and returned to the Pirates for several years as a coach.

Billy Goodman
Atlanta Braves (NL) 1968–70
Two-time All-Star.

Goodman played for 16 seasons at a variety of positions. His versatility caused teams, especially the Boston Red Sox, to move him around the infield as well as the outfield, but he always performed well both at the plate and with a glove. He led the American League several times in various fielding categories and was a .300 lifetime hitter. He hit over .300 five times and won the 1950 batting title with a .354 average.

He ended his career with the Houston Colt .45s in 1962 and later became a coach with the Braves.

Joe Gordon
Detroit Tigers (AL) 1956
See Managers section.

Johnny Goryl
Minnesota Twins (AL) 1968–69, 1979–80; Cleveland Indians (AL) 1982–88, 1997–98
See Managers section.

Goose Gossage
Colorado Rockies (NL) 2003
Outstanding relief pitcher who played 22 seasons.

Rich "Goose" Gossage was used as a starter by the 1976 Chicago White Sox, but he never started another game after that season. He had started only 8 games in the four seasons prior to that, started 29 in 1976, and spent the rest of his 1002 career contests out of the bullpen.

Gossage notched at least 20 saves 10 times, leading the American League on three of those occasions. He was named to nine All-Star teams. In 1986 he became the last pitcher to face Pete Rose, and he struck out the all-time hit king, who had come to the plate as a pinch-hitter. In 1988 he became only the second pitcher in history to record 300 saves, and he would finish with 310.

Following the 1989 season he did not catch on with a major league team, so he went to Japan to play. He returned and continued to play from 1991–94. In 2003 he coached one season with the Rockies.

Hank Gowdy
Boston Braves (NL) 1929–37; Cincinnati Reds (NL) 1938–42, 1945–46; New York Giants (NL) 1947–48
See Managers section.

Milt Graff
Pittsburgh Pirates (NL) 1985
Second baseman with a degree in accounting.

Graff played only 61 major league games in 1957 and

'58 with the Kansas City Athletics and hit just .179. He served in the Army during the Korean War, and after his baseball career he went into accounting for a time and then hooked on with the Pirates as a scouting director, eventual coach, and director of stadium operations. He later worked as a scout for the San Francisco Giants and Cincinnati Reds.

Brian Graham
Cleveland Indians (AL) 1999; Baltimore Orioles (AL) 2000
Minor league second baseman for five seasons.

After his playing career Graham became a minor league manager in the Indians' system, and in 1991 he was named the Carolina League Manager of the Year with the Kinston Indians. In 1998 he served as Cleveland's defensive coordinator before being promoted to the major league staff the following season. He coached the Orioles in 2000 and then moved to the Florida Marlins' organization as a minor league coordinator. He returned to the Pirates in 2002 as their director of player development.

Alex Grammas
Chicago Cubs (NL) 1964; Pittsburgh Pirates (NL) 1965–69; Cincinnati Reds (NL) 1970–75, 1978; Atlanta Braves (NL) 1979; Detroit Tigers (AL) 1980–91
See Managers section.

Mike Greenwell
Cincinnati Reds (NL) 2001
Lifetime .303 hitter.

A consistent outfielder who played his entire 12-year career with the Boston Red Sox, Mike Greenwell hit over .300 seven times and in 1988 slugged 22 home runs. His first three major league hits, which came in 1985, were longballs, in fact. A two-time All-Star, he hit for the cycle in a game in 1988 and in 1990 hit his second inside-the-park grand slam off Greg Cadaret of the New York Yankees. His first had also been off Cadaret. In 1996 he drove in nine runs in a 9–8 victory over the Seattle Mariners, the most RBIs by any player who has accounted for all of his team's runs. At the end of that season he went to Japan to play for the Hanshin Tigers, but he broke his leg in May and was out of action.

In 2001 he coached for the Reds.

Glenn Gregson
Los Angeles Dodgers (NL) 1998; Boston Red Sox (AL) 2003
Worked for many years in the minor league systems of the Dodgers and the Philadelphia Phillies.

Glenn "Goose" Gregson reached the big leagues with Los Angeles in 1998, but in June was reassigned as pitching coach with the Class A San Bernardino Spirit when

Fox Entertainment purchased the Dodgers and made Glenn Hoffman manager. In 1999 he returned to the Phillies as a minor league pitching coordinator, then worked with the Zulia Eagles in Venezuela before being hired by the Red Sox. He served as Boston's minor league pitching coordinator from 2002–04, but in May of 2003 filled in as pitching coach for Tony Cloninger when Cloninger was recovering from treatment for bladder cancer. The substitution was made necessary by the fact that the Red Sox were preparing to travel to Toronto to face the Blue Jays, and the city of Toronto was facing an outbreak of severe acute respiratory syndrome (SARS), which Cloninger's immune system may not have been ready to handle.

In 2006 Gregson became the pitching coach of the Gulf Coast Red Sox.

Ken Griffey, Sr.
Seattle Mariners (AL) 1993; Colorado Rockies (NL) 1996; Cincinnati Reds (NL) 1997–2001
Right fielder on Cincinnati's Big Red Machine of the 1970s.

Griffey fashioned a 19-year career during which he hit .296, accumulating 2143 hits, 152 home runs, and 200 stolen bases. He was the Most Valuable Player of the 1980 All-Star Game when he went 2-for-3 with a solo home run in the National League's 4–2 victory, and he was named an All-Star on two other occasions as well.

On August 31, 1990, Ken played left field for the Mariners while his son, Ken, Jr., manned center, and the two thus became the first father-son combination in major league history to play together. Two weeks later the pair hit storybook back-to-back home runs in Seattle's 7–5 loss to the California Angels.

Ken, Sr. became a coach following his playing career, and had the opportunity to coach his son with both the Mariners and the Reds. After coaching in Cincinnati he remained with the organization as a special consultant.

Alfredo Griffin
Toronto Blue Jays (AL) 1996–97; Anaheim Angels (AL) 2000–04; Los Angeles Angels of Anaheim (AL) 2005–
Co-Rookie of the Year in 1979.

Griffin reached the major leagues with the Cleveland Indians in 1976, but he still qualified as a rookie in '79 because he had played only 31 big league games the previous three seasons. He hit .287 in 1979 and won the American League award along with John Castino of the Minnesota Twins.

A switch-hitter who was a far better fielder than hitter, Griffin played 18 seasons. In 1980 with the Blue Jays he tied for the AL lead with 15 triples, and in 1984 he became an All-Star. He won a Gold Glove the following season. He played until 1993, and during his career he was on the wrong end of three perfect games—Len Barker's in 1981, Tom Browning's in 1988, and Dennis Martinez's in 1991.

In 1993 he was hired by the Blue Jays as a roving minor league instructor, and was promoted to Toronto in 1996. He later became a coach with the Angels.

Burleigh Grimes
Kansas City Athletics (AL) 1955
See Managers section.

Charlie Grimm
Chicago Cubs (NL) 1941, 1961–63
See Managers section.

Marv Grissom
Los Angeles Angels (AL) 1961–64; California Angels (AL) 1965–66, 1977–78; Chicago White Sox (AL) 1967–68; Minnesota Twins (AL) 1970–71; Chicago Cubs (NL) 1975–76
Right-handed pitcher from California.

Grissom pitched for 10 seasons, debuting five years after his brother Lee had pitched his last major league game. Marv won 12 games in 1952 with the White Sox, and in 1954 was named an All-Star with the New York Giants. In 1956 he posted a 1.56 earned run average in 43 games, and his lifetime ERA was 3.41. He went on to coach for a number of teams when his playing days were over.

Johnny Grodzicki
Detroit Tigers (AL) 1979
Pitched 24 major league games.

Five of those games came in 1941, and Grodzicki then served in the military during World War II. He was wounded and never completely recovered. He pitched 19 more games from 1946–47 and posted a 2–2 lifetime record with a 4.43 earned run average. He eventually coached a single season with the Tigers, and he died in Daytona Beach, Florida in 1998.

Greg Gross
Philadelphia Phillies (NL) 2001–04
Named Rookie of the Year by *The Sporting News* in 1974.

Gross hit .314 that year and would bat over .300 on four other occasions, topping out at .333 in 1979. He struck out only 150 times in 3745 at-bats and hit .287 lifetime. Toward the end of his career he was valued as an extraordinary pinch-hitter. He started and ended his career with the Houston Astros, and played for the Chicago Cubs and the Phillies in between. It was to the Phillies that he returned as a coach in 2001.

Epy Guerrero
Toronto Blue Jays (AL) 1981
Minor league third baseman who became a scout extraordinaire.

The brother of Mario Guerrero, a shortstop who played eight major league seasons, Epy never reached the major leagues as a player but did so as a coach with the Blue Jays in 1981. He became much more highly valued as a scout, however, working primarily in his native Dominican Republic for several organizations and being responsible for signing well over a hundred players to contracts with major league clubs. He and his son Mike also started a baseball academy in the Dominican.

Ron Guidry
New York Yankees (AL) 2006–
One of the most successful pitchers in Yankees' history.

Guidry debuted in New York in 1975 and two years later won 16 games for the Bronx Bombers. In 1978 he had his best season when he went 25–3, leading the American League in victories as well as in shutouts with 9 and in earned run average at 1.74 en route to winning the league's Cy Young Award. His 2.78 ERA the following season was also the circuit's best. He was a four-time All-Star, and in 1983 he went 21–9 while leading the AL with 21 complete games. In 1985 his 22 victories topped the league.

Nicknamed "Louisiana Lightning," Guidry struck out 18 California Angels on June 17, 1978, a game he called the highlight of his career. He also won 13 consecutive games that season. From 1982–86 he earned five consecutive Gold Gloves.

Guidry last played for the Yankees in 1988, and after elbow surgery caused him to start the 1989 season on the disabled list and he did not fare well in a minor league rehabilitation assignment, he decided to retire. He began serving as a spring training instructor with the Yanks in 1990, and he was named to the major league coaching staff in 2006.

An amateur drummer, Guidry once played with the Beach Boys in a concert following a game at Yankee Stadium. In 2003 the Yankees retired his number 49.

Ozzie Guillen
Montreal Expos (NL) 2001; Florida Marlins (NL) 2002–03
See Managers section.

Don Gullett
Cincinnati Reds (NL) 1993–2005
Critical member of Cincinnati's Big Red Machine.

Gullett debuted with the Reds in 1970 at the age of 19. A hard-throwing left-hander, he won 16 games in 1971, 18 in 1973, 17 in 1974, and 15 in 1975. He lost two months of that '75 season when a line drive off the bat of the Atlanta Braves' Larvell Blanks broke his thumb.

In the second game of a doubleheader on August 23, 1970, Gullett struck out six New York Mets in a row, tying a record for relief pitchers. In 1971 he led the National League in winning percentage at .727 with his 16–6 record. His lifetime earned run average was 3.11, and he never recorded one above 3.94.

In 1977 Gullett signed with the New York Yankees as a free agent, but after winning 14 games he developed rotator cuff problems and pitched only one more season. He later returned to the Reds as an instructor and a longtime coach.

Don Gutteridge
Chicago White Sox (AL) 1955–66, 1968–69
See Managers section.

Eddie Haas
Atlanta Braves (NL) 1974–77, 1984
See Managers section.

George "Mule" Haas
Chicago White Sox (AL) 1940–46
Outfielder and first baseman from Montclair, New Jersey.

A .292 lifetime hitter, Haas hit over .300 on three occasions. He played for the Clairmont Baseball Club in 1920 when the team decided to become semipro, and during a three-year period Haas helped it go 105–31 while winning back-to-back town championships in 1921 and 1922. As a major leaguer his main claim to fame came during the 1929 World Series, when, in Game 4, his Philadelphia Athletics were trailing the Chicago Cubs, 8–0. Mule hit a three-run inside-the-park home run to spark a 10-run rally in the seventh inning resulting in a 10–8 Athletics' victory, then hit a two-run homer in the ninth inning of Game 5 to tie the Cubs in what soon became a Philadelphia victory and World Championship.

Haas retired in 1938, and in 1939 he managed the minor league Oklahoma City Indians before becoming a coach with the White Sox, for whom he had played five seasons. He later returned to managing in the minor leagues, and in 1967 was inducted into the New Jersey All Sports Hall of Fame.

Stan Hack
St. Louis Cardinals (NL) 1957–58; Chicago Cubs (NL) 1965
See Managers section.

Rich Hacker
St. Louis Cardinals (NL) 1986–90; Toronto Blue Jays (AL) 1991–94

Shortstop who played 16 games in the major leagues.

Those games came with the Montreal Expos in 1971, and Hacker hit a mere .171. After concluding his minor league career Rich served as a coach at Southeastern Illinois College from 1976–78. From 1979–86 he was a scout and minor league manager in the organizations of the San Diego Padres, the Blue Jays, and the Cardinals. He was then elevated to a Cardinals' coach under Whitey Herzog, and later as a third base coach for the Blue Jays before returning to the Padres' system as a scout from 1996–2000. In 2001, the year he retired, he was inducted into the Midwest Professional Baseball Scouts Association Hall of Fame.

Harvey Haddix
New York Mets (NL) 1966–67; Cincinnati Reds (NL) 1969; Boston Red Sox (AL) 1971; Cleveland Indians (AL) 1975–78; Pittsburgh Pirates (NL) 1979–84
Pitched one of the most heart-breaking games in major league history.

In 1959 Haddix tossed a 12-inning perfect game before losing not only the perfect game, but the no-hitter, the shutout, and the game itself in the thirteenth inning.

But Harvey had plenty of success before that. In 1947 he had pitched a seven-inning no-hitter for the Winston-Salem Cards over the Danville Leafs in an 8–0 victory while striking out 14 batters. In 1950 he had led the American Association in victories, complete games, strikeouts, and earned run average before serving in the military in 1951 and then reaching the St. Louis Cardinals in 1952. In 1953, the first of his three All-Star seasons, he led the National League with six shutouts. From 1958–60 he earned three Gold Gloves.

His fateful game in 1959 came on May 26, when, pitching for the Pittsburgh Pirates, he retired every Milwaukee Brave he faced through the first nine innings. The Pirates failed to score, and in extra innings Haddix continued to be perfect through three more innings. In the thirteenth the Braves' Felix Mantilla reached on an error by Don Hoak, and after he was sacrificed to second base Haddix intentionally walked Hank Aaron. Joe Adcock then hit what should have been a three-run home run. In a bizarre twist, Aaron left the field after Mantilla scored, and as a result Adcock passed him on the bases. Adcock was therefore called out and was credited with a double instead of a home run. Mantilla's run was the only one that counted, and Haddix and the Pirates lost the game, 1–0.

Harvey retired in 1965 with a lifetime 3.63 earned run average and later became a pitching coach with several major league teams.

Jesse Haines
Brooklyn Dodgers (NL) 1938
Hall of Fame right-handed pitcher.

Haines pitched one game for the Cincinnati Reds in 1918 before joining the St. Louis Cardinals in 1920 and pitching 18 more seasons for the Redbirds. A 210-game winner, Haines won at least 20 on three occasions, topping out with 24 in 1927. He fashioned a lifetime 3.64 earned run average and led the National League once in games pitched and once in shutouts and also tied once in complete games and once in shutouts. A hard thrower, he added a knuckleball to his repertoire that helped his cause on the mound. In 1924 he pitched a no-hitter against the Boston Braves, and in 1926 he shut out the New York Yankees 4–0 in Game 3 of the World Series while hitting a two-run home run. He retired in 1937 and coached the Dodgers the following year.

Haines was inducted into the Hall of Fame by the Veterans Committee in 1970.

Sammy Hairston
Chicago White Sox (AL) 1978
Outstanding Negro League catcher and infielder.

Hairston played for the Birmingham Black Barons and the Indianapolis Clowns between 1944 and 1950. In 1948 he was named to the Negro League East-West All-Star team. In 1950 he won the Negro League Triple Crown, and in 1951 he played four games for the Chicago White Sox, going 2-for-5 for a .400 average.

The father of major leaguers Jerry Hairston, Sr. and Johnny Hairston and the grandfather of major leaguers Jerry Hairston, Jr. and Scott Hairston, he returned to the White Sox as a coach in 1978.

Chip Hale
Arizona Diamondbacks (NL) 2007–
Infielder who attended the University of Arizona.

A .277 hitter in a reserve role for the Minnesota Twins and Los Angeles Dodgers, Hale spent many years as a minor league manager following his playing career. In 2006 he guided the Tucson Sidewinders to the Pacific Coast League championship in his third year at the helm of that club, and as a result was named the PCL's Manager of the Year.

Following that success he was promoted to the Diamondbacks as a coach.

DeMarlo Hale
Texas Rangers (AL) 2002–05; Boston Red Sox (AL) 2006–
Minor league first baseman and outfielder.

Hale played in the minor league organizations of the Boston Red Sox and Oakland Athletics for five seasons. In 1989 he became an instructor at the Bucky Dent Baseball School in Boca Raton, Florida, then became a minor league coach in the Boston Red Sox' system. In 1993 he turned to managing, and two years later was named the Midwest League Manager of the Year with the Michigan Battle Cats. In 1999 with the AA Trenton Thunder he earned Eastern League Manager of the Year accolades when his club finished 92–50, and he was also named Minor League Manager of the Year by *Baseball America*, *The Sporting News*, and *USA Today Baseball Weekly*.

He managed two years in the Rangers' organization before being promoted to the major league staff, then returned to the Red Sox at the big league level.

Tom Haller
San Francisco Giants (NL) 1977–79
Three-time All-Star catcher.

Formerly a quarterback at the University of Illinois, Haller spent 12 years as a catcher in major league baseball. He averaged .257 and never hit over .286. While playing for the Giants on May 31, 1964, he caught all 23 innings of a game against the New York Mets. On July 14, 1972, during his final season while playing for the Detroit Tigers, he was the catcher while his brother Bill was the umpire, a major league first. The Tigers dropped that game to the Kansas City Royals, 1–0.

After coaching the Giants from 1977–79, Tom became the club's vice president of operations, serving from 1981 until 1986.

Mike Hamilton
Colorado Rockies (NL) 2003
Videographer listed as an official coach for one season.

Hamilton worked for the Major League Scouting Bureau for 10 years before joining the Rockies in 2000. While listed officially as a coach only in 2003, he has served as a "video coach" and "video coordinator" since joining the club. His role has been to put together video scouting reports on opposing players as well as to record the at-bats of Rockies' players so that they can, in essence, scout themselves. Some, such as first baseman Todd Helton, would download Hamilton's video records onto personal iPods so that they could view and study themselves at their leisure.

Steve Hamilton
Detroit Tigers (AL) 1975
Former basketball player with the Minneapolis Lakers.

A sidearmer, Hamilton pitched in relief for 12 seasons, spending more than half of that time with the New York Yankees. He posted a lifetime 3.05 earned run average, his best being 1.39 in 1965 in 46 games. His career record was 40–31, and he garnered 42 saves.

Buddy Hancken
Houston Astros (NL) 1968–72
Birmingham native who played one major league game.

A catcher, Hancken did not even get a chance to bat in that 1940 contest with the Philadelphia Athletics. During World War II he served in the U.S. Marine Corps, and he would eventually spend five seasons as a coach with the Astros.

Fred Haney
Milwaukee Braves (NL) 1956
See Managers section.

Larry Haney
Milwaukee Brewers (AL) 1978–91
Light-hitting backup catcher.

Despite hitting a game-winning home run in his very first major league game with the Baltimore Orioles, Haney would never become a regular because of his bat. He averaged only .215 lifetime with 12 home runs, but he did last 12 big league seasons in a reserve role. He finished his career with the Brewers and then became a longtime coach with them.

His son, Chris Haney, was a major league pitcher for 11 years.

Guy Hansen
Kansas City Royals (AL) 1991–93, 1996–97, 2005
Minor league pitcher for four seasons.

Hansen played in the Royals' system and was a California League All-Star in 1970. In spite of that success he never pitched on a big league level. From 1975–76 he served as pitching coach and head recruiter at Pepperdine University, then worked until 1980 as a scout with the Major League Scouting Bureau. He was simultaneously an associate scout for the Royals and the Baltimore Orioles, and from 1981–83 worked solely for Kansas City. He then spent two years as pitching coach at UCLA before returning to the Royals' organization as a minor league pitching coach.

He was promoted to Kansas City on an interim basis in September of 1991, but shortly thereafter was awarded the full-time job. From 1994–95 he worked in the team's scouting department before rejoining the big league club as a coach. He then spent the next few years in the Atlanta Braves' organization before returning to the Royals again in 2005.

Roger Hansen
Seattle Mariners (AL) 1992
Minor league catcher who became a catching coordinator.

Catching is a passion for Hansen. Roger was playing in the Kansas City Royals' organization when he realized he was not going to reach the major leagues. Mariners' general manager Dick Balderson hired him with the idea of making him a coach in the Seattle system, and Hansen responded with zeal. He served one year on the Mariners' major league staff as a bullpen coach, but has spent most of his career working with young players as a minor league catching coordinator.

Ron Hansen
Milwaukee Brewers (AL) 1980–83; Montreal Expos (NL) 1985–89
American League Rookie of the Year in 1960.

A light-hitting but excellent defensive shortstop, Hansen batted .255 with the Baltimore Orioles that season with 22 home runs and 86 runs batted in while being named an AL All-Star for both games. On only one other occasion as a full-time player would he hit 20 home runs and top that batting average, but he was consistently among league leaders in a number of fielding categories. In 1965 he had 28 total chances in a doubleheader, a major league record. He missed most of the 1966 season due to a ruptured spinal disk, but was back the following year. While playing for the Washington Senators in 1968 he turned an unassisted triple play in a game against the Cleveland Indians.

Hansen finished out his career in a reserve role with several teams, and he later became a coach with the Brewers and Expos.

Mel Harder
Cleveland Indians (AL) 1948–63; New York Mets (NL) 1964; Chicago Cubs (NL) 1965; Cincinnati Reds (NL) 1966–68; Kansas City Royals (AL) 1969
See Managers section.

Larry Hardy
Texas Rangers (AL) 1995–2001
Pitcher from the University of Texas at Austin.

A Texas native, Hardy had a respectable first major league season in 1974 with the San Diego Padres when he went 9–4 in relief with a 4.69 earned run average. He faltered in 18 big league games over the next two years and did not win another contest. He later coached the Rangers for six years.

Mike Hargrove
Cleveland Indians (AL) 1990–91
See Managers section.

Mike Harkey
Florida Marlins (NL) 2006
Pitched for eight major league seasons.

The Sporting News named Harkey its National League Rookie of the Year in 1990 when he went 12–6 with a 3.26 earned run average for the Chicago Cubs. He went 36–36 lifetime with a 4.49 ERA.

He played until 1997 and became a minor league pitching coach in 2000 in the San Diego Padres' minor league system. In 2006 he was hired by the Marlins to be their bullpen coach, but he was let go at the end of the season when manager Joe Girardi was fired.

Tom Harmon
Chicago Cubs (NL) 1982

Nine-year minor league player and longtime college coach.

Harmon played for five years in the Kansas City Royals' organization and another three in the St. Louis Cardinals' system. In 1978 he became a player-coach with the Oklahoma City 89ers, the Philadelphia Phillies' AAA team, then he went into managing. In 1979 he guided the Central Oregon Phillies to the Northwest League championship. In 1982 he was promoted to the Cubs as a coach.

Harmon went back to minor league managing in 1983 before leaving baseball for the private sector. In 1989, however, he returned to the University of Texas, his alma mater, as an assistant coach. In 1997 he was named the Longhorns' recruiting coordinator and third base coach, and eventually became associate head coach. Along the way he helped the Longhorns reach the College World Series eight times and win five league titles and two national championships.

Tommy Harper
Boston Red Sox (AL) 1980–84, 2000–02; Montreal Expos (NL) 1990–99

Speedy outfielder who played for 15 seasons.

Harper broke in with the Cincinnati Reds in 1962. In 1964 he stole 24 bases, and the following season he swiped 35 while leading the National League with 126 runs scored. His numbers began to decline after that, and in 1968 he was traded to the Cleveland Indians, but things did not improve. In 1969 the Seattle Pilots selected him in the expansion draft, and he promptly led the American League with 73 stolen bases and in 1970 was named an AL All-Star while playing for the club, which had become the Milwaukee Brewers. In 1973 with the Red Sox he led the league with 54 steals.

Harper retired in 1976 with 408 stolen bases lifetime. He later returned to Boston as a coach, then moved on to the Expos and back to the Red Sox thereafter.

Toby Harrah
Texas Rangers (AL) 1989–92; Cleveland Indians (AL) 1996; Detroit Tigers (AL) 1998; Colorado Rockies (NL) 2000–02

See Managers section.

Bud Harrelson
New York Mets (NL) 1982, 1985–90

See Managers section.

Lum Harris
Chicago White Sox (AL) 1951–54; Baltimore Orioles (AL) 1955–61; Houston Colt .45s (NL) 1962–64

See Managers section.

John Hart
Baltimore Orioles (AL) 1988

See Managers section.

Chuck Hartenstein
Cleveland Indians (AL) 1979; Milwaukee Brewers (AL) 1987–89

Pitched for the Texas Longhorns from 1962–64.

After his college days Hartenstein enjoyed a six-year major league career as a relief pitcher. He played for five teams and fashioned a 17–19 record with a 4.52 earned run average. He then became a minor and major league pitching coach, spending one year with the Indians and three with the Brewers. He retired in 1990.

Grover Hartley
Cleveland Indians (AL) 1928–30; Pittsburgh Pirates (NL) 1931–33; St. Louis Browns (AL) 1934–36; New York Giants (NL) 1946

Catcher for 14 seasons.

Excellent at handling young pitchers, Hartley had two stints with the Giants and two with the Browns. In between he also played for the Indians and the Boston Red Sox, and he spent two years in the Federal League with the St. Louis Terriers. A .268 lifetime hitter, he became a coach with the Tribe in 1928, then served as a player-coach in 1929 and appeared in one game in 1930. After coaching the Pirates he was a player-coach for the Browns in 1934, appearing in five contests and garnering three at-bats. He later became a minor league manager and returned to the Giants as a coach in 1946.

Gabby Hartnett
Chicago Cubs (NL) 1938; New York Giants (NL) 1941; Kansas City Athletics (AL) 1965

See Managers section.

Roy Hartsfield

Los Angeles Dodgers (NL) 1969–72; Atlanta Braves (NL) 1973
See Managers section.

Bill Haselman

Boston Red Sox (AL) 2004, 2005–06
Catcher for 13 seasons.

A reserve backstop, Haselman played in the major leagues from 1990–2003, excluding 1991, and in 1996 was Roger Clemens' catcher when The Rocket struck out 20 Detroit Tigers on September 18. In 2004 he became a scout and instructor for the Red Sox, and filled in as first base coach on an interim basis when Lynn Jones suffered an eye injury. He returned as full-time bullpen coach in 2005, and was moved to first base coach in 2006.

Ron Hassey

Colorado Rockies (NL) 1993–95; St. Louis Cardinals (NL) 1996; Seattle Mariners (AL) 2005–06
Only major league player to catch two perfect games.

Before his big league career began Hassey had played on the U.S. National Team in 1974 and 1975. A .266 hitter, he caught Len Barker's perfecto in 1981 with the Cleveland Indians, and Dennis Martinez's in 1991 with the Montreal Expos. He developed bad knees but lasted 14 major league seasons.

In 1992 he joined the New York Yankees as a scout, then became a coach with the expansion Rockies and later with the Cardinals. Beginning in 1997 he worked in the Arizona Diamondbacks' organization helping that franchise prepare for the expansion draft. He was a special assistant to the general manager, a roving catching instructor, a field coordinator, and a scout before joining the Mariners as a coach. He resigned from Seattle in mid-September of 2006 when he was informed that he would not be retained for the 2007 season.

Billy Hatcher

Tampa Bay Devil Rays (AL) 1998–2005; Cincinnati Reds (NL) 2006–
Outfielder who stole 218 bases lifetime.

Hatcher played for seven teams during a 12-year career, and six times stole more than 20 bases in a season. In 1990 he helped the Reds go wire-to-wire, then set several records in the World Series, hitting .750 for the highest batting average in a four-game Series, collecting the most consecutive hits in a Series with seven (tying Thurman Munson), and hitting the most doubles in a four-game Series with four.

After concluding his playing career Hatcher went to work in the Devil Rays' organization, spending one year as a roving minor league instructor and one as a minor league coach before joining the big league staff. After eight years in Tampa Bay he returned to the Reds in a coaching role.

Mickey Hatcher

Texas Rangers (AL) 1993–94; Los Angeles Dodgers (NL) 1998; Anaheim Angels (AL) 2000–04; Los Angeles Angels of Anaheim (AL) 2005–
Pacific Coast League batting champion in 1979.

Hatcher hit .371 that year and earned a call-up to the Dodgers. In a 12-year major league career he hit .280, his finest season coming in 1983 with the Minnesota Twins when he batted .317 with 9 home runs and 47 runs batted in. The following season he hit .302, and in 1985 he once put together nine straight hits. In 1989 he even made one pitching appearance.

In 1991 he was a minor league player-coach, and the next year became a full-time coach. He coached the Rangers the next two seasons before returning to the minors and later becoming a manager. In June of 1998 he rejoined the Dodgers, this time as a coach, under new manager Glenn Hoffman. He then returned to the minors for one season as a hitting instructor before the Angels hired him as a coach in Anaheim.

Fred Hatfield

Detroit Tigers (AL) 1977–78
Descendant of the Hatfields of the Hatfield-McCoy feud fame.

This Hatfield was an infielder who spent nine years in the major leagues and hit .242. His glove kept him in the big leagues, because his versatility allowed him to play any infield position. One of the teams with whom he played was the Tigers, and he returned to them as a coach for two years in the 1970s.

Grady Hatton

Chicago Cubs (NL) 1960; Houston Astros (NL) 1973–74
See Managers section.

Bill Hayes

Colorado Rockies (NL) 1998
Catcher who played five major league games.

Those games came with the Chicago Cubs, with four in 1980 and one in 1981. He had two hits, one of which was a double, but spent 10 years playing in the minor league systems of the Cubs and the Kansas City Royals. He then became a minor league manager in the Cubs' and Rockies' organizations. Following the 1995 season, he guided the Maui Stingrays to the Hawaiian Winter League title. In 1998 he was bullpen coach for the Rockies, and the following year managed their AAA Colorado Springs Sky Sox club. He then joined the San Francisco Giants' organization, where he continued to skipper minor league teams until being named the Giants' bullpen catcher in 2003.

Joe Haynes
Washington Nationals (AL) 1953–55
Solid relief pitcher for the Nationals and Chicago White Sox.

Haynes played 379 major league games and had 147 starts. He debuted in 1939 and spent his first two seasons in Washington before going to Chicago. In 1942 he led the American League with 40 games pitched, and in 1945 came within one hit of a perfect game when a batter singled in the third inning of a contest on May 1. In 1947 he went 14–6 for the White Sox with a league-leading 2.42 earned run average. The following season he was an AL All-Star.

Haynes was married to Thelma Griffith, whose father Clark owned the Nationals. Clark traded for his son-in-law after the 1948 campaign, and Haynes returned to Washington for four more seasons. After retiring from the playing field in 1952 he stayed on as a coach, and later served as general manager and vice president. He was still with the club when it moved to Minnesota and became the Twins.

Ray Hayworth
Brooklyn Dodgers (NL) 1945; Chicago Cubs (NL) 1955
Excellent defensive catcher.

Hayworth was decent with a bat as well as a glove, hitting .309 in 1935 and .265 lifetime. He spent 15 years in the major leagues and once set an American League record for catchers by handling 439 consecutive chances without an error. That record was later broken by Yogi Berra.

Besides coaching one season for the Dodgers and one for the Cubs, Hayworth also worked in the organizations of the Milwaukee/Atlanta Braves and the Montreal Expos. Having played most of his career with the Detroit Tigers, he was honored by throwing the ceremonial first pitch in the last game at Tiger Stadium on September 29, 1999. He died in 2002 at the age of 98, at the time the oldest surviving major league player.

Richie Hebner
Boston Red Sox (AL) 1989–91; Philadelphia Phillies (NL) 2001
Third baseman/first baseman and native of Boston.

Hebner began his 18-year career with the Pittsburgh Pirates, with whom he hit .301 in 1969 to lead all National League rookies. He hit .300 in 1972, the only other time he would break that mark in a full season, although he was dependable at the plate. In 1973 he slugged a career-high 25 home runs. During the offseasons, Hebner worked for his father at a cemetery digging graves.

He never played for his hometown Red Sox, but he did join them as a coach in 1989. He later went to the Phillies, a team with whom he had played two seasons, in the same role.

Don Heffner
Kansas City Athletics (AL) 1958–60; Detroit Tigers (AL) 1961; New York Mets (NL) 1964–65; California Angels (AL) 1967–68
See Managers section.

Jim Hegan
New York Yankees (AL) 1960–73, 1979–80; Detroit Tigers (AL) 1974–78
Five-time All-Star catcher.

Below average with a bat but excellent defensively, Hegan was skilled at throwing out baserunners. He spent most of his career with the Cleveland Indians and caught three no-hitters: Don Black's in 1947, Bob Lemon's in 1948, and Bob Feller's in 1951. In 1960 he joined the Chicago Cubs at the request of manager Lou Boudreau, who had been his skipper in Cleveland and asked him to work with his young pitchers. He was later hired by the Yankees as a bullpen coach, and was still in that role when his son Mike joined the club in 1964. When manager Ralph Houk went to Detroit to take over the Tigers, Hegan went with him, although he later returned to the Yankees.

Hegan had a heart attack while pitching batting practice for the Tigers, but recovered. He eventually died in 1984 while being interviewed in his back yard.

Harry Heilmann
Cincinnati Reds (NL) 1932
Hall of Fame outfielder who won four batting titles.

In a 17-year career Heilmann hit over .300 twelve times. In 1923 he batted .403. He spent 15 seasons with the Detroit Tigers, and besides those four batting crowns he led the American League in 1921 with 237 hits and in 1924 tied Joe Sewell with 45 doubles.

In 1916 he once saved the life of a woman who was drowning in the Detroit River. He spent some of 1918 in the Navy, and he was suspended once in 1922 for arguing with an umpire. He also missed part of that season with a broken collarbone. He sold life insurance and once sold a policy to Babe Ruth in 1923.

Heilmann hit .342 lifetime, but toward the end of his career he developed painful arthritis in his wrists. He retired following the 1930 season, which he spent with the Reds, but he returned in 1932 as a player-coach. He then became a longtime Tigers' broadcaster, and he was inducted into the Hall of Fame in 1952.

Al Heist

Houston Astros (NL) 1966–67; San Diego Padres (NL) 1980
Excellent defensive outfielder who spent most of his career
in the minor leagues.

Heist once hit .326 with the Redding Browns of the Far
West League, but that was far from his norm. He made his
mark with his glove, not his bat, which was probably the
main reason he never stuck in the major leagues. He did
become a Western International League All-Star in 1954
with the Lewiston Broncs, and with the Sacramento Solons
of the Pacific Coast League he was frequently among
league leaders in fielding and went the entire 1958 season
without committing an error.

Heist spent parts of three seasons in the majors with the
Chicago Cubs and Houston Colt .45s. He was 32 when he
made his big league debut, but he was soon back in the
minors until he retired from the playing field and then returned to Houston as a coach. He later became a scout for
the Padres and also coached with them for one year.

Tommy Helms

Texas Rangers (AL) 1981–82; Cincinnati Reds (NL) 1983–89
See Managers section.

Rollie Hemsley

**Philadelphia Athletics (AL) 1954; Washington Senators (AL)
1961–62**
Catcher for 19 major league seasons.

Hemsley overcame alcoholism and in doing so saved
his career. He played for many clubs and was a .262 lifetime hitter. He was named to five All-Star teams, and in
1940 with the Cleveland Indians caught Bob Feller's no-
hitter on Opening Day.

He became a minor league manager after his retirement, and in 1950 was named Minor League Manager of
the Year by *The Sporting News* when his Columbus Red
Birds took the American Association title and then defeated the Montreal Royals of the International League in
the Junior World Series. He coached one season for the
A's and two for the Senators, and continued to spend many
years as a minor league skipper. In 1963 *The Sporting
News* once again named him Minor League Manager of the
Year when his Indianapolis Indians won the IL championship.

Solly Hemus

New York Mets (NL) 1962–63; Cleveland Indians (AL) 1965
See Managers section.

Ramon Henderson

Philadelphia Phillies (NL) 1998–
Minor leaguer who spent eight years in the Phillies' system.

Henderson played until 1989 and then became a coach
with the Princeton Patriots the following season. He
coached the Clearwater Phillies from 1991–92, then was
promoted to manager of the Martinsville Phillies, a position he held until 1996. In 1997 he coached the Reading
Phillies, and in 1998 was promoted to Philadelphia as bullpen coach.

Steve Henderson

**Houston Astros (NL) 1994–96; Tampa Bay Devil Rays (AL)
1998, 2006–**
Played 12 years in the majors and hit .280.

Originally drafted by the Cincinnati Reds, Henderson
was involved in the deal that sent Tom Seaver from the
New York Mets to Cincinnati. He debuted with New York
in 1977 and hit .297, losing out by one vote to Andre Dawson for Rookie of the Year honors. In 1978 he had the only
hit—a home run—in a game against Silvio Martinez of the
St. Louis Cardinals.

Henderson started his coaching career in the Pittsburgh
Pirates' minor league system, but in 1994 was hired by the
Astros to serve at the big league level. In 1997 he was
hired by the Devil Rays to be their minor league hitting
coordinator. He served in that position every year until
2006, except for 1998 when he was made a major league
coach. In '06 he returned to Tampa Bay as the big league
hitting coach.

George Hendrick

**St. Louis Cardinals (NL) 1996–97; Anaheim Angels (AL)
1998–99; Los Angeles Dodgers (NL) 2003; Tampa Bay
Devil Rays (AL) 2006–**
Four-time All-Star outfielder.

Hendrick had problems with the press, but not with his
teammates or fans. He hit over .300 four times, peaking at
.318 in 1983 with the Cardinals. He won Silver Slugger
Awards both at first base and in right field. In 1973 he
broke up a Jim Palmer no-hitter with a single in the eighth
inning, and in 1984 spoiled a Mario Soto bid with two outs
in the ninth inning with a home run to tie the game.

After retiring he became a roving instructor in the Cardinals' organization, and in 1996 was promoted to the big
club. He then moved to the Angels, and from 2000–01
served as a minor league instructor for the San Diego Padres. In 2002 he managed the Lake Elsinore Storm, then
went to the Dodgers' system as a hitting coach for the Las
Vegas 51s. In 2003 he was promoted to Los Angeles on an
interim basis to finish out the season after Jack Clark had
been fired. He returned to Las Vegas, then served as the
Dodgers' minor league hitting coordinator before going to
the Devil Rays.

Elrod Hendricks
Baltimore Orioles (AL) 1978–2005
Catcher from the U.S. Virgin Islands.

Weak with a bat but solid defensively, Hendricks spent most of his 12 years as a player with the Orioles. He led American League catchers in fielding in 1969, and hit 12 home runs both that year and the next as a platoon player. In 1972 he set a National League record by walking five consecutive times in a game, and in 1978 he pitched $2\frac{1}{3}$ innings without allowing a run.

Hendricks was named bullpen coach under Earl Weaver in 1978, but he also appeared in 13 games that year and in one the next. He remained in that capacity for 28 years. He had battled cancer and suffered a stroke, and after the 2005 season the Orioles decided not to offer him another contract because of his health. He was instead offered a position in community relations. Disappointed, he at first turned down the offer but later accepted it. He died in December of that year, however.

Tommy Henrich
New York Yankees (AL) 1951; New York Giants (NL) 1957; Detroit Tigers (AL) 1958–59
Outfielder nicknamed "Old Reliable."

Henrich had been illegally buried in the Cleveland Indians' minor league system before Commissioner Kenesaw Mountain Landis discovered his situation and made him a free agent. Tommy signed with the Yankees and debuted with them in 1937. He promptly hit .320, and would spend 11 seasons in New York while losing the 1943–45 seasons to military service.

An eventual five-time All-Star, Henrich hit over .300 three times and led the American League with 13 triples in 1947 and with 14 triples and 138 runs scored in 1948. He also connected for four grand slams in '48. His last season was 1950, when he was again named an AL All-Star. The following season he became a coach.

Babe Herman
Pittsburgh Pirates (NL) 1951
Outfielder from Buffalo, New York.

Something of a liability defensively, Herman got by with his bat, rapping out hits to the tune of a .324 lifetime average. He hit at least .300 nine times, and in 1932 with the Cincinnati Reds led the National League with 19 triples. He and Bob Meusel are the only players to hit for the cycle three times. In 1926 he once had nine consecutive hits. He had his finest season in 1930 with the Brooklyn Robins, when he hit .393 with 35 home runs and 130 runs batted in. Herman was also the first player to hit a home run in a night game, going deep on July 10, 1935, at Crosley Field.

He disappeared into the minor leagues in 1937, but in 1945 the Brooklyn Dodgers (formerly the Robins) brought him back for 37 games. He later coached one season with the Pirates.

Billy Herman
Milwaukee Braves (NL) 1958–59; Boston Red Sox (AL) 1960–64; California Angels (AL) 1967; San Diego Padres (NL) 1978–79
See Managers section.

Chuck Hernandez
California Angels (AL) 1992–96; Tampa Bay Devil Rays (AL) 2004–05; Detroit Tigers (AL) 2006–
Minor league pitcher whose career ended when he broke his arm.

That unfortunate event occurred in 1983 in the instructional league of the Chicago White Sox. Hernandez had pitched five seasons, and in 1985 he began his coaching career with the Gulf Coast White Sox. In 1986 he joined the Angels' organization, where he would remain for 11 years. He served as a minor league coach until 1991, when he became a roving instructor, and in May of 1992 he was promoted to the big league staff. He then became a coach and minor league pitching coordinator in the Devil Rays' system, and was Tampa Bay's pitching coach from 2004–05. In 2006 he joined the Tigers.

Larry Herndon
Detroit Tigers (AL) 1992–98
Outfielder from the state of Mississippi.

Herndon had a cup of coffee with the St. Louis Cardinals in 1974, but in 1976 he became the San Francisco Giants' center fielder and *The Sporting News* named him its National League Rookie of the Year. He hit .288 that season and would average .274 over a 14-year career. He hit a career-high 23 home runs in 1982 with the Tigers, and hit 20 more the next season. In 1982 he also hit home runs in four consecutive trips to the plate.

After his playing career Herndon became a coach for the Tigers at both the major and minor league levels.

Orel Hershiser
Texas Rangers (AL) 2002–05
Winner of 204 major league decisions.

Hershiser spent his finest years with the Los Angeles Dodgers, winning 19 games in 1985 and then 14, 16, a league-leading 23, and 15 the next four years. He was a 20-game winner on only the one occasion, but garnered at least 14 victories eight times. A three-time All-Star, his best season by far was 1988, when he went 23–8 with a 2.26 earned run average and National League-leading totals of 15 complete games (tying him with Danny Jackson), 8 shutouts, and 267 innings pitched. He put together a streak of 59 consecutive scoreless innings, and unofficially made it 67 by shutting out the New York Mets for eight innings in Game 1 of the NL Championship Series. He shut them out again in Game 7 and then had a spectacular World Series against the Oakland Athletics, helping his team with his bat (he hit two doubles in Game 2 while going 3-for-3) as well as his arm. For the year he won the NL Cy Young Award and a Gold Glove as well as being named the Most Valuable Player of both the NLCS and the World Series.

After overcoming major shoulder surgery in 1990 Hershiser remained with the Dodgers until 1995, when he joined the Cleveland Indians. He won 16 games for them that year and was named the MVP of the American League Championship Series when he posted a 1.29 ERA and won two games.

In 18 years Hershiser led the league once in victories, once in complete games, twice in shutouts, and three times in innings pitched. After retiring he accepted a job as a consultant with the Dodgers, then became the Rangers' pitching coach. He resigned from that post after the 2005 season in order to take a position as executive director with the club, but in February of the following year he quit so that he could work as a baseball analyst with ESPN.

Whitey Herzog
Kansas City Athletics (AL) 1965; New York Mets (NL) 1966; California Angels (AL) 1974–75
See Managers section.

Jack Hiatt
Chicago Cubs (NL) 1981
Backup catcher for several major league clubs.

Hiatt played for nine years and even put in some time at first base. After his playing career he worked as a minor league coach and manager in the organizations of the Cubs, the California Angels, and the Houston Astros, joining Chicago's big league staff in 1981. He then moved on to the San Francisco Giants' system, where he worked as a minor league manager, roving instructor, and assistant to the minor league director before landing a longtime job as the Giants' director of player development.

Jim Hickey
Houston Astros (NL) 2004–06; Tampa Bay Devil Rays (AL) 2007–
Minor league pitcher for eight seasons.

Hickey played for several organizations and had his best year in 1984, when he went 13–5 with a 1.81 earned run average for the Appleton Foxes of the Midwest League. He then worked as a coach for many years in the Astros' system, and in July of 2004 was named interim pitching coach in Houston. In October he was given the position full-time, and he lasted through the 2006 season before moving on to the Devil Rays.

Andy High
Brooklyn Dodgers (NL) 1937–38
Nicknamed "Handy Andy" because of his versatility.

High could play second, third, or short, and he was no slouch with a bat, either. In 1924 he hit .328 with the Brooklyn Robins (later the Dodgers) and batted .302 in 1927 with the Boston Braves. In 1930 with the St. Louis Cardinals his single drove in the eventual winning run in a 20-inning contest against the Chicago Cubs.

Andy had two brothers, Charlie and Hugh, who were also major leaguers.

Glenallen Hill
Colorado Rockies (NL) 2007–
Longtime journeyman outfielder.

Hill played for seven teams in a 13-season career, one of them (the Chicago Cubs) twice. As a regular he hit 24 home runs for the 1995 San Francisco Giants, and in 99 games with the 1999 Cubs he bashed 20 homers while batting .300. When interleague play was instituted in 1997, Hill became the first National League designated hitter during a regular season game when the Giants faced off against the Texas Rangers.

He went to work as a minor league coach in the Rockies' system following his playing career, and for the last three months of 2006 he managed the Modesto Nuts before being promoted to the big league staff as a coach.

Marc Hill
Houston Astros (NL) 1988; New York Yankees (AL) 1991
Reserve catcher who played 14 major league seasons.

Hill did not wield a potent bat but was appreciated for his defense. He never hit over .261 and averaged .223 lifetime, clubbing 34 home runs. He eventually coached a season each with the Astros and Yankees, two clubs for whom he had never played.

Perry Hill
Texas Rangers (AL) 1992–94, 1995; Detroit Tigers (AL) 1997–99; Montreal Expos (NL) 2000–01; Florida Marlins (NL) 2002–
Minor leaguer who spent most of his career in the Mexican League.

Hill played only one season in the United States, and after retiring as a player he worked as a coach and instructor in the Rangers' organization. He was named to the

Texas staff during the 1992 season, and spent all of 1993 and '94 with the club. Following the 1993 campaign he also went to Japan to do some work with the Chunichi Dragons, a trip he repeated early in 1995. He returned to the Rangers for the second half of the '95 season.

He later moved on to the Tigers, the Expos, and the Marlins.

Chuck Hiller
Texas Rangers (AL) 1973; Kansas City Royals (AL) 1976–79; St. Louis Cardinals (NL) 1981–83; San Francisco Giants (NL) 1985; New York Mets (NL) 1990
Second baseman for several major league teams.

Hiller's best season was 1962, when he played 161 games with the Giants and hit .276. He was a .243 lifetime hitter and led National League second basemen in errors during that '62 campaign. He did, however, become the first National Leaguer to hit a grand slam in the World Series that season. Toward the end of his career he became a valuable pinch-hitter, even leading the NL in 1966 with 15 safeties in that role. He later coached for a number of teams.

Dave Hilton
Milwaukee Brewers (AL) 1987–88
One of the best players in the Texas League in 1972.

Hilton had a rather inconsistent career, struggling during four partial seasons with the San Diego Padres while showing flashes of brilliance in the minors. In 1974 he hit .328 with the Hawaii Islanders but continued to struggle in the majors. He overcame a bout with hepatitis in 1975, and after the 1977 season he signed with the Yakult Swallows in Japan. There he set records with eight leadoff home runs and six consecutive doubles and was named an All-Star. The following year he joined the Hanshin Tigers at the request of manager Don Blasingame, but when he struggled, Japanese fans became irate and at one point attacked him, his wife, and Blasingame as they rode in a car. Hilton shortly returned to the United States, then played a year in Mexico.

After his playing career he became a minor league manager, a scout for the Minnesota Twins, and a coach for the Brewers. In 1989 he played for the St. Lucie Legends in the Senior Professional Baseball Association.

Vedie Himsl
Chicago Cubs (NL) 1960–64
See Managers section.

Bill Hinchman
Pittsburgh Pirates (NL) 1923
Ten-year major league outfielder.

Hinchman played for several clubs but spent half of his career with the Pirates. After struggling with the Cleveland Indians, he was sent to the minors following the 1909 season. He set several American Association records with the Columbus Senators in 1914, and the following year resurfaced in the major leagues with Pittsburgh. He hit .307 for the Bucs in 1915 and .315 the next year with a National League-leading 16 triples. He broke his leg in 1917 and was never the same player.

After his playing career he coached and scouted for the Pirates.

Ben Hines
Seattle Mariners (AL) 1984; Los Angeles Dodgers (NL) 1985–86, 1988–93; Houston Astros (NL) 1994
Highly successful college and major league coach.

Well-respected for his coaching abilities, Hines is a member of the NAIA and University of La Verne Halls of Fame. He was once named National Coach of the Year with the NAIA. From 1978–82 he managed the Alaska Goldpanners, a collegiate summer team, and took them to the 1980 championship. He went to work in the California Angels' organization following the 1982 season, and soon reached the major leagues with the Mariners, Dodgers, and Astros.

His son, Bruce, also became a big league coach.

Bruce Hines
California Angels (AL) 1991
Son of Ben Hines.

Like his father, Bruce never played in the major leagues, but has done a lot of work around baseball. Originally drafted by the San Diego Padres in 1980, he was a career minor leaguer as a player. He soon became a mainstay in the Angels' organization, coaching at the big league level in 1991, managing at the minor league level, and later becoming the team's field coordinator of minor league operations.

Larry Hisle
Toronto Blue Jays (AL) 1992–95
Member of the Topps All-Star Rookie Team in 1969.

Hisle connected for 20 home runs that year with the Philadelphia Phillies, despite having just overcome a hepatitis infection from the previous year. He began to struggle shortly thereafter and returned to the minor leagues. He broke out in 1973 with the Minnesota Twins. He unofficially became the major leagues' first designated hitter that year when, in March, he appeared as a DH in a spring training game against the Pittsburgh Pirates. In 1975 he hit .314, and the next year he drove in 96 runs. In 1977 he hit .302 with 28 home runs and an American League-leading

119 RBIs, and the next year connected for 34 roundtrippers and drove home 115. He was an All-Star both years. In 1976 he hit for the cycle.

He played until 1982, and would reappear in the majors 10 years later as a coach with the Blue Jays.

Billy Hitchcock
Detroit Tigers (AL) 1955–60; Atlanta Braves (NL) 1966
See Managers section.

Don Hoak
Philadelphia Phillies (NL) 1967
Solid third baseman who was once a professional boxer.

Hoak was knocked out seven consecutive times before changing sports. As a baseball player he encountered his share of difficulties, once striking out a National League-record six times in a 17-inning game, but he also produced. In 1957 with the Cincinnati Redlegs he led the NL with 39 doubles and made the All-Star team. In 1961 with the Pittsburgh Pirates he batted .298.

When his playing days were over Hoak was a radio and television broadcaster for the Pirates for two years, then coached one season with the Phillies. He then became a minor league manager, but in 1969, at the age of 41, he died of a heart attack while driving his car in pursuit of someone who had just stolen his brother-in-law's vehicle.

Glenn Hoffman
Los Angeles Dodgers (NL) 1999–2005; San Diego Padres (NL) 2006–
See Managers section.

Bobby Hofman
Kansas City Athletics (AL) 1966–67; Washington Senators (AL) 1968; Oakland Athletics (AL) 1969–70, 1974–78; Cleveland Indians (AL) 1971–72
Reserve infielder and catcher from St. Louis.

Hofman spent seven seasons with the New York Giants playing all over the infield. He had served in the Army during World War II before his major league career began, and when he retired he was tied for the major league record (since broken) with nine pinch-hit home runs. He spent over 40 years in professional baseball in several roles, including player, coach, minor league manager, and executive.

In 1966 he began the first of three stints with the A's, who at that time were based in Kansas City. He spent one season with the Senators, then returned to the A's, who were now based in Oakland. He later went to the Indians, then back to the A's again. At one point as a coach under Charlie Finley he doubled as the team's traveling secretary in an effort to save the club some money.

Fred Hofmann
St. Louis Browns (AL) 1938–49
Catcher for the New York Yankees and Boston Red Sox.

A mere .247 hitter, Hofmann played nine seasons and became a minor league manager when his playing days were over. He later coached the Browns for 12 seasons and then became a scout. He was still with the club when it moved to Baltimore and became the Orioles.

Walter Holke
St. Louis Browns (AL) 1940
First baseman and .287 lifetime hitter.

A native of St. Louis, Holke never played for either of his hometown major league clubs. Instead he put in time with the New York Giants, Boston Braves, Philadelphia Phillies, and Cincinnati Reds. In 1920 with the Braves he was involved in a 26-inning game against the Brooklyn Robins that ended in a 1–1 tie. Holke recorded an amazing 42 putouts in that contest. In 1923 with the Phillies he hit .311, and batted .300 the following year.

After retiring he became a minor league manager, and he finally joined his hometown Browns as a coach in 1940.

Al Hollingsworth
St. Louis Cardinals (NL) 1957–58
Pitcher who played for six teams in 11 years.

Used as both a starter and a reliever, St. Louis native Hollingsworth fashioned a lifetime record of 70–104 despite a somewhat respectable 3.99 earned run average. He was 10–6 for his hometown St. Louis Browns in 1942 and 12–9 for them in 1945 with a 2.70 ERA. He once hit a grand slam for the Cincinnati Reds against his hometown Cardinals, but lost the game anyway.

He later managed in the Cards' minor league system, and joined the big league club as a coach for two seasons.

Dennis Holmberg
Toronto Blue Jays (AL) 1994–95
Minor league player and successful minor league manager.

Originally drafted by the Milwaukee Brewers, Holmberg found his niche at the helm. He both coached the Blue Jays at the major league level and managed in their minor league system. He later won four consecutive division titles as manager of the Auburn Doubledays.

Holmberg's son Kenny was also drafted by the Brewers, in 2005.

Doug Holmquist
New York Yankees (AL) 1984, 1985
Longtime college coach and minor league manager.

Holmquist coached at the University of Vermont and Florida Tech before eventually joining the Yankees' staff.

He also managed in New York's minor league system with the Nashville Sounds and the Columbus Clippers. He was the coach at Seminole Community College when he died of a heart attack in 1988, at 46 years of age.

Goldie Holt
Pittsburgh Pirates (NL) 1948–50; Chicago Cubs (NL) 1961–65
Minor league infielder who played more than 2000 games.

Between 1938 and 1947 Holt variously served as a minor league coach and skipper. He joined the Pirates' staff for three years beginning in 1948, then became a scout for the Brooklyn Dodgers. He went back to managing in the minors before joining the Cubs as a coach in 1961. He later returned to scouting with the Dodgers, who by that time were based in Los Angeles.

Rick Honeycutt
Los Angeles Dodgers (NL) 2006–
Left-hander who pitched for 21 years in the major leagues.

Honeycutt was an All-Star with the Seattle Mariners in 1980, and again with the Texas Rangers in 1983 when he went a career-best 14–8 with an American League-leading 2.42 earned run average. Between 1988 and his final season of 1997 he pitched solely in relief. His lifetime ERA was 3.72.

After retiring he worked for the Dodgers as a consultant and a minor league pitching coordinator. He was promoted to the big league staff in 2006. Rick is also a member of the Tennessee State Hall of Fame.

Burt Hooton
Houston Astros (NL) 2000–03
Pitcher from the University of Texas.

Hooton definitely turned the heads of the Chicago Cubs when he went 35–3 for UT in 1971. Signing with Chicago and reporting to the Tacoma Cubs, he struck out 19 batters in one game, tying a record for the Pacific Coast League. He pitched in three games for Chicago that season and went 2–0 with a 2.11 earned run average.

On April 16, 1972, Hooton had the fourth start of his major league career and pitched a 4–0 no-hitter against the Philadelphia Phillies. He won 18 games in 1975 with the Los Angeles Dodgers and 19 more in 1978. In 1981 he was named a National League All-Star. He posted 151 victories lifetime and put up a 3.38 ERA.

He retired from the Texas Rangers in 1985 and later coached for the Astros.

Johnny Hopp
Detroit Tigers (AL) 1954; St. Louis Cardinals (NL) 1956
Nicknamed "Hippity" by the media.

Johnny Hopp was a consistent hitter and more-than-adequate outfielder and first baseman. He hit .296 lifetime, topping the .300 mark five times. In 1944 his .997 fielding percentage led all National League outfielders. In 1946 he was named an NL All-Star while playing for the Boston Braves, and in 1950 he went 6-for-6 in a game for the Pittsburgh Pirates.

Hopp's last game was in 1952, and he later coached a season apiece for the Tigers and Cardinals.

Rogers Hornsby
Chicago Cubs (NL) 1958–59; New York Mets (NL) 1962
See Managers section.

Willie Horton
New York Yankees (AL) 1985; Chicago White Sox (AL) 1986
Four-time All-Star outfielder.

Horton spent most of his career with the Detroit Tigers, for whom he hit over .300 twice and cracked more than 20 home runs six times. He bashed 325 roundtrippers lifetime. In Game 5 of the 1968 World Series he threw out Lou Brock who was trying to score from second base on a single.

Horton battled weight problems throughout his career and was eventually relegated to the role of designated hitter. He played 18 seasons, and later became a roving minor league coach for several clubs. He coached at the big league level for the Yankees in 1985 and the White Sox in 1986. He then joined the Tigers' front office, and Detroit retired his number 23 in 2000.

Vern Hoscheit
Baltimore Orioles (AL) 1968; Oakland Athletics (AL) 1969–74; California Angels (AL) 1976; New York Mets (NL) 1984–87
Longtime minor league manager and major league coach.

Hoscheit skippered the McAlester Rockets, a New York Yankees' affiliate, from 1948–51. His club won the Sooner State League championship in both 1950 and 1951, then he guided the Joplin Miners to the Western Association championship the following season. He then managed the Quincy Gems from 1953–56 and took them to Three-I League titles the first two years, meaning he won five consecutive championships. He continued to manage in the Yankees' system, but eventually became a major league coach with several other clubs.

Charlie Hough
Los Angeles Dodgers (NL) 1998–99; New York Mets (NL) 2001–02
Honolulu native who pitched for 25 years in the major leagues.

Signed by the Dodgers as a third baseman, Hough learned the knuckleball from scout Goldie Holt and soon switched to the mound. He spent the first half of his career as a Dodgers' reliever, and the second half as a starter with several teams, beginning with the Texas Rangers. He won 216 games in his career against 216 losses, and he posted a 3.75 earned run average.

In 1986 against the California Angels he lost a bid for a no-hitter with one out in the ninth inning, and soon lost the game, 2–1. In 1993 he was the very first starting pitcher in Florida Marlins' history. He retired the next season due to a degenerative hip condition, but he later returned to the Dodgers and then went to the Mets as a coach.

Ralph Houk
New York Yankees (AL) 1953–54, 1958–60
See Managers section.

Tom House
Texas Rangers (AL) 1985–92
Former pitcher and coach with a Ph.D.

House earned his doctorate in psychology, focusing on sports psychology. He pitched for eight major league seasons and went 29–23 with a 3.79 earned run average. In 1974 with the Atlanta Braves he posted a 1.93 ERA, and he is probably most famous for having caught Hank Aaron's 715th home run ball in the bullpen that year. He later presented the ball to Aaron in a ceremony at home plate.

House has studied the art of pitching in the extreme and often experimented with different techniques to improve pitchers' deliveries. He worked in the organizations of the Houston Astros and San Diego Padres, and was pitching coach at the big league level with the Rangers. He also spent some time in Japan with the Chiba Lotte Marines.

House was an advisor with the American Sports Medicine Institute, and he is the author of many books on baseball fundamentals. He also wrote an autobiography, and he was one of the founders of the National Pitching Association, which helps players through camps, clinics, and instructional videos.

Elston Howard
New York Yankees (AL) 1969–79
Eleven-time All-Star catcher.

Howard was the Yankees' first black player, being signed from the Kansas City Monarchs of the Negro Leagues. He joined the New York organization in 1950, and in 1954 won the International League's Most Valuable Player Award with the Toronto Maple Leafs. In 1955 he joined the Yankees, where he would proceed to hit over .300 three times and club at least 15 home runs on five occasions. In 1963 he batted .287 with a career-high 28 roundtrippers and 85 runs batted in en route to being the first black player ever named American League Most Valuable Player. In 1963 and 1964 he won back-to-back Gold Gloves. In 1967 the Yankees were one out away from being no-hit by Bill Rohr of the Boston Red Sox when Howard singled to break up the bid.

Howard finished his career with the Red Sox in 1968, and the following year he returned to the Yankees as a coach. In December of 1980 he died suddenly of a heart attack. In 1984 the Yankees retired his number 32.

Frank Howard
Milwaukee Brewers (AL) 1977–80, 1985–86; New York Mets (NL) 1982–84, 1994–96; Seattle Mariners (AL) 1987–88; New York Yankees (AL) 1989, 1991–93; Tampa Bay Devil Rays (AL) 1998–99
See Managers section.

Art Howe
Texas Rangers (AL) 1985–88, 2007– ; Colorado Rockies (NL) 1995
See Managers section.

Dan Howley
Detroit Tigers (AL) 1919, 1921–22
See Managers section.

Dick Howser
New York Yankees (AL) 1969–79
See Managers section.

Walt Hriniak
Montreal Expos (NL) 1974–75; Boston Red Sox (AL) 1977–88; Chicago White Sox (AL) 1989–95
Catcher who played 47 major league games.

Those games occurred from 1968–69 with the Atlanta Braves and San Diego Padres. Hriniak collected 25 hits, all singles, and hit .253. After his playing career he became a hitting coach with the Expos, Red Sox, and White Sox, with whom he strongly emphasized the importance of a batter's timing and shifting of his weight.

Glenn Hubbard
Atlanta Braves (NL) 1999–
Infielder with an excellent glove.

Born on an Air Force base in Germany, Hubbard batted a mere .244 in 12 major league seasons but played an outstanding second base. A minor league Rookie of the Year with the Richmond Braves, Hubbard debuted with Atlanta in 1978 and helped turn a triple play in his second major league game. Three times he led National League second basemen in double plays. In 1983 he was named to the NL All-Star team.

After his playing career Hubbard became a coach in the Braves' system, and he was promoted to the big club in 1999. In 2001 he was inducted into the Utah Athletic Hall of Fame.

Jack Hubbard
St. Louis Cardinals (NL) 1993; Toronto Blue Jays (AL) 1998
Longtime minor league coach.

Hubbard never played in the major leagues, but he worked at the minor league level with several organizations. He served two seasons on major league staffs, one with the Cardinals and one with the Blue Jays. In 2006 he helped coach the Netherlands in the World Baseball Classic.

Dave Hudgens
Oakland Athletics (AL) 1999, 2003–05
Played six major league games.

Originally signed by the Cleveland Indians, Hudgens began playing for the Waterloo Indians of the Midwest League in 1979, but joined the Athletics' system in 1982. He played six games for Oakland in 1983 as a first baseman and designated hitter and went 1-for-7. In 1984 he served as a player-coach with the Albany A's of the Eastern League. He then became a minor league manager in the Oakland organization before moving on to the Houston Astros' system as a roving instructor and minor league coach.

In 1996 he returned to the A's as assistant director of player development. He was made a big league coach in 1999 before returning to his previous role in 2000, but during the 2003 season he once again became an Oakland coach.

Willis Hudlin
Detroit Tigers (AL) 1957–59
Right-handed pitcher from Oklahoma.

Most of Hudlin's 16 seasons were spent with the Cleveland Indians. He won at least 12 games every year from 1927–32, and did so nine times altogether. In 1927 he went 18–12, and he won 158 games in his career. In 1940 he became only the second player in major league history to play for four teams in the same season when he spent time with the Indians, the Washington Nationals, the St. Louis Browns, and the New York Giants.

After his playing career Hudlin served with the Tigers as a coach for three years, then became a scout with the New York Yankees.

Sid Hudson
Washington Senators (AL) 1961–65, 1968–71; Texas Rangers (AL) 1972, 1975–78
Pitcher who spent a dozen years in the major leagues.

Hudson had an impressive debut with the Washington Nationals, going 17–16 in 1940 and being named to the American League All-Star team the next two seasons. He also pitched two one-hitters in that 1940 campaign, taking a no-hitter into the ninth inning on the first occasion before losing his bid but winning the game. He lost 1943–45 to military service, but returned and played until 1954. He later coached for the Senators (a different franchise), and accompanied them to Texas when they became the Rangers. He also spent time as a minor league instructor and as a scout.

Hughes
Cincinnati Reds (NL) 1937
First name unknown.

Hughes is a mystery among major league coaches. His last name appears on Cincinnati Reds' scorecards during the 1937 season, but no other information is available.

Rudy Hulswitt
Boston Red Sox (AL) 1931–33
Shortstop from Newport, Kentucky.

Hulswitt debuted in 1899 with the Louisville Colonels, and three years later he was leading the National League in both putouts and errors, setting a twentieth century record in the latter category. In 1903 he again led in putouts. He played seven years and hit .253, and his career ended prematurely due to shoulder problems.

He then became a longtime minor league manager. He coached the Red Sox for three seasons, and also served as a scout for them and for Boston's other team at the time, the Braves.

Tom Hume
Cincinnati Reds (NL) 1996–
Solid relief pitcher and longtime coach.

Hume spent most of his 11-year career with the Reds. In 1980 he collected 25 saves and was named co-Fireman of the Year in the National League along with Rollie Fingers of the San Diego Padres. His first major league hit was a home run, and in 1981 his nine wins in relief were the NL's best. In 1982 he was an All-Star and earned the save in that game, while amassing 17 more during the regular season.

Following the 1980 season, he and teammate Bill Bonham, along with their wives, were trapped in a hotel fire in Las Vegas and had to be rescued from the roof.

After his playing career Hume briefly worked as a

Reds' broadcaster, and he eventually became the team's bullpen coach. In 1996 his title was officially "bullpen employee" because of Major League Baseball rules concerning numbers of coaches, but today the Reds do list him as a coach for that season. In 2006 he filled in as pitching coach while Vern Ruhle was undergoing treatment for cancer.

Randy Hundley
Chicago Cubs (NL) 1977
Catcher who spent most of his career with the Cubs.

In 14 seasons Hundley twice hit at least 18 home runs, but his biggest assets were his defense and his stamina. He won a Gold Glove in 1967 when he set a National League record by committing just four errors in 152 games. In 1968 he caught 160 games, a major league record, and from 1967–69 he became the first player to catch at least 150 games in three consecutive years. He hit for the cycle in a game against the Houston Astros in 1966. In 1969 he was named an NL All-Star.

Hundley appeared in two games for the Cubs in 1977, the same year he became a coach for the club.

Billy Hunter
Baltimore Orioles (AL) 1964–77
See Managers section.

Newt Hunter
Philadelphia Phillies (NL) 1928–31, 1933
Chillicothe native who played 65 major league games.

All those games came with the Pittsburgh Pirates in 1911, for whom Fred "Newt" Hunter played first base. He batted .254 while smacking 2 home runs and driving in 24. He eventually coached several seasons for the Phillies.

Dave Huppert
Montreal Expos (NL) 2004; Washington Nationals (NL) 2005
Catcher who lasted 17 major league games.

Huppert went 1-for-21 in parts of two seasons to bat a dismal .048. His main claim to fame, however, came with the AAA Rochester Red Wings, for whom he caught 31 of the 33 innings constituting the longest professional baseball game in history. That game started on Saturday, April 18, 1981, and was suspended at 4:09 the following morning (Easter Sunday) due to a league curfew (although the game had already gone past that curfew). It was resumed on July 23, 1981, and was won by the Pawtucket Red Sox. It lasted 8 hours and 25 minutes in all.

After his playing career Huppert worked in the Milwaukee Brewers' and Chicago White Sox' minor league systems. In 1988 he became the California League Manager of the Year while piloting the Stockton Ports, and in 1992 served as the White Sox' bullpen catcher. The fol-

lowing year he joined the Florida Marlins' organization. In 2001 he was named Florida State League Manager of the Year when his Brevard County Manatees tied for the league title. He then moved on to the Montreal Expos' system where, in September of 2004, he was named an extra coach and observer before landing a full-time coaching job with the team in 2005 after it had moved to Washington. In 2006 he became the manager of the Lakewood BlueClaws.

Clint Hurdle
Colorado Rockies (NL) 1997–2002
See Managers section.

Garth Iorg
Toronto Blue Jays (AL) 1996, 2001–02
Dependable utility infielder.

Iorg played his entire nine-year career with the Blue Jays, and although he batted just .258 lifetime, he hit .285 in 1982 and .313 in 1985. The Blue Jays had originally taken him from the New York Yankees' organization in the expansion draft in 1976. Iorg became a minor league manager after his playing career, and he also played for the Bradenton Explorers of the Senior Professional Baseball Association in 1989. He had two stints as a Blue Jays' coach.

Garth's brother Dane was also a major leaguer, and his son Eli was drafted by the Houston Astros in 2005.

Luis Isaac
Cleveland Indians (AL) 1987–91, 1994–
Minor league catcher.

Isaac opened his professional career in the Pittsburgh Pirates' organization in 1962, but joined the Indians' system three years later and played until 1972. From 1973–77 he was a player-coach. He then became a minor league coach and manager and then a scout until the middle of the 1987 season, when he was promoted to Cleveland as a coach. From 1992–93 he coached in the minors again, then he returned to the Indians.

Al Jackson
Boston Red Sox (AL) 1977–79; Baltimore Orioles (AL) 1989–91; New York Mets (NL) 1999–2000
Pitcher who was born the day after Christmas.

Jackson posted a 67–99 record lifetime, but he had played for some pretty bad Mets' teams, including the inaugural 1962 squad. He posted identical 8–20 records in both 1962 and 1965, but he also won 13 games on two occasions. His lifetime earned run average was a respectable 3.98, and he pitched nine games for the 1969 "Amazin' Mets" before being traded to the Cincinnati Reds. He would finish the season in Cincinnati but be released before the 1970 campaign. He later coached for several teams, including the Mets.

Grant Jackson
Pittsburgh Pirates (NL) 1984–85; Cincinnati Reds (NL) 1994–95

Solid pitcher used mostly in relief.

Jackson pitched from 1965–82, and of 692 games he started only 83 of them. His one real season as a full-time starter was 1969, when he went 14–18 for the Philadelphia Phillies and was named a National League All-Star. He posted a lifetime earned run average of 3.46.

Jackson later coached the Pirates and Reds, and in between, in 1989, he played for the Gold Coast Suns of the Senior Professional Baseball Association. He also worked for many years as a minor league pitching coach.

Reggie Jackson
Oakland Athletics (AL) 1991

Hall of Famer nicknamed "Mr. October."

Jackson had a long and storied career, his outspokenness making him at once a media darling and media villain. His almost unbelievable home run power was coupled with record-breaking strikeout tendencies, but he was always a feared hitter. Jackson led the American League four times in home runs, as well as once in runs batted in and twice in runs scored. He smashed 563 lifetime roundtrippers and was an All-Star 14 times. In 1973 he was the AL's Most Valuable Player when he hit .293 with league-leading totals of 32 home runs, 117 RBIs, and 99 runs scored. He was also the MVP of the World Series as he helped the A's defeat the New York Mets.

In the 1977 Series Jackson hit three home runs in Game 6 and hit five altogether, prompting his nickname. He played for the New York Yankees in that Series, but frequent feuds with manager Billy Martin and owner George Steinbrenner eventually caused him to leave for the California Angels. He returned to the A's in 1987 to finish out his career.

Jackson served as a coach with Oakland in 1991. Two years later he was inducted into the Hall of Fame, and the Yankees retired his number 44. In 2004 the A's retired the number 9 he had worn with them.

Ron Jackson
Chicago White Sox (AL) 1995–98; Milwaukee Brewers (NL) 1999; Boston Red Sox (AL) 2003–06

Outfielder, first baseman, and third baseman during a 10-year major league career.

A solid fielder, Jackson played for several clubs and had two stints with the California Angels. He was a .259 lifetime hitter, but batted .297 in 1978. He became a minor

league instructor and coach following his playing career, and emerged at the big league level with the White Sox in 1995. After moving to the Brewers, he worked in the Los Angeles Dodgers' organization and then joined the Red Sox for four years.

Sonny Jackson
Atlanta Braves (NL) 1982–83; San Francisco Giants (NL) 1997–2002

Washington native and member of the Topps All-Star Rookie Team in 1966.

Jackson debuted in 1963 but was still a rookie in '66 because he had played only 20 major league games over the past three seasons. He batted .292 that season, but that would be his career best by far. He also stole 49 bases, a twentieth century rookie record but, again, a career high.

Jackson finished playing in 1974 and became a minor league coach, manager, and instructor for the Braves. He spent two years on the big league coaching staff before moving to the player development department and working as a scout. He joined the Giants' system in 1996 and was promoted to their major league staff the following year. He stayed in San Francisco until 2002, then moved to the Chicago Cubs as a special assistant to manager Dusty Baker.

Travis Jackson
New York Giants (NL) 1939–40, 1947–48

Hall of Fame shortstop and third baseman from Arkansas.

Somewhat predictably nicknamed "Stonewall" because of his excellent defense, Travis Jackson played his entire 15-year career with the Giants. He hit over .300 six times and was an All-Star in 1934. He led the National League several times in multiple fielding categories, and in 1924 hit a grand slam in each of two consecutive games. Appendicitis caused him to lose six weeks of the 1927 season, but he came back the next year and in 1929 clubbed 21 home runs. After retiring he managed for many years in the Giants' minor league system and had two stints in New York as a coach.

He was inducted into the Hall of Fame by the Veterans Committee in 1982.

Brook Jacoby
Texas Rangers (AL) 2006; Cincinnati Reds (NL) 2007–

Two-time All-Star third baseman.

Jacoby spent most of his 11-year career with the Cleveland Indians. A .270 lifetime hitter, he was named an American League All-Star in 1986 and 1990. His best year was 1987, however, when he achieved career highs of a .300 average and 32 home runs.

After his playing days he worked in the minor league systems of both the Rangers and the Reds. From 2003–06 he was Texas' minor league hitting coordinator, and for two months during the 2006 season he joined the Rangers as a temporary substitute for hitting coach Rudy Jaramillo, who was recovering from prostate surgery. In 2007 he replaced Chris Chambliss as the Reds' hitting coach.

Larry Jansen
New York Giants (NL) 1954; San Francisco Giants (NL) 1961–71; Chicago Cubs (NL) 1972–73
Twenty-game winner on two occasions.

A right-handed pitcher, Jansen was playing in the minors when the United States entered World War II. Because of asthma problems he was instructed by the draft board to return to his home in Oregon and work the family farm instead of playing baseball. He did so but also played semipro ball. He returned to the professional ranks when the war was over and played nine major league seasons, all but one of them with the Giants. In his debut season of 1947 he went 21–5 for a league-best .808 winning percentage. After winning 18, 15, and 19 games the next three years, respectively, he went 23–11 in 1951, tying with teammate Sal Maglie for the league lead in victories and being named an All-Star for the second consecutive time. In 1950 he tied for the lead with five shutouts.

Jansen coached the Giants in both New York and San Francisco, and he also coached the Cubs.

Rudy Jaramillo
Houston Astros (NL) 1990–93; Texas Rangers (AL) 1995–
Outfielder from the University of Texas.

Jaramillo played four years in the Rangers' minor league system, hitting .365 his first year. He never made the majors, however, and began working with Little League baseball in 1977. From 1983–89 he served as a minor league instructor, coach, and manager for the Rangers, then joined the Astros' major league staff. In 1994 he managed in the Colorado Rockies' system before returning to the Rangers at the big league level.

In 2002 he was the hitting coach for the Major League All-Star team that toured Japan, and in 2005 *Baseball America* named him its Major League Coach of the Year. He was inducted into the Texas Baseball Hall of Fame in 2003.

During the 2006 season he missed two months because of prostate surgery and was replaced during that period by Brook Jacoby, the club's minor league hitting coordinator.

Dave Jauss
Boston Red Sox (AL) 1997–99, 2001; Los Angeles Dodgers (NL) 2006–
College player who became a college coach.

Jauss served as head baseball coach at both Westfield

State College (1982–84) and Atlantic Christian College (1985–87). He later became a minor league manager for the Montreal Expos, and in 1994 was named Eastern League Manager of the Year while piloting the Harrisburg Senators. In the winter of 1999 he took the Licey Tigers to the Caribbean Series championship. He then joined the Red Sox as a coach before becoming the minor league field coordinator, a coach again, the director of player development, and finally a scout. In 2006 he signed on as a coach with the Dodgers.

Ferguson Jenkins
Chicago Cubs (NL) 1995–96
First Canadian in the Hall of Fame.

A native of Chatham, Ontario, Jenkins pitched for 19 seasons and won 284 games. He was a 20-game winner seven times, and he led the National League in 1971 with 24 victories and tied for the American League lead in 1974 with 25. A three-time All-Star, he also topped his respective circuit three times in starts, four times in complete games, once in innings pitched, and once in strikeouts. In 1971 he won the NL's Cy Young Award on the strength of a 24–13 record, a 2.77 earned run average, and 263 strikeouts. After struggling in 1973, he won the AL Comeback Player of the Year Award in 1974 by going 25–12 with a 2.82 ERA and 225 strikeouts.

In 1980 Jenkins was arrested in Toronto for possession of cocaine. As a result baseball Commissioner Bowie Kuhn banned Fergie for life, but his decision was reversed a month later by an independent arbitrator. Jenkins continued to play through 1983.

He had spent much of his career with the Cubs, and returned to Chicago as a coach for two seasons. In 1987 he was inducted into the Canadian Baseball Hall of Fame, and Cooperstown called four years later. From 1989–90 he played for the Winter Haven Super Sox of the Senior Professional Baseball Association.

Mack Jenkins
Cincinnati Reds (NL) 2004
Longtime coach in the Reds' minor league system.

A pitcher from the University of Tampa, where he played in the mid-1980s, Jenkins later pitched in the Reds' organization before becoming a pitching coach in the same system. He served at every level of the minor leagues, and was the pitching coach for the AAA Louisville Bats in 2004 when, at the conclusion of their season, he was called up to the Reds as one of several "extra" coaches. In 2006 he became Cincinnati's minor league pitching coordinator.

Hughie Jennings
New York Giants (NL) 1921–25
See Managers section.

Trent Jewett
Pittsburgh Pirates (NL) 2000–02
Minor league catcher from Dallas, Texas.

Jewett played four seasons in the Pittsburgh Pirates' organization, but hit a mere .172. In 1992 he became a minor league skipper, and in 1995 guided the Carolina Mudcats to the Southern League championship. After managing the Calgary Cannons and Nashville Sounds he was promoted to a Pirates' coach during the 2000 season, and he would remain in that position through 2002. In 2003 he returned to the Sounds for two years. He then managed the Indianapolis Indians.

Darrell Johnson
St. Louis Cardinals (NL) 1960–61; Baltimore Orioles (AL) 1962; Boston Red Sox (AL) 1968–69; Texas Rangers (AL) 1981–82; New York Mets (NL) 1983
See Managers section.

Deron Johnson
California Angels (AL) 1979–80, 1989–92; New York Mets (NL) 1981; Philadelphia Phillies (NL) 1982–84; Seattle Mariners (AL) 1985–86; Chicago White Sox (AL) 1987
Power hitter from San Diego.

Like many longball hitters, Johnson was a frequent strikeout victim. He played all over the field, usually in the outfield, at first or third base, or as a designated hitter, and played for 16 seasons. He debuted with a cup of coffee in 1960, and played 96 major league games the following year before losing most of the 1962 campaign to military service. In 1963 he led the Pacific Coast League with 33 home runs while playing for his hometown, minor league San Diego Padres.

Johnson hit 245 home runs lifetime, topping 20 five times and hitting 19 two others. In 1965 with the Cincinnati Reds he banged 32 with a league-leading 130 runs batted in. In 1968 he once hit home runs in four consecutive at-bats.

Johnson played for many teams, and after his playing career he coached many as well.

Howard Johnson
New York Mets (NL) 2007–
First infielder to hit 30 home runs and steal 30 bases in the same season.

Johnson accomplished that feat in 1987 with the Mets when he slugged 36 roundtrippers and swiped 32 sacks while manning third base. A two-time All-Star, he tied Will Clark and Ryne Sandberg for the National League lead in 1989 with 104 runs scored, and in 1991 topped the circuit with 38 home runs and 117 runs batted in. He hit over 20 home runs five times and more than 30 three times while topping the 100-RBI mark twice and managing 99 on a third occasion.

After a 14-year playing career Johnson coached in the Mets' minor league system, spending two years as the hitting coach for the AAA Norfolk Tides. In 2007 he was promoted to the big league staff by manager Willie Randolph.

Lamar Johnson
Milwaukee Brewers (AL) 1995–97, (NL) 1998; Kansas City Royals (AL) 1999–2002; Seattle Mariners (AL) 2003
Designated hitter and first baseman with a fine singing voice.

Johnson once sang the National Anthem before a game in 1977 while playing for the Chicago White Sox. He played eight of his nine seasons in Chicago, finishing up in 1982 with the Texas Rangers. He hit over .300 four times, including his .345 average in his 1974 debut season in 10 games. In 1977 he cranked 18 home runs.

In 1989 Johnson played for the St. Petersburg Pelicans of the Senior Professional Baseball Association. He later coached the Brewers, Royals, and Mariners.

Roy Johnson
Chicago Cubs (NL) 1935–39, 1944–53
See Managers section.

Syl Johnson
Philadelphia Phillies (NL) 1939–41
Nineteen-year major league veteran pitcher.

Johnson threw for several clubs from 1922–40, mostly as a reliever, and he joined the Phillies in 1934. He won 112 games lifetime against 117 losses and posted a 4.06 earned run average. Injuries nagged at him throughout his career, usually as the result of contact with line drives. From 1939–40 he served as a player-coach in Philadelphia, and he turned to full-time coaching in 1941.

Tim Johnson
Montreal Expos (NL) 1993–94; Boston Red Sox (AL) 1995–96
See Managers section.

Wallace Johnson
Chicago White Sox (AL) 1998–2002
Backup second baseman and first baseman from Gary, Indiana.

Johnson spent nine years in the major leagues, all but one partial season with the Montreal Expos. A light hitter, he nevertheless led the National League in pinch-hits in both 1987 and 1988 and in pinch-hit at-bats in 1989. In '88, when Ron Robinson of the Cincinnati Reds was one out away from a perfect game, it was Johnson who broke it up with a single to left field. After his playing career he coached five seasons with the White Sox.

Jimmy Johnston
Brooklyn Robins (NL) 1931
Tennessee native who played many positions.

Jimmy Johnston played the outfield and every infield position. In 13 years he hit .294, peaking with a .325 average in both 1921 and 1923 and sandwiching a .319 showing in between. In a game in 1922 he hit for the cycle.

He spent most of his career with the Brooklyn Robins. He became a minor league manager following his playing days and returned to Brooklyn for one season as a coach.

Bobby Jones
Texas Rangers (AL) 2000–01, 2006
Vietnam War veteran and reserve outfielder for nine seasons.

Robert Oliver Jones played for the Rangers and the California Angels before leaving for Japan and spending the 1979 and 1980 seasons with the Chunichi Dragons. He returned in 1981 and bounced between the Rangers and their top minor league club until 1986. He hit .221 lifetime.

In 1988 Jones became a minor league skipper, and the following year he led the Charlotte Rangers to the Florida State League championship. In 1998 his Tulsa Drillers took the Texas League title, and two years later he joined Texas as a coach. Returning to the minors after two seasons with the Rangers, he was at the helm of the Oklahoma RedHawks in 2004 when he won the 1000th game of his managerial career. In 2006 he returned to the Rangers, but following that season went back to Oklahoma as a skipper.

Clarence Jones
Atlanta Braves (NL) 1985, 1989–98; Cleveland Indians (AL) 1999–2001
First foreign player to win a home run title in Japan.

Hailing from Zanesville, Ohio, Jones played 58 games with the Chicago Cubs in 1967 and 1968 but many more in the minor leagues. In 1974 with the Kintetsu Buffaloes he won the title that no foreigner had ever claimed, bashing 38 roundtrippers. He repeated the feat in 1976 by hitting 36. He also became the first player to hit at least 200 home runs in both the American minor leagues and Japanese baseball.

He later had a coaching career back in the United States.

Deacon Jones
Houston Astros (NL) 1976–82; San Diego Padres (NL) 1984–87
First black manager in the Midwest League.

Grover "Deacon" Jones played 40 games over three seasons with the Chicago White Sox and hit a respectable .286, but he gained far more renown for his minor league accomplishments. A first baseman, he set team records in 1956 with the Dubuque Packers when he hit .409 with 26 home runs and 120 runs batted in en route to winning the league's Most Valuable Player Award.

Ten years later he helped lead the Fox Cities Foxes of Appleton, Wisconsin to the Midwest League title when he batted .353 with a .484 on-base percentage and 58 extra-base hits, all league records. In 1967 he served as a player-coach for the club, and in 1973 he would return as their manager, becoming the first black skipper in league history. He later coached the Astros and Padres and worked as a scout for the White Sox. In 2006 he was inducted into the Appleton Baseball Hall of Fame.

Gary Jones
Oakland Athletics (AL) 1998
Minor league manager with more than 1000 victories.

A minor league infielder who played for seven seasons, Jones has had a very successful managerial career. He first took the helm of a club in 1990, and the following year he took the Madison Muskies to the playoffs and was named Midwest League Manager of the Year. In 1994 he won a similar award with the Southern League when he guided the Huntsville Stars to the championship. In 1996 he was Pacific Coast League Manager of the Year when his Edmonton Trappers took the title, and in 1997, when they repeated, he was named Minor League Manager of the Year by *Baseball America*.

He spent only the 1998 season at the big league level coaching the A's. He went right back to managing after that, taking the Fort Wayne Wizards to the playoffs in 2003 and winning a Southern League co-championship in 2004 while piloting the Mobile BayBears.

Gordon Jones
Houston Astros (NL) 1966–67
Korean War veteran and 11-year major league hurler.

Of 171 big league games, Jones started only 21 and posted a 4.16 earned run average lifetime. He had been signed right out of high school and spent 12 years in the minor leagues, losing 3 to the military, before embarking on his major league career. He finished his career with the Astros, then coached with them for two years. He then worked in sales for an electrical dealer, but later scouted for the New York Yankees. Jones suffered from diabetes and died at age 64 of heart failure resulting from complications due to his disease.

Jeff Jones
Detroit Tigers (AL) 1995, 1998, 1999, 2000, 2002, 2007–
Right-handed pitcher from Bowling Green State University.

Pitching almost entirely in relief, Jones spent five seasons with the Oakland Athletics and went 9–9 with a 3.95 earned run average. He did not allow a run in his first seven big league games. His promising career was cut short by arm problems, and he then went into coaching in the minor leagues. He spent many years in the Tigers' system, especially with the Toledo Mud Hens, and joined the major league club on an interim basis on many occasions before being promoted to the staff on a more permanent basis in 2007.

Joe Jones
Kansas City Royals (AL) 1987, 1992, 2005; Pittsburgh Pirates (NL) 1998–2000
Minor league second baseman from Tennessee.

Joseph Carmack Jones never reached the major leagues as a player, but did so as a coach for both the Royals and Pirates. In the Kansas City organization he had many roles, including minor league field coordinator and special assistant of baseball operations. He was a coach for the Pirates for three years, and in his third stint in that position with Kansas City he was reassigned to baseball operations when Tony Peña resigned and was replaced by Buddy Bell.

Lynn Jones
Kansas City Royals (AL) 1991–92; Florida Marlins (NL) 2001; Boston Red Sox (AL) 2005
Backup outfielder for eight seasons.

Jones hit .252 during his career, peaking with a .301 average in 47 games in 1984 with the Royals. In the 1985 World Series with Kansas City he hit a double and a triple in two pinch-hitting at-bats. He later returned to the Royals as a coach, and also coached the Marlins and Red Sox. He also spent many years as a minor league manager, making the Midwest League playoffs in both 1995 and 1997 with the Kane County Cougars.

His brother Darryl played 18 games for the New York Yankees.

Bubber Jonnard
Philadelphia Phillies (NL) 1935; New York Giants (NL) 1942–46
Nashville native who played for his hometown team.

Bubber, a catcher, and his twin brother Claude, a pitcher, formed a battery with the Nashville Volunteers from 1920–21. Bubber (whose given name was Clarence) also played six partial seasons in the major leagues and hit a mere .230. After his playing career he coached the Phillies and Giants, and also worked for many years as a scout with the Giants, the Kansas City Athletics, the Baltimore Orioles, and the expansion New York Mets.

Von Joshua
Chicago White Sox (AL) 1998–2001
Lifetime .273 hitter.

Joshua spent 10 years in the major leagues, mostly as a backup outfielder. In 1975 with the San Francisco Giants he batted .318, and on two occasions he hit 25 doubles. In 1989 he played for the St. Lucie Legends in the Senior Professional Baseball Association. He also coached in the minor leagues and spent three seasons in that position with the White Sox.

Joe Judge
Washington Nationals (AL) 1945–46
Twenty-year major league first baseman.

An exceptional fielder, Judge set numerous American League defensive records during his playing career. He was no slouch at the plate, either, hitting over .300 eleven times and averaging .298 lifetime. In a game in 1921 he hit three triples, tying an AL record.

After retiring from the playing field he became the baseball coach at Georgetown University. In 1945 he returned to the Nationals, with whom he had spent most of his career, as a coach.

Billy Jurges
Chicago Cubs (NL) 1947–48; Washington Nationals (AL) 1956; Washington Senators (AL) 1957–59
See Managers section.

Jim Kaat
Cincinnati Reds (NL) 1984–85
Outstanding pitcher for 25 seasons.

Kaat pitched for many teams during his career as both a starter and reliever. He won 283 games lifetime against 237 losses with a 3.45 earned run average. He was three times named an American League All-Star, and he led the AL once in victories, twice in starts, once in complete games, once in shutouts, and once in innings pitched. In 1966 he went 25–13, the first of three times he would become a 20-game winner. He won at least 15 games eight times, and he and Brooks Robinson share the major league record with 16 consecutive Gold Gloves won.

Kaat was hired by player-manager Pete Rose to coach the Reds during the 1984 season, and he remained through

'85. He then embarked on a long and very successful second career as a broadcaster.

Lou Kahn
St. Louis Cardinals (NL) 1954–55
Career minor leaguer from St. Louis.

Kahn never reached the major leagues as a player, but he did so as a coach with his hometown Cardinals. He also spent some time managing in the Philadelphia Phillies' minor league system with the Bakersfield Bears and the Spartanburg Phillies.

Ray Katt
St. Louis Cardinals (NL) 1959–61; Cleveland Indians (AL) 1962
Good defensive catcher with a light bat.

Despite his solid defense Katt set a National League record by allowing four passed balls in one inning in a 1954 game. Like many others, he was a victim of Hoyt Wilhelm's unpredictable knuckleball.

After coaching the Cardinals and Indians he became a high school coach and then the head coach at Texas Lutheran University from 1971–92. He died of lymphoma in 1999.

Tony Kaufmann
St. Louis Cardinals (NL) 1947–50
Good-hitting pitcher from Chicago.

Kaufmann won 14 games in 1923, 16 in 1924, and 13 in 1925. He spent 11 seasons with his hometown Chicago Cubs, the Philadelphia Phillies, and the Cardinals, going 64–62 overall. On August 25, 1922, he was the Cubs' winning pitcher in a 26–23 victory over the Phillies in a game that saw numerous offensive records broken. He retired from the Cardinals and then spent 24 additional years with the organization as a minor league manager, major league coach, and scout.

Johnny Keane
St. Louis Cardinals (NL) 1959–61
See Managers section.

Dave Keefe
Philadelphia Athletics (AL) 1940–49
Inventor of the forkball.

So the story goes, resulting from the fact that Keefe had lost part of his middle finger in an accident as a child and thus developed the pitch without even trying. He pitched five years in the major leagues but largely fashioned a minor league career. In 1932 he rejoined the A's, with whom he had spent four of his big league seasons, as a batting

practice pitcher. He later became a coach for 10 years and in 1950 was named the club's traveling secretary.

Bob Keely
Boston Braves (NL) 1946–52; Milwaukee Braves (NL) 1953–57
Catcher who played only two major league games.

One of those came in mid-1944, the other at the end of 1945, and both with his hometown St. Louis Cardinals. He got only a single at-bat and failed to obtain a hit. Keely had played a number of years in the minor leagues before leaving baseball to work as a plasterer, but he returned to the game during World War II and experienced his all-too-brief call-ups to St. Louis. In 1946 he became the Braves' bullpen coach, and stayed with the club when it moved from Boston to Milwaukee. He eventually returned to the Cardinals as a scout and later served in the same role for the Los Angeles Dodgers.

Mick Kelleher
Pittsburgh Pirates (NL) 1986; Detroit Tigers (AL) 2003–05
Light-hitting but good-fielding shortstop.

Kelleher hit only .213 but served mainly as a utilityman with a number of clubs. He never hit over .254, but he was dependable in the field. After 11 major league seasons he went to work as a Pirates' coach. He also coached the Tigers for three years and was hired by the New York Yankees as a minor league instructor.

Charlie Keller
New York Yankees (AL) 1957, 1959
International League batting champion in 1937.

Keller hit .353 that year and .365 the next with the Newark Bears, but he had trouble at first breaking into the Yankees' lineup because of the presence of Joe DiMaggio, Tommy Henrich, and George Selkirk in the New York outfield. He was finally called up in 1939, however, and made his presence felt by batting .334. He eventually played 13 seasons, 11 of them with the Yanks and 2 with the Detroit Tigers, and was an All-Star four times. He hit over .300 three times and twice led the American League in bases on balls, drawing over 100 five times. He lost all of 1944 and most of 1945 to military service.

Back problems caused him to play part-time beginning in 1947, and he retired in 1952. He later coached for the Yankees and became a horse breeder in his native Maryland.

Dave Keller
Cleveland Indians (AL) 2001–03
Career minor leaguer.

Keller managed many seasons in the minors before becoming an Indians' coach. He led the 1991 Burlington Indians to the Appalachian League playoffs and was named co-Manager of the Year in 1993 when his Kinston Indians qualified in the Carolina League. He later became a roving hitting instructor for the Chicago Cubs.

Joe Kelley
Brooklyn Robins (NL) 1926
See Managers section.

George Kelly
Cincinnati Reds (NL) 1935–37, 1947–48; Boston Bees (NL) 1938–40; Boston Braves (NL) 1941–43
Hall of Fame first baseman with an outstanding glove.

Kelly set numerous single-season major league records for fielding, but he was equally adept with a bat. He hit over .300 seven times and averaged .297 for his career. He hit at least 20 home runs three times, leading the National League in 1921 with 23, and also led with 94 runs batted in in 1920 (tying him with Rogers Hornsby) and with 136 in 1924. He topped the 100-RBI mark five times. In an April 1922 game his New York Giants hit four inside-the-park home runs against the Braves, and Kelly accounted for two of them. On September 17, 1923, he became the first player to homer in three consecutive innings, and on July 16, 1924, he became the first to homer in six straight games.

He spent most of his career with the Giants and Reds, and he later became a coach and then a scout for several clubs. In 1973 he was elected to the Hall of Fame by the Veterans Committee.

Mike Kelly
Chicago White Sox (AL) 1930–31; Chicago Cubs (NL) 1934; Boston Bees (NL) 1937–39; Pittsburgh Pirates (NL) 1940–41
Minor league first baseman.

There have been several major league players by the name of Mike Kelly, but this Mike Kelly was not one of them. A native of Indianapolis, his given name was Bernard Francis Kelly. (At times the White Sox have actually listed his name as Bernie Kelly.) This Kelly never reached the majors as a player but did coach for four different clubs at that level in the 1930s and early 1940s. He died in 1968 in Indianapolis.

Tom Kelly
Minnesota Twins (AL) 1983–86
See Managers section.

Fred Kendall
Detroit Tigers (AL) 1996–98; Colorado Rockies (NL) 2000–

02; Kansas City Royals (AL) 2006–
Light-hitting catcher with an excellent glove.

Kendall was outstanding defensively, and he made his debut in 1969 with the expansion San Diego Padres. He played for 12 years, 10 of them with San Diego, and then became a minor league manager. He led both the 1992 Utica Blue Sox and the 1994 Hickory Crawdads to their respective playoffs, then coached for the Tigers and Rockies. From 2003–05 he was Colorado's roving catching coordinator before being hired to coach the Royals.

Fred's son Jason was also a major league catcher and was a three-time All-Star.

Bob Kennedy
Atlanta Braves (NL) 1967
See Managers section.

John Kerr
Washington Nationals (AL) 1935
Infielder from San Francisco.

Kerr was popular in the Pacific Coast League, where he got to play in his hometown. In the major leagues he lasted eight seasons with three different clubs and hit .266 overall, spending just two of those years as a regular. He finished his career with the Nationals and returned to them the following season as a coach.

Joe Kerrigan
Montreal Expos (NL) 1983–86, 1992–96; Boston Red Sox (AL) 1997–2001; Philadelphia Phillies (NL) 2003–04; New York Yankees (AL) 2006–
See Managers section.

Bill Killefer
St. Louis Cardinals (NL) 1926; St. Louis Browns (AL) 1927–29; Brooklyn Dodgers (NL) 1939; Philadelphia Phillies (NL) 1942
See Managers section.

Wendell Kim
San Francisco Giants (NL) 1989–96; Boston Red Sox (AL) 1997–2000; Montreal Expos (NL) 2002; Chicago Cubs (NL) 2003–04
Minor league player from Honolulu.

Kim was an infielder in the Giants' organization in the late 1970s. In 1980 he became a coach in the San Francisco minor league system, starting out with the AA Shreveport Captains. He coached and managed several teams within the organization throughout the decade until finally being promoted to the Giants in 1989.

As a third base coach, Kim developed a reputation for aggressiveness, coming under fire for waving numerous runners home only to see them get tagged out at the plate. He must have done something right, however, because he lasted eight years in San Francisco and then four more in Boston with the Red Sox. In 2001 he managed the Indianapolis Indians, then returned to the majors as a coach with the Expos and Cubs.

Bruce Kimm

Cincinnati Reds (NL) 1984–88; Pittsburgh Pirates (NL) 1989; San Diego Padres (NL) 1991–92; Florida Marlins (NL) 1997–98; Colorado Rockies (NL) 1999; Chicago White Sox (AL) 2003

See Managers section.

Clyde King

Cincinnati Reds (NL) 1959; Pittsburgh Pirates (NL) 1965–67; New York Yankees (AL) 1978, 1981–82

See Managers section.

Bob Kipper

Boston Red Sox (AL) 2002

California League Pitcher of the Year in 1984.

Kipper was in the major leagues the following season with the California Angels, but after only two games was traded to the Pittsburgh Pirates. Pitching mainly in relief, he lasted eight big league seasons and posted a 27–37 record with a 4.34 earned run average.

After his playing career Kipper became a minor league pitching coach, and he spent many years in the Red Sox' organization. He served in Boston in 2002 as bullpen coach before returning to the minors for the Sox.

Bruce Kison

Kansas City Royals (AL) 1992–98; Baltimore Orioles (AL) 1999

Right-handed pitcher who played 15 seasons.

Kison's best years came with the Pittsburgh Pirates, for whom he turned in a number of clutch performances in postseason play in the early 1970s. In 1980 he twice lost no-hitters with one out in the ninth inning. He won 115 games overall and put up a 3.66 lifetime earned run average.

Kison pitched for the Bradenton Explorers in the Senior Professional Baseball Association before becoming a major league coach with the Royals and Orioles.

George Kissell

St. Louis Cardinals (NL) 1969–75

Minor league infielder signed by Branch Rickey.

After leading the Southeastern League with 31 stolen bases in 1942, Kissell served in the U.S. Navy during World War II. He resumed his career upon his return and in 1949 led the Pennsylvania-Ontario-New York (PONY) League with 15 triples. He became a player-manager in the Cardinals' minor league system when he realized he would never make the major leagues, and he guided the 1950 Winston-Salem Cards to the Carolina League championship. He stopped playing in 1953 but continued as a manager. He was elevated to the big league club as a coach from 1969–75, then returned to his work in the minor leagues. He spent time as an instructor and eventually became the team's senior field coordinator for player development.

Hub Kittle

Houston Astros (NL) 1971–75; St. Louis Cardinals (NL) 1981–83

Pitcher who played professionally in six decades.

Kittle pitched in the minor leagues from 1936–55, losing the 1944 and 1945 seasons to the Army. In 1939 he was a 20-game winner for the Yakima Pippins of the Western International League. He later became a minor league manager and general manager, and in 1960 was named Minor League Executive of the Year by *The Sporting News*.

In 1969, as skipper of the Savannah Senators, he ran out of pitchers during a game and inserted himself for two innings. He was 52 years of age. That marked the fourth decade in which he had played. As a coach with the Astros at the age of 56, he was allowed by manager Leo Durocher to pitch an inning in an exhibition game against the Detroit Tigers; he retired three straight batters and picked up the save while recording his fifth decade as a player. In 1980, as pitching coach with the Springfield Cardinals, he was activated before a game on Senior Citizens Night and pitched the first inning and part of the second, at 63 years of age, to mark his sixth decade.

Kittle later coached the St. Louis Cardinals and served the Seattle Mariners as a special assignment coach. As a minor league manager he had won seven pennants, four of them with the Yakima Bears. He had once been pitching coach with the New Jersey Cardinals, and that club eventually retired his number 34. Kittle died in 2004 of diabetes complications and kidney failure.

Chuck Klein

Philadelphia Phillies (NL) 1942–43; Philadelphia Blue Jays (NL) 1944–45

First National Leaguer to hit four home runs in a game in the twentieth century.

Klein was also the last player to lead his league in both home runs and stolen bases in a season. He played 17 seasons in the outfield, the vast majority of them with the Phillies/Blue Jays. Along the way he won one batting title and led the NL four times in home runs, twice in runs batted in, twice in doubles, twice in hits, three times in runs scored, and once in stolen bases. He was named an All-Star on two occasions. It was in 1932 that his 38 homers and 20 steals topped the circuit (his homer total actually tied him with Mel Ott); his 226 hits and 152 runs scored led as well, and he notched a .348 average and 137 RBIs en route to being named the NL's Most Valuable Player.

But it was in 1933 that he won the Triple Crown, batting .368 with 28 home runs and 120 RBIs. A .320 lifetime hitter, he topped the .300 threshold nine times and hit 300 career roundtrippers.

He served as a player-coach in Philadelphia from 1942–44 before retiring from the playing field, and he then coached one more season. In 1980 Klein was inducted into the Hall of Fame. In 2001 the Phillies honored him by placing a stylized *P* on the outfield wall alongside the team's retired numbers (perhaps because he played his first four seasons before the team donned numbers, even though he later wore seven different ones with the club).

Lou Klein
Chicago Cubs (NL) 1960–65
See Managers section.

Ted Kluszewski
Cincinnati Reds (NL) 1970–78
First baseman nicknamed "Big Klu."

Perhaps most famous for cutting off his uniform sleeves to allow his massive arms greater freedom of movement, Kluszewski spent most of his career with the Reds and was named to four All-Star teams. It was his actions, in fact, that inspired the team to adopt sleeveless jerseys in the 1950s. A former football star with the University of Indiana, Ted was a .298 lifetime hitter, topping the .300 mark seven times. He was also a power hitter, five times hitting at least 25 home runs and three times at least 40. In 1954 he led the National League with 49 homers and 141 runs batted in, and the following season topped the NL with 192 hits. He was also excellent with a glove, setting a major league mark by leading all NL first basemen in fielding percentage five consecutive times. He also set an NL twentieth century record by scoring in 17 straight games.

After playing for the Pittsburgh Pirates and the Chicago White Sox, Kluszewski was drafted by the expansion Los Angeles Angels in 1961, and that was his final season as a player. He later returned to the Reds as a coach, and after that he remained with the club as an instructor.

Chuck Kniffin
Arizona Diamondbacks (NL) 2002–05
Ten-year minor league pitcher in the Philadelphia Phillies'

organization.

Kniffin was named by Topps as the Western Carolina League Pitcher of the Year in 1971 when he went 13–1 with a 2.11 earned run average for the Spartanburg Phillies. He never reached the major leagues, however, except as a coach. Before that he was a minor league coach in the Seattle Mariners' organization, and also worked with an Italian team in Florence, Italy, in 1984. He later moved on to the Montreal Expos' system, then to the Tucson Sidewinders in the Diamondbacks' organization before being promoted to Arizona.

Ray Knight
Cincinnati Reds (NL) 1993–95, 2002–03
See Managers section.

Bobby Knoop
Chicago White Sox (AL) 1977–78; California Angels (AL) 1979–96; Toronto Blue Jays (AL) 2000
See Managers section.

Randy Knorr
Washington Nationals (NL) 2006
Light-hitting catcher who spent 11 seasons in the majors.

Knorr never played more than 45 games in a season at the big league level. His lifetime average was .226, but he did connect for 24 home runs.

Knorr eventually became a minor league coach following his playing days, beginning in 2005. In June of 2006 he was promoted to the Nationals as bullpen coach to replace John Wetteland, who had been fired for failing to curb the relief staff's penchant for playing practical jokes and other unsuitable behavior. He returned to the minor leagues to work when manager Frank Robinson was fired following the 2006 season.

Darold Knowles
St. Louis Cardinals (NL) 1983; Philadelphia Phillies (NL) 1989–90
Only pitcher in history to appear in all seven games of one World Series.

Knowles accomplished that feat in 1973 when his Oakland Athletics defeated the New York Mets, and he earned two saves in the process. The previous year he had broken his thumb in September and thus ruined his chances of appearing in that Series. In his career he started only 8 games out of 765, specializing in bullpen work and garnering 143 saves lifetime. He posted an excellent 3.12 earned run average. In 1969 he was named an American League All-Star while pitching for the Washington Senators.

Knowles retired after a 16-year career and later coached for the Cardinals and Phillies.

Fred Koenig

California Angels (AL) 1970–71; St. Louis Cardinals (NL) 1976; Texas Rangers (AL) 1977–82; Chicago Cubs (NL) 1983; Cleveland Indians (AL) 1986
Minor league first baseman.

A native of St. Louis, Koenig began his career in the Cardinals' system but would not make the big club as a player. He eventually coached for the Angels and then worked for the Cardinals as their director of player development before eventually coaching in St. Louis. He later moved on to the Rangers, Cubs, and Indians.

Rick Kranitz

Chicago Cubs (NL) 2002; Florida Marlins (NL) 2006–
Minor league pitcher in the Milwaukee Brewers' organization.

Kranitz pitched for five seasons beginning in 1979, and in 1981 he tossed a no-hitter while playing for the Stockton Ports. From 1984–93 he worked as a pitching coach in the Cubs' system, then served as minor league pitching coordinator from 1994–95, assistant pitching coach from 1996–98, Iowa Cubs' pitching coach in 1999, and assistant pitching coordinator from 2000–01. He then coached one season with Chicago at the big league level before returning to the minors. In 2006 he was hired to be the Marlins' pitching coach.

Red Kress

Detroit Tigers (AL) 1940; New York Giants (NL) 1946–49; Cleveland Indians (AL) 1953–60; Los Angeles Angels (AL) 1961; New York Mets (NL) 1962
Versatile major leaguer who played many positions.

Originally a shortstop, Kress had flashes of defensive brilliance, and provided examples of terrible glovework as well. He was moved all over the field over the years and adapted well, however, and at the plate he hit over .300 five times and averaged .286 for his career. After the 1940 season, which he spent as a player-coach for the Tigers, he returned to the minors. Once, in a game for the Toronto Maple Leafs, he played all nine positions. In a game in 1945, he had been used as a pitcher and came within two outs of throwing a no-hitter, losing both the no-no and the game itself in the ninth inning. He made one more major league appearance with the Giants in 1946 and then turned to full-time coaching. He also managed several minor league teams. He finished as a coach with back-to-back stints with the expansion Angels in 1961 and the expansion Mets in 1962. He died of a heart attack in November of '62.

Jack Krol

St. Louis Cardinals (NL) 1977–80; San Diego Padres (NL)
1981–86
See Managers section.

Karl Kuehl

Minnesota Twins (AL) 1977–82
See Managers section.

Harvey Kuenn

Milwaukee Brewers (AL) 1971–82
See Managers section.

Rusty Kuntz

Seattle Mariners (AL) 1989–92; Florida Marlins (NL) 1995–96, 1999–2000; Pittsburgh Pirates (NL) 2003–05
Backup outfielder for seven seasons.

Kuntz played for several clubs from 1979–85 and hit .236. In 1987 he joined the Houston Astros as a minor league instructor, and two years later joined the Mariners in Seattle. He then worked for the Marlins as a minor league coordinator between two stints as a major league coach. In 2002 he joined the Atlanta Braves as a roving instructor, then moved to the Pirates as a coach.

Art Kusnyer

Chicago White Sox (AL) 1980–87, 1997– ; Oakland Athletics (AL) 1989–95
Backup catcher from Akron, Ohio.

Kusnyer played 139 games over six seasons, one of which was as the backstop for Nolan Ryan's second career no-hitter on July 15, 1973, at Detroit. He finished his career as a player-coach with the AAA Iowa Oaks in 1979, and the following season was promoted to the White Sox. After eight years in Chicago he managed the Gulf Coast White Sox in 1988, his only season as a skipper at any level. In 1989 he started a seven-year stretch as a coach with the A's, and in 1996 worked as a scout for the St. Louis Cardinals. The following year he returned to the White Sox, once again as their bullpen coach.

Bill Lachemann

California Angels (AL) 1995–96
Brother of Marcel and Rene Lachemann.

Bill was a six-year minor league player and then a minor league manager. He began his career as a skipper in 1983 with the Clinton Giants and moved to the Angels' organization in 1985. In 1988 his Palm Springs Angels reached the postseason, and in 1990 he was named co-Manager of the Year of the Arizona League with the Arizona Angels. He managed through the 1994 season, when he was promoted to California as a coach for two years, then returned to managing in the minors.

Marcel Lachemann
California Angels (AL) 1984–92; Florida Marlins (NL) 1993–94; Anaheim Angels (AL) 1997–98; Colorado Rockies (NL) 2000–01
See Managers section.

Rene Lachemann
Boston Red Sox (AL) 1985–86; Oakland Athletics (AL) 1987–92, 2005– ; St. Louis Cardinals (NL) 1997–99; Chicago Cubs (NL) 2001–02; Seattle Mariners (AL) 2003–04
See Managers section.

Al Lakeman
Boston Red Sox (AL) 1963–64, 1967–69
Catcher and first baseman from Cincinnati.

Lakeman played the majority of his nine-year career for his hometown Reds, beginning in 1942. He failed an induction examination for the Army during World War II, but did make a Pacific tour with other ballplayers. After his playing career he had two stints as a coach with the Red Sox and also managed in the minor leagues for 10 seasons.

Gene Lamont
Pittsburgh Pirates (NL) 1986–91, 1996; Boston Red Sox (AL) 2001; Houston Astros (NL) 2002–03; Detroit Tigers (AL) 2006–
See Managers section.

Grover Land
Cincinnati Reds (NL) 1925–28; Chicago Cubs (NL) 1929–30
Catcher who played 25 professional seasons.

Twenty-one of those were spent in the minor leagues. Land spent most of his big league days with the Cleveland Naps, but in 1914 joined the Brooklyn Brookfeds (who shortly thereafter became the Tip-Tops) in the Federal League. That was his only season as a regular; he played 102 games and hit a career-best .275. He served in the military during World War I, and later coached the Reds and the Cubs.

Rafael Landestoy
Montreal Expos (NL) 1989–91; Detroit Tigers (AL) 2002
Outfielder who became a utility infielder.

Hailing from the Dominican Republic, Landestoy rarely played the outfield at the major league level, but was used all over the infield. A career .237 hitter, he stole a career-high 23 bases in 1980 with the Houston Astros. When his playing career ended in 1984 he became a longtime minor league coach and manager. In 1989 he was named an Expos' coach, and that same year he played for the Gold Coast Suns of the Senior Professional Baseball Association. He later coached one season with the Tigers.

Hobie Landrith
Washington Senators (AL) 1964
Catcher who played 14 major league seasons.

A backup catcher for most of his career, Landrith was used as a starter by the 1956 Chicago Cubs and led National League backstops in errors while hitting .221. After spending the 1961 season with the San Francisco Giants he was the first pick of the New York Mets in the expansion draft for 1962. In May of '62, however, the Mets traded him to the Baltimore Orioles for Marv Throneberry. He finished his career with the Senators in 1963, and coached that club the following season.

Rick Langford
Toronto Blue Jays (AL) 2000
Right-handed starting pitcher.

After debuting with the Pittsburgh Pirates in 1976, Langford tied for the American League lead with 19 losses in 1977 with the Oakland Athletics. He lost 13 and 16 games the next two seasons, respectively, before posting a 19–12 record in 1980. Billy Martin was his manager that year, and consequently he led the AL with 28 complete games (22 of them consecutive) and 290 innings pitched. The next year he was 12–10 during a strike-shortened campaign and led the league with 18 completions. An outstanding fielder, he also set an AL record by accepting 230 straight chances at his position before committing an error.

Langford developed arm problems in 1983, and many speculated that his woes were due to overuse. He played through 1986, however, and then became a longtime coach in the Blue Jays' organization. He spent part of 2000 as a big league coach in Toronto before being fired during the season.

Hal Lanier
St. Louis Cardinals (NL) 1981–85; Philadelphia Phillies (NL) 1990–91
See Managers section.

Carney Lansford
Oakland Athletics (AL) 1994–95; St. Louis Cardinals (NL) 1997–98
Strong, consistent third baseman.

Lansford spent 15 years in the major leagues, most of them with the A's. In 1981 with the Boston Red Sox he won the American League batting title with a .336 average, the first of four consecutive times and five times overall that he would reach the .300 threshold. In 1988 with the A's he was named an AL All-Star. He also hit 19 home runs in three separate seasons, and was a .290 lifetime hitter.

On New Year's Eve of 1990 he was injured in a snowmobile accident and would require surgery to repair several ligaments. He played only five games in 1991, but came back for one last season in 1992. He later coached the A's and the Cardinals.

Dave LaRoche
Chicago White Sox (AL) 1989–91; New York Mets (NL) 1992–93
Outstanding relief pitcher from Colorado Springs.

LaRoche started 15 out of 647 games in his 14-year big league career. A two-time All-Star, he was probably most famous for his blooper pitch, which he christened the "LaLob" and which would sometimes arc as high as 20 feet in the air. He notched 126 saves lifetime, peaking with 25 in 1978 and posting a 3.53 earned run average overall.

In 1989 he became a coach with the White Sox, and during the offseason played for the Fort Myers Sun Sox of the Senior Professional Baseball Association. He later coached two years for the Mets, and also worked for many years as a minor league pitching coach.

Tony LaRussa
Chicago White Sox (AL) 1978
See Managers section.

Tom Lasorda
Los Angeles Dodgers (NL) 1973–76
See Managers section.

Arlie Latham
Cincinnati Reds (NL) 1900; New York Giants (NL) 1909
See Managers section.

Charlie Lau
Baltimore Orioles (AL) 1969; Oakland Athletics (AL) 1970; Kansas City Royals (AL) 1971–78; New York Yankees (AL) 1980–81; Chicago White Sox (AL) 1982–83
Backup catcher for 11 seasons.

Lau was with the Milwaukee Braves in 1961 when he caught Warren Spahn's no-hitter. A career .255 hitter, he had problems at the plate until he adopted a new batting stance. He promptly hit .294 with the change, and would later be a well-respected hitting coach with several teams because of his new, scientific approach to batting.

At an Orioles' party in 1966, he and Andy Etchebarren saved teammate Frank Robinson from drowning when Robinson fell into a swimming pool.

Lau was a coach with the White Sox in 1983, and during the season he surrendered his position to scout and former coach Loren Babe, who was dying of lung cancer, so that Babe could qualify for his 10-year pension. Babe

died in February of 1984, and Lau then died in March of colon cancer.

Bill Lauder
Chicago White Sox (AL) 1925
Third baseman from New York City.

Lauder lasted five major league seasons, from 1898–1903 (minus the 1900 season), and spent the last two of them with his hometown New York Giants. He hit .261 overall, then he disappeared from the major league scene until 1925, when he coached one season for the White Sox.

Cookie Lavagetto
Brooklyn Dodgers (NL) 1951–53; Washington Nationals (AL) 1955–56; Washington Senators (AL) 1957; New York Mets (NL) 1962–63; San Francisco Giants (NL) 1964–67
See Managers section.

Vern Law
Pittsburgh Pirates (NL) 1968–69
Solid pitcher who spent 16 years with the Pirates.

Law pitched from 1950–67 in Pittsburgh, then coached two more. He missed the 1952 and 1953 campaigns due to military service. He won 162 games lifetime and posted a 3.77 earned run average. He won at least 10 games nine times, and more than 15 on three occasions. He had a spectacular 1960 season, when he went 20–9 with a 3.08 ERA while finishing in a three-way tie for the National League lead with 18 complete games. There were two All-Star Games that year, and they were held nearly back-to-back, on July 11 and July 13. Law pitched the ninth inning of the victorious first game, then both started and won the second game. He later won Games 1 and 4 of the World Series in addition to receiving a no-decision in Game 7 en route to the Pirates' championship. He was named the NL's Cy Young Award winner.

Law began to experience injuries that affected his career in 1961, but he continued to pitch and won 17 games in 1965. He retired in 1967, coached the Bucs for two years, and later became involved in the Church of Jesus Christ of Latter Day Saints. His son, Vance Law, had an 11-year major league career.

Tony Lazzeri
Chicago Cubs (NL) 1938
Part of the New York Yankees' "Murderers' Row" lineup in 1927.

An epileptic, Lazzeri was the second baseman on that famed squad. In 1925 with the Salt Lake City Bees of the Pacific Coast League, he had hit 60 home runs with 222 runs batted in and 202 runs scored in a 200-game season. He made the Yankees in 1926 and would play 12 of his 14 big league years with that club. Along the way he hit at least .300 five times, topping out at .354 in 1929. He hit at least 13 home runs nine times, and drove in over 100 runs on seven occasions. In 1932 he hit for the cycle, and the following year was named an American League All-Star. On May 24, 1936, he became the first major leaguer to hit two grand slams in one game and set an AL record by driving in 11 runs.

The Yankees released Tony following the 1937 season, and he signed on with the Cubs as a player-coach. He appeared in 54 games and batted .267, then finished out his career the following season with the Brooklyn Dodgers and New York Giants. In 1991 he was inducted into the Hall of Fame by the Veterans Committee.

Jim Lefebvre
Los Angeles Dodgers (NL) 1978–79; San Francisco Giants (NL) 1980–82; Oakland Athletics (AL) 1987–88, 1994–95; Milwaukee Brewers (NL) 1999; Cincinnati Reds (NL) 2002
See Managers section.

Joe Lefebvre
San Francisco Giants (NL) 2002–
Outfielder who homered for his first major league hit.

Lefebvre had some outstanding minor league seasons, especially with the West Haven Yankees. In 1978 he led the Eastern League with 11 triples and 102 runs scored, and in 1979 tied with Rick Lancellotti for best in the circuit with 107 runs batted in while being named an EL All-Star. In the majors he lasted six years with three clubs and hit .258, but a knee injury cut his career short.

In 1987 Lefebvre became a minor league coach in the Philadelphia Phillies' organization, but he moved to the New York Yankees' system in 1990. For the Yankees and later the Giants he worked variously as a coach and roving instructor, and in 2000 he began to work with the Giants' big league club in spring training and in an unofficial coaching capacity during the season. In 2002 he was made San Francisco's official first base coach, and he became hitting coach the following year.

Lefty Leifield
St. Louis Browns (AL) 1918–23; Boston Red Sox (AL) 1924–26; Detroit Tigers (AL) 1927–28
Pitcher who won 124 games in 12 seasons.

After winning 26 games as a minor leaguer in 1905 while leading the Des Moines Underwriters to the Western Association pennant, Leifield would win at least 15 major league games in a season six times, and was a 20-game winner in 1907 when he went 20–16 with the Pittsburgh Pirates. He posted a lifetime earned run average of 2.47,

and pitched three one-hitters. One of those came in July of 1906, when opposing starter Mordecai "Three Finger" Brown also pitched a one-hitter for the Chicago Cubs and Leifield collected the lone knock for Pittsburgh. Leifield had a no-hitter going until the ninth inning, and he lost the no-no and the game, 1–0. In September of that year he did pitch a six-inning no-hitter against the Philadelphia Phillies in the second game of a doubleheader, a game that was shortened due to darkness.

Leifield was released in 1913 and played in the minors until 1918, when he signed with the Browns as a player-coach. After the 1920 season he turned strictly to coaching, and would later coach the Red Sox and the Tigers. He then became a minor league manager, and his 1931 St. Paul Saints captured the American Association pennant. He later worked for 26 years for the St. Louis Water Department, retiring in 1962 due to failing eyesight.

Bob Lemon
Cleveland Indians (AL) 1960; Philadelphia Phillies (NL) 1961; California Angels (AL) 1967–68; Kansas City Royals (AL) 1970; New York Yankees (AL) 1976
See Managers section.

Jim Lemon
Minnesota Twins (AL) 1965–67, 1981–84
See Managers section.

Don Lenhardt
Boston Red Sox (AL) 1970–73
Part-time power-hitting outfielder.

Lenhardt served in the Navy during World War II, and had a five-year major league career beginning in 1950. He hit 22 home runs in 139 games for the St. Louis Browns that year, and hit 15 the next in 95 games for the Browns and Chicago White Sox. His career ended in 1954 when he suffered a broken leg, although he did play two more seasons in the minor leagues.

Lenhardt worked as a scout for the Red Sox from 1966–69, coached in Boston from 1970–73, and then returned to scouting from 1974–91. He also worked as a minor league manager and a broadcaster.

Dutch Leonard
Chicago Cubs (NL) 1954–56
Outstanding pitcher who played 20 major league seasons.

Not to be confused with the earlier Dutch Leonard (Hubert Benjamin), Emil John Leonard pitched from 1933–53 and won 191 big league games. Named to five All-Star teams, he won at least 12 games nine times and was a 20-game winner in 1939 when he posted a 20–8 record for the Washington Nationals. He put up a 3.25

earned run average lifetime. Leonard's final season was 1953, with the Cubs, and he remained with that club as a coach for the next three years.

Don Leppert
Pittsburgh Pirates (NL) 1968–76; Toronto Blue Jays (AL) 1977–79; Houston Astros (NL) 1980–85
Backup catcher who was a 1963 All-Star.

Leppert played only 190 games in four major league seasons, although he played 12 years professionally. A .229 big league hitter, he was named an American League All-Star while playing for the Washington Senators. He later coached the Pirates, Blue Jays, and Astros. On August 25, 1978, while he was with Toronto, a one-day umpires' strike left the Blue Jays and the Minnesota Twins short a couple of umps for their game at Exhibition Stadium. Leppert and Twins' coach Jerry Zimmerman were pressed into service, with Leppert stationed at third base and Zimmerman at second.

In 1986 Leppert became a minor league manager, and the following year he was named Midwest League Manager of the Year when he guided the Kenosha Twins to the championship.

Jim Lett
Cincinnati Reds (NL) 1986–89, 1996; Toronto Blue Jays (AL) 1997–99; Los Angeles Dodgers (NL) 2001–05; Pittsburgh Pirates (NL) 2006–
All-America football quarterback.

Lett played three years of minor league baseball before going into coaching and managing. In 1978 he was named Western Carolinas League Manager of the Year when his Shelby Reds posted an 84–75 record, and his 1990 Charleston Wheelers captured the South Atlantic League championship.

Lett spent 24 years in the Reds' organization as a major and minor league coach, minor league skipper, and minor league field coordinator. He later coached for the Blue Jays, Dodgers, and Pirates.

Leonard Levy
Pittsburgh Pirates (NL) 1957–63
Longtime Pirates' coach.

Levy never played in the major leagues, but spent many years in the Pirates' organization. He coached Pittsburgh for seven years and was credited with helping the careers of many of the team's big names, especially outfielder Frank Thomas.

Duffy Lewis
Boston Braves (NL) 1931–35
First major leaguer to pinch-hit for Babe Ruth.

That event occurred in 1914, when the Babe was a rookie pitcher for the Boston Red Sox. Lewis, an outfielder, was a dependable hitter who batted over .300 twice and averaged .284 lifetime. In 1912 he drove in 109 runs and in 1913 another 90. He missed the 1918 season due to military service during World War I, then returned the following year and played until 1921. He became a minor league player-manager for the next six years, and a full-time manager until 1929. He coached the Braves from 1931–35, then served as the club's traveling secretary until 1965. He died in 1979 at the age of 91.

Johnny Lewis
St. Louis Cardinals (NL) 1973–76, 1984–89
Outfielder who played four major league seasons.

Lewis had a quiet personality, but his main claim to fame was breaking up the no-hitter of the Cincinnati Reds' Jim Maloney on June 14, 1965. Maloney had shut the New York Mets down for 10 innings without allowing a safety, but Lewis led off the eleventh inning with a home run that proved to be a 1–0 game-winner.

Lewis eventually coached for the Cardinals and also worked as a minor league instructor for the Houston Astros.

Jim Leyland
Chicago White Sox (AL) 1982–85
See Managers section.

Nick Leyva
St. Louis Cardinals (NL) 1984–88; Toronto Blue Jays (AL) 1993–97; Milwaukee Brewers (NL) 2007–
See Managers section.

Steve Liddle
Minnesota Twins (AL) 2002–
Excellent defensive minor league catcher.

In 1983 Liddle led Eastern League backstops in games, putouts, assists, and double plays, and in 1987 topped the Southern League at his position in assists and DPs. In 1989 he began a career as a minor league manager and coach, and would eventually lead the 1992 Visalia Oaks and the 1998 Gulf Coast Twins to the postseason. In 1999 he was named minor league field coordinator for the Twins, and was promoted to the big league club as a coach in 2002.

Bob Lillis
Houston Astros (NL) 1973–82; San Francisco Giants (NL) 1986–96
See Managers section.

Julio Linares
Houston Astros (NL) 1994–96
Minor leaguer who played 15 seasons.

Linares retired from the playing field following the 1972 season and then went to work in the Astros' organization as a longtime minor league coach and manager, major league coach, and scout. He managed the Astros' Rookie League club for 16 years, coaching in Houston for three in between, before becoming director of Dominican Republic Operations for six seasons. He was then named special assistant to the general manager for Dominican scouting and development.

Jack Lind
Pittsburgh Pirates (NL) 1997–2000
Shortstop who played 26 big league games during two seasons.

Those games were with the Milwaukee Brewers, but Lind spent eight years in the minor leagues and one with the Yomiuri Giants in Japan. He was roommates at various times with both American home run king Hank Aaron and Japanese home run king Sadaharu Oh.

After his playing career Lind spent many years in the Pirates' minor league organization as a field coordinator and eventually served as a Pittsburgh coach. He then worked as a scout for the Houston Astros and a minor league manager for the New York Mets before returning to the Astros' system as a minor league skipper with the Lexington Legends.

Johnny Lipon
Cleveland Indians (AL) 1968–71
See Managers section.

Bryan Little
Chicago White Sox (AL) 1997–2000
Brother of Grady Little.

Bryan was an infielder, mainly a second baseman, who played in a backup role for five seasons, except for part of 1983 when he was the Montreal Expos' starting shortstop. He was an excellent bunter and led the National League with 24 bunt hits in 1983. He later became a coach for the White Sox and then worked in the club's scouting department.

Grady Little
San Diego Padres (NL) 1996; Boston Red Sox (AL) 1997–99; Cleveland Indians (AL) 2000–01
See Managers section.

Danny Litwhiler
Cincinnati Reds (NL) 1951
Consistent outfielder with an outstanding glove.

A .281 lifetime hitter, Litwhiler set a major league record for outfielders by playing in more than 150 games in a season without committing an error. He eventually extended that string to 187 before being charged with a miscue, a streak that lasted from September of 1941 to May of 1943. In 1942 he was named a National League All-Star.

Litwhiler played in the majors until 1951, when he became a coach with the Reds, then he continued in the minor leagues as a player-manager until 1954. He had bad knees and was turned down seven times for military service during World War II before finally being accepted for "limited service." He was charged with creating a base recreation program and did so with great and widespread success. One of his recruits was Doc Severinsen, who would later star on *The Tonight Show.*

Danny was the head coach at Florida State University from 1955–63, and at Michigan State University from the fall of 1963 until 1982, when he finally retired. He is also credited with having invented several important baseball items, such as the radar gun and a product that helps dry fields called Diamond Grit.

Winston Llenas
Toronto Blue Jays (AL) 1988
Longtime star of the Mexican League.

A renowned power hitter south of the border, Llenas joined the California Angels for six seasons and hit a mere .230 with three home runs in a reserve role. He did lead the American League in 1973 in both pinch-hits and pinch-hit at-bats, however. He then returned to Mexico and continued playing.

A native Dominican, in 1988 he coached for the Blue Jays, and later worked in the Cleveland Indians' organization in Dominican operations.

Bill Lobe
Cleveland Indians (AL) 1952–56
Cleveland native and minor league catcher.

Lobe never did reach the major leagues as a player, but he did so as a coach, and happily, did so in his hometown. Born in 1912, he also died in Cleveland, in 1969 at the age of 56.

Hans Lobert
Philadelphia Phillies (NL) 1934–41; Cincinnati Reds (NL) 1943–44
See Managers section.

Whitey Lockman
Cincinnati Reds (NL) 1960; San Francisco Giants (NL) 1961–64; Chicago Cubs (NL) 1965–66
See Managers section.

Dario Lodigiani
Kansas City Athletics (AL) 1961–62
Six-year major league infielder from San Francisco.

Lodigiani played from 1938–42 before going off to World War II. In 1946 he attempted to come back with the Chicago White Sox, but suffered an elbow injury that would end his major league career. He returned to the West Coast and played in the minor leagues until 1954, some of those years as a player-manager. In 1949 he accompanied his San Francisco Seals and a collection of major leaguers on a tour of Japan.

He then became a longtime scout for the White Sox, taking time out to coach the A's for two seasons, and retired in 1987.

Sherm Lollar
Baltimore Orioles (AL) 1964–67; Oakland Athletics (AL) 1968–69
Excellent defensive catcher.

Originally a bat boy with the Fayetteville Angels of the Arkansas-Missouri League in the 1930s, Lollar began his playing career with the Baltimore Orioles of the International League in 1943 at the age of 18. In 1945 he was the league's Most Valuable Player, and in 1946 began an 18-year major league career. He was named an American League All-Star seven times, twice hitting at least 20 home runs in a season. He led AL catchers four times in fielding percentage and won three Gold Gloves. In 1954, after allowing a stolen base in May, he threw out 18 consecutive runners, not permitting another steal the entire season. In 1955 he garnered two hits in an inning twice in the same game, becoming only the third major leaguer to accomplish that feat.

After his playing career he coached the Orioles (the major league version) and the A's and also managed in the minor leagues.

Dale Long
New York Yankees (AL) 1963
Football player who rejected an offer from the Green Bay Packers in order to play professional baseball.

A first baseman, Long won two minor league home run crowns and in 1956 set a record by homering in eight consecutive games. In 1955 with the Pittsburgh Pirates he tied for the National League lead with 13 triples, and the following year was named an NL All-Star. He hit at least 14 home runs six times, peaking with 27 in 1956. In 1958 with

the Chicago Cubs he filled in as a catcher for two games and thus became the first left-handed throwing backstop in the majors since 1924.

He finished his career in 1963 with the Yankees as a player and a coach, and later became a minor league umpire.

Kevin Long
New York Yankees (AL) 2007–
Longtime minor league manager and instructor.

Long spent 18 years in the minor leagues before reaching the Yankees as a coach. In 1997 he joined the minor league coaching ranks with the Class A Wilmington Blue Rocks, and in 1999, at the helm of the Spokane Indians, he was named Northwest League co-Manager of the Year along with Greg Sparks of the Southern Oregon Timberjacks.

He coached in the Kansas City Royals' organization from 2000–03, then worked as the hitting coach of the Columbus Clippers in the Yankees' system from 2004–06.

Joe Lonnett
Chicago White Sox (AL) 1971–75; Oakland Athletics (AL) 1976; Pittsburgh Pirates (NL) 1977–84
Catcher with a long minor league career and four partial big league seasons.

Lonnett began to play professionally in 1947. From 1956–59 he spent some time in the majors with the Philadelphia Phillies, but hit only .166. He continued to play in the minors until 1962, then became a scout for the Phillies, a minor league skipper, and a scout again before emerging as a major league coach.

Ed Lopat
New York Yankees (AL) 1960; Minnesota Twins (AL) 1961; Kansas City Athletics (AL) 1962
See Managers section.

Davey Lopes
Texas Rangers (AL) 1988–91; Baltimore Orioles (AL) 1992–94; San Diego Padres (NL) 1995–99, 2003–05; Washington Nationals (NL) 2006; Philadelphia Phillies (NL) 2007–
See Managers section.

Juan Lopez
San Francisco Giants (NL) 1999–2002; Chicago Cubs (NL) 2003–06
Six-year minor leaguer and longtime coach.

Lopez played in the organizations of the Cleveland Indians, Houston Astros, and San Francisco Giants, then worked in the Giants' system from 1990–2002. Initially a minor league coach, he served as a coaching assistant for the big club beginning in spring training of 1996 when Bob Brenly left the team to go into broadcasting. From 1997–98 he was the Giants' bullpen catcher, then became bullpen coach in 1999. In 2003 he moved to the Cubs in the same position.

Juan Lopez
New York Mets (NL) 2002–03
Longtime minor league coach and manager.

Not to be confused with the other Juan Lopez, this one played for 14 seasons in the minor league systems of the Detroit Tigers and Milwaukee Brewers. From 1985–94 he worked in the Tigers' organization as a coach and manager, then moved to the Mets. After spending several more years working in the minors he was elevated to New York as a major league coach and batting practice pitcher. In 2004 he returned to the Mets' minor league system as a hitting coach.

Q. V. Lowe
Chicago Cubs (NL) 1972
Veteran college baseball coach.

A pitcher himself in college, Lowe won consecutive All-America and All-Conference honors and helped Panama City's Gulf Coast Community College to the Junior College World Series in 1965. Two years later he went 15–1 and had a hand in bringing the Auburn University Tigers to the College World Series. He then played in the Chicago Cubs' minor league system and coached one season for the major league club as well as coaching in the organizations of the Montreal Expos and New York Yankees. His true love was college baseball, however, and in 1986 he returned to Auburn University in Montgomery and led that team to the NAIA World Series in 1990 and 1992. In 1990 he was named National Coach of the Year.

Peanuts Lowrey
Philadelphia Phillies (NL) 1960–66; San Francisco Giants (NL) 1967–68; Montreal Expos (NL) 1969; Chicago Cubs (NL) 1970–71, 1977–79, 1981; California Angels (AL) 1972
Solid outfielder and third baseman for 13 major league seasons.

Nicknamed "Peanuts" by his grandfather, who said that he was no bigger than a peanut as an infant, Harry Lee Lowrey hit .273 lifetime. In 1946 with the Chicago Cubs he was named a National League All-Star, and in 1951 with the St. Louis Cardinals he batted .303. Toward the end of his career he became a pinch-hitting specialist, leading the NL with 13 pinch safeties in 1952, when he once had 7 in a row, and again with 22 in 1953. He also appeared in the movie *The Winning Team*, in which Ronald

Reagan played the part of pitcher Grover Cleveland Alexander.

After his playing career Lowrey became a coach with several big league clubs.

Frank Lucchesi
Texas Rangers (AL) 1974–75, 1979–80
See Managers section.

Mike Lum
Chicago White Sox (AL) 1985; Kansas City Royals (AL) 1988–89
Hawaiian outfielder and first baseman.

Lum played from 1967–81 and was used extensively as a pinch-hitter. He retired with 103 pinch-hits and 418 pinch-hitting at-bats, both numbers putting him among the major league leaders all-time.

Lum became a major and minor league coach after his playing career. He spent many years in the Chicago White Sox' organization before moving to that of the Milwaukee Brewers.

Jerry Lumpe
Oakland Athletics (AL) 1971
Infielder for a dozen big league seasons.

Lumpe hit .268 for the New York Yankees, Kansas City Athletics, and Detroit Tigers. He was tried at third base by the Yankees but struggled defensively, then was moved to second by the A's and seemed to stabilize. He coached a year with that team, which had moved to Oakland at that point, after his retirement.

Don Lund
Detroit Tigers (AL) 1957–58
Outfielder from Detroit, Michigan.

Lund played seven seasons, only one of them as a regular. That was 1953 with his hometown Tigers, for whom he batted .257. After one more season he was finished playing, but returned to the Tigers for two years as a coach. He then became the head coach at the University of Michigan and in 1962 led the Wolverines to the College World Series championship. The following year he returned to the Tigers and worked for many years in minor league operations, scouting, and player development.

Dolf Luque
New York Giants (NL) 1935–38, 1941–45
Pitcher from Cuba nicknamed "The Pride of Havana."

After coming to the United States in 1912 and going 22–5 in 1913 for the Long Branch Cubans of the New York-New Jersey League, Dolf Luque embarked on a 20-year major league career that saw him win 194 games. He won at least 13 games eight times, and in 1923 with the Cincinnati Reds led the National League with 27 victories. He also led the league three times in shutouts and twice in winning percentage. He finished his playing career with the Giants and then coached for them for several years.

Joe Lutz
Cleveland Indians (AL) 1972–73
First baseman with a 14-game major league experience.

Lutz hit .167 in 1951 for the St. Louis Browns. He eventually became a coach with the Indians, then went to Japan as a hitting instructor for the Hiroshima Carp in 1974. The following season he was named the Carp's manager, becoming the first foreigner to skipper a Japanese club. He lasted only 15 games, however, posting a 6–8–1 record and alienating many for trying to impose American methods on his Japanese players. Under his successor, Takeshi Koba, the Carp reached the Nippon Series for the first time.

Lutz later became a counselor in Florida.

Greg Luzinski
Oakland Athletics (AL) 1993; Kansas City Royals (AL) 1995–97
Power-hitting outfielder and designated hitter for the Philadelphia Phillies and Chicago White Sox.

Something of a defensive liability, Luzinski made his mark with his bat in a big way. Nicknamed "The Bull," he won two minor league home run titles and one batting crown. In the majors he slugged over 20 home runs seven times and knocked in over 100 runs on four occasions. In 1975 he hit 34 homers and led the National League with 120 RBIs, and two years later he bashed a career-high 39 roundtrippers. A four-time All-Star, he also hit at least .300 four times, and he collected 307 homers lifetime.

After his playing career he coached several seasons for the A's and Royals, and he later opened a barbecue concession in the Phillies' stadium, Citizens Bank Park.

Eddie Lyons
Minnesota Twins (AL) 1976
Second baseman who played seven major league games.

A North Carolina native and career minor leaguer, Lyons managed but a .154 average for the 1947 Washington Nationals in those seven games. He eventually coached one season for the Twins before disappearing from the major league scene.

Ted Lyons
Detroit Tigers (AL) 1949–53; Brooklyn Dodgers (NL) 1954
See Managers section.

Ken Macha
Montreal Expos (NL) 1986–91; California Angels (AL) 1992–94; Oakland Athletics (AL) 1999–2002
See Managers section.

Earle Mack
Philadelphia Athletics (AL) 1924–50
See Managers section.

Pete Mackanin
Montreal Expos (NL) 1997–2000; Pittsburgh Pirates (NL) 2003–05
See Managers section.

Gordy MacKenzie
Kansas City Royals (AL) 1980–81; Chicago Cubs (NL) 1982; San Francisco Giants (NL) 1986–88; Cleveland Indians (AL) 1991–92
Catcher from St. Petersburg, Florida.

MacKenzie lasted only 11 major league games in 1961 with the Kansas City Athletics. He went 3-for-24, good for only a .125 average. After his playing career he became a major league coach and a minor league manager. In 1995 he guided the Kinston Indians to the Carolina League championship.

Joe Macko
Chicago Cubs (NL) 1964
Longtime minor league player and baseball ambassador.

Macko played in the Cleveland Indians' organization from 1948–56, then in the Cubs' system from 1957–64. He spent the 1961–64 years as a player-manager and coached briefly for Chicago in '64. He later worked for many years in the Texas Rangers' organization in various roles, including that of clubhouse manager, until retiring in 2000. Even after that, however, he continued to work for the Rangers as a "goodwill ambassador," making appearances and doing charitable work on behalf of the team.

Joe Maddon
California Angels (AL) 1994–96; Anaheim Angels (AL) 1997–2004; Los Angeles Angels of Anaheim (AL) 2005
See Managers section.

Mike Maddux
Milwaukee Brewers (NL) 2003–
Pitcher from Dayton, Ohio.

Mike and his brother Greg were both rookies in 1986, Mike with the Philadelphia Phillies and Greg with the Chicago Cubs. On September 29 of that year the pair became the first rookie brothers to face each other in a major league game.

Mike pitched for many teams in 15 years, almost entirely in relief, and he compiled a 39–37 record with 20 saves and a 4.05 earned run average. He ended his playing career during the 2000 season and became a minor league coach for the Houston Astros that same year. In 2003 he began coaching in the majors with the Brewers.

Bill Madlock
Detroit Tigers (AL) 2000–01
First major leaguer to win two batting titles with each of two different teams.

The first pair came with the Chicago Cubs, the second with the Pittsburgh Pirates. In a 15-year career Madlock hit .305 overall, and in addition to those four batting crowns he was a three-time All-Star. He hit over .300 on nine occasions. In 1974 he was named to the Topps All-Star Rookie Team, in 1975 he was co-Most Valuable Player of the All-Star Game along with Jon Matlack, and in 1976 he finished in a three-way tie for the National League lead in being hit by pitches. He was also mugged that year when he was in New York and suffered a slight concussion.

In 1980 he was suspended for 15 games and fined $5000 when he struck umpire Jerry Crawford in the face with his batting glove while arguing a called third strike. He played in the majors through 1987, then spent a year playing in Japan. He eventually coached two seasons for the Tigers.

Dave Magadan
San Diego Padres (NL) 2003–06; Boston Red Sox (AL) 2007–
Cousin of Lou Piniella.

In 1983 Magadan won the Golden Spikes Award, proclaiming him the nation's top amateur player, while at the University of Alabama. His major league career lasted from 1986 through 2001 and resulted in a .288 lifetime average. He hit over .300 several times and in 1990 with the New York Mets led the National League with a .425 on-base percentage while batting .328. He also had one of the best strikeout-to-walk ratios of his era, drawing 718 free passes while whiffing 546 times.

In 2002 he became a minor league hitting instructor for the Padres, and the following season was promoted to the big league club. He was fired in June of 2006, then was hired by the Red Sox.

Sal Maglie
Boston Red Sox (AL) 1960–62, 1966–67; Seattle Pilots (AL) 1969
One of the few major leaguers to play for three New York teams—the New York Giants, Brooklyn Dodgers, and New York Yankees.

Nicknamed "The Barber" because he liked to "shave" hitters by pitching inside, Maglie debuted in 1945 with the Giants but was banned for life the following year when he skipped out to play in Mexico. The ban was lifted in 1950 and he returned to the Giants, and later that year he put together a string of 45 consecutive scoreless innings. He tied for the National League lead with five shutouts and led with a 2.51 earned run average, and in 1951 tied for best in the circuit with 23 victories. He was an All-Star that year and the next.

In 1956 he pitched a no-hitter against the Philadelphia Phillies, and in October of that year he was on the wrong end of Don Larsen's World Series perfect game. Maglie himself was perfect through the first three innings until Mickey Mantle broke his attempt up with a home run.

After his playing career Maglie coached for the Red Sox and for the expansion Seattle Pilots.

Jim Mahoney
Chicago White Sox (AL) 1972–76; Seattle Mariners (AL) 1985–86
Good defensive shortstop who played 120 major league games.

Spreading those games over four seasons, Mahoney hit only .229 with four different teams. He spent many years playing in the minor leagues, and after his playing career became a major and minor league coach and a minor league manager.

Roy Majtyka
Atlanta Braves (NL) 1988–90
Minor league second baseman from Buffalo, New York.

Majtyka became a minor league manager in 1968 in the St. Louis Cardinals' organization with the Lewiston Broncs. He managed for many teams over the years, moving from the Cardinals' chain to the organizations of the Cincinnati Reds, Detroit Tigers, and Atlanta Braves. After coaching three seasons for Atlanta at the big league level, he returned to the minors, managing again in the Braves' system and then in the Philadelphia Phillies' organization.

Harry Malmberg
Boston Red Sox (AL) 1963–64
Played 67 games in one season for the Detroit Tigers.

A second baseman, Malmberg hit only .216 during that 1955 campaign, but in the minors he had led various leagues numerous times in many defensive categories. He had served in the Army before his career began and then spent many years in the minor leagues beginning in 1947. He played until 1962, then coached two seasons for the Red Sox before becoming a minor league manager. He eventually quit baseball and became a car salesman.

Jack Maloof
San Diego Padres (NL) 1990; Florida Marlins (NL) 1999–2001
Minor leaguer who won two batting titles.

An NAIA District All-American in 1971 when he hit .367 in his senior year at the University of La Verne, Maloof was also an excellent receiver on the school's football team. As a minor leaguer he won batting crowns in both the Carolina and Southern Leagues. He later coached the Padres and Marlins and also worked as a hitting instructor in the Atlanta Braves' organization. He is the author of the book *Hit Like a Big Leaguer*, written to assist young players with the fundamentals of batting.

Gordon Maltzberger
Minnesota Twins (AL) 1962–64
Pitcher from Utopia, Texas.

Maltzberger lasted four major league seasons with the Chicago White Sox. He got into 135 games and led the American League in saves (an unofficial statistic at the time) with 14 in 1943 and 12 in 1944 as he finished in a three-way tie. He compiled a 20–13 record with a 2.70 earned run average. He later coached three seasons for the Twins.

Gus Mancuso
Cincinnati Reds (NL) 1950
Catcher and two-time All-Star.

Mancuso had been buried in the St. Louis Cardinals' organization when Commissioner Kenesaw Mountain Landis ordered the team to either put him on the major league roster or make him a free agent. The team elected to keep him and thus began a 17-year major league career, spent with several clubs. Solid defensively but slow on the bases, he managed a .265 lifetime batting average, and hit over .300 on three occasions. He later coached the Reds for one season. His brother Frank was also a major league catcher, for four years.

Doug Mansolino
Chicago White Sox (AL) 1992–96; Milwaukee Brewers (NL) 1998–99; Detroit Tigers (AL) 2000–02; Houston Astros (NL) 2005–
Minor league player and longtime major league coach.

Mansolino began coaching in 1985 in the San Francisco Giants' organization. He also managed and worked as a roving instructor, moving to the Chicago White Sox' system in 1988. In 1992 he was promoted to Chicago and would coach several other big league teams. In 1997 he managed in the New York Mets' organization, and from 2003–04 worked as a roving infield instructor and defensive coordinator in the Pittsburgh Pirates' system. Mansolino traveled to Korea three times to help instruct teams in that country.

Mickey Mantle
New York Yankees (AL) 1970
Hall of Famer and 17-time All-Star.

A .298 lifetime hitter in 18 seasons with the Yankees, Mantle's credentials include leading the American League once in batting average, four times in home runs, once in runs batted in, once in triples, six times in runs scored, five times in walks, three times in on-base percentage, and four times in slugging average. He was named the league's Most Valuable Player three times, including the 1956 season when he won the Triple Crown with a .353 batting average, 52 home runs, and 130 RBIs. He slugged 536 roundtrippers lifetime and set a World Series record by hitting 18 in postseason play. In 1962 he also won a Gold Glove.

Mantle cracked at least 19 home runs in a season 16 times, and never hit fewer than 13. He hit at least 40 four times and at least 50 twice. He topped the 100-RBI plateau four times and hit at least .300 ten times. He scored over 100 runs on nine occasions.

Mantle retired following the 1968 season, and the Yankees retired his number 7 the next year. In 1970 he returned to the club as a coach, and in 1974 was inducted into the Hall of Fame. He passed away in 1995.

Jeff Manto
Pittsburgh Pirates (NL) 2006–
Most Valuable Player of the Texas League in 1988.

Manto played for the Midland Angels that year and hit .301 with 24 home runs and 120 runs batted in. He made his first major league appearance in 1990, but spent the entire 1994 season in the minors and was named International League MVP when he led that league with 31 homers and 100 RBIs. Used as a reserve in nine major league seasons, he hit 17 roundtrippers with the Baltimore Orioles in 1995 and once hit four in consecutive at-bats, at-bats that were spread over three games.

He played part of the 1996 season with the Yomiuri Giants in Japan, but returned to the majors that year and played until 2000. He became a minor league coach in the Philadelphia Phillies' organization in 2001, and in 2003 began working as a minor league roving hitting instructor for the Pirates. He was promoted to Pittsburgh as a coach in 2006.

Charlie Manuel
Cleveland Indians (AL) 1988–89, 1994–99
See Managers section.

Jerry Manuel
Montreal Expos (NL) 1991–96; Florida Marlins (NL) 1997;
New York Mets (NL) 2005–
See Managers section.

Heinie Manush
Washington Nationals (AL) 1953–54
Hall of Fame outfielder from Alabama.

In 17 years Manush hit .330, topping the .300 mark in 11 seasons. In 1926 with the Detroit Tigers he won the American League batting title with a .378 average, then led the league two years later with 241 hits and tied Lou Gehrig with 47 doubles. The next season he led again with 45 two-baggers. In 1933 with the Nationals he topped the circuit with 221 hits and 17 triples, at one point putting together a 33-game hitting streak. He was named an AL All-Star the next year.

Manush retired from the major league scene in 1939 but continued playing and managing in the minors until 1945. He then worked as a scout for the Boston Braves and Pittsburgh Pirates before coaching for the Nationals and then becoming a Washington scout. He was inducted into the Hall of Fame in 1964.

Marty Marion
St. Louis Cardinals (NL) 1950; St. Louis Browns (AL) 1952;
Chicago White Sox (AL) 1954
See Managers section.

Jim Marshall
Chicago Cubs (NL) 1974
See Managers section.

Billy Martin
Minnesota Twins (AL) 1965–68
See Managers section.

Fred Martin
Chicago Cubs (NL) 1961–65; Chicago White Sox (AL) 1979
One of the first players to enter the military during World War II.

Martin was a minor leaguer at the time, and he made his big league debut after his return in 1946. He then became one of a number of players to violate his contract by jumping to the Mexican League, which was raiding major league clubs for talent. As a result he was banned for life by Commissioner Happy Chandler. Martin and Max Lanier filed a $2.5 million lawsuit against Major League Baseball, but that suit was later dropped. Chandler reduced jumpers' lifetime bans to five-year bans, but dismissed them altogether in 1949 and allowed the players to come back.

Martin posted a 12–3 record in three seasons for the St.

Louis Cardinals, and later coached the Cubs. He was named a White Sox' coach in 1979, but died during the season on June 11.

J. C. Martin
Chicago Cubs (NL) 1974
Infielder who was converted into a catcher.

Joseph Clifton Martin struggled at both third base and first base, but as a catcher he finally stuck in the major leagues. In a 14-year career spent with the Chicago White Sox, New York Mets, and Chicago Cubs, he batted a mere .222 but was solid defensively and often produced in pinch-hitting situations. On September 10, 1967, he caught a no-hitter pitched by the White Sox' Joel Horlen.

Martin later coached a single season for the Cubs.

Pepper Martin
Chicago Cubs (NL) 1956
Outfielder/third baseman and four-time All-Star.

In 13 seasons Martin (whose real name was Johnny Leonard Roosevelt Martin) hit .298. He spent his entire career with the St. Louis Cardinals' "Gashouse Gang," hitting at least .300 seven times and leading the National League three times in stolen bases and once in runs scored. In 1933 he hit for the cycle, and his World Series batting average of .418 is the highest of any player with at least 50 at-bats and the third-highest overall.

After his playing career Martin became a minor league manager. In 1949 with the Miami Sun Sox of the Florida International League he was once fined $100 and suspended for two weeks for choking an umpire. He later returned to the majors for one season as a coach with the Cubs.

Jose Martinez
Kansas City Royals (AL) 1980–87; Chicago Cubs (NL) 1988–94
Infielder from Cardenas, Cuba.

Martinez lasted only 96 major league games, spread over the 1969 and 1970 seasons with the Pittsburgh Pirates. He hit .245 with a single home run. He eventually fashioned a very successful coaching career, spending 15 seasons in that capacity in the major leagues with the Royals and Cubs.

Marty Martinez
Seattle Mariners (AL) 1984–86, 1992
See Managers section.

Marty Mason
St. Louis Cardinals (NL) 2000–
Minor league pitcher signed by the New York Yankees.

Mason pitched from 1980–85, then appeared in four games as a player-coach with the St. Petersburg Cardinals in 1986. He then began to coach full-time in the Cardinals' system, working his way up gradually until he was promoted to the major league staff as bullpen coach in 2000.

Eddie Mathews
Atlanta Braves (NL) 1971–72
See Managers section.

Harry Mathews
Cleveland Indians (AL) 1926–27; New York Yankees (AL) 1929
Native of Newport, Kentucky, who was born in 1876.

Mathews was a minor leaguer who never reached the big time except as a coach. In that capacity he spent two seasons with the Indians and one with the Yankees.

Rick Mathews
Colorado Rockies (NL) 1993, 1995, 2003–
Pitcher who never played professionally.

Mathews pitched at Indian Hills Community College and Drake University, then immediately became a high school coach. From 1971–74 he worked as a part-time scout for the Kansas City Royals, and from 1974–77 in the same capacity for the Philadelphia Phillies. He eventually moved to the junior college level as a baseball coach, and in 1980 was hired to manage in the Royals' minor league system. He also worked for a time as the Royals' director of player development, but in 1987 returned to Indian Hills as their head coach. The following season he was back in the Kansas City organization as a minor league instructor.

Shortly thereafter he moved to the Rockies' organization, where he spent part of 1993 and part of 1995 at the major league level as bullpen coach. In '95 he was also a coach for the Bend Rockies, where he had a chance to work with his son Jonathan, who had been drafted by Colorado. Rick then worked as a roving pitching instructor until being promoted back to Denver in 2003.

Christy Mathewson
New York Giants (NL) 1919–21
See Managers section.

Jon Matlack
Detroit Tigers (AL) 1996
National League Rookie of the Year in 1972.

Matlack went 15–10 for the New York Mets that season, fashioning a 2.32 earned run average. He would garner at least 13 victories six times in a 13-year career and would lead the NL twice in shutouts and be named to three All-Star teams. In 1975 he and Bill Madlock were co-

winners of the All-Star Game's Most Valuable Player Award; Jon was the winning pitcher after going two innings and striking out four batters.

In 1973 he suffered a fractured skull when he was hit by a line drive, but he was back pitching 11 days later. He developed shoulder problems later on, however, that affected him throughout the latter part of his career. He retired with a 125–126 record and a 3.18 ERA.

When his playing days were over Matlack worked as a roving pitching instructor for the Tigers and spent one season as a Detroit coach.

Gary Matthews
Toronto Blue Jays (AL) 1998–99; Milwaukee Brewers (NL) 2002; Chicago Cubs (NL) 2003–06
National League Rookie of the Year in 1973.

Matthews hit .300 for the San Francisco Giants that season, cracking 12 homers and driving in 58 runs. In 16 seasons he would hit .281 lifetime, breaking the .300 mark three times and hitting 234 roundtrippers. In 1979 he was named an NL All-Star when he batted .304 with 27 homers and 90 RBIs, and that marked one of three times he would bash at least 20 roundtrippers. In 1983 he was named the Most Valuable Player of the NL Championship Series when he hit .429 with three home runs and eight knocked in. In 1984 he led the league with 103 walks and a .417 on-base percentage.

After his playing career Matthews worked in the private sector and then went into broadcasting before being hired by the Cubs as a minor league hitting coordinator. In 1998 he joined the Blue Jays as their hitting coach, then became a broadcaster in Toronto. He later coached the Brewers and the Cubs.

His son, Gary Matthews, Jr., had a five-year major league career.

Don Mattingly
New York Yankees (AL) 2004–
Outstanding hitter and first baseman for 14 seasons.

A pure hitter in every sense of the word, Don Mattingly hit .307 lifetime and batted over .300 seven times. He spent his entire career with the Yankees, with whom he won the 1984 batting title with a .343 average and was a six-time All-Star. In 1985 he was named the American League's Most Valuable Player on the strength of a .324 average, 35 home runs, 211 hits, and league-leading totals of 48 doubles and 145 runs batted in. In all he led the league once in batting average, three times in doubles, once in RBIs, twice in hits, and once in slugging percentage. In 1987 he homered in eight consecutive games, tying the AL record, and set a major league record with six grand slams. He also won nine Gold Gloves and has the highest fielding average of any first baseman in history at .996.

Mattingly retired in 1995. In 1997 the Yankees retired his number 23, and from 1997–2003 he worked as a Yankees' spring training instructor. In 2004 he was named New York's hitting coach, and in 2007 moved to bench coach.

Gene Mauch
Kansas City Royals (AL) 1995
See Managers section.

Dal Maxvill
Oakland Athletics (AL) 1975; New York Mets (NL) 1978; St. Louis Cardinals (NL) 1979–80; Atlanta Braves (NL) 1982–84
One of baseball's worst-hitting but best-fielding shortstops.

Maxvill lasted 14 years in the major leagues despite a .217 batting average. That longevity is a testament to his fielding prowess, because he never hit over .253 in a season but retired with the best fielding average in National League history to that time. He went 0-for-22 in the 1968 World Series with the Cardinals but in 1969 hit the first major league grand slam in Canada in a game against the Montreal Expos. After retiring he coached for several clubs, including the Cardinals, and then served as the Cards' general manager from 1985 until 1994.

Lee May
Kansas City Royals (AL) 1984–86, 1992–94; Cincinnati Reds (NL) 1988–89; Baltimore Orioles (AL) 1995; Tampa Bay Devil Rays (AL) 2001–05
"The Big Bopper from Birmingham."

A member of Cincinnati's Big Red Machine in the early 1970s, May was traded away to make room for Joe Morgan, Jack Billingham, and others. He, Tommy Helms, and Jimmy Stewart went to the Houston Astros and proved the adage that you have to give up something in order to get something. May was a consistent, feared power hitter, bashing at least 19 home runs in a season 12 times and collecting 354 lifetime. A three-time All-Star, he topped 100 runs batted in three times, each time with a different club (becoming one of only 10 players to accomplish that feat), and led the American League in 1976 with 109 while playing for the Orioles. He hit the last home run at Crosley Field, and in 1973 with the Astros he put together a 21-game hitting streak.

Born on March 23, Lee usually wore the day of his birth (number 23) on his back, while his brother Carlos wore his own complete birthday ("MAY 17") on his own back with the Chicago White Sox.

Lee retired in 1982 and later coached several big league clubs.

Milt May
Pittsburgh Pirates (NL) 1987–96; Florida Marlins (NL) 1997–98; Tampa Bay Devil Rays (AL) 2002–05
Son of major leaguer Pinky May, who played for the Philadelphia Phillies.

Milt was originally signed as an infielder, but the Pirates converted him into a catcher. He played 15 years behind the plate, hitting .263 and topping the .300 mark in 1981 when he batted .310 for the San Francisco Giants. On May 4, 1975, while playing for the Houston Astros, he drove in Bob Watson with major league baseball's one millionth run. Watson scored only seconds ahead of the Cincinnati Reds' Dave Concepcion.

Milt, who started out with the Pirates, returned to Pittsburgh in 1983. He finished out his playing career the following year and then became a coach with the club. He later moved on to the Marlins and Devil Rays.

John Mayberry
Kansas City Royals (AL) 1989–90
Power-hitting first baseman and designated hitter.

In 15 seasons John Mayberry slugged 255 home runs, topping the 20 mark eight times. He drove in at least 100 runs three times and twice led the American League in bases on balls. In a 1977 game with the Royals he hit for the cycle.

His hitting was not his entire game, however, for he topped all AL first basemen three times in putouts, twice in fielding average, and twice in double plays. He was named to the AL All-Star squad in both 1973 and 1974.

After his playing career Mayberry eventually returned to the Royals for two years as a coach.

Eddie Mayo
Boston Red Sox (AL) 1951; Philadelphia Phillies (NL) 1952–54
Infielder from Holyoke, Massachusetts.

Mayo started out as a New York Giants' third baseman in 1936 but was soon demoted back to the minor leagues. In 1941 with the Los Angeles Angels of the Pacific Coast League he was suspended for a year when he spit in the face of umpire Ray Snyder. In 1943 he returned to the major leagues with the Philadelphia Athletics and led all American League third basemen in fielding average. He was switched to second base by the Detroit Tigers the following season and promptly led all keystone sackers in double plays in 1944 and in fielding average in 1945. He started two triple plays off the bat of Gil Torres within a year's time, the first in July of 1945 and the second in May of 1946.

Mayo finished his playing career in 1948 and later coached the Red Sox and Phillies.

Willie Mays
New York Mets (NL) 1974–79
Touted by some as the greatest player of all time.

Willie Mays played in the Negro Leagues for the Birmingham Black Barons from 1948–50 before joining the New York Giants. He then fashioned a 22-year major league career matched by few. A .302 lifetime hitter, he was named the National League's Rookie of the Year in 1951 when he hit .274 with 20 home runs and 68 runs batted in. He won the 1954 batting title with a .345 average and topped the .300 mark 10 times. Besides winning that crown, he led the league four times in home runs, three times in triples, once in walks, four times in stolen bases, once in hits, and twice in runs scored. He never led in RBIs, but he topped the 100 mark 10 times. He was an All-Star a record 24 times (for a few years there were two games) and won 12 Gold Gloves for his defense. He hit 660 home runs lifetime and collected 3283 hits and 338 stolen bases. He also topped the circuit twice in on-base percentage and five times in slugging average. He hit at least 20 home runs 17 times.

Willie was named the NL's Most Valuable Player in 1954 on the strength of that .345 average, 41 homers, 110 RBIs, and a league-leading 13 triples. He won the award again in 1965 when he hit .317 and powered 52 homers with 112 RBIs.

Mays started his career with the New York Giants and finished it with the New York Mets in 1973. He then served with the Mets as a coach until 1979.

The Giants retired his uniform number 24 in 1972. In 1979 Willie was inducted into the Hall of Fame.

Bill Mazeroski
Pittsburgh Pirates (NL) 1973; Seattle Mariners (AL) 1979–80
Ten-time All-Star second baseman.

Originally signed as a shortstop, Mazeroski was moved to second with the Pirates by Branch Rickey, and he became one of the best in history at that position defensively. He led the National League multiple times in multiple fielding categories, and made a name for himself primarily with his glove. He won eight Gold Gloves in his career for his defense. A moderate hitter, he did have some pop in his bat, slugging at least 10 home runs six times in a 17-year career. He peaked with 19 in 1958.

In 1960 his home run was the first ever to end a World Series, propelling the Pirates to the ultimate championship over the New York Yankees. It was his second roundtripper of the Series. In 1968 he made an appearance in the motion picture *The Odd Couple*, appearing as a player who ended a game by hitting into a triple play.

Mazeroski coached for the Pirates and later for the Mariners when his playing days were over. In 1987 the

Pirates retired his number 9, and he was inducted into the Hall of Fame by the Veterans Committee in 2001.

Lee Mazzilli
New York Yankees (AL) 2000–03, 2006
See Managers section.

Leo Mazzone
Atlanta Braves (NL) 1985, 1990–2005; Baltimore Orioles (AL) 2006–
Minor league pitcher and longtime coach.

Mazzone spent nine years in the minor leagues as a player before becoming a manager at that level in 1976. In 1979 he joined the Braves' organization as an instructor and coach, and in 1985 served as Atlanta's co-pitching coach along with Johnny Sain. He then continued coaching in the minors until June of 1990, when he was summoned back to Atlanta by the newly-hired Bobby Cox.

Sam Perlozzo, a boyhood friend, coaxed him to Baltimore when he became manager of the Orioles.

George McBride
Detroit Tigers (AL) 1925–26, 1929
See Managers section.

Ken McBride
Milwaukee Brewers (AL) 1975
Pitcher whose career was cut short by arm problems.

McBride lasted seven seasons, and was an All-Star from 1961–63 (appearing in both games in '61) with the Los Angeles Angels. He fashioned a 40–50 record with a 3.79 earned run average, his record being somewhat skewed by the fact that he played for an expansion team. He played only two more years before a sore arm ended his career, and he later coached a season for the Brewers.

Larry McCall
Baltimore Orioles (AL) 2006
Pitcher who appeared in nine major league games.

McCall went 2–2 in three separate seasons for the New York Yankees and Texas Rangers, posting a 5.04 earned run average. He later worked for many years in the Orioles' organization as a coach and manager at many different levels. During the 2006 season he was called up to Baltimore to be bullpen coach; the coach at the time, Rick Dempsey, was moved to first base, and the first base coach, Dave Cash, was reassigned within the organization. The idea was to give pitching coach Leo Mazzone an aide who had spent a great deal of time working with young pitchers.

Jack McCallister
Cleveland Indians (AL) 1920–26; Boston Red Sox (AL) 1930
See Managers section.

Steve McCatty
Detroit Tigers (AL) 2002
Dependable pitcher whose career was shortened due to arm problems.

McCatty pitched in the majors for nine years. He won 14 games with the Oakland Athletics in 1980, and finished in a four-way tie for the American League lead with 14 more in strike-shortened 1981, when he was also one of four leaders with 4 shutouts and topped the circuit with a 2.33 earned run average. He never again won more than eight games in a season, and many blamed his problems on overuse by Oakland manager Billy Martin. He once pitched all of a 14-inning game in 1980, and was the fourth Oakland starter to do that that year.

In a spring training game against the San Diego Padres in 1982 Martin protested the fact that his club was not allowed to use the designated hitter in National League parks, and sent McCatty to the plate with a toy bat. McCatty was not allowed to use the toy, and with a real bat was called out on strikes.

Steve pitched for the Fort Myers Sun Sox in the Senior Professional Baseball Association in 1989, and eventually coached a season with the Tigers.

Lloyd McClendon
Pittsburgh Pirates (NL) 1997–2000; Detroit Tigers (AL) 2006–
See Managers section.

Bob McClure
Florida Marlins (NL) 1994; Kansas City Royals (AL) 2006–
Oakland native who pitched 19 major league seasons.

Mainly a reliever, McClure started a mere 73 out of 698 games pitched. He posted a 68–57 career record with 52 saves, but 2 additional saves came during the 1982 World Series for the eventual champion Milwaukee Brewers.

After ending his playing career in 1993 McClure coached the Marlins for part of 1994. He worked as a Marlins' scout before coaching his son's high school baseball team and then joining the Colorado Rockies' organization as a minor league coach. In 2006 he was hired as a major league coach by the Royals.

Frank McCormick
Cincinnati Redlegs (NL) 1956–57
First baseman from New York City.

McCormick was a nine-time All-Star who hit .299 life-time. He batted over .300 eight times and in 1939 led the National League with 128 runs batted in. He topped the 100-RBI mark four times and also led the league once in doubles and three times in hits. In 1940 he was named the NL's Most Valuable Player when he hit .309 with 19 home runs, 127 RBIs, and a league-topping 44 doubles while helping the Reds to the World Championship. From 1945–46 he set a record for first basemen by playing 131 consecutive errorless games. In 1947 he led the league with 13 pinch-hits.

McCormick spent most of his career with Cincinnati, and he returned to the organization as a minor league manager, scout, major league coach, and broadcaster.

Les McCrabb
Philadelphia Athletics (AL) 1950–54
Pitcher for the Philadelphia Athletics.

McCrabb played only one full season and four partial ones. He went 10–15 in 38 total games with a 5.96 earned run average. He pitched from 1939–42, and did not return to Philadelphia until 1950 when he began a five-year tenure as a coach and also pitched two games.

Tom McCraw
Cleveland Indians (AL) 1975, 1980–82; San Francisco Giants (NL) 1983–85; Baltimore Orioles (AL) 1989–91; New York Mets (NL) 1992–96; Houston Astros (NL) 1997–2000; Montreal Expos (NL) 2002–04; Washington Nationals (NL) 2005
American Association batting champion in 1962.

McCraw hit .326 that year, but would not approach that level of success in the major leagues. He did last 13 big league seasons, however, hitting .246. In 1968 with the Chicago White Sox he led American League first basemen in total chances per game, assists, and double plays, but also in errors. On May 3 he committed three miscues in one inning.

After retiring in 1975 he became a well-traveled major league coach.

Clyde McCullough
Washington Senators (AL) 1960; Minnesota Twins (AL) 1961; New York Mets (NL) 1963; San Diego Padres (NL) 1980–82
Two-time All-Star catcher from Nashville, Tennessee.

McCullough is believed to be the last catcher to play without a chest protector. His career spanned 1940–56, and he batted .252 during that span. He was excellent defensively, and in 1955 with the Chicago Cubs he caught Sam Jones' no-hitter, the first ever by a black pitcher, against the Pittsburgh Pirates.

McCullough became a major league coach after his

playing career and also worked as a minor league manager and instructor in the Mets' organization. In September of 1982, while coaching for the Padres during a road trip to San Francisco to play the Giants, he was found dead in his hotel room.

Mickey McDermott
California Angels (AL) 1968
Pitcher who was wild both on and off the field.

The son of a police officer and former minor league player, McDermott pitched against adults at the age of 13 and even tried out for the Brooklyn Dodgers, who were unable to sign him because of his age. He eventually signed with the Boston Red Sox at the age of 15. (His father had altered his birth certificate to make him appear 16, and Boston general manager Joe Cronin "worked it out" and gave Mickey's father $5000 and two truckloads of beer.) As a minor leaguer McDermott pitched three no-hitters, and after once striking out 20 batters in a game he proceeded to whiff 19, 18, 17, and 19 in the next four to set a record with 93 over a five-game stretch.

He was called up to the Red Sox in 1948, and in 1949 collected his first win when he replaced Ellis Kinder, who was drunk, in the first inning and went on to throw eight innings without allowing a run. He is the subject of the famous Norman Rockwell painting *The Rookie*, pictured sitting on the bench in the clubhouse suiting up with several players around him when he was first called up to the major leagues. His best season in the majors was 1953, when he went 18–10 with a 3.01 earned run average. As his career began to wane he started drinking heavily, and after the 1958 season he was back in the minors. In 1961 he caught on with the St. Louis Cardinals, but was let go when he punched a hotel detective who had insulted his future wife, having mistaken her for a prostitute. He pitched four more games for the Kansas City Athletics to end his playing career.

In 1968 he worked as a coach and pitched batting practice for the Angels, and later owned a bar. After scouting for the Oakland Athletics for a time he became an agent. In 1991 he and his fourth wife won $7 million in the Arizona state lottery. He continued to drink, but after receiving several DUIs and finally being sentenced to a jail term following an automobile accident, he gave up alcohol. He died in 2003 of colon cancer and heart failure.

Maje McDonnell
Philadelphia Phillies (NL) 1951, 1954–57
Army veteran from Philadelphia.

McDonnell was a combat infantryman in Europe during World War II, where he earned five battle stars. Having never played major league baseball, he joined the Phillies from 1947–50 as a batting practice pitcher, and coached the big club in 1951 and again from 1954–57. He then worked as a scout for many years and in the club's Speakers Bureau.

Roger McDowell
Atlanta Braves (NL) 2005–
Fun-loving relief pitcher who played 12 major league seasons.

A legendary prankster, McDowell pitched 723 games in his career and started only 2 of them. He accumulated 159 saves, garnering more than 20 on four occasions. He overcame a hernia in 1987, only his third major league season, although shoulder problems would eventually end his career. He made a couple of forays into television, appearing on *Seinfeld* and *America's Funniest People* as well as other shows.

He eventually became a minor league coach in the Los Angeles Dodgers' organization, and returned to the big leagues with the Braves as a coach in 2005.

Mel McGaha
Cleveland Indians (AL) 1961; Kansas City Athletics (AL) 1963–64; Houston Astros (NL) 1968–70
See Managers section.

Joe McGinnity
Brooklyn Robins (NL) 1926
Hall of Fame pitcher nicknamed "Iron Man."

That moniker came from the fact that McGinnity worked in a foundry in the offseason, but Joe made it apropos in quite another way. He pitched $3441\frac{1}{3}$ innings in a 10-year career, leading the league four times and setting a twentieth century record by throwing 434 in 1903. He won 246 games, averaging 24.6 per season, and paced the circuit five times in that category. He frequently pitched both games of doubleheaders, and in 1903 did just that on three separate occasions within a month's time and won all six games. He also led his respective league six times in games pitched, twice in starts, twice in complete games, once in shutouts, and once in earned run average. His best season statistically was 1904, when he went 35–8 (for an astronomical .814 winning percentage) with a 1.61 ERA. He won 14 consecutive games that year.

After the 1908 season he returned to the minor leagues as a player-manager and continued to pitch until he was 54 years of age. When he retired he had almost 500 career professional victories. He coached a year with the Robins in 1926. He died in 1929, and in 1946 he was inducted into the Hall of Fame.

Deacon McGuire
Detroit Tigers (AL) 1911–16
See Managers section.

Dave McKay
Oakland Athletics (AL) 1984–95; St. Louis Cardinals (NL) 1996–
Light-hitting switch-hitter and infielder.

McKay lasted eight big league seasons moving around the infield. A native of Vancouver, British Columbia, he started at third base for the Toronto Blue Jays in their very first game in 1977. In 1975 with the Minnesota Twins he had homered in his first major league at-bat, and then proceeded to hit safely in 21 of his first 22 games.

McKay's major league career lasted until 1982, and in 1983 he became a minor league player-manager. He then became a trusted coach for manager Tony LaRussa, serving under him for 12 years in Oakland and then following him to St. Louis.

In 2001 McKay was inducted into the Canadian Baseball Hall of Fame.

Bill McKechnie
Pittsburgh Pirates (NL) 1922; St. Louis Cardinals (NL) 1927; Cleveland Indians (AL) 1948–49; Boston Red Sox (AL) 1952–53
See Managers section.

J. R. McKee
Pittsburgh Pirates (NL) 1947
Another baseball mystery.

Not much information is available on J. R. McKee, including his first name, his birthdate, or his place of birth. What is known is that he is listed by the Pirates as one of their coaches in 1947.

Jack McKeon
Oakland Athletics (AL) 1978
See Managers section.

John McLaren
Toronto Blue Jays (AL) 1986–90; Boston Red Sox (AL) 1991; Cincinnati Reds (NL) 1992; Seattle Mariners (AL) 1993–2002, 2007– ; Tampa Bay Devil Rays (AL) 2003–05
Minor league catcher for seven seasons.

Excellent defensively, McLaren led Carolina League backstops in both putouts and assists in 1971, and led Southern League catchers in fielding average in 1973. He began coaching and managing in the minors in 1977, and also worked as a scout for several years. He led the Knoxville Blue Jays to the Southern League championship in both 1984 and 1985, and in '85 was named co-Manager of the Year. In 1986 he was promoted to Toronto and later coached the Red Sox, Reds, Mariners, and Devil Rays. The last 12 seasons, spanning time in both Seattle and Tampa Bay, were under Lou Piniella.

In 2006 McLaren was the third base coach for Team USA in the World Baseball Classic. In 2007 he returned to Seattle for a second stint as a coach.

Cal McLish
Philadelphia Phillies (NL) 1965–66; Montreal Expos (NL) 1969–75; Milwaukee Brewers (AL) 1976–82
Switch-hitting pitcher from Oklahoma.

Cal's full name was Calvin Coolidge Julius Caesar Tuskahoma McLish. He was named by his father, and Cal claimed his rather verbose moniker was the result of his mother's having named the other seven children in the family and his father's thus making up for lost time. McLish pitched for 15 seasons and went 92–92 with a 4.00 earned run average. In 1958 he was 16–8, and the following season, when he was named an American League All-Star, was his best at 19–8. He once set a major league record (since tied several times) by winning 16 consecutive games on the road.

McLish developed arm problems toward the end of his career and retired in 1964. He then became a coach for the Phillies, Expos, and Brewers.

Don McMahon
San Francisco Giants (NL) 1973–75, 1980–82; Minnesota Twins (AL) 1976–77; Cleveland Indians (AL) 1983–85
Well-traveled relief pitcher for 18 seasons.

McMahon switched teams in midseason five different times. His career spanned seven clubs, and of the 874 games he pitched he started only 2 of them. Having struggled in the minors as a starter, he had been converted to the bullpen while with the Toledo Mud Hens in 1955.

In 1958 with the Milwaukee Braves, his sophomore season, he was named a National League All-Star. He was also the first pitcher to be delivered by motor vehicle from the bullpen to the pitcher's mound when he rode in the sidecar of a motor scooter. The next year he tied for the league lead with 15 saves, and in 1971 he topped the NL with 9 relief wins. His lifetime earned run average was 2.96.

In 1973 he became a coach with the Giants, and in May of that season he was activated and pitched 22 games, posting a 1.48 ERA. He continued as a player-coach the following season before turning back to coaching full-time. In his 18-year playing career, McMahon never once spent time on the disabled list.

In 1987 he was working as an instructor and scout with the Los Angeles Dodgers and sometimes pitched batting practice. Having once undergone heart bypass surgery, he suffered a heart attack on July 22 on the field and died several hours later.

Roy McMillan

Milwaukee Brewers (AL) 1970–72; New York Mets (NL) 1973–76

See Managers section.

John McNamara

Oakland Athletics (AL) 1968–69; San Francisco Giants (NL) 1971–73; California Angels (AL) 1978

See Managers section.

Earl McNeely

St. Louis Browns (AL) 1931; Washington Nationals (AL) 1936–37

Outfielder for the Nationals and Browns.

The Nationals traded popular Wid Matthews, among others, to get McNeely from the Sacramento Senators of the Pacific Coast League in 1924. There was such a public outcry concerning Matthews' departure that Washington tried to back out of the deal, but it was too late. McNeely did not receive a warm welcome until he slapped a crucial hit in the 1924 World Series that bounced over the third baseman's head and helped the Nationals defeat the New York Giants for the championship.

He hit .330 in 43 games that season, and two years later batted .303. He finished his career with the Browns with a .272 lifetime average, then he coached for the Browns and later returned to the Nationals in the same role.

Jerry McNertney

Boston Red Sox (AL) 1988

Minor league first baseman converted to a major league catcher.

McNertney led International League backstops in fielding average in 1963, a year before he debuted in the major leagues with the Chicago White Sox. He missed the entire 1965 season due to an injury, but returned the following season and in 1969 was selected by the Seattle Pilots in the expansion draft. In 1971 he went to the St. Louis Cardinals, and he served as that team's "weekend catcher" when regular Ted Simmons had to serve in the U.S. Army Reserve.

A former standout player for the Iowa State Cyclones from 1956–58, McNertney returned to the college after his playing career to earn his degree. He then worked for the New York Yankees as a minor league coach for 10 years, and in 1988 was the bullpen coach for the Red Sox. In 1989 he returned to Iowa State as an assistant coach, his primary focus being on catchers. He worked there until

1996, and 10 years later he was inducted into the school's Hall of Fame. Both of his children eventually played for the Cyclones, his son Jason for the baseball team and his daughter Molly for the softball squad.

Hal McRae

Kansas City Royals (AL) 1987; Montreal Expos (NL) 1990–91; Cincinnati Reds (NL) 1995–96; Philadelphia Phillies (NL) 1997–2000; Tampa Bay Devil Rays (AL) 2001; St. Louis Cardinals (NL) 2005–

See Managers section.

Bobby Meacham

Florida Marlins (NL) 2006; San Diego Padres (NL) 2007–

Light-hitting shortstop from Los Angeles.

Meacham, a switch-hitter, played six seasons for the New York Yankees, mostly in a reserve role. He hit only .236, but twice led the American League in sacrifices. Following the 1988 campaign he was traded to the Texas Rangers but then was cut in spring training of 1989. He soon became a minor league manager, and in 1994 took the AA Carolina Mudcats to the league championship series. He later served as an instructor in the Pittsburgh Pirates' organization, then managed in the Anaheim Angels' system and worked as an instructor in the Colorado Rockies' chain before being hired as a big league coach by the Marlins in 2006. The following year he moved on to the Padres.

Sam Mejias

Seattle Mariners (AL) 1993–99; Baltimore Orioles (AL) 2007–

Outfielder from Santiago, Dominican Republic.

Mejias played at the major league level as a reserve for six seasons and batted .247. He later worked for several years in the Cincinnati Reds' organization as an instructor and later coached the Mariners for seven years. He returned to the minor leagues and eventually totalled 10 years managing at that level. In 2007 he was hired as a coach by the Orioles.

Sam Mele

Washington Senators (AL) 1959–60; Minnesota Twins (AL) 1961

See Managers section.

Oscar Melillo

St. Louis Browns (AL) 1938; Cleveland Indians (AL) 1939, 1942, 1945–48, 1950; Boston Red Sox (AL) 1952–53; Kansas City Athletics (AL) 1955–56

See Managers section.

Bob Melvin
Milwaukee Brewers (NL) 1999; Detroit Tigers (AL) 2000; Arizona Diamondbacks (NL) 2001–02
See Managers section.

Minnie Mendoza
Baltimore Orioles (AL) 1988
Minor league batting champion who played 16 major league games.

Mendoza won numerous batting titles in the minor leagues during a 14-year career, but his entire big league stay was comprised of 16 at-bats and 3 hits for a .188 batting average. He may have been responsible for the term "The Mendoza Line," referring to a .200 batting average. Someone hitting below .200 is said to be below the Mendoza Line. There is a great deal of dispute over exactly when and where that term appeared, however, and who originated it. Some attribute the reference to Mario Mendoza, who hit .215 lifetime but in nine seasons had five batting averages in the .100s. Regardless of the truth of the matter, Minnie hit over .300 six times in the minors and was an All-Star third baseman there. He eventually returned to the major leagues to coach one season with the Orioles.

Denis Menke
Toronto Blue Jays (AL) 1980–81; Houston Astros (NL) 1983–88; Philadelphia Phillies (NL) 1989–96; Cincinnati Reds (NL) 1997–2000
Versatile infielder with some power.

Menke debuted with the Milwaukee Braves in 1962 and two years later hit a career-high 20 home runs. In 1966 he hit 15 more, and in a 13-year career batted .250 with 101 roundtrippers while moving all over the infield. In 1969 he and Jimmy Wynn hit grand slams in the same inning, marking the first time that occurred in the National League in the twentieth century. In 1972 he was part of the trade that brought him, Joe Morgan, Jack Billingham, Ed Armbrister, and Cesar Geronimo to the Cincinnati Reds in exchange for Lee May, Tommy Helms, and Jimmy Stewart, and in essence completed the assemblage of the Big Red Machine.

In 1974 he returned to the Astros to finish up his playing career, then he became a coach with several clubs.

Orlando Mercado
Anaheim Angels (AL) 2003–04; Los Angeles Angels of Anaheim (AL) 2005–
Backup catcher who hit .199 in eight seasons.

Playing for the Seattle Mariners in 1982, Mercado collected his first major league hit in his first major league start, and that was a grand slam off Steve Comer of the Texas Rangers. He belted only six more dingers his entire career, however.

In 1994 Mercado became a minor league player-coach in the Angels' system, then turned to coaching full-time. In 2000 he was promoted to Anaheim as a bullpen catcher, and in 2003 was named bullpen coach.

Fred Merkle
New York Yankees (AL) 1926
Solid first baseman for 16 seasons.

Unfortunately Merkle will always be remembered for the play known as "Merkle's Boner." In September of 1908 during a crucial pennant race with the New York Giants, he was on first base in the bottom of the ninth inning with two outs in a tie game against the Chicago Cubs. Harry McCormick was on third. When hitter Al Bridwell singled, McCormick appeared to score the winning run, and Merkle, like many players of his day, headed for the clubhouse rather than proceeding to second base. Cubs' second baseman Johnny Evers called for the ball and tagged second, technically forcing Merkle and nullifying the run. Fans were swarming the field so play could not continue, and the Giants, believing they had won, were leaving anyway. The game eventually had to be replayed, and the Giants lost, thereby losing the National League pennant to the Cubs by one game.

Many and varied accounts describe the action at the end of that game, some claiming that fans swarmed the field so badly that Merkle had no chance of reaching second, others that he did indeed touch second when he realized Evers' ploy. Still others say that Merkle did nothing that other players did not do routinely, and still others that an umpire had assured the Giants that they had won the game. Some say Evers did not use the ball that was supposedly in play, because that ball had been thrown into the stands.

Whatever the facts, Merkle's fine career deserves better than to be linked to that single event. He was but 19 years old at the time, and he went on to fashion a 16-year career resulting in a .273 batting average and a penchant for hitting in the clutch. In 1911 he had six runs batted in in one inning, and in 1912 he hit .309. He played until 1920 and then continued in the International League until 1925, when he appeared in seven games for the Yankees. The following season he became a New York coach and played one more game, going 0-for-2.

Stump Merrill
New York Yankees (AL) 1985, 1987
See Managers section.

Charlie Metro
Chicago Cubs (NL) 1962; Chicago White Sox (AL) 1965; Oakland Athletics (AL) 1982
See Managers section.

Irish Meusel
New York Giants (NL) 1930
Brother of Bob Meusel.

Nicknamed "Irish" by someone who thought he looked the part (although he had no Irish blood in him), Emil Frederick Meusel fashioned a career similar to his brother's. He hit .310 lifetime; Bob hit .309. Both played the outfield, and both spent time playing in New York, though for different teams. In fact, for three straight years the siblings faced off in the World Series, from 1921–23 when Irish was with the Giants and Bob with the Yankees.

In 11 years Meusel hit over .300 six times. In 1923 he hit .297 with 19 home runs and a National League-leading 125 runs batted in, and in 1925 batted .328 with a career-high 21 dingers and 111 RBIs. He topped the 100-RBI mark in four consecutive seasons.

He finished his career in 1927 with the Brooklyn Dodgers, but in 1930 returned to the Giants as a coach.

Benny Meyer
Philadelphia Phillies (NL) 1925–26; Detroit Tigers (AL) 1928–30
Spent 60 years in professional baseball.

Four of those years were as a major league player, and two of those were in the Federal League with the Baltimore Terrapins and Buffalo Blues. With the Terrapins in 1914 he hit .304 with 5 home runs and 40 runs batted in.

Meyer spent the other 56 years as a minor league player, minor and major league coach, minor league manager, and scout. He coached two years for the Phillies (appearing in one game for them in 1925 and going 1-for-1 with a double and scoring a run), and coached three for the Tigers. As a coach he frequently annoyed opposing players with his constant screaming and shouting.

Russ Meyer
New York Yankees (AL) 1992
Pitcher nicknamed "The Mad Monk."

Meyer pitched for 13 years and frequently got into trouble because of his temper. He was renowned for losing his cool with umpires and opposing players, and even with his teammates when they committed errors. He pitched well, going 17–8 in 1949 with the Philadelphia Phillies and 94–73 lifetime. In 1953 he was once suspended for three days and fined $100 when television cameras picked him up using crude gestures and obscene language. In 1955 he broke his collarbone in an on-field collision and never

quite recovered from the injury.

He retired in 1959 and coached the Yankees in 1992. He passed away five years later.

Gene Michael
New York Yankees (AL) 1978, 1984–86
See Managers section.

Clyde Milan
Washington Nationals (AL) 1928–29, 1938–52
See Managers section.

Dave Miley
Cincinnati Reds (NL) 1993–94, 1998
See Managers section.

Bing Miller
Boston Red Sox (AL) 1937; Detroit Tigers (AL) 1938–41; Chicago White Sox (AL) 1942–49; Philadelphia Athletics (AL) 1950–53
Outfielder and .311 lifetime hitter.

In 16 seasons Miller hit over .300 nine times, peaking at .342 in 1924. He played most of his career with the A's, and in his final seasons turned mainly to pinch-hitting. He led the American League in pinch-hits in 1934 with the A's and in 1935 with the Red Sox, with whom he finished his career in 1936. He then became a coach for several clubs.

He died in 1966 from injuries sustained in an automobile accident.

Bob Miller
Toronto Blue Jays (AL) 1977–79; San Francisco Giants (NL) 1985
One of two Bob Millers on the 1962 New York Mets.

To further confuse matters, both were pitchers and both were in their fifth major league seasons. They were also roommates on the road. The other, however, Robert Gerald Miller, was a left-hander and was at the end of his career. This one, Robert Lane Miller, was a right-hander and would pitch for 12 more seasons.

Used mainly in relief, this Bob Miller led the National League in 1964 with 74 games pitched while playing for the Los Angeles Dodgers. He lasted until 1974, fashioning a 69–81 record with a 3.37 earned run average. He later coached the Blue Jays and the Giants.

Dyar Miller
Chicago White Sox (AL) 1987–88
Relief pitcher from Batesville, Indiana.

Dyar Miller began his professional career as a catcher but soon switched to pitching. In 1970 he pitched a shortened, seven-inning no-hitter while playing in the Texas

League. He debuted with the Baltimore Orioles in 1975 and would play seven major league seasons, starting only one of 251 games. He went 23–17 with a 3.23 earned run average.

After coaching for the White Sox from 1987–88 he was a player-coach for the Orlando Juice of the Senior Professional Baseball Association.

Otto Miller
Brooklyn Robins (NL) 1926–31; Brooklyn Dodgers (NL) 1932–36
Excellent defensive catcher.

Miller spent his entire major league career, both as a catcher and a coach, with the Brooklyn club, and saw them use five names—Superbas, Trolley Dodgers, Dodgers, Infants (an alternate name for the early Dodgers), and Robins. A .245 hitter, he was prized for his defense and his ability to handle pitchers. He was the catcher when Ebbets Field opened in 1913, and he attended the day it closed. In 1915 he was struck in the left eye during batting practice by a line drive hit by teammate Jack Coombs. The eye would trouble him throughout his career, but medical treatment did save his sight. In 1920 he led National League catchers in fielding average, and in a stunt he once caught a ball dropped from an airplane traveling 450 feet above the ground around 80 miles per hour. In 1920 he was also the third out of Bill Wambsganss' triple play, the only unassisted triple killing in World Series history.

Otto played semipro ball after leaving the majors, and in 1926 he returned to the big leagues as a coach. After 11 years in that position he worked as a stock broker and eventually managed a bar and grill.

In 1962 he was admitted to a hospital for cataract treatment on his left eye. He then either jumped or fell from a fourth-floor window and died instantly. He was 72 years of age.

Ray Miller
Baltimore Orioles (AL) 1978–85, 1997, 2005; Pittsburgh Pirates (NL) 1987–96
See Managers section.

Bob Milliken
St. Louis Cardinals (NL) 1965–70, 1976
Pitcher who spent two years with the Brooklyn Dodgers.

Milliken had pitched well in the minors and lost a couple of years to military service and another to arm problems. He reached the Dodgers in 1953 as a reliever and occasional starter, and in his two seasons he went 13–6 with a 3.59 earned run average. His arm problems then resurfaced and he would not pitch in the majors again, although he did coach several years with the Cardinals.

Art Mills
Detroit Tigers (AL) 1944–48
Pitched 19 games in two seasons for the Boston Braves.

Those seasons were 1927 and 1928, and Mills went 0–1 with a 5.36 earned run average. He started only one game, and struck out just 7 batters in 45$\frac{1}{3}$ innings. He later spent five years as a Tigers' coach.

Brad Mills
Philadelphia Phillies (NL) 1997–2000; Montreal Expos (NL) 2003; Boston Red Sox (AL) 2004–
Third baseman for the Montreal Expos.

Mills spent parts of four seasons with Montreal alternating between the Expos and the minor leagues. He hit .256 in 106 major league games, but his career was cut short by a knee injury when he was just 29 years of age. In 1983 he gained some fame as Nolan Ryan's 3509th strikeout victim, the one that sent the fireballing hurler past Walter Johnson into first place on the all-time strikeout list.

Mills played until 1986 at the minor league level, then became a minor league skipper. In 1994 his Colorado Springs Sky Sox made the playoffs, and the following year they captured the Pacific Coast League championship. The club would eventually induct Mills into its Hall of Fame and retire his uniform number 9.

Mills later worked as a coach with the Phillies, and in 2001 scouted for the Chicago Cubs. After managing in the Los Angeles Dodgers' system in 2002 he returned to the Expos as a coach for one season. In 2004 he moved to the Red Sox under his friend Terry Francona, who had been his teammate and roommate at the University of Arizona and for whom he had also coached with the Phillies.

Buster Mills
Cleveland Indians (AL) 1946; Chicago White Sox (AL) 1947–50; Cincinnati Redlegs (NL) 1953; Boston Red Sox (AL) 1954
See Managers section.

Minnie Minoso
Chicago White Sox (AL) 1976–78, 1980
Speedy outfielder who played 17 major league seasons.

Minoso had three different stints with the White Sox in a long and storied playing career. A .298 lifetime hitter, he topped the .300 mark on eight occasions and was a nine-time All-Star. He led the American League three times in stolen bases, once in doubles, three times in triples, and once in hits. He had previously played in the Negro Leagues and was the first black player on the White Sox. He won three Gold Gloves and led his league in being hit by pitches 10 times.

Minoso also played in Mexico, but perhaps his biggest

claim to fame was becoming one of only two major leaguers to play in five different decades (the other was Nick Altrock) and becoming the only professional to play in seven different decades. Having concluded his big league career with Chicago in 1964 (but then playing in the minor leagues and in Mexico until he was 50), he eventually returned to the club as a coach, and in 1976 was activated for three games. Having debuted in 1949, that gave him four decades. In 1980, once again a coach with the club, he was activated for two more games and gained his fifth and last big league decade. In 1993, however, he appeared in a game for the St. Paul Saints of the Northern League at the age of 70, giving him six decades. In 2003 the Saints once again activated him and he batted in the first inning and drew a walk. Now 80 years of age, he became professional baseball's oldest player (a record since broken) and only seven-decade performer.

The White Sox retired Minnie's number 9 in 1983.

Clarence Mitchell
New York Giants (NL) 1932–33
Pitcher and position player from Nebraska.

Mitchell pitched for 18 seasons and went 125–139. He was one of the spitballers who was allowed to continue throwing the pitch after it was outlawed, and was the last one to legally use it in the National League. He was also a good position player and was sometimes used in the field and as a pinch-hitter. He was also the one whose line drive to Bill Wambsganss started the only unassisted triple play in World Series history in 1920.

Mitchell finished his career with the Giants and coached for them for two seasons.

George Mitterwald
Oakland Athletics (AL) 1979–82; New York Yankees (AL) 1988
Catcher for the Minnesota Twins and Chicago Cubs.

Mitterwald played 11 seasons and hit .236. He was used mainly as a backup, but did play as a regular for several years and hit 15 home runs in 1970 and another 16 in 1973. In a game in 1974 he hit three homers against the Pittsburgh Pirates. He played until 1977 and later coached the A's and Yankees.

Johnny Mize
Kansas City Athletics (AL) 1961
Hall of Fame first baseman nicknamed "The Big Cat."

Having garnered that nickname because of his agility and reflexes, Mize was a 10-time All-Star despite losing three years to Navy service during World War II. A .312 lifetime hitter, he topped the .300 mark nine times and won the batting title in 1939 with a .349 average. He also led the National League four times in home runs, three times in runs batted in, once in doubles, once in triples, and once in runs scored. He hit 359 roundtrippers lifetime and set a record by collecting three home runs in a game six separate times. In 1947 he became the only player in major league history to hit at least 50 home runs (he hit 51) while striking out fewer than 50 times (he whiffed on only 42 occasions). From 1951–53 he led the American League in pinch-hits, and in '52 was named the Most Valuable Player of the World Series when he batted .400 with three home runs.

Mize spent his career with the St. Louis Cardinals, New York Giants, and New York Yankees. In 1961 he coached for the A's, having spent time in the minor leagues in Kansas City. In 1981 he was inducted into the Hall of Fame by the Veterans Committee.

John Mizerock
Kansas City Royals (AL) 2002–04
See Managers section.

Joe Moeller
Cleveland Indians (AL) 1978
Injury-prone pitcher for the Los Angeles Dodgers.

Moeller spent eight seasons in Los Angeles and fashioned a 26–36 record, having started 74 of 166 games. His earned run average was 4.01, and he never won more than seven games in a season. He played until 1971 and later coached a single season for the Indians.

Paul Molitor
Minnesota Twins (AL) 2000–01; Seattle Mariners (AL) 2004
Hall of Fame infielder and designated hitter.

A native of St. Paul, Minnesota, Molitor spent most of his career with the Milwaukee Brewers but ended it with the Twins. In between he spent a couple of years with the Toronto Blue Jays. Along the way he hit .306, batting over .300 twelve times in a 21-year career. A seven-time All-Star, he led the American League three times in hits, once in doubles, once in triples, and three times in runs scored. In the first game of the 1982 World Series he collected five hits for the Brewers, and in 1987 he put together a 39-game hitting streak. In 1993 he was named the Most Valuable Player of the World Series when he hit .500 with two home runs and eight runs batted in for the Blue Jays. He collected 3319 hits lifetime.

Molitor's playing career ended in 1998, and the following year the Brewers retired his number 4. He then became a coach with the Twins and later coached the Mariners. In 2004 he was inducted into the Hall of Fame.

Bill Monbouquette
New York Mets (NL) 1982–83; New York Yankees (AL) 1985–86
Four-time All-Star pitcher.

Spending most of an 11-year career with the Boston Red Sox, Monbouquette won 14, 14, and 15 games each year from 1960–62, respectively, then went 20–10 in 1963. In 1961 he struck out 17 Washington Senators in a game, and in 1962 threw a no-hitter against the Chicago White Sox. He posted a 3.68 lifetime earned run average.

Bill coached both the Mets and the Yankees following his playing days, and also coached many years in the minor leagues.

Alex Monchak
Chicago White Sox (AL) 1971–75; Oakland Athletics (AL) 1976; Pittsburgh Pirates (NL) 1977–84; Atlanta Braves (NL) 1986–88
Played 19 major league games in 1940.

Those games were with the Philadelphia Phillies, and Monchak hit only .143, going 2-for-14 and striking out six times. He later worked as a minor league manager and eventually coached several teams in the major leagues.

Rich Monteleone
New York Yankees (AL) 2003–04
Ten-year relief pitcher, mostly for the Yankees.

Monteleone pitched 210 major league games and did not start a single one of them. He posted a 24–17 lifetime record with a 3.87 earned run average. Used almost exclusively as a setup man, he never recorded a save.

He pitched until 1996 and then became a coach in the Yankees' minor league system. In 2001 he was the club's roving pitching coordinator, and in 2003 was promoted to New York as bullpen coach. He served in that role through 2004, then continued with the major league club as a special pitching instructor.

Wally Moon
San Diego Padres (NL) 1969
National League Rookie of the Year in 1954.

Moon debuted for the St. Louis Cardinals that year and hit .304 with 12 home runs and 76 runs batted in. That marked the first of three times he would top the .300 mark in a 12-year career en route to a .289 lifetime average. In 1957 he hit a career-high 24 home runs and was named a National League All-Star, an honor he would receive again in 1959 (in both games that were held that season). In '57 he put together a 24-game hitting streak, and in 1959 tied for the NL lead with 11 triples. In 1960 he won a Gold Glove for his excellent defense.

After retiring he spent one year as a major league coach, in 1969 with the expansion Padres.

Jackie Moore
Milwaukee Brewers (AL) 1970–72; Texas Rangers (AL) 1973–76, 1980, 1993–94; Toronto Blue Jays (AL) 1977–79; Oakland Athletics (AL) 1981–84; Montreal Expos (NL) 1987–89; Cincinnati Reds (NL) 1990–92; Colorado Rockies (NL) 1996–98
See Managers section.

Terry Moore
St. Louis Cardinals (NL) 1949–52, 1956–58
See Managers section.

Jerry Morales
Montreal Expos (NL) 2002–04; Washington Nationals (NL) 2007–
Fifteen-year outfielder from Puerto Rico.

Morales was playing in the New York Mets' minor league system when he was taken by the San Diego Padres in the expansion draft, and he made his big league debut with San Diego in 1969. A somewhat weak hitter at the major league level at first, he gradually improved and in 1977 enjoyed his best season at the plate, batting .290 with 11 home runs and 69 runs batted in with the Chicago Cubs and being named a National League All-Star. He had displayed power before, hitting 16 homers the previous season, 12 the year before that, and 15 the year prior to that.

He eventually coached for three years with the Expos, and then retired in order to take care of his wife, Maria, who was suffering from lupus. He returned to the organization as a major league coach in 2007, after the team had moved to Washington and become the Nationals, when his wife had recovered.

Jose Morales
San Francisco Giants (NL) 1986–88; Cleveland Indians (AL) 1990–93; Florida Marlins (NL) 1995–96
First baseman and designated hitter from the Virgin Islands.

Morales began his professional career as a catcher but led his respective league four times in errors before being converted to a first baseman. In 12 major league seasons he was used largely as a pinch-hitter, and in 1976 with the Montreal Expos he set major league records with 25 pinch-hits and 78 pinch-hit at-bats. He led the league three times in both categories.

He played until 1984 and then became a coach with several clubs.

Rich Morales
Atlanta Braves (NL) 1987
Excellent-fielding shortstop with a very weak bat.

Morales spent eight years in the major leagues, relying entirely on his glove. His highest season batting average was .243; his second-highest was .215. Lifetime he batted a mere .195.

After his playing career he worked as a minor league manager in the Chicago Cubs' and Oakland Athletics' organizations, then became a scout for the Chicago White Sox. He served as a Braves' coach for one season.

Joe Morgan
Pittsburgh Pirates (NL) 1972; Boston Red Sox (AL) 1985–88
See Managers section.

Tom Morgan
California Angels (AL) 1972–74, 1981–83; San Diego Padres (NL) 1975; New York Yankees (AL) 1979
Pitcher nicknamed "Plowboy."

Receiving that moniker because of his rather stooped gait, Morgan labored for 12 years as a major league pitcher, mostly in relief. He fashioned a 67–47 career record with a 3.61 earned run average. In 1954 he was 11–5 for the Yankees, and in 1961 went 8–2 for the expansion Los Angeles Angels.

After his playing career he worked as a scout, minor league manager, and major league coach for several organizations.

Vern Morgan
Minnesota Twins (AL) 1969–75
Third baseman who played 31 games in the major leagues.

In 1954 and 1955 Morgan appeared in those games for the Chicago Cubs, with whom he hit .225. A longtime minor leaguer, he played in several different organizations. He was a coach for the Twins from 1969–75, and died in Minneapolis in November of 1975.

Lloyd Moseby
Toronto Blue Jays (AL) 1998–99
All-Star outfielder who played a dozen seasons.

Moseby was a solid player with good power. He hit 169 home runs, contributing 21 of them in his All-Star season of 1986 and 26 more in 1987, when he also drove in 96 runs. Fleet of foot, he tied with teammate Dave Collins for the American League lead in 1984 with 15 triples, and stole 280 bases in his career. He topped the 20-stolen-base mark seven times, twice reaching 39.

Moseby played 10 years for the Blue Jays and 2 for Detroit Tigers, then spent 2 years in Japan with the Yomiuri Giants. He later returned to Toronto as a coach.

John Moses
Seattle Mariners (AL) 2000–03; Cincinnati Reds (NL) 2005
Backup outfielder with good defense.

A .254 lifetime hitter, Moses was utilized primarily for his glovework. He lasted 11 years in the major leagues, and eventually became a coach for the Mariners. In 2005 he was hired by the Reds as a minor league outfield and base-running coordinator, but during the season he joined the big club as a coach when manager Dave Miley was fired and replaced by Jerry Narron. Moses was to have been part of the 2006 coaching staff as well, but while he was on his way to the airport intending to leave for spring training he decided he no longer wanted to be away from his family for most of the year, so he turned around and went home and called the Reds with the announcement of his resignation.

Wally Moses
Philadelphia Athletics (AL) 1952–54; Philadelphia Phillies (NL) 1955–58; Cincinnati Reds (NL) 1959–60; New York Yankees (AL) 1961–62, 1966; Detroit Tigers (AL) 1967–70
All-Star outfielder who hit .291 lifetime.

In a 17-year playing career Moses hit over .300 seven times, and those averages just happened to occur during his first seven major league seasons. In 1943 he tied for the American League lead with 12 triples, and in 1945 led with 35 doubles and 329 putouts. He stole a career-high 56 bases in 1943, his second-highest total being 21 the following year. He was named to two All-Star teams.

Following his playing career he worked as a coach for many teams.

Les Moss
Chicago White Sox (AL) 1967–68, 1970; Chicago Cubs (NL) 1981; Houston Astros (NL) 1982–89
See Managers section.

Manny Mota
Los Angeles Dodgers (NL) 1980–
One of baseball's greatest pinch-hitters.

Dominican-born Manny Mota played 20 major league seasons and hit .304 lifetime. He topped the .300 mark 11 times and was named a National League All-Star in 1973 with the Dodgers. He had little power and was not strong defensively, but coming off the bench there were few, if any, better. He had at least 10 pinch-hits for six years in a row, and when he retired he had a .297 pinch-hitting average and was the career leader with 150 pinch-hits, a mark since surpassed by Lenny Harris.

While still playing for Los Angeles he also spent nine years as a player-manager in the Dominican Winter

League. His Licey Tigers won the league championship in 1971, 1983, and 1984, and he himself was named Caribbean Series Most Valuable Player in 1971. In 1980 he became a longtime coach with the Dodgers, and he was activated as a player for seven games in 1980 and for one more in 1982.

Curt Motton
Baltimore Orioles (AL) 1989–91
Backup outfielder with decent power.

Motton spent eight years as a reserve, never playing more than 83 games in a season. His average, in fact, was 40 per year. He did hit 25 home runs, however, peaking in 1968 with 8 in 217 at-bats. He both started and ended his career with the Orioles, playing for a couple of other teams in between, and he eventually returned to Baltimore in a coaching role.

Mo Mozzali
St. Louis Cardinals (NL) 1977–78
Longtime minor leaguer with a good bat.

Mozzali was small in stature and usually hit for a good average. He did not strike out often. A first baseman who weighed only 160 pounds, he was particularly tough against left-handers. He failed to reach the major leagues as a player, but did so as a Cardinals' coach and also worked as a scout. He died in 1987.

Ray Mueller
New York Giants (NL) 1956; Chicago Cubs (NL) 1957
Most Valuable Player of the Pacific Coast League in 1942.

A catcher, Mueller won that award with the Sacramento Solons although he had already played six seasons in the major leagues as a backup. His first major league hit, which came in 1935, was a home run. In 1943 he joined the Cincinnati Reds as their regular backstop, and he set a National League record by catching 233 straight games for them from July 31, 1943, through May 6, 1946, although he missed the entire 1945 season due to military service. Mueller was named an NL All-Star in 1944.

After his playing career ended he coached one year for the Giants and one for the Cubs.

Billy Muffett
St. Louis Cardinals (NL) 1967–70; California Angels (AL) 1974–77; Detroit Tigers (AL) 1985–94
Pitcher who spent 14 years in the minor leagues and 6 in the majors.

With the Shreveport Sports of the AA Texas League in 1955, Muffett tossed a no-hitter against the San Antonio Missions. He reached the Cardinals in 1957 and fashioned a 16–23 record with them and two other clubs over the

next six years, pitching mostly in relief. His lifetime earned run average was 4.33.

His big league career ended in 1962 and he went into coaching.

Hugh Mulcahy
Chicago White Sox (AL) 1970
First major leaguer to be drafted into the Army during World War II.

Mulcahy had already pitched from 1935–40 with the Philadelphia Phillies, leading the National League with 56 games pitched in 1937. In 1940 he was an NL All-Star but went 13–22 on the season, a record that can be attributed to the fact that the last-place Phillies had very little punch in their lineup and won only 50 games all season.

In the military Mulcahy served in many locations, including New Guinea and the Philippines, and he became ill at one point and never completely recovered. When he returned to baseball in 1945 he was no longer the same pitcher and won only three more games over the next three years while losing seven. He went back to the minor leagues for a short time and later became a coach, returning to the majors in that role with the White Sox in 1970.

Jack Mull
San Francisco Giants (NL) 1985
Longtime minor league coach and manager.

A minor league catcher for several years, Mull was reputed to be good defensively but very poor with a bat. He began playing in 1969, and in 1974 was offered a managing position, which he accepted. The Giants offered him a playing contract the following year, however, so he went back to catching for two years before retiring from the playing field for good.

As a minor league skipper Mull's teams reached the postseason or won the league championship eight times. He won three Manager of the Year Awards: in 1980 with the Fresno Giants of the California League (he was co-Manager of the Year in that instance); in 1993 with the Clinton Giants of the Midwest League; and in 1996 with the Kinston Indians of the Carolina League. His 1974 Gulf Coast Cubs took the Gulf Coast League championship, and his 1991 Clinton Giants won the Midwest League title.

Mull spent one year coaching the San Francisco Giants, then returned to the minors and continued as a manager. Beginning in 2000 he gave up managing and turned instead to coaching due to health reasons.

Greg Mulleavy
Brooklyn Dodgers (NL) 1957; Los Angeles Dodgers (NL) 1958–60, 1962–64
Longtime minor leaguer from Detroit.

After leading the Piedmont League with 15 triples in 1928, Mulleavy played 79 major league games from 1930–33 with the Chicago White Sox and Boston Red Sox. He then led the International League with 206 hits in 1933 and with 38 doubles and 131 runs scored in 1934.

He played many years for the Buffalo Bisons before becoming a minor league player-manager and then full-time manager. From 1950–54 he worked as a Dodgers' scout, then went back to managing and joined the Dodgers' coaching staff in 1957. In 1961 he returned to scouting, but in 1962 went back to Los Angeles as a coach. Following the 1964 season he once again turned to scouting, and continued in that role until his death in 1980.

Pat Mullin
Detroit Tigers (AL) 1963–66; Cleveland Indians (AL) 1967; Montreal Expos (NL) 1979–81
Two-time All-Star outfielder.

In 10 seasons Mullin hit .271. He debuted in 1940, but lost the 1942–45 seasons to military service. In 1947 he clouted 15 home runs, and slugged 23 the following year. Toward the end of his career he was used largely as a pinch-hitter. After his playing days he coached the Tigers, Indians, and Expos.

Danny Murphy
Philadelphia Athletics (AL) 1921–24; Philadelphia Phillies (NL) 1927
Second baseman who became an outfielder.

Murphy played about half his career at each position. After playing 27 games for the New York Giants in 1900 and 1901, he joined the A's in 1902. In his first game with his new club in July, he arrived late at the field, not showing up until the second inning. Despite the fact that he missed batting practice he proceeded to go 6-for-6, clubbing a grand slam and handling 12 errorless chances in the infield.

Murphy batted .289 lifetime and broke the .300 mark seven times. In a 1910 contest he hit for the cycle. He played for the A's through 1913, then deserted for the Federal League's Brooklyn Brookfeds, who became the Tip-Tops during the 1914 season. He later returned to the A's as a coach, and also coached one season for Philadelphia's other team, the Phillies.

Dwayne Murphy
Arizona Diamondbacks (NL) 1998–2003
Outfielder with good power.

Murphy played 12 seasons and hit 166 home runs, three times bashing at least 20. In 1984 with the Oakland Athletics he hit a career-high 33 while driving in 88 runs. He was excellent defensively as well, earning a Gold Glove every year from 1980 through 1985. Multiple injuries eventually took their toll on him, but after his playing days he became a coach with the Diamondbacks for six years.

One of Murphy's favorite hobbies is playing the bass guitar.

Johnny Murphy
New York Mets (NL) 1967
Excellent relief pitcher for the New York Yankees.

Originally a starter, Murphy went 14–10 in 1934 but was soon moved to the bullpen. He continued to excel there, posting a then-record 12 relief wins in 1937 (and winning 13 games total) and 12 more in 1943. He led the American League in saves four times.

Murphy finished his career in 1947 with the Boston Red Sox, and later scouted for Boston. In 1967 he was working in the Mets' front office when manager Wes Westrum resigned, and when the Mets moved coach Salty Parker into an interim role as skipper, Murphy filled the resulting coaching void. He served as the Mets' general manager in 1968 and 1969, and died of a heart attack in January of 1970, not long after the "Miracle Mets" had claimed the 1969 World Championship.

Eddie Murray
Baltimore Orioles (AL) 1998–2001; Cleveland Indians (AL) 2002–05; Los Angeles Dodgers (NL) 2006–
Hall of Fame first baseman and designated hitter.

The American League's Rookie of the Year in 1977 when he clubbed 27 home runs with 88 runs batted in for the Orioles, Murray would not hit fewer than 20 home runs in a season until 1986, when he managed "only" 17. In only one of 21 seasons did he hit fewer than 16, and that was his final year of 1997 when he hit just 3 in 55 games. An eight-time All-Star, Murray led the league once in RBIs, once in walks, and once in on-base percentage, and tied for the lead once in homers. He amassed 3255 lifetime hits and 504 home runs, becoming only the third major leaguer in history (after Hank Aaron and Willie Mays) to join the 3000/500 club. (Rafael Palmeiro later became the fourth.) He won three Gold Gloves and retired as the all-time leader in RBIs among switch-hitters.

In 1998 Murray became a coach with the Orioles, and the club retired his number 33 that same year. In 2002 he moved to the Indians, and in 2006 to the Dodgers. He was inducted into the Hall of Fame in 2003.

Danny Murtaugh
Pittsburgh Pirates (NL) 1956–57
See Managers section.

Tony Muser
Milwaukee Brewers (AL) 1985–89; Chicago Cubs (NL) 1993–97; San Diego Padres (NL) 2003–06
See Managers section.

George Myatt
Washington Nationals (AL) 1950–54; Chicago White Sox (AL) 1955–56; Chicago Cubs (NL) 1957–59; Milwaukee Braves (NL) 1960–61; Detroit Tigers (AL) 1962–63; Philadelphia Phillies (NL) 1964–72
See Managers section.

Dave Myers
Seattle Mariners (AL) 2000–04
Eight-year minor league infielder.

Myers was drafted by the Mariners and spent many years with the organization. He was offered a coaching position while a player, and he accepted it because his wife was pregnant and he needed the medical insurance. He then began a long career as a minor league manager, minor league coach, and major league coach. In 1992 his Bellingham Mariners captured the Northwest League championship.

Myers reached the majors on the coaching staffs of Lou Piniella and Bob Melvin, then was returned to the minors as a coach with and later manager of a Mariners' Class A team, the Everett AquaSox.

Ed Napoleon
Cleveland Indians (AL) 1983–85; Kansas City Royals (AL) 1987–88; Houston Astros (NL) 1989–90; New York Yankees (AL) 1992–93; Texas Rangers (AL) 1995–2000
Most Valuable Player of the 1959 Caribbean Series.

After a 15-year playing career in the minor leagues, Napoleon began a career as a minor and major league coach. After spending several seasons in that role at the big league level, he went into retirement from 2001–02. He returned in 2003, however, and became an instructor at the major league level for the Cincinnati Reds, focusing primarily on outfield defense and bunting.

Hal Naragon
Minnesota Twins (AL) 1963–66; Detroit Tigers (AL) 1967–69
Catcher from Zanesville, Ohio.

Naragon played only as a backup but spent 10 years in the major leagues. He hit .266 with 6 home runs and 87 runs batted in, spending his entire career with the Cleveland Indians and the Washington Senators/Minnesota Twins. He later coached for the Twins and the Tigers.

Jerry Narron
Baltimore Orioles (AL) 1993–94; Texas Rangers (AL) 1995– 2001; Boston Red Sox (AL) 2003; Cincinnati Reds (NL) 2004–05
See Managers section.

Sam Narron
Pittsburgh Pirates (NL) 1952–64
Uncle of Jerry Narron.

Like his nephew, Sam was a catcher, but he played only 24 major league games. All were with the St. Louis Cardinals. In 4 games in 1935 he batted .429, in 10 games in 1942 he hit .400, and in 10 more in 1943 he averaged .091. He eventually joined the Pirates for many years as a coach.

Bob Natal
Montreal Expos (NL) 2002–04; Washington Nationals (NL) 2005
Catcher from Long Beach, California.

A backup for six seasons, Natal hit a mere .197 in 120 major league games. His first five games he played with the Expos, the rest with the Florida Marlins. Natal had to endure constant wisecracks about his name, especially when he would bat in the middle of the lineup and commentators would refer to those hitting before him as "pre-natal" and those batting after him as "postnatal."

He eventually returned to the Expos as their bullpen coach, and accompanied the team when it moved to Washington.

Greasy Neale
St. Louis Cardinals (NL) 1929
Early two-sport star and member of the Pro Football Hall of Fame.

As a baseball player Neale was an outfielder for eight big league seasons. He hit .294 in 1917 for the Cincinnati Reds and in the 1919 World Series led the club with 10 hits. In football he was an end for the Canton Bulldogs prior to World War I and coached Washington and Jefferson College while he was still playing for the Reds. In 1922 he coached that team to the Rose Bowl. His baseball career ended in 1924, but five years later he would coach one season for the Cardinals. From 1941–50 he was the head coach of the Philadelphia Eagles, and he led that club to the National Football League championship in 1948 with a 6–0 defeat of the Chicago Cardinals and again in 1949 with a 14–0 win over the Los Angeles Rams. It was the only time in NFL history that a team has won consecutive titles with back-to-back shutouts.

Neale remains the only man to play in a World Series, coach a team in the Rose Bowl, and win an NFL championship.

Dave Nelson

Chicago White Sox (AL) 1981–84; Cleveland Indians (AL) 1992–97; Milwaukee Brewers (NL) 2003–06

Second baseman and third baseman with several teams.

In a 10-year career Nelson batted .244, his strongest season coming in 1973 with the Texas Rangers when he hit .286 with 7 home runs, 48 runs batted in, and 43 stolen bases and was named to the American League All-Star team. Nelson stole 187 bases in his career, peaking with 51 in 1972. In the minors he had led his respective league three times in that category.

Following his retirement Nelson went into coaching with Texas Christian University, then joined the White Sox. In 1984 with Chicago he proposed to his girlfriend via the Diamond Vision video screen between the fifth and sixth innings of a game at Comiskey Park. He took his position in the first base coaching box, the screen popped the question for him, and he then proceeded to the first base box seats and presented his girlfriend with a ring.

In 1985 he worked as an instructor in the White Sox' minor league system, then moved to the Oakland Athletics' and Montreal Expos' organizations before returning as a big league coach with the Indians and Brewers.

Graig Nettles

New York Yankees (AL) 1991; San Diego Padres (NL) 1995

Six-time All-Star third baseman.

In 22 years Nettles proved himself one of the best defensive players in the game. He won two Gold Gloves and in 1971 set major league records for third basemen with 412 assists and 54 double plays. A consistent power hitter, he hit at least 20 home runs in a season 11 times, leading the American League with 32 in 1976 and crushing 37 the next year. He ended his career with 390 lifetime, an American League record for third basemen. In 1974, however, he broke his bat during a game and six superballs came rolling out of it. As a result he was suspended for 10 days and fined an undisclosed amount.

Nettles retired in 1988 and eventually coached one season for the Yankees and one for the Padres.

Johnny Neun

New York Yankees (AL) 1946

See Managers section.

Al Newman

Minnesota Twins (AL) 2002–05

Light-hitting infielder with good speed.

A switch-hitter, Newman spent most of his career as a backup. He hit only .226 but stole 91 bases in eight seasons, swiping a career-high 25 in 1989. After his playing career he became a minor league coach and manager, then returned to the Twins, with whom he had played five years, as a coach. In 2003 he was away from the team for a time when he suffered a brain hemorrhage. He recovered and coached until 2005, when differences with team management caused him to leave and go into scouting with the Arizona Diamondbacks.

Jeff Newman

Oakland Athletics (AL) 1986; Cleveland Indians (AL) 1992–99; Baltimore Orioles (AL) 2000; Seattle Mariners (AL) 2005

See Managers section.

Gus Niarhos

Kansas City Athletics (AL) 1962–64

Backup catcher from Birmingham, Alabama.

A lifetime .252 hitter, Niarhos batted .324 in 42 games in 1950. He finished his major league career in 1955 and became a minor league manager, and he coached three seasons for the A's. He died in December of 2004 at the age of 84.

Reid Nichols

Texas Rangers (AL) 2001

Backup outfielder and pinch-hitter.

Nichols spent eight years playing for the Boston Red Sox, Chicago White Sox, and Montreal Expos. In 1982 with Boston he hit .302 in 92 games and also clubbed seven home runs.

After his playing career he coached one year for the Rangers and also spent many years in their front office as their director of player development. In 2003 he took on a somewhat similar role with the Milwaukee Brewers.

Bert Niehoff

New York Giants (NL) 1929

Dependable infielder who spent over 50 years in baseball.

In six years as a player Niehoff hit only .240, but in 1916 with the Philadelphia Phillies he led the National League with 42 doubles. His fielding was suspect, for he also led the league twice in errors although he did so once in double plays. His playing career ended in 1918 when he broke his leg during the season.

He became a longtime coach and minor league manager following his retirement, re-emerging in 1929 as a coach with the Giants. He managed 24 seasons in the minors, and also skippered the South Bend Blue Sox of the All-American Girls Professional Baseball League. From 1948–49 he scouted for the New York Yankees, and from 1961–68 for the Los Angeles/California Angels. In 1952 he was the general manager of the Mobile Bears of the Southern Association.

Randy Niemann
New York Mets (NL) 1997–99, 2001–02
Relief pitcher who played for five teams in eight years.

Niemann never spent a full season in the major leagues, and the journeyman compiled a 7–8 record with a 4.64 earned run average. He had suffered an arm injury in 1981, early in his career, and was never able to realize his previous potential. He spent most of 14 seasons in the minor leagues.

In 1989 he played for the St. Lucie Legends in the Senior Professional Baseball Association, and eventually coached several years for the Mets.

Tom Nieto
New York Yankees (AL) 2000–01
Light-hitting but good defensive catcher.

Nieto had a powerful arm behind the plate and a gift for calling games, but his .205 batting average kept him from becoming a regular. He became a minor league coach and manager following his playing career, starting out in 1992 in the Cincinnati Reds' organization. In 1995 he returned to the Yankees' fold, and in 1998 led the Class A Greensboro Bats to the league championship series. He was promoted to New York as a catching coach from 2000–01, then managed a couple more years in the minors. In 2005 he joined the New York Mets' major league club as a catching instructor.

Al Nipper
Boston Red Sox (AL) 1995–96, 2006; Kansas City Royals (AL) 2001–02
Right-handed starting pitcher from San Diego.

Nipper pitched for seven major league seasons and struggled with injuries and illnesses. He went 46–50 lifetime with a 4.52 earned run average. In 1992 he became a pitching coach in the Red Sox' minor league system, spending time in Boston from July of 1995 to April of 1996 before returning to the minors. He served as the Texas Rangers' minor league pitching coordinator from 1998–2000, then joined the Royals as their pitching coach. He then returned to the Red Sox' organization at the minor league level, and was once again elevated to Boston, this time as bullpen coach, in 2006. He temporarily filled in as pitching coach for Dave Wallace when Wallace required hip surgery prior to the start of the season.

Russ Nixon
Cincinnati Reds (NL) 1976–82; Montreal Expos (NL) 1984–85; Atlanta Braves (NL) 1986–87; Seattle Mariners (AL) 1992
See Managers section.

Irv Noren
Oakland Athletics (AL) 1971–74; Chicago Cubs (NL) 1975
Two-time minor league Most Valuable Player.

Noren won those awards in consecutive seasons, garnering the first in 1948 with the Texas League's Fort Worth Cats and the second in 1949 with the Pacific Coast League's Hollywood Stars. He then fashioned an 11-year major league career in which he hit .275, batting over .300 twice, and made the 1954 American League All-Star team with the New York Yankees. An excellent fielder, he once tied a since-broken AL record for outfielders by making 11 putouts in a single game. In a 1955 contest he hit an inside-the-park grand slam.

A two-sport star, Noren also played for the Chicago American Gears of the National Basketball League. In 1971 he became a coach with the A's and later coached the Cubs as well.

Bill Norman
St. Louis Browns (AL) 1952–53
See Managers section.

Nelson Norman
Boston Red Sox (AL) 2001
Light-hitting shortstop from the Dominican Republic.

Norman spent parts of six seasons in the major leagues, hitting .221 lifetime. He garnered 343 at-bats with the 1979 Texas Rangers, but never had more than 34 in a big league season otherwise.

After his playing career he worked in the minor leagues, also coaching one season for the Red Sox. He later served as the Red Sox' minor league field coordinator, and managed a baseball academy in the Dominican Republic for the Minnesota Twins.

He is sometimes erroneously listed as Norman Nelson.

Ron Northey
Pittsburgh Pirates (NL) 1961–63
Outfielder with a powerful arm.

Northey played a dozen seasons in the major leagues and hit .276. He hit over .300 three times, but on all three occasions saw limited playing time. His best season was 1944 with the Philadelphia Phillies, when he batted .288 with career highs of 22 home runs and 104 runs batted in. He also led all National League outfielders with 24 assists.

Toward the end of his career he became an excellent pinch-hitter, leading the American League with 15 such knocks in 1956 and hitting nine career pinch-hit home runs. Three of those were grand slams, and he is tied for the major league record in that category.

After his playing career Northey coached for the Pirates for three seasons. His son Scott played 20 games for the Kansas City Royals in 1969.

Joe Nossek

Milwaukee Brewers (AL) 1973–75; Minnesota Twins (AL) 1976; Cleveland Indians (AL) 1977–81; Kansas City Royals (AL) 1982–83; Chicago White Sox (AL) 1984–86, 1990–2003
Backup outfielder with a light bat.

Nossek was used largely as a pinch-hitter and reserve in six big league seasons spent with four teams. He became a minor league manager following his playing career, and in 1972 was named Midwest League Manager of the Year while piloting the Danville Warriors. The following season he was named a coach with the Brewers and thus began a long and successful big league coaching career.

Ed Nottle

Oakland Athletics (AL) 1983
Spent 45 years in professional baseball.

Nottle never played in the major leagues, but he came very close. He was called up once, but was never inserted into a game. In 1978 he started a minor league managing career in the Athletics' organization, and was promoted to Oakland as a coach in 1983 before returning to the minors. In 1985 he moved to the Boston Red Sox' system, where he worked until 1990. In the winter of 1989 he managed the Winter Haven Super Sox of the Senior Professional Baseball Association.

In 1993 he moved to independent baseball, managing the Sioux City Explorers of the Northern League for eight seasons and guiding them to the league's best record in 1994. He managed the Duluth-Superior Dukes in 2001, and in 2002 joined the Brockton Rox. He accompanied that club when it switched to the Northeast League in 2003 and promptly led the team to the league championship. He retired following the 2005 season. Of his 45 years in baseball, 25 were spent as a skipper.

In 1981 with the Tacoma Tigers Nottle was named both Pacific Coast League Manager of the Year and Minor League Manager of the Year. In 1987 with the Pawtucket Red Sox he was named the International League Manager of the Year.

Johnny Oates

Chicago Cubs (NL) 1984–87; Baltimore Orioles (AL) 1989–91
See Managers section.

Eddie O'Brien

Seattle Pilots (AL) 1969
Shortstop who gave new meaning to the terms "double play" and "twin killing."

On May 10, 1953, Eddie and his identical twin brother, Johnny, became the first twins to play in a major league game for the same team. Johnny was a second baseman, and for several years with the Pittsburgh Pirates the two became the club's double play tandem. They both served in the military in 1954, then returned to Pittsburgh. Both were rather light hitters, however; Johnny hit .250 and Eddie a mere .236. Eddie was even used as a pitcher on several occasions.

The two enjoyed confusing people as to which of them was which. Eddie retired in 1958, Johnny a year later. Eddie worked as athletic director at Seattle University from 1958–68, then coached the Pilots in 1969. He later became an energy consultant in Alaska.

Frank Oceak

Pittsburgh Pirates (NL) 1958–64, 1970–72; Cincinnati Reds (NL) 1965
Minor league second baseman who spent 40 years in organized baseball.

Eleven of those years were as a major league coach. Oceak first played in the minor league system of the New York Yankees, however, and eventually became a minor league manager, starting out in that role as a player-manager who not only played the infield but also pitched. He retired from the game in 1972, having coached for the Pirates during their 1960 and 1971 World Championships.

Oceak died in 1983 at the age of 70.

Danny O'Connell

Washington Senators (AL) 1963–64
Infielder and Korean War veteran.

O'Connell debuted with the Pittsburgh Pirates in 1950 and then spent 1951–52 in the Army. He returned to the major leagues and played nine more seasons, fashioning a .260 lifetime average. He was known for his hustle, and in 1956 tied a major league record by hitting three triples in a game. He finished his career with the Senators in 1962 and then stayed with them as a coach for two seasons.

O'Connell was killed in an automobile accident in 1969.

Lefty O'Doul

San Francisco Giants (NL) 1958
Solid pitcher who became an outstanding outfielder.

O'Doul, who was not of Irish but of French descent, pitched only 34 major league games from 1919 to 1923. He pitched many more in the Pacific Coast League and had much greater success, going 25–9 for the San Francisco Seals in 1921. A sore arm had already begun to plague him, and he switched to the outfield and became extremely dominant there. Returning to the major leagues in 1928 at that position with the New York Giants, he would play until 1934 and fashion a .349 lifetime average. In 1929 with the Philadelphia Phillies he won the National League batting title with a .398 batting average, and also led the league with an NL-record 254 hits and a .465 on-base percentage. He also walloped 32 home runs and drove in 122.

O'Doul hit 22 homers the next season and 21 in 1932, when he won a second batting crown with a .368 average while playing for the Brooklyn Dodgers. In 1933 he was named an NL All-Star.

From 1935–51 he served as player-manager of the Seals, even pitching on some occasions. He made yearly visits to Japan as a baseball ambassador, and eventually coached one year for the Giants. He retired as the winningest manager in PCL history.

Ron Oester
Cincinnati Reds (NL) 1993, 1997–2001
Dependable second baseman for the Reds.

Oester spent his entire 13-year playing career with Cincinnati, mostly as their starting keystone sacker. Originally a shortstop, he was moved when he was unable to crack the lineup because of the presence of Dave Concepcion. He was a solid fielder and showed occasional pop in his bat, playing as one of the few major leaguers who eschewed batting gloves. In 1987 he tore his left anterior cruciate ligament in a collision with the New York Mets' Mookie Wilson, and he spent about a year recovering.

After his playing career he worked in the Reds' minor league system, and coached for the big club in 1993. He resigned in protest when manager Tony Perez was fired, then he worked in the Detroit Tigers' system before returning to the Reds in 1997, once again at the big league level. When skipper Jack McKeon was fired following the 2000 season Oester was offered the job by general manager Jim Bowden, but he balked at the Reds' low salary offer and requested time to think it over. Shortly thereafter the Reds announced that they had hired Bob Boone as manager without notifying Oester, and the former infielder flew into a rage and had some extremely unkind words for Bowden. He remained with Cincinnati as a coach for one more season, however, and then worked as an instructor in the Philadelphia Phillies' organization.

He returned to the Reds' fold at the minor league level after two years, but only because, by that time, Bowden was gone.

Ben Oglivie
San Diego Padres (NL) 2000
Panama native who played for three major league clubs.

An outfielder by trade, Oglivie spent his career with the Boston Red Sox, Detroit Tigers, and Milwaukee Brewers. A slow-to-develop power hitter, he played 16 seasons and walloped 235 home runs. He was named to three All-Star teams, and had his best season in 1980 with the Brewers, when he hit .304 with a career-high 41 home runs (tying him for the American League lead with Reggie Jackson) and 118 runs batted in. He hit over .300 on one other occasion and cracked over 20 home runs four times. Following the 1986 season he left to play in Japan, and attempted a comeback with the Brewers in 1989 but did not make the major league club.

He eventually coached one season for the Padres.

Len Okrie
Boston Red Sox (AL) 1961–62, 1965–66; Detroit Tigers (AL) 1970
Catcher who played 42 major league games.

Okrie spread those games out over four seasons and batted a mere .218. He then became a manager in the Red Sox' minor league system, where his 1954 Bluefield Blue-Grays posted the best record in the Appalachian League and captured the championship. He had two stints as a Red Sox' coach while continuing to manage, then he moved to the Tigers' organization in 1967. He was promoted to Detroit as a coach in 1970, then returned to the minors as a skipper once again. In all he managed 15 minor league seasons.

Bob Oldis
Philadelphia Phillies (NL) 1964–66; Minnesota Twins (AL) 1968; Montreal Expos (NL) 1969
Catcher who played 135 major league games between 1953 and 1963.

Oldis hit .237 for the Washington Nationals, Pittsburgh Pirates, and Philadelphia Phillies, and managed only one home run in limited playing time. He finished his career in Philadelphia and immediately became a coach there, then later coached the Twins and the expansion Expos. He then continued to work for the Expos as a scout.

Charley O'Leary
St. Louis Cardinals (NL) 1913–17; New York Yankees (AL) 1921–30; Chicago Cubs (NL) 1931–33; St. Louis Browns (AL) 1934–37
Last active major leaguer to have played in the first decade of the 1900s.

A Chicago native, O'Leary was well-liked and teamed with Germany Schaefer on a vaudeville comedy act during the offseason. He was not a strong hitter, averaging only .226 for his career, but he played all over the infield. He coached several clubs when his playing days were over, but in 1934 as a coach with the Browns he asked for a chance to improve upon his .225 lifetime batting average. In September, at 51 years of age, he was activated and sent to the plate as a pinch-hitter in a game, and he promptly singled and scored a run, in the process becoming the oldest player to do so in the major leagues. The hit raised his lifetime batting average by a mere percentage point, however.

Tony Oliva
Minnesota Twins (AL) 1976–78, 1985–91
Minor league batting champion from Cuba.

Oliva's real name was Pedro, but he used his brother Tony's passport to get into the United States in 1961 and forever became known by his sibling's name. His missed a second minor league title by .0001, but would go on to capture three in the major leagues.

Oliva spent his entire 15-year career with the Twins, and he joined Joe DiMaggio as one of the only two players to be named All-Stars in their first six full seasons, and then set a new mark by extending that to eight straight. In addition to his three batting crowns he led the American League five times in hits, four times in doubles, once in runs scored, and once in slugging average. He hit 220 home runs lifetime, cracking over 20 in a season five times. He retired with a .304 average and won a Gold Glove in 1966. He was the only player in major league history to win batting titles in his first two full seasons. He was named the AL Rookie of the Year in 1964 with his league-leading totals of a .323 batting average, 43 doubles, 217 hits, and 109 runs scored, as well as with his 32 home runs and 94 runs batted in. His 217 safeties that year set a new AL record for rookies.

An ailing knee eventually curtailed his otherwise brilliant career, and he retired in 1976 and became a coach for the Twins. He had a second stint in that role beginning in 1985, and the Twins retired his number 6 in his final season as a coach in 1991.

Dave Oliver
Texas Rangers (AL) 1987–94; Boston Red Sox (AL) 1995–96
Played seven games for the Cleveland Indians and hit .318.

In spite of that average Oliver spent the rest of his eight-year professional career in the minor leagues. He was a minor league All-Star in both 1976 and 1977 with the Toledo Mud Hens, but would not return to the majors except as a coach.

Following his playing career he became a minor league manager in the Indians' organization in 1982, and the following season moved to the Texas Rangers' system. In 1985 he was named the American Association's co-Manager of the Year while piloting the Oklahoma City 89ers, sharing the award with Jim Fregosi. In 1987 he was promoted to Texas as a coach, and in 1995 moved to Bos-

ton.

He eventually went to the Cincinnati Reds' organization as a minor league skipper, and in 2001 was named manager of the Mudville Nine in his hometown of Stockton, California.

Tom Oliver
Philadelphia Athletics (AL) 1951–53; Baltimore Orioles (AL) 1954
Outfielder from Montgomery, Alabama.

Oliver played four major league seasons with the Boston Red Sox, for whom he batted .277 with 176 runs batted in. He never hit a home run at the major league level and he stole 12 bases but was caught 19 times. He was outstanding defensively, and in his rookie season of 1930 he led the American League with 646 at-bats.

Oliver played for many years in the minor leagues and managed for seven. He served in the Navy during World War II, and later worked as a scout as well as coaching the A's and Orioles.

Mako Oliveras
California Angels (AL) 1994; Chicago Cubs (NL) 1995–97
Also known as Max Oliveras.

A native of Puerto Rico, Oliveras never played in the major leagues. He did manage a number of minor league teams at several levels, however, including the Miami Marlins, Midland Angels, Edmonton Trappers, Vancouver Canadians, Kinston Indians, Orlando Rays, Charleston RiverDogs, and Bakersfield Blaze. He coached one season at the major league level for the Angels and three for the Cubs before returning to his work in the minors. He eventually became a coach in the Tampa Bay Devil Rays' organization.

Ivy Olson
Brooklyn Robins (NL) 1924, 1930–31; New York Giants (NL) 1932
Fiery-tempered infielder.

Olson was something of an enigma, for he played with tremendous heart and could send a team either to great heights with a clutch hit or into the doldrums with a tragic error. He was generally a solid fielder, but he hit only .258, although he did lead the National League with 164 hits in 1919. His temper got him into trouble a number of times on the field, but he refused to be bullied by anyone and was somewhat admired for his fortitude.

Olson retired from the playing field in 1924 with the Robins, but he continued as a coach with the club until the end of the season. He then worked as a minor league manager until returning to Brooklyn in 1930. In 1932 he coached one season for the Giants.

Buck O'Neil
Chicago Cubs (NL) 1962–65
Longtime Negro Leaguer.

Made famous by his heartfelt appearances on Ken Burns' miniseries *Baseball*, O'Neil was a first baseman with the Memphis Red Sox and Kansas City Monarchs. In a career interrupted by three years of Navy service during World War II, he batted .288 and won the 1946 Negro American League batting title with a .353 average. The following season he hit a career-high .358. He played in four East-West All-Star Games, and after his playing career became the Monarchs' manager. At the helm he guided Kansas City to Negro National League championships in 1951, 1953, and 1955.

In 1956 O'Neil became a scout for the Cubs, and in 1962 was promoted to Chicago and became the first black coach in major league history. He later returned to scouting and spent many years in that role with the Kansas City Royals. He also served as an honorary Board Chairman of the Negro Leagues Baseball Museum in Kansas City.

In 2006, at the age of 94, he was signed to a one-day contract by the Kansas City T-Bones of the independent Northern League prior to the league's All-Star Game. The T-Bones played in the Eastern Division, but O'Neil started off playing for the West and was the leadoff batter in the top of the first inning, thus becoming the oldest player in professional baseball history. He appeared in a Monarchs' jersey. By design he was intentionally walked, although he argued with the umpire on the first pitch, even though it was called a ball. He took his base and then even took a leadoff, as if he intended to stay in the game, but was replaced by a pinch-runner before the next batter came to the plate. Between innings it was announced that he had been traded to the East, so he led off the bottom of the first as well. Intentionally walked again, he nevertheless took a swing at one of the pitches and nearly spun himself off his feet. In the surrounding hoopla the umpire did not even notice that five balls were thrown out of the strike zone and taken before O'Neil was awarded first base.

Mickey O'Neil
Cleveland Indians (AL) 1930
Catcher from St. Louis, Missouri.

In nine major league seasons O'Neil batted .238 with 4 home runs and 179 runs batted in. He never played more than 112 games in a season and never had more than 362 at-bats, but he was prized for his ability to call games. His best season was 1920, when he hit .283 for the Boston Braves while setting his career high in at-bats.

After his playing career O'Neil coached one season for the Indians and also worked as a minor league manager.

Steve O'Neill
Cleveland Indians (AL) 1939; Detroit Tigers (AL) 1941; Boston Red Sox (AL) 1950
See Managers section.

Jack Onslow
Pittsburgh Pirates (NL) 1925–26; Washington Nationals (AL) 1927; St. Louis Cardinals (NL) 1928; Philadelphia Phillies (NL) 1931–32; Boston Red Sox (AL) 1934
See Managers section.

Jose Oquendo
St. Louis Cardinals (NL) 1999–
Versatile switch-hitter who played many positions.

Excellent with a glove wherever he played, Oquendo had a so-so bat, hitting only .256. The Puerto Rican was used all over the field, many times as a regular, and in 1988 he pitched once in relief—losing the game, unfortunately—and also caught once, thus becoming the first National Leaguer since 1918 to play all nine positions in the same season. In 1989 he led the NL in fielding average, and in 1990 set major league single-season records for highest fielding average at .996 and fewest errors by a second baseman with three.

Oquendo became a Cardinals' minor league instructor and manager following his playing days, and he joined the Redbirds' coaching staff in 1999. In 2006 he managed Puerto Rico in the World Baseball Classic.

Don Osborn
Pittsburgh Pirates (NL) 1963–64, 1970–72, 1974–76
Longtime minor league pitcher and manager.

Nicknamed "The Wizard of Oz" because of his uncanny ability to get batters out while not possessing dominating stuff, Osborn spent several years as a player-manager. His 1942 Vancouver Capilanos took the Western International League championship, and his 1949 Macon Peaches claimed the South Atlantic League title. In 1950 he guided the Nashville Volunteers to the Southern Association crown, and he continued to manage until 1957. With the Miami Marlins he was reported to have objected to the addition of Satchel Paige to his pitching staff, but changed his mind during a Paige tryout and later supposedly taught the hurler how to throw a curveball.

From 1958–76 Osborn worked for the Pirates, having three stints in the major leagues as a pitching coach and spending other seasons as a minor league instructor and a scout. He retired in 1976.

Claude Osteen
St. Louis Cardinals (NL) 1977–80; Philadelphia Phillies (NL) 1982–88; Texas Rangers (AL) 1993–94; Los Angeles

Dodgers (NL) 1999–2000
Outstanding pitcher who played 18 seasons.

Osteen won 196 games during his career against 195 losses. He won at least 14 games every year from 1964–73 except for 1968, when he went 12–18. A three-time All-Star, he was a workhorse for his era, tossing 140 complete games. He was a 20-game winner in 1969 when he went 20–15, and again in 1972, when he posted a 20–11 record. His finest years were spent with the Dodgers, and his lifetime earned run average was 3.30. In 1970 he was the winning pitcher in the All-Star Game when he threw three shutout innings for the National League.

Following his playing career Osteen became a pitching coach for several clubs, both at the minor and major league levels.

Reggie Otero
Cincinnati Reds (NL) 1959–65; Cleveland Indians (AL) 1966
Minor league batting champion.

Otero hit .364 in 1942 with the Utica Braves to lead the Can-Am League. Toward the end of the 1945 season he played 14 games for the Chicago Cubs and batted .391, but that would constitute his only major league experience. He returned to the minors and soon became a player-manager there, and he also began to manage in winter Caribbean leagues. In Venezuela he led the Valencia Industrials to three league titles and the Caracas Lions to four more. He also coached at the major league level for the Reds and Indians.

Amos Otis
San Diego Padres (NL) 1988–90; Colorado Rockies (NL) 1993
Four-time All-Star from Mobile, Alabama.

A speedy outfielder, Otis played 17 years and hit .277. In 1970 with the Kansas City Royals, his first full season, he tied for the American League lead with 36 doubles, and he led in 1976 with 40. In 1971 he topped the AL with a career-high 52 stolen bases, and he swiped at least 20 in a season eight times. He stole 341 in his career, in 1971 swiping 5 in one game and in 1975 tying a league record by pilfering 7 in two consecutive contests. He won three Gold Gloves for his defense.

Otis became a coach with the Padres and the expansion Rockies following his playing career.

Ed Ott
Houston Astros (NL) 1989–93; Detroit Tigers (AL) 2001–02
Outfielder-turned-catcher.

Ott was converted by the Pittsburgh Pirates, who had a crowded outfield and needed someone behind the plate. Ott became a AAA All-Star once he made the switch and, back in the majors, quickly established a reputation for himself as a tough opponent who was a master at blocking the plate.

Ed played eight major league seasons, then became a minor league manager and a big league coach. He was named the independent Northeast League's Manager of the Year in both 1998 and 1999 while piloting the Allentown Ambassadors.

Stubby Overmire
Detroit Tigers (AL) 1963–66
Left-handed pitcher who spent a decade in the major leagues.

Spending roughly half of his career as a starter and half as a reliever, Overmire posted a 58–67 lifetime record with a 3.96 earned run average. He then became a minor league skipper in the Tigers' organization, and in 14 years as a manager he did not win a championship but did lead both the 1957 Montgomery Rebels and the 1962 Jamestown Tigers to the best records in their respective leagues. Between managing assignments he spent four years as a coach in Detroit with the big club.

Mickey Owen
Boston Red Sox (AL) 1955–56
Four-time All-Star catcher.

Owen is unfortunately best remembered for his passed ball in the 1941 World Series with the Brooklyn Dodgers. The miscue occurred on what should have been the third strike to end the game with a Brooklyn victory, but instead resulted in the New York Yankees' Tommy Henrich reaching first base and the Yanks coming back to win the game. The Dodgers watched their 4–3 lead dissolve into a 7–4 loss, and a game that very nearly tied the Series at two games apiece set up the Yankees' World Championship the following day.

Owen was an All-Star that year and continued to be one the next three seasons, however. In 1942 he became the first player to pinch-hit a home run in an All-Star contest.

He lost part of the 1945 season to the Navy at the end of World War II, and the following year he did not return to Brooklyn but jumped ship for the Mexican League, which was pirating players away from the major leagues. Owen became a player-manager there and was blackballed from the big leagues until 1949, when he was allowed to return and signed with the Chicago Cubs. He finished his career in 1954 with the Red Sox and then coached for them for two seasons. He later became a scout and then started the Mickey Owen Baseball School in Missouri. The school still bears his name although he sold it off some time ago.

In 1964 Owen became a Greene County sheriff, and worked in that position until 1980.

Jayhawk Owens
Cincinnati Reds (NL) 2004
Reserve catcher for four seasons.

Those seasons were all spent with the Colorado Rockies, and the first was Colorado's inaugural year of 1993. Owens hit .232 in 130 games overall with 11 home runs and 36 runs batted in.

A Cincinnati native, he later joined the Reds as a minor league manager. At the conclusion of the 2004 minor league season he was called up to the Reds as one of several "extra" coaches to finish out the year.

Jim Owens
Houston Astros (NL) 1967–72
Starter and reliever who spent a dozen seasons in the majors.

Owens started less than half of his 286 big league games, and he fashioned a 42–68 record with a 4.31 earned run average. He debuted in 1955 and lost all of 1957 and part of 1958 to military service. In 1963 he became the first National League pitcher to commit three balks in one inning, and that mark was matched less than two weeks later by Bob Shaw of the Milwaukee Braves. Arm problems cut Owens' career short in 1967 while he was with the Astros, but he stayed with the club as a coach and then coached an additional five years with them.

Danny Ozark
Los Angeles Dodgers (NL) 1965–72, 1980–82; San Francisco Giants (NL) 1983–84
See Managers section.

Tony Pacheco
Cleveland Indians (AL) 1974; Houston Astros (NL) 1976–82
Cuban native who never played in the major leagues.

A minor league second baseman, Pacheco spent many years as a scout, and among his notable signings was Tony Perez, who later went on to star for the Cincinnati Reds. Pacheco later coached in the big leagues, spending one season with the Indians and seven with the Astros. He passed away in Miami Beach, Florida, in 1987.

Jack Paepke
Los Angeles Angels (AL) 1962–64; California Angels (AL) 1965–66
Minor league pitcher, catcher, and player-manager.

Paepke's professional career began in 1941 in the Brooklyn Dodgers' system. After spending 1942 with the Montreal Royals he lost the next three years to the Navy. He switched from pitching primarily to catching upon his return, and in 1953 began managing in the Pittsburgh Pirates' organization while still active as a player. He served as a player-manager through 1958, both pitching and catching. Shortly thereafter he became a big league coach with the Angels, then scouted for the club before joining its speakers bureau.

Andy Pafko
Milwaukee Braves (NL) 1960–62
Outfielder nicknamed "Handy Andy."

The moniker came from the fact that Pafko was also often used at third base, and was bestowed upon him by his manager with the Chicago Cubs, Charlie Grimm. A .285 lifetime hitter, Pafko batted over .300 four times and was named to five All-Star teams. He slugged 213 home runs, hitting at least 12 on nine occasions and at least 30 twice. In 1950 he hit .304 with 36 longballs and 92 runs batted in. He topped the 100-RBI mark twice as well.

Pafko finished his career with the Braves and then coached for them for three years.

Jose Pagan
Pittsburgh Pirates (NL) 1974–78
Shortstop and third baseman from Puerto Rico.

Pagan led National League shortstops in fielding average in 1962, but in 1966, while at third base, he once committed three errors in one inning, tying a modern league record. He spent the second half of his career as a utilityman and pinch-hitter, and in 1969 he led the NL with 19 pinch-hits, a total that was only one shy of the record. He spent most of his years with the Pirates, and became a coach for the Bucs following his retirement from the playing field.

Mitchell Page
Kansas City Royals (AL) 1995–97; St. Louis Cardinals (NL) 2001–04; Washington Nationals (NL) 2006–
Outfielder from Los Angeles.

The Sporting News declared Page its American League Rookie of the Year in 1977 when the left-handed batter hit .307 with 21 home runs, 75 runs batted in, and 42 stolen bases. The BBWAA award went to Eddie Murray, however. Page never again matched those numbers, although he would belt 17 homers on two occasions. His major league career ended in 1984, then he spent one year playing in Hawaii.

Page eventually became a minor league instructor in the Oakland Athletics' system, then coached for the Royals before working as a minor league hitting coordinator for the Cardinals. He was promoted to St. Louis as a coach from 2001–04, and spent 2005 as the Nationals' minor league hitting coordinator before being called to Washington in 2006. In 2007 he was slated to return to his previous role of minor league hitting coordinator when manager

Frank Robinson was fired, but new manager Manny Acta convinced him to remain on the big league staff.

Phil Page
Cincinnati Reds (NL) 1947–52
Pitched 31 major league games.

A left-hander, Page started 6 of those 31 over four seasons, and he recorded a 3–3 lifetime mark with a hefty 6.23 earned run average. He then became a minor league manager and scout for the New York Yankees, but returned to the majors as a coach with the Reds for six seasons. He died of a heart attack in 1958 at the age of 52.

Satchel Paige
Atlanta Braves (NL) 1968–69
First Negro Leaguer inducted into the Hall of Fame.

A colorful, extremely entertaining pitcher, Paige pitched from 1927 until 1965 at various levels of baseball. Most of those years were spent in the Negro Leagues, where he played for many teams but had his finest hours with the Kansas City Monarchs. He helped that squad to four Negro American League pennants and a 1942 Negro World Series championship.

Paige was 42 years of age when he made his debut with the Cleveland Indians, making him the oldest rookie in major league history. He pitched five years for the Indians and the St. Louis Browns and was named to two All-Star teams. In 1965 he pitched a final three innings for the Kansas City Athletics at the age of 59 and did not allow a run. He remains the oldest player ever to appear in a major league game.

Paige's major league record was a modest 28–31, but his earned run average was 3.29. There is no way of knowing exactly how many games he pitched if one includes all the Negro League, exhibition, and barnstorming totals, but some have estimated his record to contain at least 1500 victories at all levels. He was an excellent storyteller and drew crowds wherever he went.

After his retirement Paige was 158 days short of qualifying for a major league pension, so the Atlanta Braves signed him to a contract but did not use him in a game. On September 30 he was made a coach, and he stayed another season with the club in that role. In 1971 he was inducted into the Hall of Fame by the Negro Leagues Committee.

Dave Parker
Anaheim Angels (AL) 1997; St. Louis Cardinals (NL) 1998
Cincinnati native nicknamed "The Cobra."

The name came from the way Parker uncoiled his bat while hitting. A .290 lifetime hitter, he won two batting titles and led the National League twice in doubles, once in runs batted in, once in hits, and twice in slugging average.

He hit over .300 six times and was named to seven All-Star squads. In 1978 he was named the NL's Most Valuable Player when he hit .334 with 30 home runs and 117 RBIs for the Pittsburgh Pirates. The following season he was the MVP of the All-Star Game, which was won by the NL, 7–6. He slugged 339 home runs lifetime and won three Gold Gloves.

Parker was embroiled in controversy when he admitted to drug use and testified against an accused drug dealer. He was fined by Major League Baseball but, because of his cooperation, was not suspended. After his playing career he coached a season for the Angels and a season for the Cardinals, and also worked as a hitting instructor in the Pirates' minor league system.

Salty Parker
San Francisco Giants (NL) 1958–61, 1979; Cleveland Indians (AL) 1962; Los Angeles Angels (AL) 1964; California Angels (AL) 1965–66, 1973–74; New York Mets (NL) 1967; Houston Astros (NL) 1968–72
See Managers section.

Lance Parrish
Detroit Tigers (AL) 1999–2001, 2003–05
Bodyguard for vocalist Tina Turner.

That was one of Parrish's jobs; another was major league catcher, a vocation he practiced for 19 seasons. Converted from being a third baseman in the minor leagues, Parrish struggled with his new position at first, leading the American League with 21 passed balls in 1979. He quickly stabilized, however, and in 1983 won the first of three consecutive Gold Gloves. Never a slouch at the plate, he topped the 20-home-run mark in seven seasons and hit 19 two others. He cracked 324 roundtrippers all-time and was named to eight All-Star teams. In 1982, his 32 homers set a new AL mark for catchers.

After his playing career Parrish served two stints as a Detroit coach, taking 2002 off to work for the team as a broadcaster. In 2006 he joined the Los Angeles Dodgers as a minor league manager.

Larry Parrish
Detroit Tigers (AL) 1997–98
See Managers section.

Camilo Pascual
Minnesota Twins (AL) 1978–80
Outstanding pitcher from Havana, Cuba.

Pascual was an overpowering hurler who worked as both a starter and a reliever. He won at least 15 games five times and was a 20-game winner twice: in 1962, when he went 20–11 for the Twins, and in 1963, when he was 21–9 for the same club. His lifetime record was 174–170 with a 3.63 earned run average. A seven-time All-Star, he led the American League three times each in strikeouts, complete games, and shutouts. At the plate he hit two career grand slams.

When he was finished as a player Pascual eventually returned to the Twins as a coach. He also worked for many years as a scout for the Los Angeles Dodgers.

Gil Patterson
Toronto Blue Jays (AL) 2001–04
Once highly-touted minor league pitcher.

Patterson likely would have had a sensational career had a torn rotator cuff not ended it before he could pitch more than 10 major league games. In the minors he had pitched a no-hitter in 1976 and was a can't-miss prospect. He was told by New York Yankees' brass to pitch in Venezuela that winter, despite the fact that he had logged over 500 innings the past two seasons. His arm soon began to bother him, and he pitched the entire 1977 campaign with a torn rotator cuff, making 10 appearances for the Yankees and going 1–2. He eventually had eight operations on the arm and tried to come back, but was not the same pitcher.

The Yankees hired him as a minor league coach, but fired him when they thought he was being overly cautious with a pitcher who was himself experiencing arm problems. The pitcher's name was Al Leiter.

Patterson eventually coached several seasons with the Blue Jays, then returned to the Yankees' organization. After coaching a season with the AAA Columbus Clippers, he asked to be reassigned to the Gulf Coast Yankees, a rookie team, so that he could be close to his home and therefore to his seven-year-old son, who had been diagnosed with Tourette's Syndrome.

Marty Pattin
Toronto Blue Jays (AL) 1989
Worked 13 seasons as a starter and a reliever.

A right-hander, Pattin once struck out 22 batters in a college game with Eastern Illinois University. He made his major league debut in 1968 with the California Angels, then was selected by the Seattle Pilots in the expansion draft. He accompanied the team to Milwaukee, where it became the Brewers, and won 14 games each of the next two seasons. In 1971 he was named an American League All-Star. He was then involved in a trade to the Boston Red Sox, and he won a career-high 17 games in 1972. He nearly pitched a no-hitter against the Oakland Athletics in July, coming within two outs of the gem when Reggie Jackson broke it up with a single.

He eventually retired with a 114–109 record and a 3.62

earned run average, and he coached one season for the Blue Jays. He holds the Pilots' all-time records for most strikeouts in a game with 11, most earned runs allowed with 99, and most home runs given up with 29.

Mike Paul
Oakland Athletics (AL) 1987–88; Seattle Mariners (AL) 1989–91
Journeyman pitcher from Detroit.

In seven seasons Paul went 27–48 despite a 3.91 earned run average. He never had a winning record, but did go 5–5 in 1973 for the Texas Rangers and Chicago Cubs. Paul spent many years in the minor leagues both before and after his major league experience, and even pitched for a time in the Mexican League. From 1983–86 he worked as a minor league coach in the organizations of the San Diego Padres and Milwaukee Brewers. He then coached the A's and Mariners at the major league level before becoming a scout.

In that role he has worked for the A's, the Cubs, and the Colorado Rockies.

Greg Pavlick
New York Mets (NL) 1985–86, 1988–91, 1994–96
Minor league pitcher from Washington, D.C.

Pavlick never reached the major leagues as a player, but did so in three different stints as a coach with the Mets. In all he spent 26 years in the Mets' organization as a player and coach. He later become a roving minor league pitching instructor with the New York American League team, the Yankees.

Mike Pazik
Chicago White Sox (AL) 1995–98
Number one draft pick of the New York Yankees in 1971.

A pitcher, Pazik reached the major leagues with the Minnesota Twins for 13 games spread over three seasons. He started six of those games and went 1–4 with a 5.79 earned run average. In 1980 he went to work in the minor leagues as a coach and manager, then served as a pitching coordinator for the Milwaukee Brewers from 1983–87 and for the Baltimore Orioles from 1989–93. After scouting one season for the White Sox, he joined the major league club as their pitching coach. He then worked once again as a scout and as an assistant to the general manager in the organization before moving on to the Colorado Rockies and the Kansas City Royals.

Pazik also helped found Mike Toomey Baseball, an academy for eleventh- and twelfth-grade baseball players who are college-bound.

Les Peden
Chicago Cubs (NL) 1965
Minor league catcher who played nine games for the Washington Nationals.

Peden's entire big league career occurred in 1953 for Washington, when he hit .250 with a double and a home run that constituted his only run batted in. The following season he became a minor league player-manager, and he moved around from team to team over the ensuing decade. In 1964 with the Quincy Gems of the Midwest League he even pitched 15 games. The following season he gave up playing and served as a full-time coach with the Cubs, then went back to the minor leagues as a manager.

Al Pedrique
Arizona Diamondbacks (NL) 2004
See Managers section.

Heinie Peitz
Cincinnati Reds (NL) 1912, 1916; St. Louis Cardinals (NL) 1913
Longtime catcher for the Reds, Cardinals, and Pittsburgh Pirates.

Peitz hit .271 over 16 seasons, topping the .300 mark twice and hitting .299 on one other occasion in limited action. He was versatile, sometimes being used around the infield, occasionally in the outfield, and even several times on the mound. He played from 1892–1906, then rejoined the Reds as a coach in 1912. The following season he went back to the Cardinals in a similar role but was activated for three games and went 1-for-4 with a triple. He coached for the Reds again in 1916.

Not to be confused with major leaguer Heinie Reitz, who was killed in a car accident in 1914, Heinie Peitz lived until 1943, when he died in Cincinnati.

Tony Peña
New York Yankees (AL) 2006–
See Managers section.

Terry Pendleton
Atlanta Braves (NL) 2002–
Oft-injured third baseman for 15 seasons.

In spite of his injuries the switch-hitting Pendleton made quite a career for himself. A .270 lifetime hitter, he hit over .300 twice and won the National League batting title in 1991 with the Braves by hitting .319, and he led the league with 187 hits. He hit a career-high 22 home runs and drove in 86 runs en route to being named the NL's Most Valuable Player. The following season he was named to the All-Star team while hitting .311 with 21 homers and a career-high 105 RBIs. He won Gold Gloves in 1987, 1989, and 1992.

Pendleton played until 1998, and he returned to the Braves in 2002 as a coach.

Herb Pennock
Boston Red Sox (AL) 1936–39
Hall of Fame pitcher who lasted 22 seasons.

Originally a first baseman, Pennock became a pitcher in high school and pitched a no-hitter in 1911. His catcher for that game was Earle Mack, and his batterymate quickly brought notice of Pennock's skills to his father Connie and Pennock debuted with the Philadelphia Athletics the next year.

Despite his great promise Pennock was waived and claimed by the Red Sox during the 1915 season. He had just missed pitching a no-hitter on Opening Day, blanking none other than the Red Sox until Harry Hooper managed a single with two out in the ninth inning. He missed the 1918 season due to World War I, during which he served in the U.S. Navy. He pitched for the Sox through 1922, then was traded to the New York Yankees, where he had his best years.

Pennock was a 20-game winner twice and won at least 16 games on eight occasions. He led the American League with 277 innings pitched in 1925 and with 5 shutouts in 1928, and when he retired after one last year with the Red Sox in 1934 he had a 241–162 lifetime record with a 3.60 earned run average. While experiencing arm problems in 1928 he once treated his pitching arm with a swarm of bees, which he allowed to sting him repeatedly. The supposed "treatment" did not work.

After coaching several seasons in Boston he worked as the supervisor of their minor league system. In 1944 he was named general manager of the Philadelphia Phillies, and he remained in that position until he died of a cerebral hemorrhage in 1948, the same year he was inducted into the Hall of Fame.

One of his favorite hobbies had been raising silver foxes and selling their pelts.

Jeff Pentland
Florida Marlins (NL) 1996; Chicago Cubs (NL) 1997–2002; Kansas City Royals (AL) 2003–05; Seattle Mariners (AL) 2006–
Minor leaguer who was a first baseman, outfielder, catcher, and pitcher.

Pentland manned all those positions in just three seasons in the San Diego Padres' system. In 1971, after stepping down from the playing field, he became an assistant coach at Mesa Community College in Arizona, and shortly thereafter worked at Arizona State University (ASU) as a junior varsity coach and at Wichita State University as athletic director. He then spent nine years at the University of California, Riverside before returning to ASU as a hitting coach.

Pentland later returned to the professional ranks as a scout and a minor league coach in the Marlins' organization before being promoted to the major league staff. He remained at the big league level as he later moved on to the Cubs, the Royals, and the Mariners.

Joe Pepitone
New York Yankees (AL) 1982

Free-spirited and controversial first baseman and outfielder.

The story goes that Pepitone received a $25,000 signing bonus from the Yankees in 1962 and spent it all on a Ford Thunderbird, a boat, and a dog. He fashioned a successful 12-year major league career in which he hit 219 home runs, topping 20 on five occasions, was named to three All-Star teams, and won three Gold Gloves. In May of 1962, his rookie season, he once hit two home runs in an inning, but in the 1963 World Series he made a costly error that eventually cost the Yanks the championship. He made up for it in 1964 when he connected for a grand slam in that Fall Classic.

In August of 1969 Pepitone skipped out on the team due to "personal problems." He returned the next day, but shortly thereafter was fined $500. That caused him to quit altogether, although he was reinstated four days later. He retired from the Chicago Cubs in 1972, but quickly changed his mind and returned to the club. In 1973 he signed to play in Japan with the Yakult Swallows. He did not last, however, batting only .163 and feeling homesick, so he jumped ship again and returned to the United States, where he would finish his playing career with the Cubs and the Atlanta Braves.

He was a coach for the Yankees in 1982, but also in the 1980s was arrested on gun and drug charges and spent some time in prison. He worked in the Yankees' front office as part of a work-release program. In January of 1992 he was charged with assault when he got into a fight at a hotel.

Eddie Perez
Atlanta Braves (NL) 2007–

Catcher and native of Venezuela.

Perez hit .253 in an 11-year major league career. He played from 1995–2005, spending his entire career with the Braves except for the 2002 season, when he played for the Cleveland Indians. He was named the Most Valuable Player of the 1999 National League Championship Series when he hit .500, going 10-for-20 with 2 home runs and 5 runs batted in.

In 2006 Perez coached the AA Mississippi Braves, then was named to the major league staff for the 2007 season.

Tony Perez
Cincinnati Reds (NL) 1987–92
See Managers section.

Cy Perkins
New York Yankees (AL) 1933; Detroit Tigers (AL) 1934–39; Philadelphia Phillies (NL) 1946–54
See Managers section.

Sam Perlozzo
New York Mets (NL) 1987–89; Cincinnati Reds (NL) 1990–92; Seattle Mariners (AL) 1993–95; Baltimore Orioles (AL) 1996–2005
See Managers section.

Ron Perranoski
Los Angeles Dodgers (NL) 1981–94; San Francisco Giants (NL) 1997–99

Starting pitcher converted to a reliever.

By the time he reached the major leagues in 1961 Perranoski was pitching almost exclusively in relief; he started only 1 of 737 big league games. In 1963 he had his finest season, going 16–3 with a 1.67 earned run average and leading the National League with 69 games pitched, one shy of his league-leading total of the previous year. He also notched 21 saves, one more than in 1962. In both 1969 and 1970 *The Sporting News* named him its American League Fireman of the Year, for he posted save totals of 31 and 34, respectively, to lead the league in each campaign. In 13 seasons Perranoski posted a 79–74 record with 179 saves and a 2.79 ERA.

Following his playing career Ron spent eight years as a minor league pitching instructor for the Dodgers. He was then promoted to Los Angeles as pitching coach, a position he held for 14 years. In 1995 he was named coordinator of minor league pitching for the Giants, and two years later was brought up to the major league staff. Following the 1999 season he moved to the role of special assistant to the general manager with the club, working in scouting and player development for both the minor and major leagues.

Gerald Perry
Seattle Mariners (AL) 2000–02; Pittsburgh Pirates (NL) 2003–05; Oakland Athletics (AL) 2006; Chicago Cubs (NL) 2007–

Nephew of major leaguer Dan Driessen.

Perry was a speedy outfielder who played 13 big league seasons. His finest year as a regular was 1988, when he hit .300 for the Atlanta Braves while stealing 29 bases and being named a National League All-Star. The previous year he had swiped a career-high 42 sacks, and he would finish his career with 142 total. Injuries soon curtailed his playing time and he became a pinch-hitting specialist. He led the NL in 1993 with 24 pinch-hits, and he hit .337 and .325 in that role in 1993 and 1994, respectively.

After retiring in 1995 Perry became a minor league coach and hitting coordinator in the Boston Red Sox' organization. In 2000 he was hired by the Mariners to work at the big league level, and later moved to the Pirates, the Athletics, and the Cubs.

Johnny Pesky
Pittsburgh Pirates (NL) 1965–67; Boston Red Sox (AL) 1975–84
See Managers section.

Rick Peterson
Pittsburgh Pirates (NL) 1984–85; Chicago White Sox (AL) 1994–95; Oakland Athletics (AL) 1998–2003; New York Mets (NL) 2004–
Minor league player who later became a player-coach.

Peterson started out in the Pirates' organization, and he reached the big club for two seasons as a bullpen coach. In 1986 he joined the Cleveland Indians' chain as a coach, and in 1989 moved to the White Sox' system. In 1994 he was promoted to Chicago, and in addition to coaching he was also a co-director of the team's sports psychology program. Peterson had earned a degree in psychology from Jacksonville University before embarking on his playing career.

From 1996–97 Rick was the Toronto Blue Jays' minor league pitching coordinator, then he became the pitching coach for the A's and later the Mets. His father, Harding Peterson, was the executive vice president and general manager of the Pirates in the late 1970s and the general manager of the New York Yankees in the early 1990s.

Joe Pettini
St. Louis Cardinals (NL) 2002–
Infielder who hit only .203.

Pettini spent four seasons with the San Francisco Giants, but finished out his career in the minor leagues with the Louisville Redbirds, who were part of the Cardinals' organization. He then became a minor league manager and eventually returned to the Redbirds, and he guided his former club to the 1995 American Association championship. From 1997–2001 he was the Cardinals' minor league field coordinator, and he was promoted to St. Louis as a coach in 2002.

Gary Pettis
Chicago White Sox (AL) 2001–02; New York Mets (NL) 2003–04; Texas Rangers (AL) 2007–
Speedy, switch-hitting outfielder.

Perhaps "switch-batting" would be a better term, because Pettis *hit* only .236 in 11 major league seasons. He stole 354 bases, however, swiping at least 24 in a season eight times and peaking with 56 in 1985. He was also outstanding defensively in center field, copping three Gold Gloves.

He was prone to striking out, however, and in a 1991 game he was once picked off third base while a batter was being intentionally walked. In 1985 he had his younger brother sit in for him for the photo on his Topps baseball card.

After his playing career Pettis coached two years for the White Sox and two more for the Mets. He then coached the Nashville Sounds in the Milwaukee Brewers' organization before returning to the Rangers, one of the teams with whom he had played, as a coach in 2007.

Marty Pevey
Toronto Blue Jays (AL) 1999, 2005–
Catcher who lasted 13 major league games.

Pevey hit only .220 for the Montreal Expos in those 1989 games, but he had had a rather stellar minor league career. He had played in multiple All-Star Games and was named Most Valuable Player in one of them, and was also named MVP of the 1988 American Association Championship Series. He was frequently among league leaders in batting average.

Nevertheless Pevey never fashioned a big league career as a player, and in 1996 he began a second career as a minor league coach and manager. He was promoted to Toronto as a coach in 1999, then returned to the minors and in 2000 was named the Florida State League's Manager of the Year with the Dunedin Blue Jays. In 2003 he was named Eastern League Manager of the Year when he led his New Haven Ravens to the division title. In early September of 2005 he was made Toronto's first base coach on an interim basis, then was granted the position full-time at the end of the season.

Dick Phillips
San Diego Padres (NL) 1980
Pacific Coast League Most Valuable Player in 1961.

In spite of that honor, which he earned with the Tacoma Giants, Phillips would play only four major league seasons. Used mainly at first base but also at second and third, he hit only .229. Five of those games were with the San Francisco Giants, and 258 were with the Washington Senators.

After his playing career Phillips coached one season for the Padres but was a longtime minor league manager.

Lefty Phillips
Los Angeles Dodgers (NL) 1965–68; California Angels (AL) 1969
See Managers section.

Rob Picciolo
San Diego Padres (NL) 1990–2005
One of the toughest players to walk.

That dubious honor was gained by the fact that Picciolo drew a mere 25 bases on balls in a nine-year career, comprising 1628 official at-bats. Perhaps he should have been more patient at the plate, because he batted only .234, and he was used mainly as an infield utilityman. After his playing career he became a minor league manager and then a longtime Padres' coach. In 2006 he moved to the Los Angeles Angels of Anaheim as a roving minor league instructor.

Ron Piche
Montreal Expos (NL) 1976
Pitcher used mainly as a reliever.

Piche pitched for six major league seasons, during which he frequently bounced between the majors and minors. With the Milwaukee Braves, California Angels, and St. Louis Cardinals he fashioned a 10–16 record with a 4.19 earned run average and 157 strikeouts in $221^{1}/_3$ innings.

Canadian by birth, Piche eventually coached one season with the Expos.

Val Picinich
Cincinnati Reds (NL) 1934
Backup catcher for 18 seasons, 3 of them with the Reds.

In spite of his reserve status Picinich had the good fortune to catch three no-hitters in his career, with three different teams. In his debut season of 1916 with the Philadelphia Athletics, having been signed out of prep school, he caught Joe Bush's no-no. In 1920 with the Washington Nationals he was the backstop in Walter Johnson's gem. And with the Boston Red Sox in 1923, he was the catcher for Howard Ehmke's no-hitter.

Picinich hit .258 lifetime and never played more than 96 games in a season. He coached one season for the Reds upon his retirement.

Jimmy Piersall
Texas Rangers (AL) 1975
Talented outfielder who battled bipolar disorder.

Briefly tried as a shortstop after he broke into the majors, Piersall debuted in 1950 in six games but did not reappear until 1952, when his season was cut short by a nervous breakdown. He had extreme bouts of volatility, frequently fighting with umpires, fans, and even teammates, and he was renowned for silly stunts that left many scratching their heads until he sought psychiatric care. His struggle with his disease was documented in the motion picture *Fear Strikes Out*, based on his book of the same name, and in which he was portrayed by actor Anthony Hopkins. Piersall later criticized the movie, claiming it distorted the facts.

He did make a comeback, however, and put together a successful 17-year career in which he hit .272 with 104 home runs, winning two Gold Gloves and being named to two All-Star teams. In 1956 he led the American League with 40 doubles. In 1963 he began to exhibit symptoms of a possible relapse, heckling umpires, charging the mound, and once batting while wearing a Little League helmet. In 1963, when he connected for the 100th home run of his career, he ran the bases while facing backwards.

In 1967, the year he retired, Piersall moved into the front office of the Chicago White Sox, and 10 years later he became a broadcaster for the club. He was fired in 1981 for criticizing the team's management. He continued to do a radio sports show in Chicago, and wrote another book called *The Truth Hurts*, which detailed the events surrounding his departure from the White Sox.

Joe Pignatano
Washington Senators (AL) 1965–67; New York Mets (NL) 1968–81; Atlanta Braves (NL) 1982–84
Backup catcher from Brooklyn.

Pignatano hit .234 in six seasons, starting his major league career with his hometown Dodgers and following them to Los Angeles before moving on to several other clubs. In 1965 he was named the Senators' bullpen coach under manager Gil Hodges, whom he later followed back to New York. Pignatano spent 14 years as a Mets' coach, and became renowned for planting a tomato garden in the bullpen. He later moved on to the Braves for three years.

Lou Piniella
New York Yankees (AL) 1985
See Managers section.

Vada Pinson
Seattle Mariners (AL) 1977–80, 1982–83; Chicago White Sox (AL) 1981; Detroit Tigers (AL) 1985–91; Florida Marlins (NL) 1993–94
Outstanding outfielder from Memphis, Tennessee.

Pinson was a multitalented player who never spent time on the disabled list and hit .286 in 18 major league seasons.

In his second big league game he connected for a grand slam home run. A consistent hitter with speed and power, he also played an excellent outfield, winning a Gold Glove in 1961 and leading National League outfielders in putouts three times. At the plate he led the league twice in hits, twice in doubles, twice in triples, and once in runs scored. He hit 256 home runs lifetime, clubbing at least 20 seven times, and batted over .300 four times. He was named to four All-Star teams and stole 305 bases, swiping at least 21 nine times.

Pinson retired in 1975 and worked briefly in the Mariners' minor league system before being promoted to the big club as a coach. He moved on to several other teams thereafter, and in 1995 he died of a stroke at the age of 57.

Fran Pirozzolo
Houston Astros (NL) 1988–95; New York Mets (NL) 2003
Sports psychologist who served as a mental skills coach.

Pirozzolo's degrees were from the University of Chicago and the University of Rochester. The author of 14 books and more than 250 articles, he has worked as a consultant to a wide variety of collegiate sports departments and professional sports teams. He spent one year doing research and training on astronauts' responses to extreme environments at NASA's Johnson Space Center.

In 1983 Pirozzolo began to work with professional golfers on the PGA and LPGA circuits on attitudes and focus. In 1988 he was hired by the Astros under manager Art Howe to be the team's mental skills coach, a uniformed position. From 1990–98 he was a training consultant for boxer Evander Holyfield, and from 1994–97 also worked as a consultant for the Texas Rangers. From 1996–2002 he served as the New York Yankees' mental skills coach, although in this case he did not don a uniform. In 2003 he was hired by the Mets, once again under Art Howe and once again in a uniformed role. His duties were to have taken place in the clubhouse, however, and when Pirozzolo on several occasions entered the dugout during games, in violation of Major League Baseball rules (he was not one of the six approved dugout coaches), he was fired during the season.

He has also worked with other baseball players on an individual basis and with the Houston Texans of the National Football League.

Jake Pitler
Brooklyn Dodgers (NL) 1947–57
Second baseman who played 111 games for the Pittsburgh Pirates.

One hundred nine of those occurred in 1917, but Pitler batted a mere .232 overall. After retiring he spent many years in the Dodgers' organization as a minor league man-ager. In 1947 he became a coach in Brooklyn and lasted 11 seasons. When the club relocated to Los Angeles, he moved into a scouting position for the New York-Pennsylvania-Canada area rather than accompany the club to the West Coast. He died in Binghamton, New York, in 1968.

Gaylen Pitts
St. Louis Cardinals (NL) 1991–95
Played 28 major league games and 13 minor league seasons.

An infielder who played mainly at third base, Pitts spread those 28 games over two seasons, spending parts of 1974 and 1975 with the Oakland Athletics. He hit .250. Beginning in 1978 he put together a long and successful managerial career in the minor leagues, taking five years out to serve as a Cardinals' major league coach. In 1986 he was named Midwest League Manager of the Year when his Springfield Cardinals posted the best record in the league and qualified for the playoffs. They made the postseason again the following year.

In 1989 Pitts was named Texas League Manager of the Year when his Arkansas Travelers captured the league championship. In 2000 his Memphis Redbirds took the Pacific Coast League title. Having spent most of his career with the A's and Cardinals in various capacities, he joined the New York Yankees in 2006 as the manager of the Staten Island Yankees of the New York-Penn League.

Ron Plaza
Seattle Pilots (AL) 1969; Cincinnati Reds (NL) 1978–83; Oakland Athletics (AL) 1986
Minor league third baseman from New Jersey.

While he never reached the major leagues as a player, Plaza did so as a coach, debuting with the expansion Pilots in 1969. He spent several years as an instructor in the Reds' organization before being promoted to Cincinnati as a coach. He later moved on to the Athletics' organization, with whom, as early as 1951, he had served in several roles as a player, coach, and manager. He coached in Oakland in 1986 and later became a roving minor league instructor for the club.

Bill Plummer
Seattle Mariners (AL) 1982–83, 1988–91; Colorado Rockies (NL) 1994
See Managers section.

Johnny Podres
San Diego Padres (NL) 1973; Boston Red Sox (AL) 1980; Minnesota Twins (AL) 1981–85; Philadelphia Phillies (NL) 1991–96

Four-time All-Star pitcher.

After debuting with the Brooklyn Dodgers in 1953 Podres lost part of the 1954 campaign due to an appendectomy. He became most famous for his part in the 1955 World Series, however, during which he beat the New York Yankees twice—once on a shutout—and led the Dodgers to their first World Championship. He received the very first World Series Most Valuable Player Award following that performance, and *Sports Illustrated* named him its Sportsman of the Year.

Podres spent the entire 1956 season in the Navy, then came back in 1957 to lead the National League with a 2.66 earned run average and six shutouts. In 1961 he was 18–5 and led the NL with a .783 winning percentage. The following year he struck out eight consecutive batters in a game, tying the modern league record. He recorded 148 victories in his 15-year career and posted a 3.68 ERA.

Somewhat poetically, Podres finished his career with the Padres, and he later became a coach for them and also coached several other teams.

Brian Poldberg
Kansas City Royals (AL) 2004–
Minor league All-Star catcher.

Poldberg debuted in the New York Yankees' organization and eventually played in the Royals' system, but he never reached the major leagues. He became a minor league coach and manager following his playing days, and twice made the postseason as a skipper. His 1998 Wilmington Blue Rocks captured the Carolina League championship and had the league's best record.

From 1997–2003 (excluding the latter part of the 1998 campaign, when he managed the Blue Rocks), Poldberg served as the Royals' minor league catching instructor. In 2004 he was promoted to Kansas City as a coach.

Dick Pole
Chicago Cubs (NL) 1988–91, 2003–06; San Francisco Giants (NL) 1993–97; Boston Red Sox (AL) 1998; Anaheim Angels (AL) 1999; Cleveland Indians (AL) 2000–01; Montreal Expos (NL) 2002; Cincinnati Reds (NL) 2007–
Right-handed pitcher who went 25–37 lifetime.

Pole's career was virtually ruined when he was hit in the face by a line drive off the bat of Tony Muser in a 1975 game. The blow broke his cheek and caused him to go mostly blind in his right eye, but he did continue pitching in the major leagues until 1978, and in Mexico after that.

He later became a pitching coach for many teams. When he was with the Cubs in 2004 manager Dusty Baker was suspended for one game for arguing vehemently with an umpire over a batting-out-of-order call. Pole took over for that one game and won it before Baker returned.

Howie Pollet
St. Louis Cardinals (NL) 1959–64; Houston Astros (NL) 1965
Standout pitcher for several clubs.

In 1941 Pollet went 20–3 for the Houston Buffaloes of the Texas League while leading the circuit with a 1.16 earned run average and 151 strikeouts. Later that year he debuted with the Cardinals and posted a 5–2 record with a 1.93 ERA in nine games. He won 15 games over his next two seasons, leading the National League with a 1.75 ERA in 1943 and being named an NL All-Star before serving in the military during World War II, then he returned with a vengeance. In 1946 he went 21–10, and his victory total topped the NL as did his 2.10 ERA and 266 innings pitched. He was named an All-Star once again. In 1949 he had another All-Star year, going 20–9 and finishing in a four-way tie for the NL lead with five shutouts.

He never won 20 games again and spent the second half of his career as a reliever. He retired with 131 lifetime victories and a 3.51 ERA. He returned to the Cardinals for several years as a coach, and spent one with the Astros in a similar role.

Eddie Popowski
Boston Red Sox (AL) 1967–74, 1976
See Managers section.

Tom Poquette
Kansas City Royals (AL) 1997–98
Member of the 1976 Topps All-Star Rookie Team.

An outfielder who struggled with bad knees, Poquette had a memorable 1976 campaign, his first full season in the majors, by hitting .302 and collecting 104 hits in 104 games. Used mostly in a reserve or platooning role, he hit .268 lifetime and then became a minor league manager. As a skipper he was named the 1991 Northwest League Manager of the Year when his Eugene Emeralds went 42–34, and the 1992 Midwest League Manager of the Year when his Appleton Foxes reached the playoffs.

Poquette coached the Royals for two seasons before returning to the minor league organization, once again as a manager.

Bo Porter
Florida Marlins (NL) 2007–
Outfielder from Newark, New Jersey.

Porter spent most of a 10-year playing career in the minor leagues, although he got into 89 major league games over three seasons and batted .214. He played more than 1000 contests at the minor league level.

After his playing days Porter went to work as a minor league coach and outfield coordinator. In 2006 he managed the Marlins' Class A Jamestown Jammers before being promoted to the big league staff following the season.

Bill Posedel

Pittsburgh Pirates (NL) 1949–53; St. Louis Cardinals (NL) 1954–57; Philadelphia Phillies (NL) 1958; San Francisco Giants (NL) 1959–60; Oakland Athletics (AL) 1968–72; San Diego Padres (NL) 1974

Navy veteran who led the *U.S.S. Saratoga* to the Pac League championship.

Posedel pitched so well in the Navy that he was offered a professional contract. He won 20 and 21 games for the Portland Beavers in 1936 and 1937, respectively, and pitched five years in the major leagues, where he did not fare nearly so well. With the Brooklyn Dodgers and Boston Braves he went 41–43 with a 4.56 earned run average. He pitched from 1938–41, returned to the Navy during World War II, and then pitched a final season in 1946. He then spent many years as a major league coach with a number of teams.

Alonzo Powell

Cincinnati Reds (NL) 2004

Outstanding outfielder in Japanese baseball.

Powell played in the minor leagues for several years in the systems of the Colorado Rockies, New York Yankees, and Toronto Blue Jays. In 1987 he played 14 games for the Montreal Expos and hit .195, and in 1991 played 57 more for the Seattle Mariners and batted .216 for a lifetime major league average of .211.

In 1992 he departed for Japan, where he played for the next seven years. In the Nippon Baseball League he shone, being named an All-Star five times and winning consecutive batting titles from 1994–96, becoming the first non-Japanese to accomplish that feat and only the third player ever to do so. He won the Japanese equivalent of a Gold Glove twice.

Powell returned to the United States as a minor league coach and manager. At the end of the 2004 minor league season, having managed the Dayton Dragons for the first time, Powell was promoted to the Reds as one of several "extra" coaches to finish out the year.

In September of 2006 he moved to the Seattle Mariners as a hitting coordinator.

Jim Presley

Arizona Diamondbacks (NL) 1998–2000; Florida Marlins (NL) 2006–

Power-hitting third baseman for eight major league seasons.

Presley played most of his career with the Seattle Mariners. He hit at least 24 home runs for three consecutive seasons, from 1985–87. In 1986, the year he was named an American League All-Star, he once hit a two-run homer to tie a game in the bottom of the ninth inning and then connected for a grand slam in the bottom of the tenth with two out to win it. In 1990 he tied a major league record by committing three errors in one inning.

After his playing career Presley became a minor league hitting coach, and he joined the Diamondbacks' staff for three years beginning in 1998. He then worked for five years in the club's minor league system as a hitting instructor before joining the Marlins at the big league level in 2006.

Bryan Price

Seattle Mariners (AL) 2000–05; Arizona Diamondbacks (NL) 2006–

Minor league pitcher from 1984–89.

Price missed the entire 1987 season due to shoulder surgery, and he never reached the major leagues as a player. He began coaching in the minor leagues in 1989, the same year he ended his playing career, and coached through 1997. From 1998–99 he was the Mariners' minor league pitching coordinator, and in 2000 he was promoted to Seattle. In 2006 he moved to the Diamondbacks.

Luis Pujols

Montreal Expos (NL) 1993–2000; Detroit Tigers (AL) 2002; San Francisco Giants (NL) 2003–06

See Managers section.

Mike Quade

Oakland Athletics (AL) 2000–02; Chicago Cubs (NL) 2006, 2007–

Longtime minor league manager.

Quade's managerial career began in 1985 with the Macon Pirates of the South Atlantic League. His teams made the postseason or won league championships seven times. In 1991 he was named Eastern League Manager of the Year when his Harrisburg Senators made the playoffs and boasted the league's best record, and in 1993 became the International League Manager of the Year when his Ottawa Lynx reached the postseason. His 1996 West Michigan Whitecaps captured the Midwest League flag, and in 1999 his Vancouver Canadians not only were the Pacific Coast League champions but won the overall AAA title as well.

Quade spent the 2000–02 seasons as a coach with the Athletics before returning to the minor leagues as a skipper. In 2006, while managing the AAA Iowa Cubs, he joined the Chicago Cubs' staff on a temporary basis as a replacement for Chris Speier, who had taken a leave of absence after being arrested for DUI. He was named to the staff permanently in 2007 when Lou Piniella replaced Dusty Baker as manager.

Mel Queen
Cleveland Indians (AL) 1982; Toronto Blue Jays (AL) 1996–99
See Managers section.

Frank Quilici
Minnesota Twins (AL) 1971–72
See Managers section.

Jamie Quirk
St. Louis Cardinals (NL) 1984; Kansas City Royals (AL) 1994–2001; Texas Rangers (AL) 2002; Colorado Rockies (NL) 2003–
Part of the first "Q" battery in major league history.

Quirk started out as an infielder but was converted to a catcher early in his 18-year major league career. In 1980 with the Royals he was the catcher when hurler Dan Quisenberry took the mound, marking the first time players whose names started with the letter *Q* formed a battery. Quirk hit .240 in his career and played for eight different clubs, including three separate stints with Kansas City.

Quirk had a hard time catching on in 1984. Beginning spring training with the Cardinals, he was released in March and served as a coach with the team. He was eventually picked up by the Chicago White Sox, and he played three games with them and one with the Cleveland Indians before the season's end. The following year he returned to the Royals, and he would resume his playing career with them and several other clubs until 1992.

In 1994 he began a fourth stint with the Royals, this time as a coach. He later coached the Rangers and the Rockies.

Doug Rader
San Diego Padres (NL) 1978–79; Chicago White Sox (AL) 1986–87, 1997; Oakland Athletics (AL) 1992; Florida Marlins (NL) 1993–94
See Managers section.

Dan Radison
San Diego Padres (NL) 1993–94; Chicago Cubs (NL) 1995–99
Minor league player and longtime minor league manager.

Radison played in the St. Louis Cardinals' organization before becoming a college coach. He worked at Broward Community College in Florida from 1977–79, the University of Georgia from 1979–81, and Old Dominion University from 1982–83. In 1984 he became a minor league skipper in the New York Mets' organization, and over the years his teams would qualify for the playoffs six times. In

1986 he was named Appalachian League Manager of the Year when his Johnson City Cardinals made the postseason with the league's best record, and in 1991 his Albany-Colonie Yankees captured the Eastern League championship.

He served as a coach at the major league level for both the Padres and the Cubs before returning to the New York Yankees' organization and later that of the Los Angeles Dodgers as a minor league skipper.

Pat Ragan
Philadelphia Phillies (NL) 1924
Right-handed pitcher from Iowa.

Ragan debuted in the major leagues in 1909. By 1913 he was a 15-game winner, although he lost 18 contests that season. In 1914 he became the first National League pitcher to strike out an opposing side on nine pitches when he set down the Boston Braves while pitching for the Brooklyn Robins in the second game of a doubleheader. His finest season was 1915, when he was 17–12 with a 2.34 earned run average.

Ragan's big league career was basically over in 1919, but in 1923 he appeared in one game for the Phillies and then served as a coach with them the following season. His lifetime record was 77–104 despite a fine 2.99 ERA.

Tim Raines
Chicago White Sox (AL) 2005–06
American Association batting champion in 1980.

That crown was probably the least of Raines' accomplishments. *The Sporting News* named him its Minor League Player of the Year, but the speedy outfielder would go on to even greater things. In a 23-year major league career he became an All-Star seven times, won a National League batting title, and led the NL once in doubles, twice in runs scored, and four times in stolen bases.

A prolific basestealer, he swiped 808 in his career. In 1983 he became the first player since Ty Cobb to steal 70 bases and drive in 70 runs in the same season. The following year he became the first player to steal at least 70 in four consecutive seasons, swiping 71, 78, a career-high 90, and 75 between 1981 and 1984. He extended the string to six seasons with steals of exactly 70 in both 1985 and 1986. His 71 steals in strike-shortened 1981 had set a since-broken record for a rookie. He once set an American League record by stealing 40 consecutive bases without being caught. His career stolen-base percentage of .847 is the third-highest in major league history.

In 1987 Tim was named the Most Valuable Player of the All-Star Game when he went 3-for-3 and connected for a game-winning two-run triple in the thirteenth inning.

Raines overcame cocaine problems early in his career

but later began to battle leg maladies. In 1999 he was diagnosed with lupus and missed the entire 2000 campaign. He technically retired and then tried out for the Olympic baseball team, where he was one of the last players to be cut. He came back in 2001, and with the Baltimore Orioles he and his son Tim, Jr. became only the second father-son combination (following Ken Griffey, Sr. and Jr.) to play in the same game. The two appeared in four contests together for the O's.

Raines retired from the Florida Marlins in 2002 and then served as a volunteer roving minor league baserunning instructor with the club. In 2004 he became a minor league manager in the Montreal Expos' organization, and in September joined the big club to assist the coaches. The team also retired his number 30 that year. In 2005 he was hired by the White Sox as a coach at the major league level, and he lasted two seasons.

Bobby Ramos
Tampa Bay Devil Rays (AL) 1998, 2005– ; Anaheim Angels (AL) 2000–02
Backup catcher who hit .190.

A reserve for six major league seasons, Ramos both started and finished his professional career in the minors. In 1989 he became a coach and instructor in the Houston Astros' organization, then moved on to managing. In 1994 his Gulf Coast Astros captured the Gulf Coast League championship, the first in the team's history. From 1997–99 he managed in the Devil Rays' organization, spending one month as a coach at the big league level in September of 1998. From 2000–02 he coached the Angels and then worked in their organization as a roving catching instructor before returning to Tampa Bay as a coach in 2005.

Bob Randall
Minnesota Twins (AL) 1980
Second baseman for the Twins.

Randall was a Minnesota regular in his rookie season of 1976, when he promptly set a Twins' record for fielding average at the keystone sack. He hit .267, but after a couple of seasons he began to receive less and less playing time and he was through by 1980. He played five games that year and worked as a coach for the club.

Willie Randolph
New York Yankees (AL) 1994–2004
See Managers section.

Vern Rapp
Montreal Expos (NL) 1979–83
See Managers section.

Claude Raymond
Montreal Expos (NL) 2002–04
Pitcher from St. Jean, Quebec.

A French-Canadian, Raymond debuted with the Chicago White Sox in 1959. From 1961–63 he was with the Milwaukee Braves, but in October of '63 was claimed by the Houston Astros in a special, supplemental draft that was held for Major League Baseball's expansion teams. With Houston Raymond was named an All-Star in 1966, going 7–5 with 16 saves and a 3.13 earned run average. In 1969 he became the first Quebec native to play for the Expos, and in 1970 he posted 23 saves for the Canadian club.

Raymond retired following the 1971 season, and from 1972–2001 he worked as a French broadcaster for the Expos. He then returned to the dugout as a coach with the team for the next three seasons.

Frank Reberger
California Angels (AL) 1991; Florida Marlins (NL) 1993–94
Rancher from Idaho.

Reberger pitched as both a starter and a reliever. In five seasons he went 14–15 with 8 saves and a 4.52 earned run average for the Chicago Cubs, San Diego Padres, and San Francisco Giants. He later became a longtime minor league manager, and spent several seasons coaching the Angels and the Marlins.

Jimmie Reese
California Angels (AL) 1972–94
Spent over 70 years in organized baseball.

Reese began as a bat boy for the Los Angeles Angels of the Pacific Coast League when he was only 15 years old. His real name was Hyam Soloman; he changed it to Jimmie Reese in an effort to avoid the racial prejudice that was sometimes leveled against Jewish players. He eventually became a minor league player and then reached the majors for three seasons, playing second base for the New York Yankees (where he gained fame for rooming with Babe Ruth) and St. Louis Cardinals from 1930–32. He hit a respectable .278, but was soon back in the minors.

After his playing career Reese spent many years as a minor league coach and manager, and for a time worked as a scout. In 1972 he was hired as a coach with the American League Angels, and he remained in that role for 23 years. Jimmie died in 1994, still coaching, and the Angels retired his number 50 the following season.

Pee Wee Reese
Los Angeles Dodgers (NL) 1959
Hall of Fame shortstop.

Reese spent his entire 16-year career with the Brooklyn/Los Angeles Dodgers, missing the 1943–45 seasons due to Navy service during World War II. A 10-time All-Star, he frequently led the National League in several fielding categories. He hit .269 lifetime and tied for the NL lead in 1947 with 104 walks while leading in 1949 with 132 runs scored, and in 1952 with 30 stolen bases. He hit 126 home runs in his career and stole 232 bases.

A Dodger favorite, Reese was famous for his support of Jackie Robinson when Robinson broke the color line in 1947. At one point he even went onto the field and publicly put his arm around Jackie, leaving no uncertainty concerning his feelings about his teammate's presence.

Reese played his last season for the Dodgers in 1958, the club's first in Los Angeles. He coached the following year, then briefly became a broadcaster before going to work for Hillerich & Bradsby, makers of the famous Louisville Slugger.

Reese was inducted into the Hall of Fame in 1984, and the Dodgers retired his number 1 that same year. Pee Wee passed away in 1999.

Phil Regan
Seattle Mariners (AL) 1984–86; Cleveland Indians (AL) 1994, 1999; Chicago Cubs (NL) 1997–98
See Managers section.

Pete Reiser
Los Angeles Dodgers (NL) 1960–64; Chicago Cubs (NL) 1966–69, 1972–74; California Angels (AL) 1970–71
Aggressive, frequently-injured outfielder.

Reiser had incredible ability, but much of his playing time was hampered by the fact that he would run into outfield walls at full speed and suffer a wide variety of hurts as a result. By one count he had to be carried off the field 11 times in his career.

Reiser played his first full season in 1941 with the Brooklyn Dodgers and promptly won the National League batting title, hitting .343 and setting a record as the youngest player ever to win the crown. He was 22 years old. He also tied for the league lead with 39 doubles and led with 17 triples and 117 runs scored. In 1942 he topped the NL with 20 stolen bases, and after losing the 1943–45 campaigns to World War II he came back to lead again with 34 swipes.

In 1946 he stole home seven times, and that was believed to be a major league record until further research showed that Ty Cobb had swiped home eight times in 1912.

Reiser, a three-time All-Star, retired in 1952 and later coached the Dodgers (by now in Los Angeles), Cubs, and Angels.

Rick Renick
Kansas City Royals (AL) 1981; Montreal Expos (NL) 1985–86, 2001; Minnesota Twins (AL) 1987–90; Pittsburgh Pirates (NL) 1997–2000; Florida Marlins (NL) 2002
Minor league All-Star who played five seasons for the Twins.

An infielder and outfielder, Renick was used as a backup and hit only .221 in 276 major league games. Perhaps his biggest accomplishment was hitting a home run in his very first big league at-bat on July 11, 1968.

Renick returned to the minors as a player-coach for several years and then worked as a hitting instructor in the Royals' minor league system before joining the big club as a coach. He then became a skipper in the Expos' farm system and was named the Southern League's co-Manager of the Year when his Jacksonville Suns went 76–69. After coaching again at the major league level for the Expos and Twins, he went back to managing, this time in the Chicago White Sox' organization, and in both 1993 and 1996 was named American Association Manager of the Year while at the helm of the Nashville Sounds.

He later coached the Pirates, the Expos again, and the Marlins.

Grover Resinger
Atlanta Braves (NL) 1966; Chicago White Sox (AL) 1967–68; Detroit Tigers (AL) 1969–70; California Angels (AL) 1975–76
Third baseman renowned for his toughness.

Resinger never reached the major leagues as a player, but he was a hard-nosed competitor who hated to lose. He lived on a farm in Missouri and kept a wolf as a pet. He eventually coached the Braves, White Sox, Tigers, and Angels, and also worked with some minor league clubs.

He died in his birthplace of St. Louis in 1986.

Merv Rettenmund
California Angels (AL) 1980–81; Texas Rangers (AL) 1983–85; Oakland Athletics (AL) 1989–90; San Diego Padres (NL) 1991–99, 2006– ; Atlanta Braves (NL) 2000–01; Detroit Tigers (AL) 2002
International League Most Valuable Player in 1968.

Rettenmund was promoted from the Rochester Red Wings to the Baltimore Orioles that season and appeared in 31 games for the O's, with whom he batted .297. *The Sporting News* named him its Minor League Player of the Year.

Rettenmund was a halfback at Ball State and had been drafted by the Dallas Cowboys, but he opted for baseball instead. He spent most of his 13 big league seasons as a reserve outfielder, and eventually became a dependable pinch-hitter. In a game in 1977 he hit a three-run homer in the twenty-first inning for the San Diego Padres in a defeat of the Montreal Expos.

After his playing career he coached a number of major league clubs, including the Padres. He worked for the Toronto Blue Jays for several years as a roving minor league instructor, and in June of 2006 returned to the Padres to replace the deposed Dave Magadan.

Cananea Reyes
Seattle Mariners (AL) 1981
Mexican League player who became a legendary manager.

Reyes hit well but spent most of his career in Mexico's lower minor leagues. He became a player-manager and later full-time manager, even spending some time pitching, and eventually won six championships.

As a player-manager in 1969 he guided the San Luis Potosi Charros to the Mexican Center League pennant, and in 1972 took the Jalisco Charros to the Liga pennant. His greatest successes, however, came with the Mexico City Red Devils, whom he led to championships in 1974, 1976, 1985, 1987, and 1988. In 1976 he also guided the Hermosillo Orange Growers to the Caribbean Series title.

Reyes spent 1981 as a Mariners' coach before resuming his managerial career in Mexico. He died in 1991 at the age of 54 and was later inducted into the Mexican baseball Hall of Fame.

Tommie Reynolds
Oakland Athletics (AL) 1989–95; St. Louis Cardinals (NL) 1996
Light-hitting reserve outfielder.

Reynolds averaged .226 in eight major league seasons, never batting over .257. He played for four different teams in five cities (leaving the A's when they were in Kansas City and returning to them later in Oakland). He eventually joined them once again in Oakland as a coach, and also spent one season coaching for the Cardinals.

Del Rice
Los Angeles Angels (AL) 1962–64; California Angels (AL) 1965–66; Cleveland Indians (AL) 1967
See Managers section.

Jim Rice
Boston Red Sox (AL) 1995–2000
First player to lead the American League in triples and home runs in the same season.

That was in 1978 with the Red Sox, when Rice led with 15 triples and 46 roundtrippers. He also became the first major leaguer to lead any league in triples, homers, and runs batted in in the same season, as his 139 RBIs were also best in the circuit. He also hit .315 and led the AL

with 213 hits en route to being named the AL's Most Valuable Player.

In the minor leagues Rice had won the Eastern League batting crown in 1973 with the Bristol Red Sox, and the following season with the Pawtucket Red Sox had captured the International League Triple Crown with a .337 average, 25 home runs, and 93 RBIs while being named that league's Rookie of the Year and MVP.

Rice obviously did not slow down in the majors. He debuted in 1974, and besides that MVP 1978 campaign he was named to eight All-Star teams and led the AL twice more in home runs and once more in RBIs. He hit 382 homers lifetime, clouting at least 20 eleven times, and drove in over 100 runs on eight occasions. He hit .298 lifetime and batted over .300 seven times. Rice spent his entire 16-year career with the Red Sox, although he began to slow down toward the end because of various injuries.

After his playing career Rice stayed with the Red Sox in various capacities, working as a roving batting coach, a major league coach, and an instructional batting coach.

Dave Ricketts
Pittsburgh Pirates (NL) 1971–73; St. Louis Cardinals (NL) 1974–75, 1978–91
Catcher from Duquesne University.

Ricketts played 130 major league games over six seasons, spending time with both the Cardinals and the Pirates. He hit .249 overall, topping out at .273 in both 1967 (in 52 games) and 1969 (in 30 games). He remained with the Pirates as a coach after retiring from the playing field, and then returned to the Cardinals in the same role.

Johnny Riddle
Pittsburgh Pirates (NL) 1948–50; St. Louis Cardinals (NL) 1952–55; Milwaukee Braves (NL) 1956–57; Cincinnati Redlegs (NL) 1958; Philadelphia Phillies (NL) 1959
Catcher nicknamed "Mutt."

In seven major league seasons, comprising only 98 games, Riddle hit .238 and did not connect for a single home run. He played for five teams, including the Braves (when they were in Boston), the Reds, and the Pirates. He later became a coach for five teams, including the Braves in their new home of Milwaukee. Riddle died in 1998 in Indianapolis.

Greg Riddoch
San Diego Padres (NL) 1987–90; Tampa Bay Devil Rays (AL) 1998–99
See Managers section.

Mark Riggins
St. Louis Cardinals (NL) 1995

College player from Murray State.

Riggins signed with the Cardinals and spent five years in their minor league organization before becoming a minor league coach. In 1995 he was named the St. Louis pitching coach by manager Joe Torre, but when Torre departed after the season Riggins was not retained. He continued to work in the system, however, taking on the job of minor league pitching co-coordinator.

Jim Riggleman
St. Louis Cardinals (NL) 1989–90; Cleveland Indians (AL) 2000; Los Angeles Dodgers (NL) 2001–04
See Managers section.

Dave Righetti
San Francisco Giants (NL) 1999, 2000–
Outstanding relief pitcher for many years.

Having once struck out 21 batters in a minor league game, Righetti debuted with the New York Yankees in three games in 1979, but his official rookie season was 1981, when he went 8–4 with a 2.05 earned run average as a starter in the strike-abbreviated campaign and was named the American League's Rookie of the Year. In 1983 he went 14–8 and pitched a no-hitter against the Boston Red Sox on the Fourth of July.

Despite his success (or perhaps because of it) Righetti was moved to the bullpen the following season as a replacement for departed closer Goose Gossage. In 64 appearances he notched 31 saves, then garnered 29 the following season and a major league record 46 the next. In both 1986 and 1987 he was named the AL Rolaids Relief Man of the Year. In '86 *The Sporting News* also decreed him its Fireman of the Year, and he tied for the same award in '87.

Righetti was named to two All-Star teams and garnered 252 saves lifetime. In 1999 he became a roving minor league pitching instructor for the Giants, and joined the big club for three days in May to fill in while pitching coach Ron Perranoski visited his mother, who was ill. He returned to San Francisco in 2000 to stay.

Bill Rigney
San Diego Padres (NL) 1975
See Managers section.

Joe Rigoli
Philadelphia Phillies (NL) 1996–97
Minor leaguer with a brief playing career.

Rigoli became a minor league manager following his playing days, and in 1984 led the Springfield Cardinals to the Midwest League playoffs. He was a player-manager that year, pitching in four games and totaling seven innings. He later worked as a minor league coach, a major league coach with the Phillies, and a scout with the St. Louis Cardinals.

Cal Ripken, Sr.
Baltimore Orioles (AL) 1976–86, 1989–92
See Managers section.

Ray Rippelmeyer
Philadelphia Phillies (NL) 1970–78
College basketball star.

Rippelmeyer was drafted by the New York Knicks but was unable to play because he was drafted into the Army in 1955. He spent two years in the military and then played baseball in the minor leagues for many years, emerging into the majors for 18 games in 1962 with the Washington Senators. He started one of those games and went 1–2 overall with a 5.49 earned run average.

He later coached nine years for the Phillies and spent time working in several organizations, including as an assistant director of player development for the Cincinnati Reds and as a roving minor league pitching coach for the New York Mets.

Luis Rivera
Cleveland Indians (AL) 2006–
Good-fielding infielder from Puerto Rico.

Rivera signed with the Montreal Expos at the age of 17, and he debuted at the big league level with them five years later. In an 11-year career, in which he was used mainly as a backup, he hit .233 with 28 home runs. In 2000 he began coaching in the minor leagues, and then, in his rookie managerial season of 2003, was named South Atlantic League Manager of the Year when his Lake County Captains posted the circuit's best record. In 2006 he was promoted to Cleveland as a coach at the big league level.

Mike Roarke
Detroit Tigers (AL) 1965–66, 1970; California Angels (AL) 1967–69; Chicago Cubs (NL) 1978–80; St. Louis Cardinals (NL) 1984–90; San Diego Padres (NL) 1991–93; Boston Red Sox (AL) 1994
Catcher from Boston College.

Roarke did not reach the major leagues until 1961, when he was 30 years of age. He then spent four years in a backup role with the Tigers, hitting .230 with 6 home runs and 44 runs batted in. In 1963 he batted .318 in 23 contests.

Roarke's last season was 1964, and he went immediately into coaching with Detroit. That was the first of many years in that capacity with many teams.

Dave Roberts
Cleveland Indians (AL) 1987
One of four major leaguers by the name of Dave Roberts.

This one was David Wayne Roberts, and he was a versatile infielder and catcher who played from 1972–82 with the San Diego Padres, Texas Rangers, Houston Astros, and Philadelphia Phillies. He was named to the Topps All-Star Rookie Team in 1972 when he hit .244 with 5 home runs and 33 runs batted in in exactly 100 games. The following year he set career highs with a .286 average, 21 homers, and 64 RBIs.

He later coached one season for the Indians.

Leon Roberts
Tampa Bay Devil Rays (AL) 1999–2000
Outfielder signed out of the University of Michigan.

Roberts played 11 seasons in the major leagues for several clubs, debuting in 1974 with the Detroit Tigers. He had an outstanding 1978 campaign; having just joined the Seattle Mariners from the Houston Astros, his first hit for his new club was a grand slam. He went on to bat .301 for the season with 22 home runs and 92 runs batted in, totals he would never match again.

In his final season of 1984 he was called on to pitch one inning for the Kansas City Royals, and he surrendered three earned runs in that outing. After retiring Roberts became a longtime minor league hitting coach, and he spent two years at the major league level as a coach with the Devil Rays.

Mel Roberts
Philadelphia Phillies (NL) 1992–95
Minor league player for nine years.

Roberts played from 1961–70 in the outfield, spending 1965 playing semipro ball. In 1969 he was a player-coach, and he eventually became a roving minor league outfield instructor and a minor league manager. In 1988 his Spartanburg Phillies captured the South Atlantic League championship, and from 1992–95 he was a coach in Philadelphia. He then went to work as a minor league coach in the Atlanta Braves' organization.

Sherry Robertson
Minnesota Twins (AL) 1970
Nephew of Clark Griffith.

Robertson was signed by his uncle and was later brought up from the minor leagues despite some rather unimpressive statistics. He wound up playing 10 seasons for Griffith's Washington Nationals. He hit only .230, but at one point in 1946 led off two consecutive games with home runs. In 1952 Griffith sold Robertson to the Philadelphia Athletics, and Sherry finished his career that sea-

son. He then returned to the Nationals and worked in the team's front office. He spent many years as the club's farm director, and coached in 1970 when it had become the Minnesota Twins.

Bill Robinson
New York Mets (NL) 1984–89; Florida Marlins (NL) 2002–05
Outfielder and first baseman for several teams.

Robinson was a highly touted minor leaguer who never quite lived up to his potential. He did last 16 major league seasons, however, batting .258 and displaying some power by slugging at least 21 home runs on four different occasions. His finest season was 1977 with the Pittsburgh Pirates, when he hit .304 with 26 home runs and 104 runs batted in. The previous year he had batted .303 and knocked 21 out of the park.

Robinson later coached at the major league level for the Mets and the Marlins.

Brooks Robinson
Baltimore Orioles (AL) 1977
Hall of Fame third baseman.

Probably the greatest-fielding third baseman of all time, Robinson spent his entire 23-year major league career with the Orioles. He set all-time major league records at the hot corner for games played, putouts, assists, total chances, double plays, and fielding average. He won 16 Gold Gloves and was named to 18 All-Star teams. A .267 lifetime hitter, he slugged at least 20 home runs six times, a fact often lost in the shadow of his glovework. In 1964 he was named the American League's Most Valuable Player when he hit .317 with 28 homers and an AL-leading 118 runs batted in.

In 1970 he raised eyebrows across the nation with his stunning defense against the Cincinnati Reds in the World Series, robbing numerous Reds of certain base hits and helping Baltimore to the championship. He was named MVP of the Series for his performance, which also included a .429 showing at the plate with two home runs.

Robinson finished his career in 1977 in 24 games, and also served the Orioles that year as a coach. The club retired his number 5, and in 1983 he was inducted into the Hall of Fame.

Dewey Robinson
Chicago White Sox (AL) 1993–94
American Association Pitcher of the Year in 1979.

That standout season with the Iowa Oaks led to a promotion to the White Sox, with whom Robinson would eventually appear in 30 major league games between 1979 and 1981. Used entirely in relief, he posted a 2–2 record with a 4.05 earned run average.

After his playing career Robinson spent many years working at the minor league level. He coached in the bigs for the White Sox for two seasons, then went to work in the Houston Astros' system as a minor league pitching coordinator and director of pitching development. His responsibilities with the Astros included scouting at both the minor and major league levels.

Eddie Robinson
Baltimore Orioles (AL) 1957–59
International League Most Valuable Player in 1946.

Robinson won that award with the minor league Baltimore Orioles, and he would eventually finish a 13-year career by playing four games with the major league version. A power hitter and four-time All-Star, he slugged 172 home runs lifetime, hitting at least 14 on eight occasions and topping 20 four times.

After his playing career Robinson remained with the Orioles as a coach for three years, then worked in the club's player development department. He then became the general manager of the Atlanta Braves, and after several years he and Dan O'Brien served as co-GMs of the Texas Rangers. Robinson soon claimed the GM title for himself in Texas, but in 1982 he was fired following a dismal Rangers' showing on the field.

As a player Robinson had donned the uniforms of seven of the original eight American League clubs. After leaving the Rangers he worked as a scout for the eighth team, the only one with whom he had never played: the Boston Red Sox.

Frank Robinson
California Angels (AL) 1977; Baltimore Orioles (AL) 1978–80, 1985–87
See Managers section.

Sheriff Robinson
New York Mets (NL) 1964–67, 1972
Minor league catcher and manager.

Warren "Sheriff" Robinson spent many years in the minor leagues, largely as a well-respected skipper. He began managing in 1953, and the following season his Corning Red Sox captured the PONY League championship. He coached the Mets for several years and then became an advance scout for the club, and his reports on the opposition were credited as being influential in the "Miracle Mets" World Championship in 1969. He coached one more season in 1972 and continued as a scout.

Robinson passed away in 2002.

Wilbert Robinson
New York Giants (NL) 1911–13
See Managers section.

Tom Robson
Texas Rangers (AL) 1986–92; New York Mets (NL) 1997–99, 2000, 2002; Cincinnati Reds (NL) 2003
Pacific Coast League Most Valuable Player in 1974.

That year with the Spokane Indians earned Robson a call-up to the Rangers, but he would play only 23 games in Texas in 1974 and '75 despite some impressive minor league hitting. In the majors he hit only .208 in limited action.

Robson eventually coached the Rangers and the Mets. In June of 1999 he was let go by the Mets without manager Bobby Valentine's knowledge; Valentine had to read in the newspaper that several of his coaches had been fired and a new staff hired. Robson was brought back in 2000, however, and again in 2002. In 2003 he coached for the Reds.

Robson also authored a book about hitting entitled *The Hitting Edge.*

Buck Rodgers
Minnesota Twins (AL) 1970–74; San Francisco Giants (NL) 1976; Milwaukee Brewers (AL) 1978–80
See Managers section.

Eddie Rodriguez
California Angels (AL) 1996; Toronto Blue Jays (AL) 1998–99; Arizona Diamondbacks (NL) 2001–03; Montreal Expos (NL) 2004; Washington Nationals (NL) 2005–06
Minor league shortstop for six seasons.

Rodriguez played until 1981, and began coaching in 1983. In both 1984 and 1986 he was called upon to take the field in several games and therefore served as a player-coach. In 1987 he began managing at the minor league level, then served as the Angels' minor league roving defense coordinator from 1991–93 and as their field coordinator from 1994–97, except for 1996 when he coached for the big club. After coaching the Blue Jays from 1998–99 he was named manager of the Queens Kings in the Toronto system and his club made the playoffs, but he also took a leave of absence in July to work with the U.S. Olympic baseball team. In Sydney that year he was the third base coach for the squad that took the Olympic gold medal.

Rodriguez next moved to the Diamondbacks as a coach, then to the Expos. He was still with that club when it relocated to Washington and became the Nationals.

Ron Roenicke
Los Angeles Dodgers (NL) 1992–93; Anaheim Angels (AL) 2000–04; Los Angeles Angels of Anaheim (AL) 2005–

Backup outfielder who played eight major league seasons.

Roenicke hit .238 while appearing for six different teams. He became a Dodgers' coach in 1992 and lasted two seasons, then began managing in the minor leagues. In 1995 he was named California League Manager of the Year when his San Bernardino Spirit took the title, and in 1997 he became the Texas League Manager of the Year when his San Antonio Missions captured the crown.

He continued managing in the minors until 2000, when he was promoted to the Angels as a coach.

Pat Roessler
Montreal Expos (NL) 2000–01
Never played in the major leagues.

Roessler worked as an assistant coach at Old Dominion University as well as serving as a minor league hitting coach in the organizations of the Montreal Expos and the Houston Astros. From 2000–01 he coached for the Expos at the major league level.

Roessler eventually moved to the New York Yankees' system as the team's director of player development and then as a minor league manager.

Dan Rohn
Seattle Mariners (AL) 2006
Minor league infielder who played 54 major league games.

Rohn appeared with the Chicago Cubs and Cleveland Indians and hit .250 with a home run and 11 runs batted in. He then became a successful minor league manager, qualifying for the playoffs with the 1995 Fort Wayne Wizards and winning the Eastern League championship with the 2000 New Haven Ravens. In 2001 he was named Manager of the Year of the Pacific Coast League when he guided the Tacoma Rainiers to the circuit's best record and a co-championship with the New Orleans Zephyrs. (The championship series was canceled due to the terrorist attacks on the United States on September 11 of that year.)

In 2006 Rohn was named to the Mariners' major league staff as an administrative coach. He participated in pre-game activities as a uniformed coach and coordinated scouting reports, but was not in the dugout during games. He was fired in mid-September of 2006.

Cookie Rojas
Chicago Cubs (NL) 1978–81; Florida Marlins (NL) 1993–96; New York Mets (NL) 1997–2000; Toronto Blue Jays (AL) 2001–02
See Managers section.

Euclides Rojas
Florida Marlins (NL) 1999; Boston Red Sox (AL) 2003–04
Refugee from Cuba.

Rojas was an outstanding pitcher on the Cuban National Team, leading that squad all-time with 90 saves and 342 appearances when he decided to flee for the United States. He and 12 others floated on a 15-foot raft in August of 1994 until they were rescued by the U.S. Coast Guard. Rojas then spent six months on Guantanamo Bay before being allowed to enter the U.S. based on the sponsorship of former St. Louis Cardinal pitcher Rene Arocha. Rojas eventually became a citizen of the United States.

He was drafted by the Florida Marlins and spent one season and part of a second in the minor leagues before arm problems ended his career prematurely. He was offered a job as a coach immediately and immediately accepted. In 1999 he served as the Marlins' bullpen coach for two weeks on an interim basis, then returned to his work in the minors.

In 2002 Rojas worked as the Pittsburgh Pirates' Latin American pitching coordinator, then was hired by the Red Sox to coach at the big league level. He left the club in 2005 to pursue other opportunities.

Red Rolfe
New York Yankees (AL) 1946
See Managers section.

Eddie Rommel
Philadelphia Athletics (AL) 1933–34
Outstanding pitcher credited with pioneering the modern knuckleball.

In 13 seasons Rommel led the American League twice in victories, registering 27 in 1922 and 21 in 1925 (tying him with Ted Lyons in '25). Those were the only two years he was a 20-game winner, although he won at least 16 five times and at least 11 on nine occasions. He also led twice in games pitched and posted a 171–119 lifetime record with a 3.54 earned run average. He led the AL three times in relief wins.

Rommel pitched for the A's his entire career. In 1932 he pitched 17 relief innings in an 18-inning game at Cleveland, being the only extra pitcher Connie Mack brought along for what was a rare single-game trip. Mack had hoped to save train fare by bringing only one spare arm, but as it so happened he called upon Rommel in the second inning and had no one in the bullpen from that point on. The A's won the game, 18–17.

Rommel coached two years for the A's before eventually becoming an AL umpire, beginning a second career that would span 22 years. As an arbiter Rommel worked two World Series and six All-Star Games.

Gene Roof
Detroit Tigers (AL) 1992–95

Brother of Phil Roof.

Gene was an outfielder who was named an All-Star in the Appalachian League in 1977. In the majors he played only 48 games over three seasons with the St. Louis Cardinals and Montreal Expos, where he hit .267. He became a minor league manager following his playing days, beginning with the Fayetteville Generals. His son Shawn would eventually play on the same field for the Fayetteville SwampDogs.

Roof guided the Generals to a division title in his second season, and after eventually spending four years as a Tigers' coach he managed in the system again and later worked as an instructor with the organization's outfielders and baserunners.

Phil Roof
San Diego Padres (NL) 1978; Seattle Mariners (AL) 1983–88; Chicago Cubs (NL) 1990–91
Brother of Gene Roof.

A catcher, Roof put together a 15-year major league career based mainly on his excellent defense, because he hit only .215 at the plate. He and his brother Gene were two of five brothers to play professional baseball, although the duo were the only ones to reach the major leagues. Phil became a Padres' coach following his retirement and then began managing in the minor leagues. Between managerial stints he worked as a coach at the major league level with the Mariners and Cubs. In 2000 he was named Pacific Coast League Manager of the Year while at the helm of the Salt Lake Buzz, who reached the league championship series. He then coached for the Edmonton Trappers and managed the Rochester Red Wings before retiring.

Charlie Root
Chicago Cubs (NL) 1951–53, 1960; Milwaukee Braves (NL) 1956–57
Left-hander who won 201 major league games.

Root won at least 13 games 10 times in a 17-year career. His finest season came in 1927 with the Cubs, when he led the National League with 26 victories and 309 innings and tied for the lead with 48 games pitched. His final record was 26–15 that year, his earned run average 3.76. In 1930 he tied for the circuit's lead with four shutouts. He is probably most remembered, however, for an appearance in the 1932 World Series, when he was facing Babe Ruth of the New York Yankees and the Sultan of Swat allegedly "called his shot." Root always denied the called shot, claiming that Ruth was simply telling him he had one more strike before clouting the now-famous home run.

Root eventually returned to the Cubs as a coach following his playing career, and later coached the Braves before returning to the Cubs yet again.

John Roseboro
Washington Senators (AL) 1971; California Angels (AL) 1972–74
Four-time All-Star catcher.

Roseboro was extremely durable, failing to catch at least 103 games in a season only in his rookie year of 1957 and his final campaign of 1970. He won two Gold Gloves and caught two of Sandy Koufax's four no-hitters. He frequently led the National League in several fielding categories, and in 1961 hit a career-high 18 home runs.

He is probably most famous for his role in inciting a brawl on August 22, 1965, while his Los Angeles Dodgers were playing the San Francisco Giants. Giants' hurler Juan Marichal had thrown brushback pitches at a couple of Dodger batters, and when it was Marichal's turn to hit, Roseboro nearly clipped him in the face when throwing the ball back to the Dodgers' pitcher. After the second occurrence Marichal bashed him over the head twice with his bat, causing both benches to empty and opening a gash in the catcher's head that would need 14 stitches. A 14-minute fight ensued, and Marichal ended up with an eight-game suspension and a fine. The event caused ill feelings between the two combatants for many years, but in the 1980s they buried the hatchet and became good friends.

After his playing career Roseboro coached for the Senators and the Angels, then he worked as a catching and hitting instructor in the Dodgers' minor league system. He and his wife also opened a public relations firm in Beverly Hills, California.

Glen Rosenbaum
Chicago White Sox (AL) 1974–75, 1986–89
Member of the Indiana Baseball Hall of Fame.

Rosenbaum was a pitcher who never reached the major leagues. A resident of Union Mills, Indiana, he pitched in the minor leagues for 11 years and posted a 98–42 record with several organizations. Following his retirement he became a batting practice pitcher with the White Sox, and he held that position until a shoulder injury shut him down in 1989. Along the way he served two stints as a coach on the White Sox' major league staff. He then worked as Chicago's traveling secretary, and in 1991 was named Traveling Secretary of the Year by Major League Baseball.

Wayne Rosenthal
Florida Marlins (NL) 2003–04
Pitcher from Brooklyn, New York.

Rosenthal pitched 42 major league games in two seasons for the Texas Rangers. He started none of them and posted a 1–4 record with a 5.40 earned run average. After his playing career he eventually worked as a minor league pitching coordinator for the Marlins, and was promoted to the major league staff as pitching coach in 2003 under Jack McKeon. In 2004 conflict erupted on the club's pitching staff, with McKeon wanting the pitchers to throw more—against their wishes—and Rosenthal being perceived as doing little to defend them. The Marlins offered to give Wayne his old job back, and Rosenthal accepted and once again became the team's minor league pitching coordinator.

Frank Roth
Pittsburgh Pirates (NL) 1917; New York Yankees (AL) 1921; Cleveland Indians (AL) 1923–25; Chicago White Sox (AL) 1927
Catcher who eventually became an umpire.

Roth played for six major league seasons and hit .250 with a home run and 75 runs batted in. He spent time with the Philadelphia Phillies, St. Louis Browns, Chicago White Sox, and Cincinnati Reds. In 1909 he once attacked an umpire after arguing a call at home plate, in part inspiring the National League to implement a two-umpire system for each game. After his playing career he worked as a coach for several teams. Ironically, he once had to umpire in 1923 while serving as a coach for the Indians.

Larry Rothschild
Cincinnati Reds (NL) 1990–93; Florida Marlins (NL) 1995–97; Chicago Cubs (NL) 2002–
See Managers section.

Edd Roush
Cincinnati Reds (NL) 1938
Hall of Fame outfielder and .323 lifetime hitter.

Roush played for 18 major league seasons. A speedy runner and excellent hitter and fielder, he batted over .300 thirteen times and won two National League batting titles: first in 1917, when he hit .341, and again in 1919, when he batted .321. His finest seasons were with the Reds, with whom he starred in the 1919 World Series and led the NL in 1923 with 41 doubles and in 1924 with 21 triples. He never struck out more than 25 times in a season and he stole 268 bases lifetime, reaching the 20 mark six times. He hit 30 inside-the-park home runs.

Roush was renowned for sitting out spring training over salary disputes, and in 1930 he took things to extremes and sat out the entire season. His last season was 1931, when he returned to the Reds from the New York Giants, and he would return to Cincinnati again in 1938 as a coach. Roush was inducted into the Hall of Fame in 1962, and in 1970 he threw out the first pitch in the last game at Crosley Field. He passed away in 1988 at the age of 94.

Don Rowe
Chicago White Sox (AL) 1988; Milwaukee Brewers (AL) 1992–97, (NL) 1998
Minor league pitcher who spent part of one year in the majors.

Rowe pitched for 14 years in the minors, but in 1963 played 26 games for the New York Mets, starting 1 of them. He posted a 4.28 earned run average and also set a major league record for most innings pitched ($54^2/_3$) without recording a win, a loss, or a save.

Rowe became a baseball coach and teacher at Golden West College in Huntington Beach, California following his playing days, and in 1982 became a minor league pitching coach in the California Angels' organization. He eventually returned to Golden West, then coached in the Milwaukee Brewers' and San Francisco Giants' systems. He returned to the major leagues as a coach for the White Sox and the Brewers.

Rowe died of Parkinson's disease in 2005 at the age of 69.

Ken Rowe
Baltimore Orioles (AL) 1985–86
Minor league pitcher who enjoyed 26 games in the majors.

Those games spanned 1963–65 with the Los Angeles Dodgers and Baltimore Orioles, and Rowe went 2–1 with a 3.57 earned run average while pitching entirely in relief. In September of 1964, while also spending time in the minor leagues, he set a then-professional record and Pacific Coast League mark by appearing in his eighty-eighth game of the season.

Rowe later became an Orioles' coach and also coached in the minor leagues.

Ralph Rowe
Minnesota Twins (AL) 1972–75; Baltimore Orioles (AL) 1981–84
Minor league outfielder from South Carolina.

Nicknamed "Scoop," Rowe never reached the major leagues as a player, but spent many years as a minor league manager with a great many teams and reached the bigs as a coach with the Twins and the Orioles. He also worked as a minor league hitting instructor in the organizations of the Orioles, the Atlanta Braves, and the Montreal Expos.

Schoolboy Rowe
Detroit Tigers (AL) 1954–55
Excellent pitcher *and* hitter.

Lynwood "Schoolboy" Rowe, who received his nickname from opponents who found themselves beaten by a youthful hurler who looked like a schoolboy, was a three-time All-Star who went 158–101 in a 15-year career. He went 24–8 in 1934, his sophomore season, while helping the Tigers to the American League pennant, and along the way he tied the league record with 16 consecutive victories. He won 19 games each of the next two years, and in 1935 topped the AL with 6 shutouts. He lost two years to World War II, and in 1947 became the first player to play in All-Star Games with both the American and National Leagues when he joined the NL squad as a Philadelphia Phillie. An outstanding hitter, he was often used to pinch-hit. In 1943 he led the NL in both pinch-hits and pinch-hitting appearances. He hit a pinch-hit grand slam that season, the second four-run homer of his career, and thus became the first pitcher to hit a grand slam in each league. In a 1935 game he had once gone 5-for-5.

Rowe eventually returned to the Tigers as a coach following his retirement. He died of a heart attack in 1961, only three days before his fifty-first birthday.

Jerry Royster
Colorado Rockies (NL) 1993; Milwaukee Brewers (NL) 2000–02
See Managers section.

Sonny Ruberto
St. Louis Cardinals (NL) 1977–78
Catcher who played 21 major league games.

Ruberto played 13 minor league seasons for 18 different teams. In 1969 he became a catcher for the expansion San Diego Padres and appeared in 19 contests, then garnered 2 more in 1972 with the Cincinnati Reds. He hit only .125. He became a minor league manager in 1970 at the age of 24 and eventually coached two seasons for the Cardinals. Ruberto later worked as a radio broadcaster and then went into business in photography.

Joe Rudi
Oakland Athletics (AL) 1986–87
Three-time Gold Glove outfielder.

Rudi was also named to three All-Star teams and was one of the heroes of the 1972 World Series, when he made a critical backhanded catch and hit a home run in helping the A's defeat the Cincinnati Reds in seven games. He hit .309 in 1970, and in '72 batted .305 while leading the American League with 181 hits and tying for the lead with 9 triples. In 1974 he topped the circuit with 39 doubles and hit a career-high 22 home runs. He hit at least 10 home runs 11 times in his 16-year career.

Most of that career was spent with the A's, and Rudi returned as a coach with the team for two years after leaving the playing field.

Dick Rudolph
Boston Braves (NL) 1921–27
See Managers section.

Muddy Ruel
Chicago White Sox (AL) 1936–45; Cleveland Indians (AL) 1948–50
See Managers section.

Red Ruffing
New York Mets (NL) 1962
Hall of Fame pitcher who played 22 years.

Having lost four toes on his left foot in a mining accident when he was young, Ruffing converted from an outfielder to a pitcher in large part because of his injury. On the mound he won 273 games lifetime, reaching at least 20 on four occasions. In 1928 with the Boston Red Sox he led the American League with 25 complete games, and in 1932 with the New York Yankees topped all AL hurlers with 190 strikeouts. In 1938 his 21 victories topped the loop, and in 1939 his 5 shutouts were the league's best. He was named to six All-Star teams and was also an excellent hitter, cracking 36 home runs in his career.

Ruffing coached one season for the Mets in 1962, and in 1967 he was inducted into the Hall of Fame.

Vern Ruhle
Houston Astros (NL) 1997–2000; Philadelphia Phillies (NL) 2001–02; New York Mets (NL) 2003; Cincinnati Reds (NL) 2005–06
Pitcher for 13 big league seasons.

Ruhle won 11 games for the Detroit Tigers in 1975, but he lost 12. His finest season was 1980, when, with the Astros, he went 12–4 with a 2.37 earned run average. He would never approach those numbers again.

After his playing career Ruhle worked as an assistant baseball coach at Cal State Fullerton and the University of Oklahoma. He later returned to the Astros as their pitching coach, then moved on to the Phillies and the Mets.

In 2004 he became a minor league coach in the Reds' organization, but in June of the following year was promoted to Cincinnati when Don Gullett was fired. In spring training of 2006 Ruhle left the team to seek treatment for cancer, and he was replaced on the staff by bullpen coach Tom Hume in a move that was intended to be temporary. Hume was in turn replaced by Lee Tunnell, who had been slated to be the pitching coach for the AAA Louisville Bats. Ruhle returned to the Reds only briefly during the season, however, and after the 2006 campaign was reassigned within the organization so that he could remain close to his Sarasota home. He died in January of 2007.

Tom Runnells
Montreal Expos (NL) 1990–91
See Managers section.

Pete Runnels
Boston Red Sox (AL) 1965–66
See Managers section.

Bill Russell
Los Angeles Dodgers (NL) 1987–91, 1994–96; Tampa Bay Devil Rays (AL) 2000
See Managers section.

John Russell
Pittsburgh Pirates (NL) 2003–05
Light-hitting outfielder and catcher.

In the minors Russell had been something of a power hitter, bashing 27 home runs for the Portland Beavers in 1983. His highest major league total would be 13, which he accomplished in 1986 with the Philadelphia Phillies, but he never played in more than 93 games in a season. He hit .225 lifetime.

Originally an outfielder, he added catching to his repertoire in 1986, but Lance Parrish received most of the Phillies' playing time. Russell eventually became a coach with the other Pennsylvania team, the Pirates.

Babe Ruth
Boston Braves (NL) 1935; Brooklyn Dodgers (NL) 1938
The Sultan of Swat.

Many claim that George Herman "Babe" Ruth was the greatest player of all time. If he was not, it is probably still safe to say that more has been written about him and more has been said about him than any other player in history.

Ruth set many of the standards by which most later players were judged. Originally an outstanding pitcher, he posted a 94–46 lifetime record. In 1916 with the Boston Red Sox he went 23–12 while leading the American League with 41 starts and 9 shutouts, and the following season he was 24–13 while topping the AL with 35 complete games.

Moved to the outfield so that his bat could be utilized more in the lineup, the Babe would eventually become the single-season home run king, setting several new marks before swatting 60 in 1927, and the all-time home run champ with 714, a record since broken by Hank Aaron and Barry Bonds. In a 22-year career Ruth led the American League once in batting average, 12 times in home runs, 6 times in runs batted in, 8 times in runs scored, 11 times in bases on balls, 10 times in on-base percentage, and 12 times in slugging average. In 1923 he won the AL's League Award, an early version of the Most Valuable

Player Award, on the strength of a .393 average and league-leading totals of 41 homers, 131 RBIs, 151 runs scored, and 170 walks, while also banging out 205 hits and 45 doubles. He hit over 20 home runs 16 times in his career. He was named to only two All-Star teams, but that was because the All-Star Game did not yet exist for the majority of his playing days.

A controversial figure because of his love of eating, drinking, and general partying, Ruth was dealt from the Yankees to the Boston Braves in 1935 and finished out his career there in 28 games as a player and supposed assistant manager and vice president. He quit after that short stint, however. His goal was to become a major league manager, but he turned down several offers to begin managing first at the minor league level and never did skipper a team. In 1936 he was one of the first inductees into the Hall of Fame, and in 1938 was hired as a coach with the Dodgers. That hiring was mainly a publicity stunt, however, and Ruth had few actual responsibilities with the team. The Yankees retired his number 3 in 1948, the same year he died of throat cancer.

Connie Ryan
Milwaukee Braves (NL) 1957; Atlanta Braves (NL) 1971, 1973–74; Texas Rangers (AL) 1977–79
See Managers section.

Jack Ryan
Washington Nationals (AL) 1912–13; Boston Red Sox (AL) 1923–27
Light-hitting but good defensive catcher.

Ryan's skills behind the plate kept him in the major leagues for 13 years, because he batted only .217 lifetime. His career actually lasted from 1889–1903, then he became a successful minor league manager. In 1912 he became a coach with the Nationals, and he appeared in one game that season and in one more the next when manager Clark Griffith inserted himself as a pitcher and Ryan as his batterymate.

Ryan returned to work in the minor leagues until eventually coaching the Red Sox.

Mike Ryan
Philadelphia Phillies (NL) 1980–95
Weak-hitting catcher with an excellent glove.

Ryan played 11 major league seasons despite hitting a career .193. In 1969 he hit 12 home runs but averaged only .204. In May of 1970 with the Phillies he was the backup to Tim McCarver, and when McCarver broke his hand and had to be removed, Ryan was inserted into the game. Ryan then broke *his* hand in the very next inning and, along with McCarver, was sidelined until September.

After his playing career Ryan became a minor league instructor and manager. In 1980 he returned to the Phillies as a coach, a position he would hold for 16 years.

Mike Ryba
St. Louis Cardinals (NL) 1951–54
Western League batting champion in 1933.

After capturing that crown with a .380 batting average as a catcher with the Springfield Cardinals, Ryba switched to pitching and two years later went 20–8 with a 3.29 earned run average for the Columbus Red Birds. In 1940 he was named the Most Valuable Player of the International League when he went 24–8 for the Buffalo Bisons (leading the league in victories) with a 2.94 ERA. He was also a minor league manager, a ticket seller, and a front office worker before reaching the major leagues in 1935 with the St. Louis Cardinals. In 10 big league seasons Ryba posted a 52–34 record and a 3.66 ERA, although he never won more than 12 games in a season. He played the latter half of his career with the Boston Red Sox, then returned to the Cardinals as a coach.

Johnny Sain
Kansas City Athletics (AL) 1959; Minnesota Twins (AL) 1965–66; Detroit Tigers (AL) 1967–69; Chicago White Sox (AL) 1971–75; Atlanta Braves (NL) 1977, 1985–86
Of "Spahn and Sain and pray for rain" fame.

That 1948 Boston Braves' motto, which was culled from a poem that once appeared in the *Boston Post* about Sain and teammate Warren Spahn, indicated that there was little faith in the rest of Boston's pitching staff that season once they got past the first two starters in the rotation. Sain led the National League with 24 victories, 39 starts, 28 complete games, and 314^2/$_3$ innings pitched. Spahn went 15–12, and the other starters actually did not do poorly, with Bill Voiselle posting a 13–13 record and Vern Bickford an 11–5 mark.

For Sain it was his third consecutive 20-win season and the third of four overall. In 1946 he had also led the NL with 24 complete games, and in 1954 with the New York Yankees, who turned him into a reliever, he topped the American League with 22 unofficial saves. In all he was named to three All-Star teams.

After his playing career he began a long and very successful career as a pitching coach. His work was sometimes controversial, however, for on at least two occasions he vocally disagreed with his managers and was fired, and on others caused friction in the front office when he encouraged his pitchers to demand higher salaries. He was well-respected for his work with hurlers, however, and was much in demand.

Randy St. Claire
Montreal Expos (NL) 2003–04; Washington Nationals (NL) 2005–
Son of major league catcher Ebba St. Claire.

Randy was a pitcher and, although he racked up nine major league seasons, never spent an *entire* campaign at the big league level. He was used exclusively as a reliever and posted a 12–6 career record with 9 saves and a 4.14 earned run average.

He began his coaching career in the Milwaukee Brewers' organization before switching to the Expos' system. He reached the AAA level with the Ottawa Lynx in 2002, then signed with the Toronto Blue Jays to be their AAA pitching coach for 2003. The Expos called, however, and offered him a promotion to the major leagues, so he took that instead and accompanied the team when it moved to Washington and became the Nationals.

Luis Salazar
Milwaukee Brewers (NL) 2001
Highly versatile backup for 13 major league seasons.

Salazar played every position except catcher during his career, including pitcher and even designated hitter. A .261 lifetime hitter, he twice hit 14 home runs in a season and twice more hit 12. He had three separate stints with the San Diego Padres and played for both Chicago teams. He was used as a regular several times, but was an excellent pinch-hitter, retiring with a .308 average in that capacity. After his playing days he coached one season for the Brewers and also managed in the minor leagues.

Juan Samuel
Detroit Tigers (AL) 1999–2005; Baltimore Orioles (AL) 2007–
Three-time All-Star second baseman.

Samuel also played a lot of first base and outfield in his 16-year career, as well as serving as a designated hitter. His first full season was 1984, when he hit .272 with 15 home runs and 69 runs batted in for the Philadelphia Phillies while also tying for the National League lead with 19 triples and setting a new major league rookie record by stealing 72 bases. *The Sporting News* named him its NL Rookie of the Year, but his stolen base record would be broken by Vince Coleman the following season. In 1985 he once had 12 assists in a game, tying a major league record.

In 1987 Samuel again led the NL in triples, this time with 15. While he never stole 72 bases in a year again, he never swiped fewer than 23 in his first eight consecutive full seasons, and he stole 396 lifetime. He was also the first major leaguer to reach double digits in doubles, triples, home runs, and stolen bases each of his first four seasons. He missed a fifth straight year by just one triple in 1988.

In 1999 he became a coach with the Tigers, and the following year he earned a 15-game suspension for his part in a brawl with the Chicago White Sox. Both teams' managers were suspended for eight games each. Samuel stayed with the Tigers until 2005, then joined the New York Mets' organization as a minor league skipper. In 2007 he joined the Orioles as their third base coach.

Tommy Sandt
Pittsburgh Pirates (NL) 1987–96, 2001–02; Florida Marlins (NL) 1997–98; Colorado Rockies (NL) 1999
Infielder for 42 major league games.

One of those games came in 1975, the other 41 in 1976, and all with the Oakland Athletics. Sandt hit just .209 in that limited opportunity, but performed much better as a minor leaguer and carved quite a niche for himself as a hitting coach following his playing career. He both coached and managed in the minors before beginning a long tenure as a Pirates' coach, then moved to the Marlins and the Rockies before returning to Pittsburgh. In 2003 he went back to the minors as a coach, and shortly thereafter he retired and began working at the Metro Baseball Academy in Portland, Oregon.

Jack Sanford
Cleveland Indians (AL) 1968–69
National League Rookie of the Year in 1957.

A right-handed pitcher, Sanford posted a 19–8 record for the Philadelphia Phillies that year while leading the National League with 188 strikeouts and putting up a 3.08 earned run average. He would win at least 10 games for his first seven full seasons in a row. In 1960 with the San Francisco Giants he led the NL with six shutouts. His best season was 1962, however, when he went 24–7 and won 16 consecutive games. In 1963 his 42 starts tied for the league lead. A couple of years after that he began to pitch in relief, and in 1966 with the California Angels he led the American League with 12 relief wins while garnering 13 overall.

Sanford coached two seasons for the Indians following his retirement.

Rafael Santana
Chicago White Sox (AL) 2003–04
Shortstop with a good glove and so-so bat.

In seven seasons Santana hit .246. As a regular with the New York Mets in 1986 he batted a mere .218, but his glove and his arm kept him on the field. An arm injury suffered in 1988 affected his playing and eventually led to career-ending surgery. He missed the entire 1989 season and was able to come back for only seven games in 1990. He later returned to the major leagues as a coach with the White Sox for two seasons.

Hank Sauer
San Francisco Giants (NL) 1979
Power-hitting outfielder from California.

Sauer struggled in his initial call-ups to the majors and then lost several years to the military during World War II. In 1948 he arrived to stay, however, and promptly hit 35 home runs for the Cincinnati Reds. He would hit at least 30 for five straight years, in fact, and then hit 41 in 1954 and 26 in 1957. His best season was 1952, when he tied Ralph Kiner for the National League lead with 37 homers and also led with 121 runs batted in while playing for the Chicago Cubs, in the process being named the NL Most Valuable Player. Sauer cranked out 288 roundtrippers lifetime and was named to two All-Star squads. In 1958 he and Bob Schmidt teamed up for the first pinch-hit back-to-back home runs in major league history.

Sauer eventually coached one season with the Giants. The AAA Syracuse SkyChiefs also retired his number 9 symbolically, because that was the number Sauer had worn with the previous Syracuse Chiefs when he had established franchise records for home runs and RBIs and had been named Minor League Player of the Year in 1947.

Jim Saul
Chicago Cubs (NL) 1975–76; Oakland Athletics (AL) 1979
Minor league catcher and longtime minor league manager.

Saul never reached the majors as a player but began his managerial career in 1973 with the Salinas Packers, a team that tied for the best record in the California League. From 1975–76 he coached for the Chicago Cubs, then in 1978 was named Texas League Manager of the Year while at the helm of the Midland Cubs. The next year he coached for the A's in Oakland, then returned to the minors as a skipper. In 1996 his Eugene Emeralds had the best record in the Northwest League, and in 2001 his Jamestown Jammers reached the New York-Penn League playoffs.

Ray Scarborough
Baltimore Orioles (AL) 1968
Effective pitcher from North Carolina.

Scarborough debuted in 1942 but lost 1944 and 1945 to military service. In 1948 with the Washington Nationals he went 15–8 with a 2.82 earned run average, the best numbers of his career. In a July game he was arguing ball and strike calls with umpire Bill McGowan when McGowan threw a ball-and-strike indicator at him. The previous day the arbiter had thrown a ball at a player, and he ended up being suspended and fined by the American League.

In 1951 Scarborough was on first base when he was hit in the head and knocked unconscious by an intended pick-off throw.

Scarborough was named an All-Star in 1950, and he

went 80–85 in his career with a 4.13 ERA overall. He later opened an oil and supply company in Mount Olive, North Carolina, and he worked as a scout for the Orioles, California Angels, and Milwaukee Brewers, serving one season as a coach for the O's in 1968. He also helped create a baseball program at Mount Olive College.

Al Schacht
Washington Nationals (AL) 1925–34; Boston Red Sox (AL) 1935–36
"The Clown Prince of Baseball."

Schacht was originally a pitcher who played 53 major league games over three seasons. He posted a 14–10 record with a 4.48 earned run average and 38 strikeouts. His career was limited by arm problems, but he then began a long career as a coach and baseball entertainer. With the Nationals in 1925 he teamed up with coach Nick Altrock, who had already established some routines to entertain fans and players before games. Altrock had previously worked with Germany Schaefer. After 10 years with Washington, Schacht moved on to the Red Sox for two years, then took his act on the road. He became popular throughout baseball, creating clowning skits that involved mock boxing and tennis matches, mock bullfights, and invisible rowboats during rain delays. He eventually entertained at 25 World Series and 18 All-Star Games and also toured with the USO during World War II.

Schacht finally retired in 1969 and opened a restaurant in New York. He passed away in 1984.

Bob Schaefer
Kansas City Royals (AL) 1988–91, 2002–05; Oakland Athletics (AL) 2007–
See Managers section.

Jim Schaffer
Texas Rangers (AL) 1978; Kansas City Royals (AL) 1980–88
Catcher who hit just .223 in the majors.

Schaffer played many years in the minors and eight in The Show for several clubs. He was used as a backup and never hit over .255 in a season, four times failing to reach the .200 mark. He then embarked on a long and successful minor league coaching career, emerging for one season in the bigs with the Rangers and for nine with the Royals. In all he spent over 35 years in professional baseball.

Ray Schalk
Chicago Cubs (NL) 1930–31
See Managers section.

Wally Schang
Cleveland Indians (AL) 1936–38

Excellent defensive catcher.

Schang's glovework was well appreciated, even though he set an American League record for most career errors by a catcher with 218. He was fleet of foot for a backstop, stealing 121 bases lifetime, and he was no slouch at the plate, either, retiring with a .284 career batting average. Six times he topped the .300 mark. When he was not catching he was often used at third base or in the outfield so that his bat could remain in the lineup. In 1915 he once threw out six runners attempting to steal. In 1916 he became the first major league switch-hitter to homer from both sides of the plate in the same game. And in 1920 he set an AL catching record with eight assists in one game.

Schang played several more years in the minor leagues following his last big league season, then he coached three years for the Indians. He eventually retired to his farm in the Ozark Mountains.

Bob Scheffing
St. Louis Browns (AL) 1952–53; Chicago Cubs (NL) 1954–55; Milwaukee Braves (NL) 1960
See Managers section.

George Scherger
Cincinnati Reds (NL) 1970–78, 1982–86
Minor league second baseman for 14 years.

Scherger lost three additional years to military service during World War II. Nicknamed "Sugar Bear," George twice hit over .300 in the minors and twice led his league in fielding percentage. From 1947–56 he was a player-manager, then he became a full-time coach and full-time skipper. He logged five first-place finishes at the helm of various clubs.

From 1970–78 Scherger coached for the Big Red Machine under Sparky Anderson. When Anderson was fired following the 1978 campaign Scherger was named manager of the Nashville Sounds and promptly led that team to the Southern Association championship. In 1982 he took the Indianapolis Indians to the American Association title, and then rejoined the Reds as a coach at the end of the year. *The Sporting News* named him its Minor League Manager of the Year. His second stint in Cincinnati lasted until 1986.

Red Schoendienst
St. Louis Cardinals (NL) 1962–64, 1979–95; Oakland Athletics (AL) 1977–78
See Managers section.

Paul Schreiber
New York Yankees (AL) 1942, 1945; Boston Red Sox (AL) 1947–58

Jacksonville native who pitched 12 major league games.

A right-hander, Schreiber's minor league career lasted far longer than his cups of coffee in the majors. He pitched 10 games in 1922 and 1923 for the Brooklyn Robins, starting none of them, winning none of them, and losing none of them. He eventually became a coach for the Yankees in 1942, returning in the same role in 1945. Because of a dearth of players during World War II, he was activated and pitched two games in relief, once again without a win or a loss. His lifetime numbers show a record of 0–0 and an earned run average of 3.98. He had gone 22 years between big league appearances.

He later coached a dozen years for the Red Sox, and he died in Sarasota in 1982.

Rick Schu
Arizona Diamondbacks (NL) 2004
Journeyman third baseman.

Schu hit .301 for the Portland Beavers in 1984 and was the heir apparent to Mike Schmidt at third base for the Philadelphia Phillies. He failed to match those numbers in the major leagues, however, averaging just .246 with 41 home runs in nine seasons, and he wound up playing for five different teams in a backup role. After his playing days he returned to the majors for one season as a coach with the Diamondbacks.

Ron Schueler
Chicago White Sox (AL) 1979–82; Oakland Athletics (AL) 1983–84; Pittsburgh Pirates (NL) 1986
Pitcher-turned-executive.

Schueler pitched a no-hitter for the Shreveport Braves of the AA Texas League in 1970, and two years later he would make his debut with the Atlanta Braves. He was at first used as both a starter and a reliever, but eventually became a bullpen mainstay. In eight seasons he went 40–48 with a 4.08 earned run average.

Schueler was with the White Sox in 1979 when pitching coach Fred Martin died in June. Schueler, having appeared in only eight games, retired from the playing field and replaced Martin as a Chicago coach. He would eventually move on to the A's and the Pirates.

In 1987 Ron returned to Oakland as a special assistant to the vice president, baseball operations. In November of 1990 he returned to the White Sox, this time as senior vice president, major league operations.

Johnny Schulte
Chicago Cubs (NL) 1933; New York Yankees (AL) 1934–48; Boston Red Sox (AL) 1949–50
Part-time catcher for five big league seasons.

Schulte played for five teams in those five years, in-

cluding both St. Louis clubs. He actually had two stints with the Browns. He hit .262 in limited action with 14 home runs and 64 runs batted in.

Schulte retired in 1932 and joined the Cubs as a coach the following season. He then spent 15 years with the Yankees before ending his coaching run in two seasons with the Red Sox.

Barney Schultz
St. Louis Cardinals (NL) 1971–75; Chicago Cubs (NL) 1977
Successful knuckleball pitcher.

Used entirely out of the bullpen, Schultz tied a since-broken major league record in 1962 with the Cubs by appearing on the mound in nine consecutive games. His record for that year was 5–5, but he had a better season in 1964 with the Cardinals when he went 1–3 but garnered 14 saves and posted a 1.64 earned run average. His lifetime record was 20–20, his ERA 3.63.

Schultz eventually returned to both the Cardinals and the Cubs in a coaching role.

Joe Schultz
St. Louis Browns (AL) 1949; St. Louis Cardinals (NL) 1963–68; Kansas City Royals (AL) 1970; Detroit Tigers (AL) 1971–76
See Managers section.

Mike Scioscia
Los Angeles Dodgers (NL) 1997–98
See Managers section.

Tony Scott
Philadelphia Phillies (NL) 2001–03
Quick outfielder for several clubs.

Only a .249 lifetime hitter, Scott nevertheless stole a lot of bases and provided excellent defense. He committed only one error as a regular in 1980, leading National League outfielders in fielding percentage. In 1979 he stole 37 bases, and swiped 22 the next en route to 125 lifetime. In 1989, five years after his retirement, he played for the Winter Haven Super Sox of the Senior Professional Baseball Association and hit .360. He also spent many years as a minor league coach before returning to the majors in that role with the Phillies.

Ed Sedar
Milwaukee Brewers (NL) 2007–
Minor leaguer who played every position on the diamond.

After his playing career Sedar spent many years developing talent at the minor league level. He spent 15 years in the Brewers' chain, many of them as a rookie league manager. He simultaneously served as a minor league field coordinator and roving outfield and baserunning instructor before being promoted to Milwaukee in 2007.

Kevin Seitzer
Arizona Diamondbacks (NL) 2007–
Solid third baseman/designated hitter and two-time All-Star.

Seitzer nearly won the American League Rookie of the Year Award in 1987 when he hit .323 for the Kansas City Royals, leading the league with 207 hits and finishing second in the balloting to Mark McGwire, who pounded 49 home runs for the Oakland Athletics. A .295 lifetime hitter, Seitzer hit over .300 in half of his 12 seasons. Toward the end of his career he established the Mac-n-Seitz Baseball and Softball Company in Kansas City along with teammate Mike Macfarlane, a business that provided instruction to both professional and non-professional players.

After the 2006 season the Diamondbacks hired Seitzer to be their hitting coach.

Andy Seminick
Philadelphia Phillies (NL) 1957–58, 1967–69
All-Star catcher who spent most of his career with the Phillies.

Seminick debuted in 1943, joined the Cincinnati Reds in 1952, and returned to Philadelphia during the 1955 campaign before retiring in 1957. He had good power, nine times clouting at least 11 home runs in a season and reaching 24 twice. He ended up with 164. In 1949, the same year he was named an All-Star, he once hit three home runs in a game, with two of them coming in the same inning. He was the ninth player to accomplish that feat in major league history.

Seminick appeared in only eight games in 1957 and became a Phillies' coach that year. He then managed in the club's minor league system before returning to Philadelphia, once again as a coach, from 1967–69. He later became a scout and then a minor league roving instructor for the organization. In the 1990s he worked for the team as a catching instructor during spring training and also in the Florida Instructional League.

Joe Sewell
New York Yankees (AL) 1934–35
Brother of Luke Sewell.

Joe reached the Hall of Fame on his own merits, however, becoming an outstanding defensive shortstop as well as the hardest player to strike out in major league history. In the field he led the American League in multiple fielding categories multiple times. At bat he hit .312 lifetime, reaching the .300 plateau 10 times and once hitting .299. He also struck out only 114 times in 7132 at-bats. Only twice in his career did he strike out twice in the same game. In 1924 he tied for the AL lead with 45 doubles, and in 1932 he whiffed only three times in 503 at-bats. He was also durable, having once played in 1103 consecutive games.

After his playing career Sewell spent two years as a Yankees' coach, then became a scout for the Cleveland Indians and a coach at the University of Alabama. He took Alabama to the Southeastern Conference championship in 1968. In 1977 he was inducted into the Hall of Fame by the Veterans Committee.

Luke Sewell
Cleveland Indians (AL) 1939–41; Cincinnati Reds (NL) 1949
See Managers section.

Rip Sewell
Pittsburgh Pirates (NL) 1948
Master of the blooper pitch.

The pitch was also called an "eephus," as coined by Sewell's teammate, Maurice Van Robays, and it sometimes sailed as high as 25 feet in the air. Sewell made a career out of it, and a very successful one. Having been kept out of World War II because he had lost part of a foot to a hunting accident in 1940, Sewell made four All-Star teams during the war years and won 21 games in consecutive seasons, 1943 and 1944. In '43 those 21 wins put him in a three-way tie for the National League lead, and his 25 complete games were best in the league. He had a 2.54 earned run average, and the BBWAA dubbed him its NL Pitcher of the Year. His lifetime record was 143–97, his ERA 3.48. He was also an excellent fielder, setting NL pitching records in 1941 with 12 chances in a game and 11 assists in a game, and tying a record with 3 assists in a single inning.

Sewell spent all but the first five games of his career with the Pirates, and he later returned to that club as a coach for one season.

Howie Shanks
Cleveland Indians (AL) 1928–32
Highly versatile player from Chicago.

Shanks could play virtually any position and did so throughout his 14-year major league career. He spent 11 of those years with the Washington Nationals, 2 with the Boston Red Sox, and 1 with the New York Yankees. He was moved all over both the infield and the outfield, but the one time he really excelled at the plate was 1921, when the Nationals left him at third base for the entire season and he hit a career-high .302 with a league-leading 18 triples. It was the only time he even approached the .300 mark.

Shanks finished his big league career in 1925, but he later coached five years with the Indians.

Shag Shaughnessy
Detroit Tigers (AL) 1928
Football star with a brief baseball career.

His short baseball career was as a player, because Frank "Shag" Shaughnessy spent many years in the sport in other capacities. He played both baseball and football at the University of Notre Dame from 1901–04, and in 1904 served as captain of the football squad. In 1905 he got into one game with the Washington Nationals and went 0-for-3, then played eight games for the Philadelphia Athletics in 1908 and hit .310. He later coached football at Yale University and Cornell University, and coached both baseball and football at Clemson University. He coached football at Washington and Lee University.

Shaughnessy became the first professional coach in Canadian college football. In 1912 he was hired by McGill University, and by 1919 was also coaching both men's and women's hockey there. He remained in that role until 1927. At the same time, however, he was managing minor league baseball, spending the 1909–27 seasons in that capacity. In 1928 he coached a season for the Tigers in Detroit. He then went back to managing in the minors, and from 1932–34 served as general manager of the Montreal Royals. He spent 1936–60 as president of the International League.

The Shaughnessy Cup was created in his honor in 1969 as the football prize to be won in contests between McGill and Loyola University. In 1975 it became the annual award for challenges between McGill and Concordia University.

Bob Shaw
Milwaukee Brewers (AL) 1973
Solid pitcher who played for seven different teams.

Shaw had a somewhat unpredictable personality that sometimes led to friction with team management. Nevertheless he went 108–98 on the field in 11 seasons with a 3.52 earned run average. In 1959 with the Chicago White Sox he posted an 18–6 record with a 2.69 ERA. In 1962 he was named a National League All-Star with the Milwaukee Braves and went 15–9 on the season. In a 1963 game he set a major league record by committing five balks, three of them coming in one inning.

He eventually returned to Milwaukee as a coach for one season, this time with the Brewers.

Bob Shawkey
New York Yankees (AL) 1929
See Managers section.

Merv Shea
Detroit Tigers (AL) 1939–42; Philadelphia Blue Jays (NL) 1944–45; Chicago Cubs (NL) 1948–49
Good defensive catcher.

Shea hit only .220 and had little power. His defense and his ability to handle pitchers kept him in the major leagues for 11 years, all but one of them spent in a backup role. In 110 games in 1933 he tied the American League record for fielding percentage by a catcher at .933.

He became a coach with the Tigers in 1939 and also appeared in four games. In 1944 he was a coach for the Blue Jays (formerly the Phillies) and was activated for another seven. He managed one season in the minor leagues before joining the Cubs as a scout and a major league coach.

In 1951 Shea returned as a coach to the Sacramento Solons of the Pacific Coast League, a club for which he had once played. During the 1952 season he was forced to resign due to failing health, and he died in January of 1953.

Tom Sheehan
Cincinnati Reds (NL) 1935–37; Boston Braves (NL) 1944
See Managers section.

John Shelby
Los Angeles Dodgers (NL) 1998–2005; Pittsburgh Pirates (NL) 2006–
Outfielder who spent 11 years in the major leagues.

Shelby excelled in the minor leagues at outfield defense and stealing bases. In the majors he hit .239 but had some flashes of brilliance. In 1987 he hit 22 home runs, 1 of them with the Baltimore Orioles and the other 21 with the Dodgers. He never hit more than 11 in any other season. He stole 18 bases in 1986, then 16 each of the next two years.

Shelby retired in 1991 and became a minor league manager and coach in the Dodgers' organization. In 1998 he was promoted to Los Angeles as a coach, and he lasted until 2005. In 2006 he was hired to coach the Pirates.

Frank Shellenback
St. Louis Browns (AL) 1939; Boston Red Sox (AL) 1940–44; Detroit Tigers (AL) 1946–47; New York Giants (NL) 1950–55
Spitball pitcher who played 36 major league games.

Shellenback relied heavily on that pitch, and from 1918–19 with the Chicago White Sox he posted a 10–15 record despite a 3.06 earned run average. He became trapped in the minor leagues, however, because when the spitball was outlawed in 1920 Shellenback was playing in the Pacific Coast League. Major League Baseball allowed major league pitchers who used that pitch to continue throwing it for the rest of their careers, but since Shellenback was a minor leaguer at the time, that exemption did not apply to him. A PCL exemption *did* apply, however, and he continued to play there and set the record for most career wins in the league with 295. That was also the record for most career wins in *any* minor league. Shellenback's final record in the minors was 315–192. In both 1929 and 1932 he led the PCL with 26 victories.

Shellenback did eventually return to the big leagues as a coach beginning in 1939, spending time with several clubs.

Jim Shellenback
Minnesota Twins (AL) 1983
Nephew of Frank Shellenback.

Jim was a left-handed pitcher who was used mostly in relief. He debuted in two games with the Pittsburgh Pirates in 1966, and played six more with two starts in 1967. In October of that year he was badly hurt in an automobile accident, suffering a broken leg among other injuries. He returned to Pittsburgh in 1969 but after eight games was shipped off to the Washington Senators.

Shellenback retired in 1977 with a 16–30 lifetime record and a 3.81 earned run average. He then coached for many years in the Twins' minor league system, joining the big club for one season in 1983.

Derek Shelton
Cleveland Indians (AL) 2005–
Minor league catcher with a degree in criminal justice.

Shelton lasted only two seasons as a player in the New York Yankees' organization before elbow surgery ended his career. He then became a minor league coach and manager in the Yankees' system, leading the Gulf Coast Yankees to a division title in 2000 and a league championship in 2001, and the Staten Island Yankees to the New York-Penn League crown in 2002. In 2003 he joined the Indians' organization as a minor league hitting coordinator, and in June of 2005 was promoted to Cleveland to replace Eddie Murray as hitting coach.

Bert Shepard
Washington Nationals (AL) 1946
Winner of the Distinguished Flying Cross who had his right leg amputated.

Shepard lost his leg after his P-38 Lightning crashed in Germany during World War II. He taught himself to walk and to pitch with an artificial leg while in a Prisoner of War camp. After returning to the United States he tried out for the Nationals but was hired only as a batting practice pitcher by owner Clark Griffith. In August of that year, however, he was activated for a game against the Boston Red Sox and pitched 5⅓ innings, allowing three hits and one run and striking out two. It was his only major league game; he did not get the decision, but his lifetime earned run average was 1.69.

The following season he remained with Washington as a coach, and he later became a player-manager in the minor leagues. He eventually took a job in the mid-1950s as a safety engineer with IBM and Hughes Aircraft.

Larry Shepard
Philadelphia Phillies (NL) 1967; Cincinnati Reds (NL) 1970–78; San Francisco Giants (NL) 1979
See Managers section.

Glenn Sherlock
New York Yankees (AL) 1995; Arizona Diamondbacks (NL) 1998–
Minor league catcher originally drafted by the Houston Astros.

Sherlock set a New York-Penn League record for most double plays by a backstop in his very first professional season. He eventually played for seven years, serving as a player-coach in 1989 although he appeared in only a single game. He then became a minor league manager and a catching instructor, and in the winter of 1993 he managed the Canberra Bushrangers of the Australian Baseball League. He was a bullpen catcher for the Yankees in 1992, 1994, and 1995, and the club also lists him as an official coach in '95.

In 1996 he went to work in the Arizona Diamondbacks' system, working with minor league catchers two years before the major league team made its debut. He was then hired as a coach for the club for its inaugural campaign.

Larry Sherry
Pittsburgh Pirates (NL) 1977–78; California Angels (AL) 1979–80
Brother of Norm Sherry.

The pitcher with the poetic name was born with club feet, a condition that was corrected with surgery during his childhood. He made the major leagues in 1958 with the Los Angeles Dodgers, and after starting 9 of 23 games in 1959 he had a sensational World Series. Pitching out of the bullpen against the Chicago White Sox he earned saves in Games 2 and 3 and registered victories in Games 4 and 6. He allowed just one run and eight hits in 12⅔ innings, playing a major role in the Dodgers' World Championship.

In 1960 he led the National League with 13 relief wins as he went 14–10 overall. He and his brother Norm, a catcher, also became a rare brother battery and the first one of the Jewish persuasion in major league history. In 1966 Larry posted a career-high 20 saves with the Detroit Tigers.

Sherry became a minor league coach following his playing days, eventually returning to the Dodgers' organization. He later coached at the major league level with the Pirates and the Angels.

Norm Sherry
California Angels (AL) 1970–71, 1976; Montreal Expos (NL) 1978–81; San Diego Padres (NL) 1982–84; San Francisco Giants (NL) 1986–91
See Managers section.

Razor Shines
Chicago White Sox (AL) 2007–
Minor league player and successful minor league manager.

Anthony "Razor" Shines spent six years managing in the White Sox' minor league system. In 2003 he guided the Winston-Salem Warthogs to the Carolina League championship, and in 2005 was named Southern League Manager of the Year when he guided the Birmingham Barons to an 82–57 record. His 2006 Charlotte Knights started the season 31–9, and they eventually finished at 79–62 and made the International League playoffs.

He was promoted to the White Sox' big league coaching staff in 2007.

Ray Shore
Cincinnati Reds (NL) 1963–67
Pitcher from Cincinnati.

Shore appeared in only 31 major league games, spreading them out over three seasons in the late 1940s with the St. Louis Browns. He started only 4 of the 31 and posted a 1–3 lifetime mark with an 8.23 earned run average with 26 strikeouts and 67 walks in 62$\frac{1}{3}$ innings.

He eventually coached for five years with his hometown Reds.

Burt Shotton
St. Louis Cardinals (NL) 1923–25; Cincinnati Reds (NL) 1934; Cleveland Indians (AL) 1942–45
See Managers section.

Buck Showalter
New York Yankees (AL) 1990–91
See Managers section.

Sonny Siebert
San Diego Padres (NL) 1994–95
Pitcher who was also drafted by the National Basketball Association's St. Louis Hawks.

Siebert chose baseball and became an eventual two-time All-Star. He pitched for 12 years and won 16 games three times, 15 once, and 14 once. His lifetime record was 140–114, and he had a 3.21 earned run average. On June 10, 1966, with the Cleveland Indians, he pitched a no-hitter

against the Washington Senators. Siebert was also a decent hitter, launching 12 home runs in his career and hitting 2 in one game in 1971.

After his playing days Sonny became a minor league coach, and he returned to the majors in that role with the Padres from 1994–95.

Roy Sievers
Cincinnati Reds (NL) 1966
American League Rookie of the Year in 1949.

Sievers hit .306 that year with 16 home runs and 91 runs batted in for the St. Louis Browns. While he would hit over .300 only one more time in a 17-year career, he was a feared power hitter who blasted at least 19 home runs 10 times, all consecutively. In 1957 he batted .301 and led the AL with 42 homers and 114 RBIs, at one point tying a league record by homering in six straight games. He topped the 100-RBI plateau four times and was named to four All-Star teams. In 1963 with the Philadelphia Phillies he became only the second player (the first was Jimmie Foxx) to hit pinch-hit grand slams in both the National and American Leagues.

Sievers retired in 1965 and coached for the Reds the following season. He then went to work as a minor league manager.

Charlie Silvera
Minnesota Twins (AL) 1969; Detroit Tigers (AL) 1971–73; Texas Rangers (AL) 1974–75
Backup catcher for 10 seasons.

Silvera spent nine of those years with the New York Yankees, where he was mired behind Yogi Berra and Elston Howard. He played only 227 games in 10 years, an average of 22.7 per season, despite a .282 batting average. The Yankees appeared in seven World Series during his time with the team, but Silvera was inserted into only one game.

He finished his career in 1957 with the Chicago Cubs and eventually returned to the majors as a coach with several clubs.

Luis Silverio
Kansas City Royals (AL) 2003–
Minor league outfielder for many years.

Silverio spent his entire professional career with the Royals. He played in the minor league system from 1973–82, being named a Gulf Coast League All-Star in 1975. He appeared in eight games for Kansas City in 1978 and went 6-for-11, good for a .545 lifetime major league average. He then worked in the minor league system as a coach and manager, and in 1987 was named the Gulf Coast League Manager of the Year when he guided the Gulf Coast Royals to the South Division crown. He worked for many years as the general manager of the Royals' Dominican League affiliate, simultaneously serving as Latin American coordinator and a scout. From 2000–02 he was the organization's coordinator of Dominican Republic operations, and in 2003 was promoted to Kansas City as a coach.

Ken Silvestri
Philadelphia Phillies (NL) 1959–60; Milwaukee Braves (NL) 1963–65; Atlanta Braves (NL) 1966–75; Chicago White Sox (AL) 1976, 1982
See Managers section.

Al Simmons
Philadelphia Athletics (AL) 1940–42, 1944–49; Cleveland Indians (AL) 1950–51
Solid, consistent Hall of Fame outfielder.

Nicknamed "Bucketfoot Al" because of his tendency to step toward third base while batting, Simmons was actually named Aloysius Szymanski. The son of Polish immigrants, he changed his name to that of a hardware store when he saw an advertisement in a newspaper. By the time he retired from baseball he had accumulated more hits than any right-handed batter in history.

His record was eventually broken by Al Kaline, but that in no way diminished Simmons' accomplishments. A .334 lifetime hitter, he won back-to-back batting titles with a .381 average in 1930, when he also led the American League with 152 runs scored, and a .390 showing in 1931. A three-time All-Star, he also topped the AL with 253 hits in 1925 and with 216 in 1932. In 1929 his 157 runs batted in topped the circuit.

Simmons hit at least 14 home runs 11 consecutive times and 12 total, peaking with 36 in 1930. He topped 100 RBIs his first 11 seasons and 12 total. He finished his career with 307 homers and 2927 hits.

Simmons served as a player-coach for the A's in 1940 and '41, then turned to coaching full-time in 1942. In 1943 he became active again with the Boston Red Sox, but returned to the A's as a player-coach for one more season, in 1944. He then coached full-time for Philadelphia and later for the Indians. He was inducted into the Hall of Fame in 1953.

Matt Sinatro
Seattle Mariners (AL) 1995–2002; Tampa Bay Devil Rays (AL) 2003–05; Chicago Cubs (NL) 2007–
Light-hitting backup catcher.

Sinatro averaged 14 games played per year over 10 major league seasons. Being shuttled between the majors and the minors, he hit a mere .190 and managed a home run with 21 runs batted in overall.

He finished his playing career with the Mariners and then became a scout for the club. Afterwards he became a coach on the major league staff and later moved to the Devil Rays and then the Cubs.

Dick Sisler
Cincinnati Reds (NL) 1961–64; St. Louis Cardinals (NL) 1966–70; San Diego Padres (NL) 1975–76; New York Mets (NL) 1979–80
See Managers section.

George Sisler
Boston Braves (NL) 1930
See Managers section.

Sibby Sisti
Seattle Pilots (AL) 1969
Infielder from Buffalo, New York.

Sisti debuted with the Boston Braves in 1939 at the age of 18. After the 1942 campaign he served in the Coast Guard, and when he returned in 1946 the Braves had no place for him to play. He spent that season with the Indianapolis Indians of the American Association and was named Minor League Player of the Year by *The Sporting News* when he batted .343. He rejoined Boston the following season and served as a utilityman for the rest of his career.

After retiring in 1954 Sisti became a longtime minor league coach and manager, spending several years with his hometown Buffalo Bisons. He coached the expansion Pilots for their only season before moving to Milwaukee, and also had a small speaking role as the Pittsburgh Pirates' manager in the movie *The Natural*. He also worked as a consultant on that film.

Jim Skaalen
Milwaukee Brewers (NL) 2007–
Minor leaguer and longtime instructor.

Skaalen played in the minor leagues for three years after being drafted by the Baltimore Orioles, but he then spent 26 in player development before reaching the major leagues as a coach. He spent those years as a minor league coach, manager, instructor, and administrator, and from 2000–06 served as the Brewers' minor league hitting coordinator.

In 2007 he was promoted to the big league staff as a hitting coach to replace Butch Wynegar.

Frank Skaff
Baltimore Orioles (AL) 1954; Detroit Tigers (AL) 1965–66, 1971
See Managers section.

Bob Skinner

San Diego Padres (NL) 1970–73, 1977; Pittsburgh Pirates (NL) 1974–76, 1979–85; California Angels (AL) 1978; Atlanta Braves (NL) 1986–88

See Managers section.

Joel Skinner

Cleveland Indians (AL) 2001–

See Managers section.

Jim Slaton

Seattle Mariners (AL) 2005–

Pitcher who was drafted by the Seattle Pilots.

The team had become the Milwaukee Brewers by the time Slaton made his debut in 1971. In 16 major league seasons he had two stints with the Brewers, two with the Detroit Tigers, and one with the California Angels. He won at least 13 games six times, peaking in 1978 with a 17–11 record for Detroit. He had been an American League All-Star the previous year. In 1981 with Milwaukee he took a no-hitter into the ninth inning before losing it.

Slaton began his coaching career in the minor leagues in 1992 in the Oakland Athletics' system. In 1995 he moved to the Chicago Cubs' organization, then to that of the Mariners. In 2004 he served as a special assignment pitching coach in the Seattle system, and in 2005 was promoted to the big league staff.

Jack Slattery

Boston Braves (NL) 1918–19

See Managers section.

Don Slaught

Detroit Tigers (AL) 2006

Veteran catcher who played 16 major league seasons.

Slaught, who had an amiable personality, was used mainly in a reserve role but was productive and generally showed good defensive skills. An exception was 1985, when he was catching knuckleballer Charlie Hough with the Texas Rangers and committed 20 passed balls. He hit over .300 six times in limited action and averaged .283 for his career. In 1986 he suffered a broken nose and cheekbone when he was hit in the face by a pitch from Dennis "Oil Can" Boyd.

After his playing career Slaught became president of a baseball and softball training software company. In 2006 he returned to the major leagues as a coach with the Tigers. He resigned following that season in order to spend more time with his family.

Rac Slider

Boston Red Sox (AL) 1987–90

Minor leaguer from Simms, Texas.

An infielder, Slider's primary position was shortstop. He never did reach the major leagues as a player, and he then became a longtime minor league manager in the Red Sox' organization. He was promoted to Boston as a coach for four seasons, then went back to work in the minors.

Al Smith

New York Giants (NL) 1933

Coach who became a player.

Smith's career was a bit upside-down, as he coached for the Giants in 1933 and then spent 12 seasons pitching in the big leagues. He won 14 games in 1936 for the Giants and led the National League with four shutouts. He won 15 with the Cleveland Indians in 1940, and in 1943 was named an American League All-Star when he went 17–7. Smith retired with a lifetime record of 99–101 and a 3.72 earned run average.

Billy Smith

Toronto Blue Jays (AL) 1984–88

Lifetime minor leaguer.

There have been many Billy Smiths and Bill Smiths who played major league baseball, but this gentleman was not one of them. Billy Franklin Smith was a minor league first baseman and outfielder from High Point, North Carolina. He was born in 1930, and he never reached the major leagues as a player but did so as a coach, working on the staff of the Toronto Blue Jays for five seasons.

Dave Smith

San Diego Padres (NL) 1999–2001

One of several Dave Smiths to play major league baseball.

Several of them were pitchers, as well, as was this one. David Stanley Smith hailed from Richmond, California, and he pitched 13 years in the majors. He started only once in 609 games, and in that contest he committed three balks. As a reliever he anchored the Houston Astros' bullpen for many years, being named to two All-Star squads and recording more than 20 saves six times. He retired with a 53–53 record, 216 saves, and a 2.67 earned run average. He later returned to the big leagues as a coach with the Padres.

Hal Smith

St. Louis Cardinals (NL) 1962; Pittsburgh Pirates (NL) 1965–67; Cincinnati Reds (NL) 1968–69; Milwaukee Brewers (AL) 1976–77

One of two Hal Smiths to play in the majors.

The two were contemporaries, and to further confuse matters, both were catchers. This one was Harold Raymond Smith, and he was outstanding defensively and played in the bigs for seven years. He hit only .258 but was named to two All-Star teams. He played for the Cardinals from 1956–61, then stayed with the club as a coach for one season. In 1965 he was hired by the Pirates and was activated for four games, then went back to coaching full-time for Pittsburgh, Cincinnati, and Milwaukee.

Red Smith
Chicago Cubs (NL) 1945–48
One of four Red Smiths to play in the majors.

Unlike the other three, however, this one played only a single game at the big league level. Richard Paul "Red" Smith was a catcher from Sylvania, Ohio, who was born in 1904 and died 10 days before his seventy-fourth birthday, in 1978. His only major league game came in 1927 when he briefly worked in a game behind the plate. He stayed much longer as a coach with the Cubs, however, lasting four years.

Reggie Smith
Los Angeles Dodgers (NL) 1994–98
Ambidextrous outfielder and first baseman.

Smith threw right-handed while manning the outfield, but at the plate he was a very successful switch-hitter. Originally drafted as a shortstop by the Minnesota Twins, he was later converted to the outfield by the Boston Red Sox. In 17 seasons he hit over .300 seven times and crushed 314 home runs. He hit at least 21 roundtrippers eight times, reaching a high of 32 in 1977 with the Dodgers. He became the first switch-hitter to hit at least 100 homers in both the National and American Leagues. In 1968 he led the AL with 37 doubles, and did so again in 1971 with 33. In '68 he also won a Gold Glove for his defense as he topped all AL outfielders in putouts. He was named to seven All-Star teams.

After the 1982 season Smith went to Japan to play. He later returned to the United States and worked as a minor league instructor, a player development official, and a major league coach with the Dodgers. In 2006 he was the hitting coach for Team USA in the World Baseball Classic.

Steve Smith
Seattle Mariners (AL) 1996–99; Texas Rangers (AL) 2002–06; Philadelphia Phillies (NL) 2007–
Minor league second baseman and shortstop.

Smith spent the 1976–82 seasons in the San Diego Padres' organization before becoming a minor league coach and manager. As a skipper he guided the Wichita Pilots to the 1987 Texas League championship and the Las Vegas Stars to the 1988 Pacific Coast League crown. From 1992–93 he was a roving infield instructor for the Mariners, then managed in their system from 1994–95 before being promoted to Seattle as a coach. In 2000 he managed the Indi-

anapolis Indians to the American Association championship and then to a Triple-A World Series title over the Memphis Redbirds. In 2001 he served as a roving minor league infield instructor for the Milwaukee Brewers before joining the Rangers' major league staff in 2002. In 2007 he moved to the Phillies.

Brian Snitker
Atlanta Braves (NL) 1985, 1988–90, 2007–
Minor league catcher from the University of New Orleans.

Snitker retired as a player in 1980 without ever reaching the major leagues. In 1981 he became a roving instructor in the Braves' minor league system, and in 1982 began work as a manager. He initially coached twice for the big league club, first in 1985 and again from 1988–90. In 1991 he became a minor league coach, then managed and coached again for several seasons. As a skipper he took the Myrtle Beach Pelicans to a 1999 Carolina League co-championship with the Wilmington Blue Rocks when, with the final series tied at two games apiece, Hurricane Floyd canceled the remainder of the series. In 2000 the Pelicans captured the title, and Snitker was named the league's Manager of the Year in both 1999 and 2000.

In 2007 he returned to the Braves' coaching staff for a third go-round.

Frank Snyder
New York Giants (NL) 1933–41
Catcher who played 16 major league seasons.

Snyder played about half his career with the St. Louis Cardinals, then moved to the Giants, then finished out his last season back with the Cardinals. He was a .265 lifetime hitter, reaching his peak in 1921 and 1922 with the Giants when he hit .320 and a career-high .343, respectively, while helping the club to back-to-back World Championships. In 1924 he hit .302, and the following season belted a career-high 11 home runs. He eventually returned to the Giants as a coach for nine seasons.

Jim Snyder
Chicago Cubs (NL) 1987; Seattle Mariners (AL) 1988; San Diego Padres (NL) 1991–92
See Managers section.

Luis Sojo
New York Yankees (AL) 2004–05
Four-time Venezuelan Winter League batting champion.

Sojo peaked at .376 in that league, but averaged only .261 in the majors. He was a solid utilityman, however, and a good clutch hitter. In 1997 he batted a career-high .307 in limited action for the Yankees. In 1991 with the California Angels he led the American League with 21 sacrifice hits.

Sojo played through 2001 and was cut by the Yankees in spring training of 2002. He became a minor league manager for the club's AA team, the Norwich Navigators, and led that squad to the Eastern League championship. In 2003 he was invited to participate in a Yankees' Old Timers game, during which he hit the game-winning home run. In September he was signed to an active contract and appeared in three games for New York, giving him the distinction of playing in an Old Timers game and in regular season games in the same year.

In 2004 he returned to the Yanks as a full-time coach, and in 2006 returned to managing in the minors. Also in 2006 he was the manager of the Venezuelan team in the World Baseball Classic.

Denny Sommers
New York Mets (NL) 1977–78; Cleveland Indians (AL) 1980–85; San Diego Padres (NL) 1988–90; San Francisco Giants (NL) 1993–94
Minor league catcher and manager.

A native of New London, Wisconsin, Sommers was a tough competitor who prided himself on not missing games. He became a minor league skipper in the 1970s and guided the Lafayette Drillers to a co-championship with the Midland Cubs in 1975. In 1977 he became a coach with the Mets, and later moved to the Indians and the Padres. In 1992 he served as a special assistant, baseball operations with the Milwaukee Brewers, then went to the Giants as a coach from 1993–94.

Allen Sothoron
St. Louis Cardinals (NL) 1927–28; St. Louis Browns (AL) 1932–33
See Managers section.

Billy Southworth
New York Giants (NL) 1933
See Managers section.

Warren Spahn
New York Mets (NL) 1965; Cleveland Indians (AL) 1972–73
Winningest left-handed pitcher in major league history.

Spahn recorded 363 career victories, placing him behind only Cy Young, Walter Johnson, Grover Cleveland Alexander, and Christy Mathewson, and first among southpaws. He debuted in 1942 but then missed the 1943–45 seasons to military service, during which he served as a combat engineer and earned not only a battlefield commission but a Purple Heart and a Bronze Star as well.

Returning to baseball in 1946, Spahn established himself as one of the all-time greats. He was a 20-game winner 13 times and was named to 16 All-Star teams. Playing most of his career with the Braves in both Boston and Milwaukee, he led the National League eight times in wins, three times in earned run average, twice in games started, nine times in complete games, four times in shutouts, four times in innings pitched, and four times in strikeouts. In 1957 he won the Cy Young Award (at that time presented to only one pitcher who represented both the National and American Leagues) on the strength of a 21–11 record, a 2.69 ERA, and 111 strikeouts. He pitched two no-hitters, and in 1952 he once struck out 18 Chicago Cubs in a 15-inning game, a game he ultimately lost. In 1963, at the age of 42, he went 23–7, becoming the oldest 20-game winner in major league history. No slouch with a bat, he hit 35 career home runs, an NL record for a pitcher.

Spahn pitched as a player-coach for the Mets in 1965, but after going 4–12 he was released and signed with the San Francisco Giants. He went 3–4 for them before being released again. He continued to play in the minor leagues and in Mexico until 1967.

In 1965 the Braves retired his number 21. He coached for the Indians from 1972–73, and in '73 was inducted into the Hall of Fame.

Dick Spalding
Philadelphia Phillies (NL) 1934–36; Chicago Cubs (NL) 1941–43
Minor league outfielder from Philadelphia.

Spalding did reach the majors for parts of two seasons—1927 with the Phillies and 1928 with the Washington Nationals. In 131 games he batted .299, averaging .348 in 16 games with Washington. He later returned to his hometown Phillies as a coach, and also coached the Cubs for several years.

Spalding died in Philadelphia in 1950.

Al Spangler
Chicago Cubs (NL) 1970–71, 1974
Journeyman outfielder who played 13 big league seasons.

Spangler played several seasons for the Milwaukee Braves before being selected by the Houston Colt .45s in the expansion draft. His first two seasons in Houston he was the Colts' top hitter, batting .285 in 1962 and .281 the following year. He later played for the California Angels and the Cubs and posted a .262 lifetime average with 21 home runs and 175 runs batted in. In 1970 and '71 he was a player-coach for the Cubs, and he returned in 1974 as a full-time coach.

Joe Sparks
Chicago White Sox (AL) 1979; Cincinnati Reds (NL) 1984; Montreal Expos (NL) 1989; New York Yankees (AL) 1990
Minor league infielder for 13 seasons.

Sparks never reached the major leagues as a player but spent the majority of his professional career in the organization of the New York/San Francisco Giants. He spent four of those years as a player-coach, and upon retiring became an extremely successful minor league manager. Between one-year stints as a coach for several major league clubs, Sparks won nine championships and nine minor league Manager of the Year Awards in 19 seasons as a skipper. In later years he became an advance scout for the St. Louis Cardinals, then served one year as a hitting coach for the Sacramento River Cats before beginning work as an advance scout for the Oakland Athletics.

Chris Speier
Milwaukee Brewers (NL) 2000; Arizona Diamondbacks (NL) 2001; Oakland Athletics (AL) 2004; Chicago Cubs (NL) 2005–06
Three-time All-Star shortstop who spent only one season in the minor leagues.

Speier debuted with the San Francisco Giants in 1971 and was an All-Star the very next year. It was the first of three consecutive All-Star appointments, and he eventually spent 19 seasons in the major leagues with several clubs. In 1975 he topped all National League shortstops in fielding average, and despite batting only .246 in his career he hit for the cycle twice—in 1981 against the Atlanta Braves and in 1988 against the St. Louis Cardinals.

Speier became a roving minor league instructor for the Giants following his retirement, then in 1995 worked as a minor league coach in the Cubs' organization and shortly thereafter managed in the Diamondbacks' system. In 1997 he led the High Desert Mavericks to the California League championship. Three years later he joined the Brewers as a coach, and later coached for the Diamondbacks, A's, and Cubs. In July of 2006 with Chicago he was arrested for DUI, and he took a leave of absence from the club while Mike Quade, the manager of the AAA Iowa Cubs, filled in for him temporarily.

Tom Spencer
Cleveland Indians (AL) 1988–89; New York Mets (NL) 1991; Houston Astros (NL) 1992–93
Minor leaguer who played 29 games in The Show.

An outfielder, Spencer played those games in 1978 with the Chicago White Sox. He batted .185 with a double and four runs batted in in 65 at-bats. After his playing career he coached for the Indians, Mets, and Astros, and in 1989 he also played for the Fort Myers Sun Sox in the Senior Professional Baseball Association, where he hit .250 in 57 games.

Harry Spilman
Houston Astros (NL) 1999–2003
Eastern League Most Valuable Player in 1977.

Spilman hit .373 for the Three Rivers Eagles that season, which was far more than he would ever achieve in the major leagues. He did last 12 seasons, however, despite hitting only .237 and setting new standards for lack of speed on the bases. In those 12 years, which encompassed 810 games, Spilman stole only one base and hit only one triple.

Harry served as a roving hitting instructor for the Cleveland Indians following his retirement. He later worked as a minor league field coordinator for the Astros before joining their major league staff as a coach, then he became a minor league coach in the organization.

Mike Squires
Toronto Blue Jays (AL) 1989–91; Chicago White Sox (AL) 1992
Southern League Most Valuable Player in 1975.

That season with the Knoxville Knox Sox would be something of an aberration for Squires, who hit .260 in 10 major league years. Playing mostly as a reserve first baseman, he did, however, win a Gold Glove in 1981 with the White Sox. In 1980 he had caught two games, becoming the first left-handed backstop in the majors since 1958. In 1983 he led all American League first basemen in fielding percentage, and also played one game at third base, becoming a rare left-hander at *that* position. In 1984 he pitched to one batter to close out a game, a game the White Sox won.

After his playing days Squires would coach for the Blue Jays and then return to Chicago in that role for one season.

George Staller
Baltimore Orioles (AL) 1962, 1968–75
Solid minor leaguer who played 21 games in the bigs.

Staller played for the Baltimore Orioles of the International League in 1943 and led that circuit with 98 runs batted in, earning a call-up to the Philadelphia Athletics. He hit .271 with the A's, knocking a double, 3 triples, and 3 home runs as well as driving in 12. But he would never again play in the major leagues.

He went to work as a minor league manager in the Athletics' system following his playing days, and eventually moved to the major league Orioles in 1954. On two occasions he was promoted to the big league club as a coach, the second time for eight seasons.

Oscar Stanage
Detroit Tigers (AL) 1925; Pittsburgh Pirates (NL) 1927–31
Solid catcher with a rather weak bat.

Stanage played 14 seasons despite a mere .234 batting average. In 1911 he set a record for catchers with 212 assists, and also caught more games (141) than any other American League backstop that year. Except for a single game in 1906 with the Cincinnati Reds, Stanage spent his entire career with the Tigers.

While Detroit does not list him as an official coach for the 1925 season, that is likely what he was, or, more technically, a player-coach. Stanage had gained the respect of Ty Cobb in previous years, even though Cobb had cut him prior to the 1921 season. Stanage did not play in the majors again until Cobb hired him in 1925, likely as a coach, and Oscar was activated for three games and went 1-for-5. He later coached five seasons for the Pirates.

Lee Stange
Boston Red Sox (AL) 1972–74, 1981–84; Minnesota Twins (AL) 1975; Oakland Athletics (AL) 1977–79
Right-handed pitcher from Chicago.

Stange both started and relieved in a 10-year career, although approximately two-thirds of his appearances were out of the bullpen. He notched a 62–61 lifetime record with 21 saves and a 3.56 earned run average. His best season was probably 1963, when he went 12–5 for the Twins with a 2.62 ERA.

He later coached for the Red Sox (one of four teams for whom he had played), the Twins (another), the A's, and the Red Sox again.

Eddie Stanky
Cleveland Indians (AL) 1957–58
See Managers section.

Fred Stanley
Milwaukee Brewers (AL) 1991
Player-turned-executive.

A shortstop, Stanley played in the major leagues for 14 seasons, relying almost exclusively on his excellent defense. He hit only .216, on several occasions failing to reach the .200 mark. He had originally been signed by the Houston Astros but was selected by the Seattle Pilots in the 1969 expansion draft and made his major league debut for them. He accompanied the team to Milwaukee for one season, then played for several other clubs until 1982.

After his playing career Stanley went to work in the front offices of the Astros and the Mariners. In 1991 he returned to the Brewers as a coach, and in 1992 joined *their* front office as director of player development, later becoming assistant general manager. He eventually became a skipper in the minor leagues.

Willie Stargell
Pittsburgh Pirates (NL) 1985; Atlanta Braves (NL) 1986–88
Hall of Fame outfielder and first baseman.

Nicknamed "Pops," Stargell was a seven-time All-Star who hit .282 during his career and bashed 475 home runs. He reached at least 20 fifteen times, leading the National League in 1971 with 48 and again in 1973 with 44, when he was also on top with 119 runs batted in and 43 doubles. He hit over .300 three times, and in 1964 he hit for the cycle. After suffering a broken arm in 1977 while breaking up an on-field fight and being limited to only 63 games, he bounced back in 1978 and was named the league's Comeback Player of the Year.

Stargell's most memorable season by far was 1979, when he batted .281 with 32 homers and 82 RBIs and was named the NL's co-Most Valuable Player (along with Keith Hernandez), helped the Pirates to the pennant and was named the MVP of the League Championship Series, and then helped the Bucs to the World Championship and was named MVP of the World Series. Stargell not only became the oldest player ever to win a league MVP Award, he also became the only player ever to win all three MVPs (regular season, LCS, and World Series) in the same year.

After retiring Stargell returned to the Pirates as a coach in 1985, then moved on to the Braves for three seasons. In 1988 the Pirates retired his number 8, and he was also inducted into the Hall of Fame. He passed away in 2001.

Herm Starrette
Atlanta Braves (NL) 1974–76; San Francisco Giants (NL) 1977–78, 1983–84; Philadelphia Phillies (NL) 1979–81; Milwaukee Brewers (AL) 1985–86; Chicago Cubs (NL) 1987; Baltimore Orioles (AL) 1988; Boston Red Sox (AL) 1995–97
Longtime coach who pitched 27 major league games.

Starrette spent most of his career in the minor leagues, joining the Orioles for 18 games in 1963, 5 in 1964, and 4 in 1965. His major league record was 1–1, his earned run average 2.54. After playing he coached the Rochester Red Wings in 1967, then worked as an Orioles' minor league pitching instructor from 1968–73. At that point he went to the Braves and began a long and productive career as a major league coach. In 2004 he was hired to be the pitching coach of the Berkshire Dukes of the New England Collegiate Baseball League.

Rusty Staub
New York Mets (NL) 1982
Carolina League Most Valuable Player in 1962.

That season was a harbinger of things to come, as Staub played 23 major league seasons and made quite a name for himself with several teams. A six-time All-Star, he debuted in 1963 as a 19-year-old, and eventually joined Ty Cobb as one of the only two players to hit home runs both before their twentieth birthdays and after their fortieth. He swatted 292 lifetime, hitting at least 15 nine times and topping out with 30 in 1970. In 1967 he led the National League with 44 doubles, and he topped the 100-run-batted-in mark three times. During his career he became the first player to appear in at least 500 games for four different teams, and also the first player to collect at least 500 hits with four different clubs (accumulating 792 with the Houston Astros, 709 with the New York Mets, 582 with the Detroit Tigers, and 531 with the Montreal Expos).

In 1982 Staub was a player-coach with the Mets, but he continued as a full-time player for three more seasons after that. The Expos retired his number 10 in 1993, and later retired the same number for Andre Dawson.

John Stearns
New York Yankees (AL) 1989; Cincinnati Reds (NL) 1995; Baltimore Orioles (AL) 1996–97; New York Mets (NL) 2000–01
Catcher and potential football star.

Stearns was originally drafted by the Oakland Athletics, but he chose to attend the University of Colorado instead. He was later drafted by the Philadelphia Phillies and as a defensive back by the Buffalo Bills, and he chose baseball. He engaged in the national pastime like a football player, however, going all out and never shying from potential collisions, beginning several bench-clearing brawls in the process. His playing style also led to quite a number of injuries that eventually shortened his career.

A four-time All-Star, Stearns set a record for catchers in 1978 by stealing 25 bases. That record would stand until 1998, when it was broken by Jason Kendall of the Pittsburgh Pirates. He suffered an elbow injury in 1982 that would severely curtail his playing time and would end his career in 1984.

In 1986 he went to work as a scout and minor league instructor for the Milwaukee Brewers. After coaching for the Yankees in 1989 he became a manager in the Toronto Blue Jays' organization, and later worked as a Reds' scout and a broadcaster for ESPN. In 1994 he managed the Princeton Reds and led that club to the Appalachian League championship, earning the circuit's Manager of the Year Award in the process. Toward the end of the 1995 season, once again working as a Reds' scout, he was promoted to Cincinnati as a coach, but his presence was kept secret from Reds' owner Marge Schott, who would have likely objected to his increase in salary. The media even agreed not to interview him until after the season.

Stearns later coached the Orioles and worked for the Mets as a minor league manager, major league coach, and roving catching instructor. In 2006 he moved to the Washington Nationals' system as a minor league skipper.

Rick Stelmaszek
Minnesota Twins (AL) 1981–
Catcher who played 60 big league games.

Stelmaszek hit only .170 in those brief chances, spreading those games out over three seasons with four different teams. In 1978 he joined the Twins' organization as a minor league manager, and in 1980 was named the Midwest League Manager of the Year with the Wisconsin Rapids Twins, who finished in third place and made the playoffs. In 1981 he began a very long career as a Minnesota coach at the major league level.

Casey Stengel
Brooklyn Dodgers (NL) 1932–33
See Managers section.

Ed Stevens
San Diego Padres (NL) 1981
First baseman from Kansas City, Missouri.

Nicknamed "Big Ed" (and also, apparently, "Whistling Eddie" because he used to whistle a lot in an effort to encourage his teammates on the field), Stevens played six seasons, mostly in a backup role. In 1948 with the Pittsburgh Pirates he played a career-high 128 games and led all National League first basemen in fielding average. He hit only .252 in his career, but did manage 10 home runs in a season on two occasions.

Dave Stewart
San Diego Padres (NL) 1998; Toronto Blue Jays (AL) 2000; Milwaukee Brewers (NL) 2002
Outstanding pitcher who won 168 major league games.

Stewart debuted with the Los Angeles Dodgers in 1978 and was used mainly out of the bullpen for the first half of his career. He joined the Texas Rangers in 1983, and two years later was embroiled in controversy when he was arrested for soliciting a transvestite prostitute. He apparently was not aware that the prostitute was actually a male until after the arrest.

His baseball career truly took off in 1987, after he had joined his hometown Oakland Athletics. He tied Roger Clemens for the American League lead in victories that year as he went 20–13 with a 3.68 earned run average. The next three seasons he won 21, 21, and 22 games, respectively, and was an All-Star in 1989. Beginning in 1988 he led the AL four consecutive times in games started, and during that period also led twice in complete games, once in shutouts, and twice in innings pitched. In 1989 he was named the Most Valuable Player of the World Series as the

A's captured the championship. In 1990 he pitched a no-hitter against the Blue Jays, and was later named MVP of the AL Championship Series when he helped Oakland defeat the Boston Red Sox. He won the same award in 1993 while helping his new team, none other than the Blue Jays, to the pennant.

Stewart became a coach for several teams and a front office executive after his retirement.

Milt Stock
Chicago Cubs (NL) 1944–48; Brooklyn Dodgers (NL) 1949–50; Pittsburgh Pirates (NL) 1951–52
Solid infielder from Chicago.

A .289 lifetime hitter, Stock topped the .300 mark five times, four of them consecutively. In 1920 with the St. Louis Cardinals he led the National League with 639 at-bats, and in 1925 with the Dodgers he set a twentieth century major league record by collecting four hits in each of four straight games.

As the third base coach with the Dodgers in 1950 he was involved in controversy when, with his club one game out of first place during the last game of the season, he waved a runner home in a tie game only to see that runner gunned down at the plate. The runner was Cal Abrams, and the outfielder who threw him out was Richie Ashburn of the Philadelphia Phillies. That play may have cost the Dodgers the pennant, and Stock was fired a few days later. He was soon hired by the Pirates, however, and coached for them for two more years.

Wes Stock
Kansas City Athletics (AL) 1967; Milwaukee Brewers (AL) 1970–72; Oakland Athletics (AL) 1973–76, 1984–86; Seattle Mariners (AL) 1977–81
Nine-year major league relief pitcher.

Of 321 big league games, Stock started only 3. He compiled a 27–13 lifetime mark with 22 saves for the Baltimore Orioles and Kansas City A's, and his earned run average was 3.60. He pitched only one game in 1967, when he became a Kansas City coach, and that finished out his playing career. He later coached the Brewers and then returned to the Athletics while they were in Oakland. After coaching the Mariners from 1977–81 he worked as a television broadcaster for the club, then he went back to coaching, once again with the A's.

Mel Stottlemyre
New York Mets (NL) 1984–93; Houston Astros (NL) 1994–95; New York Yankees (AL) 1996–2005
Outstanding right-handed pitcher for the Yankees.

Stottlemyre played his entire 11-year major league career in New York, where he won 164 games overall. A five-time All-Star, he was a 20-game winner three times and won at least 14 games eight times. He led the American League twice in complete games and once in innings pitched. No slouch at the plate, he tied a major league pitchers' record by collecting five hits in a game in 1964, and in 1965 became the first pitcher in 55 years to hit an inside-the-park grand slam. In 1974 he set an AL record by making 272 straight starts, with no relief appearances.

Stottlemyre's playing career ended in 1974 due to a torn rotator cuff. He later worked as a roving minor league pitching instructor for the Seattle Mariners before being hired to coach the Mets. After 10 years he went to the Astros, then returned to the Yankees. After another 10 years with his old club he resigned in 2005, citing as one of his reasons for doing so disagreements with Yankees' owner George Steinbrenner.

Stottlemyre's son Todd also had a long and successful major league career as a pitcher.

Monty Stratton
Chicago White Sox (AL) 1940–41
Pitcher whose career was tragically cut short.

Stratton played five seasons for the White Sox, going 15–5 in 1937 and 15–9 in 1938. He was named an American League All-Star in '37. Perhaps not yet even having approached his peak, he was hunting rabbits in November of 1938 when he slipped and fell, and his shotgun discharged and sent pellets into his right leg, which had to be amputated.

Stratton received a wooden leg and remained with the White Sox as a batting practice pitcher and eventual coach. When the United States entered World War II he tried to enlist, but was rejected because of his disability. He then organized a semipro team and continued to play, working both with that club and at home trying to regain his coordination as a pitcher. When he practiced at home his catcher was his wife, Ethel. In 1946 he finally pitched professionally again in the minor leagues, and he won 18 games with the Sherman Twins of the East Texas League. He had difficulties, however, due to the fact that many opposing teams would consistently bunt balls out of his reach.

While he never again played in the major leagues, Stratton's struggles inspired the motion picture *The Stratton Story* in 1949, which starred Jimmy Stewart and June Allyson.

Gabby Street
St. Louis Cardinals (NL) 1929; St. Louis Browns (AL) 1937
See Managers section.

George Strickland

Minnesota Twins (AL) 1962; Cleveland Indians (AL) 1963–69; Kansas City Royals (AL) 1970–72

See Managers section.

Lester Strode

Chicago Cubs (NL) 2007–

Longtime minor league pitching coordinator.

Strode worked for 18 years in the Cubs' organization before being named to the major league staff. From 1994–95 he was with the big club as a pitching assistant, and for the next 11 served as the system's pitching coordinator. He worked with all the minor league pitching coaches as well as in spring training minor league camp, extended spring training, and the Arizona Fall League.

In 2007 he was promoted to Chicago as bullpen coach when Lou Piniella took over the reins as manager from Dusty Baker.

Brent Strom

Houston Astros (NL) 1996; Kansas City Royals (AL) 2000–01

Pitcher whose career was shortened due to an arm injury.

Strom showed great potential at the University of Southern California, helping his team to two NCAA championships. He signed with the New York Mets in 1970 and reached the major leagues two years later. He played for the Cleveland Indians the following season and then for the San Diego Padres, with whom he hurt his elbow. His last season was 1977. He eventually coached the Astros and Royals, and then worked as a minor league pitching coordinator for the Washington Nationals.

Moose Stubing

California Angels (AL) 1985–90

See Managers section.

Dick Such

Texas Rangers (AL) 1983–85; Minnesota Twins (AL) 1985–2001

Minor league pitcher who appeared in 21 games for the Washington Senators.

Such's big league cup of coffee came in 1970, when he started five games and went 1–5 with a 7.56 earned run average. As a coach he spent time with the Rangers and the Twins, and he served as the American League's pitching coach in both the 1988 and 1992 All-Star Games. Additionally, he served in that role for a special major league All-Star team that toured Japan following the 1996 season. In 2006 he signed as a pitching coach with the Long Island Ducks of the independent Atlantic League.

Joe Sugden

Detroit Tigers (AL) 1912; St. Louis Cardinals (NL) 1921–25; Philadelphia Phillies (NL) 1926–27

Switch-hitting backup catcher and first baseman.

Sugden played from 1893–1905. When teammate Connie Mack suffered an injury in 1895 that made it difficult for him to run, Sugden was his designated pinch-runner, taking his place on the bases but not in the field or at bat. It was a practice allowed by the rules of the time. In 13 major league seasons he hit .255.

Sugden's role with the 1912 Tigers is unclear, but some sources list him as a coach. On May 18 of that year, Detroit players went on strike to protest the suspension of teammate Ty Cobb, and owner Frank Navin had some amateurs signed to take their places in order to avoid a forfeit and a resulting league fine. Sugden, at 41 years of age, and 48-year-old coach Deacon McGuire were also pressed into service, and those two scored the only Tiger runs of the game in a 24–2 shellacking by the Philadelphia Athletics.

Sugden later coached the Cardinals and Phillies and then worked as a longtime Cardinals' scout.

Clyde Sukeforth

Brooklyn Dodgers (NL) 1945–51; Pittsburgh Pirates (NL) 1952–57

See Managers section.

John Sullivan

Kansas City Royals (AL) 1979; Atlanta Braves (NL) 1980–81; Toronto Blue Jays (AL) 1982–93

One of five John Sullivans to play in the major leagues.

John Peter Sullivan was born in 1941 in Somerville, New Jersey, and played parts of five seasons as a catcher with the Detroit Tigers, New York Mets, and Philadelphia Phillies. He hit .228 in his big league trials with 2 home runs and 18 runs batted in, never stealing a base but being caught twice attempting to do so. He later coached the Royals, Braves, and Blue Jays.

Champ Summers

New York Yankees (AL) 1990

Outfielder and Vietnam veteran.

Summers spent a lot of time bouncing between the major and minor leagues. He made his big league debut in 1974 with the Oakland Athletics, and he eventually spent time with six major league clubs in 11 years. In 1978 he played 13 games for the Cincinnati Reds but had a better minor league season, being named the Most Valuable Player of the American Association with the Indianapolis Indians as well as the Minor League Player of the Year by *The Sporting News*. In 1979 with the Reds and the Detroit Tigers he hit a career-high 20 home runs, and he would end his career with 54 and a .255 batting average.

In 1989 he played for the Fort Myers Sun Sox of the Senior Professional Baseball Association, and the following year worked as a coach with the Yankees.

George Susce
Cleveland Indians (AL) 1941–49; Boston Red Sox (AL) 1950–54; Kansas City Athletics (AL) 1955–56; Milwaukee Braves (NL) 1958–59; Washington Senators (AL) 1961–67, 1969–71; Texas Rangers (AL) 1972
Backup catcher for eight seasons.

George C. Susce hit only .228 in 146 games spent with five different teams. From 1941–44 he was a player-coach with the Indians, appearing in 1 game in 1941, then in 2, 3, and 29 the next three seasons, respectively. He was let go following the 1949 season when his son, George D. Susce, signed with the Red Sox as a pitcher. George C. followed him to Boston and later coached quite a few other teams as well.

Dale Sveum
Boston Red Sox (AL) 2004–05; Milwaukee Brewers (NL) 2006–
Infielder with a shaky glove.

Sveum debuted in 1986 with the Brewers, who were then in the American League, and he was named to the Topps All-Star Rookie Team although he led all AL third basemen in errors. Compounding the dubiousness of his fielding was the fact that he played only 65 games at that position all season. The next year he hit a career-high 25 home runs and drove in a career-high 95 runs, but in 1988, having moved to shortstop, he also led *that* position in errors. He suffered a broken leg and missed the entire 1989 campaign, and his playing time was severely limited after that.

In 2001 Sveum became a minor league manager in the Pittsburgh Pirates' organization, and in 2003 he led the Altoona Curve to the playoffs for the first time. *Baseball America* named him its Top Managerial Prospect for the Eastern League. In 2004 he joined the Red Sox as a big league coach, and in 2006 moved to the Brewers.

Bill Sweeney
Detroit Tigers (AL) 1947–48
Pacific Coast League Hall of Famer.

William Joseph Sweeney, whose uncle, William John Sweeney, played in the majors earlier, played parts of three seasons as a first baseman in the big leagues and hit a decent .286. He became a PCL player *after* those days, and would spend 21 seasons in the league as a player and manager. He began in 1936 as a player-manager for the Portland Beavers and led that squad to the pennant. In 1940 he

moved to the Hollywood Stars, then in 1942 to the Los Angeles Angels as a player-coach. He took that club to back-to-back pennants in 1943 and 1944.

From 1947–48 he returned to the major leagues as a coach for the Tigers. He then returned to Portland, then went to the Seattle Rainiers, back to Los Angeles, and back to Portland again. In April of 1957, still at the helm of the Beavers, he died of a heart attack during a road trip to San Diego. He was inducted into the PCL Hall of Fame in 2004.

Rick Sweet
Seattle Mariners (AL) 1984; Houston Astros (NL) 1996
Switch-hitting catcher and longtime minor league manager.

In three major league seasons Sweet hit .234 with 6 home runs and 57 runs batted in. He played for three different teams: the San Diego Padres in 1978, the New York Mets and Seattle Mariners in 1982, and the Mariners in 1983. He then coached the Mariners in 1984 and worked as an advance scout. In 1987 he became a minor league skipper in the organization, but in 1989 moved to the Astros' chain. In 1993 his Tucson Toros captured the Pacific Coast League championship, and the following season Sweet was named the PCL Manager of the Year when the Toros posted the league's second-best record. In 1996 he was promoted to the Astros as a big league coach. In 1998 and 1999 his Harrisburg Senators won back-to-back Eastern League titles (actually the third and fourth of four consecutive championships). He later became a minor league manager in the Cincinnati Reds' organization.

Bob Swift
Detroit Tigers (AL) 1953–54, 1963–66; Kansas City Athletics (AL) 1957–59; Washington Senators (AL) 1960
See Managers section.

Steve Swisher
New York Mets (NL) 1994–96
All-Star catcher who hit .216.

The number one draft pick of the Chicago White Sox in 1973, Swisher made his debut the following year. He hit .214 that season and .213 the next, and in 1976 was named an American League All-Star despite eventual season totals of a .236 average, 5 home runs, and 42 runs batted in.

He lasted nine seasons in the major leagues before becoming a minor league manager in the Cleveland Indians' organization. He managed many different teams over the years, and in 1992 was named the Eastern League Manager of the Year while piloting the Binghamton Mets. From 1994–96 he was a big league coach with the New York Mets.

In 2002 Swisher left baseball and became a regional sales manager for an aluminum company.

John Tamargo
Houston Astros (NL) 1999–2004
Part-time major league catcher for five seasons.

Tamargo hit .242 in 135 games with the St. Louis Cardinals, San Francisco Giants, and Montreal Expos. In 1982 he began a long and successful minor league managing and coaching career. His teams logged four first-place finishes and two championships, as his 1994 Binghamton Mets captured the Eastern League crown and his 1998 New Orleans Zephyrs took the Pacific Coast League title. From 1999–2004 he coached for the Astros, then returned to the minor leagues, taking the helm of the Durham Bulls in 2006.

Jesse Tannehill
Philadelphia Phillies (NL) 1920
Outstanding pitcher from Dayton, Kentucky.

Tannehill also played the outfield and pinch-hit successfully. On the mound he truly shone, however, becoming a 20-game winner six times in a 15-year career. In 1898 with the Pittsburgh Pirates he logged a career-high 25 victories, and in 1901 he led the National League with a 2.18 earned run average, although his 1.95 mark the following year was even better. In 1904 with the Boston Americans he pitched a no-hitter against the Chicago White Sox, and his brother Lee, the Chicago third baseman, went 0-for-3.

Toward the end of his career Tannehill began to play the outfield more than he pitched. In 1911 with the Cincinnati Reds he pitched on Opening Day and performed so badly that he decided to retire. He returned to the major leagues in 1920 as a coach with the Phillies.

Bruce Tanner
Pittsburgh Pirates (NL) 2001–05
Son of Chuck Tanner.

Bruce was a minor league pitcher who performed in only 10 major league games. Those occurred in 1985 with the Chicago White Sox, and Tanner started four times and recorded a 1–2 record with a 5.33 earned run average. After his playing days he became a minor league pitching coach, and then spent five years on the big league staff of the Pirates.

El Tappe
Chicago Cubs (NL) 1959–65
See Managers section.

Tony Taylor
Philadelphia Phillies (NL) 1977–79, 1988–89; Florida Marlins (NL) 1999–2001, 2004
Versatile, Cuban-born infielder who played 19 seasons.

Taylor debuted with the Chicago Cubs in 1958, but during the 1960 season he was traded to the Phillies and became a National League All-Star (in both games that season). He was a lifetime .261 hitter, but he topped the .300 mark three times, twice in limited action. He played every infield position and even manned the outfield on a few occasions. He finished his career with the Phillies in 1976 but stayed onboard as a coach for the next three seasons. He later had another stint as a Philadelphia coach, and then two with the Marlins.

Zack Taylor
Brooklyn Dodgers (NL) 1935; St. Louis Browns (AL) 1941–46; Pittsburgh Pirates (NL) 1947
See Managers section.

Johnny Temple
Cincinnati Reds (NL) 1964
With Roy McMillan, part of a top double play duo with the Cincinnati Reds of the 1950s.

With McMillan at shortstop and Temple at second, the Reds had one of the best up-the-middle defenses in the game. Temple was the stronger hitter, averaging .284 and topping the .300 mark on three occasions. He was named an All-Star six times, and in 1957 he tied for the National League lead with 94 bases on balls. At second base he led the league three times in putouts, once in assists, and once in double plays.

He was a player-coach in 1964 with the Reds, appearing in six games but not collecting a hit in three at-bats. After retiring he became a sportscaster for the Houston Astros.

Gene Tenace
Houston Astros (NL) 1986–87; Toronto Blue Jays (AL) 1990–97
See Managers section.

Wayne Terwilliger
Washington Senators (AL) 1969–71; Texas Rangers (AL) 1972, 1981–85; Minnesota Twins (AL) 1986–94
U.S. Marine Corps veteran.

A shortstop at Western Michigan University, Terwilliger became a second baseman in the major leagues and played nine seasons. In his rookie 1949 season with the Chicago Cubs he once collected eight consecutive hits. After his playing career he worked as a minor league coach and manager, spending time with the Senators and accompanying them to Texas, and also with the Twins.

Terwilliger had played for the St. Paul Saints of the minor American Association in 1952, a team that was a Brooklyn Dodgers' affiliate, and hit .312. In later years he spent eight seasons as a coach with the St. Paul Saints of the Northern League, and that club retired his number 5 in 2002. As a skipper he led the 2005 Fort Worth Cats to the independent Central Baseball League championship. He became the first base coach for the Cats the following season as the club was part of a merger that formed a new American Association (which, incidentally, also included the St. Paul Saints).

Nick Testa
San Francisco Giants (NL) 1958
Longtime minor leaguer who played one big league game.

Testa was a catcher and third baseman who served as a backstop during his one game with the Giants. He did not get an at-bat, but came very close, standing on deck in a tied, extra-inning game when teammate Daryl Spencer ended the contest with a game-winning home run. That was in 1958, and the Giants removed Testa from the active roster and made him a coach for the rest of the season.

Testa had struggled at the plate during his minor league career, and after his Giants' experience he returned to the minors and then went to Japan, where he continued to struggle. He eventually became a player-manager in the Quebec Provincial League, where he suddenly started to hit, twice topping the .340 mark and being named to four All-Star teams. He later played semipro ball and worked as a strength and conditioning instructor for the New York Yankees.

George Thomas
Boston Red Sox (AL) 1970
Likable outfielder who played 13 major league seasons.

Thomas had a high-energy personality that endeared him to fans and teammates, and he was used as a backup all over the field. In addition to the outfield he played every infield position at one time or another (logging a single game at shortstop), and even caught on several occasions. In 1970 he was made a player-coach with the Red Sox, then he continued to play for one more season.

Ira Thomas
Philadelphia Athletics (AL) 1914–17, 1925–26
Solidly-built catcher for several teams.

Thomas was a .242 lifetime hitter, but in 1908 with the Detroit Tigers he became the first successful pinch-hitter in World Series history when he singled in the ninth inning of Game 1 while batting for Charley O'Leary. He played the final 7 seasons of his 10-year career with the A's, playing two games in 1914 and one in 1915 as a player-coach before turning to coaching full-time. He later worked as a

scout for the A's and coached for two more seasons in the 1920s.

Lee Thomas
St. Louis Cardinals (NL) 1972, 1983
Player, coach, and executive.

As an outfielder and first baseman Thomas played from 1961–68 and hit .255 with six teams, including the expansion Los Angeles Angels in '61. He was named an American League All-Star in 1962 (appearing in both games) when he hit a career-high .290 with 26 home runs and 104 runs batted in. It was the second of three seasons in which he blasted at least 22 roundtrippers. In 1961 he tied a major league record with nine hits in a doubleheader, and in 1963 tied a mark by participating in six double plays in a game.

Thomas coached for the Cardinals in 1972 before becoming a longtime executive. He served as the Cards' director of player development from 1981–87, also coaching in 1983, as a Philadelphia Phillies' vice president and general manager from 1988–97, then as a special assistant to the general manager for the Boston Red Sox from 1998–2003.

Roy Thomas
St. Louis Cardinals (NL) 1922
Champion of the base on balls.

Thomas had an uncanny ability to foul off pitches at a time when such fouls did not count as strikes. He thus earned many walks for himself, and led the National League in that category seven times. He drew over 100 free passes seven times, recording highs of 115 in both 1899 and 1900. In an August 1900 game, he fouled off 12 pitches thrown by Bill Phillips of the Cincinnati Reds, prompting Phillips to punch him. It was because of Thomas that the NL changed the rule in 1901, making fouls strikes, but the rule had little effect on Roy, who continued to lead the league consistently in bases on balls. The American League adopted the same rule two years later.

Thomas also excelled at other facets of the game, leading the NL with 132 runs scored in 1900 and hitting over .300 five times. He also retired with career records for center fielders in putouts and fielding percentage.

Thomas began coaching at the University of Pennsylvania while he was still playing, and he continued to coach there after retiring from the playing field. In 1922 he coached one season with the Cardinals.

Milt Thompson
Philadelphia Phillies (NL) 2004–
Speedy outfielder who hit .274.

Thompson had a 13-year major league career during

which he hit over .300 four times and stole at least 14 bases on seven occasions. He swiped a career-high 46 in 1987 and retired with 214 career steals. In 1985, his sophomore season, he led the National League with a .433 pinch-hitting average.

After retiring in 1996 he became a minor league outfield and baserunning coordinator for the Tampa Bay Devil Rays. In 1998 he began coaching in the Phillies' minor league system, although he took 2000 off. In 2004 he joined the major league staff.

Robby Thompson
San Francisco Giants (NL) 2000–01; Cleveland Indians (AL) 2002, 2005
Two-time All-Star second baseman.

Thompson spent his entire 11-year career with the Giants, leading the National League with 11 triples in 1989 and hitting a career-high .312 in 1993. That average was something of an aberration, since Thompson was a career .257 hitter. On June 27, 1986, he set a new major league mark by being caught stealing four times in the same game. He hit 119 homers lifetime and stole 103 bases. In 1988 he hit the 10,000th home run in Giants' history, and in 1991 he hit for the cycle.

After his playing career he coached a couple of seasons for the Giants and then a couple with the Indians, for whom he also worked as a special assistant, baseball operations.

Tim Thompson
St. Louis Cardinals (NL) 1981
Catcher who played 187 games over four seasons.

A bespectacled backstop, Thompson played for three different clubs during his limited major league tenure. With the Brooklyn Dodgers in 1954 he got into 10 games and batted a mere .154. With the Kansas City Athletics in 1956 and '57 he hit .272 and .204, respectively. And with the Detroit Tigers in 1958 he played 4 games and hit .167. His lifetime average was .238.

After working as a longtime scout Thompson re-emerged in the majors for one season as a Cardinals' coach, in 1981.

Bob Tiefenauer
Philadelphia Phillies (NL) 1979
Relief pitcher who spent 40 years in baseball.

Tiefenauer played for six different teams from 1952–68, having two stints each with the St. Louis Cardinals and Cleveland Indians. He posted a 9–25 lifetime record despite a 3.84 earned run average and 23 saves. He then worked for nearly 20 years in the Phillies' organization as a minor league coach and roving instructor, spending the 1979 season on the big league staff.

Jack Tighe
Detroit Tigers (AL) 1942, 1955–56
See Managers section.

Ben Tincup
Brooklyn Dodgers (NL) 1940
Pitcher with a long minor league career.

A full-blooded Cherokee, Tincup also played 48 games in the major leagues spread over four seasons. Thirty-eight of those games occurred in 1914 and 1915 with the Philadelphia Phillies. Ben reappeared for the club in 1918 for eight games, then pitched two for the Chicago Cubs in 1928. The gaps were filled in by minor league play, and in 1917 Tincup pitched a perfect game for the Arkansas Travelers of the Southern Association.

In 1933 he worked as an umpire in the American Association, and from 1936–39 was a minor league skipper. In 1940 he coached for the Dodgers, then he served as a scout for the Boston Braves, the Pittsburgh Pirates, and the Phillies.

Lee Tinsley
Arizona Diamondbacks (NL) 2006–
Backup outfielder for five seasons.

Tinsley turned down a full football scholarship to Purdue University in order to play baseball. He eventually spent time with the Seattle Mariners, Boston Red Sox, and Philadelphia Phillies, having two stints each with the Mariners and Red Sox. He hit .241 and stole 41 bases, never appearing in more than 100 games in a season. He continued to play in the minor leagues when his major league days ended, and also played in the Mexican League and in independent baseball.

In 2001 Tinsley began coaching in the Diamondbacks' minor league system. In 2002 he was a roving instructor for the Anaheim Angels, then returned to the Arizona chain as a minor league outfield coordinator. In 2006 he was promoted to the major league staff as a coach.

Jack Tobin
St. Louis Browns (AL) 1949–51
Excellent-hitting outfielder for 13 seasons.

Tobin began his career in the Federal League in 1914 with the St. Louis Terriers. In 1915 he led the FL with 184 hits, and upon the league's demise hooked up with the Browns. He finished in a three-way tie for the American League lead with 18 triples in 1921, and also led with 671 at-bats. He hit over .300 seven times, peaking at .352 in 1921 and retiring with a .309 lifetime average.

Tobin coached several years for the Browns following his retirement and also worked as a scout.

Bobby Tolan
San Diego Padres (NL) 1980–83; Seattle Mariners (AL) 1987
Speedy outfielder from Los Angeles.

Tolan made his debut with the St. Louis Cardinals but later became a member of the early version of Cincinnati's Big Red Machine. Joining the Reds in 1969 he stole 26 bases and then led the National League in 1970 with a career-high 57. During the offseason he ruptured his Achilles tendon while playing on the Reds' exhibition basketball team, and he missed the entire 1971 campaign. The injury motivated the Reds' front office to disband the hardwood squad. Tolan returned in 1972 and hit .283 with 82 runs batted in and 42 steals, inspiring *The Sporting News* to name him its Comeback Player of the Year.

In 1973 Tolan began feuding with the Reds' front office, being involved in altercations with team personnel, disappearing for a couple of days in August, and growing facial hair, a practice banned by the team. He was traded to the Padres after the season.

Tolan played in Japan in 1978 and returned to the Padres for one final season the following year and then stayed on as a coach. He later coached for the Mariners and also worked as a minor league manager. From 1989–90 he was the player-manager of the St. Petersburg Pelicans of the Senior Professional Baseball Association.

Tim Tolman
Washington Nationals (NL) 2007–
Longtime minor league manager in the Houston Astros' organization.

Tolman managed at every level in the Astros' system between 1991 and 1996 before moving to the scouting department for six years. In 2003 he moved to the Cleveland Indians as a minor league field coordinator. While in the Houston organization Tolman had been considered a mentor by Manny Acta, who, upon being hired to manage the Nationals in 2007, hired Tolman as a member of his coaching staff.

Jeff Torborg
Cleveland Indians (AL) 1975–77; New York Yankees (AL) 1979–88
See Managers section.

Tony Torchia
Boston Red Sox (AL) 1985
Only man to serve as a player, coach, and manager for the Pawtucket Red Sox.

Torchia had a 13-year playing career, spent entirely in the minor leagues. In 1962 with the Keokuk Cardinals he won the Midwest League batting title with a .338 average, and also led the league with 477 at-bats, 161 hits, and 94 runs batted in. He was selected the MWL Player of the Year because of his accomplishments. In 1966 he led the Eastern League in RBIs, but he never did reach the majors as a player. In 1976 he began work as a minor league manager in the Red Sox' system, and in 1985 was promoted to Boston as a coach. He had won championships in 1981 with the Bristol Red Sox and in 1984 with Pawtucket. In 1986 he moved to the San Diego Padres' chain as a coach and later manager, then to the Colorado Rockies' organization. He later worked in the minor league systems of the Houston Astros and Montreal Expos, and in 1989 became a coach for the Fort Myers Sun Sox of the Senior Professional Baseball Association. In later years he also managed in the independent Frontier League.

Hector Torres
Toronto Blue Jays (AL) 1990–91
Light-hitting infielder with a good glove.

Torres was a member of the Topps All-Star Rookie Team in 1968 although he hit a mere .223 with the Houston Astros. That was his only year as a regular, although he would play eight more as a reserve before retiring with a .216 lifetime average. He got by on his defense but finished his career in the minor leagues in 1978. The Mexican native eventually coached the Blue Jays and also worked as a minor league manager. In 2005 he had the Monterrey Sultans in first place when he was let go because the club's front office disagreed with the way he used his pitching staff. After his departure the Sultans lost their grip on the lead.

Carlos Tosca
Arizona Diamondbacks (NL) 1998–2000, 2005–06; Toronto Blue Jays (AL) 2002; Florida Marlins (NL) 2007–
See Managers section.

Dick Tracewski
Detroit Tigers (AL) 1972–95
See Managers section.

Jim Tracy
Montreal Expos (NL) 1995–98; Los Angeles Dodgers (NL) 1999–2000
See Managers section.

Alan Trammell
Detroit Tigers (AL) 1999; San Diego Padres (NL) 2000–02; Chicago Cubs (NL) 2007–
See Managers section.

Tom Trebelhorn
Milwaukee Brewers (AL) 1984, 1986; Chicago Cubs (NL)

1992–93; Baltimore Orioles (AL) 2001–
See Managers section.

Ralph Treuel
Detroit Tigers (AL) 1995; Boston Red Sox (AL) 2001–02, 2006
Career minor leaguer.

Treuel coached for the Tigers under Sparky Anderson in 1995 before returning to work in the minor leagues. From 1999–2001 he served as the Red Sox' minor league pitching coordinator, then resurfaced with the Boston big league club as a coach. From 2003–05 he managed the Gulf Coast Red Sox. In 2006 he once again took on the job as minor league pitching coordinator, but he worked temporarily as Boston's bullpen coach when pitching coach Dave Wallace had surgery and was himself temporarily replaced by the regular bullpen coach, Al Nipper.

Virgil Trucks
Pittsburgh Pirates (NL) 1963
Pitcher with 177 lifetime victories.

Trucks played for 17 seasons from 1941–58, missing 1944 because of military service. He pitched four no-hitters in the minor leagues and two in the majors, both of which came during the 1952 season when he was with the Detroit Tigers. Trucks went 5–19 that year for a team that finished in last place with a 50–104 record, his earned run average a not-so-bad 3.97. His having pitched two no-hitters in the same season puts him in the same company as Johnny Vander Meer, Allie Reynolds, and Nolan Ryan. Of his other three victories that season, one was a one-hitter and one was a two-hitter.

That was not a typical record for Virgil, who had gone 19–11 in 1949 and in 1953 went 20–10. In 1954 he was 19–12. A two-time All-Star, Trucks also led the American League twice in shutouts and once in strikeouts. In the minors he had set a record in 1938 (since broken) with 418 strikeouts while playing for the Andalusia Bulldogs of the Alabama-Florida League. After his playing career he eventually coached one season for the Pirates.

Trucks' nephew, Butch Trucks, was one of the founders of the Allman Brothers Band.

Gary Tuck
New York Yankees (AL) 1990, 1996, 1998–99; Florida Marlins (NL) 2006; Boston Red Sox (AL) 2007–
Minor league catcher in the Montreal Expos' system.

Tuck played from 1977–79 and then went into coaching. As an assistant coach with Arizona State University in 1981 he helped the club to the NCAA National Championship, then he joined the Houston Astros' organization. In 1986 he was named the Southern League Manager of the Year when he guided the Columbus Astros to the league title. In 1990 he was hired by the Yankees as a catching and bullpen coach at the big league level. He then managed one season in the Cleveland Indians' organization before serving as an assistant baseball coach at the University of Notre Dame.

Tuck rejoined the Indians in 1993 as a scout and catching consultant. In 1996 he returned to the Yankees as a catching coach in addition to managing the club's short-season Class A affiliate, the Oneonta Yankees. He was with the Yanks from 1998–99 before once again working in the Indians' system as a scout. He then became a catching instructor for the Yankees before being hired by the Marlins as their bench coach for one season and later moving on to the Red Sox.

Lee Tunnell
Cincinnati Reds (NL) 2006
Pitcher for three major league clubs.

In six years with the Pittsburgh Pirates, St. Louis Cardinals, and Minnesota Twins, Tunnell compiled a 22–28 record with a 4.23 earned run average. His best season came in 1983 with the Pirates, when he went 11–6 with a 3.65 ERA. He later pitched in Japan, then returned to the United States in the minor leagues and finished his career in Mexico.

He became a minor league pitching coach and pitching coordinator in the Texas Rangers' organization after his playing days, and was hired to coach the Reds' AAA affiliate, the Louisville Bats, for 2006. When Reds' pitching coach Vern Ruhle had to leave the team to seek treatment for cancer during spring training, however, Tunnell was temporarily named Cincinnati's bullpen coach in place of Tom Hume, who was moved to interim pitching coach.

Bob Turley
Boston Red Sox (AL) 1964
Outstanding pitcher nicknamed "Bullet Bob."

In the minors Turley once set a Texas League record by striking out 22 batters in a 16-inning game. He did not slow down much at the major league level, pitching a dozen seasons and going 101–85 lifetime with a 3.64 earned run average and 1265 strikeouts. In 1954 with the Baltimore Orioles he struck out at least 10 batters in a game on 17 occasions. He led the American League with 185 Ks that year and was named an All-Star for the first of three times. He struck out 210 the next season. In 1958 with the New York Yankees he was 21–7, and his victory total and his .750 winning percentage were tops in the league, while his 19 complete games put him in a three-way tie for the best. He won the Cy Young Award and was named the Most Valuable Player of the World Series in addition to winning the Hickok Belt as the best professional athlete of the year and being named AL Pitcher of the Year by *The Sporting News.*

Turley had lost a no-hitter in a 1954 game with one out in the ninth inning, and he would never throw such a gem. He led the AL three times in bases on balls. In 1959 bone chips in his elbow began to affect his performance, and he would never again top nine victories in a season. He ended his career with the Red Sox in 1963, and he coached for the team the following year. He later became rather wealthy working for Primerica Financial Services.

Jim Turner
New York Yankees (AL) 1949–59, 1966–73; Cincinnati Reds (NL) 1961–65
Spent 51 years in professional baseball.

If the Rookie of the Year Award had existed in 1937, Turner would have been a strong contender for the prize. The right-handed pitcher debuted with the Boston Bees that season and went 20–11 while leading the National League with 24 complete games and a 2.38 earned run average, and tied for the lead with 5 shutouts with his teammate, Lou Fette, and with Lee Grissom of the Cincinnati Reds. At one point during the season he pitched 31 consecutive innings without allowing a run. He had already had a long minor league career and was 33 years of age by the time he reached the majors. In 1938 he was named an NL All-Star, but he would never again be a 20-game winner although he would win 14 twice. In his final season of 1945 with the Yankees he led the American League with 10 saves, an unofficial statistic at the time. He worked his family's dairy farm during the offseasons and thus earned for himself the nickname "Milkman Jim."

Turner managed in the minor leagues for a time and then coached the Yankees, the Reds, and the Yankees again. He died in 1998 at the age of 95.

Terry Turner
St. Louis Cardinals (NL) 1924
Rather light-hitting infielder.

Turner played 17 major league seasons despite hitting only .253. All but two of those years were spent with the Cleveland Indians, with whom he hit an anomalous .291 in 1906 and .308 in 1912. He was fast, stealing over 20 bases four times and totaling 256 lifetime. He was one of the first to use a headfirst slide because he claimed that regular slides hurt his ankles. Between 1906 and 1914 he went 3186 at-bats without hitting a home run. He connected for only eight roundtrippers in his career.

Turner coached for the Cardinals in 1924. Some sources incorrectly list Tink Turner, a pitcher who appeared in only one major league game, in Terry's place.

Ted Uhlaender
Cleveland Indians (AL) 2000–01
Pacific Coast League batting champion in 1965.

Uhlaender hit .340 that season but would not have nearly that level of success in the majors, averaging .263 over eight seasons. He did lead all major league outfielders in fielding percentage in 1967, however, chalking up a .996 mark. His playing days ended in 1972, and he worked as a minor league skipper from 1974–75. He then ventured into private business before returning to baseball in 1989, becoming a scout and minor league coach for the New York Yankees. In 1997 he helped the Arizona Diamondbacks prepare for the expansion draft, and in 1998 joined the San Francisco Giants as a special assistant to the general manager. He coached the Indians for two years and then returned to the Giants as a special assistant, player personnel.

George Uhle
Cleveland Indians (AL) 1936–37; Chicago Cubs (NL) 1940; Washington Nationals (AL) 1944
Pitcher who won exactly 200 games.

Nicknamed "The Bull" because of his stamina, Uhle pitched for 17 years and was a 20-game winner three times, peaking with a 27–11 record in 1926 with the Indians. He led the American League twice in victories, three times in starts, twice in complete games, once in shutouts, and twice in innings pitched. He won at least 15 games five times and he posted a lifetime 3.99 earned run average. A more-than-capable hitter, he also set a record for most hits by a pitcher in a season with 52 in 1923.

Uhle was a player-coach for the Indians in 1936, appearing in seven games, then he turned to coaching full-time.

Scott Ullger
Minnesota Twins (AL) 1995–
Catcher from New York.

Ullger spent nearly a decade in the minor leagues and played 35 games in the major leagues for the Twins in 1983. He hit .190, going 15-for-79 with 4 doubles. In 1988 he became a minor league skipper and in 1990 was named the California League Manager of the Year when his Visalia Oaks made the playoffs. In 1991 his Orlando Sunrays captured the Southern League championship, and in 1993 his Portland Beavers reached the championship series. In 1995 he joined the Twins as a coach at the major league level.

Del Unser
Philadelphia Phillies (NL) 1985–88
Member of the 1968 Topps All-Star Rookie Team.

The son of Al Unser (a catcher in the 1940s, not to be

confused with the race car driver of the same name), Del was an outfielder and first baseman who played 15 big league seasons. In 1968 he led all American League outfielders in assists, double plays, and chances per game, and the following year led the AL with eight triples. Unser was a lifetime .258 hitter, and the latter part of his career was spent in a pinch-hitting role. In 1979 he tied a major league record by connecting for home runs in three consecutive pinch-hit at-bats.

Unser finished his playing career with the Phillies and later coached for the club for four seasons.

Willie Upshaw
Texas Rangers (AL) 1993–94; Toronto Blue Jays (AL) 1996–97; San Francisco Giants (NL) 2007–
Outfielder-turned-first-baseman.

Upshaw was always solid defensively, and at the plate he displayed some power. He delivered 21 home runs in 1982 and a career-high 27 in 1983, when he also ran up peak totals of 104 runs batted in and a .306 batting average. He played all but one year with the Blue Jays. In 1988 he finished off his big league career with the Cleveland Indians, then he went to Japan to play before retiring. He later coached the Rangers and the Blue Jays, and eventually worked for the Giants as their coordinator of minor league hitting before joining the big league staff as a coach in 2007.

Upshaw's cousins, Gene and Marvin, played in the National Football League.

Bobby Valentine
New York Mets (NL) 1983–85; Cincinnati Reds (NL) 1993
See Managers section.

Elmer Valo
Cleveland Indians (AL) 1963–64
Solid outfielder from Czechoslovakia.

Valo played in the major leagues for 20 years, spending time with six teams. He batted .282 lifetime, topping the .300 mark in five full seasons and seven total. He lost 1944 and 1945 to military service, but did not miss a beat upon his return from the war. He hit .307 in 1946, .300 in 1947, and .305 in 1948. In 1950 while playing for the Philadelphia Athletics he hit for the cycle in a game against the Chicago White Sox.

After his playing career Valo coached the Indians for two seasons and also worked in the Cleveland system as a minor league manager. He then scouted for the Philadelphia Phillies for 13 years.

Ty Van Burkleo
Oakland Athletics (AL) 2007–

First baseman and native of Oakland.

Van Burkleo appeared in 14 major league games with the California Angels and Colorado Rockies, batting .132. He had previously played in Japan with the Seibu Lions and the Hiroshima Carp, and in 1988 was named Player of the Year when he hit .268 with 38 home runs and 90 runs batted in with the Lions.

After his playing days Van Burkleo returned to the Angels for six years as the club's roving minor league hitting instructor. He was hired as Oakland's hitting coach in 2007 by new manager Bob Geren, whom he had previously met on a cruise.

John Van Ornum
San Francisco Giants (NL) 1981–84
Minor league catcher from Pasadena, California.

Van Ornum never played in the major leagues, but he did manage in the minors. He later coached at the major league level for the Giants, then worked as a scout for many years.

Andy Van Slyke
Detroit Tigers (AL) 2006–
Three-time All-Star outfielder.

A solid and hustling player, Van Slyke hit over .300 twice and hit over 20 home runs twice. In 1988 with the Pittsburgh Pirates he led the National League with 15 triples, and in 1992 tied for the league lead with 199 hits and led with 45 doubles. He won five Gold Gloves for his defense.

After his playing days he worked as a broadcaster and television baseball analyst. In 2006 he returned to the majors as a coach with the Tigers.

Gary Varsho
Philadelphia Phillies (NL) 2002–06
See Managers section.

Joe Vavra
Los Angeles Dodgers (NL) 1998, 1999; Minnesota Twins (AL) 2006–
Minor leaguer with a long and successful managing and coaching career.

Vavra was drafted by the Dodgers in 1982, and he was a minor league coach by 1987. In 1989 and 1990 he led the Great Falls Dodgers to consecutive Pioneer League championships. In 1994 he was named the Northwest League Manager of the Year when he took the Yakima Bears to the playoffs, and in 1996 he guided that club to the title.

In 1998 Vavra worked for the Dodgers as a special assignment coach at the major league level, and in midseason was appointed minor league field coordinator. The exact same scenario unfolded in 1999, and in 2000 he worked with the Dodgers as a minor league instructor. In 2001 he briefly served as head coach at the University of Wisconsin-Stout before returning to Los Angeles as director of player development. From 2002–05 he worked in the Twins' organization as a minor league field coordinator, and in 2006 was promoted to the big league club as batting coach.

Jose Vazquez
Texas Rangers (AL) 2006–
Minor league outfielder who became a physical therapist.

Vazquez was a second team All-American at the University of Tennessee and was drafted by the St. Louis Cardinals, but he never reached the major leagues as a player. He spent three years in the minor leagues before earning a degree in education from UT and later a Master of Physical Therapy from Nova Southeastern University in Fort Lauderdale, Florida. He worked in Knoxville, Tennessee as a sports physical therapist at the Therapy Center, and in 2001 was hired by the New York Mets as an assistant fitness and conditioning coordinator. In 2005 he worked as the Mets' rehab director, and in October of that year was hired by the Rangers as their strength and conditioning coach.

Mickey Vernon
Pittsburgh Pirates (NL) 1960, 1964; St. Louis Cardinals (NL) 1965; Montreal Expos (NL) 1977–78; New York Yankees (AL) 1982
See Managers section.

Al Vincent
Detroit Tigers (AL) 1943–44; Baltimore Orioles (AL) 1955–59; Philadelphia Phillies (NL) 1961–63; Kansas City Athletics (AL) 1966–67
Minor league second baseman and player-manager.

Vincent had a long and successful baseball career in several capacities. He spent 12 years in the Texas League as a player-manager and manager, reaching the postseason 8 of those years. He managed 1879 games there, winning 974 of them, and was inducted into the TL Hall of Fame. He also managed several other minor league clubs in other leagues. He coached quite a few years in the major leagues with a number of different teams, and spent 16 years as an assistant coach at Lamar University in Texas. The university named its baseball stadium after him and Bryan Beck, so that it has been called, since 1981, Vincent-Beck Stadium.

Bill Virdon
Pittsburgh Pirates (NL) 1968–71, 1986, 1993–95, 2001–02;

Houston Astros (NL) 1997
See Managers section.

Ozzie Virgil, Sr.
San Francisco Giants (NL) 1969–72, 1974–75; Montreal Expos (NL) 1976–81; San Diego Padres (NL) 1982–85; Seattle Mariners (AL) 1986–88
First Dominican to play major league baseball.

A third baseman who eventually played every position except pitcher, Virgil played nine seasons for six different teams. He was used as a utilityman throughout his career and hit .231 lifetime with 14 home runs. In 1969, the year he began his coaching career, he appeared in one game for the Giants. He later coached the Expos and then followed manager Dick Williams to the Padres and the Mariners.

Virgil's son, Ozzie, Jr., was a two-time All-Star major league catcher.

Jack Voigt
Washington Nationals (NL) 2005
Sarasota native who played seven major league seasons.

Primarily an outfielder, Voigt played from 1992–98 and hit .235 with 20 homers in limited time with four clubs. In 2005 he became what the Nationals called a "roving coach," his primary responsibilities being keeping statistics and charting pitches. His job was eliminated following that season.

Pete Vuckovich
Pittsburgh Pirates (NL) 1997–2000
Pitcher with a rather bizarre personality.

Vuckovich was popular with fans, who seemed to enjoy his antics while he was on the mound. In addition to twitching and pacing on and around the hill, he would scream at umpires and make faces at opposing batters. Something must have worked, because he logged a 93–69 lifetime record with a 3.66 earned run average.

Used at various times as both a starter and a reliever, Vuckovich debuted with the Chicago White Sox but was claimed by the Toronto Blue Jays in the 1977 expansion draft. After joining the St. Louis Cardinals he won at least 12 games every season from 1978–82. He had joined the Milwaukee Brewers in 1981 and finished in a four-way tie for the American League lead with 14 victories in that strike-shortened campaign. The following year he was named the league's Cy Young Award winner on the strength of an 18–6 record and a 3.34 ERA. He was the second Brewer in a row to claim that prize, following Rollie Fingers.

A torn rotator cuff plagued Vuckovich the following season, and he would struggle through three more seasons, missing 1984 because of surgery, before calling it quits. He then became a Brewers' broadcaster and a pitching instructor in the Pirates' minor league system before being promoted to Pittsburgh as a coach in 1997. He later became an assistant general manager and then special assistant to the general manager for the Pirates.

In 1989 Vuckovich played the part of fictional New York Yankees' first baseman Clue Haywood in the motion picture *Major League*.

John Vukovich
Chicago Cubs (NL) 1982–87; Philadelphia Phillies (NL) 1988–2004
See Managers section.

Charlie Wagner
Boston Red Sox (AL) 1970
Pitcher nicknamed "Broadway."

Wagner played from 1938–42 with the Red Sox, and after spending 1943–45 in the Army returned for one final season in 1946. In 1941 he went 12–8 with a 3.07 earned run average, and the following season was 14–11 with a 3.29 ERA. After his return he pitched only eight games and had a disappointing 5.87 ERA before hanging it up. His lifetime record was 32–23, his ERA 3.91.

After his playing days Wagner worked as an instructor in the Red Sox' system and coached at the big league level in 1970.

Heinie Wagner
Boston Red Sox (AL) 1916–19, 1927–29
See Managers section.

Honus Wagner
Pittsburgh Pirates (NL) 1933–51
See Managers section.

Rick Waits
New York Mets (NL) 2003
Pitcher who loved to sing.

Waits pitched for 12 years at the big league level, winning 79 games against 92 losses and posting a 4.25 earned run average. His finest season was 1979, when he went 16–13 for the Cleveland Indians. He was the winning pitcher on Opening Day that year, and when he won the opener again in 1980 he became only the second Indian after Bob Feller to capture back-to-back Opening Day victories.

Waits also sang the National Anthem before several games, and was loudly applauded for doing so. From 1989–90 he played for the Fort Myers Sun Sox of the Senior Professional Baseball Association, and he eventually coached one season with the Mets.

Don Wakamatsu
Texas Rangers (AL) 2003–
Excellent-fielding minor league catcher.

Wakamatsu played 18 games at the major league level after leading minor league catchers in several fielding categories from 1985–89. In 1991 with the Chicago White Sox he hit .226 in 31 at-bats. Four years later he became a minor league player-coach, and in 1997 he turned to coaching full-time and then to managing halfway through the season. In 1998 he was named the California League Manager of the Year when he guided the High Desert Mavericks to a second-half division championship. After working in the Anaheim Angels' organization as a minor league coordinator and roving catching instructor, he was hired as a major league coach by the Rangers in November of 2002.

Dixie Walker
St. Louis Cardinals (NL) 1953, 1955; Milwaukee Braves (NL) 1963–65; Los Angeles Dodgers (NL) 1970–74
Son of the pitcher named Dixie Walker.

The father was Ewart G. Walker, the son Fred Walker. The son was an outfielder who played from 1931–49 and became a popular gate attraction at Ebbets Field in Brooklyn. He had played for the New York Yankees, Chicago White Sox, and Detroit Tigers before joining the Dodgers, however, and he finished his career with the Pittsburgh Pirates.

After hitting .401 in the Class B South Atlantic Association with the Greenville Spinners in 1930, Walker would be named to five All-Star teams in the major leagues. A .306 lifetime hitter, he tied for the American League lead with 16 triples in 1937, won the National League batting title with a .357 average in 1944, and topped the NL with 124 runs batted in in 1945. In 1949, his final season, he led the NL with 13 pinch-hits. In a game in 1942 he once hit an inside-the-park grand slam when the ball rolled under a bench in the bullpen.

Multiple injuries plagued Walker toward the end of his career, and when his playing days were over he became a minor league manager and a major league coach, as well as a scout for the Atlanta Braves and the Dodgers.

Gee Walker
Cincinnati Reds (NL) 1946
All-Star outfielder from Mississippi.

Gee Walker was a tough competitor but also had a fun-loving personality. He hit .294 over 15 seasons, topping the .300 mark six times and stealing 223 bases. In 1937 he became the only player ever to hit for the cycle on Opening Day and went on to bat .335 for the Detroit Tigers while being named an American League All-Star. He also connected for 124 home runs lifetime and on two occasions drove in over 100 runs.

Walker finished his career in 1945 with the Reds and stayed on with the club for one more season as a coach.

Greg Walker
Chicago White Sox (AL) 2003–
First baseman and designated hitter.

Walker led the American League with 163 games played in 1985 with the White Sox, tying a club record. He had debuted in 1982 and delivered a pinch-hit single in his first major league at-bat, then went on to play for nine seasons. In July of 1988 he suffered a life-threatening seizure during batting practice and ended up missing the rest of the season. He came back to see limited action in 1989 and played only 16 games in 1990 to finish out his career.

In 2000 Walker began to work with the White Sox at fantasy camps and in their instructional league, and in 2002 served as a coach with the AAA Charlotte Knights. While with the Knights in May of 2003 he was promoted to Chicago to replace Gary Ward.

Harry Walker
St. Louis Cardinals (NL) 1959–62
See Managers section.

Jerry Walker
New York Yankees (AL) 1982; Houston Astros (NL) 1983–85
Pitcher-turned-executive.

Walker debuted with the Baltimore Orioles in 1957 at the age of 18. In 1959 he was named an American League All-Star and became the youngest pitcher ever to start or win an All-Star Game. He finished the season 11–10 with a 2.92 earned run average. He lasted eight seasons and never again won more than eight games, then he became a minor league manager and scout in the Yankees' organization before joining New York and later Houston as a coach.

In 1992 Walker became assistant general manager of the Detroit Tigers, and was promoted to GM in 1993. In 1995 he was named assistant GM of the St. Louis Cardinals.

Rube Walker
Los Angeles Dodgers (NL) 1958; Washington Senators (AL) 1965–67; New York Mets (NL) 1968–81; Atlanta Braves (NL) 1982–84
Catcher who became a pitching coach.

Walker played in the majors for 11 seasons and hit .227 in a reserve role. He played for the Chicago Cubs and for the Dodgers in both Brooklyn and Los Angeles, serving as a player-coach in 1958 when he appeared in 25 games. He became a minor league manager after that, then re-emerged with the Senators and the Mets. In 1968 he took control of the team for the last four games of the season when manager Gil Hodges suffered a heart attack and had to be hospitalized for nearly a month. According to the Topp-Tiemann rules set forth in the introduction, the Mets' 2–2 record during that period is credited to Hodges.

Walker eventually continued with the Mets under Joe Torre, and when Torre left for Atlanta, Walker went with him. Rube's brother Verlon was a coach with the Cubs.

Verlon Walker
Chicago Cubs (NL) 1961–70
Brother of Rube Walker.

A minor league catcher from North Carolina, Verlon spent time as a minor league manager before reaching the major leagues in a coaching role. He was a coach for the Cubs during the "college of coaches" experiment days of 1962–63, but was apparently one of the few who did not take a turn managing. He remained on the staff when the experiment mercifully ended, coaching until 1970. He passed away in March of 1971 in Chicago.

Bobby Wallace
Cincinnati Reds (NL) 1926, 1928
See Managers section.

Dave Wallace
Los Angeles Dodgers (NL) 1995–97; New York Mets (NL) 1999–2000; Boston Red Sox (AL) 2003–06; Houston Astros (NL) 2007–
Right-hander who pitched 13 games in the major leagues.

Wallace spent most of his time in the minors, spending brief periods with the Philadelphia Phillies in 1973 and 1974 and with the Toronto Blue Jays in 1978. He pitched entirely in relief, and his big league record was 0–1, his earned run average 7.84. In the minors he was a much more impressive 47–31 with 60 saves.

After concluding his playing career in 1979 Wallace became a minor league coach and instructor in the Dodgers' organization. In 1995 he was promoted to Los Angeles, then he moved to the Mets before returning to the Dodgers' front office as a special assistant to the general manager and interim general manager. In June of 2003, while he was serving as senior vice president/baseball operations, he was hired by the Red Sox to temporarily replace Tony Cloninger, who had been diagnosed with bladder cancer. He stayed on the following season, and just prior to the 2006 campaign he himself was forced to take a leave of absence when he required surgery due to a life-threatening infection in a hip that had been replaced a decade earlier. He returned to the team in August, but was let go at the end of the season and moved to the Astros.

Tim Wallach
Los Angeles Dodgers (NL) 2004–05
Winner of the Golden Spikes Award in 1979.

Wallace won that award, which recognizes the year's best college player, while at Cal State Fullerton. In the major leagues he spent most of his 17-year career with the Montreal Expos, with whom he was named to five All-Star teams and won three Gold Gloves. He led all National League third baseman in putouts three times and in assists, total chances, and double plays twice. He led the NL in doubles in both 1987 and 1989 (tying Pedro Guerrero in '89), stroking 42 both times.

Wallach had two stints with the Dodgers and finished his career with them. He returned to the club for two years as their hitting coach.

Tye Waller
San Diego Padres (NL) 1995, 2006; Oakland Athletics (AL) 2007–
Fresno native who played 63 major league games.

Waller hit .236 in his brief call-ups, which spanned four seasons and three teams. After his playing days he worked as a minor league outfield and baserunning instructor for the Padres before becoming a minor league skipper and then coaching at the major league level. From 1997–99 he was the club's coordinator of minor league instruction, and from 2000–05 worked as the director of player development. In 2006 he returned to coaching at the big league level with San Diego, and the following season he moved to the A's.

Denny Walling
Oakland Athletics (AL) 1996–98; New York Mets (NL) 2003–04
Versatile fielder and valuable pinch-hitter.

In 18 major league seasons Walling played first base, third base, and the outfield. He came straight out of college to debut with the A's in 1975, and would eventually hit .271 in his career. In 1979 with the Houston Astros he hit .327 in 82 games, and in 1986 batted .312 in 130. After his playing career he returned to Oakland as a coach and later coached for the Mets as well.

Lee Walls
Oakland Athletics (AL) 1979–82; New York Yankees (AL) 1983
Bat boy for the Pacific Coast League's San Diego Padres in the 1940s.

From those humble beginnings Walls eventually fashioned a 10-year major league career, primarily playing first base, third base, and the outfield. He hit .262 lifetime and in 1957 hit for the cycle. He was named an All-Star in 1958, when he hit .304 with 24 home runs and 72 runs batted in for the Chicago Cubs. He never approached any of those numbers again. Walls eventually coached the A's for four seasons and the Yankees for one.

Ed Walsh
Chicago White Sox (AL) 1923–24, 1928–29
See Managers section.

Bucky Walters
Boston Braves (NL) 1950–52; Milwaukee Braves (NL) 1953–55; New York Giants (NL) 1956–57
See Managers section.

Bruce Walton
Toronto Blue Jays (AL) 2002–
Right-handed pitcher from Bakersfield.

Walton had a very successful minor league career, but he pitched only 27 games at the major league level over four seasons. In the majors he went 2–0, but his earned run average was 8.21. In 1996 he began working as a minor league coach and instructor in the Blue Jays' system, and he was promoted to Toronto in June of 2002.

Jim Walton
Milwaukee Brewers (AL) 1973–75
Minor league pitcher from Oklahoma.

A right-hander, Walton never reached the major leagues during his playing days. He did eventually become a minor league manager and coached for the Brewers for three seasons. He then worked as a scout for many years, spending over 40 years in professional baseball altogether.

Paul Waner
Philadelphia Phillies (NL) 1965
Hall of Fame outfielder and brother of Lloyd Waner.

Paul was nicknamed "Big Poison," his sibling "Little Poison." Paul began his minor league career as a pitcher, but was soon converted to an outfielder and played 20 stellar major league seasons.

A .333 lifetime hitter, Waner won three batting titles. In 1927 he won the League Award, an early version of the Most Valuable Player Award, for the National League, winning the batting crown with a .380 average and leading the circuit with 237 hits, 18 triples, and 131 runs batted in. He was named to four All-Star teams and led the NL twice in doubles, twice in triples, once in RBIs, twice in hits, twice in runs scored, and once in on-base percentage. He amassed 3152 hits in his career.

Waner's major league career ended in 1945, and the following season he was player-manager of the Miami Sun Sox of the Florida International League, with whom he hit

.325. The team finished in last place, however. An alcoholic and never one to respect authority, Waner saw his managerial career end at that point, although he did work as a coach for several teams.

Waner's presence in this volume is a bit questionable. It is known that he served as a hitting instructor of some sort for the Milwaukee Braves, St. Louis Cardinals, and Philadelphia Phillies, but none of these teams list him on their rosters of coaches. His exact title and role with these clubs is not entirely clear, but many sources do list him with the title of "coach" for the Phillies in 1965.

Gary Ward
Chicago White Sox (AL) 2001–03
Baseball Digest's choice for American League Rookie of the Year in 1981.

An outfielder, Ward had played 23 games total for the Minnesota Twins in 1979 and 1980, and in '81 he appeared in 85 contests and hit .264 with 3 home runs and 29 runs batted in. He had career highs of 28 homers and 91 RBIs the following season, and he was named an All-Star that season and in 1984, when he cranked out 21 round-trippers. In 1980 he hit for the cycle, and in 2004 his son Daryle duplicated the feat, making the pair the first father-son combination to hit for the cycle in major league history.

Gary eventually joined the White Sox as a coach for three seasons.

Jay Ward
New York Yankees (AL) 1987; Montreal Expos (NL) 1992
Longtime minor league infielder who appeared in 27 major league games.

Ward appeared in 9 games for the Minnesota Twins in 1963, in 12 for the Twins in 1964, and in 6 for the Cincinnati Reds in 1970. He hit .163 while playing all over the infield and in the outfield. He then became a longtime minor league manager, taking a year out to coach the Yankees in 1987 and another to coach the Expos in 1992. His minor league clubs, some of them in independent leagues, reached the postseason four times, and in 1986 his Vermont Reds captured the Eastern League championship.

Pete Ward
Atlanta Braves (NL) 1978
Member of the 1963 Topps All-Star Rookie Team.

Ward hit .295 that season with the Chicago White Sox, contributing 22 home runs and 84 runs batted in. *The Sporting News* named him its American League Rookie of the Year. He went one better the next season, batting .282 with 23 homers and 94 RBIs.

A native of Montreal, Quebec, Ward was the son of Jimmy Ward, a hockey star with the National Hockey League's Montreal Maroons in the 1930s. Pete had some problems with his defense, initially leading the American League in errors at third base with the White Sox, but it was a trade the Sox were willing to make because of his offense.

Pete coached for the Braves in 1978, and was elected to the Canadian Baseball Hall of Fame in 1991.

Buzzy Wares
St. Louis Cardinals (NL) 1930–52
Shortstop with a shaky glove.

Wares led all shortstops in the Pacific Coast League in errors in both 1911 and 1912, totaling 199 over those two seasons. In March of 1913 he became the subject of one of the most unusual trades in baseball history, as the St. Louis Browns dealt him to the Montgomery Rebels of the Southern Association in exchange for the use of the Rebels' stadium for spring training. Wares nevertheless returned to the Browns and appeared in 92 games in 1913 and 1914, hitting .220 overall. He later coached 23 seasons for the Cardinals.

Harry Warner
Toronto Blue Jays (AL) 1977–79, 1980; Milwaukee Brewers (AL) 1981–82
Minor league first baseman who spent many years as a minor league manager.

Warner never reached the major leagues as a player, and spent quite a few years as a minor league skipper before doing so as a coach. He began managing in 1960, when he took the Erie Senators to the New York-Penn League championship. In 1969 his Orlando Twins posted the best record in the Florida State League, and in 1971 he led the Charlotte Hornets to the Dixie Association title. He continued to manage in the minors until eventually being promoted to the major leagues as a coach with the Blue Jays. In 1980 he managed the AAA Syracuse Chiefs, but was recalled to the Toronto staff in September. He moved on to the Brewers the next season.

Dan Warthen
Seattle Mariners (AL) 1991–92; San Diego Padres (NL) 1996–97; Detroit Tigers (AL) 1999–2002; Los Angeles Dodgers (NL) 2006–
Pitcher from Omaha.

Warthen pitched in the major leagues for four seasons, starting nearly half of his games. He posted a 12–21 record with a 4.31 earned run average and 224 strikeouts in 307 innings.

He began coaching in 1981, spending time in the organizations of the Pittsburgh Pirates, San Diego Padres, and Philadelphia Phillies. After coaching at the major league level for the Mariners, Padres, and Tigers, he worked in the New York Mets' minor league system before returning to the majors as a coach with the Dodgers.

Ron Washington
Oakland Athletics (AL) 1996–2006
See Managers section.

John Wathan
Kansas City Royals (AL) 1986; California Angels (AL) 1992–93; Boston Red Sox (AL) 1994
See Managers section.

Bob Watson
Oakland Athletics (AL) 1986–88
Outfielder and first baseman who played 19 major league seasons.

A two-time All-Star, Watson hit .295 lifetime with 184 home runs. In 1975 he scored the one millionth run in major league history, narrowly beating out the Cincinnati Reds' Dave Concepción, who had hit a home run and tore around the bases, crossing the plate shortly after Watson did. In 1977 with the Houston Astros Watson hit for the cycle, and he duplicated the feat in 1979 with the Boston Red Sox, becoming the first player to accomplish it in both the National and American Leagues.

In 1993 he became the first African American general manager in major league history, being named to that post with the Astros. He had previously served as the Astros' assistant GM. In October of 1995 he moved to the New York Yankees as GM, a position he resigned in February of 1998. He then took a job as Major League Baseball's vice president in charge of discipline, rules, and on-field operations.

Earl Weaver
Baltimore Orioles (AL) 1968
See Managers section.

Bill Webb
Chicago White Sox (AL) 1935, 1937–39
Infielder who played five major league games.

Born in Chicago in 1895, Webb played those five games in 1917 with the Pittsburgh Pirates, and he hit .200 by going 3-for-15 with no extra-base hits, no runs batted in, and two walks. He eventually became a major league coach in his hometown with the White Sox.

Walt Weiss
Colorado Rockies (NL) 2002–03
American League Rookie of the Year in 1988.

Weiss was originally drafted by the Baltimore Orioles in 1982, but he chose to attend college instead at the University of North Carolina at Chapel Hill. In 1985 he was drafted by the Oakland Athletics and signed with them. He made his big league debut with them in 1987, appearing in 16 games, and the following season became the third Oakland player in a row to win the Rookie of the Year Award, following Jose Canseco and Mark McGwire. Weiss hit .250 in '88 with 3 home runs and 39 runs batted in while displaying outstanding defense at shortstop.

Weiss played in the majors for 14 years and was named a National League All-Star in 1998 with the Atlanta Braves. He hit .258 lifetime, and after his playing career coached two seasons with the Rockies.

Bob Welch
Arizona Diamondbacks (NL) 2001
Winner of the 1990 American League Cy Young Award.

Welch made his debut in 1978 with the Los Angeles Dodgers, and two years later he won 14 games and was named a National League All-Star. After some fine seasons in Los Angeles, during which he tied for the NL lead with four shutouts in 1987, he was traded to the Oakland Athletics and won 17 games in both 1988 and 1989. In 1990, his Cy Young campaign, he led the AL in victories when he went 27–6, and he posted a 2.95 earned run average. He was one of six pitchers who led the AL with 35 starts in 1991.

Welch won 211 games lifetime. He overcame struggles with alcoholism and later co-authored a book about his experiences. In 1982 he was once used in the outfield in a 17-inning game when the Dodgers ran out of position players.

Welch coached for the Diamondbacks in 2001, the year Arizona captured the World Championship. In 2006 he served as the pitching coach for the Netherlands in the World Baseball Classic.

Sam West
Washington Nationals (AL) 1947–49
Outfielder and four-time All-Star.

A .299 lifetime hitter, West reached the .300 mark eight times in a 16-year career. He topped out at .333 in 1931 with the Nationals. He was named to the first three American League All-Star teams, from 1933–35, while with the St. Louis Browns, and made the squad again in 1937. An excellent fielder, he set a since-broken record for outfielders in 1928 with a .996 fielding average.

West had two stints with the Nationals as a player, and he returned to them yet again in 1947 as a coach.

Wes Westrum

San Francisco Giants (NL) 1958–63, 1968–71; New York Mets (NL) 1964–65
See Managers section.

John Wetteland

Washington Nationals (NL) 2006
Outstanding pitcher for a dozen seasons.

Wetteland started 17 games in his major league career, and he relieved in another 601. He was a three-time All-Star and accumulated 330 saves lifetime. He garnered at least 25 saves in each of his last nine seasons, and in 1996 led the American League with 43. He was named Most Valuable Player of the World Series that year when he saved all four of the New York Yankees' victories over the Atlanta Braves. Those four saves tied a World Series record, and the seven he posted in the entire postseason set a new overall mark. He was also named the 1996 Rolaids Relief Man, and later the Rolaids Reliever of the Decade. He recorded more saves than any other pitcher during the 1990s.

After his playing career Wetteland worked as a roving pitching instructor in the Texas Rangers' organization, and in 2006 was hired to be the Nationals' bullpen coach. He was reassigned and replaced in June because, despite the requests of manager Frank Robinson, did not seem able to get his relievers to focus more and to cut down on activities such as practical jokes. Robinson expressed disappointment with the fact that he had addressed the problem with Wetteland many times, starting as early as spring training.

Pete Whisenant

Cincinnati Reds (NL) 1961–62
Reserve outfielder from Port Charlotte, Florida.

Whisenant was not a great hitter—he averaged just .224 lifetime and never hit over .239 in a season—but he was valued as a pinch-hitter and in 1957 hit five pinch-hit home runs for the Redlegs. He had two stints with Cincinnati, ending his playing days in 26 games with the Reds in 1961 and then staying on as a coach for the rest of that season and the next.

Randy Whisler

Cincinnati Reds (NL) 2004–05
College and minor league player.

Whisler was drafted out of high school by the Chicago Cubs in 1981, but he declined and instead attended Oklahoma State University on a baseball scholarship. At OSU he played in four College World Series. He then played in the Toronto Blue Jays' minor league system before returning to OSU and earning his bachelor's and master's degrees.

In 1990 he returned to the Rangers' system as a minor league coach, then became a head coach and academic counselor at Edmonds Community College in the state of Washington from 1995–96. In 1997 he joined the San Diego Padres' chain as a minor league skipper, and in 1999 was named co-Manager of the Year with the Arizona Padres of the rookie Arizona League along with Gary Thurman of the Arizona Mariners. He then coached one season in the Padres' system before being named minor league infield coordinator of the Montreal Expos, a position he also took later with the Florida Marlins. In 2004 he joined the Reds as a coach at the major league level. In 2006 he returned to the minors as a coach in the St. Louis Cardinals' organization.

Ernie White

Boston Braves (NL) 1947–48; New York Mets (NL) 1963
Pitcher whose career was cut short due to arm problems.

White pitched for the St. Louis Cardinals from 1940–43, and after losing the next two years to military service returned with the Braves from 1946–48. He spent the last two years as a player-coach. White's finest season by far was 1941, when he went 17–7 with a 2.40 earned run average, and his lifetime record was 30–21, his ERA 2.78.

He later returned to the majors as a coach with the Mets for one season.

Frank White

Boston Red Sox (AL) 1994–96; Kansas City Royals (AL) 1997–2001
Eight-time Gold Glove winner at second base.

White spent his entire 18-year playing career with the Royals, anchoring the keystone sack. He led the American League three times in fielding average and was named to five All-Star teams. He powered 160 home runs, twice cranking out 22 in a season. He hit for the cycle in both 1979 and 1982.

White and teammate George Brett appeared in 1914 games together, a tandem record until it was broken in 1995 by Alan Trammell and Lou Whitaker of the Detroit Tigers. White's playing career ended in 1990, and he then became a minor league manager for the Royals. He returned to the big leagues as a coach with the Red Sox in 1994, and returned to Kansas City in a similar role from 1997–2001 before becoming a minor league skipper in the organization.

In 1995 the Royals retired his number 20.

Jerry White

Minnesota Twins (AL) 1989, 1995, 1999–
Longtime outfielder for the Montreal Expos.

White played for Montreal from 1974–78, when he was

traded to the Chicago Cubs in midseason. In December of '78 he was traded back to the Expos, and would remain with his original club until 1983. He spent 1984 and 1985 with the Seibu Lions in Japan, with whom he hit 37 home runs and drove in 113 runs in those two years combined. He returned to the major leagues in 1986 in 25 games for the St. Louis Cardinals.

In 1987 White was hired by the Twins as a roving minor league outfield and baserunning coach. In 1989 he was promoted to Minnesota, then returned to coaching in the minor leagues. In 1995 he returned to Minnesota, then once again went to the minors. In 1997 he moved to the Detroit Tigers' system, but returned to the Twins again in 1999.

Jo-Jo White
Cleveland Indians (AL) 1959–60; Detroit Tigers (AL) 1960; Kansas City Athletics (AL) 1961–62; Milwaukee Braves (NL) 1963–65; Atlanta Braves (NL) 1966; Kansas City Royals (AL) 1969
See Managers section.

Roy White
New York Yankees (AL) 1983–84, 1986, 2004–05
Outfielder from Los Angeles.

A two-time All-Star, White played 15 seasons, all of them with the Yankees. His 1969 season was shortened due to military service, but he nevertheless appeared in 130 games and led the American League with 11 sacrifice flies. He led again in 1971 with 17, and in 1972 tied for tops in the loop with 99 walks. He led the AL with 639 at-bats in 1973, and with 104 runs scored in 1976. A switch-hitter, he hit home runs from both sides of the plate in a game five times, and once hit triples from both sides of the plate in a game.

White finished his playing career by spending three seasons with the Yomiuri Giants in Japan. He later returned to the Yankees for three stints as a coach, and also coached in the minor league system of the Oakland Athletics.

Earl Whitehill
Cleveland Indians (AL) 1941; Philadelphia Phillies (NL) 1943
Pitcher with 218 career victories.

Known for his temper, Whitehill pitched for 17 seasons with four teams. Most of his career was spent with the Detroit Tigers, with whom he finished in a three-way tie for the American League lead with 33 starts in 1925, and the Washington Nationals, with whom he led with 37 starts in 1933. In 1924, his first full season, he tied George Uhle for the league lead with 13 hit batsmen. In 1933 he went 22–8 for the Nationals, the only time he was a 20-game winner.

In a game in 1934 he took a no-hitter into the ninth inning when it was broken up by Ben Chapman of the New York Yankees.

When his career was over he coached for the Indians and the Phillies and also in the minor International League for the Buffalo Bisons. He later worked as a sales representative for the A. G. Spalding & Brothers sporting goods company.

Dan Whitmer
Detroit Tigers (AL) 1992–94
Catcher who played 55 major league games.

A 1955 native of Redlands, California, Whitmer attended Cal State Fullerton and spent most of his career in the minors. He appeared in 48 games for the California Angels in 1980 and hit .241 with three doubles, and appeared in 7 more for the Toronto Blue Jays in 1981 and batted .111. His next appearance in the major leagues would be as a coach with the Tigers from 1992–94.

Ernie Whitt
Toronto Blue Jays (AL) 2005–
Good defensive catcher with some power.

Whitt originally played for the Boston Red Sox but was selected by the Blue Jays in the expansion draft. He spent most of his 15-year career with Toronto, batting .249 overall but hitting at least 16 home runs in a season six times despite being used mainly as a platoon player. He was named an American League All-Star in 1985.

Whitt became a minor league instructor in 1997, and also began work as a minor league manager that same season. In 1998 he returned to his instructing role, and he eventually managed Team Canada in the 1999 Pan-Am Games, the 2003 Olympic qualification tournament, and the 2004 Olympic Games. In the Olympics his squad reached the bronze medal game, which they lost to Japan. He was named a Blue Jays' coach in 2005, and in 2006 managed Canada in the World Baseball Classic.

Al Widmar
Philadelphia Phillies (NL) 1962–64, 1968–69; Milwaukee Brewers (AL) 1973–74; Toronto Blue Jays (AL) 1980–89
Right-handed pitcher who played parts of five major league seasons.

Widmar played in the majors from 1947–52, except for 1949. He spent time with the Boston Red Sox, St. Louis Browns, and Chicago White Sox, but never won more than seven games in a season. He spent 1949 in the International League, where he won 22 games. In the majors his lifetime record was 13–30, his earned run average 5.21.

Widmar's professional career spanned 1942–58. He then worked as a minor league manager and coached for the Phillies, Brewers, and Blue Jays. He remained with the Toronto organization as a special assignment scout from 1990–91, and from 1992–2000 served as a special assistant to the vice president and general manager. He passed away in 2005.

Whitey Wietelmann
Cincinnati Reds (NL) 1966–67; San Diego Padres (NL) 1969–79
Infielder and native of Zanesville, Ohio.

In nine major league seasons Wietelmann hit just .232, spending eight of those years with the Boston Bees/Braves and one with the Pittsburgh Pirates. He was a switch-hitter in 1941, 1944, 1946, and 1947, but chose to bat solely right-handed in 1939, 1940, and 1942, and solely left-handed in 1943 and 1945.

His major league career ended in 1947, but he continued playing in the minor leagues and eventually became a player-manager with the Yuma Sun Sox of the Arizona-Mexico League, with whom he played the outfield and pitched. He then coached the Pacific Coast League's San Diego Padres, a team for whom he had once played, and then coached the Reds and the Padres again. In 1969 he became a coach with the expansion Padres of the National League.

Wietelmann coached for San Diego through 1979, but he remained with the organization for another 14 years, working as a scout, repairing equipment, doing laundry, and even cooking meals. He also invented a baseball-cleaning machine while with the club.

Del Wilber
Chicago White Sox (AL) 1955–56; Washington Senators (AL) 1970; Texas Rangers (AL) 1973
See Managers section.

Mark Wiley
Baltimore Orioles (AL) 1987, 2001–04; Cleveland Indians (AL) 1988–91, 1995–98; Kansas City Royals (AL) 1999; Florida Marlins (NL) 2005
Californian who pitched 21 games in the big leagues.

Wiley threw 15 games for the Minnesota Twins in 1975, mostly in relief. He went 1–3 with 2 saves and a 6.05 earned run average. He did not reappear in the majors until 1978, when he went 1–0 in 4 games for the San Diego Padres and had no decisions in 2 games with the Toronto Blue Jays. His lifetime record was 2–3, his ERA 6.06.

He then spent many years working in the minor leagues and coaching at the major league level with several clubs. In 2000 he served as the senior director, player personnel for the Colorado Rockies.

Kaiser Wilhelm
Philadelphia Phillies (NL) 1921
See Managers section.

Ted Wilks
Cleveland Indians (AL) 1960; Kansas City Athletics (AL) 1961
Fine pitcher for 10 seasons.

Wilks spent most of his playing days with the St. Louis Cardinals, debuting in 1944. He went 17–4 that year with a 2.64 earned run average. He would never again win more than 10 games (and would accomplish that only once), but he was used almost solely in relief. In both 1949 and 1951 he led the National League in games pitched and in saves. In '49 his 10 relief wins were also the circuit's best. When he retired he sported a 59–30 lifetime record with a 3.26 ERA and 46 saves.

After his retirement he eventually coached one season with the Indians and one with the A's.

Billy Williams
Chicago Cubs (NL) 1980–82, 1986–87, 1992–2001; Oakland Athletics (AL) 1983–85; Cleveland Indians (AL) 1990–91
Hall of Fame outfielder from Alabama.

Williams spent 16 of his 18 major league seasons with the Cubs, and the other 2 with the A's. In 1961, his first full season but his third overall, he was named the National League Rookie of the Year on the strength of a .278 average, 25 home runs, and 86 runs batted in. He was a .290 lifetime hitter, topping the .300 mark five times and winning the 1972 NL batting title with a .333 mark. He also led the league with a .606 slugging average that season, after leading in 1970 with 205 hits (tying him with Pete Rose) and 137 runs scored. In '72 *The Sporting News* named him its Player of the Year. A six-time All-Star, he once played in 1117 straight games, an NL record until it was later broken by Steve Garvey. In 1968 Williams hit for the cycle. He hit at least 20 home runs in a season 14 times and ended up with 426 lifetime.

His playing career ended in 1976, and Billy became a batting instructor and later coach for the Cubs. He moved to the A's in 1983 and back to the Cubs in 1986. He then worked in the Cubs' front office before coaching for the Indians and returning to the Cubs yet again in 1992.

Williams was inducted into the Hall of Fame in 1987, and the Cubs retired his number 26 that same year.

Dallas Williams
Colorado Rockies (NL) 2000–02; Boston Red Sox (AL) 2003–04
Brooklyn native and two-time minor league batting champion.

Williams' career can be considered a study in contrast. He won batting championships at the minor league level in both 1983 and 1987 while with the Indianapolis Indians of the American Association. In the majors he played just 2 games for the Baltimore Orioles in 1981 and another 18 for the Cincinnati Reds in 1983 and hit .079. Despite his minor league successes, he also set a record for futility in the longest game ever played in professional baseball. That game, between the Rochester Red Wings and the Pawtucket Red Sox, lasted 33 innings and began on April 18, 1981. It was suspended and then concluded on June 23, 1981. Williams, playing for the Red Wings, went 0-for-13 and also had two sacrifice bunts, so he totaled 15 plate appearances in the game without a hit.

Williams did eventually return to the majors as a coach.

Dan Williams
Cleveland Indians (AL) 1993
Minor league catcher and longtime coach.

Williams never played above Class A and in 1991 played just six games before becoming a full-time coach with the Kinston Indians. In August of 1993 he was promoted to Cleveland as bullpen coach to replace Dom Chiti, who had become the club's pitching coach. In 1994 he coached the Columbus Redstixx, then returned to Cleveland in 1995 as the team's bullpen catcher.

Davey Williams
New York Giants (NL) 1956–57
Good-fielding second baseman from Dallas.

Williams played six seasons, all with the Giants, and was named a National League All-Star in 1953 when he hit a career-high .297. He had chronic back problems, however, and he was not able to play beyond 1955. He stayed with the club as a coach for the next two seasons.

Dick Williams
Montreal Expos (NL) 1970
See Managers section.

Don Williams
San Diego Padres (NL) 1977–80
Minor leaguer and longtime scout.

Williams was drafted by the Brooklyn Dodgers in 1956 out of high school as a shortstop. He spent 10 years in the organization, finishing up as a player-coach. In 1969 he joined the Padres' system as a scout, and he worked as a coach at the major league level from 1977–80. In 1981 he joined the Atlanta Braves' chain in a scouting role, and he continued until 1996, when he moved to the Tampa Bay Devil Rays' organization. He worked as a scout in that system until 2006, when he was hired by the Kansas City Royals as a special assistant to the general manager.

Jimmy Williams
Houston Astros (NL) 1975; Baltimore Orioles (AL) 1981–87
Minor league player from Toronto.

James Bernard Williams (not to be confused with James Andrew Williams, the nineteenth century manager) was a 5-foot 10-inch, 180-pound outfielder who never reached the major leagues as a player. At the age of 49 he became a coach for the Astros at the big league level, however, and later coached seven seasons with the Orioles as well.

Jimy Williams
Toronto Blue Jays (AL) 1980–85; Atlanta Braves (NL) 1990–96; Philadelphia Phillies (NL) 2007–
See Managers section.

Otto Williams
Detroit Tigers (AL) 1925; St. Louis Cardinals (NL) 1926; St. Louis Browns (AL) 1927; Cincinnati Reds (NL) 1930
Light-hitting infielder from Newark, New Jersey.

Williams was mainly a shortstop who could fill in all over the infield and occasionally in the outfield. He hit only .203 as a reserve in four major league seasons. He eventually coached for four big league clubs, spending one season with each.

Rick Williams
Florida Marlins (NL) 1995–96; Tampa Bay Devil Rays (AL) 1998–2000
Son of Dick Williams.

Not to be confused with the Rick Williams who pitched for the Houston Astros for two seasons, Richard Anthony Williams never played in the major leagues. The Fort Worth native did follow in his father's footsteps as a big league coach, however, spending two seasons with the Marlins and three with the Devil Rays, and later worked in Tampa Bay's front office.

Spin Williams
Pittsburgh Pirates (NL) 1994–2005
Longtime minor league and major league coach.

Donald Ray "Spin" Williams was a minor league pitcher who threw for two seasons in the Pirates' organization before becoming a player-coach in 1981. He coached seven different teams in the Pittsburgh chain before being promoted to the Pirates and continuing to coach for many years at the big league level.

Stan Williams

Boston Red Sox (AL) 1975–76; Chicago White Sox (AL) 1977–78; New York Yankees (AL) 1980–82, 1988; Cincinnati Reds (NL) 1984, 1990–91; Seattle Mariners (AL) 1998–99

All-Star pitcher nicknamed "Big Daddy."

At six feet five inches and 230 pounds, Williams wore his nickname well. He threw hard and owned the inside part of the plate, intimidating batters with his size and his confidence. His control was always a little questionable, but he did fashion a successful 14-year major league career.

Williams was named an All-Star in both games in 1960 with the Los Angeles Dodgers, but pitched only in the second contest. He went 14–10 that year, 15–12 the next, and 14–12 the next to round out his best seasons. He was 109–94 lifetime with a 3.48 earned run average, and in 1970 tied for the American League lead with 10 relief wins. He later coached for many teams. During a game with the Reds he had to lend his jersey to Cincinnati pitcher Rob Dibble, because Dibble had cut the sleeves on his own jerseys to allow himself greater freedom of movement and the umpire had determined that the resulting flap was distracting to batters. Since Dibble had no jerseys that he had not so altered, he borrowed one of Williams'.

Walt Williams

Chicago White Sox (AL) 1988

Member of the 1967 Topps All-Star Rookie Team.

A speedy outfielder, Williams played 10 games for the Houston Colt .45s in 1964, then hit .330 in both 1965 and 1966 for the minor league Tulsa Oilers. He reached the White Sox in 1967 and stayed with them until 1973, when he moved to the Cleveland Indians and then, the next season, to the New York Yankees. In 10 seasons Williams hit .270 and displayed some solid defense. In 1973 with Cleveland he broke up Stan Bahnsen's no-hit bid with two outs in the ninth inning.

Williams returned to the White Sox as a coach in 1988, and in 1989 he played for the St. Lucie Legends of the Senior Professional Baseball Association.

Carl Willis

Cleveland Indians (AL) 2003–

Right-handed pitcher from Virginia.

Willis played at least parts of nine major league seasons, frequently bouncing between the majors and the minors until elbow problems finally ended his career in 1995. He started only 2 of 267 games and posted a 22–16 record with 13 saves and a 4.25 earned run average.

In 1997 Willis began coaching in the Indians' minor league system, and he was promoted to Cleveland in March of 2003.

Jimmie Wilson

Cincinnati Reds (NL) 1939–40, 1944–46

See Managers section.

Mookie Wilson

New York Mets (NL) 1997–2002

Speedy leadoff hitter with a penchant for striking out.

Wilson's on-base percentage frequently suffered because of his inability to make contact, but he did manage a .274 lifetime average and stole 327 bases, swiping at least 21 in a season on eight occasions. His career high was 58, which he reached in 1982 with the New York Mets. Having been married at home plate in 1978 in Jackson, Mississippi, while playing for the AA Jackson Generals, he would go on to play 12 major league seasons.

After his playing career Wilson managed in the Mets' minor league system and coached for six seasons in New York.

George "Hooks" Wiltse

New York Yankees (AL) 1925

Dominant left-handed pitcher for 12 major league seasons.

Wiltse received his nickname from his catcher with the New York Giants, Frank Bowerman, because of the way he used to reach out and "hook" line drives and bouncing balls hit back to the mound. In his rookie season of 1904 he won his first 12 games in a row, a major league record later tied by Butch Metzger. In 1906 he fanned four Cincinnati Reds in one inning because of a dropped third strike and then fanned three more the next inning to set a major league record of seven strikeouts in two innings. In 1908 he pitched a 10-inning no-hitter and missed a perfect game by a hit batsman with two out in the ninth inning. Wiltse had nearly struck out that batter, with the potential third strike being called a ball and the umpire later stating he may have missed that call.

Wiltse went 23–14 in 1908 and 20–11 in 1909, en route to a 139–90 lifetime record with a 2.47 earned run average. He finished his career in 1915 with the Brooklyn Tip-Tops of the Federal League, then became a minor league manager. In 1925 he joined the Yankees for one season as a coach. In 1934 he became a deputy assessor for the City of Syracuse, and in 1944 the president of the Syracuse Industrial Baseball League. He was elected to the International League Baseball Hall of Fame in 1952.

Bobby Wine
Philadelphia Phillies (NL) 1972–83; Atlanta Braves (NL) 1985, 1988–90; New York Mets (NL) 1993–96
See Managers section.

Ralph Winegarner
St. Louis Browns (AL) 1948–51
Pitcher who appeared in 136 major league contests.

Seventy of those were as a pitcher, but Winegarner also played third base, the outfield, and first base, as well as serving as a pinch-hitter. He batted .276 over six seasons with 5 home runs and 28 runs batted in, and on the mound went 8–6 with 89 strikeouts and a 5.33 earned run average. In 1935 he led the American League in pinch-hitting. He had a long minor league career at various positions in addition to his rather brief major league tenure.

He began coaching for the Browns in 1948, and in 1949 served as a player-coach, pitching nine games. He remained with St. Louis until 1951, then became a minor league skipper. In the 1960s and 1970s he worked as the official registrar of the National Baseball Congress, an administrative body for non-professional baseball.

Ivy Wingo
Cincinnati Reds (NL) 1928–29, 1936
See Managers section.

Bobby Winkles
California Angels (AL) 1972; Oakland Athletics (AL) 1974–75; San Francisco Giants (NL) 1976–77; Chicago White Sox (AL) 1979–81; Montreal Expos (NL) 1986–88
See Managers section.

Earl Wolgamot
Cleveland Indians (AL) 1933–35
Minor leaguer from Iowa.

Born in 1895, Wolgamot was a catcher who got as far as the Toledo Mud Hens but never reached the major leagues as a player. He did coach the Indians for three seasons, and that tenure would comprise his entire big league experience. After leaving Cleveland he continued in baseball as a minor league manager. He passed away in Independence, Iowa, in 1970.

Larry Woodall
Boston Red Sox (AL) 1942–48
Catcher who played 10 years for the Detroit Tigers.

Playing in a backup role, Woodall hit .268 lifetime and topped the .300 mark three times in limited action. His career high was .363, which he reached in 46 games in 1921. He eventually became a coach for the Red Sox and later remained with the organization as the director of pub-

licity, then worked as a scout and a director of tryout camps.

Gene Woodling
Baltimore Orioles (AL) 1964–67
Four-time minor league batting champion.

Woodling led four *different* minor leagues in hitting. He won those crowns in the Ohio State League in 1940 at .398, the Michigan State League in 1941 at .394, the Eastern League in 1943 at .344, and the Pacific Coast League in 1948 at .385. That '48 season he spent with the San Francisco Seals, and in addition to winning the batting title he led the circuit with 202 hits and 13 triples and was named the Minor League Player of the Year by *The Sporting News*.

Woodling nevertheless struggled to stick in the major leagues, but when he finally did so he lasted 17 seasons. In the bigs he batted .284 lifetime, crossing the .300 threshold six times. In 1953 with the New York Yankees he led the American League with a .429 on-base percentage, and in '52 and '53 he topped all AL outfielders in fielding average. He was a member of five consecutive Yankee World Championship teams. In 1959 with the Orioles he was named an AL All-Star.

After his playing days Woodling returned to the Orioles for several years as a coach, then he went to work in the private sector. In 1997 he suffered a debilitating stroke, and he passed away in 2001.

Al Worthington
Minnesota Twins (AL) 1972–73
Starting pitcher who became an excellent reliever.

Worthington debuted in 1953 with the New York Giants and promptly tied a major league record by pitching shutouts in his first two starts. Nevertheless he started only 1 of 10 games the next season, but was used primarily in the rotation in 1956. After that he was used more and more in relief, until by the mid-1960s he was the Twins' closer. He logged 21 saves in 1965, and a league-leading 18 in 1968 en route to 110 lifetime. He had a 75–82 record and a 3.39 earned run average.

Worthington finished his career with the Twins and later coached in Minnesota for two seasons.

Ron Wotus
San Francisco Giants (NL) 1998–
Minor league shortstop who logged 32 major league games.

Wotus played 11 seasons in the minor leagues, but had several appearances for the Pittsburgh Pirates in 1983 and 1984. He hit only .207 in Pittsburgh, and finished out his career in the minors in 1989.

In 1990 Wotus became a minor league coach, then in 1991 turned to managing and won the California League Manager of the Year Award with the San Jose Giants. In 1995 he took the Shreveport Captains to the Texas League championship, and in 1997 was named Pacific Coast League Manager of the Year when he guided the Phoenix Firebirds to AAA baseball's best record. In 1998 he was promoted to San Francisco as a coach.

Jim Wright
Philadelphia Phillies (NL) 1996; Colorado Rockies (NL) 2002
One of three Jim Wrights to play in the major leagues.

All three were pitchers, all three were right-handers, and all three spent parts of two seasons in the big leagues. This one was James Leon Wright, and he played 24 games for the Kansas City Royals from 1981–82. He started four of those games and went 2–3 with a 4.04 earned run average. He later coached at the big league level for the Phillies and the Rockies.

Mel Wright
Chicago Cubs (NL) 1963–64, 1971; Pittsburgh Pirates (NL) 1973; New York Yankees (AL) 1974; Houston Astros (NL) 1976–82
Right-handed reliever from Arkansas.

Wright pitched 58 major league games with the St. Louis Cardinals and the Cubs. He spread those out over four seasons between 1954 and 1961 and was used entirely in relief. He posted a 2–4 record with 3 saves and a 7.61 earned run average.

He became a coach after his playing days and eventually followed manager Bill Virdon around to the Pirates, Yankees, and Astros. In 1983 Virdon became the manager of the Montreal Expos, and he hired Wright to be his bullpen coach. Wright was a cancer survivor, and in spring training he suffered a relapse and had to be replaced by Joe Kerrigan. Mel passed away in May of that year from heart failure.

Whit Wyatt
Philadelphia Phillies (NL) 1955–57; Milwaukee Braves (NL) 1958–65; Atlanta Braves (NL) 1966–67
Most Valuable Player of the American Association in 1938.

Prior to that Wyatt had once struck out 23 batters in a college game, and in 1929 recorded 16 consecutive victories with the Evansville Hubs of the Illinois-Iowa-Indiana (Three-I) League. In 1938 he won the AA's MVP Award, capturing the pitching Triple Crown with 23 victories, 208 strikeouts, and a 2.37 earned run average while playing for the Milwaukee Brewers. He also topped the AA with 26 complete games, 9 shutouts, and 254 innings pitched.

That season occurred in the midst of his 16-year major league career, which lasted from 1929–45. His greatest big league successes occurred after that, because after that point he was named to four All-Star teams and tied teammate Kirby Higbe for the National League lead with 22 wins in 1941 while also leading with 7 shutouts. In 1940 he had finished in a three-way tie for the lead with 5 shutouts. Previously, in 1933, he had come within one out of a no-hitter while playing for the Chicago White Sox.

Wyatt posted a 106–95 career record with a 3.79 earned run average. He then spent many years as a coach with the Phillies and Braves.

Butch Wynegar
Texas Rangers (AL) 1999; Milwaukee Brewers (NL) 2003–06
Catcher and two-time All-Star.

Wynegar was the Appalachian League batting champion in 1974, his first professional season. His two All-Star seasons were his first two in the major leagues. In 1976, his first with the Minnesota Twins, *The Sporting News* named him its American League Rookie of the Year when he hit .260 with 10 home runs and 69 runs batted in. At 20 years and 121 days old, he was the youngest player in history to that point to appear in an All-Star Game. In 1980 he led AL catchers in double plays, and he caught Dave Righetti's no-hitter in 1983 and Phil Niekro's 300th career win in 1985.

Wynegar became a minor league manager following his playing career, and he was named the Rangers' bullpen coach for part of 1999. That assignment briefly interrupted his role as the Texas minor league roving hitting instructor, in which he worked from 1998–2002. From 2003–06 he was a coach for the Brewers.

Early Wynn
Cleveland Indians (AL) 1964–66; Minnesota Twins (AL) 1967–69
Intimidating Hall of Fame pitcher.

Wynn was not afraid to throw at batters, and once stated that he would knock his own grandmother down if she was hitting against him. Wynn pitched for 23 seasons, an American League record for hurlers, and won exactly 300 games. He had a 3.54 earned run average and led the AL twice in victories, five times in starts, three times in innings pitched, twice in strikeouts, and once in ERA. A nine-time All-Star, he won the 1959 Cy Young Award at the age of 39, when only a single award was given to represent both leagues. He copped that honor by leading the AL in wins with a 22–10 record and posting a 3.17 ERA while also topping the circuit with $255\frac{2}{3}$ innings pitched and tying for the lead with 37 starts.

Wynn played for the Cleveland Indians in 1957 and the

Chicago White Sox in 1958. In leading the league both years in strikeouts, he became the first pitcher ever to lead twice in a row with two different clubs. A solid hitter, he was also used as a pinch-hitter on 90 occasions, and is one of only five pitchers in major league history to connect for a pinch-hit grand slam.

Wynn coached for the Indians and Twins following his retirement, and he was inducted into the Hall of Fame in 1972.

Rudy York
Boston Red Sox (AL) 1959–62
See Managers section.

Eddie Yost
Washington Senators (AL) 1963–67; New York Mets (NL) 1968–75; Boston Red Sox (AL) 1977–84
See Managers section.

Ned Yost
Atlanta Braves (NL) 1991–2002
See Managers section.

Curt Young
Oakland Athletics (AL) 2004–
Pitcher from Saginaw, Michigan.

Young played 10 of his 11 seasons with the A's in two different stints. He went 69–53 lifetime with a 4.31 earned run average and 536 strikeouts. He began coaching in the minor leagues in 2000 in the Oakland system, and by 2003 had reached the AAA level. The following season he was named the Athletics' pitching coach.

Joel Youngblood
Cincinnati Reds (NL) 1994–97; Milwaukee Brewers (NL) 1998
Outfielder who was also tried in the infield.

Youngblood played most of his 14 seasons as a reserve, but when he was a regular he produced. In strike-shortened 1981 he hit .350 for the New York Mets and was named to the National League All-Star team. On August 4, 1982, he became the first major leaguer to play for two different teams in two different cities on the same day. Having collected a hit for the New York Mets at Wrigley Field in Chicago in a day game, he was traded to the Montreal Expos after that contest and flew to Philadelphia in time to appear as a pinch-hitter in the Expos' game against the Phillies. He collected a hit in that game as well.

He joined the San Francisco Giants in 1983 but encountered a crowded outfield. The Giants, wanting his bat in the lineup, tried him at second and then third, but in 1984 he led the league's third basemen in errors. He even-

tually became a solid pinch-hitter. Having started his career with the Reds in 1976, he finished with them in 1989. He went to work in the minor leagues as an instructor and manager, then rejoined the Reds as a coach and later coached for the Brewers as well.

Robin Yount
Arizona Diamondbacks (NL) 2002–04; Milwaukee Brewers (NL) 2006
Hall of Famer who played 20 years for the Brewers.

A .285 lifetime hitter, Yount became an everyday major leaguer at the age of 18. He spent his entire career in Milwaukee, hitting over .300 six times and crushing 251 home runs. He led the American League twice in doubles, twice in triples, once in hits, and once in slugging percentage. He was named to three All-Star teams. In 1982 he hit .331 with career-high totals of 29 home runs and 114 runs batted in while tying for the AL lead with 46 doubles and also leading with 210 hits and a .578 slugging average. He won a Gold Glove for his defense at shortstop and was named the league's Most Valuable Player.

He won that award again in 1989, this time as a center fielder. He thus became the third player (after Hank Greenberg and Stan Musial) to win an MVP at two different positions. That year he hit .318 with 21 homers and 103 RBIs. In 1988 Yount had hit for the cycle. In 1978 he had retired briefly to try a professional golfing career, but returned to the Brewers shortly thereafter. He retired for good in 1993 with 3142 lifetime hits.

In 1994 the Brewers retired Yount's number 19, and in 1999 he was inducted into the Hall of Fame. From 2002–04 he was a coach for the Diamondbacks, but in 2006 returned to the Brewers. He resigned following that season in order to devote more time to his family.

Al Zarilla
Washington Senators (AL) 1971
Ten-year outfielder from Los Angeles.

Zarilla started out with the St. Louis Browns in 1943, and he lost 1945 to military service. He returned following World War II and had his best season in 1948, when he hit .329 and was named an American League All-Star. He batted .325 in 1950 with the Boston Red Sox, the only other time he would top the .300 mark, and on June 8 he tied a major league record by stroking four doubles in a game.

After his playing career he worked as a scout, and in 1971 coached a single season for the Senators. He died in Honolulu in 1996.

Bart Zeller
St. Louis Cardinals (NL) 1970

Minor leaguer and former high school teacher.

Zeller was drafted by the Cardinals in 1963, but he reached the major leagues for only one game in 1970, when he was a coach for St. Louis and also caught briefly in one contest. He later became a manager in the amateur Men's Senior Baseball League, where he achieved World Championships in 1991, 1993, 2001, and 2003. In 1997 he was an inaugural member of that organization's Hall of Fame. In 2005 Zeller became a coach with the independent Sioux Falls Canaries of the Northern League, who in 2006 became part of a merger that formed the new American Association.

Don Zimmer
Montreal Expos (NL) 1971; San Diego Padres (NL) 1972; Boston Red Sox (AL) 1974–76, 1992; New York Yankees (AL) 1983, 1986, 1996–2003; Chicago Cubs (NL) 1984–86; San Francisco Giants (NL) 1987; Colorado Rockies (NL) 1993–95
See Managers section.

Tom Zimmer
St. Louis Cardinals (NL) 1976
Son of Don Zimmer.

Unlike his famous father, Tom neither played nor managed in the major leagues. He did coach for one season, however, in 1976 with the Cardinals. He also coached for the St. Petersburg Pelicans of the Senior Professional Baseball Association and worked as a scout for the San Francisco Giants.

Jerry Zimmerman
Minnesota Twins (AL) 1967, 1976–80; Montreal Expos (NL) 1969–75
Fun-loving catcher who hit just .204.

Zimmerman's superb defense and ability to handle pitchers kept him in the major leagues for eight years. He debuted with the Cincinnati Reds in 1961 but spent the rest of his big league days with the Twins, once hitting as low as .111. In 1967 he was a player-coach for Minnesota, appearing in a career-high 104 games. He continued to play in 1968, then joined the Expos the following season as a full-time bullpen coach. He later returned to the Twins as a coach for a second time.

On August 25, 1978, a one-day umpires' strike left the Twins and the Toronto Blue Jays short a couple of umps for their game at Exhibition Stadium. Zimmerman and Blue Jays' coach Don Leppert were pressed into service, with Zimmerman stationed at second base and Leppert at third.

Paul Zuvella
Colorado Rockies (NL) 1996
Light-hitting infielder from California.

Zuvella played primarily at second base and shortstop in limited duty for nine seasons with four different teams. He hit just .222 and managed only two home runs. After his playing days he became a minor league manager and instructor in the Rockies' organization, and in 1996 was promoted to Colorado as a coach.

Footage of Zuvella appears in the 1986 film *Ferris Bueller's Day Off*. When Ferris Bueller catches a foul ball off the bat of Claudell Washington, Zuvella is the runner on first base.

Dutch Zwilling
Cleveland Indians (AL) 1941
One of only two men to play for Chicago teams in the National, American, and Federal Leagues.

The other was Rollie Zeider. Zwilling appeared in 27 games for the White Sox in 1910 and hit just .184. In 1914 he resurfaced with the Chicago Chifeds of the FL, and he hit .313 and led the league with 16 home runs. In 1915 the Chifeds were renamed the Whales, and Zwilling remained with the club and hit .286 with a circuit-leading 94 runs batted in. In 1916 he played 35 games for the Cubs and hit just .113. His lifetime average was .284, those four seasons forming his entire major league career. As a major league the FL itself lasted only the 1914 and 1915 seasons, and Zwilling led all league outfielders in putouts both years.

After his playing career Dutch became a scout and minor league manager, and he piloted the Kansas City Blues to the American Association and Junior World Series championships in 1929. In 1941 he returned to the majors as a coach for the Indians.

About the Author

Thomas W. Brucato is a communications specialist and a lifelong, fiercely loyal Cincinnati Reds' fan. His previous books include *Major Leagues, Major League Champions*, and *Baseball's Retired Numbers*. Holding 8th degree black belts in both Tae Kwon Do and Kempo, he was the cofounder and is currently the president of the Tae Kwon Do Division of the Shukokai Kempo Martial Arts Academy. He was inducted into the World Martial Arts Hall of Fame in 2002 and the American Jukido-Ryu Martial Arts Union Hall of Fame in 2003. In his free time he enjoys writing, playing softball, traveling, and driving his classic 1968 Pontiac LeMans, the *Gray Ghost*. He and his wife, Julie, live in Cincinnati with their daughter, Kathryn, and their two Yorkshire terriers, Disney and Magic.